ISBN 978-0-428-61227-6
PIBN 10142922

New England Magazine

An Illustrated Monthly

New Series, Vol. 26

March, 1902   August, 1902

Boston, Mass.
America Company, Publishers
5 Park Square

INDEX

TO

THE NEW ENGLAND MAGAZINE

VOLUME XXVI.   MARCH, 1902—AUGUST, 1902

INDEX

INDEX

POETRY

COPYRIGHTED 1900 BY THE DETROIT PHOTOGRAPHIC CO

American Shrines VI

Independence Hall

" WE HOLD THESE TRUTHS TO BE SELF-EVIDENT:
THAT ALL MEN ARE CREATED EQUAL; THAT THEY ARE ENDOWED BY
THEIR CREATOR WITH CERTAIN UNALIENABLE RIGHTS; THAT AMONG
THESE ARE LIFE, LIBERTY AND THE PURSUIT OF HAPPINESS."

NEW ENGLAND MAGAZINE

NEW SERIES   MARCH   VOL. XXVI NO. 1

Mrs. Howe as Poet, Lecturer and Club-woman*

By George Willis Cooke

NO woman in this country better represents than Mrs. Julia Ward Howe the great advancement made by her sex during the present century in education, social influence, literary power and industrial opportunities. With almost every phase of this advance has she identified herself, and in several of them she has been a leader. Her career has been many-sided and broadly catholic in its sympathies. The companion and intimate friend of many of the intellectual and reformatory leaders of our country, she has lived much abroad and known the better phases of life in England, France, Italy and Greece. Though obtaining her education before women's colleges had come into existence, few women have attained a broader or more thorough culture than she or used it to nobler advantage.

In her charming book of "Reminiscences," Mrs. Howe has told the story of her life, and in a manner to delight and to instruct all who may read it. There could be no excuse whatever for presenting the facts of her life in briefer fashion, were it not that in so doing, attention may be drawn to the significance of her career in a manner that was not possible to her own pen. Not only will the book fail to reach the hands of many who would be interested and instructed by its most important incidents, but it is possible to make such a study of Mrs. Howe's life as will freshly interpret the gains women have made since she was a

* The illustrations in this article are from "Mrs. Howe's Reminiscences," published by Messrs. Houghton, Mifflin & Co., by whose courtesy they are here used.

young girl, and the part she has had in them.

Julia Ward was born in the city of New York, near the Battery, May 27, 1819. During her girlhood the family moved to Bond street, then in the upper part of the city. Her paternal ancestry included Roger Williams, Governor Samuel Ward of Rhode Island, who was very active in the opening scenes of the Revolution, and other persons of note. Her mother, who died, greatly beloved and respected, at the age of twenty-seven, was a grandniece of General Francis Marion. Her father early became a member of the New York bank-ing house of Prime, Ward and King, and took an active part in its affairs. In 1838 he established the Bank of Commerce and became its president. He was one of the founders of the University of the City of New York. The first temperance organiza-tion in the country was formed by him, and he was actively interested in many charities. A devoted member of the Episcopal church, he was severely orthodox and austere in his religious convictions, and somewhat ascetic in his daily life. He died in 1839, at the age of fifty-three.

Leaving school at sixteen, Julia Ward obtained her more advanced education at home under the direction of excellent teachers, no other means of thorough intellectual training being then open to a young woman. She was taught French, German, Italian, music, something of mathematics and still less of the sciences. Among her tutors was Joseph Green Cogswell, of the Round Hill School at Northampton, famous in its day, and later the librarian of the Astor Library. Her brothers graduated at Columbia College, as it then was, the family moved in the best social and intellectual circles, men and women of literary tastes frequented her father's house, and she grew up in an atmosphere of culture. Among the persons she met in her own home were Richard H. Dana, Bryant and Longfellow; and when Mrs. Jameson visited New York she was also a guest. More important than the studies she pursued was the atmosphere of serious thought and literary interest in which she grew up. She was, from girlhood, a student of books, albeit loving music and getting a goodly training in that and the other arts. She had a taste for the languages and skill to master them. Especially important was it that she early developed a love for good literature and read the best books in several languages. Without obtaining an education in any way so thorough as the college training of to-day, it was one well fitted to develop her literary gifts and to prepare her for her life work.

When only about sixteen, Julia Ward began to publish poems in the "American," a daily paper edited by Charles King, afterward the president of Columbia College. A familiar guest in her father's house was the younger Leonard Woods, who took much interest in her studies and who persuaded her to contribute a review of Lamartine's "Jocelyn' to the "Literary and Theological Review," of which he was the editor. It attracted much attention, and she was induced to send a short paper on the minor poems of Goethe and Schiller to the "New York Review," then edited by Dr. Cogswell, who had been her tutor. "I have already said," she writes in her "Reminiscences," "that a vision of some important literary work which I should accomplish was present with me in my early life, and had much to do with habits of study acquired by me in youth, and never wholly relinquished. At this late day, I find it difficult to account for a sense of literary responsibility which never left me, and which I must consider to have formed a part of my spiritual make-up. My earliest efforts in prose, two review articles, were probably more remarked at the time of their publication than their merit would have warranted. But women writers were by no means as numerous sixty years ago as they are now. Neither was it possible for a girl student in those days to find that help and guidance toward a literary career which may easily be commanded to-day."

In the summer of 1841 Miss Ward visited Boston and spent some months in a cottage near that city. Among the visitors were Longfellow and Sumner, and Professor Felton of Harvard. Interesting reports were given her by the two latter of the work of Dr. Samuel Gridley Howe at the Institution for the Blind in South Boston, where he was then carrying on most interesting experiments with

Laura Bridgman, then a girl of twelve. Miss Ward visited this institution and met Dr. Howe, and the acquaintance led to their marriage, which took place April 23, 1843. One week later they started for Europe, having as their companions Horace Mann and his newly wedded wife. In England they visited many charitable institutions and saw much of noted persons. They traveled through Germany, Switzerland and Italy, and spent the winter in Rome, where their first child was born in the spring. The little one was baptized by Theodore Parker, who was, with George Combe, a constant companion of the Howes during these months in Rome. Dr. Howe visited Greece to renew his acquaintance with the men with whom he had toiled for Greek independence in the years of his young and ardent manhood. The following summer was mostly spent in England, and there Dr. Howe met Florence Nightingale, then a young woman eagerly feeling her way to the philanthropic effort that has made her fame world-wide; and he was able to give her the encouragement she needed in order to start her upon her career. In the autumn they came back to Boston and found a home for many years in South Boston, where Dr. Howe was superintendent of the Institution for the Blind.

In 1824, after graduating at Brown University and the Harvard Medical School, Dr. Howe went to aid the Greeks in their attempt to secure independence from the dominion of Turkey. He served as a surgeon, but was obliged to accept the hard conditions under which the Greeks carried on their warfare. In 1827 he returned to the United States to raise funds to aid the poverty-stricken people, and he then devoted himself to the distribution of the food and clothing he was able to secure. In 1828 was published his "Historical Sketch of the Greek Revolution." In 1830 he was compelled to leave Greece, owing to an attack of swamp fever, induced by ex-

JULIA CUTLER WARD, MRS. HOWE'S MOTHER

posure and a rough soldier's life. Returning home through Paris, he was induced to carry aid to the Poles, was apprehended in Berlin and imprisoned. After some months he was liberated through the urgent efforts of his friends and by diplomatic intervention. While in Europe at this time he became interested in the efforts being made for the care and teaching of the blind, and on his return to Boston, in 1830, he began his efforts in behalf of that class of persons. Mr. Frank Sanborn has rightly called Dr. Howe one of the most romantic characters of our century, and describes him also as a hero. Mrs. Howe says that "his sanguine temperament, his knowledge of principles and reliance upon them, combined to lead him in advance of his own time. Experts in reforms and in charities acknowledged the indebtedness of both to his unremitting labors. He did all that one man could do to advance the coming of the millenial consummation, when there should be in the world neither paupers nor outcasts." He labored for the blind, the deaf, the criminals, the slaves, and for all who needed sympathy and help. He early gave encouragement to Dorothea Dix in her labors for the insane and criminal, and he quickly joined Garrison and Phillips in their anti-slavery crusade. His sympathies were with Horace Mann in his efforts for the common schools, and, becoming a member of the Boston school board soon after his return from Europe, he made his influence felt in the greatly improved school methods of the city.

During the next twenty years Mrs. Howe was the companion of her husband in his philanthropic and reformatory labors. She came to know the men and women who were his co-laborers and to share in their ideals and their humanitarian efforts. Devoted to her children, and aspiring to make for her husband a genuine home, she was also an earnest student, giving much time to literature, to the

SAMUEL WARD, MRS. HOWE'S FATHER

study of Greek and other languages, and to zealous inquiry into the realms of philosophy, being especially devoted to Kant. Having been brought up in good society, it had many attractions for her and she could not keep quite away from its demands; but her husband's example and her own studious habits would not permit her to give to it the best gifts of which she was capable.

In 1851, when the "Boston Commonwealth" was started to represent those who desired the suppression of slavery, but were not ultra abolitionists of the Garrisonian type, Dr. Howe gave it his aid and became its editor. He was assisted by Mrs. Howe, who for a year or more wrote frequently for the paper, especially on literary subjects. In 1854, soon after withdrawing from the paper, Mrs. Howe published anonymously in Boston a volume of poems bearing the title of "Passion Flowers." It attracted much attention and curiosity was aroused as to the author, who soon became known. The book was praised in many directions, but received some sharp criticism. Two years later appeared "Words for the Hour," also published without the author's name. Both these volumes were largely influenced by the questions of the day, the democratic and reformatory spirit of the time. They breathed forth an ardent desire for the extension of liberty to all peoples and for the lifting up of the oppressed and unfortunate. Mrs. Howe has said of her first volume of poetry that "it was much praised, much blamed, and much called in question." Theodore Parker quoted from it in one of his sermons, Catherine Sedgwick praised

one of its lines, and Dr. Francis Lieber recited a passage from it as having a Shakespearian ring. The poet herself calls it "a timid performance upon a slender reed;" but the second volume showed somewhat of improvement in mastery of the poetic art and in facility of expression.

The next poetical work was "The World's Own," published in Boston in 1857, having been produced in Wallack's Theatre in New York previously, the principal characters having been taken by Sothern and Matilda Heron. This poem has much interest as a literary production, but it lacks in dramatic qualities that would make it a stage success. A year after the production of this play, in 1858, Mrs. Howe wrote for Edwin Booth a tragedy called "Hippolytus," a result of her Greek studies. Arrangements were made for its production, with Booth and Charlotte Cushman in the principal parts; but the manager suddenly bethought him it was late in the season, and he dropped the play without an effort to revive it. It has never been published or in any manner given to the public.

During the first years of "The Atlantic Monthly" Mrs. Howe was a frequent contributor to its pages. In February, 1862, it published her "Battle Hymn of the Republic," which soon gained great popularity, and the story of the writing of which she has several times told. In the same magazine appeared her "Lyrics of the Street," and two of her noblest patriotic poems, "Our Orders" and "The Flag." These and other poems were in 1866 published in the volume called "Later Lyrics." In 1898 appeared "From Sunset Ridge: Poems Old and

JULIA WARD AND HER BROTHERS, SAMUEL AND HENRY WARD

New," which contained the best of the poems from the three earlier volumes, as well as a number that had not previously been given to the public.

As a poet Mrs. Howe belongs in the company of Lowell and Browning rather than in that of Longfellow and Whittier. Although her themes are often homely and familiar, her treatment of them is serious and thoughtful with Lowell, and sometimes dramatic in the manner of Browning. Familiarity with her poetry brings a growing recognition of its poetic value, its strength of expression and its fine humanity. Several of her poems written during the Civil War are of equal merit with her "Battle Hymn of the Republic," but they are too little known to receive just recognition. They show forth her ardent and profound patriotism, indicate most clearly how strong can be a woman's love of coun-

try and how just her recognition of its social worth. On the other hand, Mrs. Howe's introspective and semi-religious poems give rich expression to her inner life,—its noble ideals, its fine insight, its depths of spiritual wisdom.

As a poet Mrs. Howe is first of all a lover of mankind and gives voice to her sympathies with all its struggles and aspirations. Her earnest appreciation of homely and simple lives appears in the introductory poem to "Passion Flowers;" and well does she give utterance to her desire to comfort and to help them.

"I have sung to lowly hearts
   Of their own music, only deeper;
I have flung through the dusty road
   Shining seeds for the unknown reaper.

I have piped at cottage doors
   My sweetest measures, merry and sad,
Cheating Toil from his grinding task,
   Setting the dancing rustic mad.
        *   *   *   *   *   *

Better to sit at humble hearths,
  Where simple souls confide their all,
Than stand and knock at the groinèd gate,
  To crave—a hearing in the hall."

Again this desire for a large spiritual fellowship with mankind finds utterance:

  "Ere this mystery of Life
    Solving, scatter its form in air,
  Let me feel that I have lived
    In the music of a prayer,

  In the joy of generous thought,
    Quickening, enkindling soul from soul;
  In the rapture of deeper Faith
    Spreading its solemn, sweet control."

The one note in Mrs. Howe's poems
that is not to be heard so distinctly
elsewhere is that of motherhood.
Others have sung more sweetly and
enchantingly of home, its cares and its
joys, but none has so impressed the
motherly spirit upon her songs or more
truly interpreted the world from that
point of view. When she sings of war
and its ways it is as a mother who
watches over her babes and never loses
the brooding love of them, however
far they wander or strong they may
become. So must we read one of the
best of her war poems—that named:

OUR ORDERS.

"Weave no more silks, ye Lyons looms,
  To deck our girls for gay delights!
The crimson flower of battle blooms,
  And solemn marches fill the nights.

Weave but the flag whose bars to-day
  Drooped heavy o'er our early dead,
And homely garments, coarse and gray,
  For orphans that must earn their bread!

Keep back your tunes, ye viols sweet,
  That poured delight from other lands!
Rouse there the dancers' restless feet:
  The trumpet leads our warrior bands.

And ye that wage the war of words
  With mystic fame and subtle power,
Go, chatter to the idle birds,
  Or teach the lesson of the hour!

Ye Sibyl Arts, in one stern knot
  Be all your offices combined!
Stand close, while Courage draws the lot,
  The destiny of human kind.

And if that destiny could fail,
  The sun should darken in the sky,
The eternal bloom of Nature pale,
  And God, and Truth, and Freedom die!"

When she sings of "The Flag" not
less does she tune her song from the
home corner and its mother affection:

"There's a flag hangs over my threshold,
  whose folds are more dear to me
Than the blood that thrills in my bosom its
  earnest of liberty;
And dear are the stars it harbors in its
  sunny field of blue
As the hope of a further heaven, that lights
  all our dim lives through."

The same thought comes out even
more strongly in the concluding
stanza:

"When the last true heart lies bloodless,
  when the fierce and the false have won,
I'll press in turn to my bosom each daughter and either son:
Bid them loose the flag from its bearings,
  and we'll lay us down to rest
With the glory of home about us, and its
  freedom locked in our breast."

The mother love sings of the boy
who went out from the home at the
age of three years, in the poem that
bears the title of "Little One."

"My dearest boy, my sweetest!
  For paradise the meetest;
The child that never grieves me,
  The love that never leaves me;
The lamb by Jésu tended;
  The shadow, star befriended;
In winter's woe and straining,
  The blossom still remaining.

Days must not find me sitting
  Where shadows dim are flitting
Across the grassy measure
  That hides my buried treasure,
Nor bent with tears and sighing
  More prone than thy down-lying;

I have a freight to carry,
A goal,—I must not tarry.
If men would garlands give me,
If steadfast hearts receive me,
Their homage I'd surrender
For one embrace most tender;
One kiss, with sorrow in it,
To hold thee but one minute,
One word, our tie recalling,
Beyond the gulf appalling.

Since God's device doth take thee,
My fretting should forsake thee;
For many a mother borrows
Her comfort from the sorrows
Her vanished darling misses,
Transferred to heavenly blisses.
But I must ever miss thee,
Must ever call and kiss thee,
With thy sweet phantom near me,
And only God to hear me.

One of the finest of all Mrs. Howe's poems is "The House of Rest," and it brings out her poetical characteristics as well as her spiritual aspirations in language that fitly clothes her thought. It is a poem that only a mother's constant watch and care could fitly sing.

"I will build a house of rest,
  Square the corners every one:
At each angle on his breast
  Shall a cherub take the sun;
Rising, risen, sinking, down,
Weaving day's unequal crown.

In the chambers, light as air,
  Shall responsive footsteps fall:
Brother, sister, art thou there?
  Hush! we need not jar nor call;
Need not turn to seek the face
Shut in rapture's hiding-place.

Heavy load and mocking care
  Shall from back and bosom part;
Thought shall reach the thrill of prayer,
  Patience plan the dome of art.
None shall praise or merit claim,
Not a joy be called by name.

With a free, unmeasured tread
  Shall we pace the cloisters through:
Rest, enfranchised, like the Dead;
  Rest till Love be born anew.

Weary Thought shall take his time,
Free of task-work, loosed from rhyme."

The intent of this house of rest appears from the concluding stanza:

"Oh! my house is far away;
  Yet it sometimes shuts me in.
Imperfection mars each day
  While the perfect works begin.
In the house of labor best
Can I build the house of rest."

"Warning" may be taken as a sample of Mrs. Howe's more philosophical poems, those in which she deals with the great questions of life and eternity. In some of these her thought is subtle and dramatic, but in all of them it is human in its sympathies and loftily spiritual in its ministrations:

"Power, reft of aspiration;
  Passion, lacking inspiration;
  Leisure, not of contemplation.

Thus shall danger overcome thee,
Fretted luxury consume thee,
All divineness vanish from thee.

Be a man and be one wholly;
Keep one great love, purely, solely,
Till it make thy nature holy;

That thy way be paved in whiteness,
That thy heart may beat in lightness,
That thy being end in brightness."

These samplings may conclude with "A Spring Thought:"

"Overgrow my grave,
    Kindly grass;
  Do not wave
    To those who pass
A single mournful thought
Of affection come to nought.

Look up to the blue
    Where, light-hid,
  Lives what doth renew
    Man's chrysalid.
Say not: She is here,
Say not: She was there.
Say: She lives in God,
Reigning everywhere."

Mrs. Howe has been much of a traveller and has profited by her studies of foreign lands. In June, 1850, she went with her husband and children to Europe, visited friends in England and spent some months in Germany. Dr. Howe returned home, but Mrs. Howe spent the winter in Rome with her two sisters. She saw something of the revolutionary and democratic movements of 1848 in their reactionary effects, though her sympathies did not grow less for liberty and republican institutions. In February, 1859, the Howes accompanied Theodore Parker to Cuba; but Parker not being benefited in health, went on to Vera Cruz, then sailed for Europe, from which he did not return. Mrs. Howe wrote an account of her life in Cuba for "The Atlantic Monthly," which was continued through six numbers of that magazine, and which was published in book form in 1860 as "A Trip to Cuba." This volume was not favorably received in Cuba and its circulation there was forbidden. The book is bright and readable and brought the author an invitation to contribute to the "New York Tribune," and for several years she wrote of social and literary life in Boston and Newport.

The Cretan insurrection of 1866 renewed Dr. Howe's interest in the Greeks and he raised funds for them. In the spring of 1867 he set out for Greece, accompanied by Mrs. Howe and two of their daughters. On the way they visited England and Rome, but pushed rapidly on to Greece, where they arrived at midsummer. Dr. Howe visited Crete, although a price had been set upon his head, and he did all he could to aid the people there.

On their return home in the autumn Mrs. Howe wrote an account of this journey and of her ·life in Greece, which was published as "From the Oak to the Olive: a Plain Record of a Pleasant Journey." "I have only to say," she wrote in concluding the volume, "that I have endeavored in good faith to set down this simple and hurried record of a journey crowded with interests and pleasures. I was afraid to receive so freely of these without attempting to give what I could in return, under the advantages and disadvantages of immediate transcription." On their return to Boston the Howes organized a fair in aid of the Cretans.

In the spring of 1873 Mrs. Howe again visited England, having previously accompanied Dr. Howe to Santo Domingo, to which he had been the year before sent as a commissioner, with Benjamin F. Wade and Andrew D. White, for securing its annexation to the United States. This second visit was made to aid the people in developing their commercial interests. In 1875 they again visited the island, this time in search of health for Dr. Howe. Mrs. Howe has visited Europe several times in more recent years. The winter of 1897-8 was spent by her in Rome.

Dr. Howe died in January, 1876, after some months of failing health. The addresses and poems given at his funeral were published by Mrs. Howe, together with a memoir prepared by herself, the volume being especially designed for reproduction, in raised characters, for the blind. In concluding the "Memoir of Dr. Howe," she said that his was "one of the noblest lives of our day and generation. All that is most sterling in American character may be said to

JULIA WARD HOWE ABOUT 1861

have found its embodiment in Dr. Howe. To the gift of a special and peculiar genius he' added great industry and untiring perseverance, animated by a deep and comprehensive benevolence. Although ardent in temperament, he was not hasty in judgment, and was rarely deceived by the superficial aspect of things when this was at variance with their real character. Although long and thoroughly a servant of the public, he disliked publicity, and did not seek reputation, being best satisfied with the approbation of his own conscience and the regard of his friends. In the relations of private life he was faithful and affectionate, and his public services were matched by the constant acts of kindness and helpfulness which marked his familiar intercourse with his fellow-creatures." Bryant said of Dr. Howe, that "he was one whose whole life was

THE HOME AT SOUTH BOSTON

dedicated to the service of his fellow men."

Writing of her chief aim in life Mrs. Howe says that she might have chosen for her motto: "I have followed the great masters with my heart." She has been first and last a student, not so much a lover of books as a student of the thoughts which books interpret. In her books of travel and in many of her lectures she has seemed to be chiefly concerned with the social or superficial phases of life, but she has been in reality largely interested in philosophy and the great problems of human existence. In her youth she eagerly read Goethe, Richter, Herder and the other Germans, and then she turned to Dante. In her South Boston days she gave much time to the Latin writers, particularly to Cicero. She also plunged into Swedenborg that she

might sound the deeper truths of the spirit; and for the same purpose she turned to Hegel. She also gave much attention to Comte, and then to Kant, thus seeking help in all directions. She turned also to Spinoza and found great delight in his works; but it was in Kant she found the deepest satisfaction, being inclined to say with Romeo: "Here I set up my everlasting rest."

These philosophical studies, after being carried on for many years, led to a desire to speak to others her own thoughts on the problems she had studied. Although Theodore Parker encouraged her in this undertaking. Dr. Howe was opposed to it, and it was not until 1860 or 1861 that she found her first audience. She invited to her house, which was then in Chestnut street, afterwards famous for the meetings of the Radical Club, such of her friends as she thought would care to hear her. She spoke on "Doubt and Belief, the Two Feet of the Mind;" "Moral Triangulation, or the Third Party;" "Duality of Character," and other kindred themes. In her audience were Agassiz, Alger, Clarke and Whipple; and much interest was expressed in her lectures. A year or two later they were repeated in Washington, and there they were listened to by many persons of political and intellectual prominence.

The result of these lectures was to increase her interest in philosophical studies and to give her a desire to produce some original contribution to philosophical truth. She accordingly wrote several essays on such subjects as the "Distinctions between Philosophy and Religion," "Polarity," "Man a priori," and "Ideal Causation." The second of these papers was read before the Boston Radical Club, and the third to a meeting of scientists at Northampton. At the Radical Club she also read lectures on "Limitations" and "The Halfness of Nature;" she frequently attended that club and took part in its discussions. Some years later, when the Concord School of Philosophy was established, she was frequently invited to address it; and usually did so once or twice each year so long as its sessions were continued. The largest audiences which gathered at the school were those which listened to her. Her lectures there on "Modern Society" and "Changes in American Society" were in 1880 published in a little book bearing the title of the first of these addresses. Her lecture of 1884, on "Emerson's Relation to Society," was published in the volume on "The Genius and Character of Emerson," which included all the lectures of that year. Two of her other lectures given there, those on "Aristophanes" and "Dante and Beatrice," were in 1895 published in the volume called "Is Polite Society Polite? and Other Essays." This volume included seven of her lectures, originally prepared for the Radical Club, the Concord School of Philosophy, the New England Woman's Club, the Town and Country Club of Newport, and the Contemporary Club of Philadelphia, and subsequently read in many places throughout the country. One of the lectures published in this volume was on "The Salon in America," and it gives account of the growth of literary interest as developed in clubs. For such gatherings Mrs. Howe is an ideal lecturer, always bright, entertaining, instructive, and provocative of discussion as well as of serious thought. Her voice is not strong enough and does not have sufficient carrying power for large assemblies, but in the quiet of a parlor it finds its fit opportunity as the expression of her rich and noble thoughts. Most of her later prose writing has adapted itself to club utterance, and it has partaken of the limitations thus imposed upon it. This is one reason undoubtedly why her lectures, when put into print, receive less attention than when heard. Mrs. Howe's personality has given character and strength to her spoken words, and caused many to listen to them with deepest interest and satisfaction.

Her experiences as a lecturer, and especially her desire to aid women in securing recognition as religious teachers, led Mrs. Howe to enter the pulpit, as opportunity offered. Having early become a Unitarian, she frequently preached in churches of that religious body, but many other denominations have given welcome to her sermons.   In 1875 she succeeded in bringing together the women ministers of all denominations, and they organized an association for mutual sympathy and co-operation.   Of this organization she was chosen the president, a position she continues to hold. The sermons Mrs. Howe has delivered from time to time show how fit it is that women should occupy the pulpit, and how capable they are of the highest spiritual ministration.   It can be only a question of time when women will in a large degree become the religious teachers of mankind, such is their natural fitness for the tasks of spiritual instruction and moral guidance.

When Theodore Parker began to preach in Boston, Dr. and Mrs. Howe became members of his congregation. Mrs. Howe writes in her "Reminiscences" with the greatest enthusiasm of the preaching of Parker, saying that "it was all one intense delight."   "The luminous clearness of his mind, his admirable talent for popularizing the procedures and conclusions of philosophy, his keen wit and poetic sense of beauty,—all these combined to make him appear to me one of the oracles of God."   Great as was her admiration for Parker, when her children became of an age to attend church and Sunday-school she had a desire for a church fitted to their need, and she became a member of the Church of the Disciples, of which James Freeman Clarke was then the minister, who was succeeded by Charles G. Ames.   To this church Mrs. Howe has been warmly attached,

and she is always seen at its morning services when it is possible for her to attend.   It should be said, however, that she is no partisan in religion, and that her sympathies go out to all truly worshipful souls seeking the light. Radical in her thought, keen critic in her philosophical liberalism, Mrs. Howe is at heart conservative in her religious sympathies.   Finding little help in the formulas and rituals of the churches, she is in closest alliance with all who seek for the truths of life.   Her strong fidelity to the inward facts of the Christian ideal appears in many of her poems, as well as in her lectures. Perhaps it nowhere finds more expressive utterance than in "Near Amalfi," one of her best poems:

"Oh! could Jesus pass this way
   Ye should have no need to pray.
   He would go on foot to see
   All your depths of misery.
            Succor comes.
   He would smooth the frowzled hair,
   He would lay your ulcers bare,
   He would heal as only can
   Soul of God in heart of man.
            Jésu comes.
   Ah! my Jesus! still thy breath
   Thrills the world untouched of death,
   Thy dear doctrine sheweth me
   Here, God's loved humanity
            Whose kingdom comes."

Mrs. Howe sought the Church of the Disciples because it was a church of serious people, and free to all.   She says she had already had "enough and too much of that church-going in which the bonnets, the pews, and the doctrine appear to rest on one dead level of conventionalism."   There she found those who desired to help their fellow men, and a pulpit open to all the humanities.   It was not strange, therefore, that she grew to take more and more interest in the reform move-

JULIA ROMANA ANAGNOS

ments of the time, to identify herself with the anti-slavery party and to give her strength to advancing the interests of women. The first reform movement in which she took a leading part was that of peace. During the progress of the Franco-Prussian war she drew up an appeal of women against war. "The august dignity of motherhood and its terrible responsibilities now appeared to me in a new aspect," she writes, "and I could think of no better way of expressing my sense of these than that of sending forth an appeal to womankind throughout the world." She accordingly wrote an appeal to women, had it translated into many languages, and called a world's convention in London. In 1870 she held two important meetings in New York, and she gave two years to interesting women in the cause of peace. In 1872 was held the Woman's Peace Congress in London, and she devoted many months previous to its session in advocating in England the cause she had at heart. In London she held a series of Sunday evening services, in which were considered "The, Mission of Christianity in Relation to the Pacification of the World."

In the course of her philosophical studies Mrs. Howe arrived at the conclusion that "woman must be the moral and spiritual equivalent of man." This conviction led her to take part in the organization of the New England Woman's Club, of which she was for many years the president. Soon after she began to recognize the importance of the political enfranchisement of women, and although she was slow in accepting the necessity for this reform, she came finally to give it the strongest assent. She became one of the leaders in its advocacy, adding her abilities to those of Garrison, Phillips, Higginson, Clarke, Curtis, Hoar, Lucy Stone, Lucretia Mott, Mrs. Livermore, Mrs. Stanton and Miss Anthony in pleading for the emancipation of women. In 1869 she took part in the organization of the American Suffrage Association, of which she has since been the president. In January, 1870, she joined with Lucy Stone, Mrs. Livermore, W. L. Garrison and T. W. Higginson in the publishing and editing of "The Woman's Journal" in Boston. For many years she was one of its editors and wrote frequently for its pages, and she has ever since its founding been in closest agreement with its purpose to secure the advancement of women by educational, economic and political methods. With voice and pen she has continued for over thirty years to advocate the cause of woman, and though the suffrage has not been

granted her, she has lost none of her faith in the justice of the cause she has represented. She has steadily continued to adhere to the position she stated in the opening editorial of the "Woman's Journal," advocating co-operation with men and not opposition to them:

"Our endeavor, which is to bring the feminine mind to bear upon all that concerns the welfare of mankind, commands us to let the dead past bury its dead. The wail of impotence becomes us no longer. We must work as those who have power, for we have faith, and faith is power. We implore our sisters, of whatever kind or degree, to make common cause with us, to lay down all partisan warfare and organize a peaceful Grand Army of the Republic of Women. But we do not ask them to organize as against men, but as against all that is pernicious to men and to women. Against superstition, whether social or priestly; against idleness, whether aesthetic or vicious; against oppression, whether of manly will or feminine caprice. Ours is but a new manœuvre, a fresh phalanx in the grand fight of faith. In this conflict the armor of Paul will become us, the shield and breastplate of strong and shining virtue."

In the "Boston Globe," during March, 1894, she stated her continued adherence to the faith thus declared, and expressed her convictions as to the progress that had been made and the promise of the future:

"The wonderful advance in the condition of women which the last twenty years have brought about, makes me a little diffident of my ability to prophesy concerning the future of the sex. At the beginning of the first of these decades few would have foretold the great extension of educational opportunities, the opening of professions, the multiplication of profitable industrial pursuits, all of which have combined to place women before the world in the attitude of energetic, self-supporting members of society. Even the vexed suffrage question has made great progress. The changes which I

From a portrait by Hardy

JULIA WARD HOWE

foresee are all farther developments of the points already gained. I feel assured that, in the near future, the co-operation of women in municipal and in State affairs will be not only desired, but demanded by men of pure and worthy citizenship. The true progress of civilization is from the assumption of privilege to the recognition of right. In this country this progress already embraces the whole of one sex. The laws of moral equilibrium will speedily place the other sex in an equal condition, exalting the dignities of domestic life, and making the home altar rich with gifts of true patriotism and wise public spirit."

When the Association for the Advancement of Women was organized in 1869 Mrs. Howe took an active part, and on the occasion of the Boston meeting in 1879 she was elected the president. In 1882 the New England Industrial Exhibition opened a woman's department, this being the first time that a great fair gave women such recognition. Mrs. Howe was invited to act as the president; she explained the purpose had in view on the opening day, and this effort to advance the interests of women was an eminent success. The next year she was invited to preside over the woman's department of the Cotton Centennial Exposition held at New Orleans, and though the task involved much labor, it established the recognition of women in all future exhibitions of the industrial products of the country. A novel feature of this fair was managed by Mrs. Howe's daughter Maud, who took charge of an alcove in which were collected the books written by women.

Mrs. Howe has been a member of several famous clubs and the founder of two or three that have received wide recognition. Since 1852 she has been a summer resident of Newport, and she organized the Town and Country Club, which has been an attractive feature of life there, and has drawn together many intelligent men and women for amusement and instruction. When the women's club movement began she gave it her support, and she has been the president of the Massachusetts Federation of Women's Clubs and a director of the General Federation. It is probable that Mrs. Howe is better known as a lecturer than as an author, and yet she has published much. She has been a contributor to the "Atlantic Monthly," "Christian Examiner," "Old and New," "North American Review," "The Forum," and other well known journals. Her contributions to the "Atlantic Monthly" have been about thirty in number, and they extend through nearly the whole history of that magazine. In 1874 she edited a volume on "Sex and Education," in reply to Dr. E. H. Clarke's "Sex in Education," to which she was a contributor and for which she wrote the introduction. She also wrote for the "Famous Women" series of biographies an account of the life of Margaret Fuller, which was published in 1883.

In closing her "Reminiscences," Mrs. Howe says that on one occasion she was asked to enumerate her "social successes," and she gives them in words that cannot be omitted from this account of her life:

"I have sat at the feet of the masters of literature, art, and science, and have been graciously admitted into their fellowship. I have been the chosen poet of several high festivals, to wit, the celebration of Bryant's sixtieth birthday, the commemoration of the centenary of his birth, and the unveiling of the statue of Columbus in Central Park, New York, in the Columbian year, so called. I have been the founder of a club of young girls [Saturday Morning Club], which has exercised a salutary influence upon the growing womanhood of my adopted city, and has won for itself an honorable place in the community, serving also as a model for similar associations in other cities. I have been for many years the president of the New England Woman's Club, and of the Association for the Advancement of Women. I have been heard at the great Prison Congress in England, at Mrs. Butler's convention *de moralité publique* in Geneva, Switzerland, and at more than one convention in Paris. I have been welcomed in Faneuil Hall, when I have stood there to rehearse the merits of public men, and later, to plead the cause of oppressed Greece and murdered Armenia. I have written one poem which, although composed in the stress and strain of the civil war, is now sung South and North by the champions of a free government. I have been accounted worthy to listen and to speak at the Boston Radical Club and at the Concord School of Philosophy. I have been exalted to occupy the pulpit of my own dear church and that of others, without regard to denominational limits. Lastly and chiefly, I have had the honor of pleading for the slave when he was a slave, of helping to initiate the woman's movement in many States of the Union, and of standing with the illustrious champions of justice and freedom, for woman suffrage, when to do so was a thankless office, involving public ridicule and private avoidance."

This record of Mrs. Howe's successes might have been extended to a much greater length. She has witnessed a wonderful advance in the position and influence of women, and her own part in securing it has been considerable. If women have not gained the right to vote, they have secured the opportunity of studying any subject to which men give their attention. She has taken part in the opening of all professions to women, and she has aided women in organizing for every kind of intellectual, moral, religious and industrial improvement. These activities of hers at first closed to her in a measure the avenues of polite society, but with the result that for nearly fifty years she has been one of the best known and most influential citizens of Boston. Every good cause now seeks her approval. All her public activities and all her reformatory efforts have but made her more truly a woman. Instead of unsexing her, they have brought her into the full maturity of her womanly powers.

The Conquering of Caroline

By Eleanor H. Porter

FROM her earliest recollections, she had regarded babies with awe and unreasoning terror, a feeling which speedily grew into settled disapproval and dislike, and she—a woman child! Her dolls were never children, nor baby-dolls, but queens and princesses, occupying sumptuous palaces, and disporting themselves in silks and satins. As a child she had many a time crossed the street to avoid meeting a woman and a baby-carriage, lest she be expected to kiss the tiny, cooing creature half smothered in flannels; and she never borrowed the neighbors' babies for an afternoon, as did so many of her playmates. Being the youngest in the family, she found her own home quite free from the objectionable creatures.

As the years passed, and her girl friends married, their letters to her began to be filled with the sayings of small Tommies, and the doings of wee Marys, together with soft rings of baby hair, all of which filled Caroline's soul with distress,—and her stove with cinders. The letters remained long unanswered, and the correspondence waned. And then people began to call her an old maid, and to point out her prim little cottage as the place where "old Miss Blake" lived.

Caroline Blake's entire personality was made up of angles. There were no curves to her square chin nor kinks to her thin yellow hair. Even her flower beds in the front yard were laid out in severe diamond shape, and the Nottingham curtains at the parlor windows hung straight from their poles.

When the Smiths moved into the vacant house across the way, Caroline anxiously scanned the contents of the big wagons from her vantage ground behind the front chamber blinds. Her brow contracted into a frown when she spied the baby-carriage, and she fairly gasped at sight of two new high-chairs. Her disgust was complete, upon the arrival of the family on the following day,—a black-whiskered man, a thin, faded-looking little woman, a small girl of perhaps six years of age, two tiny toddlers—evidently twins,—and a babe in arms. Caroline pursed her thin lips tight, and descended to the kitchen with resolute step.

"Polly,"—said she, sharply, to her one handmaiden, who was trying to coax an obstinate fire into a blaze,—"I do not like the looks of the woman who is moving into the other house, at all, and I wish you to make no advances in her direction. If they want to borrow anything, tell 'em you're going to use it yourself, and use it—if it's the snow-shovel in August! You can dig in the garden with it," she added grimly.

Polly looked at her mistress in surprise, for Caroline was proverbially hospitable and generous, save only where a child was concerned. The girl opened her mouth as though to speak, when a wailing duet from the twins across the way sent a gleam of understanding into her eyes, and caused her to shut her lips with a snap; Polly did not share her mistress's antipathy to twins.

Caroline went into the parlor, and peered furtively through the lace curtains. No one was in sight at the other house save the small girl of six, who had evidently come out to view the landscape. Suddenly the woman noticed that her own gate was the least bit ajar; and with a quick jerk she turned from the window, darted across the room, opened the front door, and marched down the walk,

shutting the gate with a short, sharp snap, meanwhile sending her most forbidding frown across the expanse of dusty street. Then she walked leisurely back into the house.

In the days that followed, Caroline had a sore struggle with herself. She had been a strict adherent to the village creed of calling on all strangers, especially neighbors; but this creature—! For a time she succeeded in persuading herself that it was unnecessary that she should notice so objectionable a specimen of womanhood: yet her conscience would uncomfortably assert itself whenever she caught a glimpse of the frail little woman opposite, particularly as she was forced to admit that her new neighbor possessed a face of unusual sweetness and refinement.

Caroline finally compromised with herself by calling one afternoon, soon after she had witnessed Mrs. Smith's departure from the house. She was rewarded according to her iniquity, however, for Mrs. Smith had returned unseen for a forgotten letter, and opened the door herself in response to Caroline's sharp pull at the bell.

"You are Miss Blake, I know," said the little woman delightedly, smiling into the dismayed face of her visitor. "I am so glad to see you! Come right in and sit down—I've wanted to know you all the time."

Caroline Blake hardly knew how to conduct herself at this unforeseen outcome of all her elaborate scheming. She followed her hostess into the parlor with a sour face. There was a decided chill in the atmosphere by the time the two women were seated opposite each other, and Mrs. Smith began to be aware of it.

"It—it is a nice day," she ventured timidly, in a very different voice from the one she had used in cordial greeting a moment before.

"I don't care for this kind of weather—it's too hot!" said Caroline shortly.

"Yes—no! Of course not," murmured Mrs. Smith in quick apology. "I think there will be a shower tonight, though, which will cool the air beautifully!" she added courageously.

"Well—I hope not! If there's anything that I positively detest, it's a thunder storm," replied her guest with the evident intention of being as disagreeable as possible. "They're so—noisy and—er—wet," she finished feebly.

"Yes, they are—so," acquiesced Mrs. Smith unhappily, wondering vaguely what was the matter. Then there ensued an uncomfortable silence, during which she coughed nervously, and hitched in her chair.

"I think Norton is a very pretty place," she began at last hopefully; "I am sure I shall like it here very much."

"Do you? I don't care much for it, myself, I have seen so many prettier places. Of course, if one has never been about much, I dare say it seems quite fine," and Caroline fixed her eyes on a worn spot in the carpet from which the concealing rug had been carelessly pushed one side.

Mrs. Smith colored and bit her lip, but she bravely rallied her forces once more, on courtesy intent.

"What beautiful flowers you have, Miss Blake! I think I never saw such lovely beds."

Now this was a diplomatic stroke indeed, and a far-away smile dawned in Caroline's sombre eyes; but it quickly waned at her hostess's next words.

"My little Nellie is always talking about them. I'm sorry the child isn't here to-day, but she and the twins are out for a walk with the nurse."

Caroline stiffened. At that moment an infantile wail was wafted from the upper regions. Mrs. Smith sprang to her feet with an inspiration.

"It's baby—he's awake! I'll go right up and get him. I know you'll want to see him—he's so cunning!" and she had almost reached the door when Caroline arose with a face upon which determination sat enthroned.

"Excuse me, Mrs. Smith, but I must be going. I—I don't care for babies at all!" and she rustled toward the hall door,—"Good afternoon."

The little woman left behind stared in dumb amazement after her guest, whose parting assertion had placed her quite beyond the fond mother's comprehension. At a more insistent wail from above, she caught her breath with a smothered exclamation, and rushed up stairs.

A few days later, Caroline, weeding her flower beds, glanced up to find her small neighbor of six summers not three feet away, gravely regarding her.

"Pretty flowers!" ventured the sweet voice by way of introduction.

Caroline pulled spitefully at a big weed and said nothing.

"I like pretty flowers," came suggestively from the small maiden as she took a step nearer.

Caroline suddenly awoke to the possibilities of the occasion.

"Run away, child. I don't like little girls!" said she, sharply.

Two round eyes looked reproachfully at her.

"You don't? How funny! I like *you*," and the red lips parted in a heavenly smile.

At this somewhat disconcerting statement, Caroline started, and there came a strange fluttering feeling at her throat. She looked at the child in almost terror, then dropped her tools hastily, and started for the house. Once inside, she peered out of the window at her strangely victorious foe. Nellie stood looking in evident surprise in the direction of her vanished hostess. By and by she turned her attention to the bright-colored flowers before her.

Caroline's finger nails fairly dug into the palms of her hands as she watched the little girl bend over her pet bed of geraniums. Lower and lower stooped the sunny head, till the lips rested in a gentle kiss right in the scarlet heart of the biggest flower; then another, and another tender caress was bestowed on the brilliant blossoms, until the watching woman felt again that strange new fluttering that nearly took her breath away. She waited until Nellie, with slow and lingering step passed through the gate, then she went to her bedroom cupboard, and taking down from the shelf a large black bottle marked, "Nerve Tonic," turned out a generous portion.

The next afternoon, as Caroline sat sewing under the trees, she again found herself confronted by her visitor of the day before. Nellie advanced confidently, with no apparent doubt as to her welcome, and laid a tiny bunch of wilted buttercups and daisies in the unwilling hands of the disturbed woman.

"Go away, little girl! I don't——"

What a queer sensation the touch of those small moist hands gave her ! She must be going to be sick—such a little thing upset her so! The buttercups and daisies dropped from her nerveless fingers, and she began to feel the same overmastering desire to run away that had conquered her the day before. The child looked wistfully into her face.

"I gived you some of *my* flowers," she began insinuatingly.

Caroline refused to take the hint. Really, this was a most impossible child.

Nellie edged a little nearer.

"P'raps you'll give me some of yours," she suggested sweetly.

Caroline sprung to her feet.

"Run away, little girl! I—I don't ——" she had hurried along the path to the house, and now the door shut behind her. Peeping cautiously through the blinds, she saw Nellie gather up the discarded posies one by one, then stand long before the flaming geraniums, patting each blossom tenderly with her pudgy little fingers.

The woman straightened herself with a spasmodic jerk, dashed out of the door, and catching up her scissors, began snipping ruthlessly among her treasured blossoms, until her hands overflowed with riotous bloom.

"There, there, child—take 'em!" said she, nervously, thrusting the gay bunch into the eager outstretched fingers. "Now run right away; I don't——."

"Oh! thank you—thank you!" interrupted a rapturous voice, "You may kiss me, now," it added graciously.

With a slight gasp, Caroline pecked gingerly at the upturned rosy lips, then went straight to the cupboard and took down the nerve tonic.

The next day Caroline saw nothing of Nellie. She told herself that it was a great relief not to see the child running around, and she looked over to the other house every few minutes just to emphasize her satisfaction. Toward night the doctor's gig stopped at the gate across the way, and after Caroline had watched the man of pills and powders go into the house, she went again to her cupboard and took down the nerve tonic—somehow, she felt a little queer.

During the week that followed, Caroline grew strangely restless. Her flower beds were always well cared for, but never had they received such attention as now. The woman cast many a glance across the street, but no Nellie came to torment her weeding.

Whatever was the cause of the little girl's absence, it evidently was not serious, for a few days later she appeared—a little thin and pale, perhaps, but otherwise quite her old self.

Caroline fluttered around her flowers the greater portion of that morning, and in the afternoon carried her chair way down to the farther end of the yard nearest the fence. She suddenly decided that that was the shadiest place, and concluded to sit there, even if she could so plainly hear the children's voices as they played "housekeeping" just across the street.

Several days passed, and Caroline was still left in undisputed possession of her yard and her flower beds. Perhaps Nellie had received instructions from the tired little mother who had not forgotten her neighbor's heresy on the baby question. The child certainly gave no indication of further disturbing visits. But one day Caroline saw her looking wistfully over at the bright blossoms. Recklessly lopping off the head of a gorgeous poppy near her, she held it up enticingly. The little girl hesitated, then came straight across the road, and held out a longing hand.

"If you'll come in, I'll give you some more," said Caroline in a voice she hardly recognized as her own. And the child came.

It was not until September that the tragedy occurred which made the little town sick with horror. Mr. and Mrs. Smith were driving down on the river road where the Northern Express came thundering up through the quiet valley every afternoon. No one knew how it happened, but they found the poor quiet forms with the light of life quite gone out, and the dead horse and broken carriage to tell the tale.

When Caroline Blake heard the dread tidings her face went deathly white; then a strange gleam came into her eyes and she quickly crossed the street and took Nellie into her arms.

"Come, dear, you are going to be my little girl, now, and live with me."

The child stopped sobbing, and looked wonderingly into the transformed face of the woman.

"And the twins?" she asked cautiously.

"Yes," assented Caroline faintly.

"And baby?" demanded the small maiden, insistently.

"Y-y-es," breathed Caroline again. with a little gasp.

* * * * *

And the winter passed and the summer came. And it was noticed that fantastically-shaped flower beds ran riot all over the yard, and that the Nottingham curtains were looped back in graceful curves with gaily-colored ribbons.

A FAMILY GROUP

America's First Painters

By Rufus Rockwell Wilson

STUDY of the beginnings of our native art is a task that amply rewards endeavor, for, notwithstanding the too prevalent lack of faith in our early painters and sculptors, many admirable artists have lived and flourished in America, men of force, of feeling, and of talent often falling little short of genius, whose achievements cannot fail to command interest, respect and admiration.

Recent investigations prosecuted by members of the Massachusetts Historical Society make it clear that there

26

were painters in America more than a century before the Revolution, and there is reason to believe that the curious portrait of Dr. John Cutler, now the property of this Society, which represents that forgotten worthy contemplating a skull, was painted in Boston prior to 1680. The same date is attributed to a portrait of Increase Mather, and the quaint portraits of the Gibbs children are dated 1670. There is no clue to the origin of the portrait of John Winthrop, deposited in the Harvard Memorial Hall at Cambridge,

From the painting by Smibert

BISHOP BERKELEY

but if it was drawn from life, in Boston, it is the oldest work of native art in this part of the world, as Winthrop died in 1649. There is record of an artist named Joseph Allen, who sailed from England for Boston in 1684, and that at least one other painter made Boston his home before the opening of the eighteenth century is shown by an extract from Judge Sewall's Diary:

"November 10, 1706. This morning, Tom Child, the painter, died.

"Tom Child has often painted Death
   But never to the life before.
Doing it now, he's out of Breath,
   He paints it once, and paints no more."

However, aside from this singular epitaph, we have no record of the life and work of Tom Child, who was, doubtless, a well known character in the snug little Boston of his time. We know less of the painters who were his contemporaries, and it is not until a later period that we find ourselves on sure ground. That painting should be the last of the arts to take firm root among us is easily explainable, for its hard and narrow conditions at first denied the painter, or "limner," as he was called in the blunt speech of the fathers, a place in pioneer life.

Peter Pelham, whose name heads the roster of the pioneer painters of New England, has left us no other proof of his handiwork than likenesses of some of the Puritan divines of his

BISHOP BERKELEY AND HIS FAMILY

time. He settled in Boston in 1726, and the earliest American work yet traced to him is an engraved portrait of Cotton Mather, dated 1727. The portraits of Cotton and Richard Mather, now in the library of the American Antiquarian Society, at Worcester, Massachusetts, are by his hand, and he also numbered John Moorhead and Mather Byles among his sitters. Besides engraving his own work, he reproduced in mezzo-tinto some of the portraits painted by John Smibert.

In May, 1748, Pelham married Mary Singleton, widow of Richard Copley, and received into his family her son, the future artist, John Singleton Copley. The wife, who had kept a tobacco shop during her widowhood, added her contribution to the common fund by

continuing it after her union with Pelham. The records of Trinity church, in Boston, where Pelham had long worshipped, show that he was buried December 14, 1751. His widow survived him nearly forty years, her declining days cheered by the success of her son Copley, whose talent as a painter had brought him fame and competence. Pelham's productions on copper are executed in the deep mezzotinto so prevalent in the early part of the eighteenth century, and closely resemble the work of the well known English scraper, John Smith. As a painter in oils he had small merit. He was a man capable of giving a likeness and little more.

The same is in a measure true of John Smibert, who came to America in 1729, in the train of Bishop Berkeley, who had conceived the idea of converting the Indians to Christianity by means of a college to be erected in the Bermuda Islands. Sir Robert Walpole, then chief minister, opposed the enterprise, but Berkeley persuaded the British government to promise a grant of £20,000 in support of his plans, and, full of enthusiasm and courage, he sailed from Gravesend in September, 1728, expecting to found the college and assume its presidency. He reached Newport, Rhode Island, late in January, 1729, where he bought a farm, erected upon it a small house, engaged in correspondence and study, composed a philosophical treatise, preached occasionally, and longed in vain for the

Photograph by Baldwin Coolidge   *From the portrait by Smibert*

MRS. McSPARRAN

expected endowment. Finally, wearied by long delays and reluctantly convinced that Walpole had no intention of giving him the promised support, Berkeley gave up his residence in Newport and set sail for home, embarking at Boston in September, 1731, just three years after his departure from England.

Smibert, who was to have been professor of fine arts in Berkeley's projected college, was born in Edinburgh in 1684. The son of a well-to-do tradesman, tradition has it that he was destined by his pious-minded father for the ministry, but early evinced so strong a taste for drawing that he was allowed to follow the profession of an artist. Smibert studied his art in Lon-

don and then passed some years in Italy. Returning to England he became a portrait painter in London and, in 1729, as before stated, he came to America with Bishop Berkeley. He painted for some months in Newport, and when the Bermuda enterprise was abandoned settled in Boston. When Berkeley was made Bishop of Cloyne in 1734 he asked Smibert to join him in Ireland, but the painter, who in the meantime had won the heart and hand of Mary Williams, a rich American widow, declined his patron's invitation and lived in Boston, prosperous and contented, until his death in 1751.

Smibert's most important American work is the painting of Berkeley and his family, executed in Boston in the autumn of 1731, and presented to Yale

College in 1808. Besides the Berkeley group, there are said to be more than thirty Smiberts, about half of them well authenticated, scattered about New England and the Middle States. The portrait of Judge Edmund Quincy in the Boston Museum of Fine Arts and that of John Lowell in Harvard Memorial Hall are characteristic examples of Smibert's art. As paintings, pure and simple, they have small value. Executed with a dry brush and in severely formal style, they are cold, stiff and hard, but they are, undoubtedly, good literal likenesses of their subjects.

When Smibert landed in America, another Scotch painter, John Watson, had been plying his brush for nearly fifteen years in the Province of New Jersey. Watson, of whose early life we have no record, except that he was born in 1685, came to the colonies in 1715, and settled at Perth Amboy, which then promised to become a thriving commercial centre. There he, in due time, built a home and lived and painted until the ripe age of eighty-three. "I remember well," writes William Dunlap, himself a native of Perth Amboy, "the child's wonder that was caused in my early life by the appearance of the house this artist once owned, for he was then dead, and the tales that were told of the limner in answer to the questions asked. His dwelling house had been pulled down, but a smaller building which adjoined it, and which had been his painting and picture house, remained, and attracted attention by the heads of sages, heroes, and kings. The window shutters were divided into squares, and each square presented the head of a man or woman in antique costume, the men with beards and helmets, or crowns. In answer to my questions I was told that the painter had been considered a miser and usurer—words of dire portent—probably meaning that he was a prudent, perhaps a wise man, who lived plainly and lent the excess of his revenue to those who wanted it and could give good security for principal and interest." In other words, the Perth Amboy limner seems to have been endowed with the proverbial thrift of his race. None of Watson's portraits in oil has come down to us, but there still exist a number of miniature sketches in India ink made by him and including a series of drawings of himself at different ages, which evince considerable skill in draughtsmanship.

When Smibert and Watson came to America, another foreign-born painter had for several years been plying his art in Philadelphia. This was Gustavus Hesselius, a native of Sweden, born in 1682, who arrived in the colonies in 1711. After residing for several years in Philadelphia and Wilmington, Hesselius removed to Queen Anne's Parish, Maryland, and for its parish church of St. Barnabas painted, in 1721, an elaborate altar-piece of the "Last Supper," which long since disappeared, but which was, past question, the first work of art for a public building executed in America. In 1735 Hesselius returned to Philadelphia, where he lived and painted until his death in 1782. Some of his authenticated portraits now find a fitting home in the Historical Society of Pennsylvania. Refined in color and in treatment skilful, they show that he was a painter of no mean ability for his time, and easily the superior of either Smibert or Watson.

COL. JONATHAN WARNER

Jonathan B. Blackburn was a better painter than Smibert, Watson or perhaps Hesselius. There is reason to believe that he was born in Connecticut about 1700, and if this assumption is correct, he was the first native American painter of real ability. Blackburn settled in Boston about the time that Pelham and Smibert died, and remained there some fifteen years. When Copley's work began to receive more attention than his own, Blackburn removed from the town, but left upwards of fifty portraits behind him. These are now in various public collections and in private hands. Blackburn's finely modeled portrait of Colonel Jonathan Warner in the Boston Museum of Fine Arts shows this painter at his best. Quiet in tone and thinly painted in neutral colors, it has about it an unmistakable air of distinction. The pose is proud and assured, the costume handsome, the expression masterful. Copleys hang beside it on the wall and they look as if they had been painted by the same hand. Nothing is known of Blackburn's career after his departure from Boston in 1765.

The lives of two of Blackburn's contemporaries, John Greenwood and Robert Feke, with whom he must often have touched elbows, are also shrouded in obscurity. Greenwood's name appears as one of the appraisers of

From the painting by Benjamin West

THE WITCH OF ENDOR

Smibert's estate,—the latter left property valued at £1,387, a snug fortune for his time,—and a portrait of Rev. Thomas Prince, painted by him, was engraved by Pelham in 1750. He is believed to have been the son of Samuel Greenwood, a Boston merchant, and to have been born in that city in 1727, to have left America before the Revolution, and, after a short stay in India, to have settled in London as an auctioneer, dying at Margate in 1792. All this, however, is conjectural and none of Greenwood's portraits are now believed to be in existence.

Robert Feke is thought to have been born of Quaker parents at Oyster Bay, Long Island, in 1724. He left home when young, and is said to have learned to paint in Spain, whither he had been taken as a prisoner. With the proceeds of the rude paintings he had made in prison, he returned home and became a portrait painter, working in turn in Newport, New York, and Philadelphia. His first pictures bear date 1746. He died in the Bermuda Islands, where he had gone for his health, about 1769. Peke's portraits are in the Bowdoin College collection and in that of the Rhode Island Historical Society at Providence. He was a man of undoubted talent; and his quaint, yet charming, portrait of Lady Wanton, wife of the last royal governor of Rhode Island, now in the Redwood Library at Newport is a fine example of what he might have accomplished in his art, had his life been more favorably ordered.

While Blackburn, Greenwood and

From the painting by Benjamin West

THE BATTLE OF HAGUE

Feke were painting in New England and Watson in New Jersey, in the colony of Pennsylvania two other men, John Valentine Haidt and Benjamin West, the former among the Moravians and the latter among the Quakers, were playing a not unworthy part in the creation of American art. Haidt was born in Dantzic in 1700, and lived in Berlin where his father was court jeweler. He was carefully educated and later studied painting in Venice, Rome, Paris and London. At the age of forty, after a somewhat turbulent youth and early manhood, he joined the Moravians and devoted himself to painting portraits of their clergy and pictures dealing mostly with sacred subjects. He came to America in 1740, was ordained a deacon of the Moravian church, and preached through the middle colonies as an evangelist, at the same time continuing to paint. His last years were spent in Bethlehem where, in 1770, "he gave his soul to God."

A gallery of Haidt's portraits and several of his other pictures are still preserved at Bethlehem. These are painted in the dry, formal manner of the German painters of his time, but they show considerable feeling for color and borrow charm from the quaint and picturesque dress of their subjects, white caps and collars for the women, loosely flowing robes for the men; and an hour spent in their study aids not a little in reconstructing one of the least known but most admirable chapters in the history of the middle colonies.

The name of Benjamin West is one held in honored remembrance by every lover of art. Born at Springfield, now Swarthmore, Pennsylvania,

on October 10, 1738, West was a descendant on his mother's side of Thomas Pierson, a trusted friend of William Penn, and both his parents were sincere and self-respecting Quakers. Before he was six years old West never saw a picture or an engraving, but his placid life absorbed the beauty of nature, and the first expression of his talent was in the picture of a sleeping child drawn at this age. West's first instruction in art was given him by William Williams, a sign painter in Philadelphia who occasionally executed portraits, and his first attempt at portraiture was in Lancaster, Pennsylvania, where he painted "The Death of Socrates" for William Henry, a gunsmith. He was not yet sixteen years of age, but other paintings followed which possessed so much genuine merit that they have been preserved as treasures. In 1756, when he was eighteen years old, he established himself as a portrait-painter in Philadelphia, his price being "five guineas a head." Two years later he went to New York, where he passed eleven months and painted many portraits, after which he decided to visit Europe in order to improve himself in his art.

West arrived in Italy in July, 1760, and spent about three years in study, divided between Rome, Florence and Parma, "very profitable and enjoyable years," he called them. From Parma he proceeded to Genoa and thence to Turin, later visiting in turn Leghorn, Venice and Lucca. The art treasures of France next claimed his attention for a brief period, and finally in August, 1763, he reached London. It was then his purpose, after a few months spent in England, to return to

THE DEATH OF GENERAL WOLFE

From the painting by Benjamin West

35

From the painting by *Benjamin West*

QUEEN CHARLOTTE AND HER THIRTEEN CHILDREN

America but this plan was destined never to be fulfilled. A portrait and picture painted for the exhibition of 1764, brought him numerous patrons and induced his permanent settlement in London.

As West settled down to the new life, mingling the delights of his art with the pleasures of society, his thoughts went out to the sweetheart he had left behind him in the New World, Elizabeth Shewell, an orphan girl, residing with her brother in Philadelphia. This brother, an ambitious man, urged her to marry a wealthy suitor, but she refused, having already pledged her vows to West. Thereafter a close watch was kept upon the girl and orders given to the servants to refuse admittance to West if he ever came to the door. For five years Elizabeth waited; then, assisted by friends watching within and without, she descended a rope ladder from the window of her room, was hurried into a waiting carriage and driven rapidly to a wharf where a ship was ready to sail for England. The father of West received her, cared for her during the voyage, and delivered her to the eager lover who came aboard the ship at

From a portrait by Lawrence

BENJAMIN WEST

Liverpool. Upon their arrival in London they went at once to the church of St. Martins-in-the-Field, and were married. Mrs. West soon became known in London as "the beautiful American." Her letters, still in the possession of the family, breathe only of the kindness of all she met. West sent a portrait of his wife as a peace offering to her brother, who never looked at it, but had it stored away in the garret of his house. One of his grandchildren remembers having beaten with a switch the portrait of his "naughty aunty," who smiled upon the children playing in the attic where she had gone to weep, a lovelorn maid,—smiled upon them from her calm estate of wedded bliss in England.

West's long career in England.—he died in 1820, and sleeps in St. Paul's Cathedral, London,—gave him fame as an historical painter that made him President of the Royal Academy. But it is in his portraits that he is seen at his best. Here he sometimes challenges comparison with the ablest painters of his time and his portrait of Robert Fulton, now in the possession of one of the latter's descendants, is, both in conception and execution, a

From the painting by Benjamin West

PETER DENYING CHRIST

wholly admirable work, dignified, moving and full of charm. Praise not less hearty can be given to the family group painted by West soon after the birth of his first child, in which the beautiful young mother with tender solicitude shows her baby to the visiting grandfather and uncle, while the artist, brush and palette in hand, proudly surveys the scene from behind his father's chair. The grouping is natural and unconstrained, while the white robes of the mother and child afford a pleasing contrast to the sober gray in which the male figures are garbed, and lend effectiveness to a delicate and harmonious color scheme. Feeling and sincerity are apparent in every brush stroke of this charming composition, which shows where, had he followed it, lay the painter's true forte and his strongest claims to greatness.

Despite his long residence in London, West's love for America never waned, and his fellow countrymen.

38

when they sought him out in London, always found him a wise counselor and an unfaltering friend. The elder and the younger Peale, Fulton, Trumbull, Stuart, Allston, Sully and White were his pupils, and nearly all of the American painters of his time were his debtors in more ways than one.

One of West's first American pupils was Matthew Pratt, a gifted painter, who even in his lifetime seems to have fallen into unmerited neglect. Pratt. who was West's senior by four years, was the son of a Philadelphia goldsmith. Born September 23, 1734, Pratt early showed an inclination for drawing and at the age of fifteen was apprenticed to his uncle James Claypoole, "limner and painter in general," from whom, to use his own words, he "learned all branches of the painting business, particularly portrait-painting, which was my favorite study from ten years of age."

In 1764, four years after his marriage, Pratt went to London to study under West. His aunt had married the uncle of Elizabeth Shewell, West's future wife, and his voyage to London was made in company with that lady and the elder West. When the marriage ceremony of the reunited lovers was performed at St. Martins-in-the-Field, Pratt attended and gave away the bride. For two years and a half he lived with the Wests and was the husband's first pupil. While studying under West, Pratt painted his first figure composition, "The American School," which was exhibited in London in 1766, at the seventh exhibition

MATTHEW PRATT'S PORTRAIT OF HIMSELF

of the old Spring Gardens. This picture remained in the possession of Pratt's descendants until 1896, when it was acquired by Samuel P. Avery, who has placed it in the Metropolitan Museum of Art. It represents West's studio, with the artist instructing his pupils. The composition is good, the execution excellent and the color scheme pleasing and skillfully handled. As a whole and remembering the fact that it was painted by an American who had had less than a year's study in London, it is a remarkable work.

In the spring of 1768, Pratt returned to Philadelphia and, resuming his professional career, made that city his home until his death in 1805. Scores of Pratt's portraits are scattered through the Middle States, and many canvases cherished by their owners as the work of Copley came, in all probability, from the easel of Pratt. His

THE AMERICAN SCHOOL

portraits show knowledge of character and the ability to portray it, a refined feeling for color and a knowledge of values surprising in a painter of his period. His posing was often artificial, but that was in keeping with the taste and custom of his time, while his modeling was delicate, yet clear, and his drawing always careful and correct. At his best he was the equal and in some respects the superior of West and Copley.*

John Smibert's American wife bore him four sons. The youngest of these, Nathaniel, showed great talent in portraiture and "had his life been spared," writes one who knew him, "he would have been in his day the honor of America in imitative art." Smibert's

* The author begs to acknowledge his obligation to Mr. Charles Henry Hart for interesting details of the career of Matthew Pratt.

portrait of Dorothy Wendell, now owned by Dr. Josiah L. Hale, of Boston, in a measure confirms this prediction, but he died in 1756 at the early age of twenty-two, and his place was taken by John Singleton Copley, whose name concludes the list of the colonial painters. Copley was born in Boston in 1737, the son of Richard Copley and Mary Singleton. His father came to America from Ireland in 1736, and died in the West Indies, where he had gone for his health, about the time of the birth of his son. Eleven years later the widow married Peter Pelham, by whom she had one son. Copley began to draw when a child, but his studies were attended with every disadvantage. From his association with his stepfather, Pelham, and the latter's friend, the elder Smibert, he must have gained a tolerable knowledge of the painter's tools, and it is also possible that later he obtained some useful hints from Blackburn, but, according to his own account of his artistic career, he received no regular instruction and never saw a good picture until after he left America at the age of thirty-seven. He had neither teacher nor model, and the very colors on his palette, as well

step-father, Pelham, had died three years before, leaving his widow to the care of her sons; and how tenderly Copley discharged his share of the trust imposed in him is shown by passages in his letters, in which he mentions his reluctance to leave his mother as an objection to his going to Europe, and again in his unwearied care for her

JOHN SINGLETON COPLEY'S PORTRAIT OF HIMSELF

as the brush he handled, are said to have been of his own making.

However, nature had not only endowed Copley with persevering industry, but with rare feeling for the beauty and charm of color, and he made such steady progress that at the age of seventeen,—some of his pictures bear date 1753,—we find him regularly established as a portrait painter. His

comfort when circumstances finally induced him to leave America. In 1766, when Copley was twenty-nine years old, he sent to Benjamin West in London, but without name or address, a portrait of his half-brother, Henry Pelham, known as "The Boy and the Flying Squirrel," requesting that it be placed in the exhibition rooms of the Society of Incorporated Artists. West, delighted with the portrait, conjectured from the squirrel and the wood upon which the canvas was stretched, that it was the work of an American, and, although it was contrary to the rules of the Society to place an unsigned picture on its walls, secured its admission to the next exhibition of that body. .

In 1777 Copley visited New York and painted in that city for some months. Before that, however, his fame as a painter had become general, and for years people had come from all parts of New England to have their portraits painted by him. A calm, deliberate and methodical workman, he never hurried and never neglected any part of his task. "He painted," as Gilbert Stuart said in after years, "the whole man." But if Copley was slow, he was industrious, for three hundred portraits were painted by him between 1754 and 1774, most of which are in or near Boston to-day; and, although his prices were modest, by 1769, when he married Susannah Farnum Clarke, daughter of Richard Clarke—a leading Boston merchant, famous in after years as the consignee of the cargoes of tea which provoked the historic "tea party"—and a woman remarkable alike for her beauty and her worth, he was in comfortable circumstances. Colonel John Trumbull, who visited Copley two years after his marriage, described him as "living in a beautiful house on a fine, open common; attired in a crimson velvet suit, laced with gold, and having everything about him in very handsome style."

In 1774 Copley carried out a long cherished but oft postponed desire to visit Europe. The outbreak of the Revolution intervened to prevent his return to America, and, being joined by his family, he took up his residence in London, where he lived and painted with honor and profit until his death in 1815. His widow, surviving him twenty-one years, lived to see their son in the flush of the career that made him Lord Chancellor and a member of the English peerage.

It was Copley's own belief that his best work as a painter was done in America, and in this opinion the thoughtful student of his portraits now in the Boston Museum of Fine Arts and in the Harvard Memorial Hall cannot fail to concur. They are never commonplace and the handling is always unmistakable. Self taught, Copley's merits and faults are his own. Superior as a colorist to a majority of his contemporaries, he delighted in the brilliant and massive uniforms, the brocades and embroidered velvets, the rich laces and scarves of his day, and painted them, and the masterful men and stately women which they garbed, with sure and loving hand. He modeled a head with as much care as did Clouet, and he was especially felicitous in catching the expression of the eye, while his skill in rendering the individuality and character of the hand has seldom been excelled. "Prick that hand," said Gilbert Stuart of the hand in one of Copley's portraits, "and blood will spurt out."

Copley's faults as a painter are an occasional tendency to dryness, to hardness of outline and to stiffness in his figures. However, distinction is never lacking in his work and in his best portraits, like those of Hancock and Adams in the Boston Museum of Fine Arts, of the Boylston family in Harvard Memorial Hall and of Lady

By John Singleton Copley

KING CHARLES I. DEMANDING THE FIVE IMPEACHED MEMBERS

Wentworth in the Lenox Library, New York, the faults I have mentioned are hardly apparent. Indeed, the truth, simplicity, repose and refinement of the portraits named would have done credit to any painter of any time, and, painted as they were by a young man who never had a teacher, and who saw few, if any, good pictures save his own until he was forty years of age, they are bound to remain the marvels of our pioneer art.

Copley was essentially a portrait painter and his historical and religious pictures—an admirable example of his work in this field, "Charles I. Demanding the Surrender of the Impeached Members at the Bar of the House of Commons," hangs in the Boston Public Library—though showing no mean ability, are wanting in im- agination, and, at their best, are little more than groups of carefully executed portraits. Still, considered solely as a portrait painter, Copley's fame is secure. No painter, not even Holbein or Velasquez, ever lived in closer sympathy with the spirit of his time than did he.

Thus closes the record of the colonial painters, a study of whose efforts teaches anew the familiar lesson that the day of small things is ever worthy of respect. In the face of sore discouragements but with faith and enthusiasm, they did their work and builded better than they knew, for no human effort, however modest, is wasted and these pioneers, humbly and often blindly, hewed the way for an art that is to become the glory and the wonder of the world.

The Pilot

By Mary Hall Leonard

A NIGHT of storm! Both Faith and Hope were failing
    And even Love grew pallid with affright.
Then calm Obedience rose with brow unquailing,
    And guided safely till the morning light.

The Lesser Tragedy

By Grant Richardson

"HOW many this morning, Connors?" asked Lieutenant Sterrett, the officer in charge of the New York Recruiting Station, throwing his great coat over the back of a chair.

"Not one, Lieutenant," answered the old sergeant from his desk at which he was patiently filling out with his pen duplicates and triplicates of army reports.

"That's bad," said the lieutenant. "I wanted to get the men started to-night. We haven't had much luck so far. Those we have are not an extra good lot. There isn't the making of a decent 'non-com' among them."

"That's true, sir, the place to pick up good 'rookies' is in the country. New York gives us the worst it has. If I had my way I'd go over to Ireland and pick out a regiment or two in me own county. That's where they raise good sojers, sir."

The lieutenant laughed, and turned to the window that faced the Battery. He musingly watched the distant moving shipping on river and bay, tapping on the window pane with his fingers. The door opened and he turned to see a man standing within. The man was young, and had a tall athletic figure, clad in what had once been fashionable and expensive garments. His pale face was handsome and intellectual, in spite of the marks of dissipation that marred it, and there was pride and good breeding in his bearing; but his eyes were blood-shot, his hand trembled and he was greatly in need of sleep, food and a bath.

"I should like to enlist," he said.

"Step up here," said the sergeant gruffly, picking up a paper. "What's your name?"

"John Roakes," answered the man.

"Where have I seen that chap?" thought Lieutenant Sterrett. "Somewhere I'm sure. At a club or a dance? I've met him in New York, and his name is not Roakes. But no matter, poor devil, he is or once was a gentleman."

"What did you say your name is?" he asked suddenly, turning to the applicant.

"John Roakes," answered the man.

"H-m." said the lieutenant doubtfully. "I thought perhaps it might be something else."

The applicant looked at the lieutenant for a moment without replying. Then he said distinctly, with a force that carried conviction and yet without insolence:

"I said it was John Roakes."

"O, very well, John Roakes it is then." replied Sterrett indifferently, returning to the view of the river.

John Roakes was measured, weighed, punched and sounded, and every mark on his body was registered by the sergeant. He answered questions more or less truthfully, took the oath to defend his country, and passed

43

from the world into the army. That night, together with a dozen or more "rookies," he took a train under the guidance of a grizzled old corporal, and duly arrived at Fort Rincon, on the plains at the foot of the San Jacinto mountains, the most God-forgotten army post in America.

Private Roakes was no sooner in Fort Rincon and into the uniform of Uncle Sam, when he managed to get some smuggled whiskey. Well, he went to the guard house and, as soon as he was sober, to Captain Compton. He looked very well in his uniform, did Private Roakes, but he was not yet a soldier. His tunic was not buttoned at the neck, and was wrinkled from having been slept in. As he entered the captain's presence he carried himself defiantly.

"Now see here, Roakes," said Captain Compton slowly and dispassionately, "I am going to have a little talk with you. I don't know who you are, but I do know that you are a gentleman. No, you must not interrupt me. You are a private soldier of the United States now, and I am your captain. It is my privilege to talk to you as I see fit. I have had men of your stamp in my company before this. You are a man of education, and have probably had more money than was good for you. This is going to be the only real discipline and restraint you have ever known. I am thoroughly sorry for you, and regret the cause of your being in the army as a private, whatever it was, but you are not the first, and will not be the last. A soldier must fight, not one thing but many. You know the thing that you must fight. You can be a good soldier or a bad one. I do not believe it is in your

blood to be a bad one. So far as I may I will help you, but our relative positions are not what they might have been under other circumstances. I wish you to be a good soldier for your own sake, as well as for the sake of Company C, the regiment and the service. I am sure you understand me. If you are in trouble at any time I wish you would come to me."

The captain paused, and the two men looked each other fairly in the eyes. The private understood and, seeing that the interview was at an end, he bowed and withdrew.

"By the way, Whipple," Captain Compton said to his first lieutenant one day, "how is that man Roakes getting on?"

"I never saw his like," answered Lieutenant Whipple. "He is a born soldier. Picked up his work as if he had learned it at West Point. He is cheerful, a hard worker, reserved and gentlemanly, and a great favorite with the men. He does not go near the canteen, and shares everything he has with the men in his quarters. That chap has seen better days."

"I wish you would send him up to me at the first opportunity."

"Very well, I will do so."

When Roakes presented himself in officers' row he was as smart a soldier as there was in the army. Plenty of work and a wholesome diet had wiped the flush and the marks of drink from his face. He unconsciously bore himself like a gentleman, and his uniform fitted his fine athletic figure like a glove. As he went smartly up the walk to Captain Compton's quarters, Major Ransom, who was smoking a cigar on his veranda, looked after him and thought: "That chap has played foot-

ball and danced cotillions, or I'm a
sailor."

Presenting himself to his captain,
Private Roakes saluted and stood at
attention.

"Roakes, I want a 'striker,' and
should be glad if you would come up
here," said the captain. "The fellow I
have is stupid and untidy. There are
plenty of books here that you may use,
and the duties are not severe."

For an instant Roakes felt the full
sting of the degradation of the position
offered him, and he unconsciously
drew himself up with hauteur, but the
mood passed.

"As you wish, sir," he answered.

"Very well," said the captain. He
called a soldier from the next room.
"Murphy, you may instruct Private
Roakes in the duties you have been
performing for me and afterwards report to your sergeant."

"You're lucky," said Murphy,
when the two soldiers had retired from
the room. "The cap'n is the easiest
officer in the service. There's nothing
at all to do. It's all a bluff. All you
got to do is to sit here, and once in a
while carry a note to one of the officers' houses or up to the office. He
won't let you do a thing for him, and
he dines at the officers' club. All you
got to do is to keep his room and the
things in it tidy. I'm a pretty poor
chambermaid myself."

So Roakes became "striker" to his
captain.

He was sitting within call one afternoon, looking out of the window at
Lieutenant Slocum's wife and the
Misses Brierly, who were playing croquet in the next yard. Suddenly he
threw back his head in a bitter, noiseless laugh.

"God," he thought, "who could have
predicted that I would come to this?
What a fool is folly! I cannot stand it
much longer, then down I tumble
again. I have fought it and fought it
well. There it is on the buffet, mine
whenever I stretch out my hand for it.
Ah, how I love it! Better than I loved
her, God bless her, and I loved her
well. God help to keep me strong for
her sake. What a giant is the flesh;
full of pride and the lust of living.
Why cannot I forget it? Every day
have I seen it there, golden brown in
its shining decanter. Every day have
I had it in my hands and put it from
me, and every day has it grown more
difficult to do so." Private Roakes
shook with a great sob that seemed as
if it would tear his heart out.

"What is it, Roakes?" Captain
Compton stood in the doorway.

Roakes sprang to his feet. "I beg
your pardon, sir, nothing," he answered.

"I ask you what is it, Roakes?" the
captain repeated.

Officer and private looked into each
other's eyes as squarely as men ever
looked.

"It's the drink," cried Roakes.
hoarsely. "I cannot help it. I would
rather fight a regiment of devils than
fight it again," he said, trembling. For
a moment Captain Compton hesitated.
Then he turned to the private. his indecision gone.

"Roakes, I am going out and will
not be back to-night," he said. "You
will remain here until I return. You
are at liberty to use anything I have,
but you must give me your word that
you will not leave my quarters without
my permission."

Roakes nodded. standing fast. staring before him like one demented. He heard the captain close the door, cross the veranda and, as the echo of the last footsteps died away on the walk, turned and looked at the buffet on which stood a row of decanters full of the drink he craved.

As the captain walked to Major Ransom's house he thought, "Perhaps I have been a fool after all. But I believe in blood and I think he has it in him."

Private Roakes moved eagerly, with outstretched, quivering hands, to the buffet. His face was as white as his collar, and his eyes gleamed and glared. His trembling hand reached out and grasped the vessel that held his ruin. He shook it between his eyes and the light, watching the fires in it. Pouring the liquor into a tumbler, so fast that it choked and gurgled in the neck of the decanter, he shook it with impatience, as a child might, to make it run faster. Only when the tumbler was full to the brim did he set the decanter down. Then he raised the glass slowly to his lips.

"No!" he shouted, and threw the brimming tumbler into a corner. Staggering to a chair he buried his face in his hands and cried like a frightened child.

"I have won! I have won!" he cried over and over again.

Darkness came on; the hours slipped into midnight and so into the dawn, and still Roakes sat immovable. "If *she* were only here," he moaned. "She is all out of the past that I want back, and I drove her from me. Ah, dear heart, how I love you now, and ever have. And now I know that you loved me, dear wife of mine. God forgive me! God forgive me! But I have fought the fight, and now I want you back, my wife."

He did not hear the guard passing around the house trying the doors, nor did he hear the entrance of Captain Compton, who now stood in the doorway, framed in the glaring sunshine of the morning.

"Roakes! Roakes!"

"Here, sir." Roakes sprank to his feet. His face was pale with his vigil, but his eyes were clear and frank, honest and joyous.

"O, I thought you were asleep," muttered the captain, retreating to his room. His quick eye had seen the broken glass in the corner and the splash on the wall. Out of the captain's room came a happy, tuneless whistle. In a moment he returned to where Roakes stood.

"Your hand, Roakes," he said.

For a moment the eyes of these two met again as they clasped hands, each valuing the other as man to man.

It was not long after this that the private became Corporal, and then Sergeant Roakes. Captain Compton urged him to study for a commission, but Roakes demurred.

"Thank you, Captain, but I would rather not. I have very good reasons for not wishing to do so."

"Very well, Sergeant," the captain said, "but you could pass easily, I am sure. You have already mastered all the technical books I have, and the rest is easy. I believe that I could asssure you a welcome out of the ranks. But perhaps you know better than I."

Lieutenant Sterrett had been relieved of recruiting and other detached duties, and had in the meantime rejoined his company at Fort Rincon. One day, as he and Lieutenant Whipple were crossing the parade, Sergeant Roakes passed them.

"By Jove," said Sterrett, "that looks like a man I enlisted in New York under the name of Roakes."

"Yes," replied Whipple, "that is Roakes, and he is the best man you ever took into the service. I should be glad if he'd try for a commission. He's worth it, every inch of him, but he steadily refuses to do so for some reason or other."

"And I know why," said Sterrett. "Come to my quarters and I'll tell you all about it. It's not a bad story, if it isn't exactly new."

"Now in the first place," Sterrett said, after they had made themselves comfortable, "his name is not Roakes, it is Howard. Do you remember the mysterious disappearance from New York of Jack Howard about a year ago? It was the sensation of the day. All sorts of stories gained publicity; that he had committed suicide; that he had gone to Australia; that he had been murdered, and all that sort of thing."

"No," Whipple replied with a sigh. "Nothing ever penetrates the confines of Rincon except family letters and general orders."

"Well, you see," continued Sterrett, "this chap Howard was no end of a swell. Belonged to two of the oldest families in New York. His mother was a Courtney, sister to Lawrence Courtney. Young Howard was pretty wild. He was expelled from college for an outrage committed by some other men. He refused to 'peach' on them and they would not come forward and exculpate him. This made him more reckless than ever. His father was dreadfully cut up over his

expulsion from the university, of which he himself was an honored alumnus and a trustee, and after refusing to listen to any explanation, packed the young man off to travel for a year.

"In Egypt he met a beautiful Baltimore girl traveling with her father. That winter there was a sumptuous wedding in Baltimore with special trains full of society folk from New York. The Howards went away on the father's yacht to be gone a year, but were back in six months on a liner. The gossips said that Jack drank and neglected his wife.

"They settled down to life in New York and were great favorites. Mrs. Howard was admired for her beauty, her wit and her tact. Jack became the best known man about town. He belonged to the clubs, his horses won blue ribbons, his yacht cups, but—there can be no doubt that he neglected his wife, although unquestionably it had been a love match.

"One day his father died, leaving Jack a very tidy fortune, but the bulk of the estate went to the two girls, the mother being dead. After a decent period of mourning, Jack Howard, who had never forgotten his father's injustice, went back to his former habits, and figured in many an escapade, Then Mrs. Howard left New York and after a while it was announced that she had taken her maiden name. I knew what it was at one time, but it has escaped my memory. But, no matter.

"After that he went down hill fast. He settled a large share of his remaining fortune on his divorced wife, however. One day the papers announced him bankrupt; but he paid every dollar he owed and was left without a penny. His sisters offered him a small income which he refused. Then came his disappearance..

"One morning a man walked into the New York recruiting station and asked to be enlisted. The moment I looked at him I was convinced he was giving a false name and that I had seen him before,—where I did not know. That night I started him out here, and the next morning the newspapers were full of the accounts of the disappearance of Jack Howard, the society man whose extravagances had ruined him. There were portraits of Howard in the newspapers, and then I knew that Roakes was Howard, and that I had met him at a dinner one night at the Army and Navy Club, and had been charmed by his wit and good fellowship. Of course I kept the matter of his enlistment to myself and we three, Roakes, and you and I, are the only persons who know what became of Jack Howard."

As Sterrett leaned back in his chair and resumed his pipe and glass after his story, Whipple sighed and said:

"And the secret shall remain with us, and he shall never know that he is other to us than Roakes."

"Done," said Sterrett.

Shortly after Sterrett's return to duty at the post, Captain Compton stopped Roakes and said:

"Roakes, I am going away on leave in a few days; in short I am to be married. I am to have the new quarters at the end of the Sheridan road, and am having a lot of new furniture sent out from Chicago. I have asked the commandant that you be detailed to receive my things and prepare the house against my return. Employ such men and women as you need to do the work, but I am particularly anxious to avail

myself of your good taste in seeing that the house is made ship-shape, so that Mrs. Compton may not come to a disordered home."

"It will be a great pleasure, sir," said Roakes. "May I ask how long you will be absent?"

"My leave is only for a month."

"Very well, sir, I. will do my best."

The month passed quickly, but long before it came to an end the house was furnished and fitted, even to the Captain's striker in the hall, a cook in the kitchen, a maid upstairs and supplies in the larder.

Meantime Company C to a man had subscribed of their pay; Roakes had telegraphed to a jeweller in New York and in due time Company C's wedding gift arrived. It was a massive silver punch bowl of military pattern, engraved with an appropriate inscription and a set of cut glass cups, in which the whole garrison might toast the bride.

The Captain and Mrs. Compton came in the night from Soldier Creek. The four ambulance mules, decorated with bride's favors, galloped up the Sheridan road between two lines of cheering soldiers to the new quarters. The captain, from the doorway, thanked his men for their welcome, and sent them to the canteen to drink his wife's health.

The following evening, Sergeant Roakes, with a half dozen soldiers bearing the punch bowl, went to Captain Compton's quarters. Roakes had been delegated, much against his will, to deliver Company C's gift, and to present the congratulations of the men.

"Sergeant Roakes!" announced the striker.

"Show Sergeant Roakes in," said the Captain.

Roakes entered the parlor, saluted and was cordially greeted by the Captain. At the other end of the room Roakes observed a woman sitting before the hearth, with her chin in her hand, gazing into the fire.

"Captain," said Roakes, "I have been asked by the enlisted men of Company C to present to you their hearty congratulations on your marriage, and their respectful assurance of their homage to your wife, and to present you with a slight token of their devotion to you and in remembrance of the occasion. I believe you know my feelings too well, Captain, for me to add anything in my own behalf."

When he began to speak the woman at the fire looked up with a start. She leaned forward, a look of horror coming into her eyes. The soldier at the other end of the room talked steadily on. His face was in the deep shadow cast by the thick crimson shade on the lamp and through it she could see only the blur of his shaven face and the dark, close cropped hair above it. Her staring eyes were striving to pierce the gloom between them searching for something she dreaded to find. She passed her cold fingers across her forehead and gave a shuddering little gasp. Then a wan smile loosened the tense rigidity that bound the muscles of her mouth. She shook her head and seemed to toss off the fear that had come upon her.

"Impossible!" she muttered.

But she continued to stare into the shadowy vagueness that engulfed the other end of the room, vainly searching for the soldier's features. Other men entered, bearing between them the punch bowl, which they placed upon the table and withdrew. Then her husband began to speak formally to the tall soldier before him, thanking his company for its gift, and she took advantage of it to leave the room.

Roakes stood at attention listening to his captain, his eyes fixed on a broad band of light that shone into the far end of the room through an open doorway. His soul expanded in appreciation of the warmth, the color, the daintiness and the strangely familiar perfume of the room. It conveyed to him the presence, the very soul of a woman. His thoughts were on another room he had known, and the woman who had glorified it. Now he felt the spirit, the essence of that woman, and his soul was lulled and at rest.

Across that broad band of light which he was looking moved the slender, beautiful figure of Anita Compton. Roakes staggered, his eyes dilated and his face went white to the lips. In a moment his body resumed the rigid pose of the soldier at attention, but his fingers, the muscles hard and knotted, slowly opened and closed beside the broad yellow band of his cavalry breeches.

Mrs. Compton passed through the doorway and was gone, but in that moment Roakes had met and accepted the punishment Fate had dealt him. Slowly his eyes sought the face of his captain, and in them was, for the first time, fear, indecision, and hate also. The captain, who was not much given to speechmaking, stood with eyes cast to the floor, searching his mind for words, so that he had not observed the agitation of the private. Upstairs, with the door of her bedroom locked behind her, Anita Compton sat at the window looking into the night. Her brain throbbed painfully and she repeated to herself, monotonously: "It cannot be Jack. No, it is not Jack. But the voice was so like his." And thus she assured herself and wept softly, and soon grew calmer and slept with her head pillowed on her arms.

Out into the night went Roakes, the voice of his captain ringing in his ears, the face of his captain's wife before his eyes. He passed a word or two with the sentry at the bridge near the canteen and left the post behind him, setting out across the prairie with long rapid strides. Soon his steps grew heavy and slow, his body shrank and collapsed within itself, and with a low cry, in which was concentrated all the agony and despair in a man's life, he cast himself upon the ground and buried his white face in the grass, his body heaving with noiseless sobs.

Above, the eternal stars flashed and glittered unheeded by him. Around him sweet winds breathed softly through the grasses. A vagrant prairie wolf picking its way cautiously across the plain got to leeward of him and stopped, with paw raised and nostrils quivering, and eyes that burned yellow in the darkness.

Roakes stirred. "'Nita, 'Nita," he moaned.

At the sound of his voice the wolf scurried off a few yards, sat upon its haunches and howled. As if terrified by its own mournful call it turned tail and fled into the dark. The soldier at the bridge paused in his weary pacing at the sound and looked out across the prairie to where the mountains showed even blacker against the velvet black of the night.

It was evening. The band was playing in front of the Colonel's quarters and the officers' wives made gayly colored groups on the verandas and lawns of the row. The barracks were almost deserted and privates sprawled on the grass, smoking and chatting, while at one end of the parade the baseball club was languidly practising. The weather was heavy and sultry and broad sheets of lightning played on the southeastern horizon. The zenith was sulphur yellow. A storm was slowly making behind the hills.

Sergeant Roakes came out of his quarters to witness the dying of the day. The purpling night was descending, and faint sounds of laughter came to him from across the parade. A single star blazed in the southwest, and he looked at it for several minutes, his pale lips moving as if in prayer. He cast a long look around the post,—at the barracks, the parade, and the long line of officers' houses, faced by a row of tall, slender, dark cottonwood trees that stood like sentinels; at every familiar object in the scene. Then he turned and went within.

Captain and Mrs. Compton sat on their veranda with Lieutenant Whipple and Lieutenant Sterrett, who had called. They were all laughing gayly at an army story of Whipple's. A dark figure ran swiftly across the parade and Corporal Dunphy stumbled up the steps.

"Beg pardon, Cap'n," he gasped. "Sergeant Roakes has shot himself. He was cleaning his revolver in the barracks and—"

Mrs. Compton's laughter died away on the instant. "Poor fellow," she murmured, sympathetically, "I hope he is not badly hurt." Her hand fell affectionately on her husband's sleeve.

"I wish you two would go and learn what has happened. I suppose it is nothing serious," said the captain.

Whipple and Sterrett hurried down the steps with Dunphy at their heels.

"It's dead, he is," whispered Dunphy as they walked rapidly across the parade.

"How did it happen?" asked Whipple.

"He was out all night, sir," replied the corporal. "This mornin' he came back to quarters lookin' like a dead man; pale, blood-shot eyes and wet with the dew. All the day he's been sittin' on the edge of his bunk starin' at the floor like one that's daft. Just before dark he went out and looked about for a minute, and when he come in he took down his revolver. I kept my eye on him because I didn't like the way he was actin', but he was only cleaning the piece, so I paid no more attention to him. I had walked to the door when I heard the revolver go off, and ran back. I picked him up and he looked at me and said 'Nita,' and died."

The officers stopped short. "Whipple," said Sterrett, "do you happen to know Mrs. Compton's maiden name?"

"Yes," replied Whipple; "the wedding cards gave it Anita Robertson."

They stared at one another, comprehending.

"Poor fellow," muttered Whipple. "After all, he has chosen the lesser tragedy."

Strangers

By Emma Playter Seabury

HAND in hand, and day by day,
　　They trod the paths of life and care,
And lonely each their burden bore;
They greeted in the heavenly way,
But did not know each other there,—
Their souls had never met before.

Old Blue Plates

A. T. Spalding

THE children who were playing in John Sadler's yard in Liverpool, England, about 1750, little thought of the pictures they would help perpetuate, and the pleasure they would give thousands of people at their meals. Mr. Sadler was a potter, and the broken pieces of pitchers, mugs and plates often fell to the children's share as their toys, when they chose to play keep house. His little folks were great favorites with other children, who enjoyed these wonderful bits of ware which were arranged in the yard on make-believe shelves and tables; and great entertainments were given with these treasures.

One day when they had a few rude pictures given them, not half so pretty as any child can now pick up on cards and advertisements, they took these prints and wet them and stuck them on to the broken pieces of crockery for ornament. Mr. Sadler, passing through the yard, saw an impression which had come off upon a piece of a pitcher; and the idea occurred to him of printing on pottery instead of making the designs by hand. That evening he pondered on the matter, and more and more it seemed to him possible; and if possible, what a valuable invention it might prove! The next morning, bright and early, he communicated the new idea to Guy Green, a printer, well known to him, as Green had been formerly in the employ of Sadler's father. After a few experiments, the process of printing the picture from a copper-plate and pressing the impression on the surface of the ware, became very easy. In August, 1756, Messrs. Sadler and Green certified that on the 27th of July, in six hours, without help, they printed upward of twenty-two hundred tiles of different patterns, which would have cost months and months of patient labor by the old method.

These printers, after that time, did a very extensive business in printing for other potters. Much ware made at the celebrated Wedgwood establishment was sent to Liverpool to be printed by Sadler and Green. For some time these ingenious men kept their own secret with respect to the process, and made their exclusive business very profitable. But after a while other potters learned to do the same thing, and printed ware became very common. Pictures of historical and noted events, of public persons, or illustrations of popular books became transferred to pitchers, mugs, jugs, plates and dishes of all kinds. Political preferences imprinted themselves on wares by pictures and doggerel rhyme, and many a droll caricature found a place there.

Before the end of the last century the trade of the United States with China had assumed considerable importance; and beautiful specimens of Oriental porcelain owned by families in this country date back more than a hundred years. This is especially true in the larger towns on our seacoast, but not confined to them, for rare pieces found in the more rural districts show how early the taste for ornament came to our fathers and mothers, after the first hard struggle for subsistence.

In a biographical sketch of the late Rev. Dr. Sweetser of Worcester, Massachusetts, it is mentioned that his grandfather was a captain of artillery before the war of the Revolution. On the morning of the battle of Bunker Hill, Captain Frothingham came to his house in Charlestown, and said to his wife: "I must go to the cannon, but I have engaged a man with a cart and oxen to take you out of town." The brave woman, after seeing the cart loaded with all the necessary articles that could be taken away, started with her five children, the oldest only about nine years of age, walking by the side of the cart, and carrying in one hand a bag of bread and in the other some china wrapped in a cloth.

Among our earliest recollections of more than one household connected with our family are those of beautiful china which antedated the Revolution, almost as thin as an egg-shell in some instances, very vivid in coloring, in others with a delicate tracery, with double handles on creamers and pitchers crossed and terminating in leaves of most graceful indentures; high-shouldered tea-caddies, with sides and covers of marvellous designs; punch-bowls generous in size, and often gorgeons in ornamentation. No tea tastes to us as did that from these tiny old fashioned tea-cups used in our younger days by other generations, and no plates of modern decoration seem half so choice and inviting with us; no ceramic treasures are as jealously guarded as are the remains of some of these old

sets of china which belonged to revered relatives of four or five generations back.

During the eighteenth century Liverpool had several noted potters, among whom were Richard Chaffers, James Drinkwater, Richard Abbey and John Sadler. Richard Chaffers made important discoveries in the use of Cornish clays for pottery. An interesting story is told of his perseverance in going out with his men to find the kaoline clay, which, from certain indications, he felt sanguine of finding in Cornwall. After apparently useless expenditure of toil and money, he had concluded to relinquish the search, and return home with the feeling of a disappointed adventurer. He paid off his men, and was about starting on his way back, when a hail storm overtook him, and he retraced his steps to a rough shed which had been erected for shelter during their expedition, when one of his men came running toward him with a piece of the coveted clay as the result of his boring. It proved to be finer, softer and better adapted to take color than the hard-paste clay then in use; and the art of pottery in England was much indebted to his discovery.

After the Revolutionary war, American shipmasters carried many orders to Liverpool for patriotic designs to be executed on mugs, jugs and pitchers, and other articles of table ware. Almost every family felt that the possession of a Washington pitcher was a token of gratitude due to "The Father of Our Country." It is remarkable how well a certain kind of likeness to each other is preserved in these rude impressions of Washington, whether in the finer or coarser material. Many of these pitchers were made between 1790

THE LANDING OF THE PILGRIMS

and 1800; and on the death of Washington several designs were labeled, "Washington in Glory," or "America in Tears," with appropriate scenes and devices. Pictures of Thomas Jefferson, Benjamin Franklin, John Hancock, Samuel Adams, and other patriots were also printed on pitchers. About twenty varieties of these Washington pitchers are familiar to us, many of them bearing verses in which the patriotism is better than the poetry.*

It is curious to see in some rural districts how these relics of the past have been preserved after accident and carefully treasured in the closet of "the spare room." Some of them have been mended with putty, or paint, others by tying the pieces together and boiling them in milk. Whether or not they would stand the test of the iron weight which a well known mender in Boston attached to his mended china, it is certain they will last through the reverent handling they now receive.

During the first thirty or forty years

* See illustrated article on "The Pioneer of China Painting in America," in THE NEW ENGLAND MAGAZINE for September, 1895.

of the present century great quantities of blue English ware were imported by America from designs sent over to England. Pictures of scenery, of public buildings, of historical events, or subjects of fancy or humor were introduced on the tables of families, and served to impress upon the minds of the younger members many a fact or fiction. The portraits of all our distinguished statesmen were more or less frequently conspicuous at the tables of the people,—noted soldiers or sailors, persons who had served the country, from the first President down to heroes of a comparatively recent period. Enoch Ward and Sons gave us the "Landing of the Pilgrims," after the old traditions of the rock-bound coast, —whereas the coast was really as flat as a flounder, and the boulder on which the Pilgrims touched was itself a pilgrim, having drifted thither from a distance. On the rim of the plate is the American eagle six times repeated; and the inscription is: "America Independent, July 4, 1776. Washington Born 1732. Died 1799." On the flat surface of the plate is the ship on the ocean, while at the shore a boat is pulling in; one man has waded out to a rock, rope in hand, and on another rock near him two Indians with tomahawk in hand have already climbed up to view the proceedings and to dispute possession.

On another blue plate is the White House at Washington,—a large square house quite alone in the centre of the plate, and a garland of the thirteen original states on the rim. On a similar style of plate, the Boston State House is represented on a rise of ground, the cows quietly feeding on the Common in front. This also has a border of the names of the thirteen original states.

A handsome dark blue plate with flowers on the rim gives us, as we are told, the "Landing of Gen. La Fayette at Castle Garden, New York, 16 August, 1824." In the foreground appear two horsemen approaching from opposite directions. Beyond them is a line of soldiers and cannon first offering salute; further on, at the right, is the formidable pile of Castle Garden, and two ships and a steamboat are nearing the

popular in America, and many objects of local interest, such as "The First Hudson River Steamboat," were reproduced on it.

R. Hall manufactured a series of popular designs called "Beauties of American Scenery," embracing "Passaic Falls," "Fairmount Water-Works," "Scene on the Susquehanna," and other noted views. He issued also "Select Views" of English places, in dark blue ware, with deep border of oriental fruits and flowers surround-

THE LANDING OF GEN. LA FAYETTE

MARINE HOSPITAL, LOUISVILLE

shore, met by a great number of sail and row boats to welcome the coming hero.

A very interesting series of marine plates of rich dark blue has a uniform border of sea shells; and among the pictures in the centre are "MacDonnough's Victory on Lake Champlain," and "A Scene off Calcutta," with well drawn vessels and good perspective. The "Marine Hospital, Louisville, Kentucky," is of the same set.

Enoch Wood, who was sometimes called the Father of Pottery, began business in 1784. His ware was very

ing the central picture. These were much liked in America. One of the views is called "Biddulph Castle, Staffordshire;" another, "Paine's Hill, Surrey." Some of his fancy pictures were very pretty. Among these is one called "Sheltered Peasants." The rain is falling in the distance, and under a tree a man, woman, and child have taken refuge, and some lambs are quietly resting near them. The faces are unusually good, reminding one of some of Gainsborough's pictures.

Riley has several pretty views on

common blue ware, but he does not name them, and the localities are not always easily identified.

A set of Don Quixote pictures appear on very dark blue ware without any manufacturer's name; but fortunate is the person who secures them, for they are spirited in drawing and rich in coloring: such subjects as "The Meeting of Sancho and Dapple," and "Don Quixote's Attack on the Mill."

A plate without any manufacturer's

in dismay. We may well wonder at the taste which liked to eat off these plates every day; but they are a great curiosity.

We have seen a soup plate which bears on the back a picture of two steamers, with the words, "Boston Mails" above them and below, "Edwards." On the face is a view of the "Ladies' Cabin" in the centre, and on the rim the steamers, "Caledonia," "Britania," "Arcadia," and "Columbia." This cabin was doubtless deem-

SHELTERED PEASANTS

PAINE'S HILL, SURREY

name, and in a very ordinary blue, gives the great New York fire of Dec. 11, 1835. On the back it is labeled, "Ruins of Merchants' Exchange." On the rim of the front side are the words: "Great Fire," and "New York," parting off the divisions which contain alternately an eagle and a hand-engine. In the centre of the plate is the Exchange, presenting an unbroken front, but the flames are making rapid progress in the rear. Soldiers are patrolling the street to protect the goods that have been left there, while groups of people are huddled together

ed quite magnificent in 1840, when the line of steamships was established.

A very popular blue plate known as the Willow Pattern was issued in 1780 by Thomas Turner of Caughly, who is said to have made the first full table service of printed ware in England. It is a very mixed and grotesque imitation of Chinese designs, but fancy has associated with it a story variously told. On the upper side of the plate, at the left hand, is the humble home of a man who has become enamored of a lady of much higher rank than his own, where superiority of

LADIES' CABIN

LOVER ON THE BRIDGE

LOVERS IN THE GARDEN

wealth is indicated by the extent of the walls and the variety of trees about her home which is seen on the lower part of the plate at the right. Between these two residences is a body of water with a bridge, near the end of which is a house, with a boat near by. These are about the same on all the plates of the series. The first pattern sent out by Turner had one man on the bridge —the lover going over to see the lady. The second issue was the same composition, with "two men," as they are generally called, passing on the bridge —the lovers eloping, with the intention of hiding at the farther end of the bridge, and being taken away at nightfall by the boat in waiting for them. The third design, termed "Three Men on the Bridge," has the lovers, and the father of the lady in pursuit of them. The father carries in his hand a knotted scourge, very distinctly seen on the large platters, but he does not get the opportunity to use it; the lovers succeed in reaching the boat, and go off triumphantly to the new home, humble as it is, and live happily all their united life. At their death, as a

reward of their faithfulness, they are turned into two birds, which are seen on the plate, hovering in the air! There are tragic versions of this story, but we prefer this rendering which has just as good authority.

One plate of this series has the lover approaching the house of the lady on one side, while a servant is eagerly watching on the other to warn him that the father has found out the affair and is very angry. However, the lover goes on to his fate, as lovers have al-

CHRIST CHURCH, OXFORD   RADCLIFFE LIBRARY, OXFORD

ways done from the beginning. Another plate has the lovers in the garden, perhaps planning the elopement. These two plates are of a more muddy blue than the willow pattern series of the man on the bridge, and evidently come from a different manufacturer.

A very interesting set of plates was called "The Classic Series," and was issued by I. and W. Ridgway, whose wares came into use about 1814. They are of a clear, pretty, although not very dark shade of blue. On the rim is the same design of goats and children, alternating with flowers of the convolvulus. In the centre is an octagon defined by a distinct line of white and blue; and within this is a picture of some college or university building, and some professors or students on the adjoining ground. We are made familiar with views of "Downing College," "Christ Church, Oxford," "Trinity College, Oxford," "Sidney Sussex College, Cambridge," and "Radcliffe Library, Oxford." These pictures are spirited drawings of the buildings and of the students in their distinctive Oxford caps.

60

Even fashion has imprinted copies of textile fabrics on this blue ware; very handsome patterns of lace have been thus reproduced. About a hundred years ago, one of the reigning beauties of London was Lady Stormont. She invented a mixed pattern as the groundwork of some of her dresses, and it became very much in demand as the Stormont pattern—sometimes called, however, pepper and salt. This was copied on the blue ware, and a very pretty blue plate was made, without the name of the manufacturer, in which this fine mixed style is the groundwork, and in the center of the design a bird is eating cherries.

The "Syntax" plates are favorite objects of search among collectors of blue plates; not that they are very old or beautiful, but they are queer and amusing. I. and R. Clews, potters at Cobridge from 1814 to 1836, were very popular decorators of ware early in the present century, and they issued many American designs expressly for this market. Their Syntax plates had a very rapid sale both in England and

America, although of little merit except as copies of clever caricatures. More than sixty years ago, there appeared in England, a humorous poem by William Combe, abundantly illustrated, giving the adventures of an eccentric clergyman and schoolmaster, Dr. Syntax, who spent his vacations in search of picturesque scenery, studies in human nature, and general information. This poem was published first by instalments in the "Poetical Magazine," with a colored sketch every month by Thomas Rowlandson, who was the Cruikshank of his day. After the first number, the story was eagerly watched for, and its popularity gave a sudden increase to the subscription list of the magazine. The Doctor's name — thus identified with good-natured simplicity, credulity,

THE RETURN OF DR. SYNTAX

shrewdness, droll wrong-headedness, and recuperative patience under ludicrous mishaps—was given to hats, wigs, coats, canes and numberless articles, which sold all the better for being labeled "Syntax." Every shopkeeper had the tale at his tongue's end because it helped his business.

The "Tour of Dr. Syntax in Search of the Picturesque" was published in a volume in 1812, and it contained thirty-one colored illustrations. This volume was followed by two others, with pictures by the same spirited artist, Rowlandson. These were:

"Dr. Syntax's Tour in Search of Consolation," after the death of his wife, and "Dr. Syntax in Search of a Wife." Those shrewd potters, I. and R. Clews, availed themselves of the popularity of Dr. Syntax by transferring to their blue crockery, with remarkable fidelity, the original pictures of Thomas Rowlandson. These queer blue plates sent many a young person, fifty or sixty years ago, to the library to find the story of the eccentric Doctor Syntax; and they would sometimes say to younger generations, when "The Pickwick Papers" came out, "Ah, Dickens must have got the suggestion of Pickwick from Dr. Syntax!"

Three of these Syntax plates are very familiar to me. One is called "Dr. Syntax Returned from his Tour." The Doctor and his buxom wife are sitting before an open grate, and between them is a table on which are a bottle and glasses. Her uplifted foot and the poker with which she gesticulates, express her consternation lest he has returned with no means to meet the household expenses. The dog behind the Doctor's chair indicates his sympathy with his master in his peril, while the curious servants, one of them with scissors hanging at her side as if she had just risen from her sewing, are peeping in at the door, with open mouths of wonder, to see if the returned tourist does really intend to pay arrears. The Doctor reassures his wife by throwing down some notes on the table.

Another plate is entitled "Dr. Syntax and the Bees." While the Doctor is taking a sketch of an interesting country-seat, the servants happen to be driving a swarm of bees; and the lady of the house rushes out with her parasol to warn the stranger of his danger, while half a dozen servants armed with warming-pan, kettle, stewpan, pail and dipper try to divert the furious insects from the poor victim.

A very amusing plate is "Doctor Syntax Star-gazing." A literary lady whom he encounters while on his "Tour in Search of a Wife" urges him to look through the telescope with her and see the passage of the moon over the sun; and the instrument is taken from the observatory and placed in the balcony. The picture on the plate shows the butler first tripping as he descends the steps of the house, watching the astronomers. One foot is on the tail of the cat, which is, in our opinion, the author of the mischief, while another cat at the side sets up her back in defiance, and the hind leg of the man accidentally hits a cur, which resents the injury; the tray slips from the hand of the butler, and the dishes lie scattered in dire confusion. On the balcony is the Doctor, who has risen from his seat and is explaining the celestial phenomena to the lady, who is earnestly gazing through the telescope. It is a droll example of the step from the sublime to the ridiculous—the butler's misstep.

These studies of simple, coarse crockery open much of historical interest. The first steamboat, the first railway, the opening of a canal, public buildings which have long since yielded their treasures to more massive structures, college buildings as they stood in their primitive simplicity, benevolent institutions which sprang up so early in the growth of the country, all these imprinted on old blue plates lend an importance to ceramic search; and the value of this old ware increases every year.

Washington-Greene Correspondence

A large collection of original letters written by General Washington and General Greene has come into the editor's possession. It is our intention to reproduce in fac-simile those of the letters which present the most interesting details and side lights on the great events of the period covered, even though some of the letters may have been previously published.

The reproduction of these letters in chronological order will be continued through the following five issues. Printed copies of these letters appear on pages 68 and 69.—EDITOR.

Head Quarters Williamsburg. 28th September 1781.

Dear Sir

    I am very sorry to observe in your Letter of
the 12th they ... complaint that you had heard ...
... ... that ... ... many ...
... ... of ... ... that time and some of
very great ... experienced ... This ... quiet
has been ... to give ... full ... on the ... ...

    The last ... to ... from Philadel=
phia of the ... this ... ... inform that
the Plan of ... operation was totally changed from the
Attack of N. York which had been in contemplation, of
that ... ... with
my ... to ... and ... ...
Lord Cornwallis in Virginia, with the ... fleet, ...
was expected to ... with the ... ——— ...
were informed, that Admiral ... with ... Ships of the
line, had arrived at ... ... the force already
there under ... ... of ... ... had not heard of
the arrival of Count De Grasse ———

    I have now to inform that I left Phila...
on the ... ... the same day on my ... I ...
to ... ... News of the ... of Admiral De Grasse ...
the Chesapeake on the 26th ... with the ... fleet ...
fleet of 28 Ships of the line & 4 frigates —— and ...
had landed 3000 Troops, who had formed their ...
with the Marquis ——— ... possible Expedition
was made to ... on our Troops, Artillery and
... ... Col. ... ... to inform ...

have nearly all arrived at & near this place, with less accident or disaster, than might have been expected as I arrived myself, preceding the Troops, on the 14th, Soon upon paid a visit to the French Admiral on Board his Ship to make our Arrangements for the Enterprize; which were most happily effected, & settled to mutual Satisfaction — The Admiral has taken his Position; for our Water Communication to facilitate our Transportation, & to block the Enemy. their Operations are fast-drawing to a Point of Commencement & by that little Hope to open Trenches upon the Enemy & Works —

While these things are taking place on our Side, the Enemy are not idle on their Part — Lord Cornwallis has collected his Troops on York River, & taken two posts — One at York, the other in Gloucester; where he is fortifying with great Industry; & seems resolved to defend himself against our Siege with great Obstinacy — By Accounts, thro Deserters, & other ways, I fear we have little Hope to starve him into a Surrender — my greater Hope is, that he is not well provided with Artillery & military Stores for such Defence — not having had in Contemplation, the Situation to which he is now reduced —

By Information from N York, I collect, that Admiral Digby, with probably 10 Ships of the Line from Europe, is arrived on the Coast, & joined the British Squadron already here — This Junction, if formed, will probably make the English Fleet consist of 30 Ships of the Line — besides 50, & 40's — & a Number of Frigates; which will bring the two Fleets upon too near an Equality — I'm said also from N York, that a large

Embarkation of their Troops is formed, from their
Transports —— ...that Sir H. Clinton himself is ...
them —— their views undoubtedly both Northward...

The Count de Grasse has, most happily &
critically, effected a junction with Count de Barras
from Newport —— the combined Fleet are now in
a good Position within the bay of Chesapeak
Bay — making in Number 36 Capital Ships of the
Line —— four large french Frigates, with some
smaller Ships, ...from the English, one ...
one of which ... ... who had ...
for England ... ... Frigate, the ...
Richmond, which had been ... ...
have also been captured, & now form part of the
...

... you have a particular ...
of Circumstances ... far as this ... —— as to the
prospects & Operations, should we have ...
the present Operations, it is impossible for me
to decide in favor of your Wishes ...
your ... either of the 6... —— If the Fleet
remains so long as the Completion of the ...
Object, it is all I can expect from present ...
... —— If the ... ...
is obtained, that we may be aided in our ...
...portation towards the Point of your Wishes —

Col. Stewart, who is on his Way to
your Camp, favors the ... ... of the ...

Major Genl Greene ——

Col: Morris, who is now ill, & with me, will be detained a few Days —— by him you may expect to have further & particular accounts of your Progress with a confidential, verbal Communication of your future prospects, Views & Expectations ——

I am informed, by circuitous Means, of a very severe action which has taken place on 8th between your Army & the British under Com of Col: Stewart —— so many particulars are mentioned as give me Reason to believe these Reports are grounded in Fact —— I wait impatiently for your Dispatches ——

With very great esteem & regard

I am

dear Sir

Your most Obed t &

humble servant

G: Washington

from Genl Washington
Sept 28th 1781—
a moderate account
of the affairs passing
& leading to the siege of
York.

Major Genl Greene ——

Gen. Washington to Gen. Greene

HEAD QUARTERS, WILLIAMSBURG,
28th September, 1781.

DEAR SIR,

I am very sorry to observe in your Letter of the 6th August, that you had heard nothing from me since the first June—many letters have been written to you since that time—some of very particular Importance.—This failure gives me reason to fear some foul Play on the Route.

The last I wrote to you was from Philadelphia, of the 4th of this instant month—inform'g that the Plan of our Campaign was totally changed from the attack of N. Yorke, which had been in contemplation, & that I was then so far as that Place. advanced with my troops, to comence a combined operation against Lord Cornwallis in Virginia, with the french Fleet, w'ch was expected to arrive in the Chesapeake—I likewise informed, that Admiral Hood, with 13 ships of the line, had arrived at N. Yorke, & joined the force already there under Adm'l Graves—& that I had not heard of the arrival of Count D'Grasse.

I have now to inform that I left Phila. on the 5th inst—The same Day, on my Route, I met the agreeable news of the arrival of Admiral D'Grasse in the Chesapeak on the 26th August—with a formidable Fleet of 28 Ships of the Line & 4 frigates—and that he had landed 3,000 Troops, who had formed their junction with the Marquis—All possible expedition was made to hurry on our Troops, Artillery and Stores—which, I have the satisfaction to inform you, have nearly all arrived at & near this place, with less Accident or Disaster, than might have been expected.—I arrived myself, preceeding the Troops, on the 14th & very soon paid a visit to the french Admiral on Board his ship to make our arrangements for the Enterprize; which were most happily effected, & settled to mutual satisfaction. The Admiral has taken his Position, for our Water Security, to facilitate our Transportation, & to block the enemy. Our operations are fast drawing to a Point of Comencement—& by the 1st Octo. I hope to open Trenches upon the enemy's works.

While these things are taking place on our side, the enemy are not idle on their Part—Lord Cornwallis has collected his Troops on Yorke River, & taken two posts—one in Yorke, the other in Glouster; where he is fortifying with great assiduity, & seems resolved to defend himself against our siege with great obstinacy.—By accounts, thro Deserters, & otherways, I fear we have little Hope to starve him into a surrender—my greater Hope is, that he is not well provided with artillery & military stores for such Defence—not having had in Contemplation, the situation to which he is now reduced.—

By information from N. Yorke, I collect, that Admiral Digby, with (probably) 10 ships of the Line from Europe, is arrived on the Coasts, & joined the British Squadron already here—this junction, if formed, will probably make the English Fleet consist of 30 ships of Line—besides 50 & 40 & a number of Frigates, which will bring the two Fleets upon too near an Equality.—Tis said also from N. Yorke, that a large embarkation of their Troops is formed, & on Board Transports—& that Sir H'y Clinton himself is with them—*their* views undoubtedly look southward.

The Count de Grasse has, most happily & critically, effected a junction with Count de Bonas from Newport—the conjoined Fleet are now in a good Position within the Capes of Chesapeak Bay—mak'g in Number 36 Capital Ships of the Line—four large french Frigates, with some smaller ships, captured from the English, on Board one of which was L'd Rawdon, who had embarked for England—two British Frigates, the Iris & Richmond peeping into the Bay, have also been captured, & now form part of the Fleet of our allies.

Thus you have a particular Detail of Circumstances so far as this Time—as to future prospects & operations, should we have success in the present operations, it is impossible for me to decide in favor of *your Wishes, expressed in your Letter of the 6th August*—If the Fleet remains so long as the Completion of the present object, it is all I can expect from present appearances. I hope, however, if nothing further is obtained, that we may be aided in our Transportation *toward the Point of your Wishes*.

Colo. Stewart, who is on his Way to your Camp, favors the Conveyance of this.—Colo. Morris, who is now ill, & with me, will be detained a few Days—by him you may expect to have further & particular accounts of our Progress—with a confidential, verbal Communication of our future prospects, views & expectations.—

I am informed, by circuitous means, of a very severe Action which has taken place on the 8th between your Army & the British under com'd of Colo. Stewart—so many particulars are mentioned as give me Reason to believe these Reports are grounded in Fact. I wait impatiently for your Dispatches.

With very great Esteem & Regard,
I am,
Dear Sir,
Your most obed't &
humble servant,
G. WASHINGTON.

Major Gen'l Greene.

Gen. Greene to Gen. Washington

HEAD QUARTERS,
HIGH HILLS, SANTEE, Octob. 25th, 1781.

SIR,

My last letter was dated at Charlotte and forwarded by Lt. Col. Lee since which I have received your Excellency's favor of the 28th of September. I am happy to find the army under your command ready to commence operations against Lord Cornwallis, but I am sorry to hear you think the issue somewhat doubtful. And it gives me great pain to find that what ever may be our success in Virginia the circumstances of our ally will not permit them to cooperate with us in an attempt upon Charlestown. The great importance of their present services demands our warmest gratitude, but it is much to be regretted that we cannot improve the advantage which our signal success would give us, as hopes of our people and the fears of the enemy would greatly facilitate the reduction of Charlestown; however if you succeed in Virginia it will enable you to support us more effectually here if these states derive no other advantage from the present exertions of our ally. I will not suffer myself to doubt of your success, tho I cannot help at times being greatly agitated between hope and fear which alternately prevail from the many incidents that occur in military operations which may defeat the most flattering prospects, and I find by letters from Congress as well as from your Excellency that Sir Henry Clinton is making most rapid preparations for some important blow.

I mentioned in one of my former letters that I had been concerting with Governor Burke a plan for the reduction of Wilmington. General Rutherford is moving down towards that place with a considerable body of militia and I hear the enemy have left the place, and now occupy Brunswick about thirty miles below, and by preparations making in Charlestown of small transports I think it highly probable the enemy intend to take off the garrison. But this is only conjecture.

Since the battle of Eutaw our troops have been exceeding sickly and our distress and difficulties have been not a little increased for want of medicine and hospital stores. The malignity of the fevers begins (to) cease as the weather grows cool. The enemy are all in the lower country and nothing material has happened since my last except a number of prisoners which have been taken by our light parties sent out by General Marion. Inclosed I send your Excellency a return of our strength by which you will see our weak state. We can attempt nothing further except in the partizan way. Some rifle men have arrived in camp from the mountains; more are expected which will enable us to keep up pretty strong parties for a time.

But I look forward with pain to December, when the whole Virginia line will leave us. I hope measures will be taken to reinforce us before that period. To arrive here seasonably they must move soon. Col. Lee and Capt. Pearce I hope have given you a full state of matters in this quarter to enable you to take your measures without loss of time.

I transmitted by Capt. Pearce copies of all the letters and papers that had passed respecting Col. Hanes' (Hayne's) execution mentioned in some of my former letters; and as I had not paper to copy them for your Excellency, I desir'd Capt. Pearce to break the cover on his arrival at your camp to give you an opportunity to see them, and inform yourself respecting the matter as the business in its consequences might involve the whole Continent, and particularly the military part; and therefore would ultimately rest with you. Should he have omitted this matter of which I gave him a particular charge I will forward you copies by the first opportunity. I wrote to Lord Cornwallis on the subject but have not got his answer.

You have my warmest wishes for your success and my hearty prayers for your safety.

With sentiments of the greatest
respect and esteem,
I am your Excellency's
most obed &
humble ser.
N. GREENE.

His Excellency
General Washington.

STORM-BEATEN

BY
·· CHARLES · FRANCIS · SAVNDERS ··

SGARRED of bole and twisted of limb,
   By the beach stands an ancient tree,
Bowed by a thousand storms that have swept
   Up from the angry sea.

Blasts of the north have rent its crown
   But its vigor is unsubdued;
And it lives not in vain—there is joy in its midst,
   It is home to the wild bird's brood.

In the world's workshop toils a man,
   Misshapen through ceaseless strife;
Graceless of form, but his soul is aglow—
   He is guard of a woman's life.

A Conspiracy in St. Mark's

By David H. Talmadge

THIS is the story told of an angel of mercy who wears a shirt waist and a glorious crown of straw adorned with red roses, and who devotes the hours of her earthly sojourn to the doing of good deeds. She told the story voluntarily. She always talks that way. She is not one of those distressing women who must needs be urged to the pouring forth of words—and occasionally of thought. The story came out freely and without conditions of secrecy. She did not dream when she told it, toasting her libelously broad shoes before the cannel fire and cocking her head prettily first to one side then to the other in order to enjoy more fully the spectacle presented by the crown of straw held before her eyes by her own white hands, that the story was more interesting than the thousand which had preceded it. She was quite unaffected and altogether charming. Had she been otherwise— the fact is admitted shamelessly—it is more than probable that the natural perversity of man would have prevented its retelling.

"Such lovely old things as they are!" she began lucidly. "Sweet is no name for them! Intelligent too—so intelligent and—and soulful! I believe I'll have them changed; somehow they look cheap."

Let it be understood that the last sentence referred to the roses on the crown of straw, and had no reference whatever to the bursts preceding it. This was plainly obvious to one who could see her face. The world would have been tied into a hard knot and tossed into the universal closet long ago, had men not learned to listen to femininity with their eyes as well as with their ears.

"It was too funny," she continued without noticeable pause. "One day a week ago I was calling upon the Misses Wallingford,—such dear old creatures! So patient and cheerful! Struggling like demons to pay their own way!—and a happy idea popped into my head. They're so proud, you know, that they won't accept anything even faintly suggestive of charity, yet they are poorer than church mice, and sick too,—mercy! how pale and drawn Miss Alfaretta looks! They had their tea things spread out upon a tiny stand hardly large enough to hold a Gainsborough hat, and Miss Theresa apologized for it, saying that they could never seem to find an extension table to suit them. Extension tables, she said, were not what they used to be. They had such a lovely one at home, when they were girls, that they really couldn't get up the heart to buy one of the kind now on sale at the furniture shops. They preferred to eat from this little table which had been their mother's and their grandmother's and their great grandmother's and was of real mahogany. Miss Alfaretta proudly raised the drapery of the article so that I might see its legs. Then they entered into a chirping, tinkling, quavering series of reminiscences about the extension table that had been in the dining hall at home, and when they had finished, both were weeping and my own eyes were wet. Their father must have been very wealthy. It is so sad that they should be compelled to spend the twilight of their lives in poverty!"

It was sad indeed. The fortunes of the Wallingford family have been topics familiar to the ears of many people for five and twenty years. Colonel Wallingford, a man who had served his country with his sword when she was at war, and who had counseled wisely for her welfare when she was at peace, met with financial reverses in his old age, and at his death the homestead, with most of its contents, passed into other hands. The circumstances were well known, and were too commonplace to be absolutely interesting. A blanket mortgage is, of all literary products, the least entertaining. There was left of the colonel's belongings but one small piece of land in one of the Southern States, a melancholy remnant of the investments which had caused his downfall, and this piece of land, together with a few hundreds of dollars in personal property had comprised the wealth of his two daughters for a quarter of a century. Neither had married. Miss Alfaretta, the elder, had been an invalid even at the time of her father's passing, and Miss Theresa, with the true spirit of her blood, had remained faithful despite the urgings of numerous suitors, Van Dorken, the banker, among them. They lived in a box of a cottage bursting with ideals in the very shadow of

old St. Mark's, and drop by drop as the years went on they exhausted the principal of their income. But they did not part with their land. Some sort of sentiment attached to the worthless tract, and the dignity with which they had refused charitable offers for it was as pathetic as it was delightful.

"So," the angel of mercy went on, with a queer little catching of the breath, "a happy idea popped into my head. I thought what a perfectly sweet thing it would be if the man who owns the Wallingford homestead would present to them the old extension table about which so many happy gatherings had taken place, and upon which their revered father had done his writing during the last days of his stay on earth, for after his wife's death he had taken a strange dislike to working at his desk in the room adjoining the lady's chamber. Doubtless, I thought, the present owner attaches no value to the table beyond its intrinsic worth. Doubtless, further, he would have no objection to posing as a philanthropist if the case were properly presented to him. I resolved to see Mrs. Van Dorken and Mrs. Wilkins at once. I did so. They entered into the plan with such enthusiasm! They told me I was born for charity work, and said other things that made me feel so good!"

Mrs. Van Dorken, it may be stated, is the chief angel of the congregation which worships at St. Mark's, and Mrs. Wilkins is her right bower. They are women to whom the younger element of femininity in that social body looks up.

"Well, it was arranged between us that we should wait upon the gentleman who owns the Wallingford place, and lay the proposition before him, getting his terms and sounding his temper. Mrs. Van Dorken asked her husband about it, and he said this was the best way to do it; which we did, and we found him to be a most delightful man. 'My dear ladies,' said he, 'nothing would give me greater pleasure than to return the table to the daughters of Mr. Wallingford, but really I cannot accept money for it. I shall send it to them within a short time, and I shall write to them saying that owing to the purchase of new fittings for the dining room I have no further use for it,—no room for it in fact.' Wasn't that lovely? So cheap too! A veritable bargain in charity! And the dear man kept his word. The Misses Wallingford got the table this afternoon, and you should have seen them hovering about it for all the world like two sweet old robins that have found their nest of a summer long ago. I don't know when I have felt so happy. I seemed to be floating in a little cloud of incense. To think that I had been the cause of such pleasure was as balm to my soul."

She paused for a moment, quite overcome, gazing into the fire with eyes half closed and sparkling with holy water. The crown of straw was lowered to her lap. She drew a long breath.

"The table was dusty and lacking in lustre. One might almost have thought it had been stored in a loft or a warehouse. Perhaps the gentleman had told us the actual truth; perhaps he really did not want it; but this makes no difference. Miss Alfaretta limped away and returned with a bottle of furniture polish. Miss Theresa brought a faded silk handkerchief redolent of myrrh. And together they worked, rubbing it so tenderly, patting it here and there, gently bewailing its scratches, their lips quivering, their hands trembling. I should not have stayed, but they did not seem to mind my presence, and I did not want to go away. One is not often so favored as I have been. So I remained, saying nothing for a long time, for my hostesses were living in the past of which I was not a part. I can keep silent, sir,—when none will listen to me."

She said this so demurely that a smile would have been brutal and a laugh most diabolical. O, angel—but there, this is her story.

"They finished the polishing at last, and Miss Alfaretta involuntarily held out her arms to her sister, who threw herself into them. Then they sobbed and sobbed. It was too sweet! 'Twas like the blessed rain from heaven falling upon a parched field. I also sobbed, I could not help it. I think it was the sounds I made that restored them somewhat to their dignity. At any rate they looked at me in a surprised way, and Miss Alfaretta rearranged the bow upon her head. Then they tried to pull the table apart to wipe the dust from its internal arrangements. It stuck, and I arose to help, but they waved me back. 'We would much rather do it alone, if you please,' said Miss Alfaretta. So I sat down, watching them strain and struggle. Of course they succeeded finally: that blood either does or dies; but the exertion left them with barely sufficient breath for what followed. In the table, between the top and the extension things, was a letter, and upon this letter Miss Theresa pounced with a cry that was like a peal of rejoicing struck upon a cracked bell. 'I put it there myself—my very self,' she said, 'the day father was taken sick. The leaf was not quite level, and—and I put the letter under it. I took it from father's waste basket—no, from the floor beside the waste basket—O dear, dear, dear! Five and twenty years! Five and twenty years!' Miss Alfaretta placed her arm about her sister's waist, and together they looked at the envelope, the tears gushing in torrents down their faces. Above them was a halo—I saw it plainly—a halo of light from other days. The envelope bore no address. It was unsealed. Slowly, almost reverently, Miss Theresa drew forth the sheet it contained. 'Father's hand,' she murmured; 'dear father!' 'Dear father!' echoed Miss Alfaretta; 'read it, sister; I cannot see.' And Miss Theresa read it. It was a letter to the man who had once been his agent in New Orleans, and it had reference to the piece of land which the sweet old creatures own. It told of a discovery Mr. Wallingford had made during a recent trip to the property. It spoke of oil and development and a retrieval of lost fortunes. When Miss Theresa refolded it her eyes were round as saucers and her face was chalky white. She wavered back and forth an instant, gurgling, trying to speak. Then she fainted, and Miss Alfaretta—was ever such faithfulness! —fainted also. I realized then why I had remained; it was Providence."

The tea bell rang at this juncture, and the angel straightened herself in her chair.

"Well, I should think it was time!" she commented; "I'm simply famished! Charity is such hungry work!

When I left the Wallingfords they were seated, one on each side of that precious extension table, sipping tea and nibbling toast. The letter was upon the table between them. They hardly took their eyes from it. 'Father must have been about to seal and address it when he was taken so suddenly and so violently ill,' said Miss Theresa. 'Can you wonder that it seems almost sacred to us?' In the same breath with which I declined to stay for tea, I replied that I did not wonder in the least. And I really didn't,—dear old things! But wasn't it funny about the letter?"

She led the way to the dining room, where she discoursed charmingly over the tea urn on sundry topics utterly foreign to the Misses Wallingford. Having accomplished her good deed she was now, angel like, dwelling upon it no more. What are the wings of mundane angels for, if not to flutter from flower to flower like butterflies?

Yet her story was not finished. The end came two weeks later, and it was a fitting and a pleasing end. She sat before the fire again, her soles toasting, her face radiant. The crown of straw hung, with roses humbly drooping, on the back of a chair. She looked up.

"O I'm so glad you've come!" she cried; "so glad! I have been to see the Wallingfords, and they are going to be rich, rich, rich! Miss Theresa carried that letter to Mr. Van Dorken —or Mr. Van Dorken called to see them about it, I have forgotten which —he's such a nice man, Mr. Van Dorken—and he made a special trip to see that land and he's satisfied that there is oil there—oceans of it, though no one would ever have suspected it, of course, if it hadn't been for the letter, which means barrels of money, and—and isn't it just too lovely!"

It is, truly. The Misses Wallingford are now in receipt of a comfortable income. That piece of land in a Southern State has been the means of saving them from absolute want in their old age. But it is dreadful to think of the consequence which might ensue if they or certain of St. Mark's angels were to visit that piece of land to view the developments, for there are no developments; it is as barren and worthless as when misguided Colonel Wallingford bought it. Van Dorken and two or three other guilty wretches, all males and pillars of St. Mark's, have the secret locked tightly in their breasts. Van Dorken's weight of guilt is heaviest, for to the crimes of falsehood, deceit and conspiracy he has added that of forgery. 'Twas he who, after much overturning of old papers to find a specimen of the colonel's handwriting, wrote that letter, signing the colonel's name to it; 'twas his hand that put it between the table top and the extension things, replacing an envelope containing a patent medicine advertisement.

"Confound it!" he said, with characteristic emphasis, "we can't have two helpless old Wallingfords starving to death because of their pride. Maybe the plan will work and maybe it won't; it can do no harm to try it."

Wherefore the plan was tried, and by the excellence of chance succeeded.

Some day, if the angel of mercy survives the Misses Wallingford,—and please God she will, for they are old and she is young—she will be told the truth. She should, in common justice, know it now; but Van Dorken has sworn his fellow conspirators to secrecy. Therefore her story, while ended most happily, is not complete. She has builded, bless her helpful little heart, better than she knows

The Genesis of Standard Oil

By Will M. Clemens

THIS is the story of a small beginning, showing how in this golden age, a few hundred dollars invested in the right place, at the right time, by the right man, have increased in forty years to a few hundred millions of dollars.

There is neither adventure, romance, nor tragedy in the early history of that famous corporation known throughout the world for its wealth, power, and money-making capacity, the Standard Oil Company, sometimes called the Standard Oil Trust. It is a plain, simple narrative of business growth and development, as easy, natural and consistent as the sowing of a wheat field in early spring and the reaping of a profitable harvest in the autumn.

The Standard Oil Company never "struck oil," nor dug a well, nor owned a derrick in the early days of petroleum development. Six years after the first oil well company was established in Pennsylvania, two bright young men began to refine crude oil and manufacture a marketable product, and they are still selling that same product to-day, under the name of Standard Oil.

In 1850, the northwestern part of Pennsylvania was almost a wilderness. Titusville was a lumbering village with a general store and a saw mill. The site of Oil City was a highway tavern, where raftsmen on the Alleghany River stopped to get their liquor.

Oil in its crude state was found in the valley streams, in the early fifties, a mere floating substance known as Seneca Oil, from having long been used in the war paints and medicines of the Seneca Indians who lived in the region round about.

In 1852 a bottle of the oil was taken to Professor O. P. Hubbard, of Dartmouth College, who pronounced the product valuable for commercial purposes, if it could be found in sufficient quantities. Indirectly, the result of Prof. Hubbard's analysis was the formation, in 1854, of the Pennsylvania Rock Oil Company, capitalized at five hundred thousand dollars in shares of twenty-five dollars each. The company was composed largely of New York and New England stockholders. The enterprise was not a success. Three years later came the Seneca Oil Company, which was likewise unsuccessful. It was not until May 1, 1858, that the idea of drilling into the rock for oil was conceived, and not until August 28 of the following year was the first oil well in successful operation near Titusville. Then came the great oil land boom, with the nearest railroad station at Erie, forty miles away. Within six years there were one hundred thousand people in the oil regions, and millions of dollars were invested in wells, land, rigging, derricks, and machinery. Thousands of barrels of crude oil were soon being produced daily, but with small facilities for refining it, although that was necessary to make it a marketable commodity.

At this juncture appeared the man who seized the opportunity. His name was John Davison Rockefeller. Born at Richfield, N. Y., June 8, 1839, he removed in 1853 to Cleveland, Ohio, with his parents, and was a pupil at the Cleveland High School until his sixteenth year. Then he entered the forwarding commission house of Hewitt & Tuttle as an entry clerk. Fifteen months later he became the firm's cashier and bookkeeper. When not yet nineteen years of age, in company with Morris B. Clark he opened a commission business under the firm name of Clark & Rockefeller.

The oil discovered in the nearby Pennsylvania region attracted the attention of Cleveland business men, and crude petroleum began to find a market there, being shipped by rail from Erie. In 1860, Samuel Andrews, in company with Rockefeller and Clark, started the Excelsior Oil Refinery, a small concern that cost, at its inception, but a few hundred dollars. Rockefeller saw the opportunity to refine crude oil, and invested every dollar he possessed. The business of the firm, Andrews, Clark & Co., grew at an astonishing rate. Clark was afraid to risk his money in the enterprise, and withdrew. Then young Rockefeller sold out his interest in the commission business, placed his money to the last dollar in the development of the Excelsior Refinery, and in 1865 established the firm of Rockefeller & Andrews. This really was the genesis of the Standard Oil Company.

In 1867 the firm admitted William Rockefeller into partnership, reorganized the growing concern under the name of William Rockefeller & Co., and built a second refinery, called the Standard. William Rockefeller furnished the capital for the second venture.

Looked at from a business standpoint, the subsequent success of the Rockefellers was as natural as the growth of a tree. They purchased the entire output of various oil wells, the crude product to be shipped to the two refineries at Cleveland. Figures for four years, which I fortunately have at hand, tell the story in the simplest possible language.

The shipments of crude petroleum to Cleveland from the oil regions of Pennsylvania, and the amount of refined oil produced during the years from 1865 to 1868, were as follows:

1865.
220,000 barrels crude received.
154,000 barrels refined produced.
1866.
600,000 barrels crude received.
400,000 barrels refined produced.
1867.
750,000 barrels crude received.
550,000 barrels refined produced.
1868.
956,479 barrels crude received.
776,356 barrels refined produced.

This practically represented the growth of the Rockefeller business during four years, as fully ninety per cent. of the oil product was refined by them.

The crude petroleum was originally shipped to Cleveland and elsewhere from the oil fields in ordinary barrels in car load lots. Then wooden tanks were used, two tanks being built upon each car, with a capacity of forty-one barrels, or eighty-two barrels to the car. Later came the immense iron tanks built the length of the car and holding one hundred barrels or more.

The total output of refined oil for the year 1868 was divided as follows:

New York.........965,863 barrels.
Cleveland ....929,372 barrels.
Philadelphia ......266,912 barrels.
Boston ....129,981 barrels.
Portland .... 35,878 barrels.
Other points.......245,883 barrels.

The Rockefellers were at this time refining about 800,000 barrels out of the 929,372 barrels refined in Cleveland. Their only opposition to a complete control was in New York and Brooklyn, where some fifteen or sixteen small refineries were turning out 965,863 barrels.

William Rockefeller was sent by his firm to New York in December, 1868, and he promptly purchased as many of the local refineries as his money would buy. More capital was needed in order to control the New York end of the business, and Henry M. Flagler, Colonel Oliver Payne and others were admitted to the firm. The Rockefeller Company of New York was established and at the close of 1869 they were in control of 1,859,235 barrels, out of a total product of 2,573,889 barrels, which represented the year's production.

At first the Cleveland and New York houses were consolidated under the firm name of Rockefeller, Andrews & Flagler, but in 1870 the Standard Oil Company was legally organized, with a capital stock of $1,000,000. John D. Rockefeller was elected president of the new corporation, William Rockefeller, vice-president, and Henry M. Flagler secretary and treasurer.

Meanwhile the daily output of crude oil increased at a wonderful rate, and the Standard Company, now controlling a majority of refineries, was taxed to keep pace with the business thrust upon them. New refineries, railroads, pipe lines, tanks, and warehouses had to be built, and the Company thrived and grew and prospered beyond even the dreams of John D. Rockefeller himself. The daily output of the Pennsylvania oil wells was 15,000 barrels in 1872. At this latter date refined Standard Oil sold at an average price of $24.24 the barrel.

In this same year of 1872, the Standard Oil Company had a daily still capacity of 10,000 barrels at Cleveland, 9,700 barrels at New York, 650 barrels at Pittsburg, and 418 barrels at Oil City, making a total of 20,768 barrels produced. The whole enormous traffic of the Standard Oil Company was confined to marketing the product after the crude oil had been distilled. Refineries were worked night and day, and it mattered not whether this well or that well in the oil region went "dry," whether one oil company or a dozen went to smash. The Standard bought crude oil from nearly every well and firm, and having once secured control of the market, no other refiner dared interfere, and practically all crude petroleum flowed naturally into the Standard's tanks.

What was true of the Pennsylvania oil fields soon became true of other fields in other States and other countries. The Russian oil wells fed the Standard refineries abroad as quickly and as easily as those at Oil City and Titusville fed those at home, and thus the monopoly of the Rockefellers soon encircled the entire world of oil.

In 1882 the Standard Oil Trust was organized with a capital of $70,000,-000, which was increased two years later to $90,000,000. But in 1892 the

Supreme Court decided that the trust was illegal, and it was consequently dissolved. Since then the enormous business has been conducted under different names, the Standard Oil Company of New Jersey being the most prominent. In each of these various companies John D. Rockefeller is the leading director and heaviest shareholder. In recent years, stock in the Standard Oil Company of New Jersey has been quoted at a figure as high as $824 a share.

An idea of the magnitude of this great industry which now supplies the entire world with oil, will be conveyed by the statement that since 1860 there have been received for exported petroleum and its products, an aggregate amount exceeding the present money wealth, in gold and silver, of the United States government.

The same methods adopted by the Rockefellers in the early sixties are in vogue to-day, for the Standard Oil Company is acquiring great interests in both the new Texas and California oil fields. As I have said, the business of the Standard Oil Company is to acquire and control the oil when produced, but not to produce oil. The corporation builds pipe lines and furnishes cheap transportation for carrying the oil from the wells to the refineries or to the seaports. It is always ready to purchase the oil produced at any well, and always pays the market value for the oil. There are few companies that have sufficient capital to build their own pipe lines, and if the oil producer is dependent upon railroads, the freights are usually too high to compete with pipe lines, and as a matter of economy, most oil producers are glad to enter into a contract with the Standard Oil Company, not only to transport the oil, but to find a market for the product. The Standard Oil Company has its own ships and pipe line transportation, and its own agencies in almost every part of the world, so the most economic method for any oil producer is to contract with the company to transport and buy the oil. If the Standard Oil Company enters any new oil district, it is the best evidence of the permanency of that district.

Menotomy Parsonage

By Abram English Brown

THE New England clergyman was the one man of unquestioned authority in the town where he was settled. He was commonly known as the parson—the word from its derivation: Old French *persone*, Latin *persona*—suggesting his position in the community. Naturally enough the residence of the autocrat was the one dwelling of the town in which there was general interest, for it sheltered him to whom the people looked for spiritual guidance as well as much of their intellectual and social stimulus. Hither they brought a tithe of their increase with a consciousness of duty well performed, as did the Jews of old when they offered the firstlings of their flocks as a sacrifice to the Most High.

There was always a kindly welcome at the parsonage for every one. If laden with sorrow, here one was sure of finding the comfort of sympathy and perhaps the means of relief. If uncertain as to the path of duty, here was to be had that advice which enabled one to hasten on with confidence, assured that whatever the result it would be for the best. A home in which the whole parish had such vital interest, could not be other than sacred to the entire community. The affectionate pride in the parsonage was in no way affected by its size or appointments, although the house was generally as good as any in the town, but it was the power within that made it what it was. Had

it belonged to another class of aristocracy which flourished in provincial days in Massachusetts, the building would necessarily have been one of some colonial grandeur, decorated with the insignia of royalty as evidence that the occupant held a commission from the King.

But the influence of the parsonage was not limited to the bounds of the parish which had provided it. Here it was that the neighboring clergy resorted for hospitality and exchange of professional civilities. With a larder well stocked through the honest tithing of the parishioners, supplies were never lacking for the physical nourishment, and the spiritual stimulus was ever at home. No tavern upon the King's highway, its royal name emblazoned in golden letters upon its extending signboard, had charms for the New England parson, unless some untoward accident befell him, and he would so well time his journey as seldom to have need of other hospitality than that of a parsonage. In fact the weary traveller of any worthy calling found welcome at its door. Some, indeed, during our revolutionary period, were such common resorts for ardent patriots that the jealous tory element derisively called them "parsons' taverns."

Visits of brother clergymen must have been helpful to both visitor and host alike at a time when education in the rural districts was closely confined to the clergy and physicians, with pos-

sibly a slight smattering of law at the command of the squire. When the spiritual food for the Sabbath was to be dispensed by a neighboring pastor, it was known throughout the parish by his arrival on Saturday, for no parson, in good and regular standing, would think of journeying on the Lord's day.

A good representation of the New England parsonage was that at Menotomy. It was more simple in construction and less pretentious than some, but in all the essentials it was typical. Its first occupant was, too, a typical parson.

The inhabitants of Cambridge, on the westerly side of the Menotomy River, desired better accommodations than they were enjoying at the mother church, so much absorbed by the college, and they petitioned the General Court in 1725 to be set off as a separate precinct, but did not succeed in having it done until some years later. After duly humbling themselves and having sought Divine guidance, they were led to call a young man, Rev. Samuel Cook, to become their minister. Although a native of Hadley, where he was born in 1709, Mr. Cook was not a stranger to his people. He had spent four years at Harvard College, having been graduated in 1735. He resided for a year or more at Medford, in the home of Colonel Isaac Royall, serving as tutor to young Isaac, the son and pride of the West India merchant. The Colonel had left his home at Antigua, brought his family and retinue of negro slaves to Medford and there set up a palace indeed. During these years, before they were free to have a separate church, Mr. Cook had performed some parochial services for the Menotomy people, and had made his way to their hearts.

Life in Isaac Royall's family was entirely different from that of a New England parsonage, but the time spent there by young Cook did not turn him from his chosen path of duty. While engaged as tutor he kept close to his studies and so conducted himself as to secure the confidence of Rev. Mr. Turell, the pastor of Medford, and fast friend of Isaac Royall, and through his advice the people of Menotomy completed their obligations as a precinct, in calling Mr. Cook to become their pastor. He was settled with all the formalities of the times in September, 1739, when a church was formed by Rev. John Hancock, of Lexington. Although a single man when entering upon his work, he had his affections already centered in a young lady of his native town, and in August of 1740 he brought Sarah Porter, as his bride, to the parsonage. "The house was raised July 17, 1740, at the expense of the people; the frame was given and the cellar and well were dug and stoned gratis; the board and shingles were carted from Sudbury and Billerica free of charge to me," is his own record.

With a church well established, with a pastor and his wife located in a parsonage, the people at the west of the River felt that they were at last distinct from the mother town of Cambridge. Pride spurred them to do all in their power to have their parsonage compare favorably with those of neighboring towns and precincts, and they saw to it that the larder was well stocked. There was no family of the Menotomy Precinct that did not tithe its income, and the share left at the parsonage was of the best.

Calls from the neighboring parsons were occasions of pride to the people of the new precinct, and their only fear, at the coming of so many to extend fellowship, was that they might have in some things neglected their duty. What if the young parson's supply of wine or West India rum should give out, or his "firing" run low, when one of the older ministers was the caller! Would not he think that the Menotomy people had failed in their obligations to their pastor? But they did not allow such fears to repeat themselves. William Russell, who headed the petition of the settlers for better accommodation, looked out for the necessities. Jason Russell who had married Elizabeth Winship and set up a home in the Russell house, at about the time of the coming of Rev. Mr. Cook, was a thrifty man, and while fitting up his own house did not fail to share his supplies with the parsonage. The Whittemores, Lockes, Swans, Butterfields, Winships, Dunsters, Wellingtons and others did their duty and took delight in noting the calls of Rev. John Hancock, of Lexington; of his son-in-law, Rev. Nicholas Bowes, from Bedford; Rev. Daniel Bliss, of Concord; Rev. Samuel Ruggles, of Billerica; Rev. Thomas Jones, of Woburn Precinct, and of many of like distinction.

Thus everything started off well at Menotomy, but in less than a year after the auspicious beginning, the community was shrouded in gloom. The graceful lady, who had come to the parsonage as the bride of Rev. Samuel Cook, had passed away and the young minis-

ter, looking to his people for comfort, struggled to rise above the burden that rested so heavily upon his heart. It was a severe trial but it taught the young pastor, as nothing else could, how to sympathize with the members of his flock when called to similar experiences.

At length Rev. Mr. Cook brought to the lonely parsonage Anna, the daughter of Rev. John Cotton, of Newton. having followed the example of the ministers of that time in strengthening the aristocracy of the clerical profession through inter-marriage. The voices of children were soon heard about the place. Some remained but a short time while others were spared to add cheer to the home, and afford comfort to their father in his second bereavement. For their mother was taken away at the age of thirty-eight years.

Again the trusting parson looked about him for a helpmeet. It was at the Bedford parsonage where he found the widow of Rev. Nicholas Bowes, daughter of Rev. John Hancock. The coming of this cultured lady from Bedford to Menotomy again brought happiness to his home. The parson had made a wise choice. Mrs. Cook was born in the Lexington parsonage, presided as mistress of the one at Bedford and knew well how to perform the duties of a third home of this character. This alliance brought a different circle of visitors. Rev. Jonas Clark, of Lexington, successor of Rev. John Hancock, whose granddaughter he had married, had been friendly with his Brother Cook ever since he was settled at Lexington in 1755, but now that his wife's mother was the lady of the Menotomy household the association warmed into that of kinship.

Thomas Hancock, the successful and liberal-handed merchant, who had made frequent visits to the old home

BOWL AND TABLE ORIGINALLY OWNED BY REV. SAMUEL COOK

remembered many of his relatives, among them Mrs. Cook, his sister. She outlived her brother but four years, yet long enough to receive the legacy and appropriate it to the use and benefit of the family at Menotomy.

The members of the Royall family at Medford were visitors from the time the house was opened until the last of them fled to Halifax with the other Loyalists and the King's army on March 17, 1776. Colonel Isaac preceded them on the eve of the battle of Lexington and Concord. George Erving and Sir William Pepperell the younger, who married the Royall daughters, were also familiar guests, but these, like the Vassals and Inmans, made less frequent visits after the political excitement of the revolutionary period caused them to take sides against the patriots, of whom Rev. Samuel Cook was one of the most outspoken.

Although bereft of his third wife before the opening of the war, Rev. Samuel Cook was in full sympathy with Rev. Jonas Clark at Lexington, and many of the plans of the patriots must have been discussed in the Menotomy parsonage before the actual fighting on Lexington Green and at Concord Bridge. Here John Hancock must have heard the most positive assertions in regard to the constitutional rights of the Colonists. These clergymen, and their associates, Rev. William Emerson of Concord, Rev. Joseph Emerson, of Pepperell, Reverends Turell and Osgood of Medford, were actuated by high motives and deep seated convictions of duty. If John Hancock ever wavered there was

at Lexington, passing through Menotomy on his journeys to and from Boston, had occasion now to stop to call upon his sister Lucy. Nicholas Bowes, who was in the employ of his uncle Thomas at Boston, was also a frequent visitor upon his mother. The friendship of Thomas Hancock and his wife, Lydia Henchman, daughter of Colonel Daniel, the book dealer of Boston, was highly valued, and their stone mansion on Beacon Hill was the rendezvous for people of marked influence in business, social and ecclesiastical circles. John Hancock, the rising young man of Boston, found attractions at the Menotomy parsonage. He had not forgotten the aunt who had made his boyhood visits to Bedford so happy and now, when entering into his kingdom of honor and wealth he continued the early associations. It was through the death of John's Uncle Thomas that much of his wealth came, but he was not heir to it all, for the Boston merchant carefully family influence quite as strong as that exerted by Samuel Adams, who has been credited—erroneously I believe—with having secured the sympathy and support of the young merchant on the side of the patriots. (See John Hancock His Book, page 86.) There were those in the Menotomy parsonage who derived peculiar satisfaction from the elevation of John Hancock,—one of the family,—to the presidency of the Continental Congress, and to the positions of honor later conferred upon him by the Bay State.

Rev. Samuel Cook was a man of standing with the government officials before the lines of separation were drawn. On March 29, 1770, the "Boston News Letter" published the statement that "the Honorable House of Representatives made choice of Rev. Mr. Samuel Cook, of Cambridge, to preach on the anniversary of the election on his Majesty's council on the last Wednesday of May next."

There was anxiety in the Menotomy parsonage on the 19th of April, 1775, for Rev. Mr. Cook knew that his nephew, John Hancock, was in the vicinity of Lexington, and believed that he was with the Clarks, for Mrs. Thomas Hancock and Dorothy Quincy had halted at his door on their way out from town and had made known their fears on the subject. It was with solicitation for his family and his flock that the venerable pastor applied him-

self to the needs of the hour, until at the approach of the retreating enemy, he was taken away by his son Samuel, to a place of safety. Perhaps, thereby, his life was saved, for the British had great contempt for the local clergy, whom they denounced as leaders in the rebellion. The parsonage did not altogether escape the mark of the enemy, and the old bullet-scarred shutters are still preserved as reminders of

REV. SAMUEL COOK'S WRITING DESK

the excursion of the Kings army. The lady of the household at this time was Miss Mary Cook, the daughter, who never married. Two days after the battle of Bunker Hill the Menotomy parsonage was taken for a hospital, as were other houses in the precinct, and wounded provincials were cared for in these hastily improvised quarters. We may well imagine that when Rev. Samuel Cook again penned a sermon in that house, it was with emotions such as had not filled his breast during the thirty-six years of his ministry. In his summary of deaths during the year 1775 he says, "There have been 47, besides some Provincials and Hutchinson's Butchers slain in Concord Battle, near the meeting-house, buried here."

This pastor's ardent patriotism and devotion to his people prompted him, with others, to make frequent visits to the camp at Cambridge during the siege. After the evacuation, when the General Court held its sessions at Watertown in 1776, he was chaplain of that body, making his journeys to and from Menotomy on the back of his favorite horse. Having passed the last fifteen years of his life with his daughter as his housekeeper, Rev. Samuel Cook's long and useful life was closed on June 4, 1783, and his body was laid to rest with those of his three wives, in the burying ground near the church and parsonage. It was just as the Colonies, for which he had labored and suffered, were beginning to emerge from the cloud of Revolution in which they had been so long enveloped.

The house, built for him and in which he had dwelt for more than forty years, was his own property. It was a New England custom, when calling a minister, to give him a settlement fee, in addition to an annual salary. This was to aid him in providing a home and was often accompanied by land enough to constitute a farm, hence the dwelling did not revert to the parish and the people had no control of it. The habit of calling the home of the minister, the parsonage, was so firmly established that it was continued, and in many of our old towns to-day, may be seen a stately mansion shaded by elms and guarded by Lombardy poplars, so honored although no minister has dwelt in it for a generation or more. The people of Menotomy were not exceptions to this habit, and the parsonage was a place of interest, if not of reverence, long after it ceased to shelter a clergyman. This feeling was strengthened and continued by the occupancy of Miss Mary Cook, the maiden daughter, who became the proverbial "Aunt" of all Menotomy. Miss Cook never lapsed into a state of inactivity, to sit attired in rusty black bombazine as a relic of old times, seldom seen beyond her tansy or camomile bed. Hers was a lot of helpful activity, and while she never forgot the reviving effect of a sprig of tansy, on a hot day when inclined to be drowsy in the meeting house, she kept pace with the times, and her usefulness honored the title Aunt Cook, which she bore with graceful dignity.

The voice of childhood seemed never to have been wholly stilled in the parsonage, for before one generation had ceased its prattle, there came a second to take its place, not without sorrow however. Our joys are often mingled with tears. Hannah, who made her advent to the parsonage seven years after a welcome was extended to Mary, became the wife of Henry Bradshaw. She died at an early age, leaving four children, whose father soon followed her. They were received at the parsonage by Aunt Cook. If she ever looked upon them as a burden, their innocence and helplessness brought out her maternal instinct and she found in them that which more than compensated for all her care and trouble.

Miss Cook, like many another descendant of the New England clergy,

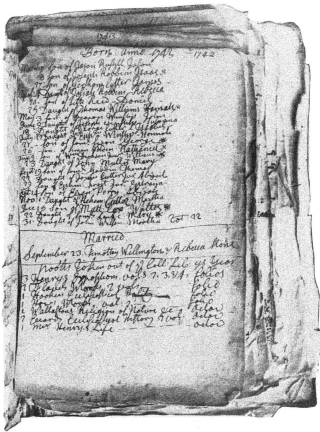

A Leaf of the Church Records

had good reason for being proud of her ancestry, but while there was satisfaction in the reality, it brought no cash to her beaded purse, and with real puritan heroism she applied herself to the sterner realities of life. Being conveniently near Harvard College the Menotomy parsonage was a desirable place of residence for students and faculty and soon others from town found a congenial home beneath the old roof-tree. Miss Cook thus maintained the dignity of the parsonage and of her position - while at the same time she added to her resources. Professional men always made their way to "Aunt Cook's" in preference to the "Black Horse" or "Cooper's Tavern" in Cambridge. In fact there was a silent influence here which had its good effect upon them. The old leather bound family Bible witnessed of the best; the ancestral portraits offered good society, silent but to be trusted, and even the old desk, with its neatly kept files of manuscript sermons told of the labor which gives true dignity to manhood.

Among the early boarders of this class was James Sullivan, a rising lawyer, who sought here a quiet retirement for himself during his inoculation for the small pox. So tenderly did Aunt Cook minister to his needs, and so rapid was his recovery, that he never forgot the Menotomy parsonage

called, accompanied by a friend, Mr. William Williamson, of North Carolina. The part of the country through which they travelled was unfrequented. The scene was rural, the air refreshing. the birds carolled on every spray and all nature was in a most agreeable humor. The hearts of the two gentlemen. which vibrated to the harmony that pervaded Creation, were open to every tender impression. In one of their excursions in South Berwick township they met a little girl, five or six years old. whose beauty and sweetness, like some little wandering wood nymph, attracted their attention; they stopped to speak to her. 'What is your name?'

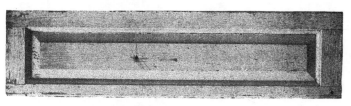

A SHUTTER FROM THE PARSONAGE, SHOWING BULLET HOLE MADE BY THE BRITISH

and its worthy occupant, and when in later years, in the fullness of his honors as jurist, statesman and Governor of Massachusetts, he made frequent visits to see her and was a friend indeed. In fact the acquaintance then formed ripened into a family association and Mrs. Amory, a daughter of Governor Sullivan, with her children passed many pleasant summers at the old parsonage.

Through the influence of Mr. Sullivan, there was brought to Miss Cook's door, one day at the dawn of the last century, a most attractive little girl. Her previous history has been told as follows: "Hon. James Sullivan, upon a tour of business and pleasure visited the District of Maine, as it was then

said Mr. Williamson, dismounting from his horse.

" 'Eunice, Sir,' returned the child.

" 'Who is your father?'

" 'I have none,' she said.

" 'Ah! that's hard, indeed. Where is your mother?'

" 'She is sick and going to die too,' cried the poor little girl. The feelings of the gentlemen were touched by the simplicity of the child. They followed up their interest by further inquiries and visited the house of the mother and found the sick woman and her friendly nurse. The nurse was talkative and in answer to their questions informed them that the mother was in the last stages of consumption, and that her

WINDOW FROM THE OLD PARSONAGE

mind was entirely occupied concerning her child who would be left, on her death, defenseless and unprotected. Entering the room where the widowed mother lay Mr. Williamson inquired if she would be willing to put the child under his protection. Her consent was given with joy; to her it seemed that this event was ordered by that Being who is the father of the fatherless and the protector of the widow. Mr. Williamson promised to send for the child as soon as the mother was no more, and they took their leave. They called upon the physician in attendance upon the

mother, and begged him to pay her every attention his professional skill could render, and write when she breathed her last.

"In about six weeks this event took place. Mr. Williamson sent immediately for the child who was accordingly conveyed to Boston. On her arrival there Maria Eunice Lord, for that was her name, was received by her Boston friends and soon after went to the old town, earlier known by its Indian name of Menotomy, now Arlington. Here she was placed in the benevolent care of a lady, Miss Mary Cook, the daughter of Parson Samuel Cook, the first minister of the parish, and in her family spent her early years."

The coming of little Eunice to the parsonage marked a new era in the life of Miss Cook. To be sure it added to her cares, but there was something in the nature of the little girl from the country, so different from that of the Boston girls whom she had known, that softened and purified her own. The voice of the child was music to the ears of all the occupants of the house, and not the least so to a young physician who had just come to enjoy the advantages of the old parsonage, and had quietly begun to make his way to a practice in the town. He had been graduated at Harvard College and its medical school, and promised to be an honor to the profession which he had chosen. Doctor Timothy Wellington became strongly attached to the pretty little girl. As time went on Aunt Cook saw that the young doctor's fondness for Eunice was ripening into love, and, liking and respecting him as she did, she could not discourage the attachment. So when at the age of eighteen Eunice went from the old parsonage as his bride Miss Cook found a solace for her loneliness in their happiness. Her ward did not go, at marriage, beyond her convenient oversight. From the parsonage door Miss Cook looked many times each day to the new home across the highway. Had it been her own daughter's she could not have done so with more evident satisfaction.

There was an occupant of the parsonage of a very different type from those already introduced to the reader. The Spanish Consul to New England in seeking for retirement from the growing city, was introduced to Miss Cook, and found a pleasant home with her. His natural characteristics served as amusement for his hostess, who at first manifested no admiration for the official, but after a time became reconciled and derived not a little pleasure from Don Juan Stoughton's society. When he was ill Miss Cook was unremitting in her faithful care and attention, and when he was laid to rest in the Old Burying Ground she felt that another grave was added to the many tenanted by those who had been dear to her in life and whose resting place was but a step from her door.

MISS ANNA BRADSHAW

Aunt Cook was not left in the parsonage alone, in her declining years, but was comforted and cared for by one to whom she had ministered when left an orphan. Anna Bradshaw was the one of the third generation to continue the family possession of the house. Faithful to the traditions of the family, she guarded it until the end of her life. When loosening her hold upon the many treasures of the parsonage, she entrusted the contents of one drawer of her lamented grandfather's study desk to one, who for name and kinship, she had a fond attachment. Maria Eunice Wellington, or Mrs. Hodgdon, even in advanced years, delighted in showing a letter penned by the Tory, Isaac Royall, while in banishment in England. This letter was written to his old tutor, Rev. Samuel Cook, pleading with him to intercede with the government of the State of Massachusetts to allow him to return to his home and estate in Medford.

True to her inherited instinct, Miss Bradshaw, the last of the family occupants of the parsonage, devised the estate to the church which she loved and over which her grandfather was settled as pastor in 1739. Now the West Precinct was no longer known as Menotomy but was duly incorporated as West Cambridge. The march of progress soon caused the removal of the old parsonage and destroyed the Lombardy poplars, but through the thoughtfulness of Timothy Wellington some interesting portions were saved. Among them is one of the window shutters which bears the mark of a British bullet, fired during the running fight of the afternoon of April 19, 1775. A glazed window sash is also treasured in the town, a gift of Mrs. Eunice L. Wellington Hodgdon, whose father had a particular interest in it. It was one of the "best room" windows, on the glass of which various autographs have been cut that give to it both historic and sentimental interest.

Naturally the first name to be placed upon this autograph window was that of the owner, the parson, and there is to be read to-day, in bold characters, the name of Samuel Cook and affixed to it is the date 1772. One pane bears the following: Madame De Neufville;

DR. TIMOTHY WELLINGTON

Nancy De Neufville; John De Neufville, Nov. 30, 1787. This trio constituted a family who shared the comforts of his home. The name is interwoven with several incidents of the American Revolution. John De Neufville, according to a rude slab in the Precinct Burying ground, was an eminent merchant in Amsterdam. His death occurred at Menotomy in 1796. It is claimed that he rendered efficient service to this country during the war, in promoting negotiations for a loan from the Dutch capitalists, and that after the war he came to the United States and established a business which was not successful. His widow petitioned Congress for relief, claiming that the family embarrassment was due to the efforts of her husband in behalf of the distressed Colonies. Alexander Hamilton, in a letter to Washington, in allusion to her claim said, "I do not know what the case admits of; but from some papers she showed me, it would seem she had pretentions to the kindness of this country." She afterwards became the wife of Don Juan Stoughton, the Spanish consul before mentioned.

THE TOMB OF REV. SAMUEL COOK

Under the date of 1811, appear the names of Rebecca Cook Bradshaw, Mary Cook, Timothy Wellington, and fancy, in careful dealing with several unfinished or unsuccessful attempts with the diamond point, may read Maria Eunice Lord. It was less than two years later that this sunbeam of the parsonage went out as the bride of the young physician.

Another pane of the window shows the name of A. C. Linzee, who was a daughter of John De Neufville and wife of Ralph I. Linzee. Andrew Boardman and Mary Boardman, the genealogist says, were prominent in the first Parish in revolutionary days; Lizzie Sullivan was a member of the Governor's family. Of the names plainly to be traced are Silvanus Bour, Nov. 30, 1787, John De Mady, Peter Curtis, Jonathan Frost, Jnr., Samuel Griffin, H. Judson and Ephraim Randall, with the initials of others, each and all of whom have shared the hospitality of the old parsonage and fain would testify of it to their children's children.

Birds of New England

By A. Henry Higginson.

AMONG the first of the feathered race to appear in the early spring are the Bluebirds. Sometimes they arrive before the first of March, willing to brave its cold and bitter winds, so eager are they to return to New England. They are found almost everywhere in inhabited districts; in old orchards, along the country roadsides, and even at times in the parks of the great cities. About May fifteenth the bluebirds build their nests in some concealed place, choosing by preference a hollow post, or a deserted woodpecker's nest. Within it they build one of grass, seaweed, rags, or anything near at hand, and there are laid four pale blue eggs. About June fifteenth the young birds are flying about with their parents.

Another early comer is the Cowbird. He has no song to speak of and little to bring him to our attention, except the fact that he is too lazy to build a home of his own in which to rear the young, and hence his mate lays her eggs in the nests of other birds. As Cowbirds' eggs hatch more quickly than those of other birds, the young interloper has generally two or three days' start of his nest fellows, with the result that he, being stronger and better developed, throws the lawful inmates out. At any rate, whatever happens, he always fares well. The eggs of the Cowbird are white, thickly dotted with reddish brown, and she usually lays them in the nests of the Yellow Warbler, Pewee, or Indigo Bird.

About April first, or a little later, some interesting birds will be met with in the thickest cedar-swamps. There the Screech Owl may be seen, blinking as if he could not quite make you out. Upon penetrating into the deepest recesses of the swamp, one may suddenly hear a gutteral croak, and looking upward the eye encounters what appears to be a pile of brush on every tree, and on each pile a dumpish bird with a long bill, more like a hen than anything else. This is the Black-crowned Night Heron, and it is likely that there may be a hundred or more nests in the colony. Each nest contains four blue eggs about the size and shape of a bantam's egg. In similar localities the Great Blue Heron, or the Green Heron make their nests.

A little later the edges of the swamps will be found alive with small birds. Near the border of some pool or brook, the Maryland Yellow-throats build their home and one may hunt for hours before it is discovered. The beautiful little nest is usually well hidden in some tussock or clump of grass, and contains three or four white eggs, dotted with brown. The parent birds will do everything in their power to divert your attention and it will be hard to resist the wiles of the handsome black-headed little yellow male.

The Black-poll Warbler and the Water Thrush will be there also, the former noticeable by his black head. Then, too, the Red-start may be found. He is a strange little chap, sometimes building his nest in low bushes, some-

BLUE BIRD

times in trees forty or fifty feet from the ground. The Redstart's plumage is not of the hue that his name implies, but of orange and black, a good deal like a Baltimore Oriole on a small scale. This latter bird will come from the South about May first, or a little earlier, and flash like a ray of sunlight from tree to tree. Presently his more sombrely dressed mate will put in an appearance and the pair will begin about the end of May to construct, at the tip of some branch overhanging the roadside, one of the nests with which we are all so familiar. It is a beautiful nest, woven out of fibres, with here and there a bit of string or gaudy cloth for ornament. Upon one occasion a patriotic person hung red, white and blue worsted near his home, hoping that an oriole, which was building near by, would use some of it; and he was highly gratified when on July Fourth, a brood of young orioles resplendent in their orange and black liveries of Lord Baltimore, for whom the bird was first named, chirped noisily from a red, white and blue nest.

Leaving the wet haunts of these birds and coming into the dry woodlands, where the ground has a peren-

AMERICAN ROBIN

nial carpet of leaves and pine needles, one will find the Water Thrush's near relative, the Oven-bird. He makes his appearance after May the first, sneaking about the woods like a burglar, a noisy one it must be said, for his song, beginning low and gradually becoming louder, ends abruptly at the top of his vocal strength. He begins to build his nest about June the first. Unless the bird is flushed suddenly, it is very difficult to discover, and one must look very closely for the four little eggs in their carefully roofed resting place.

Up in the tall pines are the rarer Wood-warblers. Oftentimes, in tramping through the woods, we hear an

YELLOW-BELLIED FLYCATCHER

BLACKBURNIAN WARBLER

apparently insignificant chirp from some tree-top, and find on careful investigation that it has come from some bird of the Warbler family for which, perhaps, we have been looking all day. Early in the spring, before the trees are well leaved out, is a very good time to see these little fellows. The Blackburnian Warbler, beautifully ar-

rayed in orange and black, the tiny Parula Warbler, with its Quakerlike dress of blue gray, set off by a saddle of old gold, the Pine Creeping Warbler and the Black-throated G r e e n Warbler will all become familiar to you in time. The one last mentioned nests in the tallest pine trees and its nest is so tiny that you will hardly find it, unless you happen to see the bird fly off.

The Yellow is the commonest of all our New England Warblers, and is known by half a dozen names—Yellow Warbler, Summer Warbler, Yellow Wren, Yellow Sparrow and Yellow Bird being the ones most frequently heard. The female is olive green and is most quiet and retiring, but the male bird in his suit of yellow sprinkled with brown, is a familiar figure on the roadside shrubbery. It nests anywhere, often in barberry bushes, when they can be found, and never over six feet or so from the ground. The nest is strongly built of plant fibres and lined usually with fern down, or some other soft material. There four white eggs are laid, splotched and dotted about the larger end with purplish brown. This is one of the birds most frequently burdened with the eggs of the Cowbird, and it often happens that the little warbler roofs over her first nest and builds on it a second one in her efforts to be rid of such an unwelcome guest.

The other familiar member of this family is the Chestnut-sided Warbler, and is one of the most beautiful—black and white, with a yellow cap, and yellow wingbars set off by its distinguishing mark of bright chestnut; this bird makes the hillsides and wooded places cheerful by its song. Its nest, generally found in some low bush on a hillside, is suspended between

CHESTNUT-SIDED WARBLER

two branches, or a small fork of a shrub, and contains usually four eggs very much like those of the Yellow Warbler in size and marking. It is one of the most perfect examples of bird architecture and does not easily escape the notice of the ornithologist.

Another variety of Warbler often seen in large numbers during the spring migration, is the Yellow Rump, a showy little bird in blue, gray and yellow. It breeds but seldom in New England, except in the more Northern States, and then sparingly.

The Warbler family is very large, and in addition to those birds already mentioned, one may see in the spring the following: Canadian, Wilson's, Hooded, Maryland Yellow-throat, Mourning, Connecticut, Prairie, Pine Creeping, Yellow Palm, Yellow Throated, Bay-breasted, Magnolia, Black-throated Blue, Cape May, Tennessee, Orange-crowned, Nashville, Golden-winged, Blue-winged, Worm-eating, Prothonotary, and Black and White. The last named, sometimes known as the Black and White Creeper, is familiar to many lovers of the woods. He is often to be seen

GREAT BLUE HERON

running up and down the bark of large trees, looking for the larvæ and bugs that form his diet. The nest, usually on the ground at the foot of some large tree, is a slight structure of grass, and contains, when complete, four small white eggs, with reddish brown dots all over their surface.

Leaving the uplands and wandering

BLACK AND WHITE WARBLER

down toward the river, along its banks Blackbirds will be discovered looking about for a suitable bush in which to build their nests, or if it is fairly late in May, one may see the male bird perched on some branch overhanging the stream, while he sings to his heart's content. Within the thick bushés, or perhaps in the long grass, the little brown female is quietly sitting on her substantial nest. In the reeds the marsh wrens are busily twittering and excitedly peeping forth at anyone who intrudes. Their nest is a wonderfully made structure, carefully woven of dead reeds and fastened to living ones. It looks more like a gourd than a nest. A tiny hole in the top ad-

mits the parent birds. It is carefully lined with feathers and soft material, in which six or eight chocolate colored eggs are deposited. This little nest of the Marsh Wren's is one of the most perfect of bird homes.

But what is that form that scuttled away so suddenly, hardly giving one a chance to determine its character? A careful search will reveal a Rail's nest, with its complement of seven or eight buff eggs speckled with black. In the northernmost state of New England may be found the Coot, which lays its eggs on a tussock in the middle of some marsh. The eggs resemble in color those of the Rail, but in size are as large as those of the bantam.

CAT BIRD

In marshy borders of lakes or ponds are found the nests of the Horned, or Pied-billed Grebes (Hell-divers they are called when they appear along the sea coast in winter). They build a platform of dead weeds, which they anchor to living ones. The Loon constructs a similar resting place for the two eggs (as large as those of the

BELTED KINGFISHER

two New England birds, I believe, that conceal their eggs in the earth, but often birds use holes in trees for that purpose. Many of them are lazy, though, and have a habit of appropriating the deserted nests of woodpeckers which make their own excavations often to the depth of eighteen inches in sound green trees. There at the bottom of the hole thus made, on a few chips, they lay their eggs, always white, but varying greatly in size according to the variety. The Woodpeckers found in New England are the Red-headed, Hairy, Downy, Pileted, Yellow-bellied, Red-naped, and Golden-winged. In winter some of the Arctic species come to us.

Along the sea-coast near fishing grounds, may be seen the common Terns hovering about, waiting to pick up any bits of fish thrown from the fishermen's boats, and sometimes taking a hand themselves in the fishing. Their near relatives, the Caspian, Arctic, Roseate and Least Terns may be met with them. These birds all breed

goose) which it lays each year, their ground color being chocolate, with black dots sparingly distributed over the surface.

Some birds build their summer homes in strange places. For instance, one would never think of finding the Kingfisher, so familiar to all who live near water, sitting on seven white eggs at the end of a burrow which would do credit to a woodchuck or rabbit, yet this is the form of seclusion which is sought. There is a gravel pit on the banks of the Sudbury River in Massachusetts that is the home of hundreds of Swallows and two pairs of Kingfishers. The steep walls of this pit are honey-combed with the little holes of the Bank-swallows that live there and each year raise their broods to add to the numbers that skim over the smooth surface of the river. One may take a trowel and dig into the bank for three feet before coming to the end of the burrow, where on a few grasses will be found at nesting time four white eggs. These are the only

WHIP-POOR-WILL

COOPER'S HAWK

dle of May the Whip-poor-wills put in an appearance, as do also their near relatives the Night Hawks. The Chimney Swallows are close connections of these two, and if you can manage to see the nest of one, you will observe an odd provision in nature which furnishes these birds with a kind of glue to fasten the basket-like nest against the side of the chimney. The Pewee is known by the constant reiteration of his own name, and you may look for his nest under old bridges and in similar places. Then the Swallows will come and build on some old barn, and if one has time to watch their nest grow bit by bit, it will be found most interesting.

Vireos nest in the woods, but as they come a little later than most birds, they may be reserved for the next article.

That gaudy woodland bird, the

in the various islands of the Vineyard Sound group, particularly Muskegat, where they are protected. Some of the Hawks will be seen there also, notably the Marsh Hawk, which in his quest for mice and shrews flies low over the wet meadows. The Red-shouldered Hawk and the Sharp-shinned Hawk are the ones that do the damage; the Marsh Hawk, distinguishable a long way off by his white rump, will not invade the poultry yard.

Toward the mid-

BLUE JAY

REDWINGED BLACKBIRD

England during the months of March, April and May is appended. This is taken from "The Birds of New England," by H. D. Minot. These dates are only approximate, as the birds come far earlier to Connecticut and Rhode Island than to the Northern States of New England.

The space allowed will hardly permit the enumeration of more than half the names of the birds which may cross one's path in the spring season.

Blue Jay, will make himself familiar with you whether you want to meet him or not. He will imitate all the other birds in addition to his own cat-like call, and at times give a cry like the squeaking of an old door on a windy day.

Sparrows without number come from the South, the early arrivals being the Fox Sparrow, the largest of his kind, and the White-throated Sparrow. Both of these pass on to the Northern limit of New England, closely followed by many others.

A calendar of the birds of New

CARDINAL GROSBEAK

March 1st-15th.

Song Sparrows and Snow Birds begin to sing. The Bluebirds and Blackbirds come from the South, and the Song Sparrows and Robins become more abundant.

March 15th-31st.

The Robins, Cedar-birds, Meadow Larks become more numerous. Blackbirds, Fox Sparrows, Bay-winged Buntings, Cow-birds, and Pewees arrive.

April.

The Kingfishers, Swallows, Chipping Sparrows, Field Sparrows, Hermit Thrushes, Pine Warblers, Red-poll Warblers,

BOBOLINK

Ruby-crowned Kinglets, and sometimes White-throated Sparrows appear.

May 1st.

About the 1st of the month the Barn Swallows, Black and White Warblers, Least Flycatchers, Night Hawks, Purple Martins, Solitary Vireo, Towhee Buntings, Yellow-rump Warblers, and Yellow-winged Sparrows make their appearance.

May 5th.

The Baltimore Orioles, Black-throated Green Warblers, Catbirds, Chimney Swallows, Wilson's Thrushes, Yellow Warblers.

May 10th.

Blackburnian Warblers, Blackcap Warblers, Black-throated Blue Warblers, Parula Warblers,

Bobolinks, Chestnut-sided Warblers, Oven-birds, Golden-winged Warblers, House Wrens, Humming-birds, King birds, Maryland Yellow-throats, Nashville Warblers, Redstarts, Rose-breasted Grosbeaks, Warbling Vireos, Water Wagtails, Wood Thrushes, and Yellow-throated Vireos arrive.

May 15th.

The Bay-breasted, Magnolia, Black-poll, Canadian, and Mourning Warblers arrive, also the Olive-sided Flycatchers, Traill's Flycatchers and White-crowned Sparrows appear.

May 20th.

About the 20th the Tennessee Warblers, the Yellow-bellied Flycatchers and the Wood Pewees may be looked for.

LARK BUNTING

A Century of Choral Singing in New England

By Henry C. Lahee

THE cause of music in New England has always received its greatest impulse from the enthusiasm of men who, while possessed of comparatively small technical ability or musical education, put the whole force of their souls into the work of helping the masses of people to a higher enjoyment of music than that in which they found them. Their accomplishments to this end must always be regarded with respect, for he who does the most for the cause of music in a nation is the man who inspires the greatest number with a love for the art and a desire for some knowledge of it, and as choral singing affords the surest foundation, we naturally look to those men who have been foremost in its cultivation.

Until the latter part of the eighteenth century there was practically no choral singing except in the church, but an enthusiast arose who not only initiated important reforms in church choirs, but also established that peculiar institution of olden times generally known as the "singing skewl," and who is said to have originated, in New England, the concert.

This enthusiast was William Billings, born in Charlestown, Massachusetts, a tanner by trade, who has been described as a mixture of the ludicrous, eccentric, commonplace, active, patriotic, and religious elements, with a slight touch of musical and poetic talent. He was deformed,—one arm somewhat withered, one leg shorter than the other, and blind of one eye, and he was given to the habit of continually taking snuff. He had a stentorian voice, drowning that of every singer near him. He was an advocate of the "fuguing tunes" then being introduced into the country from England, and he wrote many such tunes himself, using the sides of leather in his tannery on which to work out his musical ideas with a piece of chalk. With the compositions of Billings, crude as they were and amusing, we have nothing to do. Let a single sample, and that a poem (?) stand for all. This verse was written as a dedication ode to his "New England Psalm Singer," published in 1770:—

> O, praise the Lord with one consent,
> And in this grand design
> Let Britain and the Colonies
> Unanimously join.

Billings introduced the bass viol into the church and thus broke down the ancient Puritanical prejudice against musical instruments. He also was the first to use the pitch pipe in order to ensure some degree of certainty in "striking up the tune" in church. Billings gradually drifted away from tanning and became a singing teacher. As early as 1774 he began to teach a class at Stoughton, and as a result of his labors the Stoughton Musical Society, which still flourishes, was formed in 1786, and it has the record of being the first musical society of Massachusetts. The Dartmouth, N. H., Handel Society was also formed about this time, and numerous singing schools sprang up, for the example of Billings was followed by others. Indeed, Billings was able to impart so much enthusiasm to his classes and he taught them to sing with such good swing and expression, that singing became a revelation to most people. He died at the beginning of the nineteenth century, but he had given the impulse which has gathered in force with each succeeding year, and which has been carried forward and increased by other enthusiasts.

The Massachusetts Musical Society was formed in 1807 with the same object as most of the singing societies, viz., that of singing psalms and anthems. It was dissolved in 1810, but in 1815 the Handel and Haydn Society was formed, and on December 25th of . that year, gave a performance at King's Chapel in Boston of the first part of Haydn's "Creation," and airs and choruses selected from Handel's works. The audience numbered nine hundred and forty-five and the verdict on the performance was, "Such was the excitement of the hearers, and attention of the performers, that there is nothing to compare with it at the present day." There had, however, been performances of oratorio in Boston previous to this, both in 1812 and 1813 under the direction of Dr. Jackson, the organist, at that time, of the Brattle Street church. At this last performance, in 1813, part of the Dettingen Te Deum and the Hallelujah

Chorus were given by a choir of two hundred and fifty voices and an orchestra of fifty instruments, and the impulse given by this concert undoubtedly had much to do with the formation of the Handel and Haydn Society.

Thus within fifteen years of the death of Billings, choral singing, poor as it was, had reached a much higher plane than that in which he left it. Amongst his most eminent contemporaries and successors were Andrew Law, who was a better musician, though a man of less magnetism; Jacob Kimball, less original than Billings; Oliver Holden, first a carpenter and joiner of Charlestown, then teacher of singing, composer of hymns and fuguing tunes, and later a publisher; Samuel Holyoke, of Boxford, teacher of singing, violin, flute and clarinet; Daniel Read, Timothy Swan, Jacob French, Oliver Shaw, a blind singer, and many others, who all flourished and taught the "singin' skewl."

A vivid description of an old fashioned New England singing school was given in the Musical Visitor for January, 1842, by Moses Cheney, an old time preacher and singer, who was born in 1776. Elder Cheney was the progenitor of the well known family of singers of that name, who during the middle of the century traveled all over the country giving concerts.

After relating some incidents of his childhood, Elder Cheney says:

"We were soon paraded all around the room, standing up to a board supported by old-fashioned kitchen chairs. . . . The master took his place inside the circle, took out of his pocket a paper manuscript, with rules and tunes all written with pen and ink, read the rules, and then said we must attend to the rising and falling of the notes. I shall now take the liberty to call ladies and gen-

tlemen and things just as they were called
in that school, and I begin with the rules as
they were called, first:

FLATS.

The natural place for mi is in B
But if B be flat mi is in E.
If B and E be flat mi is in A.
If B, E, and A be flat mi is in D.
If B, E, A, and D be flat mi is in G.

SHARPS.

But if F be sharp mi is in F.
If F and C be sharp mi is in C.
If F, C, and G be sharp mi is in G.
If F, C, G, and D be sharp mi is in D.

"These rules as then called were all that
was presented in that school.

"The books contained one part each, bass
books, tenor books, counter books, and
treble books. Such as sung bass had a bass
book; he that sung tenor had a tenor book;
he who sang counter a counter book, and
the gals, as then called, had treble books.
I had no book. With all these things before
the school the good master began, 'Come,
boys, you must rise and fall the notes first
and then the gals must try.' So he began
with the oldest, who stood at the head,—
'Now follow me right up and down; sound.'
So he sounded, and followed the master up
and down as it was called. Some more
than half could follow the master. Others
would go up two or three notes and then
fall back lower than the first note. My
feelings grew acute. To see some of the
large boys, full twenty years old, make such
dreadful work, what could I do! Great fits
of laughing, both with boys and gals, would
often occur. . . . Then the gals had
their turn to rise and fall the notes. 'Come,
gals, now see if you can't beat the boys.' So
when he had gone through the gals' side of
the school he seemed to think the gals had
done rather the best. Now the rules were left
for tunes. Old Russia was brought on first.
The master sang it over several times, first
with the bass, then with the tenor, then with
the counter and then with the trebles. Such
as had notes looked on, such as had none
listened to the rest. In this way the school
went on through the winter. A good num.
ber of tunes were learned in this school and
were sung well as we thought, but as to the
science of music very little was gained.

"At the close of the school, and after
singing the last night, we made a settlement
with the master. He agreed 'to keep,' as
then called, for one shilling and sixpence a
night, and to take his pay in Indian corn at
three shillings a bushel. A true dividend
of the cost was made among the boys, the
gals found the candles for their part, and it
amounted to thirteen quarts and one pint of
corn apiece. After the master had made
some good wishes on us all, we were dismissed and all went home in harmony and
good union."

It would be difficult to find a more
touching or more convincing tribute to
the value of the singing school than
that given by Elder Cheney. "Think
for a moment," he says, "a little boy at
twelve years of age, growing up in the
shade of the deep and dense forests of
New Hampshire, seldom out of the
sight of his mother, or the hearing of
her voice, never saw a singing master
or a musical note—seldom ever heard
the voice of any human being except
in his own domestic circle, by the fire-
side of his father's humble hearth.
Think of it! Now he is a member of
a school—more, a singing school!
Singing the tunes by note! Singing
'We live above!' Carrying any part
all in the same high boy's voice. O,
that winter's work. The foundation
of many happy days for more than
fifty years past. The master too! Ah,
that blessed form of a man. His bright
blue, sparkling eyes and his sweet,
angelic voice—his manifest love and
care for his pupils—everything combined to make him one of a thousand."

Then comes a repetition of the story
of Elijah and Elisha, with a New England coloring. "Forty-three years ago"
(one hundred and four years from
the present date, for Mr. Cheney wrote
in 1841) "or the winter after I was
twenty-one, I followed Mr. William

Tenney, the best instructor I had ever found. He taught every afternoon and evening in the week, Sunday excepted. When he left us, he gave me his singing book and wooden pitch pipe and told me to believe I was the best singer in the world and then I should never be afraid to sing anywhere. . . . After this last school, from the time of my age, twenty-one, I have taught singing until I became fifty—that is, more or less, from time to time."

There is in the Religious Monthly of 1861 an acount of the Oxford, Massachusetts, singing school, founded in 1830, in which a good deal of human nature is revealed. The jealousies among the singers, their sarcastic remarks, at one another's expense, and the oddities of the teacher are very amusing. "Fill your chests and open your mouths. Don't squeeze your mouths as if you were going to whistle Yankee Doodle," the teacher exclaims, and then proceeds to give an example of a thunderous tone, roll it, quaver and shake it. Then he shows the opposite, in mimicry of his class. Now the pupils endeavor to imitate him, and subject themselves to the biting sarcasm of their fellow pupils,—"Now I understand being threatened with lock-jaw," says one. "She looks as if she was trying to swallow the universe," another exclaims. But these little pleasantries have become uninteresting by frequent repetition, and we may well turn to a later number of the same journal and glance at an account of "a singing school of fifty years ago," which means about 1820:

"The class arrives in a straggling stream, the meeting being held at seven o'clock in the parish vestry. The teacher takes from his pocket a yellow flute with one key, fits the parts together with much care, adjusts the instrument to the corner of his mouth and gives a preliminary flourish. With a few well considered remarks the school is open for the season.

"The pupils are marshalled according to their voices and attainments. Now he stands before a row of young ladies, gets the pitch from the yellow flute and elevates his sonorous voice. Now he listens along the line for unison or discord, as the class repeat the note or passage. From the rattle of short, diffident responses, let off at every possible grade, his quick ear is able, after some severe trials of patience, to judge of the materials offered. They are afterwards put through a series of more difficult tests. At one bench shrill tenors respond as through a comb covered with thin paper. Boys crow like young chanticleers, or fall into ruins from some high note, while basses drop into unfathomable depths of sound which seem to come up everywhere through the floor and give no hint of origin or relation to other sounds.

"Failing at his bench to govern the tones of the class by his voice, the teacher now goes to an obscure corner of the candle-lighted room and returns with a violoncello in a green bag, and after some wailings and shrieks from the upper strings, groans from the lower ones, and a little tub-tub-tubbing with the thumb and finger, the instrument is in tune and away they go at it again guided in their perilous path by the tones of the bass viol.

"As the class proceeds from week to week, Fa, Sol, La become obsolete, varieties of time and movement are noted, keynotes discovered and the class goes from "Dundee" and "Old Hundred" to more stirring music. Now they start on some ambitious fuguing tunes of Billings and Holden, in which the several parts worry and puzzle each other like half a dozen reckless fire engines in full cry to a conflagration, and the few remaining lessons are more like musical reunions."

A graphic picture is given of the bent and aged sexton, an old sailor, and his frequent dashes to the door to disperse the crowd of young street buc-cancers who gather to have some fun at the expense of the class. At them he hurls a broadside of invective, of which his sea training has made him master. The grotesque shadows of the teacher cast upon the wall by the dim glimmer of the candles afford gentle mirth. Then, too, many a running noose flung over young people unawares at the singing school was drawn into a love-knot in after months and years. Undoubtedly the singing school was a great institution in its day.

Another great factor in the development of choral singing amongst the people was the Musical Convention, and the establishment of these conventions has generally been attributed to Lowell Mason. But we must refer again to the Cheney family and quote from a letter written by Moses E. Cheney, the son of Elder Cheney.

"You know, perhaps, that the singing conventions, or 'musical conventions,' had their beginning in Montpelier, Vermont, in May, 1839, and that your humble servant was the projector, and that they were continued yearly until five very successful conventions had been held. At every convention a committee was appointed to fix upon a town within the state for the next convention and give due notice to the newspapers. The five conventions under the organization were held at the following villages: Montpelier, 1839; Newberry, 1840; Windsor, 1841; Woodstock, 1842; Middlebury, 1843. The committee made no appointment for 1844 and that ended the organization. Seven years later, when I returned to Vermont to live, I found that musical conventions had been going on for three or four years. Mason, Baker, Woodbury, Root and others were holding them; it was a new start. Plainly enough they had all rooted from the convention held in Montpelier in 1839."

Mr. Cheney then enters into the details of the origin of these conventions:

"E. K. Prouty, a broken merchant in Waterford, then a travelling peddler with a horse and wagon, came along with his cart and took me to Coventry. As he was a singing teacher there, we could meet some singers and have a great musical time. Very good. Prouty was a fine singer and also a composer, ten years my senior. Afterward I used to meet Prouty who kept me aroused to music, and soon I was teaching in Montpelier and leading the brick church choir. I was in request as a teacher for all I could do. Well, in 1836 Prouty was visiting his wife's relations at the Capital. I chanced to meet him, and he was very eloquent on the subject of music. As we parted I said to him jocularly, 'Prouty, we must have a musical convention.'

"I soon found myself seriously in thought on the subject. I spoke of it to Judge Redfield and other eminent persons, all of whom gave their approval. Judge Howes said a call must be issued, inviting the people to assemble for a convention. So I trained all my schools to the practice of unusual tunes, anthems, quartets, male quartets, duets and solos for both sexes. We used for secular music 'The Boston Glee Book' and Kingsley's two volumes. We had more than two hundred singers, half of them good and some very good. All could read music. Every one, I think, knew his or her part. The convention was held May 22 and 23, 1839. . . . Lowell Mason knew nothing of it; Henry E. Moore knew nothing of it. The musical convention was begotten and born in Vermont, not in Massachusetts; in Montpelier, not in Boston. It was suggested, nursed and trained by Moses E. Cheney and not by Lowell Mason, who stated at our third convention, held at Windsor in 1841, that that was the first day he had ever stepped foot into Vermont. Our committee invited him to come to lead our singing. He came bringing two hundred Carmina Sacras just from the press, and the convention sang the new music. He said to me that Vermont was the second state in the Union in point of musical culture. He did not think it the equal of Massachusetts, but it surpassed all other states."

The officers of the first musical convention, held at Montpelier, were:

President, Joshua Bates, President of Middlebury College; Vice-president, E. P. Walton; Secretary, E. P. Walton, Jr.; Treasurer, Solomon Durgin; Director, Moses E. Cheney; Organist, John H. Paddock.

There were also thirteen clergymen present, who spoke on thirteen different subjects, all connected with music. Their speeches were interspersed with anthems, tunes and glees which constituted the prime object of the convention.

There appears to have been a peculiar confusion of name in connection with musical meetings. The word "convention," which has been customarily applied to such affairs as that just related, means a gathering of select persons for discussion of a subject. This certainly does not apply very well to the conventions of the Cheney type, which consisted of singers gathered together from far and wide for the purpose of singing, but it does apply very aptly to the gatherings organized by Lowell Mason and called Teachers' Institutes. These were really gatherings of teachers for the purpose of discussing matters of musical education. They were held at various places and lasted a few weeks. As an institute is essentially something on a firm foundation and of a lasting nature this title seems peculiarly inappropriate, even more so than the use of the word convention for musical festival.

With all due allowance for confusion of terms, there is still evidence that Elder Cheney is mistaken as to the origin of the musical convention, for according to good authorities a similar gathering was held at Concord, N. H., in 1829, under the auspices of the Central Musical Society of that State, and

was conducted by Henry E. Moore, the same gentleman who, according to Elder Cheney, knew nothing of the Montpelier convention of 1839.

It is now advisable to go back a little for the purpose of sketching the career of Lowell Mason and his greatest works—introducing singing into the public schools, and establishing conventions—that is, "Teachers' Institutes."

Lowell Mason will always be a prominent figure in the history of music in America. He marked the transition period from the illiteracy of the beginning of the nineteenth century to the generally diffused musical information of the present time. To him we owe some of our best ideas in religious music, elementary musical education, music in the public schools, the popularization of classical chorus singing, and the art of teaching music on the inductive plan. In short, he formed the musical taste of his generation and of the next following, and has been called, "The Father of Music in America."

Lowell Mason was born in Medfield, Massachusetts, January 8, 1792, and was the son of a manufacturer of straw bonnets. As a boy he had a great fondness for music, but such a thing as devoting himself to it for a life business was not contemplated. In school he did not distinguish himself, and although he had no bad habits, he acquired the reputation of being a ne'er do well. His thirst for everything relating to musical art was great, and he amused himself by learning to play almost every instrument which came in his way. This he could do with very little trouble, and he taught singing schools, led a choir and became prominent in his native town quite early. At the age of twenty he went South with a view to making his fortune. He secured a position in a bank at Savannah, but there also his chief work became that of teaching singing and leading a choir, which soon became famous in the surrounding country, not only for the musical quality of its work, but especially for the religious spirit which characterized its singing.

In 1825 Deacon Julius Palmer, of Boston, spent a Sabbath in Savannah and was so impressed with the music in the Presbyterian church where Mr. Mason was playing the organ and leading the choir, that on his return home he interested a number of gentlemen in joining a movement to invite Mr. Mason to remove to Boston and work for the improvement of church music there. The result was that Lowell Mason moved to Boston in 1827 and took charge of the choirs of Dr. Lyman Beecher's church in Hanover Street, Dr. Edward Beecher's and the Park Street church. After a time the plan of managing three church choirs was found not to work well and he confined his labors to the first. In the same year he was elected president of the Handel and Haydn Society, a position which he held for five years.

Meanwhile his mind became occupied with schemes for the musical education of children. In 1829 he met Mr. William C. Woodbridge, who had been abroad for several years studying educational systems, and brought with him the published works of Pestalozzi and the music book on Pestalozzian principles by Nägeli and other writers. Being engaged to lecture in Boston Mr. Woodbridge wished to find

some school children to help him with illustrations of a musical nature and was referred to Lowell Mason, who had a well trained class of boys. Mr. Mason did not at first care to change his method in favor of that of Pestalozzi, and it was not until after a good deal of persuasion that he consented to teach a class upon the new system. The result, however, so far surpassed his expectations that he was permanently converted, and became a consistent advocate of the inductive method.

It was apparently this new departure which caused his resignation from the presidency of the Handel and Haydn Society, for many of the members were old fashioned, and opposed to innovations. It also caused the founding of the Boston Academy of Music in 1833.

Shortly after his conversion to the new method, efforts were made to establish music as a regular study in the public schools, and in 1832 a resolution was passed by the primary school board to the effect that "one school from each district be selected for the introduction of systematic instruction in vocal music." The experiment did not prove to be more than a partial trial and Mr. Mason became convinced that it was necessary to bring more potent influences to bear in shaping public opinion as a motive power with the educational authorities. He therefore organized gratuitous classes for children and gave concerts to illustrate their proficiency and the practicability of his scheme for primary musical education, and thus the people's interest became aroused.

This all took time and it was not until 1836 that the school board, on petitions from citizens, authorized the introduction of music into the public schools, and even then the city failed to make the necessary appropriation.

Mr. Mason, however, was not to be daunted by trifles after he had gone so far, and he volunteered to teach in one school for a year without charge. He did this and in addition supplied the pupils with books and materials at his own expense. The result was that the report of the committee on music in 1838 testified to the entire success of the experiment and said: "The committee will add, on the authority of the masters of the Hawes School, that the scholars are farther advanced in their studies at the end of this than of any other year."

Thus, seven years after the enterprise was first taken in hand by Mr. Mason, a work was accomplished whose influence has ever more been felt and continues to expand in its beneficent operation throughout the whole United States. Music was formally adopted as a public school study and Lowell Mason was placed in charge of the work. In 1839 the school committee said in their report, "It may be regarded as the Magna Charta of musical education in America."

Lowell Mason remained in charge of the music in the public schools of Boston until 1853 when he was superseded by a former pupil of his own, an event which caused him some mortification, although of a nature common in city politics.

Shortly after this, Mr. Mason went abroad where he was received with great honor and everywhere recognized as an eminent teacher and a most impressive lecturer.

Aside from his books, and occasional musical conventions, his last days were not occupied with teaching, with the exception of the Normal Musical Institutes held for several years at North Reading, Massachusetts, where he conducted the oratorio choruses and the sacred music classes, and brought them to a remarkable degree of perfection. The degree of Doctor of Music was conferred upon him by the University of Yale.

Dr. Mason was a natural teacher, full of tact, logical, handy with the black board and delightfully simple in his phraseology. He declared that teachers ought to be promoted downwards, for the real work must be done at the bottom. His great merits were his simplicity, sincerity and unaffected kindness. He died at Orange, N. J., in 1872.

The establishment of the "convention" was a part of Lowell Mason's plan for the education of the masses in singing by note. The Boston Academy of Music was founded with this object in view and in 1834, the year after its establishment, a course of lectures was given by its professors to teachers of singing schools, and others. The "others" must have been few in numbers for the lectures, we are told, were attended by twelve persons, most of whom had been accustomed to teach. In 1835 a similar course was given with an attendance of eighteen persons, besides several of the class of '34. In 1836 the membership rose to twenty-eight, besides members of the previous classes, and the gentlemen present on this occasion organized themselves into a convention for the discussion of questions relating to the general subject of musical education, church music, and musical performances, during such hours as were not occupied by the lectures.

It is not our purpose to follow the history of the convention in detail. It resembled the course of true love which never does run smoothly. Suffice it to say that the convention became a popular method for the diffusion of musical knowledge,—and sometimes also for the display of ignorance. Much good was done by it, however, and when properly conducted, with its true intentions carried out it enabled the psalm-tune teacher, the music teacher from small country towns, and members of singing societies or church choirs to hear new works rendered by a good chorus, to gather some new and much needed information, and sometimes to enjoy the inspiring performance of some noted artist.

Like every other good thing, it was subject to abuse, and many conventions were held by ignorant impostors, men of low tastes, and those whose sole object was "trade," but on the whole the convention wrought much good, and helped to make possible the Oratorio and Choral Society.

The evolution of the Oratorio Society in New England was not rapid, and we may perhaps get the best idea of it by tracing the history of choral singing in one of the smaller cities.

Let us take Salem, Massachusetts, for our example. Previous to 1814 there was an association called the Essex Musical Society, by which were held primitive festivals in different towns in the county, but the first regular society formed in Salem was the Essex South Musical Society, organized in October, 1814, with Isaac Flagg of Beverly for director, and consisting of about sixty members. It was customary in those days for the clergy to make addresses on musical subjects at the public performances and even at the rehearsals, and many of these were considered important and undoubtedly aided in developing the interest in music. This society continued to exist for ten years and a half, the last concert being given on November 20, 1829.

There were also other societies,— the Handel Society was organized in 1817 and lasted three years; the Haydn Society came into existence in 1821, but was short lived; the Mozart Association was formed in 1825 and existed nearly ten years. These societies chose ambitious names, and sang selections from Handel, Haydn and Mozart, besides minor composers, but the members were untrained in the vocal art, except for such instruction as was afforded by the old fashioned singing school.

In 1832 the Salem Glee Club was formed for the purpose of studying a lighter and more modern class of music. This society flourished for about twenty years and became very efficient. There was also the Salem Social Singing Society formed in 1839, and a new Mozart Association in 1840.

In 1846 the Salem Academy of Music was formed, with a membership of fifty persons and an orchestra of sixteen instruments, and in 1849 the Salem Philharmonic Society was organized. These two societies amalgamated in 1855 under the name of the Salem Choral Society. All these societies tended to raise the standard of music, more ambitious work was continually being done, better musicians were constantly becoming associated, and the general average of musical knowledge was greater each year.

In 1868 the time was considered ripe for the formation of a society capable of performing the greater choral works and the result was the establishment of the Salem Oratorio Society, which has always had a high reputation. The prominent names in the musical history of Salem include Henry K. Oliver, Dr. J. F. Tuckerman, B. J. Lang, Manuel Fenolosa, Carl Zerrahn and others.

Some of the most noted choral societies are the Worcester County Musical Association of Worcester, Mass., the Hampden County Musical Association of Springfield, Mass.; the Salem Oratorio Society; and the Portland Oratorio Society. New Bedford, Mass., Hartford and New Haven, Conn., Burlington, Vt., and many other cities and towns have flourishing choral societies.

In the middle of the century there was little or no earnest musical effort outside of the two or three largest cities, which was not included in the range of culture represented by Lowell Mason and his associates, who effected a great deal in the way of introducing the chief choruses from the great oratorios.

After the war the conditions changed. Many musical societies were formed, but with the increase of wealth and culture there became a wider difference between the advanced and the elementary grades of knowledge. Thus while a high class of music was cultivated amongst the few, the masses of people did not advance,—in fact they appear to have retrograded.

Nevertheless the work of the convention and the musical institute went steadily on, and made possible the Peace Jubilee of 1869.

This great musical festival was planned by P. S. Gilmore and it was intended to "whip creation." The plan included a chorus of twenty thousand voices, an orchestra of two thousand, an audience of fifty thousand, and a building to hold them all. In addition to all these wonders, there were to be soloists, both vocal and instrumental, suitable for the occasion. To give a complete history of the affair would take more space than can be spared, and would lead us beyond the limits of this paper, but some little sketch of the chorus, which actually exceeded ten thousand voices is within our province, and at the same time it may be remarked that a second Jubilee was held in 1872 in which the numbers planned for the first one were realized, and the whole program carried out with all its elaborate details, even to the importation of several of the finest military bands from Europe. The first Jubilee was financially a success, the second a failure. It will answer our purpose to glance at the first only, for the second was merely a repetition on a larger scale, the methods employed being the same, but the artistic result certainly no greater, because of the unwieldy mass of material to be managed.

From the beginning the project was worked up with consummate skill, first in the securing of financial support, second in advertising and third in the organizing of the chorus and orchestra. When Mr. Gilmore first ventilated his huge plan, he visited many of Boston's musicians and organizers, but they were appalled by the magnitude of the undertaking. Finally he suc-

ceeded in interesting Dr. Eben Tourjée, who, after a couple of days' reflection, came to the conclusion that the
scheme was feasible, and convinced
other men who were influential in musical and financial circles.

Mr. Gilmore could not have secured
a more efficient assistant than Dr.
Tourjée, who was a born organizer
and an inspirer of enthusiasm in others, whom he impressed by his inborn
grace and suavity of manners. For
many years Eben Tourjée had worked
with the desire to make possible for
the masses the best musical education.
He became impressed, during a foreign
journey, with the idea of establishing
a musical conservatory in America
similar to the great institutions abroad,
and his efforts in that direction bore
fruit in the New England Conservatory. In regard to the establishment
of this institution an amusing story is
told, which gives the keynote to Dr.
Tourjée's ingenuity and tenacity of
purpose. On unfolding his plans to a
friend from whom he wished to secure
financial aid, he was told, "You can no
more do it than you can make a whistle
out of a pig's tail." Tourjée went off,
but in a few days returned to his friend
and showed him a whistle which he
had made out of a pig's tail. In such
ways he enlisted the confidence of
moneyed men, his scheme was carried
out and the whistle is to be seen to this
day in the museum of the New England conservatory.

When Dr. Tourjée decided to co-
operate with Gilmore in the Peace Jubilee, it not only saved the Jubilee but
ensured its success, and the result of
this success was that Dr. Tourjée was
called upon to lecture all over the country. By this means he established "the

Praise Service," giving lectures and
illustrating the subject in nearly one
thousand churches, and inspiring a
vast number of people with his own
enthusiasm.

The organization of the chorus was
thus placed in the hands of Dr. Eben
Tourjée, whose great services in the
cause of musical education had already
become conspicuous. Dr. Tourjée
sent out invitations to all choral societies, clubs, choirs and conventions to
join the huge chorus. The replies came
in quickly, many new societies sprang
up and choruses were organized
for the occasion. Musical instruction
in the public schools had been unosten-
tatiously feeding all these fountains.
The program was laid out and sent to
each organization. The singers came
together in their respective towns with
enthusiasm and in the work of rehearsal, the sense of participation was inspiring and uplifting.

When the great gathering took place
and visitors streamed to Boston for the
final rehearsals *en masse* there was in-
describable enthusiasm. Perhaps the
greatest object lesson of the whole festival was the chorus of seven thousand
school children giving a concert of
simple music on the last day of the
week. No greater testimonial to the
work of Lowell Mason could have been
devised.

As far as the artistic results of the
Jubilee are concerned, there was much
that was disappointing, although some
grand effects were produced at times,
especially in the rendering of the great
chorals from the Oratorios. It gave a
new impulse to the cause of choral
singing all over the country. The first
bond of union of the new societies was
the practice of *good* music,—the great

works of Handel, Haydn, Mozart and Mendelssohn.

It will be seen by the following statistics that by far the greatest part of the chorus was recruited from Boston and its immediate vicinity, although there were representatives from states as far distant as Illinois and Ohio. In the second Jubilee the representations were from almost, if not quite, every state as far west as Nebraska, and the chorus was twice as large. In commenting upon the Jubilee, the New York Tribune said:

"The Jubilee could have been organized nowhere but in Boston. A great orchestra can be collected by anybody who has the the money to pay for it; but a great chorus, in the present state of American musical culture, is impossible except in the capital of New England. Children in Boston learn music with their alphabet. Singing by note —not the mere screaming of tunes—is taught in the most thorough and systematic manner in all the public schools. This is why Boston has such magnificent choruses; and shall we not say that the charming good order, good temper, and enthusiasm which were so conspicuous in the motley crowd that overflowed the Coliseum were also attributable in no small degree to the refining and elevating influence of an early musical education. Here New York and all the great cities of America may find their lesson of the Jubilee."

The following list of organizations which took part in the Peace Jubilee of 1869 is taken from Dwight's Journal of Music. We copy simply the matter referring to the Chorus:

MASSACHUSETTS.

	Directors.	Members.
Boston Chorus—Bumstead Hall Classes	Carl Zerrahn, P. S. Gilmore, and Eben Tourjée	2934
Handel and Haydn Society, Boston	Carl Zerrahn	649
Boston Choral Society, South Boston	J. C. D. Parker	278
Chelsea Choral Society	John W. Tufts	504
Newton Choral Society	George S. Trowbridge	221
Worcester Mozart & Beethoven Ch. Union	Solon Wilder	202
Salem	Carl Zerrahn	269
Randolph	J. B. Thayer	101
Spingfield Mendelssohn Union	Amos Whiting	113
Georgetown Musical Union	E. Wildes	51
Newburyport	Charles P. Morrison	92
Haverhill Musical Union	J. K. Colby	132
Fall River Chorus Society	C. H. Robbins	75
Medford	W. A. Webber	84
Weymouth	C. H. Webb	188
Athol Musical Association	W. S. Wiggin	40
Quincy Point Choral Society	E. P. Heywood	30
Groton Centre Musical Association	Dr. Norman Smith	49
Malden Chorus Club	O. B. Brown	56
Plymouth Rock Choral Society	John H. Harlow	29
South Abington Choral Society	William A. Bowles	46
Waltham Choral Union	J. S. Jones	143
Fitchburg Choral Society	Moses G. Lyon	73
East Douglas Musical Society	John C. Waters	25
Quincy	H. B. Brown	60
Lawrence	S. A. Ellis	167
Abington Centre	Henry Noyes	45
Yarmouth Chorus Club	Jairus Lincoln	28

Sandwich Choral Society ....H. Hersey Heald.................   21
Hyannis ....R. Weeks.......................   24
Mansfield ....George E. Bailey...............   35
Holliston ....W. L. Payson...................   50
Melrose Musical Association.................H. E. Trowbridge...............   29
Northfield ....Miss M. A. Field   24
Springfield Choral Union ....J. D. Hutchins.................   24
North Abington.............................J. F. L. Whitmarsh.............   21
East Somerville.............................S. D. Hadley....................   29
Sherborn Musical Association...............Augustus H. Leland............   22
South Braintree Choral Society...........H. Wilde......................   140
Whitinsville ....B. L. M. Smith.................   13
New Bedford................................J. E. Eaton, Jr..................   75
West Acton Schubert Choral Union..........George Gardner   40
Middleboro ....A. J. Pickens...................   23
East Boston Choral Society ....Dexter A. Tompkins............   54
Hopkinton ....E. S. Nason....................   31
Methuen ....Jacob Emerson, Pres............   30
Natick ....J. Asten Broad.................   102
Milford ....C. J. Thompson.................   38
Woburn ....P. E. Bancroft.................   58
Lowell ....Solon W. Stevens...............   148
Amesbury Musical Ass'n.....................Moses Flanders   65
Belmont Musical Ass'n......................F. E Yates, Pres...............   37
Acushnet Musical Ass'n......................Ammi Howard   24
Framingham ....L. O. Emerson..................   40
Winchester Choral Society...................J. C. Johnson..................   48
Webster ....Carl Krebs   23
Ashland ....C. V. Mason....................   41
North Bridgewater..........................Dr. G. R. Whitney.   138
Reading Musical Ass'n ....D. G. Richardson, Pres..........   43
Sterling ....Birney Mann   18
Andover ....George Kingman   32
Groveland ....L. Hopkins   25
Taunton Beethoven Soc'y....................L. Soule   97
Lynn ....Rufus Pierce   133
Westfield ....J. R. Cladwin, Pres.............   36
Roxbury ....H. W. Brown, Pres..............   35

NEW HAMPSHIRE.

Manchester ....E. T. Baldwin..................   40
Nashua ....E. P. Phillips..................   49
Wolfeboro Union Chorus and Glee Club......M. T. Cate....................   31
Plaistow Choral Soc'y.......................Mrs. J. T. Nichols..............   23
Keene ....G. W. Foster and C. M. Wyman..   33
Farmington ....B. F. Ashton...................   20
Lebanon ....J. M. Perkins..................   39
New Hampton.................................Z. C. Perkins..................   29
Salmon Falls.................................George W. Brookings............   30
Exeter, Rockingham Mus. Ass'n.............Rev. J. W. Pickering, Jr..........   82
Concord Choral Soc'y.......................John Jackson   96
Francestown ....G. Epps   31
Dover, Strafford Co. Mus Ass'n............W. O. Perkins..................   193

Laconia, Belknap Mus. Ass'n . . . . Ralph N. Merrill.   34
Suncook Choral Soc'y. . . . . J. C. Cram.   31

VERMONT.

Randolph, Orange Co. Mus. Soc'y. . . . . George Dodge   18
Rutland . . . . R. I. Humphrey.   50
Middlebury . . . . C. F. Stone.   26

MAINE.

Damariscotta . . . . G. M. Thurlow.   32
Farmington Choral Society. . . . . C. A. Allen.   27
Augusta . . . . Waldemar Malmene   23
Saco . . . . G. G. Additon.   69
Lewiston, Androscoggin Mus. Soc'y. . . . . Seth Sumner   61
Bangor . . . . F. S. Davenport.   57

CONNECTICUT.

New Haven Choral Union. . . . . J. H. Wheeler.   83
Thompsonville. Enfield . . . . E. F. Parsons.   14
Waterbury . . . . J. W. Smith, Pres.   42
Wallingford . . . . J. H. Wheeler.   40
Lakeville, Salisbury. . . . . D. F. Stillman.   20

RHODE ISLAND.

Pawtucket Choral Society. . . . . George W. Hazelwood.   33
Providence . . . . Lewis T. Downes.   82

NEW YORK.

Granville . . . . D. B. Worley.   28
Malone Musical Ass'n. . . . . T. H. Attwood.   21
Saratoga Springs. . . . . S. E. Bushnell.   48

ILLINOIS.

Chicago Mendelssohn Soc'y. . . . . J. A. Butterfield.   95

OHIO.

Mansfield . . . . W. H. Ingersoll.   20
Cleveland . . . . S. A. Fuller.   28

Total 10,228

From the time of the Jubilee the work of educating the masses to sing at sight went steadily foward and efforts have been continually directed to improving the musical taste of the people. In the higher branches of musical education and enjoyment immense progress has been made. Boston to-day possesses an orchestra said to be the finest in the world, and there is no city in America in which great musical artists are more highly appreciated. or where more is being done for music students. All this is actually a testimonial to the work of those who have labored for the masses.

Notwithstanding all this, there is still room for more foundation work, and a lesson has been learned from New York, where some nine or ten years ago Mr. Frank Damrosch established Sunday singing classes for all people. The experiment was highly successful, for the opportunity was eagerly accepted by the people for whom it was intended.

In the fall of 1897, a similar plan was adopted in Boston under Mr. Samuel W. Cole, a well educated musician, who has for many years been a teacher of sight singing in the public schools of Dedham and Brookline and at the New England Conservatory.

The same feeling of enthusiasm with which the singing school filled Elder Cheney in the days of his youth, inspired Samuel W. Cole when he attended a convention at Concord, N. H., as a boy. Always fond of music and the son of a musically inclined father, the impression made on him by the singing of the grand choruses from the oratorios by a large choir directed by Carl Zerrahn was such that he determined to make music his life work. The hymn singing at Mr. Cole's class was under the direction of L. O. Emerson, and Mrs. Martha Dana Shepard presided at the piano skillfully supporting and coaching the somewhat nervous choir.

Mr. Cole now entered seriously upon musical studies and secured the best education available for the purpose in view. He began life as a music teacher in Portsmouth, N. H., and has since been continually engaged as organist, choir director and as teacher of sight singing in the public schools. A few years ago he gave up his position as organist at the Clarendon Street Baptist Church in order to travel abroad, and on his return, his Sundays then being free, he was able to accept the suggestion of the committee of the Massachusetts Emergeny and Hygiene Society to establish and direct the People's Singing classes. These classes meet at four o'clock on Sunday afternoons. Each person pays ten cents towards the rent of the hall and the purchase of music. The instructors give their services, and consider that their reward lies in the moral and intellectual good gained by the chorus.

In a very short time after the establishment of the first class in Bumstead Hall, it was found necessary to provide for the overflow, and other classes were formed in different parts of the city, until there were five large choruses.

Mr. Cole declares that people like the music that they know, and the aim of the People's singing class is to enable them to know good music in the belief that when they know it they will like it. In answer to the statement that the people always want a "tune," he says that certainly they will have the approval of all good musicians in this, if they will only like good tunes, and such they learn in these classes. This work may be considered in some respects the most important movement since sight singing was established in the public schools, for it enables people to enjoy the inspiration of choral singing, whose means and occupation prevent their gaining it in any other way, and makes it possible for them to continue the study which they began in the schools. In New York, where the plan has been in existence for several years, the classes are immense, and have been so judiciously managed financially that they have a good balance at the banker's. In Boston the scheme is not less successful, and will doubtless gain financially as long as the present system is maintained. There is no doubt that the movement will spread into the smaller cities and towns of New England, just as all schemes for choral singing have done. There is, however, this difference,— that while at the beginning of the century few, very few, of the singers could read the simplest music at sight, today no one who has attended school is without a moderate knowledge of the elements of sight singing. In what better manner can the working people spend their Sunday afternoons than in the manner prescribed by the old hymn :—

"All people that on earth do dwell,
Sing to the Lord with cheerful voice."

Hoosac Tunnel's Troubled Story

By Edward P. Pressey

"A pathway cleft beneath Old Hoosac hoary!
How few will climb the mountain's weary stair;
And future years will hand its troubled story
From child to child as olden legends are."

THE Mohican name Hoosac means far-over-the-mountain. The Indians called the streams just west of Hoosac the Mayunsook and Ashuwillticook, while the winding torrent to the east, under the beetling rocks, was the Pocumtuck. Over the mountain, from the western to the eastern waters runs an ancient roadway. This was first known to the white settlers as the Mohawk warpath, and many a brave found it the short cut to the happy hunting grounds. In the name of St. Croix, for a junction of streams, there is the single trace of an early Jesuit missionary's hopes.

By 1744, the Hoosac Mountains became famous in the military operations in New England. The Mohawk warpath, directly over the modern tunnel, was becoming rutted with the wheels of English cannon, while captives from Deerfield and Charlemont fainted on their forced marches up its weary stair, straight and unsoftened by any engineering triumphs of zigzag approaches.

By 1759, the year of Wolfe's capture of Quebec, the exigencies of the French wars had made necessary the construction of a rude road following this trail. The western gateway of the valley, near the spot where twice rose Fort Massachusetts, became the Thermopylæ of New England, in consequence of the repeated defeats there of Dutch, French and Indians. In 1797 the commonwealth ordered a fine turnpike, of the easy, whiplash type, built over the mountain across the eastern end of the trail, but by 1825 the abruptness of the mountain's slope had worn out so many good horses and men that a tunnelled canal uniting Pocumtuck and Hoosac waters was proposed.

The original trail was still open in 1848; and college boys often ran up and down it ahead of the lumbering Williamstown stage. It was traceable in 1893. There was an inn during

stage days where the paths crossed at the top of the mountain, "way up there, out of sight of land," and near a typical New England school house. On a sign board, which once stood at the foot of the trail, the traveller read, "Walk up, if you please," and on another at the summit, "Ride down, if you dare." In the heyday of staging four milk white horses drew motley humanity and its baggage over the mountain. There still lingers the memory of the last of the stage drivers of the '50's, Morris Carpenter. I once sat on his garden wall in the twilight looking down over the Hoosacs to the Berkshires and heard strange tales of his turnpike days. Much wealth at one time and another passed over this east and west thoroughfare; and some of the "hold-ups" became famous in the legends of the road. One night in mid-summer Carpenter, armed to the teeth, had just rounded the ledge at the summit going west, when, in the moonlight suddenly appeared two fig-

118

ures covering his approach with four enormous pistols. Under the circumstances nothing could be done but to parley. The knights of the road believed that there was a clear ten thousand in booty or ransom inside the stage. But when upon thorough investigation a few half-empty bottles were all they could find, they refused to take the gentlemen's small change, broke the bottles over the passengers' heads, and wishing them God-speed and a good surgeon, departed. The old driver had an almost sacred memory of the still, sunny winter days on the mountain. In his seventieth year he could not speak of their splendor without emotion. Then there were days of hurricane and cold when no living thing could cross the ridges of the hill. Legends of startling blow-aways abound, and they say that the bells from church steeples rolling down the ledges at midnight made fiendish music above the roar of the tempest. There is a reminiscence, almost the last, of staging in 1871. Late in September General Butler arrived in great haste at the "east portal" and was hurried up and down the mountain stair to North Adams in the record time of one hour and seventeen minutes.

There was a time when the old trail was a famous route for the polite mountain climber. In Thoreau's description of the view from the summit he says:

"I had come, over the hills on foot and alone in serene summer days, plucking the raspberries by the wayside, and occasionally buying a loaf of bread at a farmer's house, with a knapsack on my back which held a few traveller's books and a change of clothing, and a staff in my hand. And that morning I looked down from the Hoosac mountain on the village of North Adams in the valley, three miles away under my feet. A stream ran down the middle of the valley. It seemed a road for the pilgrim to enter who would climb to the gates of heaven. Now I crossed a hay-field, and now over the brook on a slight bridge, and ascended with a sort of awe. It seemed as if he must be the most singular and heavenly minded man whose dwelling stood highest up the valley. The thunder had rumbled at my heels all the way. I half believed I should get above it. I passed the last house. And at last I reached the summit (of Greylock) just as the sun was setting, and overlooked the woods. I was up early to see the day break. As the light increased, I discovered around me an ocean of mist. I was floating on this fragment of the wreck of a world, in cloud land. It was such a country as we might see in dreams, with all the delights of Paradise. The earth beneath had passed away like the phantom of a shadow. But when its own sun began to rise on this pure world, I found myself drifting amid saffron-colored clouds, in the very path of the sun's chariot, and sprinkled with its dewy dust. I saw the gracious God

Flatter the mountain-tops with sovereign eye,

Gilding pale streams with heavenly alchemy."

SITE OF THE MOUNTAIN TOP INN

Up the Pocumtuck, in the borders of Rowe, are Prospect and Pulpit rocks. Here, a thousand feet above the waters, in tunnel building days, were rustic arbors and tables and a register of names of pilgrims from all over the world. A little to the south of the eastern portal of the tunnel is a half-moon cave in the rock, the only record of vain aspirations. On this spot a mechanic, who had invented a huge rock-bit, that, like a ship worm, was to bore the ribs of Hoosac, endeavored dramatically to fulfill Mother Shipton's prophecy:

"Men through the mountains shall ride
Without horse or mule at their side."

His failure, legend tells, drove him
mad. The records show that during
the long period of construction the
slow-crawling process of drill and blast
was thrice abandoned in order to test
different ambitious inventions.

At the top of the mountain, scattered
about in huge ridges of gneissic rock,
lie samples of the depths within. Professor Edward Hitchcock, the eminent

"THE EVIDENCE OF A DREAM"

geologist, had been engaged to foretell the probable mineral treasures of
the Hoosacs and in spite of the unpromising nature of his reply nearly
every block of this *débris* has been
scanned by expectant eyes and every
hill and mountain for leagues around
has its pit of some hastily abandoned
gold mine.

In the midst of perils of chill and
damp and suffocation, the belief crept
into the hearts of the tunnelers that
the waters that drenched them were
curative. Rheumatism ceased to be

complained of. Chronic ills were dissolved in the daily forced bath. The
contractors had hitherto been compelled to advertise attractive wages to
keep the work moving. Now men
came from far and near to offer their
services. The old belief in the fountain of youth had almost been revived.

A dream of wonderful times to come
to western Franklin County upon the
completion of the tunnel arose in 1867.
It was near the end of the period of
failing contracts
and little summer
spurts of triumph
and advance. In
vision was seen,
at the eastern
portal, a new city.
The chief works
o f construction
were there, on the
crescent of the
Deerfield where it
sweeps from
north to east after
threading the dim
nether world of
the Hoosacs. Near
this point the
chief peaks rise
sheer in a long splendid wall of
green. Opposite, within gun shot
and towering a thousand feet sky-
ward rises the craggy southwest
bastion of Rowe. Eastward, between abrupt woody mountains, the
meadows stretch along their broken
waters. A hundred paths and ancient
roadways go up from here into the
mystery of the hills. Some of these
are still well worn, but many are overgrown. Even to a casual observer
there appear for miles around traces of
the work of man. Fern-grown levels,

moss-grown walls, choked-up conduits, and a thousand other such marks arrest attention and give a hint of a busy world of workmen, where now is left little more than the original solitude of the romantic wild wood of the Mohican. Hereabouts, in 1867, was a population of a thousand in an actual embryo city. There were miniature thoroughfares up the mountain sides where now you see the cattle-paths running up to the hedge-like border of beech and maple. Whole families came down from the hills to help dig the tunnel, attracted by the high wages or the hope of cure. A great hotel arose at the head of the sweet meadows. Soon the western terminal of the Greenfield and Troy Railroad arrived with its great round-house; and thou-

sands of tourists came by coach and rail to visit the most famous engineering feat of the continent. The State, to further its work, had built a dam and dug a long canal down the western bank of the mad-running Deerfield, the Pocumtuck of the Indians, and here, in the heart of the glen, a substantial stone factory was erected. A glowing picture of the city that was to be appeared at that time in the county paper. In imagination the whole meadow was peopled. Brilliant shop windows and *cafés* lined a grand avenue along the southern river front. On the mountain sides north and south and west gleamed windows and gilded spires at the rising and setting of the sun. The mountain tops of Rowe, Savoy and Florida sent down their butter and milk into this city, and over its housetops floated the June fragrance of their orchards, matchless pastures and wild-woods. The strength of the youth of the hills came down also in a stream that made glad. The suburbs of the city spread up every valley, along Cold and Chickley rivers; up Bosrah and Dunbar and Fife and Mill brook and old Pelham.

The towns were roused to action. The State allowed them to subscribe three per cent. of their valuation to hasten the completion of the tunnel. Some citizens put in a good part of all they had. Altogether five hundred and twenty shares were thus disposed of. Industry was actually quickened at Beacon Hills and in m a n y mountain h a m l e t s besides. There was a sense of new life after a long period of

THE CASCADE

stagnation. Population increased, as did property values. By 1872, when the tunnel was nearing completion, a condition of prosperity was reported at Beacon Hills such as had never been known in this little hamlet in the mountain tops. The manufacturing of Venetian shades, baskets, baby carriages, chairs, furniture and many other things fairly lined the banks of

Pelham brook for a great distance with a series of miniature factories, whose broken dams and sluices and penstocks may be seen to-day in part and can be reproduced in their entirety by imagination. Now there is not a single industry active enough for the name.

In 1871 the centre of activity shifted westward and gathered about the meeting place of the sweet Indian waters of Mayunsook and Ashuwillticook. That locality had a broader valley and was the original Hoosac, or "faraway-land." Here the city of North Adams arose in a night. In prospect of the speedy completion of the tunnel many a hilltown farm was wholly abandoned as were, in many cases, the better homesteads. Every family was anxious to choose a house lot in the c i t y that n o w guards the western gateway.

During July and August of that year the bore had extended westward one thousand feet; and the half-way figures had long since been passed. And now we come to the consideration of conflicting interests that led to trouble. Two routes for a draft canal through the Hoosac Mountains were surveyed by a commission of the Commonwealth

A CHURCH AND CHURCHYARD ON THE MOUNTAIN

in 1825. One was through a tunnel in line with the present one. The railroad company that actually began the tunnel was incorporated in 1848 with a capitalization of three and a half million dollars. Denizens of the hills originated the scheme as a whole. It was a descendant of that Eleazer Hawkes, who a hundred years before had traded the first wheat of the upper Deerfield meadows in Charlemont to garrisons in Forts Pelham and Massachusetts, who suggested the canal under Hoosac. Major Samuel H. Reed, of Beacon Hills, was prominent in the Greenfield and Troy Railroad Company, which in 1825 broke the first soil for the construction of the tunnel. A native of Deerfield, on that occasion, the Rev. Dr. Crawford, used the ceremonial spade. The work came many times to a standstill. Unforeseen difficulties dispelled illusions in regard to the efficiency of patent borers. Discouraged and incompetent contractors, and frightful loss of life caused long delays and pauses. Under three successive contracts in the first six years only a little more than a thousand feet of tunnel, wide enough for a single track, had been opened. And in the ninth year the Greenfield and Troy Railroad Company failed and abandoned its work. The State foreclosed its mortgage and in the tenth year work was again begun. Nitro-glycerin was introduced and became a new source of accident, which in the end exceeded all others in fatal results, but made the tunnel possible. The work now proceeded fitfully but more successfully until the fearful winter tragedy of 1868 on Florida Mountain, when the central shaft buildings and pumps were burned and about a score of workmen, crushed by falling *débris,* were smothered or drowned at the bottom of the well several hundred feet down. Their bones were not found till the following spring. In sixteen years less than two-fifths of the length of the tunnel had been opened. At

THE CENTRAL AIR SHAFT

that rate it would barely be completed at the end of the century. The execution of the wild scheme of the Charlemont farmer and his visionary neighbors was prolonged beyond all reasonable limits and was growing very costly and dangerous; but still its was practical and possible to realize.

A new era began in the summer of 1868, when two Canadian engineers, Francis and Walter Shanly, took what proved to be the last contract; and in five years penetrated the remaining fifteen thousand feet of rock. But even their surprising success was not won by any new discovery, such as sometimes proves the solution of mechanical problems. They did a half more work in one-third the time of their predecessors, chiefly through sheer heroism and patient continuance. Their trials were also as great.

They had little more than cleared away the wreckage of the last contractors when there came the memorable flood of 1869. Half a million dollars' damage in this sparsely settled region was done, showing that nearly everything along the water courses must

have been lost. The state's works by the Deerfield were flooded and largely swept away. The three thousand dollar bridge, a few miles below the tunnel, was hurled bodily from its piers and wrecked along the banks. Every bridge on the Pelham was carried away. Six human lives and innumerable sheep and cattle were lost by drowning in these mountain tops. Fellows' Mill, on the Pelham, was then owned by a Mr. Hyde. At eight o'clock Mrs. Hyde had got the children off to school and Mr. Hyde went to work about his mill. At that time there was no cause for apprehension, but before the middle of the afternoon the heavens seemed to part and let down all the waters of the firmament upon the Hoosac range. Pelham brook, which falls by continuous rapids a thousand feet in four miles, spouted with a treacherous smoothness down its bed. Hyde and his wife began to lash cables around their buildings and anchor them to trees up stream. The water was rising, not as the tide rises, but with fresh avalanches of water from above. Hyde was caught by one of these and swung out into the stream, clinging to a limber sapling, which momentarily threatened to be uprooted. Mrs. Hyde crept out and a neighbor saw her throw him a line. At the same moment the great building was lifted bodily by a terrible burst of waters and hurled with its owners like a straw towards the Deerfield, and no man to this day knows the Hydes' sepulchre. Two little orphans came home from school that night, one running ahead in childish glee at the rushing waters just in time to see home and father and mother whirled into the fearful thunders and foam of the gorge. In their native hamlet far over the mountain, touching services were held the next week, in the church where, as children, these two worthy persons had received another baptism.

"THE STRENGTH OF THE HILLS"

Another problem than flood had been left over to the Shanlys from the last contractors, namely, staying the demoralized and shattered rock in the western section of the tunnel. Before they had completed the work they encountered a surface requiring, since the work began, twelve millions of bricks to overarch it, six years' labor and the sacrifice of many lives. The last brick was laid July 5, 1872, a little more than a year before the completion of the bore. Another of the perils encountered was from the great pockets

of water, which kept the miners drenched and sometimes caused fatal accidents. At any moment a flood of unknown force and volume might leap upon them out of the darkness. There were frequent fatalities from premature or mismanaged blasts. Circumstantial accounts appeared from week to week in the county paper, of heads and arms blown off, of tools and trucks and men hurled through the narrow darkness, of bursting air pipes and suffocated men, of falling boulders and sudden destruction from all the variety of causes that beset miners' lives. But all these sources of accident were aggravated by the necessity for haste. Water and fire, crushing rocks, suffocation and explosion, accidental falls and disease, hardship and disaster in the twenty years that the Hoosac tunnel was building cost the lives of one hundred and thirty-six men.

And last of all came the abandonment of the town at the east portal. The population of Florida in a few years after the completion of the bore fell to almost nothing. And now to the careless observer little is visible of the great city that was the dream of the sixties. Meanwhile, however, there had been a marked increase in social life in all these hills. Two churches have had a most interesting history and witnessed an unusual number of picturesque changes. They are the old First Parish of Beacon Hills and the ancient Baptist Church on the eastern top of Florida Mountain. It happens that the present temples are of one model, the creation of the locally noted Amidon brothers of Beacon Hills. It is they who are responsible for a good part of the most dignified architecture and love for things beautiful in all these mountains. The Beacon Hills Church stands sixteen hundred feet and the Florida Church nineteen hundred feet above sea level, their respective slopes some six or eight miles apart as the bird flies. One faces the warm south down Pelham brook, and the other toward Pocumtuck water and the rising sun. At Beacon Hills, where now in winter there are barely five hundred souls, were once evening gatherings that brought four hundred people together.

The cheerful ring of industry, that for long years was heard in these solitudes, is still remembered, — l i k e a song that has never died away. When the work was at its height seven hundred men were delving in the rocky ribs of the mountains, whilst above, a hundred more supplied them with their needs. There were over half a million dollars employed in the capital of . the contractors. The yearly wages were about the same sum. Twenty-one 400-horse power engines and a locomotive burned more than thirteen hundred tons of coal in a year besides sixteen hundred cords of wood hewn from the hitherto unbroken silences of woods now ringing with the axe. Four

COL. ALVAH CROCKER

160-horse power water wheels brought old Pocumtuck into service to aid in running nineteen air-compressors, fifty-two Burleigh drills and machinery of that sort in the eastern heading. More than one-eighth of a million pounds of explosives were used in a year. With such an equipment the Shanlys removed annually about a half mile of rock.

The evolution of the applied machinery reads like the story of many a human life, from the hand drills and black powder of the fifties t h r o u g h t h e heavy, complicated machine drills and removal of the *débris* block by block, to the simplified drills run in gangs. Black powder was exchanged for nitro-glycerin; the awkward, old fashioned fuse for electric discharge. In the eastern heading, w h e r e t h e greatest work was done, compressed air was introduced by a twelve-inch pipe. And with numerous improvements of a sort of which these may stand as illustrations, the accomplishment of the work leaped forward from thirteen hundred feet in six years and ten thousand feet in sixteen years to more than fifteen thousand feet in five years. The new progress had all the difference in spirit between living despair and living hope. In this way the great engineering romance that began in the imagination of an obscure farmer of the upper Deerfield in 1825, ended on Thanksgiving day, November 27, 1873, an ac-

ENTRANCE TO THE HOOSAC TUNNEL

complished fact. A hole four and three-quarter miles lóng had been pierced from base to base of the Hoosac range, and where the main headings of the famous Mt. Cenis tunnel in Switzerland swerved in alignment more than half a yard, these varied only five-sixteenths of an inch.

During the last weeks of March, 1867, the bore had proceeded four feet a day. In May, Dull & Gowan, of Chicago, contracted for two years' work to remove sixty-four hundred feet of rock, that is, to advance at the average rate of ten feet a day. They never made half that distance. There were some spurts of work in June, and on the last day of that month they removed thirty-six feet of rock, but the methods used could not be advantageously employed. Their largest record for a whole month, one hundred and twenty-three feet, was in August. It was during their contract that the problem of staying the areas of demoralized rock in the west end, after many fruitless experiments, began to be

solved. But the contract was never completed. The plant lay crippled and idle for the best part of a year until the Shanlys took it.

They began with the modest record of forty feet a month, and by improvements in method, machinery and organization advanced until in the summer of 1871 they were moving along at the rate of five hundred feet a month, or about double the rate before contracted for. In the spring of 1872 there was a mile and a half still to bore so that in the last year and a half the work advanced at the rate of a mile a year, or at a sustained speed of four hundred and forty feet a month. But during the three months in the spring the record progress of half a mile was burrowed into the stubborn darkness.

We are now entering upon the last chapters of the romance. On October 14, 1872, workmen in the central and eastern sections were calculated to be exactly six hundred feet apart. They could distinctly hear each other drilling at the core and bottom of the mountain. A month passed in excited expectation. By November 18 they were stated to be three hundred and fifty-six feet apart; but the miners believed the engineers had miscalculated, so distinctly could they hear the drilling and terrible explosions of each other's blasts. On December first one hundred and twenty-three feet remained in the eastern end. And twelve days later at half past four o'clock in the afternoon a rift was opened by a blast and light shone through these tragic cells eleven hundred feet below the sunlight. A tool was first passed through and received with hurrahs. In a short time a small hole was cleared and a boy crept through from the east and was borne westward in triumph through the smoky corridor upon the shoulders of the workmen, singing and shouting as they went. At the central shaft, where a tiny spot of wholesome blue and gold shone down upon their heads, the lad was swiftly drawn up to the mountain top. He was the first being who had ever thus found himself above the "mountain's weary stair."

On February 1, 1873, there was still half a mile to open in the western end. They had worked eastward from the foot of the central shaft fifteen hundred and sixty-three feet; and westward they now went two thousand and six. By April 14 only a third of a mile remained. One day in August the greatest record was made, a fifty foot plunge back for daylight. On September first an eighth of a mile remained to open and by November first two hundred and forty-two feet were still unbroken. The contractors then made their first boast,—"We shall eat Thanksgiving dinner in North Adams coming by way of Hoosac Tunnel." On November 27, 1873, with snow flying in the air, but a glow in their hearts, a company of gentlemen passed under the mountain straight from old Pocumtuck to Hoosac waters and fulfilled the letter of this promise.

The work had proceeded night and day except Sundays for some years. It was originally estimated to cost three and a half million of dollars but the actual cost was $12,700,000. The first train passed under the mountain February 9, 1875.

𝔄merican 𝔖hrines VII

Charter Oak

"THOU MONARCH TREE!—AND WORTHY OF THY CROWN;
FOR HANDS OF FREEMEN PLACED THE SIMPLE GUARD
THAT MARKS THEE FROM THY FELLOWS—GUARDIAN TREE,
TO MAKE THY TRUNK THE SANCTUARY SAFE
OF SACRED PLEDGE WHICH TYRANNY WOULD WREST."

[This half tone is from the only photograph extant of the Charter Oak, and was obtained through the courtesy of Mr. F. G. Whitmore, Secretary of the Board of Park Commissioners, of Hartford, Conn.]

NEW ENGLAND MAGAZINE

NEW SERIES   APRIL   VOL. XXVI NO. 2

The True Story of Paul Revere's Ride

By Charles Ferris Gettemy

PAUL REVERE performed a great and lasting service to his country when he took his famous midnight ride on the 18th of April, 1775. It remained unsung, if not unhonored, for eighty-eight years or until Longfellow, in 1863 made it the text for his Landlord's Tale in the Wayside Inn, clothing it with all the matchless beauty and witchery of his imagination. Some one signing himself "Eb Stiles" had, to be sure, written a poem about 1795 which he called the "Story of the Battle of Concord and Lexington, and Revere's Ride Twenty Years Ago," and in which he said:

"He spared neither horse, nor whip, nor spur,
     As he galloped through mud and mire;
He thought of naught but liberty,
     And the lanterns that hung from the spire."

But Stiles did nothing else in a literary way to perpetuate his name, and he failed to find a publisher capable of rescuing his poem from obscurity.

It is to Longfellow's simple and tuneful ballad that most persons undoubtedly owe their knowledge of the fact that a man of the name of Revere really did something on the eve of the historic skirmish at Lexington which is worth remembering.* Indeed the

(*Bancroft mentions the incident of Revere's ride in the edition of his history published in 1858; Hildreth says the alarm had been given, without mentioning Revere's name; Palfrey, whose History of New Eng-

April, 6, 1860

Paul Revere's Ride.

Listen, my children, and you shall hear
Of the midnight ride of Paul Revere,
On the eighteenth of April in Seventy Five;
Hardly a man is now alive
who remembers that famous day and year!

land is brought down to the Battle of Bunker Hill, says: "They [the British] were watched and, by signals before agreed upon, the movement was made known to the people on the other side." He does not allude to Revere.)

true character of Revere's services, both on the occasion of this particular ride, and during the period preceding, has been a matter of comparatively recent recognition, and from the majesty of the closing lines of the poem:

"For, borne on the night-wind of the past,
Through all our history, to the last,
In the hour of darkness and peril and need,
The people will waken and listen to hear
The hurrying hoof-beats of that steed,
And the midnight message of Paul Revere."

it might seem that we are indebted to Longfellow for some instinctive appreciation of the historic significance of the episode, independent of its poetic value.

But poetry and history sometimes become sadly enmeshed, and the language in which such a combination is clothed often remains fixed and is fin-

ally accepted as a record of fact. It is one of the missions of poetry and fiction to give glimpses of things in the intellectual and physical worlds and an insight into the beginnings of great movements in history which vast numbers of people would get in no other way. It ought not, therefore, to be improper or impertinent to inquire whether the poet and romancist, in so far as they deal with historic events and personages and with matters of verifiable record, might not find it possible to hew with greater fidelity, sometimes, to truth, without in any degree detracting from the poetic quality or interfering seriously with that license whose exercise may be essential to artistic literary expression. Such an inquiry is suggested in the common tendency of historical narrative to draw upon poetry for embellishment and for the stimulation of a certain human interest in a story which otherwise might possibly make dull reading.

Upon how many thousands of

schoolboys who have declaimed the stirring lines of Longfellow's description of Paul Revere's ride, and upon how many thousands, too, of their elders, has the picture drawn by the poet left its indelible impression? Certainly it is the sum and substance of all their knowledge of the subject to hundreds of visitors, who, every summer, wander through those old,

challenged, it being urged that Revere's own allusion to the North church steeple probably referred to another North Church, located at that time elsewhere in the vicinity. This allegation was met and exhaustively examined by William W. Wheildon, and his view, which is in accordance with the tradition in favor of Christ Church, is now generally accepted. Another claim brought forward at about the same time, to the effect that Revere's friend, whom he selected to display the signals, was one John Pulling,

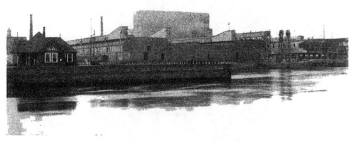

WHERE PAUL REVERE WAITED FOR THE SIGNAL

narrow streets of the North End of Boston, and gaze with reverence upon the graceful spire of Christ church. The stone tablet, placed in the wall of the tower by order of the city government in 1878,* tells them that:

THE SIGNAL LANTERNS OF
PAUL REVERE
DISPLAYED IN THE STEEPLE OF
THIS CHURCH
APRIL 18, 1775,
WARNED THE COUNTRY OF THE
MARCH OF THE BRITISH TROOPS
TO LEXINGTON AND CONCORD.

(*The proposition for the placing of this tablet, when brought forward in the Boston city government, precipitated a lively controversy, the echoes of which have not yet entirely died away. The right of Christ Church to the honor in question was stoutly

likewise deserves to be rejected. Revere has not left us the name of this friend, but a mass of traditionary evidence supports the belief that he was Robert Newman, the sexton of the church. Many of the parishioners were loyal to their Church of England instincts and adhered to the King's cause, but Newman was a consistent and fervent American patriot.)

And from the summit of Copp's Hill, in the ancient burial ground nearby, surrounded by tombstones marked by indentations which the guide books say were caused by Revolutionary bullets, one may look across the mouth of the Charles, opening just at the foot of the height into the harbor, and—shutting out from present view the ugly grain elevators, the black coal wharves, the masts of the ships, and Charlestown's brick walls beyond—try to conjure up the vision of the poet's fancy: the stout-hearted messenger of the Revolution ferried across the stream under the shadow of the forbidding man-of-war Somerset, his safe landing on the opposite shore, his impatient and fretful slapping of his horse's side as he stands booted and spurred, and strains his eyes for a glimpse of the signal rays from the steeple of the old church; then the ride out through the villages and farms of Middlesex until, in the lines of the poet,—

"It was two by the village clock,
When he came to the bridge in Concord town."

It is a pity to mar this work of art by the homely daubs of fact; yet a faithful limning of the scene, as it was really enacted, would necessitate some retouching. But it ought not to be difficult to do this without in any essential respect spoiling the liveliness or romantic spirit of the picture. To be sure, the statement that Revere reached Concord was long ago shown to have been incorrect; but its persistent virility only goes to prove that

INTERIOR OF THE BELFRY OF CHRIST CHURCH

truth is not the only thing which, crushed to earth, will rise again. The impression, however, is yet more general that the signal lanterns were placed in the North Church steeple for Revere's benefit, and that he waited on the Charlestown shore for the message they were to convey before he was able to start on his journey. The facts are that Revere had all the desired information before he left Boston, and that the lights were hung out at his instance as a warning to others, who might know by them the necessity of arousing the country in the event of his capture while being rowed across the river.*

(*These accounts of the hanging of the lanterns, those written both before and since Longfellow's poem was published, are, most of them, curiously inaccurate. John Stetson Barry in his History of Massachusetts, (p.509) published in 1856, makes an allusion to Revere, saying "a lantern was displayed by Paul Revere in the upper window of the tower of the North Church in Boston," and George Lowell Austin in his History of Massachusetts (p. 300) published twenty years later, copies Barry's statement. Even John Fiske, usually as accurate in detail as he is safe in his generalizations, did not take Revere's

VIEW OF CHARLESTOWN FROM THE BELFRY OF CHRIST CHURCH.*

narrative as his authority, else he would hardly have said (The American Revolution, Vol. I, p. 121) : "Crossing the broad river in a little boat, under the very guns of the Somerset man-of-war, and waiting on the farther bank until he learned, from a lantern suspended in the belfry of the North Church, which way the troops had gone, Revere took horse," etc.

The looseness with which Lossing allowed himself to write is nowhere more apparent than in his allusions to this historic episode. In his Pictorial Field Book of the Revolution he says (Vol. I, p. 523) : "Paul Revere and William Dawes had just rowed across the river to Charlestown with a message from Warren to Hancock and Adams at Lexington." Dawes, of course, did not accompany Revere, and Lossing, in Our Country, p. 775, corrects himself in this respect, but still serenely careless of statement, says:—"William Dawes had gone over the Neck to Roxbury on horseback, with a message from Warren to Hancock and Adams, and Warren and Revere were at Charlestown awaiting developments of events." Such a statement can be reconciled with itself only upon supposition that Warren,

after despatching Dawes, went over to Charlestown and there joined Revere,—a supposition purely gratuitous. Lossing not unnaturally also follows the other writers in giving the impression that Revere engaged a friend "to give him a timely signal" from the North Church, when as a matter of fact, Revere personally had no use for such a a signal.)

It so happens that for the account of the events of that night we have the highest possible authority. Revere himself was not so modest and self-effacing as to fall short of appreciating, at something like its true value, the importance of his services to the cause of liberty on the 18th of April, 1775, and posterity fortunately has a circumspect and detailed narrative of his movements on that occasion, written down by himself. One must not, indeed, forget that the real worth of personal reminiscences, as authority for history, is frequently a matter of doubt and that inaccurate

* We are indebted to Mr. Will C. Eddy, of the Mystic Camera Club, for many of the photographs used to illustrate this article.

THE NEWMAN HOUSE. HOME OF THE SEXTON
WHO DISPLAYED THE SIGNAL LANTERNS

refuted, and one cannot turn its pages in the publications of the Massachusetts Historical Society, to whose secretary, Dr. Jeremy Belknap, it was written in the form of a letter, over a century ago, without a conscious feeling that here indeed is a document from the historic past which will preserve a patriot's fame from the iconoclasm of the modern investigator, even though it may itself make a little iconoclastic havoc among poets and historians.*

(*In preparing this letter Revere undoubtedly refreshed his memory of incidents which happened so many years previous, from an account written by him, supposedly about 1783, and which was found among his papers. This in turn was based upon other memoranda, so that the letter to Dr. Belknap does not stand alone. The earlier accounts may be found in Goss's Life of Revere, the originals being in the possession of the family of the late. John Revere of Canton, Mass.)

statements, due to a treacherous memory or a faulty perspective, are common occurrences in autobiography, But when there is no indisputable and unprejudiced record which can be cited to controvert an autobiographical narration and when there is no reason to doubt the truthful purpose of the author, such an account is entitled to stand and does stand, as an authority outranking all others. Revere's own story of his midnight ride, though written after a lapse of twenty years, has this quality. None of its assertions in all the warfare of antiquarians and pamphleteers has been successfully

Boston was in a ferment, during the winter of 1774-75. The long series of

PAUL REVERE'S HOME IN NORTH SQUARE

GENERAL GAGE'S HEADQUARTERS

grievances endured from the mother country had led to the adoption of the Suffolk Resolves* in September.   In

(*The spirit of the Suffolk Resolves is set forth clearly in these two of its numerous declarations: "That the late Acts of the British Parliament for blocking up of the harbor of Boston, and for altering the established form of government in this colony, and for screening the most flagitious violators of the laws of the province from a legal trial, are gross infractions of those rights to which we are justly entitled by the laws of nature, the British Constitution, and the charter of the province;" and "That no obedience is due from this province to either or any part of the Acts above mentioned; but that they be rejected as the attempts of a wicked Administration to enslave America." The full text of the Resolves is printed in Warren's Life by Frothingham, pp. 530-531.)

October the Provincial Congress was organized, with Hancock as president; a protest was sent to the royal governor remonstrating against his hostile attitude and a committee of public safety was provided for. In February this committee was named, delegates were selected for the next Continental Congress, and provision was made for the establishment of the militia. Efforts were then made by the royal governor to seize the military stores of the patriots and to disband the militia, but they proved futile, and the fire of opposition to the indignities heaped upon the people by the crown was kept alive by secret organizations. "Sons of Liberty" met in clubs and caucuses, the group which gathered at the Green Dragon Tavern becoming the most famous. They were mostly young artisans and mechanics from the ranks of the people, who in the rapid succession of events were becoming more and more restive under the British yoke. No spirit among them chafed more impatiently or was more active in

HEADQUARTERS OF LORD PERCY

THE OCHTERLONY HOUSE

taking advantage of each opportunity
that offered to antagonize the plans of
the royal emissaries than Paul Revere,
aged forty, silversmith and engraver
on copper of famous caricatures. Within the twelvemonth he had ridden hundreds of miles on horseback, as the
trusted messenger of the plotters
against the peace of King George,
making four trips to New York and
Philadelphia and one to Portsmouth.

In the early months of 1775, Revere
was one of a band of thirty who formed themselves into a committee to
watch the movements of the British
soldiers and the Tories in Boston. In
parties of two and two, taking turns,

* The "Ochterlony house" is still standing, though
the front wall has apparently been rebuilt, at the
corner of North and North Centre Streets, Boston.
The Ochterlonys were royalists, but a tradition exists in the Revere family that one fair member of
the household was in sympathy with the rebel
plans, and that one of Revere's friends, while the
party was on their way to the boat on the night of
April 18, 1775, stopped in front of this house and
gave a signal. An upper window was raised and
presently, after a hurried conversation in whispers,
a woolen undergarment was thrown out. This was
the petticoat used to muffle the oars of Revere's
boat while he was being rowed across to Charlestown. The story was told by Drake in his history
of Middlesex County, and John Revere, a grandson
of Paul, in a letter written in 1876 said that it was
authentic. This picture is from a photograph, reproduced by permission of W. H. Halliday.

they patrolled the streets all **night**.
Finally, at midnight of Saturday, **the**
15th of April, the vigilance of these
self-appointed patrolmen was rewarded. It became apparent then that
something unusual was suddenly
transpiring in the British camp. "The
boats belonging to the transports were
all launched," says Revere in his narrative, "and carried under the sterns
of the men-of-war. (They had been
previously hauled up and repaired.)
We likewise found that the grenadiers
and light infantry were all taken off
duty. From these movements we expected something was to be trans-
acted." The following day, Sunday,
the 16th, Dr. Warren despatched Revere to Lexington with a message to
John Hancock and Samuel Adams.

This ride of the 16th has never received much attention. It is not famed
in song and story and Revere himself
alludes to it only incidentally. He
probably made the journey in the day-

"HE CROSSED THE BRIDGE INTO MEDFORD TOWN."

Reproduced from an old photograph.

MEDFORD SQUARE

time, jogging out and back unnoticed and not anxious to advertise the purpose of his errand with noise and publicity. Yet there cannot be much doubt that, in its relation to the portentous events which followed three days later, it was at least of as great importance as the more spectacular "midnight ride" of the 18th. The movements of the British on the night of the 15th aroused the suspicion of the patriots, of whom Warren was chief, who had remained in Boston. They meant to him one thing,—an intention to send forth very soon an expedition of some sort. The most plausible conjecture as to its object, even had there been no direct information on the subject, suggested the capture of Hancock and Adams at Lexington, or the seizure of the military stores at Concord, or both.

The two patriot leaders, upon whose heads a price was fixed, were in daily attendance upon the sessions of the Provincial Congress at Concord but they lodged nightly in the neighboring town of Lexington at the house of the Rev. Jonas Clarke, whose wife was a niece of Hancock. It was of the utmost importance that they and the Congress be kept fully informed of what was transpiring in Boston. But when Revere called on Hancock and Adams in Lexington, on Sunday, he found that Congress had adjourned the day before to the 15th of May, in ignorance, of course, of the immediate plans of the British. It had not done so, however, without recognizing "the great uncertainty of the present times, and that important unforseen events may take place, from whence it may be absolutely necessary that this Congress should meet sooner than the day aforesaid."* The delegates indeed had

(*Journal of the Second Provincial Congress, p. 146.)

139

scarcely dispersed before the news brought by Revere aroused such apprehension that the committee which had been authorized to call the convention together again met, and on Tuesday, the 18th, ordered the delegates to re-assemble on the 22nd at Watertown.

Meantime, the committees of safety and supplies had continued their sessions at Concord. Friday, the 14th, it had been voted:

artillery company, to join the army when raised, they to have no pay until they join the army; and also that an instructor for the use of the cannon be appointed, to be put directly in pay."

It was also voted:

"That the four six pounders be transported to Groton, and put under the care of Col. Prescott."

"That two seven inch brass mortars be transported to Acton."*

(*Journal, ɔ. 515.)

THE CRADDOCK HOUSE, MEDFORD

"That the cannon now in the town of Concord, be immediately disposed of within said town, as the committee of supplies may direct."*

(*Journal of Committees of Safety and Supplies; p. 514.

Monday, the 17th, however, with John Hancock—to whom Revere had brought on Sunday information of the preparations being made in Boston for the expedition of the British—the committees on safety and supplies, sitting jointly, voted:

"That two four pounders, now at Concord, be mounted by the committee of supplies, and that Col. Barrett be desired to raise an

On the 18th, the committees continued their preparations in anticipation of the descent of the British upon the stores which had been collected. Numerous votes were passed, providing for a thorough distribution of the stock of provisions and ammunition on hand; a few of these may be cited to tell the graphic story:

"Voted, That all the ammunition be deposited in nine different towns in this province; that Worcester be one of them; that Lancaster be one, (N. B. Col. Whitcomb is there); that Concord be one: and, that Groton, Stoughtonham, Stow, Mendon, Leicester and Sudbury, be the others.

Voted, That part of the provisions be removed from Concord, viz: 50 barrels of beef, from thence to Sudbury, with Deacon Plympton; 100 barrels of flour, of which what is in the malt house in Concord be part; 20 casks of rice; 15 hogsheads of molasses; 10 hogsheads of rum; 500 candles.

* * * *

Voted, That the vote of the fourteenth instant, relating to the powder being removed from Leicester to Concord, be reconsidered, and that the clerk be directed to write to Col. Barrett, accordingly, and to desire he would not proceed in making it up in cartridges.

* * * *

Voted, That the musket balls under the care of Col. Barrett, be buried under ground, in some safe place, that he be desired to do it, and to let the commissary only be informed thereof.

Voted, That the spades, pick-axes, billhooks, shovels, axes, hatchets, crows, and wheelbarrows, now at Concord, be divided, and one third remain in Concord. one third at Sudbury, and one third at Stow.

* * * *

Voted, That two medicinal chests still remain at Concord, at two different parts of the town; six do. at Groton, Mendon, and Stow. two in each town, and in different places; two ditto in Worcester, one in each part of the town; and, two in Lancaster, ditto: that sixteen hundred yards of Russia linen be deposited in seven parts, with the doctor's chests; that the eleven hundred tents be deposited in equal parts in Worcester, Lancaster, Groton, Stow, Mendon, Leicester, and Sudbury."*

(*Journal, pp. 516-517.)

The transporting of the six pounders to Groton and the brass mortars to Acton carried an inference and a message of its own. It helps to account for the presence at the fight at Concord Bridge, on the 19th, of the minute men, from these and other towns, who could not readily have covered the distance within so short a time, had their information been due solely to Revere's alarm of the night before. But that the blow might be expected at almost any moment, Revere's tidings, brought on Sunday, made quickly apparent to the committees in session at Concord on Monday, two days before it fell.

No one in Boston knew better than Revere what the plans of the British were on the night of the 18th of April. He was in the thick of everything that was transpiring. "On Tuesday evening, the 18th," he writes, "it was observed that a number of soldiers were marching toward the bottom of the Common," which meant that they were to be transported across the river to Charlestown or Cambridge, instead of making the long march around by way of Boston Neck. He continues:

"About ten o'clock, Dr. Warren sent in great haste for me, and begged that I would immediately set off for Lexington, where Messrs. Hancock and Adams were, and acquaint them of the movement, and that it was thought they were the objects. When

two friends rowed me across Charles River a little to the eastward where the Somerset man-of-war lay. It was then young flood, the ship was winding, and the moon rising. They landed me on the Charlestown side. When I got into town, I met Colonel Conant and several others; they said they had seen our signals. I told them what was acting, and went to get me a horse; I got a horse of Deacon Larkin."

Revere thus makes it quite plain that the signals were agreed upon for the benefit of the waiting patriots on the Charlestown shore, who when they

THE HANCOCK-CLARK HOUSE, LEXINGTON

I got to Dr. Warren's house, I found he had sent an express by land to Lexington—a Mr. William Dawes. The Sunday before, by desire of Dr. Warren, I had been to Lexington, to Messrs. Hancock and Adams, who were at the Rev. Mr. Clark's. I returned at night through Charlestown; there I agreed with : Colonel Conant and some other gentlemen, that if the British went out by water, we would show two lanthorns in the North Church steeple; and if by land, one as a signal; for we were apprehensive it would be difficult to cross the Charles River, or get over Boston Neck. I left Dr. Warren, called upon a friend, and desired him to make the signals. I then went home, took my boots and surtout, went to the north part of the town, where I kept a boat;

should see the light or lights, might be trusted to carry the news to Lexington and Concord in the event of no one being able to cross the river or get through the British lines by the land route over Boston Neck. From the spot where Revere landed on the Charlestown shore, the steeple of Christ church was plainly visible, yet he does not mention seeing the signals, though taking pains to record that others had seen them. Certainly curiosity could have been his only motive for looking for the lights in any event. Had Revere and Dawes both been captured or

THE MERRIAM HOUSE, LEXINGTON

ance, preceding the first act in the great drama of the Revolution to be played next day on Lexington Green and at Concord Bridge, executed his part well, with courage, skill, intelligence and patriotism.

otherwise prevented from starting on their journeys, the signal lanterns were to tell their story just the same, and it is fair to assume that some other rider would then have carried the news out through the Middlesex villages to Hancock and Adams. But to say this is not to detract from the value of the services rendered by Revere and Dawes. It so happened that the three-fold safeguard taken to insure the alarming of the country was not, in the event, necessary. All three served their purpose and any one without the others might have served, but as a matter of fact all three succeeded. To Revere must be awarded the possession of the foresight which suggested and arranged for the display of the signal lights ; and to Dr. Warren, after having despatched Dawes with the important news, belongs the credit for providing against the contingency of his capture by sending Revere on the same errand by a different route. Each of the actors in this little curtain-raising perform-

And in view of all these facts, for which Revere himself is our chief authority, we are forced to the conclusion that Mr. Longfellow drew liberally from his imagination, when he wrote the lines :

"Meanwhile, impatient to mount and ride,
Booted and spurred, with a heavy stride
On the opposite shore walked Paul Revere.
Now he patted his horse's side,
Now gazed at the landscape far and near,
Then, impetuous, stamped the earth,
And turned and tightened his saddle-girth;
But mostly he watched with eager search
The belfry-tower of the Old North Church,
As it rose above the graves on the hill,
Lonely and spectral and sombre and still.
And lo! as he looks, on the belfry's height
A glimmer, and then a gleam of light!

THE BUCKMAN TAVERN

LEXINGTON COMMON

He springs to the saddle, the bridle he turns,
But lingers and gazes, till full on his sight
A second lamp in the belfry burns !"

Revere's story is to the effect that as soon as he could procure a horse, he started upon his journey, without further delay. "While the horse was preparing," he says, "Richard Devens, Esq., who was one of the Committee of Safety, came to me, and told me that he came down the road from Lexington, after sundown, that evening; that he met ten British officers, all well mounted and armed, going up the road. I set off upon a very good horse; it was then about 11 o'clock, and very pleasant." He had not gone far, when he discovered just ahead of him two British soldiers, but he turned quickly about, and, though pursued, made good his escape, passing through Medford and up to Menotomy, now Arlington. "In Medford," he records, "I awaked the captain of the minute men; and after that, I alarmed almost every house, till I got to Lexington." This quite agrees with the stirring description of the poet:

144

"A hurry of hoofs in a village street,
A shape in the moonlight, a bulk in the dark,
And beneath, from the pebbles, in passing, a spark
Struck out by a steed flying fearless and fleet:
That was all ! And yet, through the gloom and the light,
The fate of a nation was riding that night."

Revere aroused Hancock and Adams at the Rev. Jonas Clarke's house in Lexington.* No one has told the

(*Among the depositions of the survivors of the Battle of Lexington, printed in Phinney's history of the fight, published in 1825, is one signed by William Munroe, an orderly sergeant in Capt. Parker's company of minute-men. Munroe says he learned early in the evening of the 18th that British officers had been seen on the road from Boston. "I supposed," he continues, "they had some design upon Hancock and Adams, who were at the house of the Rev. Mr. Clark, and immediately assembled a guard of eight men, with their arms, to guard the house. About midnight, Col. Paul Revere rode up and requested admittance. I told him the family had just retired, and had requested, that they might not be disturbed by any noise about the house. 'Noise!' said he, 'you'll have noise enough before long.

The regulars are coming out.' We then permitted him to pass." p. 33.

Dorothy Quincy, Hancock's betrothed, whom he married the following autumn, was also in the house.)

story of what occurred after that better than Revere himself:

"After I had been there about half an hour, Mr. Dawes came; we refreshed ourselves, and set off for Concord, to secure the stores, &c., there. We were overtaken by a young Dr. Prescott, whom we found to be a high Son of Liberty. I told them of the ten

in nearly the same situation as those officers were, near Charlestown. I called for the Doctor and Mr. Dawes to come up; in an instant I was surrounded by four;—they had placed themselves in a straight road, that inclined each way; they had taken down a pair of bars on the north side of the road, and two of them were under a tree in the pasture. The Doctor being foremost, he came up; and we tried to get past them; but they being armed with pistols and swords, they forced us into the pasture; the Doctor jumped his horse over a low stone wall, and got to Concord.

CONCORD SQUARE

officers that Mr. Devens met, and that it was probable we might be stopped before we got to Concord; for I supposed that after that night, they divided themselves, and that two of them had fixed themselves in such passages as were most likely to stop any intelligence going to Concord. I likewise mentioned that we had better alarm all the inhabitants till we got to Concord; the young Doctor much approved of it, and said he would stop with either of us, for the people between that and Concord knew him, and would give the more credit to what we said. We had got nearly half way; Mr. Dawes and the Doctor stopped to alarm the people of a house; I was about one hundred yards ahead, when I saw two men,

"I observed a wood at a small distance, and made for that. When I got there, out started six officers, on horseback, and ordered me to dismount;—one of them, who appeared to have the command, examined me, where I came from, and what my name was? I told him. He asked me if I was an express? I answered in the affirmative. He demanded what time I left Boston? I told him; and added, that their troops had catched aground in passing the river, and that there would be five hundred Americans there in a short time, for I had alarmed the country all the way up.*

(*Lossing, in Our Country, p. 777, says:— "Revere and his fellow prisoners were closely questioned concerning Hancock and

Adams, but gave evasive answers." This is another of Lossing's wholly gratuitous statements, there being no authority for saying that questions were asked concerning Hancock and Adams, while from Revere's account of the colloquy he appears to have been exceedingly frank in his replies to the British officers. Lossing made the mistake of supposing that the story would read better by crediting Revere with displaying a certain amount of Yankee shrewdness in attempting to deceive his captors. With a pistol to his head, it is quite likely Revere thought discretion the better part of valor; if such a suggestion be unjust, then it may

about one mile, the Major rode up to the officer that was leading me and told him to give me to the Sergeant. As soon as he took me, the Major ordered him, if I attempted to run, or anybody insulted them, to blow my brains out. We rode till we got near Lexington meeting-house, when the militia fired a volley of guns, which appeared to alarm them very much."

So much so, in short, that the major ordered the sergeant to take Revere's horse from him, and the officers rode quickly off together leaving their prisoner free. It was then about two

WHERE PAUL REVERE WAS CAPTURED

surely be said that his remarkable candor in truth-telling is a tribute at once to his courage and audacity. In either view, he was anything but evasive.)

"He immediately rode towards those who stopped us, when all five of them came down upon a full gallop; one of them, whom I afterwards found to be a Major Mitchell, of the 5th Regiment, clapped his pistol to my head, called me by name, and told me he was going to ask me some questions, and if I did not give him true answers he would blow my brains out. He then asked me similar questions to those above. He then ordered me to mount my horse, after searching me for arms. He then ordered them to advance and to lead me in front. When we got to the road, they turned down towards Lexington. When we had got

o'clock in the morning, and Revere went across lots, returning to the Rev. Mr. Clarke's house, where upon narrating his adventures to Hancock and Adams, it was decided that they ought to retire to a safer place. Revere went with them toward Woburn, where they found lodging, Dorothy Quincy and young Mr. Lowell, Hancock's clerk, accompanying them. There Revere left them, and with Lowell returned to Lexington "to find what was going on." Great things, indeed, fraught with momentous consequences were "going on" when Revere and his companion reached the village green.

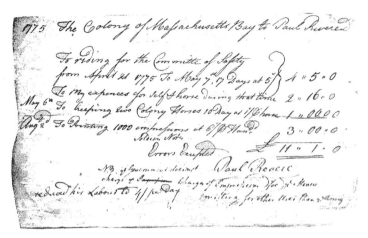

FAC-SIMILE OF THE BILL PRESENTED BY PAUL REVERE FOR HIS SERVICES AS MESSENGER

The 19th of April had dawned. It was daylight and messengers were hurrying through the town with the news that the British troops were coming up the road from Cambridge.

"Mr. Lowell," writes Revere, "asked me to go to the tavern with him, to get a trunk of papers belonging to Mr. Hancock. We went up chamber, and while we were getting the trunk, we saw the British very near, upon a full march. We hurried towards Mr. Clark's house. In our way, we passed through the militia. They were about fifty. When we had got about one hundred yards from the meeting-house, the British troops appeared on both sides of the meeting-house. They made a short halt; when I saw and heard a gun fired, which appeared to be a pistol. Then I could distinguish two guns, and then a continued roar of musketry; when we made off with the trunk."

This was the "Battle of Lexington" —fifty men exchanging a few volleys of musketry with eight hundred of the King's disciplined troops, who then marched on to Concord, only to find, after a bloody encounter, that the most valuable of the stores they had come to seize or destroy, had, thanks to the timely warning of Paul Revere three days before, been already removed to places of safety.

On the day following these events, Revere was permanently engaged by Dr. Warren, president of the Committee of Safety, "as a messenger to do the outdoors business for that committee." * It would be a mistaken idea

(*Revere's narrative.)

for any one to cherish that Revere was willing to tender these services without expectation of something more substantial in the way of reward than the mere satisfaction of having performed patriotic duty. There was much self-sacrifice on the part of the Revolutionary patriots, whose only remuneration was ingratitude from their countrymen, but the men whom history holds as heroes were by no means lacking, nevertheless, in that quality of thrift which holds even patriotic service to have a

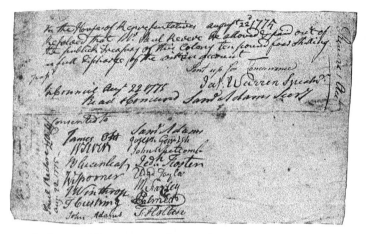

commercial value which the state should recognize. Revere, at this period, was prospering fairly well in his business, and he doubtless felt that he was not called upon to neglect it for the public service without some financial recompense. That his employers took the same view of the case one may feel assured, from the promptness with which his bill was approved by the legislative body and the executive council. That the authorities thought Revere disposed to place too high a valuation upon his services is equally evident, for they reduced his charge for riding as a messenger from the amount asked, five shillings a day, to four shillings. This bill, a fac-simile of which is produced for the first time, is carefully preserved among the Revolutionary archives at the State House in Boston.* The paper is faded with time, but the handwriting of Revere and the endorsement on the back with

(*Mass. Archives Vol. 164 p 3.)

the signatures of James Otis, Samuel Adams, John Adams and other members of the council in approval, stands out clear and distinct. The bill, with the council's comments, is as follows:

1775. The Colony of Massachusetts Bay to Paul Revere,
Dr.
To riding for the Committee of Safety from April 21 1775 to May 7th, 17 Days at 5/.................... 4 5 0
To my expenses for self & horse during that time 2 16 0
May 6th To keeping two Colony Horses 10 Day at 1/ pr horse 1 00 0
Aug. 2d, To Printing 1000 impressions at 6/ pr Hundd, Soldiers Notes............. 3 00 0

Errors Excepted........£11 1 0
PAUL REVERE.

N. B. ye Government does not charge ye charges of Impressions for ye Money emitting for other Uses than ye Army.
reduced his Labour to 4/ per Day.

The comments of the council upon the original bill, as made out by Re-

148

vere, show the care with which the expenditures were guarded. Revere evidently did not designate the purpose for which the "impressions" printed by him and charged up to the colony was intended, so a memorandum was made at the bottom of the bill calling attention to the fact that only the printing of money for the use of the army would be paid for. Doubtless inquiry developed that Revere's charge was in accordance with this understanding, though he had neglected to indicate it in the item in question, and the explanatory words, "Soldiers Notes," were afterward added.

The record of the appropriation made to cover the bill, after the total had been reduced to ten pounds four shillings, is inscribed on the back of the original, and is to this effect:

In the House of Representatives August 22d 1775
Resolved that Mr. Paul Revere be allowed & paid out of the publick Treasury of this Colony ten pound four shilling in full discharge of the within account

Sent up for concurrence

JAS. WARREN Speakr.
SAML ADAMS Sec'y

In Council Aug 22 1775
Read and concurred

Consented to

James Otis	Saml Adams
W. Sever	Joseph Gerrish
B. Greenleaf	John Whetcomb
W. Spooner	Jedh Foster
J. Winthrop.	Eldad Taylor
T. Cushing	M. Farley
John Adams	J. Palmer
	S. Holten

WHERE HE MANUFACTURED POWDER IN CANTON

149

From a steel engraving from the portrait by Gilbert Stuart.
PAUL REVERE

After the British had evacuated Boston, Revere made himself useful to Washington and on April 10, 1776, he entered the regular military service, being commissioned a major in the First Regiment; Nov. 27 he was made a Lieutenant-Colonel of Artillery. He served in the Rhode Island campaign and was in command of Castle William in Boston Harbor; but with his subsequent career we need not concern ourselves here. He retained throughout his life an intelligent interest in public affairs, and on one occasion probably used his influence in an important and lasting manner. When the fate of the Federal Constitution was trembling in the balance in 1788, and the support of Massachusetts was vital,

Samuel Adams, who had been the leading critic of the document, as drawn up at Philadelphia, is credited with having turned the scales in its favor. It is pleasant to think that he was induced to do so by the impression made upon him by a procession of those plain people, to whose voice Adams never failed to listen, led by Paul Revere, from the old Green Dragon Tavern, where resolutions enthusiastically approving the new Constitution had been adopted. Daniel Webster, in a speech delivered at Pittsburg, July 9, 1833, alluded to this incident, and represented a colloquy as having taken place between Adams and Revere somewhat after this fashion:

"How many mechanics," said Adams, "were at the Green Dragon when these resolutions were passed?"

"More sir,' was the reply, "than the Green Dragon could hold."

"And where were the rest, Mr. Revere?"

"In the streets, sir."

"And how many were in the streets?"

"More, sir, than there are stars in the sky."

For many years, Revere continued to follow the business of coppersmithing and bell founding, establishing an industry at Canton, Massachusetts, which still bears his name. When he died, in his eighty-third year, in 1818, he left a considerable fortune. He was twice married, and the father of sixteen children, eight by each wife. His remains lie in the Old Granary Burying Ground, a quiet spot in the midst of the rushing tide of business in Boston's commercial section, and where they keep company with the dust of Peter Faneuil, the parents of Benjamin Franklin, and three signers of the Declaration of Independence,— John Hancock, Samuel Adams and Robert Treat Paine.

International Sweethearts

By Edgar Fawcett

"I SHOULD never suppose him to be an American," said Lady Innismore.

"Why not, mamma?" asked her daughter, the Honorable Miss Vane.

Her mother, who was thin and pink and high-nosed, after a certain type of patrician Englishwoman, laughed lightly.

"He hasn't, for one thing, any dreadful twang when he talks. For another, he's graceful, and dresses like our own men . I don't like his legs, somehow," drawled the lady in conclusion, "but his figure is very good, and his face manly, if not handsome."

"You don't like his legs because they have calves to them," said Cicely Vane. "Our men's never do, unless their possessors are of the old John Bull pattern, which, for some reason, is rapidly disappearing."

"My dear, how unpatriotic! By the way," pursued Lady Innismore, taking a red rose from a vase and putting it into the front of her black lace dress, "who got him out?"

She was going to six or seven afternoon receptions, and had just met her daughter in one of the drawing-rooms of their Portman Square home, which they occupied not longer than about three months every season. Her carriage, with its powdered coachman and footman on the extravagantly high front seat, and its huge colored coat-of-arms painted on one of the panels, waited for her outside. She knew very well that her daughter, who stood hatless before her and very simply gowned, had chosen to stay away from all entertainments, this afternoon, because of an expected visit on the part of this same young American gentleman whom they had just been discussing.

"Who got Clement Madison out?" Cicely replied. "Why, he knew the American Ambassador, I believe—"

"Nonsense, my dear. The American Ambassador is charming. I wish they'd always send over such nice specimens. But this official, as you perfectly well know, doesn't occupy his time in seeking to thrust fellow countrymen down the throat of British society."

"Mr. Madison met at one of the European watering-places," proceeded Cicely, as if recollecting, "that pretty Mrs. Macnamara."

"Oh, the little woman whom two or three of our Royalties beam on? That makes the affair altogether different. I *thought* I saw him talking with her at the Vandeleurs' garden-party. He's—er—very rich, isn't he, by the bye?"

"They say so," answered the girl, rather vaguely. "I've never made inquiries."

"Oh, you haven't?" said her mother, with a smile dim but sharp. "And yet you have grown rather rapidly intimate, I should gather."

Cicely flushed and started. "By the way," she heard Lady Innismore add, "your father will see you presently; he said that he would join you here."

In the hall Lady Innismore met her husband. He was a grizzled and very spare man, unerringly tailored, with deep-set eyes from which, of late days, troubled flashes would sometimes leap.

Eighteenth Baron Innismore of Ormolow, sprung from a race no less rich than patrician, he found himself at the present time in galling financial straits. There was no reason why this condition of things should be otherwise. Lord Innismore was not the victim of misfortune, but rather of his own violent extravagance. Ormolow, in Devonshire, had for several years been heavily mortgaged, because of gambling debts. This June his winnings at the Ascot races had been very large, but debt had left him only a few thousand of these after they were reaped. Like so many of his compeers in rank, he lived a false, vain, selfish life, and, like numbers of them, as well, he scarcely gained one annual half-hour of happiness. His wife he had never loved, though at the time of their marriage, she was very much in love with him. So much, indeed, that she had "lent" him almost half of her jointure, never seeing a penny of it again. She now hugged the remainder greedily. Cicely was their one child. The girl was so handsome, with her profuse amber hair and sea-blue eyes, that when her first London season began there were many prophecies as to her making a great match before its end. Yet this was her third season, and though offers had come to her, some of them highly approved by her parents, she resisted all suasion from any source but that of her own heart and spirit.

"She's an odd girl to be ours," Lady Innismore had said repeatedly to her husband, in varying forms of phrase. "I don't know where she gets her sentiment from, really." This mother, now so ossified in worldliness, had forgotten the sentiment of her own girlhood and the bitter disillusions which had cruelly gorgonised it.

"Cicely's there in the front drawing-room, if you want to see her," the lady continued. Then, looking coolly into her husband's face, she went on: "I think I guess the truth, Innismore. The American has asked you for her. I saw you reading that long letter this morning in the library, and something in your face made me suspect. Perhaps you may have seen him since. I've heard he's enormously rich."

Lord Innismore pulled his gray moustache and nodded twice or thrice. He had long ago given up all confidential dealings with his wife, but this time he doubtless felt that she deserved full tribute to her shrewdness in a matter of such momentous family import.

"Yes, Adela, there's no question about his wealth. I'll tell you everything later. I shan't have a very long time to talk with Cicely, for Madison's coming this afternoon."

He was moving past his wife when her next words made him pause.

"How we hate it, don't we?"

"Hate it? You mean—?"

"Marrying our daughters to foreigners. But if Cicely takes him, as I've strong suspicions that she will, we should remember his Americanism as a very small fact. He'll live here with her most of their time, if not all—I'm convinced of it. As if he could possibly prefer one of those provincial Yankee towns after being accepted by our great English world! I shouldn't be at all astonished, indeed, if he had himself Anglicised."

Lord Innismore gave a dubious little grimace as his wife passed him on her way downstairs. At once he went in and joined his daughter.

"So, Cicely," he said, taking her hand and holding it for a moment, Mr. Clement Madison tells me that he wants you for his wife. He believes that you like him. Do you?"

"Yes, papa."

Cicely was perfectly accustomed to her father's matter-of-fact way. He seldom kissed her; he had rarely scolded her, though he had once or twice told her she was a precious little fool for refusing So-and-So or Thus-and-Thus. His manner had never seemed to her brusque or heartless, for she knew so many Englishmen of their aristocratic set who behaved precisely as he did. With one of them she had indeed narrowly escaped falling in love. They were nearly all very much alike. They waxed talkative, even enthusiastic, over horses and dogs and races; they had long periods of silence when this woman or that did her best to amuse them; they spent hours in the hunting-field or in shooting grouse, and often at country-houses their feminine admirers were expected to follow them into the billiard-rooms and attempt some travesty of conversation punctured by the frequent clicks of ivory balls. Without realizing it, Cicely knew in every detail the ungallant modern swell of her race.

"He wrote me," said Lord Innismore, dropping into a chair, pocketing either hand and crossing his slender legs. "Then I went to his chambers and we had a chat." Seeing a look of surprise, here, on the girl's face, her father added: "I—er—went to *him*, you know, because his letter was —er—very polite indeed. He offers handsome settlements—I may say, exceedingly handsome." Here Lord Innismore rose. He hated long talks, and he had a card-playing appointment at one of his clubs. "I don't know much about our ancestral line, Cicely, but I don't think that in any instance we've married other than Englishfolk for surely two hundred years."

"In 1620," said Cicely, with a demure recitational manner, "Edmund Gordon Waynfleete, Baron Innismore, married a Venetian lady belonging to the famous family of Gradenigo."

"Brava!" replied her father, with the rasp that he usually gave instead of a laugh. "That's where you get your yellow locks from, I haven't a doubt. Well, my consent, please understand, is given. I'd like the marriage to take place before the shooting-season, and I suppose you'd prefer St. George's, Hanover Square."

"Yes, papa, though the preference isn't strong."

His lordship gave a shrug, and took out a cigarette, which he rolled unlighted between his fingers. "I hope your preference in another direction is more decided."

"Oh, certainly," said Cicely, laughing.

"Upon my word, I've sometimes believed you'd marry a pauper if you were fond of him," declared her father. "But Madison, luckily, is very far from being that. The truth is, he's richer than some of our dukes. I've verified his statements absolutely. They know all about him at Coults's. One of the American agents happened to be there to-day when I called. He left no doubt in my mind as to Madison having a million and a half of pounds (I never can remember how you put pounds into dollars), besides holding a very respected position."

Lord Innismore departed, that afternoon, without having mentioned to his daughter a fact which he wished to remain inviolably secret, and which Clement Madison, on his own part, had promised to keep so. The latter had received a daring proposal that he should make Lord Innismore a large loan within the next few days. Only to call this proposal daring would be to invest it with an insufficient blame; for it was also the very essence of hidcous taste. But Innismore felt desperate enough to deport himself thus, even after having accepted this young man as a son-in-law and received from him, as well, an assurance that Cicely should be generously dowered.

Clement mused rather sombrely after the father of the girl he loved had left, that morning, his agreeable chambers in St. James's Street. He did not like his prospective father-in-law; he liked few of the fashionable, dawdling men with whom Lord Innismore mingled. All in all, titled and untitled, they were a great throng, and they stood for a most lamentable arrogance. Love for Cicely made much of her surrounding, at least temporarily, rose-color, but even so halcyon a necromancy could not tinge it all. Except for Lord Innismore's daughter, he would have gone back to America soon after the feverish fascination of Mrs. Macnamara had perished. He was by nature cool-headed, firm of purpose, and an abominator of vice. Especially did he loathe vice when blent with so-called culture. He had begun to look, in his reticent, clear-visioned way, upon the English aristocracy as the curse of a noble country. He was young—barely twenty-seven—and his opinion may have been open to refutation in many of its most important details. I leave that to the arguments of the comparative social analysts. Nevertheless, it was his opinion, and he clung to it with hardy, concealed stubbornness. For many days before telling Cicely that he loved her, he had undergone much severe anxiety. He had never dreamed of marrying an Englishwoman at all, and if such an idea had ever entered his head, it must have been totally disconnected with becoming the husband of any woman who belonged to Cicely's class. He was deeply fond of his own country; he came of New England stock, though for several generations his family had made their home in New York. Now he had no near relations, and had found himself, when scarcely twenty, the master of a great fortune. It had always been his wish to enter a political life on returning home, and already he had concerned himself not a little with primary meetings and other governmental questions in his huge native town.

Of all this he had scarcely spoken a word, as yet, to Cicely. His love for her was the truest of passions, but like so many attachments of the sort, it never concerned itself with the girl's mental strength or weakness. He felt that she was complaisant and yielding, and that she resembled hundreds of Englishwomen, old and young, who consented without a murmur to play passive parts toward the other sex. These made of themselves voluntary backgrounds, and took it for granted that they were to be amused rather

than to amuse, smiled upon rather than even hint self-assertion, obey and conciliate, rather than direct and counsel. All this Clement disliked; he had a furtive conviction that some day he would see Cicely delicately Americanized. Such a change could not add to her a single charm in his eyes, but it would still bring him an elusive, yet vital cheer.

To-day his meeting with her in Portman Square dealt only with the divine frivolities of love-making. That evening, at a certain very large dinner in Mayfair, the fact of their engagement was caused to transpire. Later, at a great crush in Belgrave Square, Clement and Cicely received many gratulations. From the English of both sexes, they mostly came in the characteristic, reserved way. But there were several American women present, and their cordiality was, to Clement, rich in refreshing contrast.

"What will you do when you bring her to New York?" whispered one of these, "and have to put on your cards 'Mr. and Lady Cicely Madison'?"

"She isn't 'Lady' anything," said Clement; "she's a baron's daughter, you know."

"True; I'd forgotten. But 'Mr. and the Honorable Mrs.'? Won't that look even stranger still?"

"It may," returned Clement, with an oracular smile. "It certainly ought."

At this same entertainment a slender, comely young man found his chance to glide into the little crowd which surrounded Cicely. "Is it true?" he asked, carelessly, with his lips close to her ear. He spoke with such speed and in a voice so deftly modulated, that almost no one caught his words.

"Yes, it's true," she answered, looking full into his earnest eyes.

"Will you come and talk with me about it for a little while?" he said, in his quick, yet wooing voice. Somewhat later, as they moved away into whatever coign of privacy the thronged apartments would grant, Cicely met the gaze of Clement Madison. It did not look at all jealous, though he was well aware that her present companion, Sir Chetwynd Poyntz, had been among her former suitors and that he stood well outside the black list of detrimentals.

It was not until the next day that Clement had untrammelled possession of his sweetheart's company. By prearrangement he drove her in one of his smart traps to Hampton Court, which they reached in time for luncheon at the drowsy and picturesque Mitre inn, only a step from the river. After lunching, they strolled among the imperial oaks and chestnuts of old Bushey Park, sought to pat the shy deer and fawns, laughed at their own repeated failures, and then moved onward among the glorious trees.

"You haven't told me anything about your talk last night with Sir Chetwynd Poyntz," Clement presently said. "Did he tear me all to pieces as an impudent usurper?"

"Fancy my allowing him!" she replied. They sank, as if by mutual wish, on one of the infrequent benches. All about them was a voluminous melody of high tossed leafage, whose rifts revealed the brilliant blue and the rounded, rolling clouds of a perfect midsummer English day.

"No," Cicely continued, "there's nothing mean or double about Chetwynde. "If I'd loved him as much as I respect and like him, no doubt we'd be to-day Sir Chetwynde and the Honorable Lady Poyntz."

"You'd have called yourselves after that funny fashion?"

Cicely drew herself up a little. "Don't you know yet," she asked, "about the rigid etiquette of our titles?"

"I haven't thought very much about some of their intricacies," laughed Clement, perhaps a trifle nervously. "Why, if you married him, should you not be simply 'Lady Poyntz'?"

Her sweet eyes widened. "Because I _could_ not. It would be against all custom, all precedent. I am above him in rank; I am the daughter of a baron; he is only a baronet."

"M-m, I see. And then he's an Englishman."

Her head gave a bird-like start. She looked at him across one shoulder, with slanted eyes. "An Englishman, of course. If he were a _real_ foreigner, like a Frenchman, a German, an Italian, then it would of course be different."

"A real foreigner," Clement repeated, as if to himself. "Do you call an American a real foreigner, Cicely?"

"No," came her brisk response.

Clement spoke very softly. "Then you would expect to call yourself the Honorable Mrs. Madison after you married me?"

"Call myself?" she exclaimed, with a tang of irritation in her tones, wontedly so suave and mellow. "One never _calls_ oneself that. One is never addressed as 'Honorable' even by servants, as of course you know. But one always put it on one's cards."

"Still, to us, in America, it would seem absurd; no matter how employed.

During our visits to England, I should not have the least objection. But as residents of New York I should not desire it, and no less for your sake than my own."

"As residents of New York!" The words were harshly given. "You can't mean that you've intended to drag me over there! You surely don't wish me to *live* there!" The face of Cicely was pale as her puffed and broidered white frock.

"I do wish it." And very gravely, but very tenderly, Clement leaned toward her. "All my future lies there, Cicely. You come of a race and a set that despise my country—"

"We don't despise her! We don't think enough about her to do that!"

"Could contempt go farther?"

"It isn't contempt," she persisted. "We admit her enormously large and prosperous. In certain respects we're prepared to call her refined. But we do not often feel like doing so. As a rule (you must pardon me), it has been our experience that she is very vulgar."

In a swift mounting surge the color stained Clement's blond face, then slowly faded. She had hated to speak as she had spoken, and she dearly loved the man at her side. But it must be now or never. She must make him yield. Here and forthwith must the fight be fought out—a veritable fight to the finish. Here and forthwith must be crushed down and forever annihilated this horrid peril of becoming an American through marrying one.

"You call my country vulgar," Clement said, after he had held for some time his chin buried in one hand, whose arm rested on his knee. "How, pray, is it in the least more vulgar than yours? Assuredly, judged by size, it has far fewer paupers, and these sink to depths of degradation that ours rarely reach. Is not ignorance vulgarity? Go among your peasantry, your mechanics, your fisherfolk, your miners, all your working-classes, and see what ignorance abounds there! Many of them dwell in pretty cottages, and through summer these are overmantled by flowering rose-vines. But inside they are often comfortless, ill-ventilated, unwholesome. The question of pensions for your aged poor has long cried to your parliament and received from it no pitiful answer. The education of your masses at the present hour is below that of Germany, France, Austria and even Denmark. It is so far below that of our United States as to make any comparison almost ridiculous. Is knowledge, then, your definition of vulgarity?"

Cicely evaded his clear, mild eyes. "Your people flock here in droves, and we judge of them by their loudness, their pushing deportment, their braggadocio."

"But your people—your common people, as perhaps you would phrase it, Cicely—cannot flock to us in droves. They are too poor. The Irish flock that way, and do so still, but only because starvation has driven them to our shores. However, I have no desire to talk politics."

"I do so wish that you would drop the entire subject," she flashed impatiently.

"I cannot," said Clement, with placid seriousness, "for the time has come when it must be threshed out thoroughly between you and me."

"You mean, then—?" murmured the girl, growing pale.

"THEY SANK . . . ON ONE OF THE INFREQUENT BENCHES."

"That all must be arranged, dear Cicely, and the sooner the better."

"All arranged?" she faltered.

"That I should never consent to your not living with me as my wife in my native land. That however we may transiently wander to this or to other lands, from time to time, our real home must be overseas. That I concede the faults of the great Republic in which I was born, but that these faults, in a sense, only make her dearer to me, since I believe them always fraught with a promise of betterment. That I see in this Republic the noblest and purest idea of human government yet conceived by man. And finally, that it would cover me with shame to forsake her for any protracted period."

"This—this," the girl stammered, "covers *me* with a sort of horror. You never told it me before. You waited till now, when everybody knows we are engaged!"

"And pray," asked Clement, a note of sternness creeping unawares into his voice, "what did you expect from me?"

"Expect? Why, that you'd already pitched your tent here, for good and all! We'd received you," she fired on, her eyes moistly flickering, her pure-curved lips curling with disdain. "We don't receive everybody, you know!"

"Yes, I do know," he answered. "You receive nearly every American who is rich, you British aristocrats, and who is willing first to fawn upon you a little and then to spend money on you in showers. You bow specially before the American women who marry your dukes and earls, my angry Cicely. And very often these marriages are horribly unfortunate, being made with the most sordid motives. One foolish little woman gives thousands to mend the old broken-down "historic" abode of His Grace This. Another little woman, equally foolish, pays the huge debts of Lord That. The list of Anglo-American marriages has grown very long by this time. How many of them have been happy? How many of them have contained, during the early days of courtship, a spark of actual love— of the rich, devout love which I feel for you now, and which I am certain you feel for me as well?"

Cicely rose, trembling. "You insult the class to which I belong!"

"I could not," said Clement, while he also rose. "It is beneath insult. It is too lazy, selfish and vicious. However, I speak only of what are called its smart sets, and by this time I think I ought to know them."

"Why, then—why, then," she gasped, "did you go among us after you saw our depravity?"

"Because of *you*, Cicely. Nothing as yet had tainted *you!* Your purity was like a star which I loathed to see blurred."

"Are you sure it was not Mrs. Macnamara who kept you handling such pitch as you describe us?"

Clement's features grew tense. "That is not worthy of you. And I resent your 'us.'"

She laughed high and gratingly. "Ah, don't idealize me, please. It sounds anomalous enough after you've abused my place in the world, my associates, even my kindred. Still, all's over now." She swept past him, having grown deadly pale. "Good-bye," he just heard, no more.

As she began to walk rapidly onward he sprang after her. "Are you not going home in my carriage?"

"No; I've been here often," she said, in husky tones, her head almost imperceptibly turned toward him. "I'm quite familiar with the place. I shall go back by train."

"One moment, please. You said 'all's over.' Did you mean by that——?"

"I meant that our engagement is at an end." She hurried on, and he stood with one lifted hand pressing hard against the furrowed bole of a giant tree.

On her return, that afternoon, Lady Innismore met her with marked surprise. "So early, my dear! I thought you and your new sweetheart were to feast upon all the finest paintings in Hampton Court. You look queer. Did the horses run away—or what?"

"*I* ran away," said Cicely.

Lady Innismore stared at her child in that stolid, languid style with which years had made Cicely conversant. "Good gracious, my dear, I hope you haven't been quarrelling!"

At once Cicely told everything. She was in great mental pain, and now her mother's throwing of the head from side to side and intolerant curling and recurling of the lips, by no means lessened her distress.

"This is quite preposterous," Lady Innismore declared, when the recital was ended. "You never knew the word diplomacy, and you'll never learn it till you're an old maid with scores of wrinkles."

"Ah, you say that, mamma, because Clement Madison is rich!"

"I say it because he's an admirable match, certainly. What on earth was the sense of your breaking with him because he chose to be a little pompous about his own country and rather impudent about yours? Didn't your common sense tell you that he'd never be contented with Yankeedom after having really been taken up and smiled on by *us?* I hear he's a good sportsman—has ridden to the hounds more than once in Leicestershire and elsewhere. And then he's seen our country houses, a few of the very best. You played your rôle idiotically."

"I had no rôle to play, mamma."

"Yes, you had. It was marriage first and talk afterward. Wouldn't you have had your assured settlements, you goose?"

"Oh," cried Cicely, "you counsel such deception as that!"

"Bosh! How would we women ever get on without it? Besides, no special deception would have been needed. *C'etait la moindre des choses* —it was all such a trifle! You could have smiled and looked a little sad—and got married. Men are all alike. Oppose them in a pet idea and they turn granite. Yield (or seem to yield) and they're wax. Hadn't you the weapons of your beauty and the fascination it exerts upon him? And why in heaven's name should you bore yourself by taking a heroic pose on the subject of the British aristocracy? My silly girl, are you a conservative newspaper wrangling with an Irish parliamentary member? He said we're a sorry lot, did he? Well, he's quite right; so we are. We've nothing to do except spend money, and we haven't half enough money to keep up the impudence of our idleness. What Clement Madison said we've all heard a thousand times before. The Radical gangs are always flinging it at us, and (for that matter) we're always flinging it at one another."

Lady Innismore paused. She was very indignant, but she had not once raised her voice above a tart, stinging drawl. Cicely had dropped upon a sofa, and she now went up to her, and with a touch of something in her tones that might relatively be termed softness, she recommended:

"Come, now, let me write Madison a note. You shall sit beside me while I write it. I'll tell him that you were secretly feeling quite nervous and unstrung, this morning, and that you regret——"

But here Cicely flew up from the sofa. "No, no! Clement isn't the fool you paint him, mamma. He at least meant what he said. He has the dignity and honesty of his opinions, however I deplore them. He loves me, and he would not lie to me. I love him, and I will not lie to him. You once told me, while you scolded me because I wouldn't marry that odious Mr. Cavendish-Pomfret, that you were sorry you'd ever sent me for three years to Wye Seminary under the care of dear old Mrs. Holme. But she taught me at least what truth and honor mean, if she taught me nothing in your eyes more noteworthy."

Here Cicely hastened from the room, and went upstairs to her own. By degrees her anger against Clement died, but its passing left her determination still firm. She would not expatriate herself. It was bred in the bone that she should not. Let her mother talk insincerely and flippantly of the whole affair. If pride and love of country were myths, if there were nothing worth having on earth but wealth and caste and splendor, then she meant to live as if this were all a fabulous affirmation and the complete reverse were true.

She dreaded to meet her father, for she was dearly fond of him despite flaws but too manifest. In a little while, however, Lord Innismore, fresh from a talk with his wife, appeared; and Cicely had cause never to forget the interview that ensued. Lord Innismore began by looking at his daughter as if she were a dish of something that he didn't like and was impelled to push away. But instead of pushing her away he went closer to her. His air was horribly grim; his bushy eyebrows were so drawn down that they almost veiled his eyes; he stood planted before Cicely with red face, legs apart, hands deep down in his pockets, and a general air of commonness which suggested its having been borrowed from one of his most plebeian grooms.

"Well, my girl, you *have* made a mess of it!"

Cicely was not in the least afraid of him. She had long ago learned that his bark was far worse than his bite. She was excessively fond of him, as already recorded, however much or little he may have deserved it. He had once saved her life when her horse bolted with her on the hunting ground, and had been laid up for weeks with a fractured thigh in consequence. He had never complained afterward, in spite of much suffering, and repeatedly he had said, with hand tight-clasped about her own: "Thank God I *got you* safe through it, anyhow, Siss, old girl!"

"You've come to scold me," she now said, receding from him a few steps. "I'm miserable enough, surely, without that. No doubt mamma has been telling you just what happened at Hampton Court."

He suddenly veered away from her, and went to a table, from which he snatched up a book. Staring down at the volume, he turned over its leaves with such rapidity that each twist of thumb and finger threatened to tear one of them from its binding.

"Take care, please," ventured Cicely, with veiled satire. "That's a Mudie book, and if you mutilate it the damage must be paid for."

"*I* can't pay for it," he shot out, flinging the book with a slam back on the table. "I can't pay for anything. I'm about as well ruined, now, as a man can be. I don't see anything that I can raise money from. I'm brutally in debt; you're not mean, and would have helped me with a small slice of your settlements, or enabled me, before you got 'em, to put myself on my legs again—I know how, perfectly well."

Cicely said with sadness, then: "Papa, if I had married Clement, and if I had lent you anything, you'd simply have gambled it away. And so——"

Lord Innismore struck the table with his clenched fist. "I wouldn't have done anything of the sort! I tell you I would *not!* I've made up my mind never to touch a card again or gamble in any way, as long as I live!"

"*Serment d'ivrogne,*" thought Cicely. But this was certainly better than to be scolded after the manner of her mother. Aloud she promptly answered: "Bravo, papa! I wish, all the more, now, that Clement Madison hadn't tried to use so high a hand with me."

He looked at her, quite abruptly, with a certain mildness and melancholy which he never showed to any-one else. "If I made you a sacred oath, Cicely"—he began. But then he stopped dead short.

"I should love to have you make the oath," she said, perfectly understanding his incomplete sentence. "But not on the terms which I feel confident you desire—no, no!"

Lord Innismore gave a great sigh. With lowered head he moved toward the door. Then he turned and looked at her again, with great steadiness.

"I—I oughtn't to have spoken of the settlements he promised, Cicely. It was shabby of me, I grant. But you don't know the madness that comes over a man placed as I am. Your mother will do nothing for me. She's never forgiven me—you recall for what. She'll help you, but she'll let this house go, she'll see me in the gutter, before she helps me with five hundred pounds—or even less. Only fools babble of suicide, and then don't commit it. Look at Rotheraye, last month. He staid till four o'clock at the St. James's Club, merry as a linnet over baccarat. By ten his valet found him ——"

"Papa!" cried Cicely. She sped to her parent and struck him sharply on the shoulder, then kissed him almost violently on both cheeks.

He caught one of her hands, pressing it with vehemence. "Take my oath that I'll never gamble again!"

"I'll take it."

"There's nobody on earth I'd make it to but yourself."

"I'll take it," repeated Cicely. "But not on the condition that I marry Clement Madison."

"Never mind." He gave her the oath, and in his rough, lowered voice, he made it very sacred.

"Now," he broke off, with his old bluff manner returning, "will you do a favor for me?"

"A favor?"

"Yes. See Madison once more. Oh, you needn't look so stern. It's nothing about marriage. Perhaps it's harder than would have been any offer to take him back."

"Harder?" Cicely creased her brows.

"What is it?"

"This: Madison agreed to lend me a certain sum of money during the next day or two. Of course he'll think it all off, now. Will you see him and ask him (remember, my girl, the solemn oath I've sworn you!) to let the agreement hold good?"

Cicely gave a great start. Then she hurried away, sank into a chair and covered her face. She felt the hot crimson shame steal against her delicate palms.

Lord Innismore's voice went on. "If he lends me that sum I can pay him back every penny inside of two years. Living my new life, which I've sworn to you that I *will* live, I can get from my Devonshire rents and my Scotch property twice the sum he offered."

There came a pause. Cicely still sat with covered face. Presently her father's voice again sounded, mournful, but not reproaching.

"Oh, well, I see it's no use. You won't do it. All right. You're the only woman I ever loved, Sissy, old girl. I don't blame you. I've been a bad lot in my day and you've stuck by me more than once. It's asking too much, though, this time; it's asking too much!"

She heard the door close, and staggered to her feet. Yes, her father had gone. She flung herself into the chair again, racked by a torrent of tears.

*   *   *   *   *

"I am sorry," said Clement Madison to his visitor, "that you did not send for me instead of coming here yourself."

Cicely was darkly clad and looked all the paler on this account. For a moment her eyes wandered about the pretty room, full of curious, tasteful and costly things. "You were afraid to have me come like this, all alone?" she said, absently. "Well, I didn't know whether you'd answer any message I might have sent. How should I know?"

"Cicely!" He motioned toward a chair close at her side.

"No thanks; I'll stand. So you think I've compromised myself by coming here? Well, we'll assume I'm a typewriter, or a girl with some sort of subscription, or an artistic damsel with a portfolio of barbaric water-colors. But my mission is more serious." For an instant there came into her eyes a kind of frenzied light. She slipped one hand toward her throat, rubbing it restlessly below the chin. "I—I don't come on my own account," she pursued, and then seemed unable to speak the next words.

But effort prevailed, and soon she brought them out with clearness and calm. Her entire appeal to the man with whom that morning she had broken faith was meant to be set in the key of intense entreaty. But she never reached the end of it. With trenchant ardor Clement cut her short.

"I hadn't dreamed, Cicely, of withdrawing my word to your father. How could I?"

She stared at him wonderingly. "But the marriage?"

"Our marriage has nothing to do with the affair. If you will not, you will not. Your father, meanwhile, shall receive his cheque to-morrow.

A gladdening light seemed to pour itself over Cicely's face. "Oh, how I thank you! Many another would not have acted like this, Clem—excuse me, Mr. Madison!" Her eyes glittered with tears, and some of them fell. "I— I told you, didn't I, of papa's oath to me? And he'll keep it—he'll keep it! In two years' time, he will have gathered together——"

"Yes, you told me about that, too."

"Did I? My head's so confused, I——"

"You'd better let me go home with you, in that case," proposed Clement.

"Oh, no, thanks." Here Cicely sank her voice to a whisper. "I—I didn't tell you that I feared papa might commit suicide!"

It occurred to Clement that there wasn't much danger of anything so ghastly. "In that case," he said, however, "I'd better bring the cheque myself at once. "Provided," he went on, solemnly, "you'll allow me to appear in your house."

"Oh, it isn't my house," fluttered Cicely. "You may do precisely as you please."

He dismally laughed. "You didn't speak like that this morning."

Cicely moved toward the door. Resting her hand on its knob, she gave him a look replete with mystery. Half of it seemed gratitude and half belligerence.

"Don't mar your noble conduct," she murmured, "by allusions to this morning."

Clement somehow slipped much nearer to her without being himself quite aware of the approach.

"I might allude to them—er—apologetically, you know."

"Oh," cried Cicely, "you want to make me appear a perfect fiend by deporting yourself like an angel! Come, now; you meant every word you said."

"That doesn't prevent me from apologizing. Suppose *you* did the same."

"Never! "But she softened in every feature while this little exclamatory crash was effected.

"I'm sorry," Clement answered. "Because that, you know, would make

us quits. You certainly were not very polite in Bushey Park. Neither was I. We might each apologize for that. Then we could begin all over again. I see your eyes ask me how, dearest! Well, this way: you could be my wife and spend three years with me in America——"

"Three years!"

"Wait. You could go back with me every summer. Summer's the only decent time in England, anyway."

"Pray," she said, with a pensive haughtiness, "don't revile poor England any more! Surely I've had a surfeit!"

"Is that reviling her? Good heavens! I've heard you vituperate the fogs and the dampness for hours at a stretch. Well, if not hours, appreciable periods. After we'd spent three years in New York you would have the right to command that I should spend three years with you in England. It would ruin my career, but I'd do it, provided you so insisted."

"Ruin your career?" she repeated. as he slightly turned away.

"Oh, yes; I had hoped for a political future in the States. Not on my own account, but because I've felt that I might do some good in a land where legislation, God knows, needs honest men far more than rich ones."

"Oh," burst from Cicely, "so your beloved United States are not *perfectly* faultless, after all?"

"Did I ever say they were?"

"No, you were too occupied in upbraiding England. I must go now; it's growing dusk." She turned the door-knob, slightly opening the door. "I would never ruin your career," she continued. shutting the door again, yet still keeping a stout hold on the knob. "But you mustn't believe I'm not immensely thankful for your great goodness to papa. It would trouble me greatly if I thought otherwise."

Clement drew backward several steps. He folded his arms, and drooped his head. There was silence. Cicely's hand dropped from the knob; she took some faltering paces toward the man she loved.

"Clement."

He lifted his eyes, but gave no other response.

"I—I think I might try to live in your country for—for three years. But if I should grow very homesick before they were ended, wouldn't you take pity upon me, and——?"

She did not finish her sentence, for with eager haste he had caught and crushed her in his arms, and pressed his lips to her own.

*   *   *   *   *

They were married in London that autumn; and when they went to America, a few weeks later, Cicely found her fear of homesickness drifting away with unexpected speed. The gay world welcomed her, and its novelty, freshness and individualism became, as month followed month, a deepening charm. Clement's political impulses were exploited with determination, and their first result was a winter residence in Washington. But every summer the young pair would sail for England, and at these times all the old remembrances were brightened for Cicely by realization that her father was not only keeping his oath, but would still keep it while he lived. If possible, this realization endeared her to Clement all the more. It seemed like a continual testimony, shining and precious, of the high and sweet boon that his love had brought into her life.

The U. S. Naval Torpedo Station[*]

By Grace Herreshoff

A S our late war with Spain has quickened the interest and increased the activity in our new Navy, so the greater Civil War set on foot more ambitious projects and offered wider opportunities for inventions, "changing the old order and giving place to the new." A wonderfully able navy was that of the sixties; but one of the most essential elements the present day organization possesses, it lacked: the torpedo, which, previous to the Civil War, was in the most embryonic state, needing the activity of actual warfare to bring it into prominent notice. In the general revitalization of all governmental departments, a spirit engendered by the final demonstration of the Nation's power, attention was turned to the powerful explosives then recently brought into use by the Navy, and the subject seeming to open up unknown possibilities, it was thought wise to pursue a special course of study and experiment upon torpedoes. To this end, Admiral Porter selected, as the home of the "Torpedo Station," Goat Island, forming one of the protections of the harbor of Newport, Rhode Island, convenient to and yet removed a safe distance from the city. The little island—it is hardly a mile and a half long—was the property of the Army, however, and had hitherto been known only for its disused Fort Wolcott, where the Naval Academy boys had been drilled during war-time; but Admiral Porter's scheme was too excellent to pass unnoticed, and the value of Goat Island was finally fixed at $50,-000, a yearly rental of $5,000 being decided upon.

Accordingly, on July 29, 1869, the island was transferred from the War to the Navy Department, only by lease, however, for the possession of anything so stable as dry land is denied those whose domain covers all the seas of the earth; a torpedo corps was organized, and under the direction of Commander E. O. Matthews, as Inspector in Charge, took possession of Goat Island in September. Until

[*] It was by the courtesy of Commander Mason that the writer was enabled to visit the Station.

THE COMMANDANT'S HEADQUARTERS

the routine should be regularly established and adequate working-space
provided, the old army barracks were
transformed into lecture-rooms and
laboratories, while a machine shop and
store house were evolved from the few
shelters the naval cadets had left behind.

During the first five years of the station's growth, were erected its most
important buildings, which are those
in present use; they were the machine
shop, store house, electric and chemical laboratories, several cottages for
the officers, and the inspector's house,
which latter was built over the old
barracks and includes also various offices. In 1881 a comparatively large
gun-cotton factory was built on the
west shore, and for a period of years
that explosive was manufactured exclusively at Goat Island, though of
late only a small quantity for experimental use is yearly turned out. It
being found impracticable to mass in
one building so great a quantity of
sensitive explosives—the factory was

destroyed by fire, with some loss of
life, in 1893—a number of small buildings were erected along the west shore,
and built into the embankment which
was cut out to receive them. This
scheme was rendered the more necessary by the introduction of smokeless
powder into general use; for, in each
little building, only one step in the
transformation of the raw cotton can
be effected, thus reducing to a minimum the danger of explosion.

Goat Island, or the Torpedo Sta-
tion, as it is invariably called, is entirely surrounded by a heavy sea-wall of
stone and masonry, begun under the
direction of Captain, then Commander,
Converse; and it was only by the
timely construction of this barrier
that the island was saved from the
uselessness to which the constant wear
of the waves threatened to reduce it.
From its northernmost point—Goat
Island, long and narrow, extends almost due north and south—a heavy
stone breakwater stretches some one
thousand six hundred feet up the bay,

ending in a light-house of the usual neat, white-plastered variety. Both the breakwater and "Goat Island Light" were built long before the creation of the Torpedo Station,—about 1840, in fact; while even previous to that date a small light had been maintained on the point, its keeper inhabiting a house near by.

the station. Even a few tenderly cared for trees flourish before the commandant's quarters directly opposite the landing-pier, though elsewhere the neatly marked paths and roads gleam white in the sunlight. And let it here be noted that the extreme neatness prevalent at the Torpedo Station is such as to remind one forcibly of the

THE ELECTRIC LABORATORY

The aspect which the station presents, as one approaches it on a summer's day, is not without its beauty; with the winter days it is best not to concern one's self, for then the bleak winds, sweeping up and down the bay, seem to render even one's foothold insecure. In the summer, the ground is grass-covered, and vines embellish the six severely plain cottages, marshalled in a row along the south part of the island, which are occupied by the officers constituting the personnel of

"holystoned" and orderly appearance of a great battle-ship. Over in front of the machine shop a number of ponderons torpedoes and tubes of obsolete make, with other objects of that nature, are regularly disposed on the lawn, and clumsy old submarine mines (one "ancient" example is dated 1880, such is the haste of modern invention!) mark the corners of the paths.

And here, north of the inspector's quarters and scattered over the widest part of the island, within and about the embankments of the old fort, stands the little group of buildings which shelter the forces that go to make up the Torpedo Station,—that little speck on the great map of the United States which exercises on the Navy an influence out of all proportion to its size. For the purpose of the Torpedo Station is to manufacture, instruct, and primarily, to experiment. Every invention of use to the Navy, and the power which these insignificant objects possess is symbolical of the importance of the Torpedo Station. They are, generally speaking, small round receptacles of brass, one or two inches in length, filled in the case of primers and fuzes, which ignite gun powder, with a very fine meal powder; but the contents of exploders and detonators, which explode the gun-cotton in a torpedo and are of necessity

OFFICERS' COTTAGES

except in the line of propelling machinery and heavy armament or "ordnance proper," passes through or has its birth at the station. Here also a large number of officers and men receives instruction on matters of vital importance.

Though gun-cotton and smokeless powder are no longer manufactured exclusively at the station, there are produced here the primers and fuzes, exploders and detonators, which fire the charges of guns and torpedoes; more powerful, are composed mainly of fulminate of mercury. A recent invention at the Station was the combination primer, which, as the name indicates, unites in one primer the forces of two different classes: so that if, say the electricity, should fail to act, the charge would still be fired by virtue of the power of friction which the primer also possesses—and vice versa.

On the floor above the machine shop is the torpedo lecture room, a large hall in which officers and men are instruct-

ed, fairly lined with torpedoes, most of which are the modern automobiles; but in one corner hang three obsolete forms, one of which possesses an historic interest in having been taken from the Spanish war-ship "Maria Teresa." The Whitehead automobiles, however, predominate in interest, for they are the torpedoes in common use at the present time. The Howell—also an automobile—is occasionally used, to be sure, and is most successful in actual warfare; but its delicate and complex mechanism (it is propelled by a revolving disc instead of by compressed air, as is the Whitehead) renders it impracticable for instruction or "exercise" use.

The modern torpedo is a cylindrical case of steel, 11 feet 8 inches, or 15 feet, long (the Whitehead is used in two sizes) and nearly 18 inches at its greatest diameter, tapering to the bluntly rounded "head" at one end and to the slender pointed "tail," carrying the rudder and propellers, at the other. Into three sections is the wonderful torpedo divided: the head, holding the explosive; the air flask—which is the middle section—containing the driving power of air at a high pressure; and the after-body, in which are the engine, shaft and steering-gear, together with various appliances controlling the idiosyncrasies of this miniature submarine vessel. For such the torpedo really seems to be, guiding itself, and entirely independent of any outside agency from the time it leaves the tube, until the little war-nose projecting from the head touches a solid substance, when the gun-cotton with which the war-head is packed explodes and the torpedo, with its target, is blown to atoms.

But in carrying out its purpose of destruction upon the opposing force what an exquisite piece of workmanship is sacrificed in the torpedo! Its interior is filled with numerous delicate and complicated mechanisms which automatically regulate its course, every possible contingency being provided for.

That it may the more resemble an actual boat, one small compartment is called the engine-room; within this the little engine, occupying a space hardly a foot in diameter and driven by the force of compressed air, accomplishes thirteen hundred revolutions every minute. Though racing at this tremendous rate, it can and does stop on the instant without injuring in the slightest, without even jarring the delicate machinery surrounding it. The speed made by the miniature ship in passing through the water, which, it must be remembered, offers resistance to its entire surface, is twenty-six knots an hour for a run of eight hundred yards, and amounts to about thirty knots when half that distance is to be covered. As a matter of comparison, let it be noted that the engines of the torpedo boat "Dupont," gigantic in contrast to the dainty mechanism under consideration, cannot make more than four hundred revolutions to the minute; yet with this power the boat, encountering to be sure, less resistance, can make over twenty-eight knots an hour—nearly the greatest speed of which the torpedo is capable. What, then, would be the speed of the "Dupont," could her powerful engines, without destroying themselves, even approach the high rate reached by a torpedo's machinery!

As torpedoes are in constant use for both instruction and experiment, it would of course be dangerous and even impossible for them always to carry their charge of gun-cotton; each one is accordingly provided, besides the war-head, with an exercise-head, which is filled with water, in order that its weight may equal that of the former.

A torpedo is fired from a tube, the upper half of which projects, roof-like, over the mouth, as a shell from a gun, that is, by a charge of powder ignited by a primer; but with this difference, that the torpedo travels under its own propelling power, whereas the shell gains its momentum from the force of the ejecting charge. It requires, however, great care and skill to set correctly the different regulators in a torpedo, preparatory to the run; and it is both interesting and ludicrous to watch the proceeding of the novices at "target-practice," for they are prone to forget the most important adjustments. A "surface-run" is most remarkable to witness: then the huge cigar-shaped object goes skimming across the water, occasionally leaping several feet into the air, looking and behaving exactly like a porpoise, it is said, while making a great rushing and whirring noise, like the sound of a train speeding through a tunnel, a fact not at all strange when one remembers that the fifteen-foot torpedo is running at a rate of twenty-six to thirty knots an hour. Perhaps the steering gear is left to its own devices: immediately the torpedo proceeds upon a course most bewildering and even terrifying to the beholder, turning in circles, running up against some object, only to be headed off in another direction, and, when the compressed air is finally exhausted, describing an arc in the air before ending its gyrations at the most unexpected spot. Occasionally a torpedo will be lost, burying itself in the mud or following so eccentric a course beneath the water as to evade the vigilance of the searchers; but it is usual-

A TORPEDO TUBE FOR PRACTICE WORK

ly recovered eventually, as was the case with a torpedo found recently by the divers under instruction at the station. Though having lain a year and five days beneath the water, it was found to be intact, and will perhaps be used eighty or a hundred times for exercise purpose during its future existence.

It is hardly possible to realize that this remarkable mechanism is the result of so humble a beginning as the primitive spar torpedo. This explosive, it can hardly be called a missile, came into existence about the time of the Civil War, and was nothing more or less than a cast-iron box filled with coarse gun powder, and fastened to the end of a long spar, or "boom," which was carried alongside a launch, though projecting some distance in front of the bow. As this torpedo could not be exploded until the launch was beside the object of attack, and as this act was accomplished by means of a primitive friction primer, manipulated by a cord, the danger to the operators was nearly as great as to the enemy. Though spar torpedoes have been superseded by automobiles they have been constantly improved: the shell is now of steel, the charge has become gun-cotton, ignited by an electric detonator. At a recent experiment in the waters near Goat Island, four of these modern spar torpedoes were exploded, sending great beams of wood two hundred feet into the air, while the solid column of smoke and debris seemed to extend up into the clouds themselves.

The next step from the spar was the towing torpedo, dragged by careful manipulation of two lines at some dis-

U. S. Torpedo Boat "Porter" Making 35 Miles an Hour

tance off the quarter of a vessel, and made to dive beneath her adversary. An approach to the automobiles were the Lay, Lay-Haite, Ericsson and Edison-Simms torpedoes; but these, although propelled by their own power, were hampered by the cables controlling them from the boat or shore. In 1870, before the adoption of the Whitehead by our Navy, the so-called Station torpedo, resembling the English one, was constructed and experimented with at the island; it gave way, however, to the Howell, which, though a later invention, was introduced here at about the same time as the Whitehead, the most recent and by all odds, the best.

It is a remarkable, and perhaps not fully realized coincidence, that during the Spanish War not a single torpedo was fired by our vessels, the torpedo boats having been mainly useful as despatch boats, defending themselves, when necessary, with the small guns with which they were provided. Consequently the first explosion of a Whitehead under actual conditions of

174

war took place only year before last in Narragansett Bay, when the United States Torpedo Boat "Porter," running at full speed, fired the torpedo at a distance of eight hundred yards from the target, the beach of Prudence Island; then immediately turned about and fled to a safe distance. Several other torpedo boats were assembled, with a number of officers on board to witness the experiment, which resulted most satisfactorily, effectually proving that with the discharge of a single torpedo the "Porter" could destroy the enemy's ship and herself escape with practically no damage.

Mines were originally intended to receive as much attention at the station as torpedoes; but shortly after its beginning the mine department was removed to Willett's Point, not however before Captain Converse had made an important invention in that line. The Naval Defense mines are invariably loaded at the station, and at the time of the Spanish War the employees were kept very busy filling the countermines.

FIRING A WHITEHEAD TORPEDO

Not only are mines and torpedoes loaded there, but it is at the Torpedo Station that the torpedo outfit of every vessel in the Navy is assembled; and on going out of commission it is there a ship returns her outfit, to be repaired or, if necessary, replaced. The regulations, moreover, provide that an overhauling of the outfit shall take place every three years. With the "rush in business"entailed by the tremendous growth of the Navy during recent years, it is not surprising to find the pay-roll of the employees at the Torpedo Station increased from about $100 per month in 1872 to about $400 per day in the present year.

The experiment manœuvres at the island are by no means confined to torpedoes. Back of the machine shop stands the electrical laboratory, a neat little building crowned by the search light tower, in which is given practical instruction on this weapon of the new Navy. In the lecture rooms are to be found examples of every kind of electric light used on board a vessel, from the huge search light, down to the minute one-half candle power incandescent, with which the inside of a torpedo is illuminated for examination. The dynamo room is also the place of particular investigation and practical instruction to both officers and men.

Leaving the electric laboratory, one approaches an archway cut through the high embankment which formerly surrounded the fort; one approaches, but may not pass through, for within the enclosure stand two buildings closed to the outside world. The larger is the chemical laboratory, in which are conducted experiments in the line of explosives; in the small building to the right of the entrance the blocks of wet gun-cotton are shaped, by means of a circular saw, to fit snugly into the oval war-heads. Sawing gun-cotton sounds as if it were a decidedly hazardous proceeding; but as the material is saturated with water and every possible precaution taken, the workmen are nearly as safe as are those in the machine shop,—more so than the workers on detonators, perhaps, for a careless blow, be it ever so light, on the sensitive fulminator may result in the serious, if not fatal, wounding of the workman.

In one wall of the white plastered archway is cut the name of the French engineer, very modestly, thus:— "Rochefontain Enginr." He it was who threaded the embankments with passages, partly underground; leading into these are little doors at intervals in the walls, one of which, in a corner of the enclosure, opens into an old prison in the tunnel.

Again, back of the enclosure is another, but solid embankment, which extends thence along the west shore nearly to the breakwater; it is this embankment that shelters the six guncotton and smokeless powder houses, entrance into which, it is hardly necessary to state, is strictly forbidden.

Buildings 1, 2 and 3 comprise the guncotton factory. In the first of these the raw cotton is picked apart and dried, a certain brand of English cotton being always used, as it is the most successfully treated in the manufacture of the powder. The second step is the nitrate bath, out of which the cotton, now nitrocellulose, is wrung and washed, then carried to building 3 to be reduced to a soft pulp; after a final wringing the gun-cotton is ready to be taken to building 4, which, with 5 and 6, is the smokeless powder factory. From building 4 the cotton emerges transformed into smokeless powder, and having the appearance of sticks of glue; but a process of drying and seasoning, accomplished in the next building, is now necessary, and after that the powder undergoes a final test, lying stored in the last building,

under different degrees of temperature, before it is issued for use.

The preparation to which the guncotton is subjected, the ingredients of which are known to very few, is of course constantly experimented upon and, as the results show, greatly improved, for the smokeless powder of the present day has obtained a considerable advance in velocity over that of a few years ago. Many of the experiments in the action of gun-cotton and smokeless powder are conducted on Rose Island, which lies to the northwest of the station, and where a guncotton magazine is also situated. The subject of nearly as much study as the powder itself is the elimination of danger from explosion during its manufacture, and of disease to the workmen; and to that end the buildings have been so constructed that they may be frequently and thoroughly cleansed, while some progress has been made in protecting the men from the "noxious vapors" arising from the chemicals.

As a place of instruction, the Torpedo Station holds a position of importance in the Navy. Not only are classes of officers engaged there every summer in practical study on torpedo work, electricity, the chemistry of explosives, etc., but each year two classes of seamen, the pick of the enlisted men, are thoroughly trained in electricity and torpedo work, and, if they so desire and are physically fit, in diving. The course in torpedoes renders the men capable not only to fire the missiles, but to give them proper care and to repair them, to some extent, when disabled. A lasting proof of the excellence of the Station's diving course was furnished by the work and condition of the men diving on the wreck

THE EFFECT OF THE EXPLOSION OF A TORPEDO

177

of the "Maine" in Havana harbor. So thorough had been their physical training, that after 50 days of continuous work in the filth and stench of the harbor, in a hot and oppressive climate, not one of the naval divers suffered any ill effects or was in any way injured—a most unusual occurrence in any wrecking company. As to their ability, though the New York press was at first inclined to criticise, comparing the "sailors" unfavorably with the professional divers, at the last it was eager to admit their undoubted skill and bravery.

With their previous six months' training in the gun-shops at the Washington Navy Yard the men qualify as seamen gunners after this seventeen weeks' course, and are usually ordered at once to sea; later, those who possess sufficient ability rise to the rank of warrant officers.

A small portion of their time of study at the station is spent on board torpedo boats, the men thus becoming somewhat accustomed to sea-duty, though of course the majority are sent on board battle-ships and cruisers, gun-boats and other smaller vessels, whose numbers predominate over those of torpedo boats. Life on the latter, it must be understood, is quite a different matter from that on any other ship in the Navy. In the first place, torpedo boats are not built for men to live on, far less with a view to comfort; in fact, the question of ex-

THE MACHINE SHOP

In the foreground may be seen many torpedo tubes taken from the Spanish vessels at Santiago.

istence on board was so far forgotten in the cases of the "Craven" and "Dahlgren," that no spaces were allowed for the galleys, and on their completion it was necessary to construct them between the stacks on deck! It is however, well known that these boats were not the result of American talent.

Beyond the primary purpose of discharging her missiles, the objects of a torpedo boat are facil-

"THE ARCHWAY"

ity of control and speed, speed that will enable her to outstrip any other class of vessels whatsoever; save only the torpedo boat destroyers, which are merely torpedo boats raised to a higher power, size, armament and speed increased, but not altered.   But to attain this speed a torpedo boat must be of a slender shape and lie low on the water, in order to escape observation as well as to offer the least possible resistance; further she must not be uselessly encumbered with elaborate fittings, but every portion of her make-up must be reduced to the least weight, while her machinery must embody in a compact form a tremendous amount of power. Fully as high as her speed qualifications must be her ability to respond to the lightest touch on the wheel, to reverse, stop, or start her engines at a second's notice; for she depends in battle not upon the material protection of heavy armor-plate, which would weigh her down and detract from her swiftness, but upon her own insignificance and cunning in escape.

A torpedo boat is, in proportion to her size, without an exception the fast-

est vessel afloat. Though the "Dupont" is but 175 feet in length, with a displacement of 165 tons, the 3,800 horse power of her engines is equal to that of the Sound liners, such as the "Plymouth," for instance, a boat of vastly greater tonnage and perhaps 150 feet longer. Yet the "Plymouth's" speed is hardly two-thirds that of the torpedo boat. A comparison with a modern ocean liner, whose proportions more nearly approach those of a torpedo boat, is also interesting. Roughly speaking, the "Deutschland"—fastest of the ocean greyhounds—measures about four times the "Dupont's" length and breadth; but against a hundredfold increase of tonnage, the "Deutschland" can develop only a nine times greater horse power, with the result that her speed lacks about five knots of the "Dupont's." The latter craft, be it noted, was built to attain a speed of only twenty-six knots; but on her official trial she exceeded this contract rate by about two and one-half knots.

The power of endurance against the ceaseless battery of waves and ice in

A Recent View, Showing the New Administration Building at the Left

our northern waters is not considered one of the requisites of a torpedo boat; but the "Dupont," with the smaller "Morris," refuted the idea that these vessels must be hauled up or sent south during cold weather. Both of these boats successfully weathered the hard winter of 1898-99, moored to a dock in a sheltered cove of Bristol, R. I., harbor; the "Dupont" going there directly after the terrible November storm of that season, while the "Morris" joined her later—in good time, however, to pass through the novel experience of being frozen in the ice for many weeks. But though the boats stood the test well, the crews endured untold discomforts.

Two members of the latter, nevertheless, seemed to enjoy life in the cold weather to which they were so unaccustomed. Both of southern birth, they were "Chic," the lively little fox terrier mascot of the "Morris," captured from some Spanish merchantship; and "Dupont Bill," basely kidnapped in infancy from his Cuban home, a goat which gladly devoured the candy, with its paper bag, so frequently offered him by the sailors, as well as, on one occasion, the feathers decorating a visitor's hat! For a short time last winter, the "McKee" was rejoiced with "Bill's" presence as a guest, and it was on one of her trips that he narrowly escaped a watery grave. The trip was memorable in the boat's career as well as in "Billy's."

The "McKee," which is the smallest of her class,—hardly one hundred feet in length and of only sixty-five tons displacement—left New York one stormy day for Newport, expecting to arrive in about eight hours. A short distance along the Sound, however, her blowers gave out and she was forced to proceed under natural draft, crawling along at about three knots an hour, while the seas literally swept over her, nearly sweeping poor "Billy" overboard. At last he was lashed to the smokestack, and though half smothered by the water, weathered the twenty-four hour nightmare of a trip; meanwhile the executive officer, "Bill's" only companion on deck, was forced to grasp the supporting stack in a close embrace.

Innumerable are these unofficial records of runs bravely accomplished under conditions with which no torpedo boat was designed to cope; but so enjoyable can warm, fair weather render a short trip, that one would forever scorn the most luxurious steam yacht after a single rapid, exhilarating run on a torpedo boat.

The "McKee" has been mentioned as the smallest vessel of her class. Still smaller is the "Stiletto," the only wood torpedo boat in the navy; be the other slips crowded or deserted, she is always to be found at her dock at the Torpedo Station. Moored near her, last summer, was that representative of a new type, the submarine torpedo boat "Holland;" and very strange and weird, like some deep-sea monster newly dragged into the light of day, appeared that part of her fifty feet of length which is visible when she rises to the surface. As far as the question of life on board (or is it within?) is concerned, the "Holland" is a little more comfortable than a diving-suit, and can be stored with sufficient air and food to support her crew of five for forty-eight hours; as to the question of destruction upon an outside force, this submarine vessel is an undoubted success, as was proved in the fleet and harbor defense manœuvres held at Newport last summer. It was reported on this occasion, that the "Holland" could have "torpedoed" (synonymous with "destroyed") probably three ships of the blockading fleet. In strange juxtaposition to this modern invention, an old submarine boat, designed by Admiral Porter, lies near the docks at the Station. It is a box-like structure of iron, divided within into compartments, one of which contains an ancient smooth-bore gun, and intended to be sunk to a stationary position.

It has been almost entirely through the ceaseless activity of its many excellent commandants and assisting officers that the Torpedo Station has attained its prestige. The present Inspector is Commander N. E. Mason, the well-known executive officer of the U. S. S. "Brooklyn" during the Spanish War, who distinguished himself at Santiago; Lieutenant - Commander Rees, formerly executive officer of the island, but ordered to sea duty August, 1901, most ably performed the duties of executive officer on no less a ship than the "Olympia," at Manila, under Admiral Dewey. It is hardly necessary to add that the Department strenuously endeavors to appoint the personnel of the Station from among the most active and efficient officers of the navy.

Many years ago Rear Admiral Sampson was Inspector at the Station, and little known to the general public. With the increase of the new navy he has come into prominence, and by his ability has shown to the world her power in war,—a power the growth of which is typified by the progress made at our Navy's Torpedo Station.

Handsome Felix

By I. McRoss

"WHAT is the use, Felix, in being the handsomest man in all Madawaska, if you care nothing for the girls? You might as well be as homely as Sol Boulier, for all the use your good looks are to you!"

"Perhaps better, mother, for Sol has just married as pretty a girl as ever confessed a sin to Father Marchand; you see good looks have nothing to do with it. Now give me one of your aprons to put across my knees and I will shell the peas for you, before I go down town to hunt up a table girl."

"You'd better hunt up a wife; remember you are thirty years old; when your father was your age we had been married ten years."

"Whom shall I marry? Susie Michaud? Delphine Dionne? Rosie—"

"Shame on you, Felix St. Thomas! To think of such creatures! No, no, marry some one like yourself, pretty and slender, straight and tall, though not quite so tall as you; you stand six feet in your high-heeled boots, your wife's forehead should just reach the tip of your ear; she must be dark, too, just a trifle lighter than you; hair a good, warm brown, eyes brown or hazel, color enough to stain her cheeks a rich red. Never, Felix, never marry a washed-out, light-haired, blue-eyed girl,—she'd be faded before thirty. Your wife must be French, too; I'd like a Canadienne, but she must speak English as well as you or I. Yes, and her hair might curl a trifle that your children's hair be not too straight. Sometimes I think of the children while I am here at work, until this kitchen seems swarming with the dear, bright-faced little fellows; they jostle my elbows, they get their little hands into my flour, and I put out my hand to box their ears—but not hard, I wouldn't hurt them—just to get them from under my feet. Madame rested the rolling-pin upon the piecrust and looked at Felix with happy, smiling lips.

"Well, mother, you pick out the one you want me to marry, and I will get her if I can."

"Of course you can get her! What girl would not be proud to be the wife of handsome Felix? Then see what a good business you are doing; twice you have been obliged to enlarge this hotel, yet it is always full."

"That is because of your famous cooking."

"Partly, and partly because the liquors you sell are the best, so they say, that were ever sold in spite of the Maine liquor law."

"There, mother, the peas are shelled." Felix rose and put the pan of peas upon the table. "Now I must go and look up the table girl."

His mother watched him as he walked down the street—tall and straight, head upheld, eyes bright, complexion clear—he cared too much

for his good looks to drink the liquor
he handled. His new suit of dark
gray cheviot fitted perfectly his fine
figure, and his boots had just the high,
pointed heels dear to a Madawaska
Frenchman. Apparently he looked
neither to the right nor the left, but
from the corner of one eye he saw two
girls looking at him from the opposite
side of the street, and heard the ripple
of a few syllables in French. Intent upon his errand, he crossed the
street.

"Do either of you girls want to work
out? I need a table girl at the St.
Thomas hotel." He directed his question to the elder of the two, a girl about
twenty. "How pretty she is!" he kept
thinking. "But mother would not think
so, she is so fair; and not tall enough,
either; her head would scarcely lie
upon my shoulder." He had the grace
to blush at the thought, as she smiled
into his face.

"Yes, I came to town to find a
place."

"What is your name?"

"Julie Le Vasseur."

"And your home?"

"In Canada, near the Chaudière."

His questions had been put in
French, now he spoke English:

"Can you speak English?"

She answered in English as perfect
as his own:

"O, yes; I went to an English school
and my mother is an Englishwoman."

"That is the reason you are so fair;
you do not look like a French girl. Can
you come to the hotel now, with me?
Our girl left this morning and we need
you now."

"Yes; but my trunk is at my cousin's, Pete Thibbedeau's."

"I will send for it, if you will come

with me." They walked together to
the hotel and into the kitchen.

"Mother," said Felix, "this is Julie
Le Vasseur; she will wait upon the
table."

"Come with me, then; I will show
you what to do," said Madame.

"What a white head!" was Madame's
inward comment, though she could
not deny that it was a pretty head, with
its glistening waves of fair hair breaking into tiny curls wherever a strand
became loose. "She would be pretty
if only she were darker, and I am glad
she is not. Felix will never fall in love
with such a light girl." So hard it is
to abdicate a throne that Madame forgot, for a moment, what she had been
preaching to Felix for ten years.

Madame watched Julie very closely
for many days; she always kept her
eye upon the table girls, they were so
eager to get a word or glance from
Felix; but Julie, to Madame's surprise,
seemed utterly indifferent to Felix's
charms, and that was something that
neither he nor his mother could quite
understand. Madame tried by hints
and questions to get Julie's opinion of
Felix; at last she asked outright:

"Do you not think my Felix very
handsome, Julie?"

Julie was polishing silver in the dining room, and she looked at a fork
critically, before answering:

"O, yes, Madame, for such a black
man."

"Black man! My Felix!" Madame
almost screamed.

"Yes, Madame, such black eyes and
hair, and such dark skin, you know."

"Of course! W'at else will you have
for ze man? Ze white hair an' skin,
like ze foolish girl?" Madame never
lost her perfect command of the Eng-

lish language except under stress of great mental excitement. "Where ever did you see one ot'er such han'some man, like my Felix?"

"My Triflis is handsomer," said Julie, her eyes bent upon a tea spoon.

"Your Triflis! So zat ees eet, ze mattaire! Your Triflis! Bien, w'at do he look lak?"

"Triflis? O, he is tall—six feet and two inches."

"Zat ees too much; ma Felix ees just six feet."

"In his stocking feet;" said Julie, as though she had not heard, "my Triflis does not need to wear boots with high, pointed heels, like a fine lady's."

"Zat ees ze style, an' ma Felix have ze leetle, pretty feet zat look so nice."

"Triflis is broad across the shoulders, thick in the chest and strong."

"So is ze ox."

"His hair is just a little darker than mine, and it curls around his white forehead; the rest of his face is tanned quite dark, but his cheeks are red as June roses. And Triflis's mouth— O, it is handsome! He does not need any mustache to hide it."

"Ma Felix does not wear hees mustache to hide hees mout', his mout' ze pretties' you evair saw."

"Perhaps his teeth—"

"His teet'!" Madame was quivering with rage. "His teet' are perfee'! Yes, look at you'se'f in ze spoon; you see you upside down, zat w'at you are! W'at you t'ink you see, anyhow? You t'ink you pretty wit' you tow-head an' you putty face? Felix can have any girl he want for marry heem."

"Oh!" Incredulously, "he'd better be hurrying a little, he's getting pretty old."

"Old! Ma Felix! He iss young! An'

listen; he will marry one hen'some girl like heemse'f—black eyes an' hair an' red cheeks, tall an' fine, wis ze proud head like hees own, zat is ze wife I choose for heem."

Julie shrugged her shoulders, disdainfully.

"Well, that would be best. It will save spoiling two families."

Madame was too angry to answer this, and went into the kitchen banging the door after her. Julie could hear her slam the stove covers. "Ma Felix! Black! Old! Wear mustache to hide his mouth! Bad teeth! Make fun of his pretty boots!" She could not keep it to herself, but found Felix and poured the story into his ears.

"She shall leave, the baggage! To-morrow, to-day she shall go!"

"No, no, mother; I should be ashamed to send her away for that, and you know she is the best table girl we ever had."

Madame's anger continued many days, but Julie did not pay any attention to it, nor did she seem to notice that Felix's mustache and the high heels of his boots had disappeared.

One day word came that the governor and his staff, with their wives and daughters, were going through the Upper Madawaska and would be at the St. Thomas hotel for six o'clock dinner. Then Madame forgot her anger and turned to Julie:

"O, Julie! Only to-morrow! Thirty of them! And such a dinner as they will expect! Many governors have taken dinner here, and have always been served with the best, but now— not twenty-four hours' notice, and bread, cake, pies, puddings to be baked, chickens and turkeys to be killed, dressed and cooked, fresh meat to be killed and made ready for oven and broiler!

"Go quick, quick, Felix! Get Pete Thibbedeau's wife to come and help!"

Pete's wife was nursing a sore hand and could not come, but by the time Felix returned Julie had encouraged Madame, and she had become a little more calm.

"I will help, Madame; the chore boy and I will get the fowls ready for your hand; I can do lots of things, you shall see." Her voice was so cheerful, and her face so bright and sunny that before Madame thought what she was doing she patted the girl's shoulder:

"You are a good girl, Julie, the best that ever worked for me; you do not mind the extra work and look cross, as most girls would. Now while I get my canister of herbs you go into the yard and pick out the fattest chickens and the tenderest young turkeys for Joe to kill." She took a chair to climb upon, to reach the canister; there was a crash, and Julie ran back. Madame lay upon the floor, groaning with pain.

"O, Madame, what is the matter?" She tried to help Madame to rise, but she screamed:

"My leg is broken! I took that old chair and it let me down! What will we do? It was bad enough before, but now—we will lock the doors, pull down the shades and let no one in."

"No, no, Madame; I will get the dinner. You shall lie there in your bedroom, just off the kitchen; the bed can be pulled close to the door and you can tell me everything to do. Come, Felix, we must put her in bed and send for the doctor." It was Julie who alone retained a cool head; Julie who directed and commanded, waited upon the doctor, soothed Madame and ordered Felix.

"Now, don't you worry, Madame, the dinner will be so like yours that no one will be able to tell the difference." After the doctor had gone, Julie went to work; until eleven o'clock that night she baked and boiled and made preparations for the next day. At five the next morning she was again at work, so deft, quick and capable that Madame watched her in amazement.

"Julie, where did you learn to cook so well? I believe you have taken the mantle from my shoulders."

The dimples came to Julie's pink cheeks: "O, Madame, have I not been watching you for three months? Then I knew a little before, and you lie there telling me, and I have your recipes. Now taste this dressing for the turkeys, then I will fill them."

"It is good; just a trifle more summer savory and it cannot be told from mine."

When the governor and his party arrived, everything was in readiness; cups of bouillon, hot, rich and fragrant; trout from a mountain lake— John Therrault had caught them while the governor was taking his morning nap; broiled chickens, young turkeys with Julie's nice dressing; baked spareribs of tender young pork; then there were pies, and puddings with foamy sauces, and coffee rich with yellow cream.

"Tell Madame," said the governor, in his kindest, most courteous manner, "that those who expect a good dinner here are never disappointed, but today Madame has fairly surpassed herself."

Felix would have explained, had not Julie silenced him with a glance.

The governor and his party had gone; Julie and John Therrault's wife were putting things in order, when Felix came into the kitchen. The tired droop at the corners of Julie's pretty mouth went to Felix's heart.

"You look so tired, Julie, sit down and rest. I will help Susanne." Madame heard; the tone more than the words opened her eyes to her son's feelings. Not even when Felix had sacrificed his beloved mustache and his cherished high heels had she suspected. If she could have looked into Julie's eyes she would have read her secret, too, that secret which dear little Julie had guarded so well.

Madame's heart filled with anger— not against Felix or Julie, but—Triflis! What business had he with Julie's heart? "I wish he'd drown in the Chaudière! I wish he'd tumble over on his big head and break his neck! The gawky hulk! O, my, the wicked woman I am!" She reached for her rosary and said a pater-noster, then listened again:

"Come into the dining room, Julie, and let me wait upon you; I do not believe that you have eaten a mouthful since morning."

"Yes, I have, and I am not very tired." She raised her blue eyes to Felix and his heart gave a great bound.

"Triflis! There is Triflis!" she cried the next moment and ran out to meet him.

"Felix," cried Madame.

"What, mother?"

"Is—is it really Triflis?"

"Yes, mother."

"Did—do—you think—was she very glad to see him?"

"Yes, mother."

"She—she—did not kiss him, did she?"

"Yes, mother."

"The shameless tyke! Send her home! She shall not stay here another hour!" Felix did not hear; he was out of reach of his mother's voice, out of sight of Julie and Triflis.

"And all he could say was, 'Yes, mother,' sighed Madame.

"I wish that Triflis may choke with the next mouthful of bread he takes! O my, O my!" And she said another pater-noster.

It seemed to Felix that hours had passed, though Susanne had just finished washing the dishes and gone home, when Julie walked into the office with Triflis's hand clasped in hers:

"Felix—I mean Mr. St. Thomas, this is my brother, Triflis," she said demurely, though her eyes were twinkling.

"What! Triflis your brother!" With outstretched hands Felix sprang toward the tall young man. "You big, handsome boy!" was his thought, while he tried to shake the large, heavy hands.

"We must give him a good dinner, Julie; there is enough left to feed a dozen like him. Sit here, Triflis, and rest with Julie while I put on the table a dinner as good as the governor ate."

But Julie would help, and together they loaded down a table with fish and meats, bread and cakes, pies and puddings, until Triflis, giant that he was, declared that if he ate steadily for two whole days he would not be able to clear the table. Yet Felix was not satisfied; in the hiding place, behind the cellar wall, were a few bottles of wine; his father had put them there to await Felix's wedding. Felix brought out a bottle of this precious wine and filled the largest goblet he could find.

"There, Triflis, that is something that the governor could not get, no, or even the president, not if they should beg for it upon their knees."

"He left Triflis smacking his lips over the rich, mellow wine, and went into the kitchen to find Julie.

"Julie, he has not come for you?" He took both her hands and drew her toward himself.

"Yes; they are lonesome at home without me."

"You cannot go, Julie; I must have you always, dear; I have never wanted anybody else, and I must have you. Stay, Julie, and be my wife."

Madame forgot her broken leg and all the doctor's instructions and raised herself upon one elbow, to hear better.

"But you know I am too fair; your mother says that you must marry a dark, handsome girl; she does not like my light hair and blue eyes."

"Yes, I do," cried Madame. "I want you, Julie, who else would be so good? I like you just as you are, with your shiny, curly hair and blue eyes. I love you, too, Julie, dear."

Julie's happy laugh sounded as though it had been smothered against something.

Madame sank back, contentedly, upon her pillows, hardly noticing the twinge of pain. She closed her eyes and a happy smile played over her handsome old face.

Memories of Daniel Webster in Public and Private Life

By William T. Davis

SOME of the incidents in the life of Daniel Webster narrated in the following paper have come to my knowledge from my own observation, from communications made to me by my uncle, Isaac P. Davis, of Boston, and Charles Henry Thomas, a native of Marshfield, and from information obtained from my father-in-law, Mr. Thomas Hedge, and his brother, Hon. Isaac L. Hedge, both of Plymouth. To these incidents I have added such of a general charac-

ter as secure a continuity of narrative. So far as my own opportunities of observation are concerned, I met Mr. Webster at his home in Marshfield and at his home in Washington; and in my native town of Plymouth, eleven miles from Marshfield, his figure was a familiar one.

It may perhaps with truth be said that no person outside of Mr. Webster's family was more familiar with his social habits and every day life, than my uncle, and in the second volume of Mr. Webster's speeches, published in 1851, the following dedicatory letter to him may be found:

"My Dear Sir:

A warm private friendship has subsisted between us for half our lives, interrupted by no untoward occurrence, and never for a moment cooling into indifference. Of this friendship, the source of so much happiness to me, I wish to leave, if not an enduring memorial, at least an affectionate and grateful acknowledgment. I inscribe this volume of my speeches to you.

DANIEL WEBSTER.

Mr. Charles Henry Thomas was for many years his agent and man of affairs, and Mr. Webster in his will requested his executors and trustees "to consult in all things respecting the Marshfield estate with Charles Henry Thomas, always an intimate friend, and one whom I love for his own sake and that of his family."

Messrs. Isaac L. and Thomas Hedge, above referred to, were intimate friends of Mr. Webster, and his frequent companions when fishing in Plymouth Bay or hunting in Plymouth woods.

Mr. Webster was born January 18, 1782, in that part of Salisbury, New Hampshire, which is now Franklin, and graduated at Dartmouth College in 1801. He entered, as a student, the law office of Thomas W. Thompson of Salisbury, where he remained three years, teaching school a part of the time in Fryeburg, the first earnings from which were devoted to the education of his brother, Ezekiel. On the 20th of July, 1804, he entered the office of Christopher Gore, in Boston, remaining there until March, 1805. At that time his brother was teaching a school in Short street, now Kingston street, in Boston, with Edward Everett

as one of his pupils, and for a short time in August, 1804, Mr. Webster taught the school during his brother's absence. In March, 1805, he was admitted to the bar of the Court of Common Pleas in Suffolk County, and opened an office in Boscawen, N. H., adjoining his native town. In May, 1807, he was admitted as counselor in the New Hampshire Superior Court and removed to Portsmouth.

On the 24th of June, 1808, he married Grace, daughter of Rev. Elijah Fletcher of Hopkinton, N. H., who died January 21, 1828. His courtship was a romantic one. Grace Fletcher was visiting her sister Rebecca, wife of Israel Webster Kelly of Salisbury, and on a stormy Sunday morning in preparing for church her sister told her that she need not be particular about her dress, as she would see no one to mind. After church she reminded her sister of what she had told her, and said, "I did see someone, a man with a black head, who looked as if he might be somebody." Mr. Webster noticed her, as well. One day, not long after, a package was received at the Kelly home with a string about it tied in a hard knot, and Mr. Webster and Miss Fletcher by their united efforts succeeded in untying it. He then said to her: "We have been successful in untying a knot, suppose we try to tie one which shall last through life." Taking a piece of ribbon and partially tying a knot, he handed it to her to finish, which she did, and thus was the offer of marriage made and accepted. His love never faded. Near her death, while sitting at a generous tea-table at the home of Albert Livingston Kelly, a nephew of Mrs. Webster, he

From a drawing made by Healy in 1843; owned by Benjamin F. Stevens.

DANIEL WEBSTER

said, "Albert, you live luxuriously," and Mr. Kelly replied that it had been his wish to imitate the delightful tea-table of his dear Aunt Grace. Tears at once started from Mr. Webster's eyes and it was with some effort that he recovered his composure. On his death-bed, finding on one occasion Mrs. James William Paige by his bed-side, he said, "If dear Grace could look . . . ' . . ' . . ven, how grateful she would be to y. . . William for ministering to my comfort." Mr. Paige was a half brother of Mrs. Webster, her mother, Rebecca (Chamberlain)

Fletcher, having married for a second husband Rev. Christopher Paige and become Mr. Paige's mother.

He was chosen, in Portsmouth, a member of the Thirteenth Congress, taking his seat May 24th, 1813, and being re-elected to the Fourteenth Congress. In June, 1816, while having an annual income of about two thousand dollars from his practice, he removed to Boston, where he occupied a house in Mt. Vernon street near the State House, and a law office on the corner of Court and Tremont streets over the store many years occupied

189

by S. S. Pierce & Co. Though John P. Healy occupied the office with him for some years, the only law partner he ever had was Alexander Bliss, one of his pupils, who was the first husband of my aunt, Mrs. George Bancroft, and who died July 15, 1827.

In 1818, at the age of thirty-six, by his argument in the Dartmouth College case he established a reputation as one of the ablest constitutional lawyers in the Union. The words, "Dartmouth College case," probably slip from the pen of a writer without conveying to those of the present generation any idea of their meaning. A case so important that the argument of Mr. Webster, in the words of his biographer, "caused the judicial establishment of the principle in our constitutional jurisprudence, which regards a charter of a private corporation as a contract, and places it under the protection of the Constitution of the United States," should be more generally understood.

In 1769 a corporation was established by charter to consist of twelve persons, and no more, to be called the "Trustees of Dartmouth College," to have perpetual existence and power to hold and dispose of lands and goods for the use of the College, with the right to fill vacancies in their own body. The New Hampshire Legislature by acts passed June 27th and December 18th and 26th, 1816, changed the corporate name from "The Trustees of Dartmouth College," to "The Trustees of Dartmouth University," and made the twelve trustees, together with nine other persons, to be appointed by the Governor and Council, a new corporation, to whom all the property of the old corporation with its rights, powers, liberties and privileges was to be transferred, with power to establish new colleges, and an institute subject to the power and control of a board of twenty-five overseers. The conversion to the new corporation of the records, charter, seal and other property was made on the 6th of October, 1816, and an action of trover was brought by the old trustees to recover them, on the ground that the acts of the Legislature were repugnant to the Constitution of the United States. By consent, the action was carried directly to the Superior Court of New Hampshire in May, 1817, and argued at the September term of the Court in Rockingham County, Jeremiah Mason, Jeremiah Smith and Mr. Webster appearing for the trustees. At the November term of the Court in Grafton County, Chief Justice Richardson delivered the opinion of the Court sustaining the constitutionality of the acts. By a writ of error, the case was carried by the plaintiffs to the United States Supreme Court in February, 1818, and argued in March by Mr. Webster and Joseph Hopkinson, of Philadelphia, for the plaintiffs, and by John Holmes, of Maine, and William Wirt, United States Attorney General, for the defendants. In February, 1819, the opinion of the Court was delivered, reversing the action of the State Court and declaring the acts of the Legislature unconstitutional. Though assisted by Mr. Hopkinson, a leading Philadelphia lawyer, popularly better known as the author of "Hail Columbia," the burden of the case rested on the shoulders of Mr. Webster. John Holmes, one of his opponents, was nine years his senior and, as the ablest lawyer in the District of Maine, was selected, when in 1820 that district became a state, as one of its first two United States Senators. William Wirt, his other opponent, was ten years his senior and had by distinguished service at the bar won the appointment of Attorney-General in the Cabinet of President Monroe, which he continued to hold until the accession to the Presidency of Andrew Jackson, in 1829. Against such men Mr. Webster won the title of "Defender of the Constitution."

On the 22d of December, 1820, Mr. Webster delivered his memorable address at the invitation of the Pilgrim Society of Plymouth, in commemoration of the landing of the Pilgrims. The Pilgrim Society had been incorporated on the 24th of the preceding January, and in view of the fact that the celebration of 1820 would be its first public act, and would occur on the two hundredth anniversary of the landing, it was determined to make the occasion a notable one. The desire to hear Mr. Webster was widespread, and throughout the day before the celebration the roads leading to Plymouth were dotted with stages and carriages of all kinds, crowded with visitors.

The company was a distinguished one. At the dinner, held in the Court House, then building and far enough advanced to be used for that purpose, the parchment sheets, since framed and kept in Pilgrim Hall, were passed along the tables to receive the autographs of those present.

Mr. Webster was the guest of Mr. Barnabas Hedge, and on the eve of the celebration a reception was held at the home of my grandfather, William Davis. He was visiting Plymouth for the first time. With Pilgrim associations clustering around him, he was about to speak the next day in the meeting-house of the first New England church, organized in Scrooby, England, in 1606, and in the presence of those whose criticism he would fear as much as he would value their approval, and throughout the evening he was depressed, as he said, by a sense of the responsibility resting upon him.

During the delivery of his address he stood in front of the pulpit. He wore small clothes, with silk stockings and a black silk gown. As is well known, the most marked feature of his address was its eloquent and scathing denunciation of the slave trade. Though that trade had been prohibited by the British Parliament in 1807, and by Congress in 1808, it still survived, and even within the limits of the Old Colony was profitably carried on. With this fact in mind Mr. Webster uttered the following words:

"I deem it my duty on this occasion to suggest that the land is not yet wholly free from the contamination of a traffic, at which every feeling of humanity must forever revolt—I mean the African slave trade. Neither public sentiment nor the law has hitherto been able entirely to put an end to this odious and abominable trade. At the moment when God in his mercy has blessed the Christian world with an universal peace, there is reason to fear that to the disgrace of the Christian name and character new efforts are making for the extension of the trade by subjects and citizens of Christian states, in whose hearts no sentiments of humanity or justice inhabit, and over whom neither the fear of God nor the fear of man exercises a control. In the sight of our law the African slave trader is a pirate and felon; and in the sight of heaven an offender far beyond the ordinary depth of human guilt. There is no brighter part of our history than that which records the measures which have been adopted by the government at an early day, and at different times since, for the suppression of the traffic; and I would call on all the true sons of New England to co-operate with the laws of man and the justice of heaven. If there be within the extent of our knowledge or influence any participation in this traffic, let us pledge ourselves here upon the rock of Plymouth to extirpate and destroy it. It is not fit that the land of the Pilgrims should bear the shame longer. I hear the sound of the hammer, I see the smoke of the furnace, where manacles and fetters are still forged for human limbs. I see the visages of those, who by stealth and midnight labor in this work of hell, foul and dark, as may become the artificers of such instruments of misery and torture. Let that spot be purified, or let it cease to be of New England. Let it be purified, or let it be set aside from the Christian world; let it be put out of the circle of human sympathies and human regards, and let civilized man henceforth have no communion with it. I would invoke those who fill the seats of justice, and all who minister at her altar, that they execute the wholesome and necessary severity of the law. I invoke the ministers of our religion that they proclaim its denunciation of these crimes and add its solemn sanction to the authority of human laws. If the pulpit be silent, whenever or wherever there may be a sinner bloody with this guilt within the hearing of its voice, the pulpit is false to its trust."

The clergy had not at that time been more emphatic in condemning the slave traffic than they were at a later period in condemning slavery itself, and I was told by a witness of the scene that the ministers, who had taken part in the service and were leaning over the reading desk of the pulpit, retreated abruptly to the rear while the above closing words were spoken. The peroration was worthy of the address:

"Advance then, ye future generations! We would hail you as you rise in your long succession to fill the places, which we now fill, and to taste the blessings of existence, where we are passing, and soon shall have passed, our own human duration. We bid you welcome to the pleasant land of the fathers. We bid you welcome to the healthful skies and the verdant fields of New England. We greet your accession to the great inheritance, which we have enjoyed. We welcome you to the blessings of good government and religious liberty. We welcome you to the treasures of science and the delights of learning. We welcome you to the transcendant sweets of domestic life, to the happiness of kindred and parents and children. We welcome you to the immeasurable blessings of rational existence, the immortal hope of Christianity and the light of everlasting truth."

In 1822 Mr. Webster was chosen Member of Congress from the Boston district and re-chosen in 1824. In January, 1824, he made an important speech on the Greek question, advocating the passage of a resolution by Congress:

"That provision ought to be made by law for defraying the expense incident to the appointment of an agent commissioner to Greece, whenever the President shall deem it expedient to make such appointment."

In February, 1824, Mr. Webster won a second victory in the United States Supreme Court, and confirmed his reputation as a Constitutional lawyer, in the case of *Gibbons vs. Ogden*. In the light of today this case appears an extraordinary one. The Legislature of New York had passed laws securing, for a term of years, to Robert R. Livingston and Robert Fulton, the exclusive navigation by steam of all waters within the jurisdiction of the state. Aaron Ogden, to whom was assigned Livingston and Fulton's right to navigate the waters between Elizabethtown, in New Jersey, and the city of New York, secured an injunction in the Court of Chancery against Thomas Gibbons, who was running two steam-

WEBSTER'S HOME AT MARSHFIELD

boats in said waters in alleged violation of his exclusive privilege, and the injunction was affirmed by the highest court of law and equity in New York, the court for the trial of impeachments and correction of errors. From that court the case was taken, by appeal, to the United States Supreme Court. Mr. Webster and William Wirt, the United States Attorney General, appeared for the appellant and Thomas Jackson Oakley and Thomas Addis Emmet for the respondents. It seems now strange that the Ogden claim could have been seriously entertained, and yet Mr. Webster himself began his argument by "admitting that there was a very respectable weight of authority in its favor." He argued that the laws of New York, on which the respondents' claim rested, were repugnant to that clause in the constitution, which authorizes Congress to regulate commerce, and to that other clause, which authorizes Congress to promote the progress of science and useful arts. The respondents' counsel claimed that:

"States do not derive their independence and sovereignty from the grant or concession of the British crown, but from their own act in the declaration of independence. By this act they became free and independent states, and as such have full power to levy war, conclude peace, contract alliances, establish commerce and to do all other acts which independent states may of right do."

The decision of the State Court was reversed, and, as a result of the argument of Mr. Webster, it was established for all coming time that the commerce of the union was a unit, and that no state can grant a monopoly of navigation over waters where commerce is carried on. In this case also Mr. Webster had to contend against powerful adversaries. Mr. Oakley was Attorney General of New York and became at a later date Chief Justice of the Superior Court; and Mr. Emmet, the brother of Robert Emmet, the Irish revolutionist, had been Attorney General of the same state.

193

On the 17th of June, 1825, Mr. Webster delivered the oration at the laying of the corner-stone of Bunker Hill Monument, parts of which are familiar to every schoolboy in New England. The following passage in the oration is the only one to which I shall refer:

"Let it rise till it meet the sun in his coming; let the earliest light of the morning gild it and parting day linger and play on its summit."

This passage is often quoted with the article "the" before the word "parting," but Mr. Webster's ear for rhythm would have been disturbed by the use of that word. Whatever the form of the passage may be in some publications of his speeches, in the editions of his works published in 1830 and 1851 the article "the" does not appear.

No one would dare to charge Mr. Webster with plagiarism, but he sometimes borrowed thoughts and ideas, to which he added force and beauty by a more brilliant clothing of words. A figure of speech like that quoted above may be found in an ode written by Rev. John Pierpont for the Pilgrim Celebration at Plymouth on the 22d of December, 1824, six months before the Bunker Hill Celebration, as follows:

"The Pilgrim fathers are at rest;
  When summer's throned on high,
And the world's warm breast is in verdure
    dressed,
  Go stand on the hill where they lie.

The earliest ray of the golden day
  On that hallowed spot is cast,
And the evening sun as he leaves the world,
  Looks kindly on that spot last."

There can be little doubt that Mr. Webster had seen the ode, and I think that there is as little doubt that Mr.

Webster's prose is the better poetry. There is also that passage in his speech in the Senate, in 1834, on the Presidential protest, where, in speaking of the American colonies, he said:

"Oh this question of principle, while actual suffering was yet afar off, they raised their flag against a power, to which for purposes of foreign conquest and subjugation, Rome in the height of her glory is not to be compared—a power which has dotted over the surface of the whole globe with her possessions and military posts, whose morning drum-beat, following the sun and keeping company with the hours, circles the earth with one continuous and unbroken strain of the martial airs of England."

I have heard it said that Mr. Webster constructed this passage in Quebec, after witnessing a parade of British troops. There is, however, a poem written by Amelia B. Richards entitled "The Martial Airs of England," in which these lines occur:

"The martial airs of England
  Encircle still the earth."

But I have been unable to learn when this poem was written, whether before or after the speech. It is certain, however, that the grandeur of the passage is Mr. Webster's alone.

On the 2d of August, 1826, Mr. Webster delivered, in Faneuil Hall, his eulogy on Adams and Jefferson, by which his reputation as an orator, established at Plymouth in 1820, and at Bunker Hill in 1825, was fully sustained. In 1825 he saw for the first time the estate in Marshfield, which was destined to become his home. He was then living in a house which he had built in Summer street, Boston, opposite the entrance of South street, and which he continued to occupy a part of each year until 1839, when he sold it and made Marshfield his permanent home. For several years prior to 1825, it had been his custom to spend a part of the dog-days in Sandwich, shooting and fishing with John Denison, familiarly called "Johnny Trout," as his helper and guide. It having been suggested to him by Mr. Samuel K. Williams that Marshfield, with its marshes, its boat harbor and its brooks, would be a pleasant summer resort and much nearer to Boston than Sandwich, he stopped there on his next return from the Cape. Mr. Williams told him that Captain John Thomas, an intelligent farmer occupying a comfortable house and estate, would doubtless be glad to accommodate him. Late one afternoon in early September, in 1825, accompanied by his wife, in a chaise with a trunk lashed to the axle, and his son, Fletcher, a lad of twelve or thirteen, following on a pony, he drove down the avenue leading to the house of Captain Thomas, and drew up at the piazza where the Captain, with his oldest son, Charles Henry, was sitting, resting after putting into the barn a load of salt hay. Neither had ever seen the other, but when Mr. Webster said "I am Webster." "I thought so," said the Captain, for he knew very well that no other living man possessed the majestic personality which he saw before him. The hospitality of the house was at once extended to the party, and for several days Mr. Webster was a welcome guest, passing his time in shooting on the marshes and fishing in the waters of the bay.

Mr. Webster had, mingling with and softening his gravity of demeanor, a quiet vein of humor, and on his departure, as he was about to drive away, he saw Nathaniel Ray Thomas, the younger son of the Captain, standing nearby holding a fine looking horse by the halter. "I like the looks of that halter," said Mr. Webster; "I should like to buy it." "Ray," said the Captain, "take off that halter and put it in Mr. Webster's chaise box." "Oh, but I want the head in it," said Mr. Webster. The horse was bought, and when hitched behind the chaise, the procession, with Fletcher on the pony bringing up the rear, started for Boston.

This younger son of Captain Thomas afterward entered largely into the life and affections of Mr. Webster. He was at that time attending a school in Duxbury, taught by George Putnam, afterwards the distinguished Unitarian divine, and was later taken by Mr. Webster to Boston under his special guardianship. He finally became a secretary of the great statesman whose love he shared with his own children. In 1840, at the age of twenty-seven, he died at Mann's Hotel in Washington, of bilious fever, and on the testimony of Dr. Sewall, the attending physician, Mr. Webster, though pressed with the burdens of public business, was with him for a week almost constantly, day and night. The letters which he wrote to the family of the young man during his sickness and after his death reveal a sympathetic heart and a tenderness of spirit which illuminate and beautify the grandeur of the man. Between the 10th and 18th of March he wrote no less than eleven letters, some of them long and in detail, to Charles Henry Thomas, Ray's older brother, full of anxiety for his young friend and sympathy for his family at home. No one can read these letters without

awakening to a higher admiration for their writer than his intellectual qualities had ever kindled.

After annual visits to the Thomas homestead, in the year 1831, Captain Thomas asked Mr. Webster to buy his estate, which, after repeated requests, he consented to do, upon the condition that Captain Thomas would occupy it as his home, free of rent, as long as he lived. Captain Thomas died in 1837, and after that time his widow lived with her son, Charles, in Duxbury, until her death, in 1849. Though the purchase of the estate was made in 1831, the deed, in which the consideration was $3,650, was not passed until April 23, 1832, and included the house and outbuildings and one hundred and sixty acres of marsh, tillage and woodland.

The estate was an historic one. William Thomas, one of the merchant adventurers who assisted the Pilgrims in their enterprise, came to New England in 1637, in the ship "Marye and Ann,"

and on the 7th of January, 1640-1641, received from the Plymouth Colony General Court a grant of a tract of land in Marshfield containing about twelve hundred acres. Adjoining this tract, another of about the same number of acres had been previously granted under the name of Careswell to Governor Edward Winslow. The Thomas estate descended to Nathaniel Ray Thomas, who built the house which finally became the Webster mansion. Before the revolution, Marshfield was a town of aristocratic pretensions, and at the beginning of the war a majority of its people were loyal to the crown. For the protection of these from the indignation of patriots in the neighboring towns, General Gage sent down a company of soldiers called the "Queen's Guard," under Captain Balfour, who, with his officers established headquarters in the Thomas House. On the evening of the 19th of April, 1775, a body of militia had marched from various towns in Plymouth County and occupied the outskirts of Marshfield, with the intention of attacking the Guard the next morning. In consequence, however, of the disastrous results of the Lexington fight on that day, General Gage dispatched a messenger with orders for Captain Balfour's immediate return to Boston. On the morning of the 20th the militia discovered the flight of the enemy, and thus Marshfield narrowly escaped being the first battle-ground of the war. When I was a young man I heard a lady say that she remembered that on the 19th of April the older members of her family in Marshfield were engaged in moulding bullets and making bandages and lint in anticipation of the coming battle.

A number of the leading citizens of Marshfield went to Boston after the retirement of the Queen's Guard, and among them Nathaniel Ray Thomas, the owner of the Thomas estate. Nine of them returned later and were imprisoned at Plymouth by the Committee of Correspondence and Safety. I have before me an unpublished petition of the prisoners, headed by Cornelius White, one of my own kinsmen, to be released, which was finally granted. Nathaniel Ray Thomas remained in Boston, and at the Evacuation went with the British troops to Halifax, leaving in Marshfield his wife and son, John. His estate was confiscated, an allowance being made to his wife of the house and one hundred and sixty acres of land, which at her death fell to her son John, the grantor to Mr. Webster. Mr. Webster, at the time of his death, had by twenty-two deeds bought twelve hundred and fourteen and three-quarters acres, and by one

other deed an unknown quantity of land with a water privilege and claim in Duxbury. These purchases included nearly all of the original William Thomas grant and a part of the Edward Winslow grant, and their total first cost was $34,644.20, and, including improvements after deducting receipts, $87,144.20.

In 1827 Mr. Webster was chosen United States Senator and remained in the Senate until he resigned, in 1841, to become Secretary of State in the Cabinet of President Harrison. Upon Mr. Webster had devolved the duty of negotiating with Lord Ashburton the Northeastern Boundary Treaty, and he patriotically refused to resign his post until that treaty was concluded. On the 8th of May, 1843, he retired to private life, but in 1845 was again chosen Senator, remaining in the Senate until he was appointed Secretary of State by President Fillmore, July 23, 1850, a position which he held until his death.

In December, 1829, Mr. Webster married for his second wife Caroline, daughter of Jacob Le Roy, of New York, who survived him. In 1830 he made his celebrated speeches in reply to Senator Robert Young Hayne of South Carolina. Though the question under discussion was the adoption of a resolution of inquiry concerning the distribution of public lands, introduced by Senator Foote of Connecticut, Mr. Hayne seized the opportunity to attack New England on account of its advocacy of a protective tariff, which he believed to be unconstitutional, and to take the position that a state had the right to nullify the operation of a law which it believed to be repugnant to the constitution. Mr.

Webster had established, by his Dartmouth College argument, the limit of the functions of states concerning chartered rights, and by his argument in the case of *Gibbons vs. Ogden,* their limited functions concerning commerce.   Now the duty devolved on him to define the exact position of states in the mosaic framework of the Federal Union.

Though nine years younger than Mr. Webster, Mr. Hayne was no mean antagonist.   He had been four years longer in the Senate, and had taken his seat with a reputation in his own state perhaps second only to that of Mr. Calhoun.   He had been a member of the State Legislature, Speaker of the State House of Representatives and Attorney General.   His defeat by Mr. Webster was so overwhelming that the present generation are inclined to think of him only as the fly in the amber of Mr. Webster's speeches.   He was sustained by his state in the position he took, and in 1832 was chosen Governor.   When, on the 10th of December, in that year, President Jackson issued a proclamation against the nullification acts which a South Carolina convention had passed on the 24th of November, Governor Hayne replied with a proclamation of his own.   Congress, however, modified the tariff which had led to the nullification, and the acts of the convention were repealed.

And now I come to the time when I first heard and saw Mr. Webster.   It was in the presidential campaign of 1836.   Prior to 1840, when the first presidential convention was held, there was, in the Whig party, at least, a diversity of candidates.   In the election of 1836, Mr. Van Buren, who had been Vice-President under Jackson, received one hundred and seventy democratic votes and the whig votes were: for William Henry Harrison seventy-three, Hugh L. White twenty-six, Daniel Webster fourteen, from Massachusetts, and Willie P. Mangum eleven.   At the time to which I refer Mr. Webster spoke standing in the rear doorway of the court house in Plymouth, and though I was only a youth of fourteen, his appearance has never been effaced from my memory. Standing, as he always did, with neither legs nor body ever bent, his portly, but not corpulent, frame surmounted by a massive head, with eyes looking out from beneath overhanging brows, he seemed to me godlike indeed. When, in 1839, he visited England Sidney Smith said he was a fraud, for no man could be as great as he looked.   Lord Brougham said he was a steam engine in breeches. Thomas Carlyle, after breakfasting in his company, wrote to an American friend:

"He is a magnificent specimen.   You might say to all the world—'This is our Yankee Englishman; such limbs we make in Yankee land.'

"As a logic fencer advocate or parliamentary Hercules one would incline to back him at first sight against all the extant world. The tanned complexion; that amorphous, craglike face; the dull black eyes under a precipice of brows, like dull anthracite furnaces needing only to be blown; the mastiff mouth, accurately closed; I have not traced so much of silent Berserker rage that I remember of in any other man.   I guess I should not like to be your nigger."

It was said that when he appeared in the streets of London the crowds on the sidewalk, without knowing who he was turned and gazed with wonder at the majestic human specimen in their midst. I can easily believe it, for even in Boston, where he was known, his public appearance always caused a sensation. I have seen him many times walking down Court or State street, or along Washington and down Summer street, always in the middle of the sidewalk, with a slow and stately gait, the crowd meeting him turning to the right and left as the waves divide before a battleship.

It was my good fortune to stand very near Mr. Webster and hear his speech in Faneuil Hall on the 30th of September, 1842. He was still in President Tyler's cabinet, and the Whigs of Boston had, in their hasty and unwarranted disapproval of his refusal to resign, committed themselves at an early period to the nomination of Henry Clay as their candidate for the Presidency in 1844. The hall was crowded, and at the start the audience was unsympathetic. Jonathan Chapman, Mayor of Boston, presided and his opening speech, which I well remember, was sagacious and eloquent. He said, in connection with the anomalous attitude of Mr. Webster, a cabinet officer of a President, from whom his party had departed, "that amidst the perplexities of these perplexing times, he who has so nobly sustained his country's honor, may safely be trusted with his own." Mr. Webster's speech was in no sense an explanation or a defence. It was a rebuke rather to the party which had deserted him, a rebuke which touched the hearts of all who heard him and revived their allegiance to their idol. He probably never came so near speaking in anger as on that occasion. In a rasping voice, which is still ringing in my ears, he exclaimed, "What are you going to

do with me? I am a Whig, a Massachusetts Whig, a Faneuil Hall Whig;" and every man present responded in his heart, "We will make you President." It is a sufficient answer to the charge that he selfishly sought the gratification of an unconquerable ambition to become President, that he must have known that by remaining in the cabinet he was taking issue with the very men by whose aid alone his nomination could be possible.

Again I heard him deliver his oration at the dedication of Bunker Hill Monument on the 17th of June, 1843. As a member of the Boston Cadets, the body guard of the Governor of Massachusetts, it was my fortune to be stationed immediately in front of the platform. He had in the previous month resigned his place in the cabinet, and President Tyler, having in view the debt which he owed to the orator, had accepted the invitation of the committee of arrangements to be present. With the President were several members of his new cabinet, among whom was Mr. Legaré, who succeeded Mr. Webster as Secretary of State, and who died in Boston a few days after the celebration.

In the winter of 1843-44 Mr. Webster appeared in the United States Supreme Court in the case of the heirs of Stephen Girard against the executors of his will, which came to that court by appeal from the Circuit Court of the United States, sitting as a court of equity for the Eastern District of Pennsylvania. The plaintiff for whom he appeared, assisted by Colonel Walter Jones of Washington, sought to have the will set aside for three reasons, one of which was that the plan of education prescribed for the college, which the will established, was repugnant to the law of Pennsylvania and opposed to the provision of Article 9, Section 3, of the constitution of that state, that "No human authority can in any case whatever control or interfere with the rights of conscience." The will in its reference to the college "enjoined and required that no ecclesiastic, missionary or minister of any sect whatsoever shall ever hold or exercise any station or duty whatever in the said college; nor shall any such person ever be admitted for any purpose, or as a visitor within the premises appropriated to the purposes of said college." Horace Binney and John Sergeant of Philadelphia appeared for the defendants, and their position was sustained unanimously by the court, that Mr. Girard did not intend to exclude the teaching of Christianity by preventing its being taught by ministers, for it might nevertheless be taught by laymen without violation of the terms of the will.

It has always seemed to me that the argument of Mr. Webster in this case, with its display of biblical learning and its eloquent exaltation of those principles of the Christian religion, which should mould and direct the education of youth, was the profoundest forensic effort of his life. In recognition of its importance as a contribution to Christian literature, at a public meeting of citizens of Washington regardless of sect, resolutions were passed declaring "that it demonstrated the vital importance of Christianity to the success of our free institutions, and that its general diffusion among the people of the United States was a matter of deep public interest."

In September, 1849, I heard Mr. Webster again. Early in that month he said one day to my uncle, Judge Charles Henry Warren, "Charley, I wish you would get together a hundred of my friends and we will take a special train to Plymouth and celebrate with a dinner at the Samoset House the anniversary of the final departure of the Pilgrims from Plymouth in old England." The plan was carried out, and as the 16th of September occurred that year on Sunday, the party went to Plymouth on Monday, the 17th. Through the kindness of Judge Warren, I, then residing in Boston, was permitted to join the party. It was indeed a notable company, made up, with the exception of myself, of men, who were distinguished in either public, mercantile or professional life. Mr. Webster presided, and seated at the tables were: President Quincy, Josiah Quincy, Jr., Edward Everett, Rufus Choate, George S. Hillard, Sidney Bartlett, Benjamin R. Curtis, William Sturgis, Nathan Appleton of Boston, Charles A. Davies of Portland, Joseph Grinnell and John H. Clifford of New Bedford, Nathaniel P. Willis of New York, and others equally well known. I was the youngest member of the party, and I am now its only survivor. Mr. Webster's opening speech was a little heavy, but after the addresses of the other speakers he made a closing speech, tender and touching, and more eloquent than any I ever heard from his lips.

He was then sixty-eight years of age. He was beginning, he said, to feel the weight of years, and the grasshopper was becoming a burden to him. He was surrounded by friends, whom he loved and trusted, and who, he be-

From a daguerreotype taken in 1849.

DANIEL WEBSTER

lieved, put their trust in him. Probably for the last time he would address in grateful affection those, who in the perplexities of public life had stood manfully by him, and on whose arm he had leaned for support.

Mr. Willis, who was then one of the editors of the *New York Mirror,* wrote to his journal a letter descriptive of the scene, from which the following is an extract:

"Unable from illness to join in the conviviality of the evening, he (Mr. Webster) was possibly saddened by a mirth with which his spirit could not keep pace; and at the same time, surrounded by those who had met there from love of him, and whose pride and idol he had always been, his kindest and warmest feelings were uppermost. and his heart alone was in what he had to say. His affectionate attachment to New England was the leading sentiment, but through his allusions to his own advancing age and present illness, there was recognizable a wish to say what he might wish to have said, should he never again be surrounded and listened to. It was the most beautiful example of manly and restrained pathos, it seemed to me, of which language and looks could be capable. No one who heard it could doubt the existence of a deep well of tears under that lofty temple of intellect and power."

In 1850 I saw for the first time Mr. Webster trying a case in court. It was a patent case in the United States Court in Boston, with Mr. Choate on the other side. A two-thirds length portrait by Willard, in Pilgrim Hall in Plymouth, represents him as he then appeared in face, posture and dress, and on the whole furnishes a more correct conception of the man than any other portrait I have seen. In this trial the contrast between the antagonists was striking,—Mr. Webster, calm, serene and stately, Mr. Choate nervous, energetic and fiery; the one simple in his vocabulary, the other making heavy drafts on the dictionary for words unfamiliar to the ear; the one so natural in his gestures as to leave his hearers forgetful whether he had gestured at all, the other lashing the air with his arms and making the table resound with his blows. Mr. Webster was not, as many who never heard him suppose, a fluent speaker. Fluent speakers are rarely concise, but conciseness was his chief characteristic. Often in extemporaneons speech he would hesitate, and he had a trick of scratching his right ear until the word he wanted came to his tongue. On this occasion he was in a playful mood and during the short re-

cess after Mr. Choate had finished his address to the jury, he took the latter's brief during his absence from the court room, and distributed the sheets, which no one but Mr. Choate could read, and which he often found illegible after the writing had got cold, as he once said, among the ladies, who had crowded the seats behind the rail to hear the thunder and witness the lightning of those wonderful men.

The last important speech of Mr. Webster in the Senate, on the 7th of March, 1850, on the compromise resolutions introduced by Henry Clay, caused intense disappointment to his friends in the North, and for a time clouded his reputation. By some it was charged that he had betrayed the North and was bidding for Southern presidential votes. But now, since time has cleared the atmosphere, the injustice of such a charge is apparent, for by opposing the sentiment of Northern friends, by whose aid alone his nomination could be made possible, he was really sacrificing his political prospects on the altar of his country, as he did by remaining in the Cabinet of President Tyler. More lenient critics took the ground that his fears of disunion were groundless, but the events of 1861 demonstrated that he was better informed than they. In a conversation I had a few years ago at his house in Augusta with Hon. James Ware Bradbury, who died January 6, 1901, at the age of ninety-eight years, the last survivor of the Senate of 1850, he told me that the North was totally unaware of the danger which threatened the union when that speech was made. He further said that it was well known among Senators that the middle states, looking on a refusal to accept the compromises as an aggression on the part of the North, would have followed the Southern states out of the Union. When, however, secession finally came in 1861, those states, looking on the South as the aggressor, sent more soldiers into the Union army than all New England. The speech was a plea for the Union. Mr. Webster believed that the hope of republican institutions rested on the perpetuity of the Union, and that disunion would not only check their progress, but would also result in the permanent establishment of slavery in a confederacy, within whose limits no influence would exist looking to its abolition. How far the people of the North misunderstood the position of Mr. Webster is shown by the statement made as late as 1881, in the "Memorial History of Boston," that "he opposed the exclusion of slavery from the territories by law," when one of the very compromises advocated by him was the admission of California as a state, which the South opposed, with a constitution forbidding slavery within its limits. The speech was in line with the consistent efforts of his life to defend the Constitution and uphold the Union.

"When," he said, "my eyes are turned to behold for the last time the sun in heaven, may they not see him shining on the broken and dishonored fragments of a once glorious union, on states dissevered, discordant, belligerent, on a land rent with civil feuds, or it may be drenched with fraternal blood."

By his early death he was spared the sorrow of witnessing the miseries of civil war. If, during that conflict, he could have looked down from heaven on the scenes of earth he would have beheld the armies of the North, gathered under the inspiration of the lessons of patriotism which he had taught, yielding up their lives in defense of the union he loved so well. It is a question no man can answer, if that speech had not been made, if the compromises had been defeated, and if the people of the North had rightly or wrongly refused to aid in the rendition of slaves, whether a Southern confederacy would not have been established in 1850 and slavery been continued to this day. But in some inscrutable way, followed either under the guidance of Providence or of the wisdom of man, the result for which Mr. Webster prayed has been achieved, not liberty without union, nor union without liberty, but liberty and union now and forever, one and inseparable.

As an aftermath of the 7th of March speech, was the refusal by the Aldermen of Boston of the use of Faneuil Hall to the friends of Mr. Webster for the purpose of hearing him on the topics then agitating the public mind. The refusal was based on the ground that the hall had been refused to the Abolitionists, and that the advocates and opponents of the compromise measures should be treated alike. In the following week the city government, under the pressure of public indignation, reconsidered their action and extended an invitation to Mr. Webster to address his fellow citizens in the Hall, which he declined.

Turning now from the public to the private life of Mr. Webster at his Marshfield home, much may be found that is new to those who have known of him only as the lawyer, orator and statesman. There among his neighbors he was the true, simple, transparent, tender-hearted man. Among

THE WEBSTER ESTATE AT THE PRESENT TIME

them he assumed no superiority, interested himself in their families and farms and became their counselor and friend. Of these neighbors only one remains, Mr. Charles Porter Wright, who for a number of years was the manager of Mr. Webster's landed estate. To him the memories of the great man are blessed ones, and even now, after the lapse of fifty years, he can scarcely speak of him without a tear. Released from the cares of state, the playful side of Mr. Webster would often asserts itself, as the following ineident shows, which illustrates as well his familiar and kindly intercourse with the farmers of Marshfield. Once, on his return from Washington, a neighbor called with a bill for hay. Mr. Webster told him that he had just reached home and that if he would call on the next Monday he would have the money ready for him. After the man left Mr. Webster said to his son Fletcher, "I think I have paid that bill, and I wish you would see if you can find a receipt." The result of the search was that two receipts were found. "Let those bills lie there," he said, "and when our friend calls next Monday we will have some fun with him." On Monday the farmer called just before dinner, and Mr. Webster said, "Come, neighbor, get your dinner with me, and then we will talk business." After dinner they went out and sat under the shady elm-tree near the house, accompanied by Fletcher, and after a little general conversation, Mr. Webster said, "Mr. N., do you keep books? I advise you by all means to keep books; now if you had kept books you would have known that I had paid this bill once," and he handed him one of the receipts. Mr. N. was mortified beyond measure and accused himself of inexcusable negligence and forgetfulness. After further conversation, Mr. Webster again said, "Mr. N., you don't know how important it is to keep books," and handing him a second receipt added, "If you had kept books you would have known that I had paid this bill twice. Now I am going to pay it just once more, and I don't believe that I shall ever pay it again." Poor Mr. N. was overwhelmed with surprise and protested that when able he would refund the money. "No, Mr. N.," said Mr. Webster, "you are a poor man and I know you to be an honest one. Keep the money, and when you have any more hay to sell, bring me a load and I will buy it."

Mr. Webster in Marshfield was always up before sunrise, attending to correspondence or strolling about the farm, petting his horses and oxen, or arranging for the farm work of the day. "I know the morning," he said. "I love it fresh and sweet as it is, a daily new creation, breaking forth and calling all that have life and breath and being to new adoration, new enjoyments and new gratitude." He thought the rising of the sun the grandest spectacle in nature and wondered why people were willing to forego the pleasure of beholding it.

His style of living was unostentatious and his habits were plain, regular and unexceptionable. He did not use tobacco in any form, and considered an oath unfit for a gentleman. He never gambled; at whist, the only game of cards he ever played, he was not proficient; he never indulged in telling stories, and was a far from patient listener to those of others. His drinking habits, which those without knowledge have exaggerated, I have been assured by my uncle, were only such as prevailed in his day among refined and educated gentlemen. At dinner he confined himself to two glasses of Madeira wine.

Mr. Webster was a man of deep religious feeling and was as familiar with the Bible as with the Constitution of the United States. On Sunday morning he would gather his household in his library and, after reading scriptural passages, would address them on the responsible duties of life. In answer to the questions often asked concerning his theological views, it seems to me that the facts bear out the statement that during the larger part of his life they were those of the Trinitarians. In Salisbury he joined the orthodox Congregational Church under the pastorate of Rev. Thomas Worcester. When he removed to Portsmouth he carried a letter to the orthodox Congregational church in that town, under the pastorate of Rev. Dr. Joseph Buckminster. At that time Unitarianism was receiving large accessions from the ranks of conservative theological thinkers, and among those who found their way into the new fold was Dr. Buckminster's son, Joseph Stevens Buckminster, who was ordained pastor of the Unitarian Brattle Street Church, in Boston, in 1805. It is not improbable that the theological discussions between father and son modified Mr. Webster's views for a time, for when he went to Boston, in 1816, he became a worshipper at the Brattle Street Church. His connection with that church, however, terminated in 1819, when he became one of the founders of St. Paul's Church, Episcopal, attended the meetings of its organizers and was one of the committee for building its place of worship in

Tremont street.   The pew occupied
by him was Number 25, and his continued association with that church is
shown by the fact that his son Charles,
who died in 1824, his first wife, who
died in 1828, and his son Edward, who
died in Mexico in 1848, were buried in
its vaults, though later removed to
Marshfield.   His belief in Christ as
mediator and intercessor was shown
by the prayer uttered by him in his last
hours,—*"Heavenly Father, forgive my
sins and receive me to thyself through
Christ Jesus."*

No sketch of Mr. Webster would be
complete without a reference to his
habits as a sportsman.   Of fishing in
the bay, shooting on the marshes,
dropping his line in a trout brook and
hunting in Plymouth woods, he was
inordinately fond.   He was a good
shot and in marsh shooting was undoubtedly skillful, but in hunting and
fishing too often his reveries permitted
the game to escape and the fish to
nibble away his bait, until he had completed the construction of some passage or solved some law point in the
speech or argument he was soon to
make.   On the trunk of a maple tree
standing on the margin of Billington
Sea, one of the large ponds in Plymouth, I have seen the initials "D.
W.," which were cut by him while
waiting for the sound of the dogs in
pursuit of the quarry.   On that occasion a noble buck passed him without warning, but seizing his gun, he
brought him down with a bullet as he
ran hock deep in the water along the
shore.

Of one of his hunts his son Fletcher
told me the following story.   Reaching home in the early evening of an
October day, in answer to the question

of Fletcher, "What luck, father?" he
said, after seating himself at the supper table:

"Well, I met the Messrs. Hedge and
George Churchill at Long Pond Hill, which
you know is about eight miles beyond
Plymouth, and there also was Uncle
Branch Pierce with his hounds, and
he had already found a fresh deer
track to the eastward near the Sandwich road. Uncle Branch told us that
as nigh as he could make up the vyage, the
critter would run to water in little Long
Pond. So he put me on the road as you
go down the hill, and told me to keep my
ears open and my eyes peeled, and not to
stir till he called me off. For two hours I
stood there under a red oak tree, expecting
every moment either to hear the dogs or see
the deer, but without a sound or a sight.
I then put my gun against the tree and took
a lunch. When it got to be one o'clock,
I made a speech, and about three o'clock a
little song sparrow came and perched on a
limb over my head, and I took off my hat
and said 'Maoam, you are the first living
thing I have seen today. Permit me to
pay my profoundest respects.' Pretty soon
Uncle Branch came up and said the dogs
had gone out of 'hearth' and the hunt was
up 'by golly.' So here I am, Fletcher, tired
out and as hungry as a cooper's cow."

Before he left the hunting grounds
he drove his knife into a pitch pine
tree and said, "Gentlemen, we meet
here to-morrow morning at eight
o'clock." After riding home and back,
thirty-six miles, taking supper, a
night's sleep and breakfast, he pulled
the knife out of the tree precisely on
the hour.   As I was told by the
Messrs. Hedge, the morning coming
on wet, and he having a slight cold, he
told his companions to go on their hunt
and he would go up to Uncle Branch's
house and await their return.   After
a successful hunt, they went to the
house and found old lady Pierce sitting in the common room, with the

breakfast dishes still unwashed, listening to Mr. Webster as he paced the floor, repeating some of the grand old lyric poems of Isaac Watts:

"Keep silence all created things,
And wait your maker's nod;
The muse stands trembling while she sings
The honors of her God.

"Life, death and hell and worlds unknown,
Hang on his firm decree;
He sits on no precarious throne,
Nor borrows leave to be."

Uncle Branch, as everybody called him, was the most skillful

" UNCLE BRANCH "

hunter ever raised in Massachusetts. He and Mr. Webster were frequent companions, and though I have never seen them together, I have been told that it was interesting to see them in company. He was too far removed from social life to feel embarrassment in the presence of any man, and as king of the woods on his own domain, no one was his superior. He signed and made oath to an affidavit that he had killed in Plymouth woods with the gun shown in his portrait two hundred and forty-eight deer,—three at a shot once, and two at a shot twice.

Reference has been made in an earlier part of this article to one of the many portraits taken of Mr. Webster. It is probable that no other man has been so often portrayed on canvas and in marble. I have a list of forty-five portraits, five drawings, eight miniatures, five statues, one statuette and six busts, exclusive of daguerreotypes, seventy in all, representing the work of thirty-three artists.

On the 8th of May, 1852, while on his way to Plymouth with Mr. Charles Lanman as his companion, for a days' fishing with his friend, Mr. Isaac L. Hedge in the latter's trout pond, at Seaside, near Plymouth village, in going up the hill from Smelt Brook, in that part of Kingston called Rocky Nook, the linchpin of his carriage broke and he was thrown to the ground, receiving bruises on his head and left arm. Though not unconscious, he was faint and chilled by the shock and was carried into the house of Mr. Benjamin Delano, who happened to be a political friend and one of his ardent admirers. Under the sympathetic and kindly care of Mr.

Delano and his family, he was in three or four hours sufficiently recovered to be carried home. While Dr. Nichols, of Kingston, was dressing his wounds and just as an attack of faintness was passing off, Mrs. Delano came into the room, and he said, "Madam, how very diversified is the lot of humanity in this our world; a certain man passing from Jerusalem to Jericho fell among thieves and was illy treated; a man passing from Marshfield to Plymouth fell among a very hospitable set of people and was kindly taken care of."

From the effects of this accident Mr. Webster never fully rallied. He addressed the citizens of Boston in Faneuil Hall on the 22d of May, in a speech which I heard, full of eloquent pathos. In June he was in Washington and there, on the 16th of that month, endorsed the nomination of Winfield Scott for the Presidency. On the 9th of July a public reception was tendered him in Boston, and he addressed his fellow citizens on the Common. On the 12th of July he was in Franklin, and on the 25th was received by his neighbors and friends at the station in Kingston and escorted to Marshfield, where, to those who had lived near him and loved him, his last speech was made. In August he went to Washington, where he remained until the 8th of September. After his return he gradually failed, and died on the morning of Sunday, the 24th of October. The story of his death was told me by Mr. Charles Henry Thomas, on whose bosom his head was resting when he breathed his last. The scene was an impressive one. There were gathered around his bed Mrs. Webster, his son Fletcher and wife, James William Paige and wife, his son-in-law Samuel A. Appleton, Peter Harvey, Dr. J. Mason Warren, Dr. John Jeffries, and George T. Curtis of Boston, Edward Curtis, Mr. Le Roy and Miss Downs of New York, Mr. W. C. Zartsinger and Mr. George J. Abbott of the State Department in Washington, and Mr. Thomas. Mr. Webster had entertained the idea that there was a point of time between life and death when the spirit was conscious of both the scenes of earth and of heaven. After a period of silence, he opened his eyes and said, "I still live." Dr. Jeffries, not understanding the meaning of his words, repeated the scripture passage, "though I walk through the valley of the shadow of death I will fear no evil." Again he opened his eyes and said, "No, Doctor, tell me the point, tell me the point," and died. An autopsy was held which disclosed a disease of the liver as the cause of death accompanied by hemorrhage from the stomach and bowels and dropsy of the abdomen. In a report made to the Massachusetts Medical Society, it was stated that his brain exceeded by thirty per cent. the average weight, and with the exception of those of Cuvier and Dupuytren was the largest on record. It was also stated that there was an effusion upon the arachnoid membrane, the inner of the triple membrane of which the Dura Mater and the Pia Mater are the other two lining the cranium and covering the brain and spinal marrow.

I attended his funeral on Friday the 29th of October, the services at which were conducted by the Rev. Ebenezer Alden, pastor of the Trinitarian Congregational Church in Marshfield. He had stated in his will that he wished "to be buried without the least show or ostentation, but in a manner respectful to my neighbors, whose kindness has contributed so much to the happiness of me and mine, and for whose prosperity I offer sincere prayers to God." His wishes were complied with, and on a beautiful Indian summer day, his body, clad in a blue coat with brass buttons, buff waistcoat and, I think, white trousers, lay in its coffin exposed its whole length to view, under the elm in whose shade he had loved to sit, and, like the autumn leaves falling about him, having performed his mission, he was borne by loving neighbors to his final rest.   On his tomb in the ancient Winslow burial ground, not far from the Webster mansion, is the following inscription by himself:

DANIEL WEBSTER,
Born January 18th, 1782,
Died October 24th, 1852.

Lord, I believe. Help thou mine unbelief.

"Philosophical argument, especially that drawn from the vastness of the universe, in comparison with the apparent insignificance of this globe, has sometimes shaken my reason for the faith which is in me; but my heart has always assured and reassured me that the Gospel of Jesus Christ must be a Divine Reality. The Sermon on the Mount cannot be a mere human production. This belief enters into the very depth of my conscience. The whole history of man proves it."

In An Old Garden

By Elizabeth W. Schermerhorn

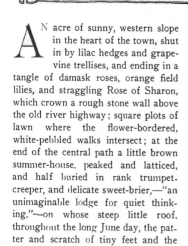

A N acre of sunny, western slope in the heart of the town, shut in by lilac hedges and grape-vine trellises, and ending in a tangle of damask roses, orange field lilies, and straggling Rose of Sharon, which crown a rough stone wall above the old river highway; square plots of lawn where the flower-bordered, white-pebbled walks intersect; at the end of the central path a little brown summer-house, peaked and latticed, and half buried in rank trumpet-creeper, and delicate sweet-brier,—"an unimaginable lodge for quiet thinking,"—on whose steep little roof, throughout the long June day, the patter and scratch of tiny feet and the dropping of fruit and pits from an

overshadowing cherry-tree, betray the pilfering robin and oriole, and the taciturn cedar-bird; two sturdy evergreens to break the force of the west winds, and to spread tents of slanting branches for a refuge from the midday sun; beyond them, two twisted apple-trees, to make cool circles of shadow, and strew the ground with a fragrant drift of snowy petals or dot it with shining golden fruit,—and to bend and crook their hollow old arms into nooks where the wrens can play hide-and-seek, and the woodpecker may set up his carpenter-shop; below the summer-house, on a gentle descent toward the wall, an orchard of pear and quince and cherry-trees, where bunches of scarlet berries,—stray waifs from an

Illustrated from photographs by Thomas E. Marr, Clifton Johnson and Baldwin Coolidge.

ancient strawberry bed,—lurk in the tall, tasselled grasses, and blue violets reflect the changing tints of the sky:— this is the garden I love, where I have played as a child, labored as a woman, where,—if anywhere,—the shapes and memories of the past will gather at the summons of backward-glancing old age.

In the heart of the town! Or rather, in its lungs;—one of those open spaces which even a growing city always manages to leave for breathing-places. For a garden, a real garden, is a denizen of the town, an adopted child of civilization; mellowing and uplifting by its fresh beauty and innocence, the heart of its labor-worn, brain-sick foster-parent.   Those who live in the country, before whose very door the pageant of forest and field is ever outspread, do not need to mimic the panorama of the seasons; the original is free to all.   Cultivated plants look tawdry and artificial when wild flowers are at hand to invite comparison, as hothouse flowers cheapen beside garden blossoms.   Then, too, the *sine qua non* of a garden is seclusion,—a quality not to be found in the boundless privacy of tranquil nature, but only to be realized when Edom is at your very gate, and you must encounter him whenever you venture outside the bulwark of your hedge.   What beauty in a trellis or arbor unless it screens something, unless it shuts out the "cark and clutch of the world"—

"Doves defiled and serpents shrined,
"Hates that wax and hopes that wither?"

An ivy-draped wall has a *raison d'être* when it muffles the discordant noises of traffic; soft green stretches of well-kept lawn are a respite to eye and foot when the distant hum of the

trolley calls up faint memories of jostling, perspiring crowds, and hot, glaring pavements.   Thoreau was merely theorizing when he declared that "Man has sold the birthright of his nose for the privilege of living in towns."   The consciousness of contrast is the seasoning of enjoyment.   The dew-sweet fragrance of old fashioned flowers, the cool depths of trees, the uplift of waving vines give keenest satisfaction to senses weary of staring advertisements and gaudy wares, of ugly bricks and noisome odors, of networks of wires overhead, and darting bicycles and lumbering carts below.   What Meredith says of one of his heroines, is also true of a garden,—"She could make for herself a quiet centre in the heart of the whirlwind, but the whirlwind was required."

The Island Garden of Celia Thaxter possessed this charm of seclusion,— though it was far from civilization,— because it nestled in the rough embrace of booming breakers, on the barren bosom of the gray, old rocks, encompassed by a dreary desolation of reef and ocean; because every barrow of earth, every pound of fertilizer, every seed, every root was brought with infinite labor from the mainland, and its whole history was a struggle against sea bird and sea wind, untempered sun and destroying tempest. We prize most what represents difficulties overcome.   There is no primrose path leading to the real garden.

Moreover, our human limitations can comprehend beauty only in little. We long for a lodge in a wilderness, a tent on the lonely sea-shore, a tabernacle on the Mount, but of all the grandeur at our very feet, we can take in only a limited quantity.   Who has

not actually suffered with the sense of futility and incapacity, when standing on the summit of Kaaterskill Mountain, or watching a wild tempest on the cliffs at Newport, or a fine sunset over an Adirondack lake? Except for an occasional broadening of the horizon, all the more effectual because rare, it is better to use the microscope than the field glass,—to take our glimpses of nature in homœopathic doses, small but frequent.

The Japanese make dainty miniatures of nature in the wild. In small compass, their little imitations of gardens possess tiny lakes and islands, mimic forests and meadows, fairy rills and grottoes. This is not childish mimicry but a thoughtful and reverent selection and combination of natural effects. As we hang landscapes and sunsets on our walls, adorn our houses with Turkish smoking-rooms and Moorish parlors, decorate our churches with evergreens and lilies,—so we do well to bring into our grounds living pictures of the great garden of the world.

Though a long way from Japanese ideals, the garden I know best contains many quotations from the book of nature, and by the aid of a healthy imagination I am able to make a "wilderness of handsome groves." For it has many patches dedicated to sylvan things,—tall, rippling grass that has never known the lawn mower, where trailing blackberry vines and elusive wild strawberries and early violets can multiply unmolested; where a handful of daisies and a clump of golden-rod by the fence suggest the white capped billows and gay shores of the open meadow. One shady nook,

where the cultivated summer plants would not thrive, is kept for the few spring wild flowers I can coax to grow. There columbine's doves arch their purple necks over the edge of their swinging nest, the bright pink stars of the wild geranium nod to the drooping purples of the deadly nightshade, and clumps of gray-green sage and hairy mint wait for my feet to bruise them into fragrance. Clusters of ferns, cool to the touch, inexpressibly sweet when wilted or broken, encircle the foot of a tree or border a wall, and gives a woodsy tinge, soothing the eye with the soft blending of their greens, which range from the light yellow-green of the common brake, through the deeper shades of the sweet-fern, bronzed by the fruit on its sides, to the dark, glossy evergreen of the acrostichoides.

In the centre of the garden is the "Jungle," a thicket of rose bushes, old fashioned single pink roses, that open fresh buds in the June mornings and fade and shed their petals under the midday sun. Beneath them, where thorny branches defy the would-be weeder, gay parrot tulips flaunt their harlequin garb in spring, the scarlet Oriental poppy flashes and flutters like some gigantic tropical butterfly, and tangled bachelor's buttons swing their blue and pink fringes; or in August, the curious cardinal torches of the balm light up the "Jungle" and spread their flames until the smouldering hips on the rose bushes are kindled into a blaze.

Besides these bits of field and forest thus brought into the heart of the town, cultivated flowers are scattered through the grass in conventional

beds, or border the paths in stiff and dignified rows. Petunias and Drummond's phlox, candytuft and lacy sweet alyssum are near the veranda, where their kaleidoscopic variations of color and form, and their delicate perfume may be readily perceived. The showy hardy phlox, purple and white and crimson, a-murmur with bees and a-flash with butterflies,—the brilliant sheaths of gladioli, the great crumpled globes of the marigold, the pink and white stars of the cosmos shining through a waving background of green smoke, are most effective at a distance as a foil for the more subtle harmonies of balsams and zinnias and asters. The nasturtiums spread a crisp mantle of green over the beds where the daffodils are enjoying their mid-summer nap and the sweet peas serve as a screen to the only "vegetable shop" the garden can boast, the staunch and faithful tomato, which betrays an ancient and aristocratic lineage in its old name of "Golden Apple." I always keep some precious blossoms in the farthest corner of the garden to lure me on frequent pilgrimages of inspection. The varied markings of the China aster, the evanescent rainbow silks that fringe the poppies,— Iceland, Shirley, and all the rest,—the splendid surprises unfolded from a few prize bulbs of gladioli, the curious crimpings and streakings of some particularly choice petunias, draw me irresistibly to thrill over the unfoldings of every hour.

The old fashioned flowers are by

themselves, as is befitting. An exclusive atmosphere of ancestral dignity surrounds them, that accords not with the fancy strains and ambitious names of the seedsman's collections. "How the flowers would blush if they could know the names we give them," exclaimed Thoreau. The simple names of our grandmothers' posies expressed their character or habits. Four-

hocks peeping primly over the fence, and their cousin, the healing Mallow-rose, with great broad cups of pink or white splashed with crimson, and with odd clusters of pointed buds shut up in little green cages,—these survivors of the quaint nomenclature of our grandmothers are gathered in the plot set apart for them, aloof from the pretentious newcomers,—hardy abo-

o'clocks, and London Pride, Mourning Bride and Prince's Feather, Bleeding Heart and Widow's Tear, Sweet William with the Honest Eye, Canterbury Bells in chimes of blue and pink and white, Fox-gloves that the Germans call "Fingerhut," Fraxinella with the fragrant oily bean, baneful Aconite in its monk's hood of purple and white, shining Primroses as yellow as butter, and pale Cowslips "sick with heat" under the summer sun; stately Holly-

rigines penned up in a Government Reserve.

The poets are all agreed that the presence of running water is indispensable to the perfection of a beautiful scene. The birds, too, love the spot where drinks and baths are abundant, and the proximity of a fountain or spring is a great consideration to them in selecting a summer resort. In the swooning heat of July, when the garden is parched and scorched and no dew falls at night, and the great piled up, white thunder-clouds have rumbled by, day after day, without a passing visit, then a rubber hose, though more far-reaching in its ministrations, is no substitute for the cool trickle and splash of a fountain, to soothe the mind with dreams of cold, brown Adirondack trout-brooks, or crashing, foaming surf on the breezy New England shore. Who ever heard of a poet's garden without a brook or a pool, a spring or a fountain? Keats's lush nook was kept moist by a "babbling spring-head of clear waters;" Bacon gave elaborate and explicit directions for the arrangement of fountains which were to furnish "beauty and refreshment" in his ideal garden; Solomon "made himself pools of water to water therewith the trees of his orchards and gardens;" a river flowed through Eden, that first garden of the world, and Milton tells us it rose in fountains on the Mount of Paradise. Delicious to the ears of those first gardeners must have been the murmuring of that

"Crispèd brook, rolling on Orient pearl and
    sands of gold,
"With mazy error under pendent shades;"

but it cannot compare for somnolent qualities with those "welles" that Chaucer tells us trickled down by the cave of Morpheus, and "made a dedly, sleping soun'," nor with those "slow-dropping veils of thinnest lawn," in the Lotus-eaters' land, that

"Like a downward stream along the cliff
"To fall, and pause, and fall again did
    seem."

What slumbrous music that, to tinkle in my ears, and lull my senses to poppied oblivion, on a drowsy summer afternoon, as I swing to and fro in the hammock, blinking up at the idle clouds that float quietly in the wide blue above, while the sleepy whirr of the grasshopper "runs from hedge to hedge," and the shadows slowly lengthen and stretch across the lawn, and the lazy vines sway and curtsey in the soft south breeze, and all my senses go a-wool-gathering.

But honesty forces me to confess that the music is in Tennyson's verses, not in my garden. The nearest approach to that which "no garden should be without," that I can offer, is an old well,—not a mossy sweep but a neat square curb with a latticed roof. Yet the well is deep, defying the most obstinate drouth, and it has a wide circle of acquaintances among heated pedestrians and tired workmen. All day the slow shuffle of heavy feet, the creak of the rusty chain, the muffled splash of the bucket, the swish and drip of the water, the clink of dipper and slam of lattice testify to the comforting properties of this unromantic spring. And in spite of the unpromising curb, a goodly company of birds "their quire apply," and brave unnumbered dangers from bandit cats that infest the neighborhood, in order to bring up their families here.

The list begins of course with the robin. The robin, like the garden, really belongs to the town. He looks best on a smooth-shaven, velvety lawn; it is the proper background for his trim, erect, and strictly up-to-date figure. He is a Utilitarian, a Philistine, and prefers the comforts of city life to the primitive ways of the country. Though affecting exclusiveness, his plebeian self-consciousness and fondness for posing demand that he shall be seen of men. Brisk, alert and busi-

ness-like, nothing escapes him; yet he has his contemplative moods, and then his glowing breast shows off well on the top of a stake or pole. Of course the tidy little chipping sparrow, with his innocent air and corkscrew trills, is on the list; and the pugnacious, hysterical blackbird, though he leaves early; the indefatigable vireo, the lighthearted goldfinch, the nervous little hummingbird, the nasal voiced nuthatch, "answering tit for tat," the downy woodpecker flitting noiselessly from tree to tree. The great golden-winged woodpecker, a giant among the others, has frequented the garden

for several summers, his discordant laugh and clarion calling from the trees early and late. It is not uncommon to see four of these splendid creatures together, industriously engaged in hammering the turf for grub; punctuating their labors with frequent upward glances, for they are very shy. The scarlet on their heads and black crescents on their breasts are very showy when they are feeding, and when they spread their gold-lined wings and fly in alarm to the lower branches of the evergreens under which they feed, the snowy patches on their backs make them dangerously conspicuous. That impertinent little busybody, Jenny Wren, I could never spare. Her ecstatic, bubbling melody, which seems to gush from every corner of the garden at once, is silent before the end of August, and leaves a great void in the summer song that

the ubiquitous insect voices cannot fill. The flashing contralto of the oriole, the pure sweet melancholy of the thrush, "like a mower whetting his scythe," says Thoreau, the spring whistle of the Peabody sparrow, the catbird, **practis**ing broken bars of her medley song,— these are the voices that blend in the great jubilee chorus of the old garden. And last summer the crooning of a pair of wood-doves was added. On a pear tree limb directly over the path, their frail, careless nest of twigs was placed. The male cooed mournfully from an elm down on the highway, and as often as I walked by the nest, the timid mother would twist her long iridescent neck, to look at me with her bright frightened eye, until she had endured me as long as she could,— then with a rush of her strong wings that shook down a shower of tiny pears, she would fly to the protection

of her mate. The more sophisticated robin would have clung to her nest, though with palpitating breast, and pretended she did not see me.

The spring flowers and the ferns are not the only wild flavor my garden boasts. More and more the sylvan life is seeking the society and protection of man. Besides the flicker and the wood-dove, the oven-bird skulks every spring and fall in the shade of a snow-ball bush, among the lilies of the valley, uttering its querulous, metallic chirp, like a fine wire spring. And the "oologizing" squirrel plays tag all day in the treetops, stares me out of countenance as he straddles head downwards on the trunk, not a yard from my seat, or skips about the piazza vines, where the robins' nest is concealed, on his unholy errands. When the dusk is gathering and all is quiet, I hear the trills and moans of the for-

lorn little screech-owl. I find him often in the lilac bush, staring in blank amazement at my intrusion, and, as I walk past him, turning his head as if it were on a pivot, until he resembles a mask at a "Looking Backward" party. Once I discovered his two fluffy babies snuggled up close together and fast asleep almost within my reach. And so the "feathered tribes" themselves help on the illusion of the garden.

I have never shared the general enthusiasm over that popular book, "Elizabeth and Her German Garden." There is a "stand-offishness" in her attitude towards flowers, a lack of the intimacy of every-day association, and of knowledge of their "true inwardness," that make the book artificial in tone. "Go to! I will now be a lover of Nature!" she seems to say; and thus she secures the *point de départ* for her picturesque moods and her pretty ad-

jectives, her petulant self-analysis and her "gay malevolence." The flowers whose color scheme she elaborates so exuberantly are no more hers, than the Groliers and *éditions de luxe* which adorn his Gothic library, are the possessions of the upstart millionaire. We possess only that which we earn. The flowers this cold hearted, cynical poseur strolled out to admire, and opened her note-book to exploit, belonged not to her, but to the surly gardener, contemptuous of her interferences, who had himself nursed and trained them. Celia Thaxter, fostering the tiny seeds in her sunny window through the long bleak winter, transplanting the fragile roots in eggshells, building little barricades of lime to ward off the slugs, weeding and hoeing through the hot summer days, rising at midnight to satisfy herself that everything was

well in the moonlit garden by the sea,
—what secrets of the flowers has she
not surprised! For neither a fat
pocketbook nor a graceful vocabulary,
nor yet a fastidious nature, is the key
that opens their hearts. They have no
affinity for selfishness or indolence.
He who would love and be loved by
them, must not only cultivate a generous enthusiasm for humanity, but
must "know the history of his barn-
floor."

Neither do I find my ideal in Mrs.
Wheeler's "Garden of Content." She
strikes, to be sure, a truer note. She
is thoroughly genuine in her enthusiasms, and to the trained and sensitive
perceptions of an artist, she adds a
practical knowledge of plant life, and
brings to her pen-picture a sweetness
of spirit and gentle sympathy that are
charming in themselves. But her garden lacks the seasoning of age; it
didn't *grow*, but was made,—and in a
short time. Like painters' studios and
the houses of people with "an eye for
color," the picturesque and apparently
careless confusion have an air of calculation and deliberate intent, like the
best clothes that the Thrums villagers
laid out on the spare room chairs when
visitors were expected.

The garden I know was doubtless
indebted to the hand of man a half
century ago, for its present plan and
the germs of its present glory; but the
slow growth of years has changed and
adapted and added to it, till its way-
wardness is genuine, its antiquated air
unassumed. Moreover I have known
it as long as I have known anything.
I can close my eyes and see it as it was,
and as it is, in every detail. I know
every leaf and root, every weed to
which each spot is liable, the pedigree

of every plant, and the waxing and
waning of every blossom.

"The spirit culls unfading amaranth when
    wide it strays
"Through the old garden ground of boyish
    days."

The perfume of rockets after a
shower, the crash and thud of great
windfall pears, the sweet, sad psalm of
the thrush on warm, damp evenings,
the distant cries of newsboys on Sunday mornings when I stood under the
blossoming apple trees,—these are the
warp and woof of all my present love
of poetry, and happiness in outdoor
life. My earliest experience of sorrow
was on being taken to my city home
after the long happy summer in this
garden, standing wistfully at a window which overlooked a bricked-in
back yard, and sobbing softly for
"Grandma's pink clouds and pretty
garden."

What a curious commentary on
child-life and child-lore could be gathered in a record of garden games! If
we grown-ups could all unite to collect and compare the "Let's pretends"
of ingenious little brains, the priceless
treasures that Nature's toy shop offered in indulgent abundance to the
buoyant imagination of healthy childhood! The black and yellow anthers
folded away in the buds of the Crown
Imperial were packages of kid gloves
for the dolls. The scarlet trumpet-
flowers were finger protectors. The
big hips from the rose bushes, when
furnished with straw handles and
spouts, made tiny tea-sets for the play-
house under the trees; and the pantry
shelves for their accommodation were
the gnarled roots which projected here
and there from the carpet of smooth

brown needles. The seeds of plantain and dock, when mixed with water, furnished the kind of oatmeal that made little dolls grow. The strawberry-shrub blossoms were cabbages, the drooping yellow racemes of the barberry were grapes for dessert, and yellow catkins were bananas. Sometimes the cruel fickleness of the age that knows not pity betrayed itself in sham battles, wherein were decapitated the violets just tenderly culled from the wet grass. How we exulted in the possession of some triumphant, stiff-necked Roland who had resisted the onslaught of many a weaker Saracen. To suck the honied throats of lilacs, to weave fragile garlands from the stars of the rocket, and necklaces of pine-needles, and fringe with a pin the white stripes of the ribbon-grass into waving plumes; to ask the dandelion-down if mother wanted us, and festoon our heads with pale curls fashioned by artful tongues from the stems of the dandelion;—these were some of the occupations of the busy little folk, who trudged all day up and down the paths, peeped from the low, smooth branches of the spruce, or bobbed their sunny heads above the tall, waving grass in the orchard.

When I am alone in my garden it seems a Paradise of blossom and color; I take my visitors there and a sinister spell seems to fall upon it. There is nothing to see; everything has "just stopped blooming," or is "late this year," or is "not doing well." I suppose this blight falls upon the spirit of every connoisseur at times. The collector of old furniture, of rare books, bric-a-brac or porcelain; the biologist, entomologist or ethnologist; the painter or musician; nay, even the stamp-collector and amateur photographer;—how sorely are they sometimes troubled by blindness to the beauties, or superficial praise of the trivialities, of their art, or disappointed hy the stolidity with which their treasures are viewed. And so I am shy and nervous when I exhibit my flowers, shrinking and wincing in anticipation of the rebuff my enthusiasm is pretty sure to meet. My guest strides rapidly down the path, sweeping, with eyes that see not, the borders full of expectant, welcoming faces, discoursing the while on foreign topics, or at best describing another garden he has visited, or some rare flower he has seen elsewhere. If by any chance he stops to admire, it is probably before the flowers that have been popularized by the florist and his fashionable patrons,—valued chiefly for the prices they bring. Nearly all my guests who betray any interest whatever, express a dislike for the zinnia,—that artist's color-box of quaint, harmonious tints. The whole gamut of mediæval and Oriental colors may be found in the exquisite rosettes of this strong, simple plant. Bits of rare old Persian rugs; fragments of painted cathedral windows; ashes-of-roses shading to amethyst, violet and purple; pale flesh tints melting into rose, madder and carmine; brilliant vermilion and scarlet, that blend with orange, crimson and chestnut; dingy ochres, siennas, cinnamons, umbers;—all tarnished and oxidized, bronzed and stained, as with long exposure to sun and air. Embalmed blossoms, they seem to be, old as the seed in the mummy's hand. Some people dislike the pungent smell of the marigold; and others refuse garden room to the lady-slippers,—though I proffer them my finest seed,—because, forsooth, they are not effective in vases in the house!

As the book-lover throws himself into the mood of each author he reads, finding some traces of beauty and truth in all, so the true lover of flowers will perception of universal beauty should apply to flowers more than to literature, for their author is not subject to lapses of inspiration,—has never been detected in a failure or mistake. Sir, in flowers I love everything!

After all, the real lovers of flowers

deem nothing that blooms to be common or undesirable, and will shift his point of view for every specimen, in order to detect its inward as well as its outward character. *"Monsieur, en littérature j'aime tout,"* was Taine's response to a curious questioner who asked his preferences in books. This are naturally few. How can people admire when they do not know what to look for? And how can they know without practical experience? Once let my indifferent visitor get his dainty fingers in the moist, cool earth, let him make the acquaintance of spade and hoe, of weed and insect,—be it but once,—he will be an interesting companion when next he comes. Sir Thomas Browne tells us that "Cyrus was not only a lord of gardens but a manual planter thereof." Dismiss the gardener! The great general does not cry "Fight on, my brave boys!" from a commanding hill, but bivouacs with his men and fights in the front. He who lets any one do for him what he can do for himself, cheats himself out of an inexpressible pleasure. Perhaps the outward results may not be as satisfactory as if a trained hand had been at work, but the pleasure has been in the labor. Industry is its own wage, as the parable of the workers in the vineyard teaches us. The "joy of the doing" is a reward that blight and drouth cannot cheat us out of. When you have digged and spaded, watered and weeded; when you have known the eager zeal of acquisition, the joy and pride of possession, the anxieties incident to the bug and blight period; when you have experienced cares as harrowing as the mother's through the dangerous months of baby-teething,— then you can walk with me in my garden and recognize the hopes and fears, the disappointments and anticipations, —the tireless vigilance and tender solicitude that have made it what it is.

Preparation

By Charles Hanson Towne

HOW long the violets 'neath the snow
　　Toiled ere they breathed the Spring;
How long the poet dreamed his song
　　Before his heart could sing.

Ode to the Organ

By Lucy C. (Whittemore) Myrick

This poem was written about 1875 in response to a request from her fellow members of the famous *Conversazioni* instituted by Ralph Waldo Emerson. The poem speaks for itself, and additional interest is given by the many associations which cluster about it.

Organ, King among the clan
Of mechanisms complicate,
Through which the cunning skill of man
Doth silence make articulate
    Harmonious sound,
    Melodic measure!—
Say, who conceived the wondrous plan
To build a palace for this treasure?—
    With chambers round,
    Whence, at the pressure
Of a human finger light
On ivory or ebon gate,
Shall hasten many an aery sprite,
With sudden consciousness elate,
    To answer "Here!"
    With ready voice.

Whence came ye, viewless spirits?   Where
Lurked ye before ye found these cells?
From blue illimitable air?
In labyrinth of tinted shells,
 Where erst ye breathed
 Your songs of ocean?—
From forests, 'mongst whose ancient pines
Ye sang—and trembled with devotion?
 From cascades wreathed
 In archéd motion
Like silver web Arachne twines?
From rolling cloud—the Thunder's lair—
From Ocean caves—from Ocean waves—
Cataract and storm! Spirits of Air,
 Ye answer "Here,"
 With ready voice.

Organ!   Grand epitome
Of Pipe and Sackbut, Lyre and Lute;
Tabor, Timbrel, Psaltery;   ,
Viol, ten-stringed Harp and Flute;
 The Trumpet's blare,
 The Cymbal's clashing,—
Sounds of grief and sounds of glee;
Dirge funereal,—Triumph flashing;
 All, all are there;
 Wailing—dashing.
From distant clime, from ancient time,
They speak anew in harmony.
Organ, instrument sublime!
All meet, all culminate in thee,
 And answer "Here,"
 With ready voice.

Did Pan, among Arcadian hills,
While Syrinx still his suit evaded,
Hear hints of thee in murmuring rills
Whilst yet the charm'd reed he waded?
 Did Love infer
 The quaint invention?
Or, while the Psalms of Nod were young,
Did Jubal catch some sweet intention
 From insect whirr
 Or bow-string's tension,
Voice of winds, or bird's clear song?
To thee, Cecilia, taught of Heaven,
Thee, raptured by the angelic throng,
The banded organ pipes were given
 To answer "Here!"
 With ready voice.

Organ, Instrument sublime!
Thy feeble infancy began
In the midst of dateless time,
With the infancy of man.
    Harsh and few
    Thy first inflations.
But as broad and broader ran
The life-stream down through generations,
    Sweeter grew
    Thy intonations;
Till to-day, thou standest, King!—
Climax of all that men applaud;—
That out from spheral silence bring
The echo of divine accord;—
    Aye answering "Here!"
    With ready voice.

O Builder! build the Organ well!
Bring soundest metal from the mine;
And fragrant wood from forest dell;
And deck with carvings, quaint and fine,
    Sweet Music's shrine.
    Paint Angels' faces
On the silver pipes that shine
In front; and in the panelled spaces
    Garlands twine,
    And nymphs and graces;
While caryatides unweary,
Like the basses of the chord,
On either side the burden carry;
Seeming still to praise the Lord,
    Still answering "Here!"
    With ready voice.

Happy they, the Master Souls,
Who wrote undying symphonies;
Hieroglyphics—magic scrolls—
Full of wondrous mysteries.
    'Tis thine to tell
    Their mystic story,
Worthy Organ! and as rolls
Through pillared aisles the varied, unseen glory,
    That now doth swell
    "Memento Mori,"
And now "Te Deum Laudamus,"
We know not which is most entrancing—
The skill that brings the sound to us,
Or those sweet sounds themselves advancing,
    Still answering "Here!"
    With ready voice.

Humbly sit I at thy portal;
With a sense of awed surprise,
That to me, a sinful mortal,
Should approach such harmonies.
    Grief, care and fear,
    And doubt and sorrow,
All that pains the soul immortal,
All that makes it dread the morrow,
    All disappear;
    I seem to borrow
Wings from ye, ye wingéd tones,
And with ye my heart ascends,
Till with songs of blesséd ones
Perchance the Organ-Anthem blends,
    And answers "Here!"
    With ready voice.

House of Music! Organ Grand!
Temple templed; Shrine enshrined!
Let the Poet-King's command
Now in thee fulfilment find;
    "Praise the Lord!"
    Let thine oblation,
Wreathing up with solemn chord.
Represent a world's oration,—
    "Praise the Lord!"
    Let thy vibration
Thrill through space with worship's hymn,
Till, about the Great White Throne,
With Cherubim and Seraphim,
Sounds the far-aspiring tone,
    Still answering "Here!"
    With ready voice.

Washington-Greene Correspondence

A large collection of original letters written by General Washington and General Greene has come into the editor's possession. It is our intention to reproduce in fac-simile those of the letters which present the most interesting details and side lights on the great events of the period covered, even though some of the letters may have been previously published.

The reproduction of these letters in chronological order will be continued through the following four issues. A printed copy of this letter appears on page 233.—EDITOR.

Camp before York
6th Oct. 1781

How happy am I my
dear Sir, in at length having
it in my power to congratulate
you upon a victory as splendid
as I hope it will prove important. — Fortune must have
been coy indeed had she not
yielded at last to so persevering a pursuer as you have
been — I hope now she is yours
she will change her appellation
of fickle to that of constant. —

I can say with sincerity
that I feel the highest degree of
pleasure the good effects which
you mention as resulting from
the perfect good understanding
between you the Marquis and
myself. — I hope it will never be
interrupted, and I am sure it
never can while we are all
influenced

influenced by the same pure
motive – that of love to our coun
try & interest, and interest in
the cause in which we are em
barked. — I have happily had
but few differences with those
with whom I have the honor of
being connected in the Service
– with whom, and of what nature
these have been, you know. —
I bore much for the sake of peace
and the public good — My consci
ence tells me I acted rightly in
these transactions, and should
they even come to the knowledge
of the world, I trust I shall stand
acquitted by it.

The Baron, from the warmth
of his temper, had got disagreea
bly involved involved with the
State, and an enquiry into part
of his conduct must one day take
place, both for his own honor and
their satisfaction. — I have for
the

the present gives him a com
mand in this army, which
makes him happy —

I shall always take plea
sure in giving Mr Greene's
letters a conveyance and if
they persist in the resolution
of undertaking so long a jour
ney as that from New England
to Carolina I hope she will
make Mount Vernon (where
Mrs Knox now is) a stage of
more than a day or two

With much truth and
sincere affection
I am D Sir
Yr obedt
G Washington

Majr Genl Greene.

Gen. Washington to Gen. Greene

6th Oct. 1781.

How happy am I, my dear Sir, in at length having it in my power to congratulate you upon a victory as splendid as I hope it will prove important.—Fortune must have been coy indeed had she not yielded at last to so persevering a pursuer as you have been—I hope now she is yours, she will change her appellation of fickle to that of constant.—

I can say with sincerity that I feel the highest degree of pleasure the good effects which you mention as resulting from the perfect good understanding between you, the Marquis and myself.—I hope it will never be interrupted, and I am sure it never can while we are all influenced by the same pure motive— that of love to our Country and interest in the cause in which we are embarked.—I have happily had but few differences with those with whom I have the honor of being connected in the Service—with whom, and of what nature these have been, you know.—I bore much for the sake of peace and the public good. —My conscience tells me I acted rightly in these transactions, and should they ever come to the knowledge of the world I trust I shall stand acquitted by it.

The Baron, from the warmth of his temper, had got disagreeably involved with the state, and an enquiry into part of his conduct must some day take place, both for his own honor and their satisfaction.—I have for the present given him a command in this army which makes him happy.—

I shall always take pleasure in giving Mrs. Greene's letters a conveyance and sh'd she persist in the resolution of undertaking so long a journey as that from New England to Carolina I hope she will make Mount Vernon (where Mrs. Knox now is) a stage of more than a day or two.

With much truth and sincere affection,

I am, Dr Sir,
Yr. Obed't,
G. WASHINGTON.

Maj. Genl. Greene.

On the Wharf

By E. L. Pearson

"ELLEN! Ellen!" Mrs. Phinney pounded on the door till Ellen opened it and stood staring at her. "Ellen, have you heard? Short's boat swamped goin' over the bar this mornin', an' Dave an' your husband threw over their bait an' went to pick 'em up. Two of 'em jumped in to catch Fred Short who was goin' down, but they couldn't swim 'count of their oil-skins, an' they all three was drowned!" Mrs. Phinney backed away from the door, and stood, stammering, among the rose-bushes in the little garden of the fisherman's cottage. Ellen tried to speak twice, before she said, "Which two?" "That's it," said Mrs. Phinney, "they don't know. They telephoned this up from the life-saving station, an' then the storm got so bad they couldn't make out what they said, an' now the wires are down. They said that both the boats' crews,—the ones that ain't lost, are comin' up the river as soon as they can. Don't look so, Ellen, I guess Jim's all right."

Ellen disappeared into the house, then came out with a shawl over her head. "Where are you goin'?" said Mrs. Phinney. "Down on the wharf," Ellen replied. "Land sake, there ain't no use doin' that; they may not come for hours, an' at any rate the boat will be sighted 'fore it gets up,—you'll get your death!" shrieked Mrs. Phinney, as Ellen got farther away. Mrs. Phin-

ney stood and watched her till she was out of sight in the driving mist of the northeast storm. Then she went on to tell the other neighbors.

Ellen kept on to the head of the wharf. One or two men were standing there and she spoke to them. "Do you suppose he's all right? How soon will they be up? Where are they now, do you think?" One of the men took his pipe out of his mouth and answered with maddening deliberation, "I dunno,—p'raps they are, and p'raps they ain't. They was fools," he went on with more energy, "trying to get outside in weather like this." Ellen could get no more out of him, so she continued alone to the end of the wharf.

Here the force of the wind was such that she could hardly stand, and she had to cling to one of the big posts. The tide was nearly high, and the wind drove the water against the wharf so that it struck with a slapping sound and splashed over the planks. The mist was thick, like a fine rain, cold and stinging to the cheek, though the month was April. Ellen thought she had never seen the river looking so black and rough. The sky and water were of the same dark color; but here and there circled a few storm-beaten gulls, standing out against the sky as did the white-caps against the dark body of the river. The storm had shut down and the line of white breakers which had marked the river's mouth and the bar beyond, plainly visible on clear days, were hidden behind a gray curtain of mist.

She could hear the pounding of those waves, however,—a ceaseless grumble that rose to a roar, as the violence of the storm increased. She always hated that sound, as did all the women of the fishing village. Now it seemed to her something terrible. She shut her eyes and tried not to see, or hear, or think. But always before her was that white wall of breakers, forever towering one above the other only to come crashing down in their ceaseless fury.

She thought of the life that her husband led in his seine-boat. He laboured unceasingly, in all kinds of weather, suffering every hardship, and at the end of it all the work was often thrown away; for the fishing schooners seemed never to come for bait when the porgies were in the river. The bait would not keep unless salted down on the schooners right away. Often it was caught three or four miles up the river and if schooners were waiting out at sea, there was a race between the seiners. A race, not in a light shell for a silver cup, but a race, or rather a struggle, in an overloaded dory, manned by five or six tired men, rowing for food and clothing for their wives and children.

Such a race had taken place this morning, and for her husband's crew the end of it was to heave over the bait and go to the rescue of their rivals,—men who wouldn't say "thank you," but who, nevertheless, would do the

same for them if need came. Two were drowned,—which two? The roar of the breakers arose again in her ears, and she almost screamed in her helpless agony.

It was much darker now. Although only the middle of the afternoon, the storm hastened the darkness. She was numb with cold, but still waited there, alone. The other women were willing to stay in their houses till the boat should be sighted.

A long time passed, till, as she watched, a speck grew out of the mist. It was a boat, and a seine-boat, as she knew by the long oars. It came on with great strides like a water-spider. Soon she could count the men,—two, six, eight. Was he there? They were all dressed in oil-skins, and their "sou'-westers" were pulled over their faces. She heard the people come running down the wharf. Some of the women spoke to her, but she did not answer. She tried to make out if he was in the boat,—he usually rowed in the bow, she knew. She looked at the man there. The figure was short and thick set—not the tall, straight one that she had longed to see.

Dizzy and faint, she clung to the post, and for a moment neither saw nor heard anything. The boat was in under the wharf, when suddenly she heard some one calling her name. In a daze she looked down. A man was crouched in the stern, steering. A moment later she felt a hand on her shoulder and heard a voice say:

"Hello, Ellen. What are you doin' down here?"

How Young Lowell Mason Travelled to Savannah

By Daniel Gregory Mason

I HAVE before me two letters nearly a hundred years old, and full of quaint suggestions of the habits and customs of their writers, so different from our own. In the first place our grandfathers never used envelopes, but wrote on large double sheets of stout paper which they deftly infolded and sealed. My specimens are turned a deep brownish yellow with time, and well frayed at the edges, nearly ready to disintegrate altogether. One is addressed to "Mr. Lowell Mason, present"; the other bears the superscription, in fat deeply shaded letters, "Johnson Mason, Esqʳ., Medfield, Mass," and the postmark, legible only by the aid of inductive reasoning, "Savannah, Jan. 24." In the corner where we should put the stamp is scrawled the number 25. Two round holes indicate where the seal was placed, and by experimenting until they coincide one discovers the mode of folding. The first letter, which has no postmark, scrawled figures, or seal, was probably delivered by messenger.

Lowell Mason, who in due time became famous as a musical educator and as the composer of "Nearer, My God, to Thee," of the "Missionary Hymn" and other church tunes, was in 1812 a young man not quite of age, preparing to journey southwards to seek his fortune. His letter to his father will tell us some interesting details of his journey, but first we must turn for a moment to his father's anxious words of advice and warning on the eve of departure. Johnson Mason was a rude, shrewd, and upright man, keen of eye, dishevelled of hair, and firm of jaw, a straw-bonnet maker in the town of Medfield, and a radical in the matter of spelling. He reveals in his letter the combination, so frequent in his contemporaries, of a canny and circumspect business sense with indefatigable piety and the habit of scriptural allusion. He hopes his son may "accumulate a small property," but fears the presence of "Wolves in Sheaps Clothing to devower it." He advises him, should he be at first unsuccessful, "not to dispond but maintain steady habbits and have A particular eye to devine providence in all you say and all you do."

But the reader will be anxious for the letter itself, which I shall give with all its eccentricites of orthography and punctuation. Johnson Mason was a man of integrity and self-respect, quite able to ignore the subtleties of grammar and sentence-structure without losing dignity. Any lapses he makes are more than counterbalanced, I think, by the sincerity of his ethics, even if we say nothing of the keenness of his observation, shown in such remarks as that about the especial danger of the "cience of Music."

MEDFIELD Novr 22 1812—

My Son As you are about seting out on a long and I fear furteagueing journey I cannot refrain from makeing a few observations to you by way of advice before your departure—your abilities and address in many particulars I think sufficient to recomend you (at least) to the second class in sosiety the prinsipal indowments in which I think you defisient in (as it respects the present life) is *Prudence and Economy* in the first of these particulars I should not only include a prudential care of your own property but a strict Assiduity and carefull attention in whatever you may be called on to transact for others— by Economy I do not mean to be understood selfisness but a mediom between extravigence and meanness which are both detestable in the minds of the wise and good If it should please a kind Providence to prosper you in any undertaking so that you should be accumulating a small property to your self you will find plenty of Wolves in Sheaps Clothing to devower it if by inticing flattery, or fals statements it can be obtained but especially in the cience of Music for that will probably make your circle of acquaintance large in a short space of time so there will not be that chance to distinguish the real charracters of your acquaintance that there would be in some other occupations where you would be more deliberate and longer in forming connections. In a word you cannot be too cautious about joining parties and I should recommend you to evade them as much as possable—You will find the manners of the People very different at the Southward from what it is here or in New York I expect Gaming and Sabbath Braking are among the many bad practices which you will find. prevalent in Georgia and the Southern States which I hope by the care of a kind Providence you will be able to withstand also numerous other Vices which it is not necessary to enumerate—If you should not meet with the success at your journeys end which you expect (which I am fearfull may be the case) you ought not to dispond but maintain steady habbits and have A particular eye to devine providence in all you say and all you do

Nov 25

I hope there will be some opening here next Spring which will be to your advantage and mine If so I shall inform you but if things should not prove more favourable in the Spring than they are now should not advise you by any means to stay at the Southward dureing Summer shall write you as soon as I can be informed of your Arrival in Savannah—wish you to write me without fail from New York and Alexandria give my respects to Mr Kellogg and request Mr D Metcalf to give you the proceeds of the last Box of Bonnets if they are sold—I am with esteem your

Affectionate father
JOHNSON MASON

Mr Metcalf will give you all the proceeds of my Bonnets except 50 Dollars which I owe Mr Baxter of Boston

Two days after this was written, Lowell Mason set out on his journey. He estimates the distance from Boston to Savannah to be a little over a thousand miles. Nowadays we think nothing at all of a jaunt like that. We buy our railroad ticket and our novel, and sit comfortably in our upholstered seat, learning nothing about the country we travel through, to be sure, but suffering no fatigues or dangers. In 1813 it was very different. Lowell Mason describes his journey, with his characteristic love of paradox, as "unpleasant, agreeable, fatiguing, fine, long, tedious." He travelled in a wagon, with two companions, taking fifty-five days and spending about one hundred dollars, which was in that day a sum of money. But on the other hand he had the experience of journeying, by a natural and primitive method, through a noble country. He did not merely leave Boston and arrive at Savannah; he traversed the places between them. With businesslike accuracy he recounts his itinerary, and it will not prove dull, I hope, if I quote it in detail, especially as it is frequently enlivened by idiosyncrasies of phrase and by picturesque bits of incident. I adhere for the most part to his own punctuation:

SAVANNAH January 21. 1813
Thursday

Dear Parents I am at length able to inform you of my arrival this day at this place after an unpleasant, agreeable, fatiguing, fine, long, tedious journey of fifty five days. Having left you on Friday 27th Nov. 1812—we passed through Medway and Belingham to Mendon 17 miles. We staid the night with Mr Jackson. Saturday 28th. Passed through Uxbridge and Douglass to Thompson in the state of Conecticut 21 miles. Sunday 29th. Went to meeting & heard Rev. Daniel Dow—a high calvinist. Monday 30th. Through Pomfret & Ashford to Mansfield 23 miles. Tuesday Dec. 1st. Through Coventry, Bolton and East Hartford to the city of *Hartford* 23 miles. Wednesday 2nd Through Weathersfield and Berlin to Marridon 17 miles. Thursday 3rd Through Walingford, Hamden and North Haven to the city of *New Haven* 17 Miles. Friday 4th. We remained at N. Haven on account of rain. Saturday 5th. Through Milford and Stratford to Bridgeport 18 miles. Sunday 6th. Went to meeting. Monday 7th. Through Middlesex, Sokunteek, Norwalk, Stamford, Greenwich, Rye, to Mamaroneck in the State of New York 32 miles. Tuesday 8th. Through New Rochel, East Chester, West Chester, Harleim, to the city of New York 22 miles. 9th and 10th we staid in New York. Friday 11th. Crossed Hudsons river in a steam boat and passed through Powlershook in the State of New Jersey—Barbadoes, Elizabethtown, Bridgetown, Woodbridge to the city of New Brunswick the capital of New Jersey, 32 miles. Satur-

day 12th. From New Brunswick to Trenton 27 miles. Here we saw the ground on which the famous Battle was fought in the revolutionary war. Sunday 13th. Crossed Trenton bridge across the Delaware river & passed through Morrisville & Bristol to the city of Philadelphia in the State of Pennsylvania 30 miles. Evening went to church. Monday 14th. Remain in Philadelphia. Tuesday 15th. Crossed the Schuylkill—passed through Darby, Ridley, Chester, to the city of Wilmington the principal place in the State of Delaware. Bristol, Stanford, Cristiania to Elktown 36 miles. Wednesday 16th. North East, Charlestown, Crossed the Susquehannah to Havre de Grace 31 miles. As we were ascending a very steep hill in North East Town Mr. Bosworth's Trunk fell out unperceived by us. We proceeded about three quarters of a mile before we discovered our loss—and we had met only one Negro—we knew it must have fell out [sic] at the hill—accordingly we turned about and drove immediately to the place —but behold the trunk was gone—there were two houses in sight—we enquired at both of them but without effect—We therefore concluded that the Negro we had met must have hid it in the woods—which were on all sides of us. Mr. Bosworth took the Pistol, Mr. Hall a club & myself a Dagger and we went in different directions in the woods—after about two hours search I found it in a Ditch covered up with leaves—but no negro—we were in a great hurry or we should have hid ourselves and taken him when he came after it—Thursday 17. Through Bush and Abbington to the city of Baltimore in the State of Maryland 36 miles. Friday 18th. remained in Baltimore—went to see the remains of the house that the Federalists defended in Charles Street against the fury of a Democratic mob, and the spot where Genl Lingan was barbarously murdered. Saturday 19th. Through Blensburgh to the City of Washington in the District of Columbia—the capitol of the U. States. Sunday 20th. At Washington. Monday 21st. Through Georgetown, crossed the Potomac river, through Alexandria, by Mount Vernon to Colchester in the State of Virginia 25 miles. At Mount Vernon we saw the seat of Genl Washington which is beautiful beyond any description I can give—it is on a high piece of ground on the banks of the Potomac. The tomb of the American hero stands under a cluster of cedars about one hundred yards from the house. There is no monument of any description whatever—it is 8 miles from Alexandria and 16 from Washington city. William Lee a black man, servant of Genl Washington in the American army is yet living. The seat is now occupied by Judge Bushrod Washington. Tuesday 22nd. Through Dumfries and Aqua to Stafford 25 miles. Wednesday 23rd. Falmouth, crossed the Rappahannock to Bowling Green 31 m. Thursday 24th. Through Hannover to [illegible] 31 miles. Friday 25th. Passed through no town today untill we arrived at the city of Richmond 26 miles. Here we saw the ruins of the Theatre that was burnt in Decr. 1811. A Church is now building on the spot—and directly underneath it is the tomb of about 60 of the unfortunate persons who perished at that time. Saturday 26th. Through Petersburgh 26 miles. Sunday 27th. (no town to-day) 31 miles. Monday 28th. Crossed the Roanoke into the State of North Carolina 24 miles. Tuesday 29th. Went a-hunting. Wednesday 30th. through Warrenton 24 miles. Thursday 31st. Through Louisburg 31 miles. Friday January 1st 1813. Through the city of Raleigh the capitol of North Carolina 30 miles. Saturday 2nd. To Averysborough 18 miles. Sunday 3rd. To Fayetteville 25 miles. Here Mr. Hall concluded to stay and teach musick we left him on Monday 4th. (no town today) 23 miles. Tuesday 5th (no town) 26 miles. Wednesday 6th. Hunting Deer. Thursday 7th. (No Town) passed into the State of South Carolina. 15 miles. Friday 8th. Crossed Pede river. Passed through Greenville over Long Bluff 20 miles. Saturday 9th (No Town) 23 miles. Sunday 10th to Stateburgh on the high hills of Santee 15 miles. 11th and 12th. Staid at Stateburgh. Wednesday 13th. Crossed the Lakes [?], the Congree and Wateree rivers and went to Belle Ville 23 miles. 14th. Staid at Belle Ville on the

account of rain. Friday 15th. To Orangeburgh 25 miles. Here we found Mr. Cummins. 16th. Staid with Mr. Cummins. Sunday 17th. Went 23 miles (No Town). Monday 18th. went 30 miles—through water so deep that it came into the waggon. Tuesday 19th. Went 33 miles (no town, house, or any thing else). Wednesday 20th. Crossed Savannah river at the Two Sisters ferry—went 27 miles. Thursday 21st. Arrived at Savannah 16 miles.

The whole distance if I have added it right is one thousand and eightyeight miles. Although we have generally found good entertainment on the road—yet we have several times put up at a little log house where there was but one room, a large family of children and fifteen or twenty negroes—this was not altogether comfortable. Our horses have held out remarkably well and are in good order at present. I board at a very good house kept by Mrs. Battey. Mr. B. and myself occupy three rooms—one apiece for a bed and one between us for musick. I have called on Doc. Kollock—who is an extremely fine man. He thinks I shall meet with encouragement. I find however that my prospects are materially different from what I expected by Mr. Bosworths account—if I make two hundred dollars in all I shall think I do well—indeed I have offered to let myself for $150 to Mr. B. and he will not give it. But it is certain I must make 2 or 300 before I can return home. I wrote to you from New York and informed you of the money I had received there on your account. When we got to Alexandria we found we should be deficient and I got $20 of Mr. Metcalf which I shall consider myself indebted to you for. I shall expect to receive a letter from you as soon as this reaches you [illegible] write on one sheet to prevent postage. I hope by the time I write you again I can give you a more pleasant account of my business. It is very warm here—so as to be some days quite uncomfortable—and amongst imprudent people it is unhealthy (there has a number died within a few days after having been sick but two or three days) I suppose there is about 8 or 10 die weekly. I shall not think of staying in the city next summer if I do not come home—but shall probably return as far as some part of South or North Carolina. From New York we shipped the guns by Water and they arrived here in four days. Mr. Bosworth is willing to acknowledge now that it would have been much better if we had come by Water. N. Underwood is at No. 30 North 2nd St. Philadelphia—he said he would attend to my business you wished him to do.—I wrote to Mr. Hill from Washington and requested him to give you this information. Lucretia will remember me to all my young friends and thank Mary Prentiss for the Poem.

Goodbye for the present   L. MASON.

It is to be regretted that Miss Prentiss's poem, probably valedictory and pathetic in nature, has not been preserved to us. Nor have we any of the answers of Johnson Mason. We know only that Lowell suc- ceeded in finding a place as teller in a bank, and remained in Savannah until he was called, in 1827, to be choirmaster in the three principal churches of Boston. Thus began his musical career the further history of which is too well known to need repetition.

As for his journey to Savannah, though he has made, I think, a mistake of sixty miles in his addition (of which he himself suggests the possibility) it was certainly arduous beyond anything we know of travelling to-day. If any reader doubt the statement, let him merely copy the letter on a typewriter, as I have just done. He will become devoutly thankful for the introduction of modern conveniences.

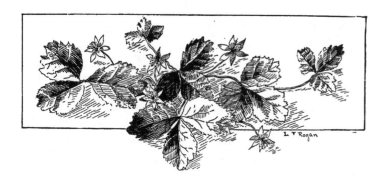

L. F Rogan

Early Churches at the North End, Boston

By William I. Cole

THE first church gathered within the limits of Old Boston was, paradoxically speaking, the Second Church. The First Church of the town had been organized in Charlestown, under a tree, by John Winthrop, Thomas Dudley and others, before they and their followers crossed over to the peninsula of Shawmut, or "Trimontaine," and found, at last, "a place for our sitting down." For nearly twenty years after their removal hither, the church which they had brought with them was the sole church of the community; and its meeting-house, originally a small, low building of mud walls and thatched roof,—later a larger and more pretentious wooden structure—was the only place of public worship. In 1649, however, "by reason of the popularity of the town, there being too many to meet in one assembly," the people living at the northern end of the peninsula were gathered into a separate church body.

North Boston, as this part of the town was called, the North End of the present day, had undergone considerable change since Anne Pollard, the impulsive young woman who was the foremost to leap ashore from the first boat load of colonists, had found it a place "very uneven, abounding in small hollows and swamps, covered with blueberries and other bushes."

The narrow neck joining it to the main part of the peninsula had been cut through by a canal, which was bridged at one or two points. Three main traveled ways crossed the island thus created, one to Snow Hill, now Copp's Hill; one to the Winnisimmet ferry; and one to the present North Square, where the "long wharf" reached out into the water. These rough paths were the beginnings of what are now Salem, Hanover and North streets. A windmill for the grinding of corn stood on Snow Hill; and near by, on the slope of the hill, a strong battery had been built of timber and earth. Houses, for the most part small, unpainted, and unimposing, followed the coast line at irregular intervals, or were gathered in a cluster around the hill, or in the neighborhood of the "long wharf." Although the population at this time did not include over thirty householders, business was rapidly increasing and removals hither from south of the canal were becoming more and more frequent.

A meeting-house was built by the new religious society, which became known as the North Church, at the top of a gentle slope where now is North Square. No description of this building has come down to us. Probably it was a plain square structure, not very large, with the usual high pulpit and wall pews. Some of these pews, it is said,

NORTH SQUARE

had private doors opening into the street. Ladders, branded with the town mark, hung on the outside for use in case of fire. These ladders, be it observed, were not for the protection of the sacred edifice alone—which, devoid as it was of all heating apparatus, was in little danger of fire from within—but of the entire neighborhood. Thus the meeting-house was a primitive fire station as well as a place of worship. One wonders whether attendants upon its services discovered any symbolism in the fire ladders suspended without. Did they see in them a figure of the church as a means of escape from eternal flames? Such a use of material objects to illustrate spiritual truth was especially congenial to the Puritan mind.

But the ladders did not save this building from destruction by fire; for in 1676 it was burned in a conflagration that swept away all the houses in the vicinity. The next year it was replaced by a larger edifice, also of wood, with a rather low belfry. This second structure, which was looked upon as "a model of the first architecture in New England," after serving its purpose as a church home for almost a hundred years, in the winter of 1775-76 was pulled down by the British for firewood. Whether this building, like its predecessors, combined the office of fire station with that of meeting-house, is uncertain; but for many years it was a public arsenal, the powder of the town being kept here. What a variety of solemn thoughts must have filled the minds of the worshippers within its walls! To the reminders from the pulpit of spiritual perils were added from the storage under the same roof those of physical perils.   In view of this strange storage, any references to the uncertainty of life must have had peculiar point and force!

The first regular minister of the North Church was the Rev. John Mayo. Of his personality and labors little, if anything, is known to-day. The records of the church give one item, however, concerning his funeral which, unintentionally perhaps, lights up for a moment contemporary customs. According to this entry, the whole cost of the funeral was ten pounds and four shillings, of which only six shillings were paid for the grave and six shillings for the coffin, while three pounds and seventeen shillings were spent for wine and five pounds and fifteen shillings for gloves.

The two succeeding ministers were Increase Mather, and his son, colleague, and finally his successor—the more famous Cotton Mather. The combined pastorates of these two men extended over a period of more than sixty years, during the greater part of which time the pulpit of the North Church was the most conspicuous pulpit not only in Boston but in America. If father and son were contrasted, it might be said that the former was more the man of affairs, the latter more the scholar and preacher. To the duties of his ministry, Increase Mather added those of the presidency of Harvard College, from 1684 to 1701. He was also for several years the agent of Massachusetts at the court of James the Second and of William and Mary. When the lineal descendant and present representative of the North Church selected an incident in the life of this man of many activities to depict in a "minister's window," it chose that

of his appearing before the English Commissioners to protest against the surrender of the colony charter. The window, which adorns its house of worship on Copley Square, shows him standing, a tall, commanding figure, in the act of addressing the royal commissioners, who are seated at a table, the simple austere garb of the Puritan priest being in marked contrast to the rich dress of the Englishmen.

But as a minister alone, Increase Mather would still be a conspicuous character in the early annals of New England. His appearance in the pulpit is described as having been peculiarly apostolic. His voice was strong and he sometimes used it with great effect, delivering sentences which he wished to make especially impressive "with such a tonitrous cogency," to use the words of his son, "that his hearers were struck with awe like that produced by the fall of thunderbolts." The same authority affirms, also, that it was his custom to "back everything he said with some strong or agreeable sentence from the Scriptures."

If an incident in the life of Cotton Mather were singled out for representation as being peculiarly characteristic of the man, probably it would be one suggested by the part he took against the witches. It might be that described by Calef in connection with the hanging at Salem of the Rev. George Burroughs. According to this writer, the sympathy with the condemned man was so great that at one time the spectators seemed likely to hinder the execution. "As soon as he was turned off," he goes on to say, "Mr. Cotton Mather being mounted upon a horse, addressed himself unto the People, partly to declare that he (Rev. Mr.

Burroughs) was no ordained minister, and partly to possess the People of his guilt; saying, that the Devil has often been transformed into an Angel of Light; and this did somewhat appease the People and the Executions went on." Probably an incident of this kind would be chosen to perpetuate the memory of Cotton Mather; for, strange as it may seem, his persecution of the witches, although ot short duration and far less fanatical than that of some of his contemporaries, is more frequently dwelt upon than any of the other activities of his long life, many of which were of a beneficent character, unquestioned even to-day. Without doubt few historical characters are less understood than Cotton

Mather. Self-conscious to an unusual degree he undoubtedly was; but what else could be expected of a man of his natural parts reared in the days when, to quote Barrett Wendell:

"As soon as children could talk, they were set to a process of deliberate introspection, whose mark is left in the constitutional melancholy and the frequent insanity of their descendants."

The belief in witchcraft, for which he is especially censured, was well-nigh universal at that time. In England alone, more witches were hanged or burned every year, for many years, than were put to death during the whole period of the Salem frenzy. To his weakness and eccentricities, of which he possessed not a few, were

COTTON MATHER

added qualities of the highest character. Although a persecutor of witches, he was at the same time a scholar of immense learning, a powerful preacher, and, what few familiar with his life can really doubt, a good man.

Early in the eighteenth century the population of the North End had increased to such an extent that the North Meeting-house was overcrowded and the need of a second place of worship began to be felt. In 1713, Cotton Mather, foreseeing that another religious society must be formed because of the "swarming brethren," wrote characteristically in his diary:

"God calls me in an extraordinary manner to be armed for the Trials which I may undergo in a church breaking all to pieces, through the Impertinences of a proud crew, that must have pues for their despicable Families."

Nevertheless, his wounded vanity did not prevent him from advising with those about to start a new church, and preaching to them two appropriate sermons in a private house. The following year the associates, consisting primarily of "seventeen substantial mechanics," built for themselves a church house at the corner of Hanover and Clark streets. An interesting fact in connection with its erection is that permission to build it of wood had to be obtained from the General Court, a law having been passed two or three years before prohibiting other construction than brick or stone.

This meeting-house, of small dimensions, but enlarged later, was put up without assistance from the more wealthy part of the community, excepting what was "derived from their prayers and good wishes." So difficult was the undertaking that several years afterward, by way of compensation to the builders, the church voted:

"That if by any means this house should be demolished, they shall have the privilege, by themselves and their heirs, to rebuild the same with such others as they please to associate with them in the work."

The contingency provided for by this action occurred in 1802, when the building was taken down to make room for a larger and finer structure; but the privilege graciously conferred was not claimed.

The later building, it may be interesting to know, was after a design by Charles Bulfinch. Enlarged and otherwise altered, it is still standing, although no longer the home of its original owners.

The new organization was called the New North Church to distinguish it from the North, henceforth the Old North Church. Among its first deacons was John Dixwell, a son of one of the judges of Charles the First.

The early history of this church was marked by a dissension leading to a permanent division and engendering between the two opposing factions a bitterness of feeling that was many years in dying out. The cause of so great a dissension was the calling and installation of a Rev. Mr. Thatcher as a colleague with the pastor. Rev. Mr. Thacher was settled pastor of the church in Weymouth, and the real point at issue was the propriety of taking him away from his flock. In view of modern church methods in securing pastors

the mere raising of such a question seems well nigh absurd, still more so allowing it to become a subject of fierce altercation. In justification of their course, the supporters of Mr. Thacher gave, among other reasons, if an old writer is to be believed, that: "He was afflicted with the asthma, which was attributed to the local situation of the place. The air of Boston was more congenial to his health." To this his opponents replied, according to the same authority, that "his disease was not very alarming till he was tampered with about changing his parish." Thus early in the history of New England were ministers accused by their detractors of making the need of a more salubrious climate an excuse for accepting a call to a larger field.

Those who had resisted the calling of Mr. Thacher, when they found that their efforts had been in vain, set themselves to work to prevent his settlement. The council, in which were represented but two other churches, the church at Milton and the church at Rumney Marsh, now a part of Chelsea, met at the house of the pastor, which was situated at the corner of Salem and North Bennet streets. The "aggrieved brethren," on the other hand, met at the house of one of their leaders, at the corner of Hanover and North Bennet streets, by which, under ordinary circumstances, the council would pass on its way to the meetinghouse. Their purpose in this was to intercept the council and prevent it, by force if necesasry, from entering the sacred doors. The pastor, however, learning that such a plot was on foot, conducted the council by a back way through what is now Tileston street, thus getting it into the building with-

COTTON MATHER'S TOMB IN COPP'S HILL BURYING GROUND

out disturbance. Both factions assumed, apparently, that possession of the pulpit was all the points of the law.

Active opposition now ceased, but the disaffected members left the church and formed a separate organization, the third of the same faith and order in the North End; and built a place of worship on the upper part of Hanover street. In the first stress of wrathful resentment, they proposed to call the new society the "Revenge Church of Christ," but milder counsels prevailing they allowed themselves to become known as the New Brick Church, from the construction of their meeting-house, which was of brick.

But one fling they must have at the church from which they had come out, and especially at the direct cause of all the trouble. As a vane for their steeple they chose a gilded cock in derisive reference. so it is said, to Mr. Thacher whose first name was Peter. To make this reference unmistakable, when the cock was put in place, a "merrie fellow," if an old chronicler is trustworthy, climbed upon it and, turning it in the direction of the New North Meeting-house, crowed lustily three times! This vane gained for the edifice which it surmounted the sobriquet of the "cockerel church," a name surviving in "Cockerel Hall" by which the building occupying the same site is known to-day. When the New Brick Meeting-house was taken down at the time of the widening of Hanover street, the cock was transferred to the Shepherd Memorial Church in Cambridge, where it still can be seen facing the direction from which the wind blows, a perpetual symbol of changeableness.

Individual expressions of bitter feeling toward the New North, on the part of the seceders, were not lacking. One man nailed up his pew in his former church home, that at least one pew there would always be empty. For several years the pew remained nailed up, until certain persons entering the meeting-house by night sawed out the section of the floor upon which the pew stood and, carrying the whole away, placed it at the shop door of its owner, where it excited much mirth among the passersby.

As time went on, however, the feeling grew less and less bitter and the occasion of it became the subject of many a joke. A rather grim illustration of this has been preserved. It seems that Mr. Thacher died at night, in the midst of a severe storm accompanied by thunder and lightning, which was very unusual at that season of the year. The next morning, according to the story, a member of his church passing along the street met an acquaintance and asked him if he knew that Parson Thacher was dead? "No," said the other, "when did he die?" "In the midst of the storm," was the reply. "Well," rejoined the friend, "he went off with as much noise as he came!"

Strangely enough, the character and ability of Mr. Thatcher appear to have played no part in this historic quarrel. So far as is known he was personally acceptable to those opposed to his call and settlement. The question so violently in dispute was one of church polity exclusively. As a matter of fact, Mr. Thacher proved to be a popular preacher, and was greatly beloved. His ministry also was far from unfruitful. From his installation till his death in 1736, a period of sixteen years, 383 persons were admitted into the full communion of the church; and 92 were given the covenant, without admission into full communion. When the somewhat severe conditions of church membership in those days are remembered, such figures appear quite remarkable.

Following Mr. Thatcher in the ministry of the New North, after an interval of a few years, came Andrew and John Eliot, perhaps its two most eminent pastors. Like Increase and Cotton Mather, they were father and son; and their pastorates, separated by a few months only, comprised a term of seventy years. The most salient characteristic of the elder Eliot seems to have been circumspection, for he bore the nickname of "Andrew Sly." One of his maxims is said to have been:

"When your parishioners are divided in sentiment, enjoy your own opinion and act according to your best judgment; but join neither as a partisan."

Although suspected during his earlier life of being a Tory at heart, because of his friendship for Gov. Hutchinson, in his later years he proved that he was not wanting in true patriotism. With the exception of Mathew Byles, the pastor of the Hollis Street Church at the South End, he was the only Congregational minister who remained at his post during the siege of Boston.

A sermon of his, still in existence, has a peculiar interest because of the circumstances under which it was given. These are indicated by the title page: "A Sermon Preached the Lord's-Day before the Execution of Levi Ames, who suffered Death for Burglary, Oct. 21, 1773, Act. 22." A foot-note explains still further: "This discourse was preached at the desire of the Prisoner, who was present when it was delivered." The subject was, pertinently, "Christ's Promise to the penitent Thief," from the text, "To-day shalt thou be with me in Paradise."

The closing words were addressed rather to the general audience than to the condemned man:

"Let me exhort and intreat all who may attend the execution of this poor condemned criminal, to lay to heart such an affecting sight, and to behave with decency and seriousness on such a solemn occasion. And may the awul spectacle be a means of instruction and amendment to sinners."

Doubtless this exhortation to due propriety of conduct at the hanging was needed at a time when a public execution was looked upon as the greatest of diversions, imparting to the day of its occurrence the character of a holiday.

The younger Eliot's most distinguishing trait was, apparently, catholicity of spirit, as the epithet of the "liberal Christian," often applied to him, seems to imply. Of him it was said:

"Good men he loved and associated with, although they differed from him in senti-

THE MATHER HOUSE

ment, and excluded none from his pulpit on that account."

For this spirit of tolerance he received many a reproof from some of his ministerial brethren. Once in particular was he chided—perhaps reprimanded would be the exacter word—for "inviting Mr. Hill, an amiable man, to preach for him, who belonged to the church called the Church of New Jerusalem." On another occasion he gave offence by acting as pall-bearer at the funeral of a Methodist minister who had been a neighbor of his. He was on intimate terms with the Universalist minister whose church building was not far from his own meeting-house, which likewise was frowned upon.

During the ministry of the two Eliots the New North reached the point of its greatest prosperity. In the period directly preceding the Revolution, the population and prosperity, if not the fashion, of the town were centered at the North End; and the congregations gathering Sunday after Sunday in the New North Meeting-house were the largest and most influential in Boston. After the departure of the British, however, social deterioration set in here, which went on with increasing rapidity nearly up to the present time. Of course the churches quickly felt the change. At the very beginning of the century just closed, a writer deplores the altered aspect of the "face of the assembly" at the New North and attributes it to "the local situation of the meeting-house." "The young gentlemen who have married wives in other parts of the town," he goes on to say in explanation, "have found it difficult to persuade them to become so ungenteel as to attend worship at the North End; while the ladies of the society, as they have become wives, have affected to consider it a mark of taste to change their minister."

Even most of the pastors had become non-resident. According to this same writer, only one out of the six or more lived in his field of labor.

This single exception must have been John Eliot; for both he and his father always dwelt in the midst of those among whom they worked. It is pleasant to read also of these two pastors that they went among the people of their church, "not only when duty called them, as in cases of marriage, sickness and death, but in a social manner as friends." Their parishioners in turn visited them on Sunday evenings, "at which times their studies were filled with them, not for the sake of religious conversation only, but here the common topics of the day were talked over, much information given and received relative to the polities of the time and the interest of the country." Many men not belonging to the parish were in the habit of joining these circles. Surely the two Eliots are worthy of imitation by all pastors of all times.

The house in which the Eliots lived, and where these Sunday evening gatherings were held, had been, curiously enough, the home at one time of Increase and Cotton Mather. A section of the original building is still standing on Hanover street.

After the Revolution, the Old North Church people, whose meeting-house had been demolished by the British soldiers, were invited to worship with the New Brick, the membership of the latter having been greatly reduced by the war. The result was a formal union of the two societies, mother and daughter, or, more exactly, mother and granddaughter, in 1779, under the name of the Second Church.

The middle period in the history of the church thus reorganized was distinguished by the ministration, for a brief time, of Ralph Waldo Emerson, called in 1829 as colleague to the pastor. Mr. Emerson soon succeeded to the full pastorate, discharging its duties until 1832, when he resigned the office. The reason for this act was the radical difference between his view of the Lord's Supper and that generally held by the church and the Congregational body at large. This rite, he declares in his farewell discourse, ought not to be observed, inasmuch as it confused the idea of God by transferring the worship of Him to Christ. Christ is the mediator only as the instructor of man, he explains. In the least petition to God "the soul stands alone with God, and Jesus is no more present to your mind than your brother or child." This entire sermon was an epoch-making utterance in the Unitarian movement.

After withdrawing from the church, Mr. Emerson left the city to live henceforth in Concord. It was in connection with his departure from Boston at this time that he wrote the well known poem beginning:

"Good-bye, proud world; I'm going home."

For sixty-four years the North Church was the only church in the North End, with one exception. This exception was a small body of Baptists, meeting in a little wooden structure in the neighborhood of Salem street, on the edge of what was called the "mill-pond." Organized in Charlestown in 1665, this church had removed hither by the way of East Boston fifteen years later. Its reception in the town had been very far from friendly, the governor and council promptly ordering that the doors and windows of its scarcely finished meeting-house be boarded up. This proceeding on the part of the civil authorities is less surprising, in view of the fact that only thirty-six years before a man had been publicly whipped at Hingham for refusing to allow his child to be baptized, the belief in infant baptism being one of the car-

CHRIST CHURCH

dinal heresies of the Baptists. Less than forty years after the boarding up of these doors and windows, at the ordination in the very same edifice of a pastor of the church, Cotton Mather was present and preached the sermon. In this sermon, whose subject was, "Good men united," the speaker condemned "the withdrawal of fellowship from good men," and "the disposition to inflict uneasy circumstances upon them under the wretched notion of wholesome severities." Thus the plant of religious tolerance had already taken root in the somewhat stony soil of New England and was beginning to grow.

For one hundred and fifty years the church worshipped by the side of the "mill-pond," a larger edifice replacing the original one; then removed to the corner of Hanover and Union streets. One of its pastors during this period, the Rev. Samuel Stillman, gave the church considerable dignity and influence, being regarded as one of the able preachers in the Revolutionary days. People of the town and strangers alike, so it is said, many of them men and women of distinction, thronged the aisles of his obscure little meeting-house, drawn hither by his eloquence.

In 1743 a division occurred in this church which led to the formation of a new society, as the separation in the New North had resulted in the New Brick. In this case, however, the division was mainly over a question of theology rather than of church polity. The pastor was accused of holding unsound religious views, and also of opposing "the work of God in the land." "The work of God" was the Great Awakening, which, begun by Jonathan Edwards in 1735, had received a fresh impulse from the opportune arrival in this country of George White-field, the Wesleyan preacher. The unsoundness of the pastor's views consisted in his tendency to Arminianism, the essence of which was repudiation of the doctrines of "election" and "reprobation." Now this very heresy, as it extended in New England, had prepared the way for Whitefield's won-

METHODIST ALLEY

derful work; as it later made possible the establishment of Methodism in Boston and elsewhere. Therefore the opposition of the Baptist pastor to the "work of God," of whatsoever nature it was, must have been on other than theological grounds.

The seceders built a place of worship near that of the parent church, in what is now Baldwin Place. By the end of the century the society had so increased that the building was enlarged, and a few years later was taken down to be replaced by a still more commodious edifice. The early history of this Second Baptist church was comparatively uneventful.

The Methodist as well as the Baptist form of faith gained its first foothold in Boston at the North End. Among the British soldiers who came in 1768 were some Methodists who made the beginning of a society. About 1772 a small organization was formed, which soon after became extinct. While there was some preaching in the interval, it was not until 1790 that Methodism was fairly established

REVEREND JOHN MURRAY

here—its founder, the Rev. Jesse Lee, holding his first public service in the town in July of that year. This service took place under the historic old elm on the Common, at the close of a Sabbath day. The appearance of the preacher and the effect that he produced have been thus described:

"Upon a rude table a man of powerful frame and of a serene but shrewd countenance, took his stand. Four persons approached, and curiously gazed while he sung. Kneeling he prayed with a fervor unknown in the Puritan pulpits, attracting crowds of promenaders from the shady walks. Three thousand people drank in his flowing thoughts, as, from a pocket Bible without notes, he proclaimed a free salvation. . . . It was agreed, said one who heard him, that such a man had not visited New England since the days of Whitefield."

Five years later the first meeting-house of the denomination was built. It was situated on Methodist Alley, now Hanover avenue, and was a small, plain, wooden building, rough and unfinished within, benches without backs serving for pews. The society at this time numbered about forty, all of whom were poor. While in no sense persecuted, they suffered at first many

petty annoyances similar to those that the Salvation Army endures to-day on its appearance in a new community. Within thirty years their numbers had so increased that a larger meeting place became imperative, and in 1828 they finished and dedicated a new house of worship on North Bennet street.

One other important form of religious faith came into Boston through the North End. In 1785 the first society of Universalists in the town was gathered by the Rev. John Murray, the "father of Universalism" in this country. A house of worship for the new sect was ready at hand in the sacred edifice at the corner of Hanover and North Bennet streets recently vacated by the followers of Rev. Samuel Mather.

To account for this structure it is necessary to go back a period of fifty years. In 1732, Samuel Mather, a son of Cotton Mather, was dismissed from the Old North, after a service of nine years as colleague of its pastor. The reasons for this action on the part of the church are vaguely stated as his being "not entirely sound in doctrine, and not entirely proper in conduct." The latter charge was based solely on his attitude toward the Great Awakening already referred to. Wherein his heresy lay is not given. With him went ninety-three others of the church, who put up the building in question. This they and their successors occupied until the death of their pastor, in 1785, when most of them returned to the Second Church.

Of Samuel Mather, it may be said in passing, that he was accounted a man of learning although not a powerful preacher. In spite of the opposition that he aroused, there is no good reason to doubt his uprightness. That he was generally esteemed, appears from the title pages of two sermons preached by him, one on the death of Queen Caroline, "in the audience of his excellency the governor;' the other on the death of "the high, puissant, and most illustrious Prince Frederick Lewis, Prince of Great Britain." The latter was "in the audience of the honorable Spencer Phips, Esq., lieutenant-governor and commander in chief, and

The Universalists, acquiring the property left when the church of Samuel Mather was disbanded, made it their church home..

A dramatic contrast was involved in this change of ownership and occupation; for Samuel Mather had been a strong opponent of Universalism. His best known if not his only controversial book bears the title:

"All men will not be saved forever, or an attempt to prove that this is a Scriptural

THE FIRST UNIVERSALIST CHURCH

the honorable his majesty's council, of the Province of Massachusetts Bay."

A third sermon of his which has been preserved was prepared and preached for the benefit of the same Levi Ames that Andrew Eliot addressed, both discourses being given on the Sunday before the man was hung for burglary. The subject of Mather's sermon was "Christ sent to heal the broken-hearted." Poor Levi Ames; one cannot but hope that these two sermons of his last Sabbath on earth brought peace to his heart!

Doctrine; and to give a sufficient answer to the Publisher of the Extracts in favor of the Salvation of all Men."

Nevertheless, within a few months of his death, in the very pulpit which for so many years he had occupied, the voice of the Rev. John Murray was lifted up in the exposition of the doctrine of ultimate universal salvation!

The building was enlarged in 1792, repaired and partially remodeled a few years later; and in 1838 demolished preparatory to the erection of the brick structure still standing.

One more early church at the North End remains to be spoken of. In 1723 Christ Church, the second Episcopal church in the town, dedicated a stately house of worship on Salem street, near the two Baptist meeting-houses. At one period it was a large and prosperous society, and is to-day the sole survivor at the North End of all the churches worshipping there previous to the nineteenth century; but it is less famous for its history than for its house of worship, which it has occupied from the first. The edifice, erected one hundred and seventy-five years ago, from a design by Sir Christopher Wren, if report is to be believed, retains generally its original appearance. Externally the body of the building is plain and uninteresting, differing little from that of all old houses of worship in New England; but the steeple gives dignity and distinction to the whole structure. The interior resembles that of an old English church, and is at once quaint and beautiful.

Around this venerable sanctuary are gathered many associations, not a few of them having to do with important events in American history. In the steeple, according to tradition, were displayed the signal lanterns of Paul Revere, "which warned the country of the march of the British troops to Lexington and Concord." From the tower General Gage witnessed the battle of Bunker Hill; and in one of the burial vaults beneath the nave, for after the English custom the space under the floor was used in the early days for sepulchre, the remains of General Pitcairn reposed until they were transferred to Westminster Abbey.

A GLIMPSE OF ST. STEPHEN'S CHURCH

Among the treasures and curiosities of the church are parts of a communion service presented by George the Second and bearing the royal arms; a copy of the "Vinegar" Bible, in which, by a misprint, the word "vinegar" is substituted for "vineyard" in the parable; prayer-books in which all the prayers for the king and royal family are covered with pieces of plain paper, pasted on after the Revolution; and, as one of the mural decorations, a bust of Washington by Houdon, the distinguished French sculptor.

Services are held here every Sunday morning, attended by a small congregation made up chiefly of sightseers; and a Sunday-school of a few members meets in the afternoon. This Sunday-school dates back to 1815, and is perhaps the oldest Sunday-school in the country.

With the exception of Christ

Church, as has been said, not one of the early churches at the North End is to be found there to-day. The North, or Old North, which was merged into the New Brick Church, now has a house of worship on Copley Square; the New North Church, after removing to Bulfinch street, became extinct; the First Baptist Church is occupying a stately edifice on Commonwealth avenue; the Second Baptist is housed on Warren 'avenue, and is known as the Warren Avenue Baptist Church; the First Methodist Church is continued in the Grace Methodist Episcopal Church, worshipping on Temple street, and the First Universalist Church was dissolved in 1864. Of the Protestant churches established in this part of Boston since the beginning of

THE BALDWIN PLACE SYNAGOGUE

the century just ended, two or three only remain. The Hanover Street Church, of which Lyman Beecher was pastor at one time, removed to Bowdoin street and later went out of existence, and the Salem Street Church merged into the Mariners' Church.

Those that still are to be found here comprise three societies for carrying on work especially among sailors, and a Methodist Episcopal Church of Italians in charge of an Italian pastor.

Protestantism has all but disappeared from the North End and in its place have come alien forms of faith. Within a stone's throw of the site of the Old North Meeting-house, stands the church home of an Italian Roman Catholic body; the former meeting-house of the New North is now occupied by Irish and that of the First Methodist Church by Portuguese Roman Catholics; while what was once the church home of the Second Baptist Church has become an orthodox Jewish synagogue.

In a word, the religious situation at the North End to-day, broadly considered, departs more and more widely from that in each remoter period, until it presents the most amazing contrast to what it was two hundred and fifty years ago when Puritanism was the dominant and sole form of faith. Puritanism departed with the Mathers and Protestantism has all but disappeared, while alien faiths have increased more and more. In its religious aspects at the present time the North End can be likened only to a palimpsest on which over the half erased annals of Protestantism are written in large characters the records of Roman Catholicism and orthodox Judaism.

American Shrines VIII

Lexington Common

" LAY DOWN THE AXE, FLING BY THE SPADE:
LEAVE IN ITS TRACK THE TOILING PLOUGH;
THE RIFLE AND THE BAYONET-BLADE
FOR ARMS LIKE YOURS WERE FITTER NOW."

NEW ENGLAND MAGAZINE

NEW SERIES   MAY   VOL. XXVI NO. 3

Flower Folk in the Boston Reservations

By Elsie Locke

MARCH is not only nursing April's violets; she also brings to us the first wild flower of the year. And what is it?—for poets and naturalists disagree. The honey bees know. If, about the middle of March, we see them returning home laden with pollen and could follow them, they would take us, I think, to the swamps and bogs of the Middlesex Fells, there to find the symplocarpus—the country folk call it skunk cabbage because of its unpleasant odor. But, for all that, it is a near relative to our cherished calla lily. Hamilton Gibson gives it a prettier name, "the hermit of the bog," and says that it is not without honor, save in its own country.

In March the pussy willows are coming, ten or twelve different kinds of them,—for there are as many dif-

ferent species of the willow hereabouts. Some of them, indeed, are later with their leaves, but first and dearest are the silvery gray pussies peering out of scaly buds on the bare, brown twigs. Heralding the earliest blossoms of spring, they bring gladness to the hearts of all true lovers of nature, a golden gladness which pierces the films that wrap the inner sense, until, for a time, we become like Asgard who sat and listened at the rainbow bridge and could hear the grass grow, leagues away.

Leaving the hermit of the bog to the botanist and the bees, let us find the first blossom that is also a flower. It is not the trailing arbutus; for, although that once grew in the Fells, it has gone with the great pines, and the beautiful fringed gentian that once could be found there. But in the Cas-

HEPATICA   BLOODROOT   ANEMONE

cade Woods the hepatica is coming, that dear little first flower sometimes called squirrel-cup, and with it, the anemone, swaying on its stem.

And the violets! Sweet white violets—the *viola blanda* with rounded leaves, and the long-leaved *viola lanceolata;* and on higher ground the downy yellow violet growing at the root of some old tree. On Bare Hill, and by Beaver Brook, still grows the beautiful bloodroot. And the anemonella, differing from the true anemone by its cluster of flowers, is found throughout the Fells.

By the brookside, beneath the red maples, look for the early saxifrage; and, in wetter places, the marsh marigold—marsh gold, some of us call it— and with it wild callas, and the sweet flag *acorus calamus* known to some people only as a confection. And, later, growing by these same brooksides, we shall find the wild forget-me-not, golden saxifrage and the white crowfoot, its finely dissected leaves floating on the water.

Somewhere east of Hawk Hill the little goldthread is found, and on rocky places everywhere look for the delicate meadow rue, and for the columbine swinging its scarlet bells,

"Like clear flames in lonely nooks."

On these same rocky ledges grow the wild geraniums and the pale corydalis.

In the moist woods Jack-in-the-pulpit preaches to the Solomon's seal, the baneberry, the sweet cicely, and the nodding trillium hiding its pretty blossom beneath its three broad leaves. Everywhere we see the drooping white clusters of the shadberry, with the tiny yellow blossoms of the spicebush.

Late in May the flowering dogwood tree is blooming in the eastern part of the Blue Hills, and the Middlesex Fells south of Spot Pond. Only here and there may the rare rhodora be found; while far less shy are its sisters, the swamp azaleas, lovely—and sticky!

In open, moist, grassy places you will find the Houstonia that delicate little flower with so many pretty local names, bluets, innocence, Quaker-ladies, and sky-bloom—

"Sky-bloom on the hillside,
Sky-bloom in the meadow,"
*   *   *   *   *

"Like a cherub crowd astray
For an earthly holiday."

There may be found pyrolas, mediolas and the yellow dog-tooth violet. And on the wooded hillsides the smilacina, the maianthemum and oakesia are common in both the Blue Hills and in the Fells; but the *uvularia*—the real straw lily—is very rare.   Common enough, yet with a golden-starred beauty of its own, blossoms the faithful dandelion, that friend of the merry children.   Later, when

"June bids the sweet wild rose to blow,"

those growing in its ponds, swamps, or bogs fringing the swamps; the wild cranberry, and, growing with roots matted together, the clethra, cassandra —swamp rose—and the "sacred Andromeda" are among these. Sometimes this last, pushing out into the pond, lifts its dark green leaves and lovely flowers up out of the water.   The drooping flower stalks are white, the calyx white tipped with rose, and the petals all rose color.   Not far away you

MARSH MARIGOLD

WILD GERANIUM

we shall find on these hills the dwarf wild rose, *rosa humilis;* and the sweetbriar escaped from cultivation.

There are fields full of daisies and buttercups, and knee-deep clover. Barberry bushes are in blossom along the wayside, agrimony with its elegantly cut leaf, and the pretty, starry stitchwort.   And as we go on, we drink in with delight the fragrance of the wild grape blossom. Hiding in deep woods are the lady's-slippers, and the rare, ragged-fringed orchids by Hoosicwhisick Pond.   Some of June's loveliest flowers in the reservations are

may find an early *iris versicolor,*—our native fleur-de-lis. And here, also, are the pink spikes of the water smartweed, *polygonum;* and, on the banks, the delicate, blue-eyed grass, and the lilac-colored, fragrant whorls of the wild mint.

Queen of all, is the white pond lily, our Lady of the Lake.   In the same pond is its cousin, in yellow, better named frog lily, because it loves the mud, and blooms contentedly there from May until August, unheeding the general indifference to the useful properties of its root.

WILD COLUMBINE   MEADOW LILY   JACK-IN-THE-PULPIT

Other very interesting bog and water plants may be studied at this season—the pitcher plant, the sundew and the utricularia. Most familiar is the pitcher-plant with its leaves shaped so wonderfully into woodland pitchers and its flowers so queerly constructed that somebody thought it looked like a sidesaddle—hence its name. A strange little plant is the sundew. It will close its round leaf about the end of your finger,—in the vain attempt to eat you, no doubt, thinking you a marvellous kind of spider! The utricularia is appropriately called bladderwort for its finely dissected leaves are covered with curious little glands filled with water while the plant is immersed, and until the time of flowering. Then, in some mysterious way, these bladders eject the water, fill with air, and so raise the plant to the surface of the pond, where it floats and rests in the sunshine until the time of its flowering is over and it wishes to ripen its seed. Then these wonderful contrivances eject the air, fill again with water, and the plant once more sinks to the bottom of the pond. These little organs have other duties beside keeping the flower afloat, they go fishing to catch the carnivorous food

which seems to be part of the *utricularia's* diet. It is well worth while to take Darwin's fascinating "Insectivorous Plants," and go to the Fells some August morning to interview this queer genus.

Some of the parasite flowers to be studied in June—and occasionally to be found in the Fells—are the dodder, tangling its golden threads about the nearest plant; the chestnut-colored squaw-root under some old oak tree in the southwestern part of the Reservation; the coral-root, with blossoms mottled with red, in Virginia Wood; and, in deep, moist woodlands, the Indian-pipe, sometimes called the ghost flower. The last is common in the Blue Hills.

On hot July days as we walk or drive along the wooded roads, we shall see the shining-leaved wild rose—*rosa lucida*—often hiding beneath the broad disks of the common elder. And all along in the wayside thickets are yellow hop clover, meadow sweet, white, feathery sprays of the New Jersey tea —*ceanothus*—downy hardhack, the tall meadow rue, and the pretty pink dogbane—*apocynum*. And there in the shelter of a stone wall stands the mullein wrapped even in July in wool,

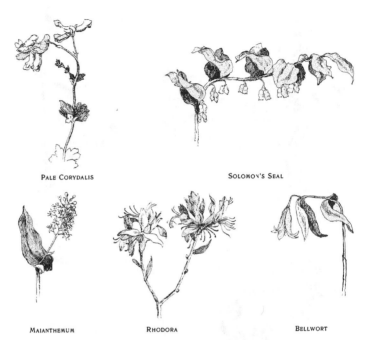

PALE CORYDALIS

SOLOMON'S SEAL

MAIANTHEMUM

RHODORA

BELLWORT

and sunning itself near the sumach bushes. By the way we find no less than four kinds of St. John's-wort, two of the species with their leaves dotted with oil glands, and their stamens done up in little parcels. And near by, it may be, appears the paler yellow of the linaria. The blue linaria and the thyme-leaved speedwell grow beside the wooded paths, in sunny places; and the dear little pinky-gray pussy clover runs fearlessly into the cart roads. In low, moist places we can gather monkey flowers, snake-heads—*chelone*— the fragrant heads of the button bush, and the bright yellow loosestrife. And, although we miss the harebells, we may expect to find a rare marsh bell-flower, if we search well for it. In moist, rich woods the partridge vine is at its prettiest now, bearing on the same sprays bright red berries and waxy white flowers.

On the sunny hillsides are the blue spikes of the wild lobelia, the yellow and purple Gerardias, and blue patches of the vetch—*vicia sativa*. The sleepy catchfly is common among the Blue Hills; and the little corn-speedwell is blooming in the Fells on Bear Hill.

Here is a partial list of the August flowers blooming only a little way out from the city.

In the fields and in the roadside thickets, mingling with, and following close after those we have been studying, are the wild clematis, appro-

PITCHER PLANT   NEW JERSEY TEA   LADY'S SLIPPER

TRILLIUM.

priately called the traveler's joy; the evening primrose, so beautiful at twilight time; and the day primrose, called sundrop, just as beautiful at daybreak; the wild carrot, better called, queen's lace; the white thoroughworts; the purple Joe-Pye weed; and those two little plants that grow the wide world over,—brunella and yarrow. Then comes all the golden glow of the wild sunflowers, the early goldenrods, black-eyed Susans, coreopses, tansy, groundsel, and fall dandelions.

Later come the tick trefoils—*desmodiums*—and the beggar ticks—*bidens,*—that in late August and early September ripen such interesting and troublesome fruit. Thoreau says of them,

"Though you were running for your life, they would have time to catch and cling to your clothes. Whole coveys of desmodiums and bidens seeds steal transportation out of us. I have found myself often covered, as it were, with an imbricated coat of the brown desmodium seeds, or a bristling *chevaux de frise* of beggar ticks, and had to spend a quarter of an hour, or more, picking them off in some convenient spot. And so they got just what they wanted— deposited in another place."

The twining wild bean bears its violet-scented blossoms at this time; and have you ever tried to disentangle it, endeavoring to get a perfect specimen, from its tuber root to its topmost clinging tendril, and not lose a single chocolate-colored blossom? And perhaps, further on in your drive, on a sandy patch in some old field you will find the *polygala sanguinea,* the blue curls, and

the sand spurrey, all so easily pulled up by the roots.

Down in the meadows, growing among the reeds and rushes, is the fragile arrowhead with its three white petals and its arrow-shaped leaves. And here are cardinal flowers; and that pretty little orchid, *spiranthes,* called ladies' tresses; and the nodding meadow lily; and, on higher ground the wild red lily erect and stately, with robes more rich than those of Solomon.

In late August and early September days we admire the lovely succory, generally blue as the sky, yet sometimes running the gamut of color through lavender to pink as delicate as that of the Gerardia. So friendly is it that it comes even into our dooryards. Yet it is so shy and wild, it will not have much to do with us, drooping when picked, like its contemporary, the blue curls, a kind of wild mint that cannot be domesticated as we have the catnip, for the benefit of our pussies.

Let us try to see how many we can find of the twenty or more different species of asters, and fifteen of golden-rod growing in the reservations about Boston. We all know the New England aster, and the heart-leaved, the zigzag-stemmed, the frost, the heather, and the lavender-colored swamp asters. The anise-scented goldenrod blossoms by the dry, woodland paths. It is common in both the Blue Hills and the Middlesex Fells; while the elmlike goldenrod,—*solidago ulmifo-lia,*—is rare, being only occasionally found in certain localities.

There are no gentians, although, as has been said before, the beautiful fringed gentian once grew in the Fells, upon land that is now filled in.

When we get into the late September and the October days, the pretty berries of autumn add to the beauty of the woods, although these berries have such a way of hiding! In George Macdonald's delightful story, "At the Back of the North Wind," the little boy, Diamond, calls the berries the birds' barn or storehouse.

In our search for the berries, the crimson bitter-sweet climbing over stone walls near Bear Hill shall not es-

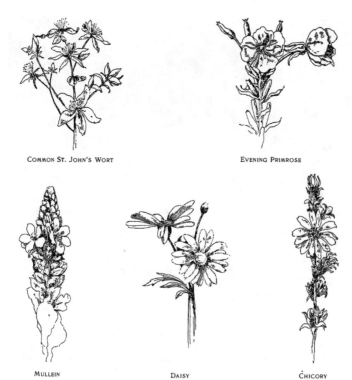

COMMON ST. JOHN'S WORT   EVENING PRIMROSE

MULLEIN   DAISY   CHICORY

cape us; nor the red berries of the mountain holly and the mountain ash. And here are the white berries of the kinnikinnik and the green briar; the blue of the woodbine, the sassafras and the alternate-leaved cornel with their blue berries on red stalks; and the dockmackie doing better than that, as it has berries that are at first red, then, afterward—as if discontented with the brighter color—changed to purple.

And now we come to the last flower of the year—the witch hazel. This is common at the feet of rocky slopes, in moist, shady places,—a bright lit-

tle blossom greeting us cheerily and almost as if it were wishing us a pleasant winter. Hamilton Gibson gives this charming description of the witch hazel:

"The waving pennants coiled for weeks within their patient buds, are now swung out from thousands of gray twigs in the copses, and the underwoods are lit up with the yellow halo from their myriads of fringed petals. These luminous blossoms are very well known to most dwellers in the country, but there is something else going on there among the twigs which few observers have suspected. It is a mischievous haunt out there among the witch hazels about this time. I shall never forget the caper it

NEW ENGLAND ASTER   WITCH HAZEL

played upon me years ago. While admiring the flowers I was suddenly stung in the cheek by some missile, and the next instant shot in the eye by another, the mysterious marksman having, apparently, let off both barrels of his gun directly in my face. I soon discovered him, an army of them, in fact, a saucy legion. These little sharp-shooters are the ripe pods of last year's flowers now opening everywhere among the yellow blossoms. Each pod contains two long, black, shining seeds of bony hardness. The pod splits in half, exposing the two white-tipped seeds. The edges of the horny cells contract against the sides of the seeds and finally expel them with surprising force, sometimes to the distance of forty feet. A branch of the unopened pods brought home and placed in a vase upon the mantel will afford considerable amusement, as the seeds rattle about the room singling out their whimsical targets, or perhaps career about from walls and ceilings to the glass lamp shade upon the table, or the evening news-paper of *pater familias,* or, possibly, the bald spot on his head."

With the passing of the witch hazel our procession of flowers in New England is over. And as we go home through the cool November woods, we say reverently, with Helen Hunt,

"I never knew before what beds,
Fragrant to smell and soft to touch,
The forest sifts and shapes and spreads;
I never knew before how much
Of human sound there is in such
Low tones as through the forest sweep
When all wild things lie down to sleep."

And as, through autumn storms and winter snow we await the buds and blossoms of another year, a happy sense of security makes sweet these days of waiting. For we know that the axe of the woodman will spare the magnificent forest trees of our reservations, and that no plough of tillage, or builders' tumultuous industry will invade these hills and dales in which the flowers of wood and field may bloom in their fragile beauty with none to make them afraid.

Honor to the men and women to whose long years of ceaseless labor in the cause we owe these reservations with their treasures of field and stream and forest. When Fame is writing names in letters of light, theirs will be among those she thus delights to so honor.

As It Was Written

By H. Knapp Harris

"I THOUGHT we were to give no more of these confounded formal dinner parties this season," growled Colonel Wentworth Billingham, pulling his mustache and looking bored and uncomfortable in his dress suit. Billingham was one of those men to whom a dress suit is so unbecoming that one almost wishes mankind had clung to the aboriginal loin cloth.

"I believe I did say so in a rash moment. But this is a special number, by request. Where do you like this rose best, Wentworth?"

Mrs. Billingham stood before the long pier glass meditatively pinning an American Beauty rose first in her hair, then in the corsage of her low-cut dinner gown and turning her small, well-poised head from side to side. It was in truth as scheming and far-seeing a little head as was ever set coquettishly upon a pair of very white shoulders. She had fine eyes, a vivacious manner, and the art of making one believe her much better looking than she really was. Part of it was due to her dressmaker, but more to her inborn tact, and that strain of French blood in her veins. Her American birth accounted for her fine eyes; her French blood taught her how to use them. On the stage she could have played the *ingénue* to perfection. On the stage of life she did a far more difficult part: she managed her husband with such

fine and subtle diplomacy that he went through life unconscious of the fact. No one would have resented it more vociferously than he, had he ever become conscious of being in leading strings. So delicate was the compliment he paid her finesse that he frequently alluded laughingly, in his bovine, bulky way, to a man he considered under petticoat tyranny with contemptuous irony. On these occasions little Mrs. Billingham's long lashes were always lowered demurely over the glint of humor that *would* shine from her big expressive eyes.

"There—I like it best in my hair," she said finally, fastening the rose with a long, vicious-looking hair-pin of the harpoon variety. "Right behind my ear, where Calvé always wears *hers.*"

As an instance of Mrs. Billingham's managerial tactics, they had taken a London house and had spent the past six months in the American colony. Billingham didn't really want to spend even six weeks in what he termed "this beastly English maelstrom." But his wife made him believe he did, which comes to much the same in the end. She convinced him that his liver was much more active in London than in New York. Though, in point of fact, Billingham's liver was less influenced by the climate than his temper, and his face always suggested a faded Naples yellow. What she really meant was that the damp and fog of the climate cleared out her own complexion, and the gayety and frivolity of life in the American colony suited her.

Billingham had made his money in pork, while his millionaire brother had made his in the manufacture of fine toilet soaps. Before leaving America, Mrs. Billingham felt on one occasion that she had run against her social Waterloo, when she chanced to overhear two women say in a spiteful aside: "Which Mrs. Billingham do you mean? Mrs. *Soap*—or Mrs. *Pork?*" But surely now, she thought, after six months abroad, and returning with a French maid and a valet with a heavy English accent, those snobbish Chicagoans would never dare speak of her so.

In another fortnight they would once more hear the American eagle flap its wings. Billingham was secretly as down with nostalgia as only a Western man can be who has lived and moved and had his commercial being in a sphere as far removed from formal London drawing rooms as the breezy heights of a cloud-capped mountain is from the artificial atmosphere of a horticulturist's force-house.

"The dinner is for that pretty little American heiress—Miriam Turner—you know, dear," said Mrs. Billingham.

She came up close and stood on tiptoe to straighten her liege lord's tie. "No one would suppose you had a valet, Wentworth," she laughed. "You always look so thrown together. There's always such a catch-as-catch-can air about the way your clothes are put on."

"You can't expect a man to accommodate himself late in life to a valet as he does to rheumatism and a bald head," growled the weary colonel, with a yawn. "I suppose, of course, that invertebrate little English lord will be here. That scheming Anglomaniac mother of Miriam's has at last succeeded in bowling him over. What other bores are to be on hand?" Mrs. Billingham smiled amiably.

"Lord Ainsley *will* be here, of course—it's a sort of an engagement announcement dinner, you know."

"Think of a bright little American girl like that marrying a brainless cad like Ainsley—with a monocle and a lisp. It's only because he's holding up a title that's bigger than he is. And it's only by the accident of birth that he got *that*."

The colonel glowered and sniffed with democratic disgust.

"Cigarettes," said he, "seem to be his only intellectual stimulant and he takes 'em regularly. Mrs. Turner has held Miriam like a broker does his stock until the quotations are raised. Those startling English waistcoats he wears are the only things with any character about him. If he ever amounts to anything in the House it will be because his wife injects a little American "go" into his four-century-old veins." He ran his hands through his stiff, upstanding bristle of grey hair as he mounted his favorite hobby and ambled off.

"I'd rather a daughter of mine should marry a wild and woolly Westerner with a rapid-firing career behind him—yes, by gad, than a titled nonentity with a glass screwed into one eye and a huge *boutonnière* in his coat lapel. It's a thundering shame! Why doesn't she marry a good, live, hustling American? Lord knows she's had chances enough. Miriam has simply been knocked down to the highest bidder," he raved.

Billingham had a great deal of that quality that made our ancestors plant their feet wide apart, and expand their chests, and invite George III. to come on. His Americanism was of the dyed-in-the-wool sort that is as pronounced as a Southern drawl.

Mrs. Billingham laughed softly and changed the rose from her hair to her corsage. She herself had none of those aggressive Americanisms. But it was part of her infinite wisdom and tact never to contradict her husband when he aired his favorite fads.

"If you made an exhaustive search for that little Englishman's brains," said he, "they'd be as hard to find as the man inside the Automaton Chess Player. He's the most aimless ass of my acquaintance. A fellow that screws a monocle into one eye, and sucks the head of his cane—"

"Why, I think *that's* when he's the very least objectionable," laughed Mrs. Billingham. "Because, you see, of course, he *looks* awfully stupid, still— you don't feel at all sure that he *is* till he takes his cane out, and opens his mouth."

"Humph," grunted Billingham as he stooped and stirred the logs on the hearth to a brighter flame. "Who else is coming? Any more Americans? A little leaven will lighten the whole loaf, you know."

"I depend upon Miriam," said Mrs. Billingham, "for my leaven. Oh, yes, and that bird-of-passage, your nephew, John Churchill. I'm sure *John's* democratic and American enough to leaven a whole bakery! He's promised to come. But a message at any moment saying he's off to South Africa or the North Pole would not surprise me. He's as nomadic as the Wandering Jew. Did you ever see so restless a soul? John always impresses me as a man searching frantically for something he never finds and can't be happy without. Like Sir Galahad and the Holy Grail, you know. I never knew a man who had had more attractive heiresses thrown at his head than John has. And he's as indifferent to them as a graven image. He doesn't seem to care for anything on earth but his old electrical inventions. Sir Henry Van Wick will be here, too."

"Great Scott! Another titled Englishman, and with my liver in the anæmic condition it's in now?"

"And the French Minister."

"He's the fellow who looks as if he ought to have been born in the days of frilled shirt bosoms and powdered wigs. And who else?"

"And his young wife. You're sure to like her, Wentworth. And then there's young McVeigh—he has just published those clever stories of Parisian-Bohemian life that have made such a hit, you know. He's my lion. The only one in the literary menagerie I've been able to get hold of. He doesn't *look* like a celebrity at all. In fact, in America, you'd probably pick him out as a clerk at the ribbon counter. And Mrs. Hemminger will be here. She's the widow of the Secretary of Something-or-other. I asked her because she is an aunt of Lord Ainsley. She has just emerged from crepe to heliotrope chiffon, and is awfully blue-stockingy and intellectual."

"It's all right for a woman to be intellectual," struck in the colonel, "if she didn't always *look* it so confoundedly, you know. Why can't a woman be intellectual and frizz her hair?" he added.

"Is it a conundrum, Colonel?" came the laughing query of a tall, superbly formed girl, who came toward them across the long room, having handed her wraps to a maid in the hall.

She walked with a peculiarly graceful undulating movement, trailing her long draperies with a silken swish behind her.

"Is it a conundrum, Colonel?" she laughed, with a flash of white teeth and a pretty uprising of her straight brows. She was a striking looking girl, Gibsonesque in her contours, and with a vivid coloring that suggested tropical skies. You wondered how she came by it; till you knew that her mother was of Spanish-American birth.

"By George! They have to import this sort of thing over here," said Billingham to his inmost soul. "Beauty like that isn't indigenous to the soil of the foggy little island."

*   *   *   *   *   *   *

A half hour later, Mrs. Billingham, taking her seat at the long table, cast an approving eye down its shining length. Though she was apparently engaged in animated conversation with the French Minister, who sat on her left, her all-seeing eye took in the smallest detail of the perfectly , appointed table. And in her inmost soul she sang a pæan of praise to her priceless *chef*. She wished she might take him home with her to that dear "land of the free," where they have a hundred religions and only one gravy. Out of the corner of her eye she watched Billingham tuck his napkin into the top button-hole of his waistcoat in that maddening way that always proclaimed his early Western environment and gave her inward qualms.

Mrs. Billingham was an undoubted genius in the rare art of getting the right people together. They had all met before except John Churchill, who had run the gamut of introduction in the drawing room. There was no embarrassing pause as they took their places at table and broke into a low murmur of perfectly-at-ease conversation.

Miriam Turner's low ripple of laughter at a *bon mot* of young McVeigh, who sat on her left, was like the soft throat-note of a thrush. She had known and liked him first when he was merely an impecunious reporter on one of the big dailies. And now that he had waked and found himself famous in a small way, the spirit of *camaradarie* was none the less pronounced between them.

The din of the down-town Babylon was muffled and afar off. Through the long French windows came the odor of mignonette from the tiny garden. The rumble of cabs over the asphalt and the sound of a passing band which brayed out "God Save the Queen" came softened by the distance. The candles flared under their ruffled shades. The sharp-visaged wife of the defunct Secretary, who wore her hair pushed straight back from a high, intellectual forehead, was well launched on her latest hobby and prosing on peacefully when Sir Henry Van Wick was heard contending amiably with Churchill. "But I didn't suppose *any* one really believed in elective affinities any more in this enlightened day and generation. I supposed *that* went out with crinolines, and powder, and patches, and periwigs, you know."

"What has John been saying?" laughed Mrs. Billingham, not catching the remark which had roused Sir Henry's spirit of controversy.

"John always has such debatable theories. They form part of his unique charm."

She favored Sir Henry with that madonna smile of hers.

"Mr. Churchill affirms his unshaken belief in the *outre* theory of the universal working of the principle of affinity."

Sir Henry hid a cynical smile behind his raised napkin.

"Seems to me that's as out of date as a discussion as to who wrote the Letters of Junius or on which side of Whitehall Charles the First was beheaded," beamed the French Minister, who was given to paying closer attention to the menu than to the exchange of conversational small change.

"Oh, I say, isn't that theory a trifle *passé*, you know," drawled Lord Ainsley, with his strident little cackle of a laugh.

Churchill's dark eyes shot a quick glance across the table at the little Englishman and the American girl, his fiancée. who sat next him. Her heavy-lidded eyes were hidden under the dark sweep of her long lashes.

"Are the principles that underlie all science and the immutable laws of nature ever *passé?*" asked Churchill dryly.

Lord Ainsley adjusted his monocle and gazed vaguely into space. Then he turned upon the severe-looking young man a smile that was childlike and bland. These aggressive Americans were always so frightfully in earnest.

"Really, you have me there, you know"—he lisped, and turned undivided attention to his dinner.

"I supposed those laws acted only upon chemical atoms and molecules," vouchsafed the intellectual widow, beaming amiably through her *pince nez* and scenting a battle afar, after the manner of the traditional warhorse. She liked young Churchill.

John was certainly a noticeable man, swarthy as a Spaniard and *distingué* in appearance. He had a temperament too imperious for modern social life, and he never scrupled to yield to its influence. He was wholly original and unconventional in his views, and, with no special contempt for the tenets of social. morality, he had a way of snapping his fingers and shrugging his shoulders at conventionalities that distinguished him from most men. He had a few theories that were peculiarly his own. Born in an earlier age of the world he might have made either a brigand or a martyr. He was distinctly alive to his finger tips, and not in the least that deplorable spectacle. a blasé young man. But always, through the veneer and polish of modern social luxurious life, shone the strong, marked personality of the man pure and simple. There coursed no milk-and-water in John's veins. Those deep-marked lines about the corners of his handsome mouth bespoke both tenderness and strength.

"Perhaps John made the remark in the same spirit which prompted young Emmerson to propose to Miss Van Flint"—laughed Mrs. Billingham, nibbling daintily at her ice. "You know he says that the reason was because he couldn't think of anything else to say, and the silence was becoming appalling."

When the laugh which followed had subsided, Churchill, who sat twisting the stem of his wine glass between his thumb and finger, shot a strange look, alert and watchful, across the table at the American girl opposite him. Her eyes were lowered and she was nervously fingering the violets which lay beside her plate.

"Yes," said Churchill, still with that fixed look on his thoughtful face—"yes, I certainly have an unshaken belief in the theory of elective affinities. Possibly because a strange little incident in my own life cemented the belief."

"Oh, how perfectly delightful!" gushed the petite, vivacious wife of the French Minister, bringing the full battery of her dimples into play. "You're going to give us the story, aren't you, Mr. Churchill?"

"And that at last accounts for John's declining to become a Benedict!" ejaculated Mrs. Billingham. "He has been waiting all these years for his affinity."

Her voice had a touch of amused incredulity. John was really her favorite nephew and she had always wondered how he would bear up under matrimonial trials.

"And you never found her, John?" she asked, her eyes shining with mirth.

"Yes, I found her," said Churchill.

His dark saturnine face flushed. All eyes were turned toward him as he leaned back in his chair, one hand still twirling his wine glass.

"'Tis better to have loved and lost than never to have loved at all," quoted Sir Henry inanely, in an abortive attempt to dispel the vague, indefinable impression that the situation was portentous.

"It was on one of the Italian lakes," said Churchill, in his soft, low-pitched voice. His expression was retrospective, and he seemed looking into a long vista of the past. The American girl leaned forward to pin the violets in her gown and her fingers trembled nervously.

"The night was divine," went on Churchill. "A harvest moon sailed in a sky as clear and translucent as only an Italian sky can be. I had been drifting about in a small row-boat for hours, basking in the moonlight, and had taken up the oars to row ashore. Just ahead of me a flight of stone steps ran from the water's edge up to a vine-covered villa on the shore. A tall, slender girl in a white gown stood, balancing herself in a small boat a few feet from shore. She had an oar in her hand and was trying to turn the boat about. Some one singing snatches from Il Trovatore on the shore trilled out in a high sweet tenor, 'Non ti scordar di me.' The girl turned her head to listen. The heavy oar fell splashing from her hand. She lurched forward to recover it and losing her balance fell with a smothered scream into the water. I dropped my oars and sprang in after her. We were only a few feet from the foot of the steps, but the water was deep and she clung about my neck with the sob of a frightened child."

The girl across the table made a strange sound in her throat like an indrawn breath that chokes down a cry. She had the frightened look of a trapped bird that struggles to escape the snare.

"As I struggled up on to the lower step," went on Churchill, still with that air of dreamy retrospection—"she still clung with one bare arm about my neck. And in that trance-like moment and only in that one moment in life have I—lived. And by a strange and subtle intuition—vague and indefinable—I know that she too was conscious that the wind of destiny had swept us thus together. There are sub-conscious moments in life when spirit is paramount. She is the one woman in the world whose soul's harmony is attuned to mine."

Churchill's voice had taken on a peculiar, vibrating quality as of one recalling an exquisite memory. His eyes had never once left the face of the girl opposite him. She lifted her wine glass to her lips. With a sudden turn it fell from her hand, snapped at its slender base.

"Oh, how unpardonably awkward of me!" she gasped in a choking voice, as its contents went in a red splash upon the cloth.

A servant behind her, leaning forward, quietly took up the broken glass.

"Then you found her only to lose her?" asked Sir Henry, with his enigmatical smile. He was secretly horrified in his British conservative soul at what he considered the escapade of a young man sowing a flourishing field of wild oats.

"Only to lose her," said Churchill. "She slipped from my arms with a laugh that was more than half a sob and disappeared like a wraith up those shadowy steps. Under the olive trees she paused, looked back, and waved me a farewell with her white hand. The notes of that soft-voiced singer on the shore came clear and soft, '*Non ti scordar di me.*' Was it my overwrought fancy, or did I hear the girlish voice echo the line, I wonder?"

Churchill paused. Though the eyes of all at table were upon him the girl opposite him, who had slowly lost her color, kept her heavily fringed lids lowered.

"Wasn't it on that tour through the Italian lakes that you met with that accident to your foot?" asked Mrs. Billingham as Churchill paused.

"That very night. In springing from my boat a half hour later I slipped and fell, wrenching my ankle in a way that kept me a prisoner in my room for weeks. The first day that I could painfully hobble out on crutches I made inquiry at the villa. I found that it was a one-time private residence converted into a tourists' hôtel. 'How should he know to whom the Signore referred'—asked the gesticulating little landlord with a broad sweep of his pudgy hands, 'since the Signore did not know himself the name by which she was known.' I believe they thought me a harmless lunatic, escaped from my keeper. I haunted the place for weeks and made untiring inquiry. Then I started in search of her."

A strange indefinable change had come over the face of the American girl, who raised her eyes to her hostess as if asking permission to go; then lowered them swiftly again as Churchill continued:

"I have always known that I should some time find her," with an intense look at the girl across the table, "and wherever she is, and by whatever claim another holds her—she is *mine.*"

Even Sir Henry's well-disciplined old heart gave a little jump under the thrill in Churchill's voice.

The sparkling eyes of the little Frenchwoman were shining and aglow with changing lights like an opal.

The wife of the defunct Secretary

leaned forward excitedly, forgetful of her theory of molecules and atoms.

Mrs. Billingham was thinking that she had never before realized what a handsome fellow John was. He had more force and *empressement* of manner than any man she had ever known. Contrasted to that colorless little Englishman, he gave her a glowing feeling of pride in her own countrymen.

"I shall hold out my hand to her," said Churchill, "and she will come to me. By every law of love and life—she is *mine.*"

The face of the girl across the table, which had been white to the lips, suddenly flushed with a wave of color. She raised her face and their eyes met. The look that passed between them was like a flash of fire.

With a little embarrassed laugh Mrs. Billingham gave the signal to rise, and with a soft rustle and swish of draperies the ladies left the room. When the men had again taken their seats in the dining room, and cigars and liqueurs were passed, Churchill, who sat leaning back silently in his chair, turned his head suddenly and listened. His face was tense with repressed excitement. Muffled and soft from the piano in the drawing room came the tender refrain:

"Non ti scordar di me."

He got to his feet and tossing aside his cigar started impulsively for the drawing room. Then suddenly realizing the unconventionality of the action turned and came back. With his elbow on the table he sat listening, still with that strained, alert look. A girl's voice, with a peculiarly vibrating note in its plaintive quality, followed the accompaniment of the Italian love song. Clear and sweet it trilled the familiar refrain. Churchill raised his head from his hand. His lips parted, and the smouldering light in his sombre eyes leaped into sudden flame.

When they entered the drawing room, the American girl stood turning over the loose music on the piano. Lord Ainsley, with his jaunty little walk, which bordered upon a swagger, strolled over and stood beside her. Churchill, after wandering aimlessly about the room a moment, stepped out through one of the high open windows onto the balcony which overhung the garden. With his hands clasped behind his head he stood leaning against a vine-covered pillar in the moonlight. He was watching the face of the girl by the piano. Through the high French window he saw her flush with sudden color as she slipped a diamond band from her finger, stammering with embarrassment broken words of explanation and apology. The ring slipped from her nervous fingers and rolled with glittering scintillations across the floor. The little Englishman's face wore a look of blank amazement. He picked the ring up with a stiff little bend of his immaculately groomed person and held it out to her. Churchill could not hear her words, but her face was a study. She stepped back and held her hands behind her. Her lips moved in a singular way. She drew them in and held her full lower lip with her teeth.

Lord Ainsley looked as if he were balancing between the Scylla of doubt and the Charybdis of horrible certainty. She stepped back and spoke again chokingly as he offered the ring to her. He evidently understood *then*, beyond a peradventure. He dropped the ring into his waistcoat pocket and took his *congé* with the same stilted ceremonious smile with which he would have accepted an invitation to dine. He was the sort of fellow who, if given a deadly stroke in battle, would have saluted his officer before he fell.

Like a somnambulist, the girl walked slowly to the open casement. Standing there, the moonlight white on her bare shoulders, she caught her breath in a quick sob. Churchill, whose swarthy face was illumined with a sudden inward light, saw her start, hesitatingly, toward him. He stepped forward and held his hands out with an imperious gesture.

"I have always known that I should some time find you again. It was written," he said, breathlessly. His face had grown strangely white as she came straight toward him across the moonlit veranda.

"Oh why—were you—so long?" she half laughed, half sobbed, as he caught her hands and drew her to him, silencing her lips from further question.

Steel Ship-building in Massachusetts

By Ralph Bergengren

THE proverbial readiness and energy of American shipbuilders—qualities that in the War of 1812 produced a victorious fleet at hardly more than a day's notice and for many years delayed the growth of the present United States Navy on the assumption that the feat could be repeated at will—are illustrated anew in the building up in less than a year and a half of a new steel shipyard at Quincy, Massachusetts, by the Fore River Ship and Engine Company, which is already engaged in the construction of two first-class battle-ships, two torpedo boat destroyers, a protected cruiser, and the first seven-masted schooner ever constructed, an aggregate of 44,500 tons.

The rapid growth of so great an enterprise is naturally picturesque. Its broader interest, however, lies in the fact that the new yard has reestablished shipbuilding as an important Massachusetts industry, providing the State, almost at a single stroke, with a shipbuilding plant that is to be compared only with Cramp's, the Newport News Company, or the Union Iron Works of San Francisco; with one, that is, of the four most important in the country. Two years ago it was supposed that shipbuilding was almost a dead industry in the old Commonwealth, lingering only in the construction of an occasional wooden barque or schooner and in the building in and about Boston of yachts, small torpedo boats, a revenue cutter or two, and the like minor craft. It had become practically a thing of the past in its old haunts at New Bedford, Scituate, Gloucester, where the first schooner was launched early in the eighteenth century, or at Germantown, near the present Fore River Yard, where in 1789 the Massachusetts, at that time the largest vessel ever constructed in America, first took the water.

Various causes had contributed to this decline. The chief one was the increased freight charges upon the raw material of the wooden ship as delivered at Boston and nearby ports, which had first handicapped the industry and then slowly put Massachusetts shipbuilders—North Shore and South Shore alike—quite out of all practical competition with more favored places. It was at first expected that the same conditions would affect the building of steel as well as of wooden vessels, but steel, it appears, can now be delivered in Boston at a cost that in our modern steel-building age eliminates all advantages which the rate on wood had previously given to other localities.

In answer to these new conditions the Fore River yard has arisen as by magic, although the new plant, while equipped with all the essentials of the work in progress, is still in an intermediate state between the open meadow of two years ago and the final completion of the plans of the company. Enough, however, has been done to assemble all its parts and departments in active and effective cooperation. More interesting still is the fact that as it comprises an entirely new equipment it is not only the youngest but in many respects the most modern and up-to-date of American shipyards, and as such is attracting the attention of shipbuilders the world over.

The plan and operation of the new yard are naturally an exceptionally interesting object lesson in the development of the ship from wood to steel. The great trees of the forest, the raw material of former shipyards, have been replaced by enormous steel ingots which a 20-ton hammer pounds into preliminary condition. The smell of pine and cedar has been replaced by that of oil and laboring steel, the sound of the axe by the reverberation of metal upon metal, the "gee" and "haw" that once directed the lazy movements of slow-footed oxen by the puffing of a locomotive, and the buzz of augers by the incisive whirr of drills biting into steel. Nevertheless, for those who seek romance, there is the same magic of human activity as in the days gone by; the difference lies in the increased size of the ship, in the problems of handling the masses of metal that must be pounded, forged, bent, and moulded to the work of construction; and in the control of the great machines, still man-built and operated, that the modern shipbuilder has enrolled like so many captive Titans to do his hauling, lifting, and hammering.

The Fore River yard, whether in present or in prospective equipment like all the great plants with which it has entered into competition, is an excellent example of the almost human dexterity with which the man behind the machine may seem to endow the machine itself. At the plate yard is a great crane with a span of 150 feet, to pick up the plates of steel and carry them where they are wanted. In the forge another crane, operated by five

electric motors controlled by a man who directs them from a cage suspended from the crane itself, will soon carry a 75-ton forging straight ahead from one end of the big building to another, or diagonally in any direction—lifting, lowering, turning it end for end, or tipping it bottom up. Along the still uncompleted seawall of the receiving basin the foundations are being laid for a powerful gantry crane to be used for carrying boilers or engines to their exact places in the ships under construction. This gantry crane, moving on tracks 50 feet apart at a rate of 500 feet a minute, promises, indeed, to be one of the interesting novelties of the yard, superseding the old fashioned stationary crane which made it necessary for each ship to be moved to and fro under it to receive its armor plate, engines, and other equipment. When erected the crane will have an elevation of 108 feet, its arm extending 80 feet beyond the edge of the wharf so

288

as to reach every part of the ship, and capable of bearing a load of 25 tons at that distance, or of 75 tons when the reach is of 50 feet and the heaviest material—that intended for the centre of the ship—is being handled. Tipped upward to an angle of 45 degrees the arm still serves as a "shears" for setting up military masts or the stacks of battleships, and then take an upright position so that the ship may pass by. The gantry crane will be the giant of the yard, but eight other cranes, hardly less remarkable for the ingenuity with which they will do their work, are soon to be added to the present equipment, by means of which each of four ships, in process of construction side by side, will have the exclusive service of two cranes capable of carrying tons of steel as rapidly as a workman could run.

No less interesting are the big hammer and anvil of the forge, the mechanism of which is simply that of the old fashioned smithy grown so enormously big that if the force were received directly on the ground surface a single blow of the hammer on the anvil would make the workmen topple like so many tin soldiers when a croquet ball is dropped on the floor of a play room. The largest hammer, weighing some 20 tons, and, with the exception of the Midvale hammer, in Pennsylvania, which is about the same feet apart, rest upon independent granite and solid timber foundations, so that altogether the effect of the anvil vibrations is reduced to a minimum. None of this foundation is visible when one enters the forge house, a lofty building lit by the fires of a half dozen furnaces and by the daylight that struggles dimly through the smoky windows. The anvil apparent-

BUILDING A SEVEN MASTED SCHOONER

size, the largest in operation in the country, rises 30 feet above the anvil, which in turn extends 20 feet below the ground and rests finally upon a ledge of granite which conveniently underlies the forge house. From this natural foundation rises a complication of hard pine timbers to a height of eight feet, supporting a pyramid of seven 30-ton plates of cast iron. The legs of the hammer frame, 14 ly rests directly upon the ground and the fall of the hammer upon glowing steel suggests rather relentless determination than its own great weight. The actual blow may range, moreover, from a mere touch to the impact given by 20 tons of metal dropping nine feet and further aided by steam pressure at 100 pounds to the inch.

In systematizing its work Fore River follows the plan adopted by the

United States Navy Department, separating the vessel in process of construction into "hull" and "machinery," although the whole plant, including for convenience seventeen distinct departments, can be called upon for service by either the superintendent of hulls or the superintendent of machinery, both of whom are under the general manager and general superintendent of the yard. The hull division is con-

chinery to the required size. It then passes through a planer which smooths the edges and trims them to the nicety of proportion necessary to make a watertight joint between connecting plates. Then the plate goes to another building where it passes under a heavy roll of steel that bends it to the curve of the part of the ship that it is to cover, following a wooden pattern already constructed from the lines laid

FORGE AND ANNEALING PLANT

cerned with the plates, frames, and general construction of the ship, and the machinery division with the engines, boilers, and other machinery; the one, it might be said, prepares the body, the other the vital forces, of the ship. The progress of a plate from its arrival at the yard to its final place on the side of a ship illustrates very well this division of labor and detail in modern ship construction. This plate is first "pickled" to remove dust and dirt, and then cut by special ma-

down in the mould loft. If it is destined to become part of the bow or stern it must be made pliable by heat and beaten with sledges until it attains the proper shape. When it has roughly achieved this shaping it is reheated and again beaten until the surface is perfectly smooth and regular and the plate itself is ready to be riveted on, when the car of a small gravity road carries it to the ship's side.

The machinery department receives its raw material not in plates but in

steel ingots, castings, rods, tubings, and the many other forms of material that are to be transformed into engines, cranks, shafts, and other machinery. This material must pass through the forge, where the ingot loses its identity and assumes roughly its final shape, and from there to the machine shop, in which the largest lathes are capable of handling a 100-foot shaft, and where, in the case of the 55-foot pieces required by the battleships now building, a five and one half inch tool bites its way from one end of the solid steel shaft to the other. From the machine shop the shaft goes to the annealing plant, where it is first heated in a 52-foot vertical furnace and then transferred to an oil bath of similar proportions.

Then it is ready to undergo the government test, which requires that a square inch of the metal, so ductile that a test bar from it can be bent almost double on a short radius, must be able to resist a pulling force equivalent to a suspended weight of 95,000 pounds.

Under the machine shop, which stands on the seawall, an open subway is in process of construction that is intended to cooperate with the gantry crane in transporting machinery from shop to ship. The usual practice has first been to set up an engine, for example, in the shop, and then, the engine having been pronounced perfect, to take it to pieces and set it up again, like a great puzzle, in the ship itself. Crane and subway will in

MOULD LOFT AT FORE RIVER

a great measure obviate this necessity. An ordinary engine, set up and tested in the shop, will be lowered through a trap into a flat car in the subway and so moved outside the building to the crane. The crane will pick it up bodily, carry it along the wall to the ship, and there gently lower it into its resting place.

All these activities, of course, require their motive power, and it is not surprising in our electrical age and in so new a plant to find that electricity almost entirely supplies this need. An aggregate of 1400 horse power is distributed from the power house to the yard by over one hundred motors. Nearly every machine, including the three 116-foot lathes already mentioned as unique in the manufacturing plants of the United States, has its own motor, so that the absence of belts and steam jets is one of the essential

evidences of the difference between the modern shipyard and the shipyard of even ten years ago, not to speak of fifty or a hundred. All riveting, however, is done by pneumatic power, and for this purpose compressed air at 100 pounds pressure to the square inch is carried all over the yard, some eighty acres in area—much as the water companies of the modern city convey water to each separate house. Electricity is supplied to the floating machine shop, an idea suggested by the Vulcan which the government fitted out during the Spanish War for the purpose of repairing navy vessels in active service. As practically employed, however, it is to be reckoned as still another of the mechanical novelties which make the new yard so notable an expression of Yankee energy. Unlike the Vulcan, the floating shop is intended for economy

BUILDING BERTHS

rather than emergency, and is practically a complete workshop that may be moored beside a vessel undergoing repairs, thus not only providing for a greater number of vessels but moving an entire repair outfit to the spot where its services are most immediately required and can be most economically employed.

The working force of the yard, it is estimated, will eventually number about three thousand men. The settlement now includes about half that number, and it is interesting to know, in view of the expected growth of the colony, that the company officials, not as a corporation, but as individuals, have bought an old estate which will be sold in lots to the workmen. The shipworkers, machinists, pattern makers, woodworkers, blacksmiths, laborers and seamen, draughtsmen, paint-

ers and foundrymen may themselves buy stock in this experiment, which is not a speculation but intended rather to be a form of loan and building association with capital already provided.

It has already been said that the Fore River yard has been busy developing its own resources at the same time that it is busy with government and other contracts amounting in the aggregate to about $9,000,000, and including two of the most important vessels in the United States Navy, the great battleships New Jersey and Rhode Island. The question arises naturally, how could the newest shipbuilding plant in the country have obtained such contracts in competition with her long established rivals? The answer might, indeed, be said to lie partly in the ledge of Quincy granite that outcrops so fortunately under the

great anvil of the forge, but it is more exact to attribute it, first to the plans outlined for the erection and carrying on of the plant; second to the possession of resources sufficient to insure the probable success of the plans; and finally to the excellence of the site as a whole, which is remarkably adapted to the purposes of shipbuilding. Originally it was a big meadow separated from the ocean by a beach of hard pan gravel and intersected by a small river, the Weymouth Fore River, whence the Company takes its name, and a tributary creek. The nature of the beach has made it possible to lay down the granite and concrete ship ways for the big battleships without the customary use of piles, and the water which it skirts leads directly and immediately to the deep water of Boston Harbor, while creek and river are well adapted for the building of smaller craft. In addition to the gran-

284

ite ledge that, as already pointed out, seemed placed on purpose for the forge, there was a natural soft bottom for the outfitting basin, and the famous Quincy granite for foundations and seawall was within easy teaming distance. The spot itself is only two miles from the centre of Quincy,—still remembering its two sons, John and John Quincy Adams, who became Presidents of the United States, but nowadays taking on more and more the character of a bustling centre of business and manufacturing—and is within the limits of metropolitan Boston. Being new-born, moreover, the Company has no accumulation of old and only partly serviceable machinery for which to make allowance in its contracts and promises, and could plan for its equipment without reservations; that is to say, it could look forward to quick, economical and efficient construction on a

THE TWENTY TON HAMMER

basis of completely modern mechanism. The plant was hardly more than planned when the Company entered its bids for Government work, and was so well under way when the government experts were sent to investigate it, they were able to report that first-class battleships could be constructed at the new Massachusetts yard as well, and perhaps more economically, than at any other.

Aside from purely commercial reasons, the revival of Massachusetts shipbuilding, signalized by the erection of this new shipyard at the southernmost inlet of Boston Harbor, is of more than local, or even sectional, interest. Not only is it a very large straw among the many now blowing toward a re-awakening of American maritime endeavor, but it continues the industry in Massachusetts in a straight line of descent from so long ago as 1631, when the Blessing of the Bay was built in Medford. The poorness of the soil and the absence of precious minerals and metals were doubtless the determining forces that almost immediately turned the early colonists to fishing and navigation, and it is a curious coincidence that this first vessel was launched on July 4th, just 145 years before that date received its permanent importance in American history. Ten years later, in 1641, Edward Bangs launched at Plymouth the

autumn of 1625 on a trading voyage to the Kennebec River. At the mouth of the Kennebec itself was built in 1607—that is, even before the landing of the Pilgrims at Plymouth—a "fair pinnace of 30 tons," named the Virginia, the first New England built craft. She was big enough to have crossed the Atlantic. Of the smaller vessels of that period there remains,

THE FORE RIVER BEACH

bark, of some 40 or 50 tons, which was recorded as being the "first vessel of size" built in the colony, and was estimated to cost £200—perhaps $5,000 today. Of smaller boats, the record has practically vanished. In 1624, however, it is known that a sloop carpenter came over to Plymouth, dying soon after, but not until he had built at least two shallops, one of which, laden with corn, sailed in the

as just said, hardly any definite description, but we know from the old records that coasting, fishing and trading were increasingly important industries, and that shallops, sloops, pinnaces, barks, and ketches were built and navigated, although it would be difficult to reconstruct the exact details of masts, spars, sails or rigging.

The history of Massachusetts ship-building, though the first vessel must

be credited to the shores of the Kennebec—which, after all, was at least
nominally a Massachusetts river—
contains also several events that were
the first of their kind in the larger history of the whole nation. Thus, in
1645, the "Rainbowe" commanded by
one Captain Smith sailed out of Boston for Madeira, and on her way back
touched on the coast of Guinea for
slaves. The venture involved a false
pretense of quarrel with the natives,
a murderous attack upon them, and
two slaves as a part of the cargo of the
returned "Rainbowe," which accordingly is recorded as the first American
craft engaged in the slave traffic. It
is interesting to know, however, that
Boston returned the slaves to their
original home, and only the fact that
the court decided that it had no jurisdiction over Captain Smith's actions
on the African coast saved him from
a conviction for "murder, manstealing,
and Sabbath-breaking." About 1714
the first schooner ever built was

launched at Gloucester. She was a
development of the earlier and now obsolete ketch, and tradition still points
out the wharf where she took the
water. The name schooner, suggested
by a bystander who exclaimed, "Oh,
how she scoons!"—an exclamation
that will have meaning to anyone who
remembers that peculiar motion of a
flat pebble skipped or "scooned," over
the surface of a large body of water—
was perhaps intended first as an individual designation, but the craft was
of a new type, and the name soon
gained its present significance. The
Great Republic, in her time the largest
sailing vessel in the world, must be
mentioned as another noteworthy product of Massachusetts ship-building,
and the new seven master, now building at Fore River, looks back to both
of these achievements in that she will
be the first seven masted schooner and
the largest of all contemporary sailing
craft, competing in size, not only with
the old-school square rigger, but with

the modern ocean steam ship. The first water line model, invented in 1794 by Mr. Orlando B. Merrill, of Belleville, now a part of Newburyport, belongs also to the above category, and was an important step from the eighteenth to the nineteenth century yard. as at Fore River, where practically every problem is worked out in the preliminary models of which this is the first recorded instance. In the old yard which produced the host of wooden vessels, sloops, schooners, pinkeys, pinnaces, brigs, Chebacco boats, jiggers and all the others that made possible the merchantmen, whalers, slavers, pirates and ships of war that figure so picturesquely in the annals of the eighteenth century, the master workman, it will be remembered, lined out each piece to fit its final place in the ship. The stem and stern posts were first set up and the workmen began amidships, working fore and aft as the timbers were filled in. The broad axe, whipsaw, adze, and pod auger were the tools and wooden tree nails—"trunnels" as they

were, and are pronounced—were the means of fastening the ship together.

There is an amusing tradition, which well illustrates the general distribution of old time shipbuilding, that the first Chebacco boat, a craft once much used in the New England fisheries, was built in a barn and could only be launched after the absentminded builder had removed part of the roof and walls. The story shows also the custom of building these earlier and smaller craft often a mile or more from water, and then mounting them on wheels to drag them to the place of launching. This condition naturally disappeared rapidly with the increase in the size of sailing vessels, dating from the early nineteenth century. The growth of the schooner is the most concrete example of this increase in size, continuing to mount but two masts until well into the nineteenth century, and now, at the beginning of the twentieth, about to appear, in this great Fore River craft, with seven masts and 43,000 square feet of sail area and to extend one hundred feet beyond the cruiser Des

Moines building alongside. Not only that, but in her the schooner is apparently entered definitely in the class of steel constructed vessels, with battleships and ocean steamers. Indeed, if a craft is to survive, it is almost a case of steel or nothing nowadays, although less than three-quarters of a century ago, the chief architect of one of the English yards exclaimed indignantly, "Don't talk to me about iron ships; it's contrary to nature!"—a statement on which the seventy-five acres at Fore River are in many ways the most interesting because the most purely modern commentary.

The Regeneration of Young Hawley

By Neill Sheridan

S HE came to Manila with the first consignment of Red Cross nurses, as the correspondent of an American newspaper, and in one day she drove her calesa up and down the Luneta through the golden dusk, and over the hearts of the whole mess of the First Volunteer Infantry. She was young, small, and not beautiful. She had no color at all. Her figure owed so much to art, the Red Cross nurses said—though that might have been envy—that the little nature had done was overlooked in the total result altogether. But her gowns, sheer white for the most part, were perfect after their kind, her green eyes were the large eyes men fall into and drown, and her smile the revelation of unutterable things. And although she was young, as years went, she had been born old in that measureless guile that comes from the serpent.

She had all the officers of the transport that brought her across the Pacific at outs before the boat reached Hono-

lulu, and all the women on board hated her with perfect ferocity. The mess of the First called upon her, and went down to a man. Even the Adjutant, who had a dragon and some well-grown nestlings at home, quartered at the Presidio, and who was regarded as proof, struck his colors and took her for a ride on one of the regimental Tagalog ponies out beyond the Pasay cross-road. That was the scene of his gallant action during the siege of Manila.

But the worst hit were the Major-doctor and young Hawley. That was plain from the first. And she was impartial. Also, she rode and drove, at odd times, with naval officers from the fleet, and she was not averse to receiving, now and again, a private who came well recommended. There were the sons of millionaires in the ranks f the First, and Lydia Fairish could gild brass buttons and a plain blue coat with paternal gold as well as another. More than that, she was a young woman who had not been born with any illusions, which are apt to be troublesome things to an enterprising spirit.

Miss Fairish rode out with the Major-doctor in the morning, and even went one day to the smallpox hospital with him, upon the plea that she wanted to get a story for her paper. The Colonel raved when he heard about it, and the whole mess sent the Major-doctor to Coventry and the brandy bottle for daring to risk her life—but Miss Fairish came to dinner at the mess that night, and laughed at the Colonel and sent glances from her soft eyes so straight into the heart of every man there that not one of them but would have jumped off the balcony into the Pasig, and taken her with him if she had ordered it. Each man reprobated not the less the conduct of the Major-doctor. Moreover, he had a wife and a family of small children at home, as every man there knew.

It befell, therefore, that Miss Fairish presently heard all about the domestic concerns of the Major-doctor, with the result that she made not the slightest difference in her treatment of him. It was at this juncture one of the Red Cross nurses said that she had been born wicked as well as wise. Women are malicious, but that seems to be the usual human combination.

But if the Major-doctor found favor in the morning, young Hawley found favor and also a seat in her calesa when she drove on the Luneta in the tropic dusk. The Spanish women, disdainful of their conquerors, were driven there in the dusk also by liveried coachmen, but if one of them deigned a glance at the bold young woman who outraged the proprieties by sitting beside a man and herself trying the paces of her fast pony, Miss Fairish never knew it.

"The poor things must have a stupid time of it," she said to young Hawley, flicking her pony, and that youth would have laid his whole prospect of the paternal millions at her feet if she had let him. No man knows how, but a girl not yet out of her teens can keep a lover skating along the thin edge of a proposal for months, and not let him break through. Miss Fairish was a long way out of her teens, and also she had been born wise.

Now it chanced that young Hawley had also some domestic responsibilities at home. The story was told in various ways. Miss Fairish soon heard it, in all its variety, as she heard most things—and she let it make not the slightest difference in her treatment of young Hawley. That innocent youth never really knew how wise she was. There is a strong repressive force about the woman men know to have claws, even though she keeps them in sheath.

The larger portion of the mess dropped out after awhile, leaving the running to the Major-doctor and young Hawley, with a navy lieutenant or two whom nobody considered. The comedy went on, for a couple of months, to the intense amusement of the spectators, and to the enjoyment, as it appeared, of the principals. Her mornings were given to the Major-doctor and her afternoons to young Hawley, with rigid impartiality. The rivalry became the subject of betting in the mess, at last. Everything did, sooner or later. In the meantime transports were coming and going across the sea to San Francisco, and these ships sometimes carried tales not of war. It was in September, and the monsoon was sweeping the black clouds against the hills that lie close about the Laguna de Bai, and the hush of the coming rains was in the air, when the curtain went up on the last act.

The First had been relieved from duty at the Palace of Malacanan, and removed across the river to the old barracks of the Spanish Marine Infantry. The transport Senator came up the bay one afternoon, driving ahead of the monsoon, and the men at headquarters were counting upon getting their letters at dinnertime. Miss Fairish dined at the mess that night. She had no chaperon—but, then, she needed none. She had made that fact patent from the first. The letters came in with the dessert, and the Major-doctor, who had got her seated at his end of the table and consequently scored in young Hawley's time (leaving that youth scowling among the juniors), was observed to become greatly perturbed upon reading one of the missives brought to him. It was the custom to read home letters as soon as they were brought in, at Manila, and even Miss Fairish had her mail sent to headquarters that night. The Major-doctor read his letter, excused himself hastily, and then went out and called the Colonel after him. Young Hawley, smiling once more, slipped into the doctor's vacant seat, and the discussion of the home news became general. The Colonel came back presently, smiling.

"The Major's family is on board the Senator," he said.

The whole table smiled. Young Hawley fairly beamed, but he said nothing. The lad was a thoroughbred.

"How pleasant for him," Miss Fairish said, and every man there saw that she honestly meant it. Also, it began to dawn upon the dullest, even, that her hand was visible in this thing. The expression on young Hawley's face was cherubic. The Major-doctor rejoined the company when they had adjourned to the Colonel's room, having been unable to board the transport that night, and Miss Fairish went straight up to him.

"I am so glad, for your sake, Major," she said. "You need not be lonesome now. Will you not let us go on board with you to-morrow to welcome them to Manila?"

Young Hawley glared, but the Major-doctor jumped at it. You have perhaps observed how frail a straw sometimes serves the purpose of a drowning man.

"You should head a delegation from the mess, Colonel," she went on. "Mr. Hawley would be glad to go, I am sure, and the Adjutant, and Captain Jones and Mr. Smithers." The elect testified their delight, and young Hawley was again in the clouds.

The whole party was on hand next morning at the office of the Captain of the Port, where the Government launches lay, and they were very gay as they steamed down the Pasig and out upon the rough waters of the bay— very gay, all but the Major-doctor. Gaiety is not in the part when a man is being led to execution. The Major-doctor behaved well, on the whole, but chastened. One would have thought that the *Mrs.* Major-doctor was going to smother Miss Fairish with the fervor of her embraces. And young Hawley stood apart and chewed his moustache and grinned. That was in appreciation of his own superior acumen in fathoming the manner of the undoing of the Major-doctor.

The Senator had a saloon and state-rooms between decks, and presently Miss Fairish, breaking away from the embraces of the Mrs. Major-doctor and the narration of the last bit of interesting domestic experience, fluttered like a bird down the companion-way into the saloon, with young Hawley in her train. It was dark in the saloon, after the tropical sunlight, and nobody noticed the little woman seated at the piano, strumming softly, until Miss Fairish bent over her and kissed her. Then the little woman arose; there was a cry, "Oh, John!" and she had her arms around the neck of young Hawley. He had to stand and hold her up. She would have fallen otherwise. But he looked unutterably foolish; and he said things, softly.

"Speak to me, John," the little woman said, between laughing and crying. "You are not angry? The doctor's wife wanted a nurse, and I had to come. I could not stay away any longer.

Young Hawley was not exactly a brute. He was taken by surprise—and Miss Fairish was present. Matters adjusted themselves after a little.

There were three women and three children in the launch that took the party back to the city, but neither the Major-doctor nor young Hawley so much as looked at Miss Fairish on the way. There are some things the boldest men may not venture to do. But she was dangerously sweet to the other two women.

The Major-doctor took up separate quarters at once, and presently obtained his discharge and went home. Children do not thrive in that climate. Young Hawley also took up separate quarters. That was proper. But it is a curious thing that within a week neither of those women would speak to Miss Fairish. They had got on swimmingly before that.

She did not seem to mind it in the least. "I am used to the ingratitude of my own sex," she said plaintively to the Colonel. Then she married a navy lieutenant, and went off with him to the China station, leaving the First desolate. They attended her farewell in a body, and looked their reproaches.

Two Foreign Schools and Their Suggestions

By Daniel S. Sanford

I. ILSENBURG.

WE had devoted the winter to the study of German education, had spent long hours in the classroom, following recitations of monotonous excellence. We had read school programmes and courses of study and talked with German teachers until we had grown weary of the superbly organized Prussian school system and had come to long for the variety, the flexibility, and the uneven results of our American schools. A letter written by a nine-year-old American boy, who was born in Florence, struck a responsive chord in our hearts. His little life had been clouded by the apprehension that he might die before he should see his "native land," as he expressed it, but now he was on a visit to his grandparents in Pennsylvania. He wrote to his father, who was still in Europe: "Dear Papa: I love you very much. I want you to come over here quick. This is a good, lively country. I like *freedom*. Aunt Mary is teaching me to sing 'My Country, 'tis of Thee.' Jack."

THE HERR DIRECTOR

With somewhat the same craving for freedom, activity and life, we took the train one May morning for the Hartz mountains, intending, so strong was the sense of duty within us, to visit still another school, at Ilsenburg, of which we had heard strange rumors. "*Eine idealische Schule*," remarked a Berlin teacher to me, with a shrug of his shoulders that betokened at once amusement and disdain.

Ilsenburg is charmingly situated in the midst of the Hartz mountains, with the Brocken full in view. A red-tiled roof, appearing among the trees a mile and a half from the village, was pointed out to us as our destination. Our road took us along the side of a mountain brook, the Ilse, which was fringed with willows and hundreds of growing things. All nature throbbed with the fulness of life. We had left huge piles of brick and mortar, veritable prison houses reared in the name of education. We had inspected armies of well drilled, super-obedient

AT WORK IN THE GARDEN

schoolboys, from whom every vestige of spontaneity had been eliminated. Another chapter of the same sort on such a day and amid such surroundings would have ill suited our mood. But no such disappointment awaited us. The low-browed farmhouse, emerging from a wealth of shrubbery, just at the point where the Ilse tumbles over a ledge of rock, seemed a part of the landscape itself. Certainly this was no prison. The Herr Director, who, hatless and in bicycle costume, met us at the gate, gave no suggestion of the traditional German pedagogue; and the boys, full of life and animal spirits, and yet all at work constructively and in ways that somehow seemed singularly in keeping with the spirit of the place and season, were a still more gratifying surprise. The first that we noticed were in the garden, all busily employed, now hoeing between the rows of vegetables, now on their knees pulling the weeds by hand. Like the director, they were in easy dress, some had even pulled off their shirts and were browning their little backs in the warm sun-

shine. In a neighboring thicket, two were cutting pea brush, and beyond, there were others sawing into proper lengths, and sharpening, posts for a fence which they were building. The teachers worked side by side with the boys, but the animating spirit of them all was the director, who passed from group to group, and caught up hoe or spade or saw, to illustrate practically how the work should be done.

Not a great privilege, some one may be prompted to say, to weed a garden and build a fence, and not in the highest degree educational. That depends entirely upon the purpose with which it is done, and the relation that such work bears to the general scheme of education. Gardening and farming, which we soon found played so important a rôle in the life of the school, have at least these merits, they provide a variety of occupation, changing with the seasons, and are in themselves helpful and interesting; they take the child out of doors and relate him to the soil, the sky, animal and vegetable life, and familiarize him with the processes of nature as no laboratory course indoors, however skil·

A CLASS IN MATHEMATICS

fully devised, can possibly do. There is a lingering impression in the minds of not a few persons with whom I am acquainted, that the New England farm of their youth was the best educational institution that America has known, affording opportunities which are scarcely duplicated by the most carefully planned courses in manual training of our urban schools.

However that may be, it took us but a few minutes to discover that we were in the domain of an idealist, and that the most prosaic pursuits were in his philosophy of education freighted with far reaching consequences. The open drain at the back of the house, which one of the young shirtless citizens was cleaning out, not as a

CLEANING A DRAIN

meaningless task, but as his contribution to the health of the school community, was made to suggest such important topics as the great sanitary problems of city life. The factory which we had passed on the way to the school and from which come the manual training instructors, furnishes an object lesson for the study of manufacturing processes and of industrial conditions. In other words, the con-

ception of the school as a social and a socializing institution, where all are learning to work constructively, is a fundamental principle in the policy of this progressive schoolmaster. All this we discovered before the day was over, and it saved us from condemn-

SHAPING FENCE POSTS

ing much that might otherwise have seemed trivial and worthless.

Let me return to our first impression. Given the freedom of the place, we continued our walk and at every step made new discoveries. Across the street, on a knoll beneath the trees, was a group sketching from nature. In the yard, an arithmetic class was estimating the cost of painting the house by computing its superficial area. Two of the boys had already begun the painting. In the shops, hard by, still others were busily employed, not slavishly following a prescribed course, but making such articles as a boy delights in,—sleds, a case for books, a mineral cabinet, a spring board for diving. The general arraignment of German boys that they lack initiative cannot be true of these youngsters.

We entered the schoolrooms, where there were classes reciting in litera-

IN THE SHOP

ture, in history, and in English. The teaching was characterized to an unusual degree by ingenuity and fertility of resource in making direct and immediate application of what is taught. Wherever this can be done, it increases immeasurably the fruitfulness of academic instruction. These boys were not seeing hazy, indistinct pictures of past events; they were dealing with living realities. They were reënacting in their own experiences, as all imaginative children who are given a chance will, those episodes from literature and history which appealed most powerfully to them. Contrary to the prevailing custom in Germany, the modern languages are taught by native teachers, an Englishman and a Frenchman being enrolled among the instructors for that purpose. Vital interest is added to these subjects by correspondence with schools in France and England, and by vacation visits to those countries. A reciprocal relationship is maintained with an English school of the same sort, Abbotsholme, with which they exchange not merely letters, but at certain seasons of the year, teachers and visits.

More feasible and indeed quite practicable for American schools would be the excursions, lasting from two days to a fortnight, which are an established custom at Ilsenburg and in many German schools. I know nothing which yields a richer return in realistic and practical knowledge of

A CLASS IN SINGING

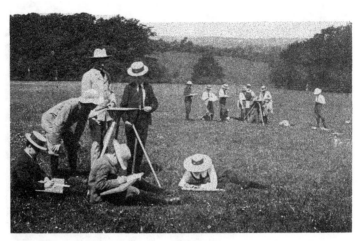

A CLASS IN SURVEYING AT BEDALES

every sort—scientific, historical, sociological and industrial,—and, I may add, in sympathy and good comradeship between the· teacher and the taught than these trips on foot and by bicycle to different places of interest.

Time will not permit me to describe at length all the incidents of that day at Ilsenburg—the swim in the river, the supper under the trees where we all sat down together, boys and teachers and guests, the free time after supper, an hour for recreation which the boys filled with bicycling, games and gymnastic practice, and finally, the twilight hour of evensong, a most fitting close for a busy day.

As might naturally be expected, music fills an important place in the school. One of the large boys played the violin while we were at supper.

This is a common practice, we were told. Had we been in the house, there would have been the accompaniment of a piano. Frequently some one is appointed to read an interesting book at meal time. Reading aloud is not a lost art in this school, and its practice by one for the entertainment of the others is a common form of social service. The systematic pursuit of literature in the classroom has in this way been supplemented by readings from a wide range of classic authors.

Not less interesting are the attempts of the director to broaden the sympathies and increase the social consciousness of these boys by introducing them through familiar talks to many of the unsolved social and economic problems of the day. I have already referred to their visits

to factories. That they are apt pupils is proved by the questions which they discuss in their debating club and by their amusing social experiments in inviting the servants to their musical and literary entertainments or to join them at dinner, and in sharing with the stone breakers on the road the contents of their Christmas boxes.

The following quotations from a report by one of the older boys give characteristic features of their school life:

"On Sunday evenings, after supper, during the first week of the new year, a review was made of the chief political events of the year just past, and their significance pointed out. For this purpose, Dr. Lietz drew up a table, giving the chief facts of a political, economic and social nature for all the principal countries. From this review it could be seen that the year 1898 was of as great importance as

any belonging to ancient or mediæval history."

"Dr. Lietz thinks it important that all the boys, at least of the upper classes, shall each week take a review of the current political and social happenings in the world, and to this end, the oldest of the boys should read the newspapers under advice and direction."

"In our debates, we attack for the most part serious political and social questions of the day, such as, What is the Social Democracy trying to do and how is it to be judged by us? How are we to regard the different political parties in Germany? The alcohol problem. How is the want in our great cities to be relieved? What should be the attitude of the employer of labor toward the employee? How should we, as members of the body politic, conduct ourselves toward our fellowmen? Many may wonder that problems of such a nature should be undertaken by us, but these debates have certainly had this result, that they have made us more serious and thoughtful, wiser, more sym-

pathetic in our attitude toward our fellow-men, less controlled by party watchwords, more independent in our thinking."

"But we try to be practical as well as theoretical. As from the beginning we have invited the servants to our evening service in the chapel, so we finally decided to ask them to sit down with us to our common meal. In this way they could share with us the advantage of the music during supper and the readings during dinner. Our next step was to carry our social politics into the garden by giving work to the beggars and tramps who came along, and these in return set us an example all day long of diligence and hard work and we came to realize that we had here to deal with real human beings, after all. From the proceeds of our collections on Sunday evening, we have saved fifty marks for the support during illness or need of some Ilsenburg workman."

II. BEDALES.

"We can imagine a school in the country where hardihood of life can be culti-

vated amid fresh air, open windows and cold water, where life is simple and varied and the evils of excessive subdivision of labor are avoided."

"We can imagine a school where the masters lead a common life with the boys, dressed like them for practical activity in the field, . . . working at gardening or ploughing, directing the boys at work with them; where the child is not isolated from the society of adults out of lesson time, and where adults find a real and not a pretence or toy occupation in utilizing the child's force as far as it goes in work which is useful for the establishment. We can imagine that time at this school will . . . consist of interchange of occupation, continuous but varied, some lighter, some severer, some taxing muscle, some brain."

"We can imagine that in such a school there would be established a collective, corporate life, in which, however juvenile, each member would learn self-reliance and individual responsibility . . . and constant adjustment of the relation of self to other people. The virtue that here grows up

GARDENING

will not be negative, as of those who are good because they are constrained to be good by force external to themselves, but active virtue, such as springs from having lived in a society where good lives are lived and where a good life has been lived, thanks to the environment of a well organized community."

These extracts from an article on Individualism in Education in *The Parents' Review* were suggested, as the author has since confessed, by Bedales, one of two English schools which are as unique among English institutions and as much of a protest against traditional academic methods as is Ilsenburg among the German schools. Like Dr. Lietz's school, it derives its inspiration from Abbotsholme, where Mr. J. H. Badley, the head master, had formerly taught, and

like that, it exemplifies a healthy, natural development, and a broad, many-sided, realistic training, in which books, though not wholly neglected, play but a subordinate part. What then are the *materia pedagogica*, the instruments of culture, if books are to be relegated to a second place? Why, things, actualities, the results of direct contact with external nature, and, more important than this, of intimate association with cultivated men and women, young enough and broad enough to feel a sympathetic interest in all that appeals most strongly to growing boys and girls.

One does not look for radical experiments in education in England, and so, although forewarned, we

were not fully prepared for all that we found at Bedales. Recall all that has been said of Ilsenburg, making of course generous allowance for the less idealistic, more practical character of the English mind, substitute for the forty German boys, some sixty English lads, more vigorous and enterprising than their German cousins, with an inherited fondness for sports and life in the open air, include girls, freely participating in the life—the studies, the outdoor work, the excursions, and many of the sports of the boys, an extreme form of co-education; put in charge of them a fine-grained, scholarly gentleman, aided by a corps of assistants, devoted men and women who believe in him and in his educational ideals, and count no sacrifice of time or effort too great to be made for the

school's success; leave out all cramming for examinations and early specialization for scholarships, the bane of English schools; give due weight in your thought to the refining influence of woman in this community, something which is wholly lacking in Dr. Lietz's school; and finally, imagine as the setting for this somewhat rare combination of circumstances, a stately English manor house, commanding far-away stretches of English landscape, and surrounded by the greenest of close-clipped lawns, by boxwood hedges and fine old trees, and you must admit that the conditions for such an experiment in education are ideal.

We arrived Saturday afternoon, a half holiday, while the boys were still at lunch, and under the guidance of one of the masters, we visited the dor-

MAKING BUTTER

mitories and study rooms, the cricket field, the bathing pool, the garden, the shop, and a house which the boys themselves had made for bicycles, photography, and natural history specimens.

At Ilsenburg, the Herr Director carried his arm in a sling, because of a fall from his bicycle while touring with his boys through the Thuringian forest; here we found the head master lying on a couch under the trees, disabled with a twisted knee, the painful reminder of a recent cricket match. There could be no better proof that the authorities of these schools participate in the boys' pastimes. Incapacitated for active work, Mr. Badley was still the central figure of the school life. It was interesting to sit by his side and watch the boys and girls come and go, all with some word of greeting from their chief. First, there passed the natural history enthusiasts, with butterfly nets and botany boxes, off for an excursion along the river; next came the haying squad

on their way to the farm, to be followed by a party of bicyclists, setting out to visit a Norman church some miles away. So varied are the interests which claim the attention of these boys and girls. And yet it is not a haphazard election which determines how the half holiday shall be passed. All is prearranged by the ever watchful and ever present masters. Hay is to be made when the sun shines, the cows to be milked at sundown, butter to be churned when the cream has risen, berries to be picked when they are ripe, and bees to be hived when they swarm. There are to be no drones in this human hive. Idleness is not to be tolerated. Even lolling about the cricket field when the team is playing is tabooed. The school motto cut on the fine old mantle of the dining-room is, "The work of each for the weal of all." This seems to be interpreted literally by masters and scholars. We were prepared for good comradeship between English schoolboys and their teachers; we had seen it at Rugby. But such unremitting consideration as prevails at Bedales was quite new to us. "What are your hours?" I asked one of the masters. "From seven in the morning until nine at night," was his rejoinder. "What time do you have to yourself?" "None whatever, except after nine P. M."

Seated on the grass by the disabled head master, I took occasion, before following the haymakers, to question him about the school and his educa-

They should become adepts in all manly sports, sure of hand and foot, strong of limb and quick of movement, to run, to ride, to swim, winning for themselves that physical endurance and courage which will stand them in good stead later in life. There should be a wide range of interests and the freest opportunity for self-revelation, for the supreme end during the early stage of the child's education is to discover, if possible, his bent, his dominant interest, that

HAYING

tional theories. "Until fourteen years of age," said he, "all children, boys and girls alike, should have a happy, free development, close to the heart of mother Nature, from whom they should learn the secrets of the woods and fields, the habits of animals and of plants, that they may have eyes to see and ears to hear, and be in sympathetic communion with all life. They should plant seeds in their own gardens, and learn to make things with their hands, that they may share with omnipotence the joy of creation.

his subsequent training may be shaped accordingly.

"Books are at first but little used. Formal instruction should be based on objects and given orally. So much of literature or of history as the child learns should be addressed to the ear rather than to the eye. The classics should not be begun too early, Latin not before a child is twelve years old, Greek certainly not before he is fifteen. After sixteen, he should specialize upon some one subject, without wholly neglecting the rest.

CARPENTRY

"When his more serious academic life begins, there is without doubt a difficult period of transition—that is, from fourteen to sixteen—when he must learn the use and value of books. But this difficulty once surmounted, he will with strong physique and well-established habits of observation and application be able to work harder and do more than the child who has been introduced prematurely to the study of books. He may even read for honors at the university, neglecting everything but his chosen subject, and do it with a minimum of harm. Indeed it would be a mistake to continue the broad, discursive training at this time, since now having acquired a breadth of interest which will always save him from becoming a narrow specialist, it is not only safe but highly desirable that he should deepen his education by following his natural aptitude."

"What can you tell me of the school's discipline?" I asked.

"Discipline should be an apprenticeship to liberty. Without a doubt, the most valuable training that is given in the school is the training in self-government. This is provided in many ways. In the schoolrooms a

monitor is responsible for the paper and ink. Certain boys must maintain order in the dormitories. And in the farm work, there are still others whose duty it is to see that there is no shirking. The dairy and butter-making are in the hands of three responsible lads. Furthermore, the boys manage their sports and exercise no little authority over their mates. A single incident will illustrate this. A squad of youngsters

SEARCHING FOR QUEEN BEES

was sent to roll the cricket field. They shirked and were reported to the older boys, who decided that the offenders should devote the entire half holiday to rolling the field, and that certain other boys who might have prevented the shirking should be caned, and they were caned forthwith, for the members of the upper form may whip the younger boys for their misdeeds, and, although somewhat keen in administering this form of punishment, they never seriously abuse their authority."

"But the most unique feature of your school and the greatest innovation from the English standpoint is the presence of girls here to whom you are giving the same training as the boys."

"Yes," said he, "I believe in co-education. We need the girls. The school was counted a success before they came, but we were not satisfied. I am convinced that ideal conditions can exist only when boys and girls are educated together. It is natural and right that they should be so educated. Life in our little community is less abnormal since the girls came. They save our boys from undue rudeness and the girls are themselves the gainers for the freer life they are leading. The best of good comradeship exists between them. Our experiment is only a year old, but thus far it has been a splendid success."

These were strange sentiments to come from the lips of an English schoolmaster. We could not but admire the courage of the man who in the face of most deep-seated prejudices was determined to follow his convictions.

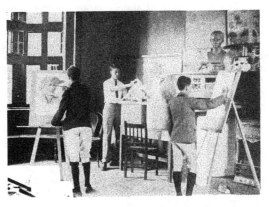

IN THE STUDIO

The National Pike and Its Memories

By Rufus Rockwell Wilson

THE coming of the railroad a generation and a half ago consigned the National Pike to the limbo of abandoned things; but for more than fifty years that now half-forgotten highway was the artery along which the country's life blood of commerce and travel ran from the East to the West and back again, its history part and parcel of that of a dozen states. Henry Clay has often been called the father of the National Pike, and he was its friend from the beginning; but as a matter of fact its origin goes far beyond his period. The proceedings of the convention which framed the Federal Union show that the chief objection made by Maryland, Delaware and some of the other smaller states to the adoption of the proposed Constitution was that Virginia, which then comprised a vast territory northwest of the Ohio, if allowed to come in with this immense area, would at no distant period exercise an overwhelming influence in national politics. To obviate this objection Virginia agreed to cede to the general government its territory north of the Ohio, with the condition, among others, that a stated percentage of the public lands sold in such territory should be set apart for the building of a road through the domain for public uses. Out of this reservation and percentage originated the National Pike.

One finds no serious opposition to it in the Congressional debates of the period; while, on the other hand, there is a tradition of a speech made by Congressman Beeson in its behalf, in which it was demonstrated that the horseshoes it would wear out would keep the smithies of the country ringing and that the horseshoe nails it would require would furnish work for all the idle population. It is doubtful, however, whether such figures as these were needed; for the road became a fixed fact from the time the cession of the reservation was accepted, and every appropriation by Congress in its aid provides that the money shall be paid out of the fund which accumulated by reason of this reservation. The road was, therefore, practically built, so far as it was built, from Cumberland to St. Louis, by Virginia, Congress simply discharging a trust assumed when the cession of Virginia's rights in the Northwest territory was accepted; and reference to the source of the fund is found in every appropriation for its laying out, making, extension and repair, from 1806 to 1837.

From Baltimore to Cumberland the road was laid out by Maryland banks, which were rechartered in 1816 on condition that they should complete it. In 1806 Congress ordered that the road be laid out and built from Cumberland, Maryland, to the Ohio River. On the third of March, 1811, $50,000 was appropriated to carry the road from Cumberland to Brownsville, Pennsylvania. On the sixth of May, 1812, $30,000 more was appropriated; and on the sixteenth of February, $100,000 was voted. From Cumberland to Uniontown, Pennsylvania, the trend of the mountains made only one route

possible, but beyond that the line was a matter of discretion tempered by political influence, as in the case of Wellsburg and Wheeling. The route by way of Wellsburg offered superior advantages to one by the way of Wheeling; and Philip Doddridge, who was then a man of national prominence, made a strong fight to secure the passage of the road through the former town. He was opposed, however, by Henry Clay, who had many friends in Wheeling, and, the Kentuckian's influence proving the stronger, Doddridge was worsted in the fight. It was in token of this service that Colonel David Shepherd erected a monument to Clay, that still stands beside the pike a few miles east of Wheeling.

From Cumberland to Wheeling the road was constructed in the most substantial manner. It was designed to be thirty feet wide, timber to be cut sixty feet, and twenty feet to be covered with stone to a depth of twelve inches, no stone larger than three inches being used. The road was first located by Joseph Kerr and Thomas Moore, and was built in the main by Kincaid, Beck & Evans. Its many bridges were of stone, with carefully turned arches; and their present condition attests the thoroughness of the work on them. The mileposts and tollgates were of iron, and the tollhouses, erected every fifteen or twenty miles, were of uniform size and shape, angular and durably built. Between Cumberland and Uniontown they were all of stone, while those west of the latter place were of brick. The road from Cumberland to Wheeling was finished as originally designed in December, 1820, but was not macad-

amized until 1832-36, when the original roadbed was taken up and stone
broken very small, not to exceed one
and a half inches, was laid and com-
pactly rolled, making it, length and
location considered, the finest road in
America and one of the finest in the
world.

Years before that, steps had been
taken for its extension from Wheeling
to St. Louis. On the fifteenth of May,
1820, Congress voted $10,000 to sur-
vey the road through Ohio, Indiana
and Illinois; and on the third of
March, 1825, $150,000 was appropri-
ated to build it from Canton (now
Bridgeport), opposite Wheeling, to
Zanesville on the Muskingum. On
the second of March, 1829, $50,000
was voted to build the road in Indiana,
east and west from Indianapolis to
the boundaries of the state. The following day, $100,000 was appropri-
ated to be spent east of the Ohio
River; and in 1831, a $75,000 appro-
priation was passed for Indiana, and
$66,000 for Illinois. In truth, this was

an era of internal improvement; legis-
lators vied with one another in introducing bills into Congress for improvements to be carried on in their
districts, and the government's alleged extravagance in this respect
became an issue in Presidential can-
vasses. President Monroe was one
of those who took a firm stand against
this growing tendency, and in a state
paper vetoing an annual appropriation for the maintenance of the National Road took occasion to deny
the constitutionality of the jurisdiction which the government assumed
over it.

The bill was passed over Monroe's
head, but was not without its later
effects; for in 1836 Congress gladly
accepted an offer from Pennsylvania,
Virginia and Ohio to receive and care
for the portions of the road within
their respective boundaries, and at
the same time sought to induce the
other states interested to make a
similar agreement. Two years before
this it had voted $200,000 for continu-
ing the road in Ohio, $150,000 for
continuing it in Indiana, $100,000 for
Illinois, and treble that amount for
improvements and repairs east of the
Ohio River, ordering that when these
appropriations were expended the
road should be surrendered to the
states through which it passed, and
not be subject to further expense on
account thereof. This sounds per-
emptory, yet on the third of March,
1835, Ohio got $200,000 more from
Congress for continuing the work
within her limits, Indiana half that
sum, and the section east of the Ohio
River, $346,000, the money to be
withheld until these states accepted
the road and took the burden off the

general government. In spite of the restriction, the contractors were able to get all this money before the road was fully turned over, and three more appropriations were made by Congress. The one granted on the second of July, 1835, gave the Ohio section $200,000 and Illinois $150,000. By that of the third of March, 1837, Ohio got $190,000, Indiana $100,000, Illinois $100,000, and the section east of the Ohio River $183,000; while by the act of the twentieth of March some $460,000 was divided in about equal parts among the several states. This, however, was the last appropriation made by Congress for the repair and improvement of the road, the section lying between Cumberland and Wheeling passing into the hands of the state authorities of Maryland, Pennsylvania and Virginia, and being cared for very much as it is to-day. Maryland has since turned her share of the road over to the two of her counties through which it passes, Allegheny and Garrett; but the others retain control in their state governments, except the share of Virginia, which fell to West Virginia when the state was divided. Ohio and Pennsylvania formally accepted the road from the general government in 1831, and Virginia did the same two years later. All of these states provided for commissioners to take charge of the portion given them, to fix tollgates and rates, to appoint a superintendent and collectors, and generally to supervise matters connected with their charge. The schedule of tolls fixed by the first Virginia commissioners lies before me as I write, and affords a vivid picture of our grandfathers' days.

Where the tollgates were placed at intervals of twenty miles, the charge for "every chariot, coach, coachee, stage or phaeton with two horses was eighteen and three-quarters cents, and for every dearborn, sulky, chair or chaise with one horse, twelve and one-half cents." Where the tollgates stood closer together, the rates were proportionately less; and in all cases it was intended that they should be no more in the aggregate than was sufficient to keep the thoroughfare in condition. Vehicles having tires not less than six inches in width got through free. Persons riding or driving on their way to or from divine worship and funerals were then, as now, passed free. So were persons on their way to or from court meetings and general musters, or going and returning in the ordinary course of their business to and from farm or woodland, mills or common place of trading and marketing, while the general government was given free way for its mails and the passage of troops and military stores.

The National Road was no sooner completed than traffic on it became general. Mail and passenger coaches, freight wagons, private conveyances, and droves of sheep and cattle formed, in the summer season at least, an almost continuous line from the rising till the going down of the sun, so that often the highway resembled the main street of a busy town, save that a few yards from its side the country was a wilderness. No accurate data is available as to the freight and passenger traffic which passed over the pike in its palmy days, but both grew steadily with each extension of the road until

THE GERMAN D. HAIR HOUSE

the coming of the locomotive super-seded slower modes of travel. I find in a Cumberland newspaper of 1849 a paragraph to the effect that between the first and twentieth of March in that year, 2,586 passengers were carried in coaches through that city; and the late George W. Thompson, of Wheeling, once told me that, standing on the porch of his house, formerly a famous hostelry on the National Road, he had counted fifty-two six-horse wagons in sight at one time, and had known as many as four thousand head of cattle en route to the East to be quartered over night on the place, adding that at times the freight wagons seemed like a continuous procession.

Nor were these ordinary wagons. On the contrary, they were built to meet the requirements of the time, and the long beds sloping from the centre and rising high at either end held under their white canvas covers a load that would confound a modern teamster. Eight thousand pounds was no unusual burden, and often loads weighing 10,000 pounds and called by the wagoners "a hundred hundred," were hauled over the road by the six big-boned horses attached to each blue-painted van. Eighteen

days from Cumberland to the Ohio River was the time allowed in the old bills of lading and, barring accident, was amply sufficient. The freight drivers, who were called wagoners, carried their beds with them, and slept in the public room of the inn where evening found them. There were two classes of wagoners, the regular and the sharpshooter, the former being engaged in the business throughout the year, and the latter made up mainly of farmers, who put their teams on the road only when freight was high. A regular averaged fifteen miles a day, while a sharpshooter would make twenty or twenty-five.

Coaching on the National Road in the old days was a delightful pastime. There were three lines of passenger coaches conducted respectively by Moore & Stockton, of Baltimore, James Reeside, of Cumberland, and Kincaid, Beck & Evans, of Uniontown. Moore at that time lived in Wheeling and died only a few years ago in Baltimore. Stockton was a native of Washington, Pennsylvania. Reeside was also a Pennsylvanian, a handsome man, with a bluff, hearty way about him that made him many friends, while his sagacity and indus-

THE TEMPLE OF JUNO

try won for him the title of "Land Admiral." One thousand horses and four hundred men were employed by him, and he was the largest mail-coach owner of his time. The first coaches used were built at Cumberland and held sixteen passengers; but these were soon found too cumbrous, and the Trenton coach, which had an egg-shaped body, was substituted. Then came the Troy coaches, which held nine passengers inside and two out; and after them the Concord coaches, in use when the lines were discontinued. These were massive vehicles with panelled landscapes, damask upholstering and springs so delicate that they bent beneath the slightest weight.

All the lines had first-class horses and plenty of them. Ten miles an hour was ordinary speed; and the twenty-six miles between Frederick and Hagerstown, where the road was particularly good, is said to have been regularly covered in two hours. Such dangers as the road presented were exceptional, yet there was no wearying of the constant change of scene and adventure presented to the traveller. There were long stretches of level or gently undulating highway, along which the coaches bowled as smoothly as over a paved floor, and in pleasant weather nothing could be more delightful than the balmy air and ever varying panorama presented. Nor was there wanting an occasional mishap to lighten the tedium of the road. When other diversions failed them, the passengers would sometimes amuse themselves by holding letters at arm's length out of the windows, and calling to the villagers, who, supposing that the missives were for them, would follow the coach for many a weary mile. One day the trick was played upon one Daniel Oster, who, to the delight of the hectors, pursued the coach up a long and steep hill. The distance was so great that it did not seem likely he could reach them; but Oster was not to be trifled with. He knew they had no letter for him, but was determined to make an example of the inconsiderate wag. "Who has a letter for me?" he fiercely demanded, when he had overtaken the mail and ordered the driver to stop. No one answered, and Oster, hastily gathering a dozen stones from the roadside, declared that, unless the offender was pointed out, he would pepper and salt

them all. Whereupon, finding that the actual transgressor was willing to let them suffer for his sins, his companions surrendered him to Oster, who dragged him out of the coach and gave him a hearty trouncing. "Now," he said, as he lighted his pipe and walked down the hill, "don't fool me any more," a warning to which subsequent travellers gave careful heed.

Travellers on the National Road had little to fear from highwaymen. Passenger coaches seldom travelled singly, mail coaches never; and the robber's only chance was to cut the rear boots of the stage and allow the baggage to drop out on the road This was attended with considerable risk, however, and a dark night, a sleepy driver and a rough piece of road, to drown the sound of the falling baggage, were necessary adjuncts. Stealing cautiously up behind the coach, it was the work of a moment to cut the leathern boots, the platform of which was suspended by iron chains from the roof of the

coach. Still, such cases were few and far between, and it was other features of the drivers' calling that nurtured a deftness and courage which sooner or later made them as hardy and intrepid as trained veterans. Most of these men—stagers and pike-boys they were called in the vernacular of the road—had native wit and intelligence, and their occupation bred in them signal skill and steadiness of nerve. Often they had need for both, for in the winter season, when snow and ice covered the roadbed, to guide the coaches safely down the mountain sides demanded a sure hand and a cool head, as well as good judgment and discretion. To try to pick the way slowly along these dangerous inclines would, in many cases, result in sliding the stage over the embankment at every turn and corner. The only safety was to put on speed and keep the vehicle moving in exactly the same direction as the horses; and to hold the road and preserve a perpendicular, adjusting the speed to the incline and the friction to the curve, required an adroitness that at times seemed miraculous. Again, the existence of competing lines engendered hot rivalry among the drivers. This rivalry was amiable and well meant, as a rule, but led now and then to accidents and fisticuffs. Heavy trunks were strictly forbidden, each passenger being limited to fifty pounds of baggage; and "never be passed on the road," was the begin-

abetted by the passengers. Their strength and fistic skill proved to be as well balanced as the speed of their horses, and they buffeted one another for an hour or more before a decisive point was reached. A hardy set were these pike-boys,—honest, polite, temperate and fond of the sound of their own voices. We shall not see their like again.

At first the mails were carried on

THE BURIAL PLACE OF GENERAL BRADDOCK

ning and end of the driver's gospel. Indeed, there were few members of the craft who would not test the mettle of a rival's horses whenever opportunity offered, and at least one instance is recorded of a race which ended in an impromptu battle on the turf. So well matched were the teams on the occasion in question that, strained to the utmost, one could not defeat the other, and when the drivers had come to the end of a large and varied vocabulary of invective, they decided to settle their differences by a combat—a resolve gleefully

the passenger coaches; but as these grew heavier mail wagons were substituted, and it was in their dispatch that the greatest speed was attained on the National Road. Relays were established at a distance of from ten to twelve miles, and stories are told of quick changing that would appall a modern Jehu, one old driver boasting of having harnessed four horses in as many minutes, and changed teams before his coach had ceased rocking. One is apt to associate staging with slow travelling; but such was not the case with the mail

coaches on the National Road. A through mail coach left Wheeling at six o'clock each morning and just twenty-four hours later dashed into Cumberland, a distance of one hundred and twenty-three miles. There were occasional delays, but these were not permissible after the completion of the Baltimore and Ohio Railroad to Cumberland. Following that event, a way mail coach, which both received and deposited mail at all stations, left Wheeling at seven o'clock each day, and, despite its extra duties, never failed to overtake the through mail before the latter reached Cumberland.

Nor did the mail coaches hold all the honors of quick passage over the National Road. Frequently Ohio River steamboats arrived at Wheeling as late as ten o'clock in the forenoon, with passengers booked for the train leaving Cumberland at six o'clock the next day. One hundred and twenty-three miles up hill and

down dale lay between, with rivers to ford and mountains to cross; but connection must be made, and it was, though at a heavy cost to the stage company.

The severest test, however, of a driver's mettle was the delivery of the President's message. The letting of contracts by the post office department hinged on these deliveries; and if a driver failed to make fast time it meant the cancellation of the contract with his employers and its transfer to a rival company. David Gordon, a noted driver, once carried the President's message from Washington, Pennsylvania, to Wheeling, a distance of thirty-two miles, in one hour and twenty minutes, changing teams three times on the way; while William Noble, another famous pike-boy of the period, once drove from Wheeling to Hagerstown, one hundred and eighty-five miles, in fifteen and one-half hours. Small wonder then that the position of stager on the pike was held in as high esteem by the youngsters who dwelt along it as that of pilot among the boys of the Mississippi, or that in their eyes a driver was of more importance than the President.

Travel on the National Road early developed the business of innkeeping to such an extent that a hostelry was always in sight, Each had its gayly painted signboard, spreading porch and spacious wagon-yard. All were models of cleanliness, and there was no bustle or disorder. Meals were timed to suit the arrival of the coach, and long before it was due preparations were making for the coming guests. As the time to spare grew shorter, landlord and servants doubled their activity and the tempting odors from the kitchen became more distinct. Finally the villagers gathered before the door to watch the arrival of the coach, which soon dashed into view around the curve at the foot of the hill, swaying and pitching perilously, the horses at full gallop, and the driver swinging his whip, with a pistol-like snap, over their heads. No sooner did mine host hear it than, with a final word to the kitchen, he hastened to the porch, and stood there, with smiling face, the picture of welcome, ready to lead the weary, dust-stained wayfarer into the inn.

And such inns as they were! Never before on one thoroughfare were there so many roomy and capacious taverns, such bursting larders, such generous kitchens, such well-stocked tap-rooms. The ride in the open air bred keen appetites as a rule, and, if further appetizers were indulged in, there was no headache in the whiskey which stood upon the shelf or the sugar bowl that rested on the counter. Each guest quenched his thirst as suited his individual taste, and sat down to the table never doubtful of his capacity. The cooking at these roadside inns was fit for a king, and if one were to repeat half that is told him by those who ate them of the savoriness of the dinners and suppers, the tenderness of the venison, the flavor of the mountain trout, the succulence of the grouse, and the creaminess of the corn cakes, epicures would grow envious at the recital. "I tell you, sir," said one veteran to me, "though it's half a century since I ate them, the recollection of the buckwheat cakes and mountain honey served in those road houses makes my mouth water yet, when they come up in memory." The meal ended, there was no haste to be gone. The guest had time to look about him, and literally took his "ease in his inn." If he journeyed by chartered coach or in private conveyance, he gave his own orders as to resuming his journey; if he travelled by the regular stage line, he found in summer a resting place on the shady side of the porch, or in winter in a snug corner of the tap-room, until a fresh relay of horses was put in, and then took his departure, at peace with himself and the rest of mankind.

Most of the travellers over the National Pike were the farmers, stock raisers and merchants of the West, garbed in homespun cloth and buckskin; yet over it journeyed at one time and another nearly all of the best known men of the middle period of our history. Western public men going East and Eastern officials go-

THE BROWNFIELD HOUSE *

ing West; Presidents-elect, senators, congressmen, judges and governors on their way to assume their official duties; ex-Presidents and lesser officials returning to the shades of private life; aged men and gray-haired women journeying to the frontier homes of their children,—all these and many more were among the patrons of the stagecoaches passing over the great highway. In truth, a volume of absorbing interest could be written on the guests of a single tavern on the pike,—the old Globe Inn at Washington, Pennsylvania. Monroe, when he made his celebrated tour in 1817, stopped there over night; and so did Lafayette during his second visit to America in 1825. Jackson was a guest at the Globe on many occasions; and Harrison, Taylor, Polk, Benton, Crittenden and Bell were often there. A good story used to be told in connection with one of Jackson's visits to the Globe. Those were the days of training bands, and one morning the commander of the local battalion called on Jackson in all the panoply of his office, introducing himself with a great deal of dignity and not a little vanity as "Major Simon, of the militia, sir." Jackson, who was quietly smoking his pipe, surveyed his visitor with grave deliberation, and then said: "I know of your militia, but I'll be d——d, sir, if I ever heard of you." Simon was vanquished at this rejoinder; but it was the most eventful incident of his life.

Henry Clay was one of the most popular of the Globe guests. On one occasion, so the story runs, he reached there in the evening and was compelled to remain over night. The Whigs could not let the occasion pass without a speech from their hero, the dining-room of the hotel being selected as a hall. The room was crowded early in the evening; but

* The sketches of the old taverns herewith are from "The History of Old Pike," by Thomas B. Searight.

THE JOHNSON-HATFIELD HOUSE

hour after hour passed with Clay still missing, and those who had come to hear him were finally forced to accept one of his travelling companions as a substitute. Meanwhile, in Clay's room above stairs was a crowd of Democrats, who, having made escape impossible by bolting and barring the door, had so cleverly engaged and held the statesman in conversation that he forgot all about his friends in waiting below.

Not long after this an accident occurred to Clay near Monongahela City, Pennsylvania, which for years formed one of the stock stories of drivers on the pike. As the stage-coach was dashing down a hill the wheels encountered a rut, and Clay was pitched through the window and into the mud outside. It was some minutes before he was extricated from his unfortunate position; but when the driver finally came to his relief, he observed with a laugh that never before had he known of "Kentucky Clay mixing with Pennsylvania limestone."

In these days, however, public men of power and repute journey to and from the capital by rail and in their private cars, and neglect and decay have fallen upon the National Pike. As the railroads advanced, the coaching and wagon business declined. This ebb of fortune was at first stubbornly resisted by the stagers and wagoners, many prominent men, who were friends of the road, lending them their aid,—but all in vain. In 1853, the Baltimore and Ohio Railway was completed to Wheeling; and in the same year the coaches ceased running on the pike. During a recent trip over it, few travellers were to be met with. Old taverns fast falling to ruins gape on either side; and the tollkeeper has little to do, while most of the pike-boys are dead or bending under the weight of years.

Our trip began at the fine old town of Frederick, in itself one of the romances of the National Pike, for there once dwelt Francis Scott Key, author of the "Star Spangled Banner," and aged Barbara Frietchie, the lion-hearted dame made immortal by Whittier's verse. All that is mortal of Key reposes in Mount Olivet Cemetery in the south end of the town; while

sturdy Barbara, who dared to reprove Stonewall Jackson for shooting at "his country's flag," sleeps in another burial ground in the northwest section of the place. Barbara's house no longer exists in Frederick. It was purchased by the corporation after her death, in 1862, and torn down, in order to make room for a widening of the creek that passed alongside of it. In that home she had lived for many years, and her husband, by industry and thrift, had accumulated a little property, by which he left her on his death in 1849 in comfortable circumstances. Aside from the episode of which the poet has made her the heroine, Barbara's life was a remarkable one. Born in 1766, she remembered the signing of the Declaration of Independence and the events of the first war with England. When Washington visited Frederick in 1791, she contributed her modest share to the reception given in his honor; and later she was one of the pallbearers at the ceremony by which her townsmen gave token of their grief at the death of the first President. A portrait of her made in war

times shows an intelligent grandmotherly face of the New England type, and local tradition has it that, while "an active, capable woman, mistress of many generous enthusiasms, she had also a sharp tongue, of which she made frequent use."

The journey westward over the National Pike, especially if it be taken in the green and fragrant month of June, is one sure to dwell long and pleasantly in the memory. From Frederick placid meadows stretch away on either side to the horizon line, while to the south the distant, azure-tinted Blue Ridge looks like a low-lying, truncated cloud. Locusts, chestnuts and poplars line the road, which finally leaves the bottom lands and climbs a hill, from whose crest one obtains a noble and wide-reaching prospect of the Middletown valley, its meads and steads as green and fertile and beautiful as on that "cool September morn" of the long ago, when Lee came "winding down, horse and foot into Frederick town." The Union artillery did deadly work up here in the buried years, and beyond that gap in the mountains lies

the river-flanked hamlet of Harper's Ferry, where the melodrama in which John Brown was the chief actor had its strange unfolding and its heroic close. All the way across the valley, in the centre of which lies sleepy, oak-embowered Middletown, we were lured onward by the purple beauty of lordly South Mountain, up which we finally toiled through a dense, prolific growth of pine and chestnut, resting for a time in the old post town of Boonsborough on the farther side and spending the night at Hagerstown, which still enjoys much of the prosperity that came to it in palmy post days.

From Hagerstown to Clear Spring, the pike is level and uninteresting, save for the roomy, dolorous taverns and the stables and smithies which time has left standing; but between Clear Spring and Hancock it rivals in beauty and grandeur the noblest passes of the Sierras; ridge flanking ridge until earth and sky meet and blend in cloud and mist. Clear Spring lies at the base of the Alleghanies, and the road when it first begins to climb away from the village is over-arched with oaks, chestnuts and sugar maples. A little farther up these give way to pines, and near the summit little grows save the balsamic and hardy evergreen. The descent of the steep farther slope carried us past Indian Springs, the site of a once noted post-house, and down into a narrow valley cut in twain by the Chesapeake canal, with the Potomac glinting in the distance. Hancock, formerly a busy and bustling burg, is now as silent and somnolent as the thoroughfare which gave it birth, while from that point to Cumberland the pike is almost deserted, there being no tavern in over forty miles of a wild region, that during the war was a favorite ground of the bush-whackers West of Cumberland the pike pushes through a hill country, closely following as far as Uniontown, Pennsylvania, the route of General Braddock,—who has left an interesting old milestone at Frostburg,—passing by the ruins of Fort Necessity and skirting the spot where the British commander was buried.

Our ride ended at the little town of Brownsville, just without the shadow of the Alleghanies' western slope. The story of this almost forgotten hamlet is another romance of the National Pike. Time was when the name of Brownsville was as familiar to the people of the West as that of Pittsburg, for it was then the point from which a voyage down the Ohio and Mississippi was begun. Brownsville claimed the first steamer that ever ascended these rivers, and for the better part of two decades was a strong rival to Pittsburg, sixty-five miles to the north of it. Travellers coming from the South and West by water took passage over the pike at Brownsville, and wayfarers from the East began their river voyaging at that point. The older residents of the village retain many interesting recollections of that vanished time. For instance, when a steamboat from the West came within two miles of the town, the pilot blew his whistle, as many times as he had through passengers for the East, thus notifying innkeepers and pike-boys how many people they would have to provide for. The signal also served to notify the townsfolk that a boat was about to arrive, and by the time it reached its wharf a great crowd was usually gathered to greet the incoming passengers.

James G. Blaine, then a boy, often made one of the throng which gathered on the wharf to meet the steamboats, he having been born in Brownsville, where still linger grateful memories of his family. The elder Blaine owned the ferry across the Monongahela River, and tradition has it that he made money easily and spent it with a free hand. However, others helped to enjoy it, and, to his credit be it said, he died without leaving behind him a legacy of debt, as many a man has done. More than this, when he "came into his fortune," he paid the debts of his father before him; and this manly and high-minded act is not yet forgotten. His illustrious son, while still in his teens, left his birthplace, never to come back as a resident; but until his death half a century later, the little town and its inhabitants had a secure place in his affections. More than once the younger Blaine went back to visit the house in which he was born,—it is still standing on the west bank of the Monongahela,—and above the graves of his parents in the village cemetery there is a monument raised by him in their honor.

Brownsville rose and fell with the National Pike, and the decline of the latter left it stranded on the shore that is washed by the sea of Buried Hopes. Nothing happens now in Brownsville, and never will. Grass is growing in its streets, and time and the elements are hastening its decay. I can think of it only as a silent watcher over the dead artery of trade from which it had its being.

Washington-Greene
Correspondence

A large collection of original letters written by General Washington and General Greene has come into the editor's possession. It is our intention to reproduce in fac-simile those of the letters which present the most interesting details and side lights on the great events of the period covered, even though some of the letters may have been previously published.

The reproduction of these letters in chronological order will be continued through the following three issues. Printed copies of these letters appear on pages 327 and 328.—EDITOR.

Head Quarters near York 24th Oct. 1781

Dear Sir

      I wrote you on the 16th inst. giving a detail of occurrences to that time — on the next day, a proposal was received in writing from Lord Cornwallis, for a meeting of Commissioners to consult on terms for the Surrender of the Posts of York & Gloucester — This proposition the first that passed between us led to a correspondence which terminated in a definitive Capitulation which was agreed to and signed on the 19th. In which his Lordship surrenders himself and Troops prisoners of War to the American army — marched out with Colours Cased & drums beating a British march, to a post in front of their lines, where their arms were grounded — the public Stores, Arms, Artillery, Military Chest &c — delivered to the American army — The Ships with their Guns, Tackle, Apparel &c with the seamen surrendered to the Naval army under the Count De Grasse — Lord Cornwallis, with a Number of his officers, to have liberty to go on parole to Europe, New York or any other American Maritime post in possession of the British Forces, at their option his Troops to be kept in Virginia, Maryland or Pensylvania — these are the principle articles

P.S.
The Number
surrendered will
be little extra
29 — prisoners
of British — & I
with 7324 m—
surrend'd &c the
exclusive of
Count's ship
& army or gar—

a more particular account will be transmitted to you, when I have more leisure, and a better opportunity which will probably soon present by Colo. Lee, who will be returning to you

I congratulate you my dear Sir on this happy event which has been produced at an earlier period than I expected

With much Regard and Esteem

I am
Dear Sir

Yours &c --

G: Washington

P.S.
The number of Prisoners is not accurately collected — but from the best estimation will amount to 7,000, exclusive of Seamen — 74 Brass — 8,140 Iron Cannon with 7320 Musquets are already from Genl. Washington returned — The number of Seamen exclusive of those on board the Private Ships, will amount to 800, or 900

October 24th 1782

Oct 24

From Genl Washington
Octr 1782

Head Quarters
Novembr 21. 1781.

Sir

Your Excellency's letters of the 16.
24." and 30." of October containing an account of the
operations of the combined Army against Earl Cornwallis
and of the surrender of his army afford me the highest
satisfaction and I beg leave to congratulate Your
Excellency again upon this important and happy event.
I contemplate its advantages with infinite satisfaction
and feel a relief upon the occasion that is difficult to express.
Count Rochcambeau's stay in Virginia and the march of
General St Clair if he arrives speedily I am in hopes will
place us upon an eligible footing - The Reduction of Charles
Town is an event much to be wished but to be able to cover
the Country and confine the Enemy to that place will be
a great object. However I am not without my apprehensions
that Sir Henry Clinton will endeavor to push some
vigorous operations in this quarter this Winter to efface
if possible their late losses both here and in Virginia.
General Lesly is arrived to take command here, and it
is said reinforcements are expected - I have sent one of
my Aids to haisten the March of Genrl St Clair

and as Lexington is vacated there is nothing to prevent an immediate junction. after which if the Enemy's reinforcements are not very large they shall purchase their advantages at an expensive rate —

I would have a return made immediately of the prisoners of war in this department but Major Hyrne the Commissary of prisoners has lately met with an unhappy fall which has disqualified him for business by disordering his understanding from which I am not a little apprehensive he will never recover. as soon as it can be done by another hand it shall be forwarded. But before a General exchange is gone fully into, I wish something decisive may be done respecting Coll. Haynes. As retaliation necessarily involves the whole Continent. I wish Your Excellency's orders and the order of Congress thereon—The latter have signified their approbation of the measures I took. But as retaliation did not take place immediately nor did I think myself at liberty on a matter of such magnitude but from the most pressing necessity and as the Enemy did not repeat the offence, I have remain at a loss how to act with respect to the original not having any officer of equal Rank with Coll. Haynes in my possession—I am ready to execute whatever may be thought advisable.) It would be proper something should be done to put a stop to the practice of burning both in the northern States and here also; and to prevent these I wrote the Enemy a letter on the subject a copy

335

of which I have inclosed and if they do not disapprove it will put
the war on the footing I mention —

    We are on our march for your holes
Col. Mayum brought off upwards of 80 Convalescents
prisoners from one of the Enemy's Hospitals near Fair
town — these and some small skirmishes of little
consequence and a few other prisoners are all the
changes which have taken place since my letters
by Cap.t Pierce. I am happy that Wilmington is
evacuated as it leaves North Carolina perfectly at
liberty to support this Army and fill up their line —

        I am with great respect
        and attachment
        Your Excellency's
        most obedient
        humble Serv.t

        Nath Greene

His Excellency
General Washington

Gen. Washington to Gen. Greene

HEAD QUARTERS NEAR YORK, 24th Octr., 1781.

DEAR SIR,

        I wrote you on the 16th inst. giving a detail of occurrences to that time—on the next day a proposal was received in writing from Lord Cornwallis, for a meeting of Commissioners to consult on terms for the Surrender of the Posts of York & Gloucester—This proposition, the first that passed between us, led to a Correspondence which terminated in a definitive Capitulation which was agreed to and signed on the 19th—in which His Lordship surrenders himself and Troops prisoners of War to the American Army—march'd out with Colours Cased & drums beating a British march, to a post in front of their lines, where their arms were grounded—the public Stores, Arms, Artillery, Military Chest &c—delivered to the American Army—The Ships with their Guns, Tackle, Apparel &c with the seamen surrender'd to the Naval Army under the Count De Grasse—Lord Cornwallis, with a Number of his officers, to have liberty to go on parole to Europe, New York or any other American Maritime post in possession of the British Forces, at their option his Troops to be kept in Virginia, Maryland or Pennsylvania—these are the principal Articles. A more particular account will be transmitted to you, when I have more leisure, and a better opportunity—which will probably soon present by Colo. Lee, who will be returning to you—

        I congratulate you my dear Sir on this happy event—which has been produced at an Earlier period than I expected—

With much Regard and Esteem,

I am,

    Dear Sir,

Yours &c

G. WASHINGTON.

P. S. The number of Prisoners is not accurately collected—but from the best estimation will amount to 7,000, exclusive of Seamen—74 Brass & 140 Iron Cannon with 7,320 musquets are already return'd—the Number of Seamen exclusive of those on board the private Ships, will amount to 800 or 900—

Gen. Greene to Gen. Washington

HEAD QUARTERS,
November 21st, 1781.

SIR,

Your Excellency's letters of the 16th, 24th and 30th of October containing an account of the operations of the combined army against Earl Cornwallis and of the surrender of his army afforded me the highest satisfaction and I beg leave to congratulate Your Excellency again upon this important and happy event. I contemplate its advantages with infinite satisfaction and feel a relief upon the occasion that is difficult to express. Count Rocheambeau's stay in Virginia and the march of General St. Clair if he arrives speedily I am in hopes will place us upon an eligible footing. The reduction of Charles Town is an event much to be wished but to be able to cover the Country and confine the Enemy to that place will be a great object. However I am not without my apprehensions that Sir Henry Clinton will endeavor to push some vigorous operations in this quarter this Winter to efface if possible their late losses both here and in Virginia—General Lesly is arrived to take command here, and it is said reinforcements are expected—I have sent one of my aids to hasten the march of General St. Clair and as Wilmington is evacuated there is nothing to prevent an immediate junction, after which if the Enemy's reinforcements are not very large they shall purchase their advantages at an expensive rate—

I would have a return made immediately of the prisoners of war in this department but Major Hyrne the Commissary of prisoners has lately met with an unhappy fall which has disqualified him for business by disordering his understanding from which I am not a little apprehensive he will never recover—As soon as it can be done by another hand it shall be forwarded—But before a General exchange is gone fully into, I wish something decisive may be done respecting Col. Haynes—As retaliation necessarily involves the whole Continent I wish your Excellency's own and the order of Congress thereon—The latter have signified their approbation of the measures I took. But as retaliation did not take place immediately nor did I think myself at liberty on a matter of such magnitude but from the most pressing necessity and as the Enemy did not repeat the offence, I have been at a loss how to act with respect to the original not having any officer of equal Rank with Col. Haynes in my possession—I am ready to execute whatever may be thought advisable. It would be happy for America if something could be done to put a stop to the practice of burning both in the Northern States and here also; and to prevent it here I wrote the Enemy a letter on the subject a copy of which I here enclose and if they do not desist I will put the war on the footing I mention—

We are on our march for Four Holes. Col. M— (Mayum?) brought off upwards of 80 Convalescent prisoners from one of the Enemy's Hospitals near Fair Lawn—These and some small skirmishes of little consequence and a few other prisoners are all the changes which have taken place since my letters by Capt. Pierce. I am happy that Wilmington is evacuated as it leaves North Carolina perfectly at liberty to support this army and fill up their line—

> I am with great respect
> and attachment,
> Your Excellency's
> most obedient
> humble Servt,
> NATH. GREENE

His Excellency
General Washington.

Cape Cod Notes

By a Returned Native

STRETCHING out into the Atlantic from the eastern side of Massachusetts like a bent arm, the forefinger at the end curved inward, is Barnstable County, more commonly known as Cape Cod, although that name really belongs only to the extremity along whose inner shore lies quaint and interesting Provincetown. Buzzard's Bay is the arm pit. On its western shore lie Marion and Mattapoisett, well known to summer tourists, and just around the corner, so to speak, is New Bedford, once the old whaling port, now a thriving manufacturing city. To the eastward Chatham is at the elbow; thence, northward, to Wellfleet and Truro, at the wrist, the land makes another bend to the west and then comes the beckoning finger of Cape Cod. Twenty miles or so in width at Buzzard's Bay, the land narrows gradually until at Provincetown the finger is less than a mile wide. From end to end of the Cape the distance is not far from sixty miles. Fifteen or more towns occupy this territory, some including all the land from shore to shore, from Cape Cod Bay on the north to Vineyard or Nantucket Sound on the south; others dividing between them shore and woodland. Each has, of course, its town meeting, its town officers, its town administration, alike but separate; but most of them are divided into many villages, each with its own post office and its own name. These, as we go from east to west, lie near one another along the shores, but, from north to south are separated by miles of woodland, with scarcely a house to be seen, except, it may be, the town-house and the poor-house, which, to avoid quarrels as to location, are often placed in the geographical centre of the town, which often means in the woods. Almost every village has its little harbor, once lively with a fleet of fishermen, now silent and deserted, save for a few pleasure craft. Comfortable homes, almost entire absence of signs of poverty, and yet no indication of great wealth, intelligent faces, a certain kind of sturdy independence, meet the eye of the observant traveller everywhere.

From Cape Cod came more than a generation ago those able seamen and capable ship-masters who took the American flag into all parts of the world. In every one of these many villages every male inhabitant, with few exceptions, as soon as he was big enough to haul on a rope, went to sea. Perhaps he only got as far as the Banks for cod, or to the Bay of Chaleur for mackerel, but his life was passed on the sea. from the time the ice left the harbor until it came again in the fall, almost as much so as was that of his neighbor who went on the "long voyage" to China and Calcutta and around Cape Horn, and who renewed acquaintance with his family only once in two or three years. The railroad, a generation ago, came down from Boston as far as the town of Barnstable, forty miles or so from the end of the Cape. Thence four-horse coaches twice a day ran to Provincetown and back, and their arrival at the village post offices was the event of the day. Most people, when they travelled, which was seldom, went to Boston by "packet," a roomy vessel which sailed, perhaps, twice a week from nearly every village.

All over the Cape, on the fair hills overlooking the sea, were the windmills which pumped the sea-water into wooden vats for the making of sea-salt by evaporation, and on the lowlands were acres of these vats, their conical shaped roofs forming a picturesque feature in the landscape. When it rained, day or night, men and boys hastened to the salt works to close the vats and keep out the fresh water. Along the shores were the "fish flakes" on which the cod were spread to dry, and at the wharves the summer days were busy with culling and inspecting and packing the mackerel. Vessels were continually coming and going, and a rivalry, not unlike that between owners of crack yachts nowadays, often sprang up over the merits of some fast schooner, and the big fare it could bring home.

The population was remarkably homogeneous. Certain families occupied certain villages, and their descendants are found there today, with no more foreign admixture than of old. In Barnstable were the Hinckleys and the Scudders; in Dennis the Howes, the Searses and the Crowells; in Brewster, the Freemans, the Crosbys and the Snows; in Harwich, the Nickersons and the Smalls; in Orleans, the Higgenses; in Truro, the Riches; in Provincetown, the Atkinses. It is tolerably safe to say that most people of these names now scattered over the country can claim descent from some one of these few old Cape Cod families, all of whom are of pure English blood. In each village they married and intermarried, until a professional genealogist would be puzzled to unravel the tangled skein of kinship. Intelligence of a high order was the rule. The men saw the world and learned its ways in long voyages; the women read and learned at home. The girls, having no women's colleges, went to normal school and taught the summer village school. The winter district-schools were conducted by college students from Amherst, or Dartmouth, or Harvard, who had a delightful three months' life of it, and left behind many hints to the boys and girls of things heretofore beyond their ken. The sewing circle, the quilting-bee and the spelling-match were the social events, while ice-boats on the fresh water ponds took the place in winter of the pleasure-boat on the bay in summer. Strangers seldom came except as family visitors, when they were warmly welcomed, and the summer boarder was unknown. Foreigners were rarely seen so far from Boston. Most of the towns and villages were connected by the bonds of relationship, and the population of the Cape was like one great family, whose members were far enough apart not to quarrel. In the villages every one called everybody else by the christian name; where so many had the same surname it was useless to say Mr. Sears, or

Mr. Howes; while "Uncle John," or "Aunt Persis," no one could misunderstand. Such was the Cape of forty years ago. Then came, about thirty-five years ago, the extension of the railroad to the lower part of the peninsula, and its entire supplanting of the great four-horse coach.

Ships, fast and famous clippers, had been built in Dennis by the Shivericks, some of them becoming noted for their swift voyages from Calcutta and San Francisco, and every Cape boy of any ambition wanted to sail the seas over on them. But the civil war came to overturn all this and change everything. No more ships were built on Cape Cod, or anywhere else in this country, for that matter. The fishing interests were all concentrated in Boston and Gloucester and a few such centres. Nobody went to sea any more, excepting in a coasting schooner or, now and then, as officer of a steamship. The salt works disappeared and the windmills no longer reminded one of Holland. Cape Cod was left with little visible means of support. There were the small farms, to be sure, which grow to be very small as one travels down towards the elbow of the Cape; the clam flats and the oyster beds were not damaged by war or tariff; but what were these among so many? The miracle of the loaves and fishes was not likely to be repeated, and when the young men sought other fields in which profitably to expend their native energy, something must be done for those left behind. Then came the cranberry culture, and the summer boarder. Somebody discovered that the wild cranberry which had always been found in certain spots could be made to yield a return to the industrious cultivator. All at once, about 1860, the old peat swamps, which as such had scarcely any market value, were cleared of trees, bushes and peat, and cranberry vines were set out and watched and tended, at first like rare plants. Success was immediate. More swamps were cleared, and, in a few years cranberry culture became one of the important sources of income all over the Cape. Families who had struggled with poverty and used the old swamp only to get the peat for winter fuel, and that because they could not afford to buy wood or coal, found themselves in comparative affluence. Widows, and they were very numerous on the Cape in those days, who had been barely able to keep out of the poorhouse, were surprised to find themselves in receipt of an almost certain income of hundreds and, sometimes, thousands of dollars. A retired sea-captain whose little fortune was invested in a cranberry bog, as it is called, was getting richer from the once worthless old swamp, where, forty years before, he had chased foxes, than he would have done as master of a fine ship. As you drive along the sandy, winding roads through the low forest of scrub oaks and stunted pines, you pass now and then in a clearing a low, perfectly level expanse covered with the cranberry vines, which in the month of August, when the stranger is most likely to see them, are just beginning to be spotted with the bright color of the ripening berry. Sometimes it is only a patch; sometimes acres will stretch out as level and as green as a billiard table. One of the sights of the early autumn is the cranberry picking, done chiefly by women and children, and it is worth a journey to behold. Then are shipped the barrels, which one sees in the markets of Boston, New York, Chicago and St. Louis, where the branded name recalls at once the lovely green and red and white of the Cape bogs: the green rows of fresh-looking vines, the berries red and shining, suggesting always the New England thanksgiving dinner, and the white lines of sand in which the vines are set. I do not know the yearly value of the hundreds or thousands of acres of cranberry meadow; but it is many thousands of dollars, and has gone very far to make up for the loss of ships and fishing fleets and salt-works.

The summer boarder is not peculiar to Cape Cod. The eastern coast, from Nova Scotia to Cape May, is thronged with such in search of rest and recreation and change of scene, as are also, indeed, the lake shores of Michigan and Wisconsin and the wilds of Colorado. In very many places, however, we find nothing but the boarders, and the houses built for them. When autumn comes, loneliness descends upon the scene, lately so full of life, and all is desolate until the next summer's heat, or the call of fashion, entices the crowd once more to sea and lake and mountain. But not so on the Cape. There the ordinary life goes on quite undisturbed, although somewhat modified at times, in summer and winter. The old village adds, it may be, a hotel or two near the shore; some ancient houses are enlarged, sometimes by curious additions; the variety store spruces up and puts in a lot of fancy articles which "city folks" will like; cool drinks of a strictly temperance brand and ice-cream soda are added;

a few cigars of a better brand than the "two for five" in which the natives inclined to be dissipated and extravagant on Sundays sometimes indulge, are temptingly displayed; the parson of the village church surpasses his winter efforts in the battle against evil and in the eloquence of his sermon; and the girls watch eagerly and copy industriously the latest fashion of sleeve or hat. But the village turns aside only a very little from its usual plan of existence, and fall and winter and spring see the old ways go on as before the summer boarder came. Forty years ago a stranger coming to our Cape village to seek board merely to get a change of air and surroundings, was unknown, and would have been looked upon had he appeared as an odd, not to say suspicious, character. Now of all the four-score communities that line the shores on both sides of the peninsula, from Buzzard's Bay to Provincetown, only one is uninvaded by summer boaders. In that village, one of the prettiest on the Cape, the people, strange to say, do not want them, and make no effort to atract them.

The south side of the Cape and the eastern shore of Buzzard's Bay are the favorite resorts. There the water is warm for bathing, the temperature being usually at seventy, or higher. The prevailing southwest wind is soft and balmy, laden with the aroma of the sea, and yet, coming as it does over the shoal and warm water of Vineyard Sound, without the harshness of the sea-breezes of the north shore. The roads are unusually good, especially for a section popularly supposed to have no soil but sand, if sand may be called soil. The drives through the pines and scrub-oaks are charming; the small lakes, or ponds, so numerous one almost never loses sight of one, tempt the angler to try for the big bass which tradition says is lurking in the deep places. Every village is full of history of its own, and nowhere has the quaint old stock died out. Old houses, curious furniture, rare articles brought home in sea-going days from foreign lands, in the fast ship, once commanded by the master of the house, the model of which now ornaments a table or mantel-piece, a fish, or vessel under full sail, for a weather-vane; the odd sayings one hears, the peculiar ways of the people—all these are full of interest to a visitor. There is, to be sure, the same salt sea on the shore and in the air to be found by the ocean anywhere; there are the large hotels and the same gay summer life, with the numerous summer girls and the rare men on the Cape as elsewhere; but one who chooses may find much more. He may see phases of life and character among the people of these towns as interesting as he could find in a novel; vastly more so, indeed, than in most of the modern stories with which the piazza dawdler tries to while away the heavy days.

To the villages themselves comes ample return for the cost and pains expended. Ready money flows into the landlord's pocket and to every family in the village. Lands and houses increase in value and larger taxes are more easily paid than were the small ones before. Many sons of the Cape who have amassed fortunes in the cities or in the far West return to their ancestral towns, build handsome summer homes, or more frequently restore and beautify the old

mansions, and often give to the village a hall, or a library. Many an old homestead has been thus rejuvenated and the community correspondingly benefited, both by the actual money spent and by the new sympathy given to every good work of the town. Thus much of the influence of the summer life is made permanent and of lasting value. Old ties are renewed, family affections are strengthened, local pride is stimulated. People often return to the same place season after season and form strong attachments to the good towns-folk, so that the summer's return is anticipated with pleasure by natives and foreigners alike. The village life is quickened for the other nine or ten months in the year, without being disturbed or revolutionized or losing its native flavor and strength.

And so the lovely vine bearing its handsome fruit, and the summer boarder of infinite variety, may share the honor of rescuing historic Cape Cod from poverty and comparative oblivion.

Looking more carefully at one of these Cape villages, one finds a type of all. With its two or three principal streets; its Baptist and Methodist meeting-houses; the post office, where natives and foreigners mingle nightly in a good-natured crowd to wait for the evening mail; several village stores where can always be found the things you don't want as well as some things which you must have; old houses, stored with furniture and curios which would delight the soul of an antiquarian; its families who have lived here for generations, all connected by marriage, and all calling everybody by their christian names. Then there is

the little village library, with a charming reading-room, supported generously by the summer visitors, but
used continually and profitably the
year round; and the village hall,
where some sort of entertainment goes
on almost every night, from a pretentious dramatic performance by a
strolling company to a local concert in
aid of the library fund.   The houses
are all, almost without exception, neat
and comfortable one-story-and-a-half
cottages.   No signs of poverty are
seen anywhere, nor any indications of
wealth.   The people seem to have
reached the enviable state prayed for
by Agur, when he said, "Give me
neither poverty nor riches."   One
wonders how the people live; where
the income to satisfy needs never so
modest can be found.   There is no
manufacturing interest anywhere on
the Cape below Sandwich, and the
glass industry which once made that
town so lively has practically disappeared like the shipping and the salt-
works.   The old sources of revenue
have gone.   Not every family has a
cranberry bog or keeps boarders, but
all seem comfortable and happy.
Money taken in large sums by certain
people sifts down through the mass
somehow.   And then the savings-
banks still pay the semi-annual divi-
dends from old-time savings, when
Captain Crosby or Captain Lovell
went to sea, or had his share from the
fishing voyage. Besides, two or three
hundred dollars go farther here than
as many thousands in the great city.
On the bluff overlooking the blue
waters of the Sound, a mile or so from
the village, in the midst of odoriferous
pines, is a charming hotel, with cottages all about, making a little colony

by itself.   West of the village, a quarter of a mile down the shore of a
lovely bay surrounded by wooded hills,
is the more modest establishment, half
hotel, half boarding-house, where
some of us returned natives love to
stay. A mile or more further on is a
passage called "The Narrows," entering a still larger bay whose waters
wash the shore of a pretty village
perched on the hill overlooking the
Sound, the entrance to which is at the
lower end of the bay.   Boats abound,
especially that variety known as the
"cat," broad and shallow for shoal
water sailing, with a centre-board to
drop in the deeper water, and one great
sail, enormous in proportion to the
size of the hull.   These boats, many
of which are built in the shops near
our pier, are famous for speed and
ease of management, and many a
friendly race takes place on the waters
of the bay when the breeze freshens in
the afternoon.   We are seven miles
from a locomotive, and the electric car
has as yet spared us, although a projected line threatens soon to invade
our peace.   Sometimes, when far out
from shore, we are startled by the distant rumbling of a railway train,
brought to our ears through the unusually clear atmosphere.   The swish
of the water against the boat, the flap-
ping of the sail, the sighing of the
breezes have driven out of mind the
clang of gongs, the rattle of the electric car, and the bang on the granite
streets.   We seem so far away from
noise, and dirt, and dust, and care, that
one almost forgets they will ever annoy us again.   All villages, by the sea
or in the country, have their peculiar
people, their odd characters, who seem
to be numerous out of all proportion

to the size of the community; but it really seems as though the Cape has more than its share. Everybody has read Mrs. Stowe's "Oldtown Folks" and remembers Sam Lawson, the shrewd Yankee villager. There is a Sam Lawson in any Cape Cod village which we may study; a town oracle, a gossip, in a good-natured way always, the friend of the children and of all the dumb animals, the defender of those whom malicious tongues may wound, the lover of all good things. Our village has its share of interesting characters. There are so many families of the same name that all the elderly men are *Uncle,* the women, *Aunt.* Captains are as numerous as colonels in Kentucky. There is Captain Y., who is old enough to have celebrated his golden wedding some years ago; a perfect type of the old time sailor; honest, sturdy, kindly disposed to all, who has been at sea, on long voyages or coasting, for sixty years, until he has now taken up the lighter duty of skipper of the big catboat that takes the pleasure parties to the bathing-beach or to the fishing grounds. He is unlike the typical sailor in that he has never tasted liquor or tobacco and he never swears, except in quotation marks, thus differing somewhat from his stage prototype, who is always saying something condemnatory of his eyes. He is a genuine Baptist Christian, who would rather not take a party out for a moonlight sail on "prayer meetin'" night and who alters the crowd's Sunday bath hour to afternoon, because he must go to church in the morning. Of great strength, even now that he is past seventy, he is never easy when the wind is light, but

pulls out his long oar, and poles or rows over the shallows and through the deeps. In his prime he has been known to stand in the hold of a vessel all day and pass the barrels of flour up to the deck hands, lifting them as easily as most men would a peck measure. And unwilling as he has always been to have any trouble with a fellow man, he has more than once silenced and shamed the big bully who was trying to provoke a quarrel, by picking him up and throwing him into the street, as gently as possible, but with a meaningful force after all. The village would not seem the same without his genial company.

Down to the boat-house comes daily, leaning heavily on his stick, Uncle Daniel, gray-headed, with a venerable beard, he looks like an old picture. With a merry twinkle in his bright eye, which his "specs" do not conceal, he inquires how our day is going, and gives his opinion of men and things, of philosophy and religion, of politics and social questions, in a manner and in language not to be described. Woman, her virtues, her usefulness, her many graces, her infinite superiority to man—is his pet theme; and when he gets well warmed up on a Sunday morning with an appreciative audience of natives and boarders about him, the boat-house resounds with his eloquent periods. He loves to provoke a discussion, especially with our host of the boat-house, another uncle, who professes to be an out-and-out atheist, while Uncle Daniel is an enthusiastic Christian in his own peculiar way. But the wary free thinker rarely rises, however tempting the bait, and while Uncle Daniel shouts and saws the air with his arms, only whittles, and at the end of the oration quietly says: "While you have been getting out of breath, Uncle Daniel, talking of what you don't know nothin' about, I have made this cleat for a boat." That usually breaks up the service for the day.

Uncle Sam drops in almost every morning when he is not sailing with a party from the hotel. He wears a patch over one bad eye, and is not very well physically, but his will is as strong as it was twenty years ago when he knocked off using tobacco. He tells the story of his victory over the weed now and then. "Ye see, I had smoked and chawed for a good many years, and I knew it was hurtin' me. One day I was all out of tobaccer and I wanted a smoke terrible; so I went to the store, got a pound of navy plug and a new clay pipe and put 'em on the mantel-piece in my settin'-room. Then I stood up and said to 'em, 'Now we'll see who'll conquer! I or tobaccer!' and when I wanted to smoke so I couldn't sleep nor rest I went to that mantel-piece and said: 'We'll see who'll be the boss!' and I hain't smoked nor chawed these twenty years."

The Cape villages differ from those in the interior in the flavor which a sea-faring life for generations has given to all the life of the people, to the village gossip, to the idioms and illustrations brought into daily talk. The old Cape Codder asks you to "fleet" over to the other side of his boat or of his parlor; he will say of a village beauty who has more than one beau to her string that she "will git ashore trying to tack in a narrer channel between two pints." The village ne'er-do-well is described as one who has "lost his rudder;" the flippant, careless fellow

"lacks ballast." On the other hand the boats are spoken of as elsewhere are women. The *Sallie* is an able boat; the *Billow* is cranky; the *Cygnet* is dependable.

And what stories of life these villagers conceal! Often they would supply writer and dramatist with plot of thrilling interest. So it is that to the student of human life and its strange problems no Cape Cod village is dull and monotonous. He sails his boat, he dips in the refreshing waters of the bay, he enjoys to the utmost the *dolce far niente,* which the Cape sailor used to call "taking a quish"; and yet the greatest interest of his summer outing may come from the people and the life about him.

Vacation life in a place like this, where we give ourselves up to the spirit of rest which is all-pervading, seems monotonous in the telling of it, but this is its charm. We should not want it the year round; we want work and familiar faces and places by and by, and are glad at last when the time comes to return to them; but here, for the brief days which are ours to enjoy, we think nothing could be better than the daily round of busy idleness. And this is about the way that the days go: breakfast, a late one, over, comes the hour's smoke and chat; at ten o'clock the sail to the bathing beach in the Narrows. One big cat-boat carries twenty-five or thirty, and is followed by a fleet of smaller craft each with its load of passengers. The water is warm, delicious for floating or swimming, and the bath is a leisurely one. Then comes a sail on the bay, or perhaps across the Narrows to the rustic building opening upon the water, where we have served to us in the shell on wooden plates little-neck clams or oysters just out of the water, toothsome and appetizing. The genial old man who serves us is a study, one of the characters here, with whom we love to chat as he opens the reluctant clam or oyster. Then, hungry with the edge that has thus been put upon our appetites, we hurry home to dinner. Driving through the woods, golf on the links hard by, a stroll along the shore, or a cast in one of the ponds for that big bass, if haply we may be able to tempt him, follow, and for those who love the water and would avoid dust and noise there is always the boat to sail, perhaps out into the bay and through the Narrows to the deeper and rougher waters of the Sound. Hours pass as minutes, and the sun begins to get near the western hills before we think of the return. Then in the cool of twilight comes the walk to the village, the visit to the post office or the reading-room, or the store, to meet the natives and hear the village gossip. We go to bed early and get up late. It must be granted that this is a dull and uneventful programme for summer pleasure-seekers. So it is, indeed; and some of us are just dull enough and old-fogyish enough to like it far better than the fashionable summer hotel with its music, and its dancing, and its jealousies, its rivalries, and its disappointments. So year after year the same people come again, and each summer seems better than the last. The company is congenial, the life independent and free-an-easy, full of health and honest, simple enjoyment. It is absolutely different from that which we have left behind us in the city, and we store up this delicious sea air to neutralize for the next nine months the vitiated atmosphere of Boston, or Philadelphia, or Chicago, or St. Louis.

One of the odd things about the topography of Cape Cod is the number of ponds of fresh water which one sees, no matter in which direction he drives. Indeed, there is more than one drive through the woods which the boarders in our village take, when for miles one is never out of sight of the gleaming water. The number of ponds on the Cape is variously estimated, but it is safe to say that there are hundreds of them. Most of them are set most beautifully within high banks, thickly wooded. They are of all sizes, from Nine-Mile Pond or Lake Wequaket, as the fashion now is, where yachts and a steam launch are kept, to Aunt Tempie's Pond, near our house, only two or three acres in area. Fed by cool springs, the water is deliciously refreshing and very clear. Sometimes these little lakes are so near the sea that an unusually high tide makes the water brackish; but in a few days it is pure and sweet again. I remember one of these on which we used to sail our toy ships in summer and swift iceboats in winter, so near the waters of Cape Cod Bay that I have seen the spray during a northeaster dash over the narrow barrier of sand, and make us boys think that the pond would never be fresh again. I recall a curious phenomenon which was an annual occurrence in Sheep Pond, very near the home of my ancestors. This pond was nearly two miles from the sea, shut in by high hills all about it. The water, as in many of these lakelets, was cold and deep. No stream flowed into it, and it had no visible outlet. In the spring, during a period of two or three weeks, salt-water smelt were found here in great abundance. We fastened willow wythes between the teeth of hay-rakes, and in the darkness of night raked in the fish by the bushel along the shore. In a few days they disappeared, not to be seen again until the following spring. The views from the high banks of some of these ponds is lovely beyond description. There is no view more beautiful in the famed English Lake Country than that which one may have from the top of a hill overlooking one of the largest of these lakes, called Wakeby. This is in the queer village of Mashpee, inhabited by a remnant of the old Mashpee tribe of Indians, once rovers all over the Cape, now settled down and civilized. It is rather odd, however, to see from the hotel piazza two Indian maidens coming down the hill on brand-new bicycles. Ancient mariners, the redmen of the forest, the summer boarder, the old and the new, get strangely mixed up on Cape Cod nowadays.

These random notes on a bit of Massachusetts coast have purposely omitted mention of that shore which is washed by the beautiful sheet of water called Buzzard's Bay, the western boundary of the Cape. It is lined with villages, the summer homes of fashion and wealth, but there is less of the old-fashioned flavor, less individuality, than is found in Barnstable, or Hyannis, or Brewster. The nearness of locomotive and steamboat makes a difference, and the summer villages are more numerous and more crowded than farther down on the Cape, where he who wants a few weeks of a life quite unlike anything which the city or its neighborhood can afford, and different from the life of most watering places, can so happily find it.

Sunset

By Alice Van Leer Carrick

THE West flares up as if some giant hand
  Flung into castle-clouds a jealous brand
To set the whole sky-world aflame. Below,
All gold and crimson, lies the burnished land.

The Lakes of Cape Cod

By S. W. Abbott

MASSACHUSETTS is unusually well supplied with abundance of fresh water, distributed with considerable uniformity throughout the state. Two great rivers, the Merrimack and Connecticut, with their sources and principal water sheds in New Hampshire and Vermont, traverse portions of the state, furnishing power to several cities and many towns. Besides these, there are scattered here and there more than one thousand lakes and ponds with an area of more than ten acres in each. These are so well distributed as to give almost every town at least one within its limits, but the seacoast towns are the most favored and have a greater number of lakes than those of the western counties. The town of Plymouth alone has at least fifty-three ponds or lakes of more than ten acres, and with a total area of nearly four thousand acres of water surface, while the town of Lakeville has more than six thousand acres in its magnificent lakes.

Many of these bodies of water are pure and wholesome and well adapted for use as the public reservoir of cities and towns whose citizens enjoy the privilege of a constant, never-failing supply in their houses, ready for instant use at the mere turning of a faucet. In no other state does the population thus supplied reach so high a percentage as in Massachusetts where, by the last census, it is shown to be 90 per cent. of the total. The states next upon the list, with from 80 to 90 per cent., are Rhode Island, New Jersey and the District of Columbia. Sentimentally considered, the "old oaken bucket, the moss-covered bucket," as it came up dripping with the cold and crystal draught from the depths of the open well, is a delightful memory; but the keen and accurate analysis of its contents by the chemist, coupled with the great frequency of hitherto unexplained illness in the farmer's family, and the prevalent proximity of the well to an environment, which, to say the least, was of doubtful advantage, shows that public supplies are, as a rule much safer for drinking purposes than the ordinary farm-house well. In 1886 the Board of Health began a careful analysis of the waters of Massachusetts, especially those used as public supplies, and, in the course of the examination of several thousand samples, a very interesting fact was gradually developed. The relative amount of chlorine represented by common salt actually existing in the uncontaminated waters of the State diminishes with considerable uniformity as one leaves the sea-coast and proceeds inland. Even in the most exposed portions, it rarely exceeded 2 parts per 100,000, or about 1/1000th as much as in sea-water. It is to this minute quantity of chlorine, together with other mineral salts, that spring waters owe their pleasant, sparkling taste, as compared with the flatness of rain or distilled water. Up to a certain amount the presence of salt renders them more agreeable, but when the proportion rises as high as 1/10th of one per cent. the water, in common parlance, becomes "brackish." The percentage of chlorine is also an index of considerable value in the determination of the amount of sewage pollution in water, and by examining the results obtained by analysis and connecting, upon the map, points where equal quantities of chlorine are found in the uncontaminated sources of supply, a chart has been obtained showing with comparative accuracy the standard of purity of the water to be found in any given district. In the case of the lakes and ponds of Cape Cod, as we leave the tip of the Cape at Provincetown and proceed south and west toward the mainland, this rule applies with considerable precision, as will be seen by the following table arranged in that order:

Name of Lake or Pond	Location	Ratio of Chlorine in water per 100,000 parts	Areas in Acres
Shank Painter Pond,	Province- town,	2.42	83
Clapp's Pond,		2.39	72
Great Pond	Eastham,	1.98	112
Long Pond,	Brewster,	1.44	778
Nine Mile Pond	Barnstable.	1.05	700
Mashpee Lake,		.85	770
John's Pond,	Mashpee,	.81	240
Ashumet,		.77	226
Long Pond,	Falmouth,	.87	205

Of such lakes and ponds having areas of more than ten acres in each, there are in all one hundred and seventy-four in the fifteen towns comprised in the region known as Cape Cod, that is in Barnstable County. Twenty-one of these lakes have areas of one hundred, and three have areas of seven hundred acres or more in each. Twenty-seven of the whole number are in the *town* of Barnstable, while the remainder are scattered throughout the county with a considerable degree of uniformity, no town having less than five within its limits. In consequence of the topographical character of the Cape none of the large ponds are at elevations of more than one hundred feet above the sea.

The highest, according to the topographical sheets of Massachusetts published at Washington, is Peters Pond in Sandwich, with an elevation of about ninety feet. Next are Mashpee Lake, Spectacle, Triangle, and Lawrence Ponds in Sandwich, with elevations of from sixty to eighty feet. Santuit Pond in Mashpee, Cotuit, Shubael and Round ponds in Barnstable, forty to sixty feet. Great or Nine Mile Pond in Barnstable, and Mill Pond in Brewster, about thirty feet. Mill and Pollins ponds, tributaries of Bass River in Yarmouth, Long and Swan ponds in Yarmouth, Swan Pond in Dennis, Long Pond in Brewster, and Hinckley's Pond in Harwich, have elevations of from ten to twenty feet, while few if any of the larger ponds in the easterly towns of the Cape beyond Brewster have elevations of more than fifteen feet above the sea.

A considerable number of the fresh water ponds which are quite near the sea level along the south shore, as well as those on the shore of Nantucket, are probably nothing more than shallow inlets from the sea which were cut off by the formation of bars at their mouths, the annual rainfall being sufficient to convert them into fresh water lakes in a few years. Considering the geological formation of this region, it would hardly seem reasonable that any of its depressions should have greater depths than are found in the neighboring waters of the sea. The extreme depth of the Sound and of Massachusetts Bay at distances of five miles from the shore is scarcely more than twenty-five fathoms, at any point. It is not probable therefore that any of these ponds have greater depths than that, although local tradition often accredits them as bottomless. The writer was once informed by a native that Peters Pond in South Sandwich was six hundred feet deep in parts. On making many soundings, with a ship's lead and line, the extreme depth was found to be fifty feet. According to the report of the Massachusetts Fish Commission of 1900, Great, or Nine Mile Pond, in Barnstable, has a maximum depth of twenty-five feet, and at Follin's Pond in Yarmouth the "depth in the northern part varies from four to seven feet in the deepest sections."

Mashpee, which is the largest of the Cape Cod lakes as well as the most picturesque, is probably the deepest in the county. This beautiful sheet is surrounded by bolder and higher shores than the others, yet several soundings, taken both in the northern and southern halves, show the deepest place to be but sixty-one feet and at a point about one-third of the distance across from the eastern shore in the southern half. The lake is divided into two nearly equal portions by a peninsula, across whose narrow neck, as tradition says, the earlier Indian inhabitants were wont to drive the deer and other game which are still to be found in greatly diminished numbers. The lake abounds in fish of many kinds, including the delicious trout for which this region is famous. At its southern end the town of Mashpee has its principal village, the largest and almost the only settlement in the state in which the descendants of the Massachusetts Indians have lived, since the state reserved this tract for their use. Nearly if not all of these people have become so mixed by intermarriage, either with whites or with negroes, that the Indian type is modified. They have their town government, church, and schools the same as other Cape towns. The church, a Baptist one, is largely supported by an ancient fund, the distribution of which is entrusted to the authorities of Harvard College. Its meeting-house is located a mile from the village in the forest with an Indian grave-yard near it. Along the lake shore traces of the earlier tribes are often found in the shape of implements, arrow-heads and other weapons, which are ploughed up from the light sandy soil of the region; while nearer the sea, often within a few rods of the water, heaps of broken oyster, clam, scallop and quohaug shells are found in scores, showing that the aborigines evidently appreciated their contents for food. A dam in the outlet at the road makes a little mill-pond a few acres in extent, and here the Egyptian lotus, planted there by the proprietor of the neighboring hotel, grows and thrives luxuriantly.

The climate of the southern shore of Cape Cod is generally milder than that of other portions of the state, as indicated by the fact that the lakes and ponds of this region rarely freeze in winter to a thickness of more than five or six inches. The shallower ponds are everywhere studded with water lilies of unusual size and brilliancy, and some of them of varied colors, which command a good price at the flower stores in Boston. The sea water along the shores of Vineyard Sound and Buzzards Bay has a temperature during the summer months of about 75 degrees. The surface temperature of the fresh water lakes is a little high-er, or about 80 degrees from July 1st to September 1st. Observations made upon Jamaica Pond and other fresh water ponds in the summer of 1889 by the State Board of Health, showed that the temperature of the water un-dergoes a uniform decrease in the lower strata, until at depths below sixty feet a temperature of about 40 degrees is reached. But as water con-tracts down to a temperature of 40 de-grees and then expands until it reaches 32 degrees, the temperature of the lower strata does not fall much below 40 degrees. So that in October or November when the temperature at the surface is 40 degrees, a change takes place in all the ponds which have a depth of twenty feet or more and the lower strata of water rises to the sur-face, the whole body of water thus be-coming of a nearly uniform tempera-ture and remaining so throughout the winter.

The reason that Thoreau, in his charming description of Cape Cod, says so little about these beautiful lakes, is probably because in his visit he selected a route which lay along the seashore. He writes:

"Our host took pleasure in telling us the names of the ponds, most of which we could see from our windows, and making us repeat them after him, to see if we had got them right. They were Gull Pond, the largest, and a very handsome one, clear and deep, and more than a mile in circum-ference; Newcomb's, Swett's, Slough, Horse-leech, Round, and Herring Ponds, all connected at high water, if I do not mistake. The coast surveyors had come to him for their names, and he told them of one which they had not detected. He said they were not so high as formerly. There was an earth-quake about four years before he was born, which cracked the pans of the pond which were of iron, and caused them to settle. I did not remember to have read of this. In-numerable gulls used to resort to them, but the large gulls were now very scarce, for, as he said, the English robbed their nests far in the north, where they breed."

The ponds here referred to are in Wellfleet, which like those in Orleans, Eastham, Truro and Provincetown, the northern towns of the Cape, are the least interesting and picturesque of them all. They are mostly shallow ex-cavations in the soil, and are at a slight elevation only above sea level, a cir-cumstance which has given rise to a popular theory that their source is the sea water, which is deprived of its salt by filtration. This theory, however, is not tenable, frequent experiments, notably by the late Prof. W. B. Nich-ols of the Massachustts Institute of Technology, showing that sea water might be passed through sand filters over and over again without losing a particle of its salt. The fresh-water springs, which appear at intervals along the seacoast, are nothing more than the expression of the rainfall, which falling upon the higher lands makes its way toward the sea. This rainfall, amounting to over forty inches a year, is amply sufficient to ac-count for all the water in the ponds, for a single inch of rain upon an acre of water-surface amounts to one hundred tons of water, and a year's rain would therefore amount to more than four thousand tons of water per acre. Even were they near enough the cities of eastern Massachusetts, the quantity of water which these lakes could furnish would be entirely inadequate to supply the wants of a metropolitan population, since no one of them has a large contributing water-shed or streams of considerable size running into them. The great pumps of the Boston Water Works at Chestnut Hill would pump any one of them dry in a few days.

The most picturesque series of lakes upon the Cape is that which extends from Long Pond in Falmouth to Great or Nine Mile Pond in Barnstable, Coonemosset, Ashumet, John's, Mashpee and the Cotuit Ponds. Several of these lie in deep hollows, and are surrounded by forests of ash and pine. A fine view of Coonemosset Pond may be had from the south, across cultivated fields and meadows, or glimpses of its silvery surface may be caught here and there through the trees along the road upon its northern border. Ashumet also lies near the road leading from Falmouth to Mashpee, while the next of the series, John's Pond in Mashpee, is entirely concealed from view, being remote from any habitation or traveled road. The water of all these lakes is exceedingly pure, although, like all surface waters, it is subject to the growth of *algae* during the summer. It is remarkable that the microscopic flora of these lakes, Ashumet and John's, although separated by a ridge of scarcely a half mile in width, is quite as distant as though they were a thousand miles apart. Each of the ponds in this series is connected with Vineyard Sound by brooks; that of Nine Mile Pond being an artificial outlet, made by the town of Barnstable several years ago to allow the herring to ascend to the fresh water of the pond for the purpose of spawning.

The persistence of Indian names is more noticeable in this county than in any other part of the state. Nearly all of the names of the towns are of English origin, but those of the lakes, streams and localities are largely the Indian ones by which they have been known for centuries. Such are Coonemosset Pond and River, Ashumet, and Wakeby or Wakepee Lakes, Poponesset Bay, Waquoit Bay, Chapoquoit Harbor, Wenaumet, Cataumet, Nauset and Monomoy.

An Old Letter From a New England Attic

By Almon Gunnison

SOME day the wise writer will tell the story of the New England attic, and will weave into verse or song the romances of the heirlooms that are gathered there,—the discarded cradle whose rockers are footworn by those whose grave stones were long ago gray with moss; the broken chairs in which, by the fireside, aged parents slumbered into the sleep which has no awakening; the rude bedstead in which boys who are now bowed with age slept beneath the rafters and heard the pattering of the rain upon the attic roof, looking out upon the stars and weaving their dreams into visions and songs; the old garments bearing the fashion of an age long gone, while unspent odors of the bleached floor and roof mingle with the scent of the house wife's herbs which once hung in the great room. How curiously childhood made its little mysteries of the half darkened attic, what strange figures used to hide behind chimney and press, what voices spoke from the old chests and what curious ancestors crept at night into the old garments and awed the childish imagination of those who made the attic the half haunted chamber of dreams and visions. The novelist who is hunting in town and country archives for the story of colonial days has somehow missed the richest treasury of the New England attic,

and the true history of the Civil War will never be told until the yellowing letters hidden in attic chests have been read again and the chroniclers from field and camp and battle field have told their eventful and vivid tale.

Central Massachusetts is rich with old houses whose attics will some day furnish a rare field for the antiquarian and story teller. Great cities have not swept away these homes with the tides of surburban enterprises and the jar of industry's whirling wheels has not shattered the mysteries and memories of a long past. The great religious agitation which shook New England more than a century ago and resulted in the Unitarian movement was hardly more felt in Boston than in Central Massachusetts. Nearly every Congregational church in the valley of Nashua was on Unitarian lines. Heterodoxy became Orthodoxy and parish churches which had been dedicated to the triune God became Unitarian. Elsewhere than in New England this sect has had its social and religious ostracism, but in Massachusetts, in places not a few, the social and intellectual life of the community was largely centered in the Unitarian church, and for a little time at least, the prestige, the wealth and influence of the town were with the church whose new faith had well nigh shattered New England Orthodoxy.

The town of Lancaster, Massachusetts, very early became Unitarian, and has been until this day one of the strongholds of this faith. Many of the old and influential families are still associated with that church and its influence is felt in the refined social and intellectual life for which the town is famous. The present pastor, Rev. Dr. Bartol, white bearded like a patriarch, has completed a pastorate of many years and is still in active service. He is a fine type of the Unitarian minister for which the last century was famous: scholarly, refined, courtly in manner, he has some of the literary accomplishments of his more distinguished brother, Dr. Cyrus A. Bartol, of Boston, recently deceased.

In 1780, in Lancaster, Sampson V. S. Wilder was born. Later in this paper some particulars of his eventful life will be given. After a long absence he returned to his native place in 1823. He was a man not only of indomitable enterprise but of a stalwart and uncompromising faith. He saw with alarm the growth of the new heresy and with relentless determination sought to overcome it. The new faith had become the orthodoxy of the town and he found himself in the unwonted rôle of a heretic. So persistent and pestilent did his opposition seem to his neighbors that he was visited with a social ostracism and at length, in the interest of the community's peace, he was by formal petition asked either to cease his agitation or to remove from the town. This petition, signed by forty-four men of the town, was presented to him in the form of a letter. There is no record of it in the history of the town, but in a trunk in the attic of one of the old houses of Lancaster

the original letter has recently been found. It makes a unique chapter in the history of Unitarianism in New England. The letter is as follows:

August 20, 1831.

To Sampson V. S. Wilder:

Sir: The undersigned inhabitants of South village in the town of Lancaster, deeply impressed with a just sense of that duty which they owe to their families, to the rising generation and to society in general, and believing it to be a paramount duty incumbent on them, to use all honorable means in their power to preserve and transmit to posterity, unspotted and uncontaminated, those blessings which they so highly appreciate: Religion, Morality and Public Order, which they have hitherto rationally and peacefully enjoyed. Therefore entertaining these views of those sacred privileges which have been transmitted to them, they cannot refrain from expressing their abhorrence and solemnly protesting against everything which tends to corrupt those principles and virtues, and to disturb that peace and harmony which can alone adorn the human character.

Having long watched with painful anxiety the unhappy effects produced by your fanaticism and zeal, we feel it our duty to inform you that we look upon your coming and view your presence among us as a calamity of no ordinary kind. That we believe the course which you are pursuing is productive of little or no good, but much evil. That we think it calculated to corrupt the morals and disseminate vice among the people. That you are sowing contentions, hatred and discord, where peace, happiness and good order have hitherto prevailed. That family hatred, strife and abuse of every kind have been the effects in every family where you have made proselytes and we look upon the fruits of your zeal as worse than the pestilence that stealeth at noon day. We pity your ignorance so far as that directs your zeal, but we fear something worse than ignorance guides your operations against the peace and harmony of this town. We look upon the course you are pursuing towards the inhabitants of this place as insulting in the highest degree and were we to form an opinion from your conduct we would think you a fit person to inhabit a mad-house or a workhouse. In short, we view your character and conduct as disgraceful to any person professing decency and common sense and we shall hail your departure from this section of the country as a blessing to the people, which we hope may long be continued to them.

(Signed by forty-four men.)

The life of Mr. Wilder is so unique and eventful that its story can profitably be retold, being summarized from his biography published by the American Tract Society in 1865.

He was born in Lancaster, May 20, 1780. His maternal ancestors came from the west of England and were brought up in the Whitefield Orthodox School. The Socinian Controversy was raging at that time, and it is possible that his almost fanatical hatred of Unitarian views was a birth inheritance from his ancestors. His mother was a woman of fervent piety and brought up in the principles of strictest morality. In a public address, the son thus alluded to her: "If I have any right to the endearing title of Evangelical Christian, it is to the faithful, untiring admonition impressed line upon line, precept upon precept, by this devoted mother." His father died when the son was thirteen years old. He was a man of great integrity and his funeral was the largest ever held in Lancaster. The boy Sampson was overwhelmed with grief and could only by force be prevented from throwing himself into the open grave.

Entering a store kept by Squire Flagg, a form clerk to his father, he remained one year; and after two years' work in Gardner, ne went to Boston. He was partially engaged to work for a prominent firm when, accidentally learning they were believers in the Socinian faith, he refused a salary of one hundred and fifty dollars, engaging with another merchant whose compensation was smaller, but whose orthodoxy was sound. He at once attached himself to the congregation presided over by Rev. Jedediah Morse, the father of the inventor of the magnetic telegraph. His ardent piety at once arrested the attention of his pastor, who tendered him the use of his library and became his instructor. On the death of his employer, he carried on the business for the widow, going into business, however, for himself after a few years, his store being located on Court Street. One day a merchant, Allan Melville, came into his store and told him that he had received an invoice of thirty thousand dollars' worth of French goods on which he desired to realize at once. Young Wilder, on examination, saw that the goods were invoiced at nearly twenty per cent. less than their value. He had no ready money. A friend told him that William Gray, a millionaire of Salem, had money which he was always ready to loan. Gray was interviewed and promised one third of the profits of the sale for the loan of the thirty thousand dollars, the transaction to be closed in sixty days. The rich merchant gave his note payable in ten days. Getting the note cashed, the purchase was made. The next morning the goods were displayed and advertised. Customers came, and in nine days Mr. Wilder called on Mr. Gray with one thousand eight hundred and seventy-five dollars in money as his share of the profits. The incident is so peculiar that it is quoted from the papers of Mr. Wilder:

"On reaching the office," he says, "instead of being cordially received, Mr. Gray exclaimed: 'Ah, young man, I did a very foolish thing in assisting you to go into that operation, in which they say much money will be lost; and besides it is only the ninth day and you told me you would not need the money for ten days. I shall not pay you one cent to-day, sir. Call tomorrow and I suppose I must give you the money. And, now, as I am very busy, I bid you good morning.' Said I: 'Mr. Gray, before leaving your office I must request you to do me the favor to sign this paper.' Said he: 'Young man, I shall sign no papers until at least tomorrow.' 'Well,' said I, 'You must excuse me, sir, but I do not leave your office until you sign this paper.' Mr. Gray turned to me and said: 'It is no use, young man, for you to stand there, as I shall sign no papers.' 'But,' said I, 'Mr. Gray, do you object to casting your eye on the paper and seeing its purport?' 'Why,' said he, 'It is really too bad to have one's time taken up in this way; there are two ships I have to despatch to sea this afternoon. Here,' said he, reaching out his hand and putting on his specs, 'let me see the paper.' He then began to read it aloud: 'Received of S. V. S. Wilder,—received!' said he, 'I've received nothing,' and was on the point of handing back the paper. Said I: 'Read on, if you please, Mr. Gray.' 'Received eighteen hundred and seventy-five dollars,—eh! eh!—it being my proportion of profits.' 'Yes,' said I, 'I've sold the goods and here is the money,' handing it to the clerks to count. 'What?' said he, 'And you want no money from me tomorrow?' 'No, sir,' said I, 'I sold for ready cash, with which I paid

Mr. Melville. You have one-third of the profits counted down, sir.' 'And you want no money from me?' 'No, sir; it's all settled as you perceive.' 'Why, Mr. Wilder, walk into my private counting room. Do you ever come to Salem?' 'No, sir,' said I, 'and all I ask of you, sir, is to sign the receipt and as I have other pressing engagements, excuse me from coming into your counting room.' 'Well,' said he, 'come down and pass a week with us and let me introduce you to my family.' Thanking him, I left him exultant."

This led Mr. Gray to propose to Mr. Wilder to be his agent in Europe. Accepting the position, he sailed for Europe in the ship *Elizabeth* from Boston. He reached Paris on the day and

hour when Napoleon was proclaimed Emperor in the twelve squares of the city. The fountains ran wine from morning till night. Thousands of legs of mutton were distributed to the eight hundred thousand people who witnessed the imposing pageantries. He set at work at once to learn the French language, engaging as his tutor Latour Maubrey, who afterwards became the private secretary of Napoleon, and who died of a broken heart because he was not allowed by the government to share in the exile of his chief. In eighteen months Mr. Wilder cleared for Mr. Gray sixty thousand dollars. Returning home he accepted agencies for Mr. Gray, Israel Thorndike and William Bartlett of Newburyport, the three wealthiest merchants in New England. With occasional returns to America, he resided in Paris for several years, an intimate friend of Talley-

rand and other French notables, representing the United States at the marriage of Napoleon and being a witness of his triumphs after the battle of Austerlitz and the festivities which followed the birth of the King of Rome. He entertained with lavish hospitality, and was one of the centers of the American colony, but, while he was an enthusiast in his admiration of Napoleon, he was an ardent lover of his own land.

His enthusiasm for Napoleon was a passion. He had seen under his sway religious freedom come; the Code Napoleon, afterward to be adopted in the main by every leading nation, was his creation; a new era of larger liberty and progress had been brought to France by the man of destiny, and when the final crisis came in his career, Mr. Wilder proposed a plan for Napoleon's escape and tendered him

an asylum at his residence in Bolton. The plan was that Napoleon should disguise himself as a valet, for whom Mr. Wilder had already a passport, and hasten with him to the coast, where there would be one of his ships with a large cask on board, in which the Emperor would be concealed until the ships had sailed beyond the limits of danger. This scheme, the Wilder biography narrates, Napoleon seriously considered and declared feasible, but finally declined because he would not desert friends who had been faithful to him through prosperity and adversity. He wished Mr. Wilder to arrange for their flight also, but Mr. Wilder said this was impossible, so the project fell through, and soon after, other plans for escape failing, the Emperor surrendered himself to the officers of the *Bellerophon*. Edward Everett Hale, in alluding to the incident,

wittily said: "Who knows but that he might have been selectman of the town of Bolton, had he chosen to take out naturalization papers."

The following incident occurred during Mr. Wilder's stay in Paris. During the Elba exile, the Bourbon king had a law passed that no picture, statue, statuette, figure or resemblance of General Bonaparte, as he was called, should remain in any public or private place or any native or foreign residence. Mr. Wilder's turn for inspection came. Not even his friend Talleyrand could have protected him. An officer, with secretary and attendants, came into his counting room, saying in a pompous manner: "Have you any image, statue or likeness of any kind of that man?" "Of what man," said Mr. Wilder, "I am a stranger here." "Why do you keep me, you know whom I mean; that usurper, that

Bonaparte, if you will have it," said the officer. "Have you any likeness or representation of him?" "Certainly I have," said Mr. Wilder, "Gorrgain, bring me a bag of Napoleons." Then, pouring them out on the desk before him: "Here, they are, sir." The official stared. At first he could make no answer, but then said: "That money is not what I want. You can keep that." "Go and tell your master," said Mr. Wilder, "that the whole specie currency of the realm must be called in before he can keep from the eyes of the people the features of the Emperor Napoleon." "You are right," said the officer, but continuing aside to his comrades, "It is ridiculous, this business we are about, but the stupid Bourbons cannot see it."

The entire life of Mr. Wilder is characterized by his passionate devo-

tion to the evangelical faith. He was willing to spend and be spent in his service to historic orthodoxy. While in Europe, he met one day Mr. Collins of the London Tract Society. Being asked by him if he could not dispose of some French tracts in Paris, Mr. Wilder took from his pocket a ten pound note saying: "Send me the worth of that and I will see what I can do." In a short time he was notified that a bundle awaited him at the public buildings of Paris. He went to the place, which chanced to be the very building where Marie Antoinette and Josephine had been incarcerated. The huge bundle contained his tracts, which had been detained as suspicious literature. Mr. Wilder asked the privilege of reading aloud some of them. At the conclusion of his readings the superintendent said: "I thank you.

These teach good morals. Will you give me some?" Within a month the great supply was exhausted and more were ordered. A translator was secured, a printing establishment set up and this was the beginning of the French Tract Society, which was formed under Mr. Wilder's roof in 1818.

In 1812 Mr. Wilder crossed the Atlantic, bearing dispatches from France. President Madison anxiously awaited him. Relays of horses speeded him on his way to Washington. Arriving there at eleven o'clock at night he went to the house of the Secretary of War, Monroe. "We must go immediately," said the secretary, "to the President." Ringing the bell, an old man with nightcap on and candle in hand came to the door. It was the President. Mr. Wilder, accustomed to the etiquette and formalism of the French court, was shocked at first, but was proud of the simplicity of this ruler whose authority was larger than that of the King of France.

In 1823 Mr. Wilder came home to live in the United States, to the regret of many of his friends in Europe. He had owned the house in Bolton for many years, but had given the rent of it to a friend in Boston. He was grieved to find upon the tables, Unitarian books and pamphlets and attributed to the hateful doctrine the laxity which he found in his native town. He reconsecrated himself to the extermination of the hated heresy, and while he planted the vines and fruit trees which he had brought from Versailles and beautified his home, he instituted a relentless propaganda against the new faith which had banished Orthodoxy. His zeal was not always tempered with discretion, nor softened by charity. The old bitterness was revived among neighbors who had forgotten the enmities of doctrine and where there had been peace, discord came. It was at this time that the letter found in the attic chest was written, rebuking the proselytism of the rich citizen and, with words which left nothing to be imagined, gave the fanatical defender of the old faith the assurance that he must moderate his zeal or increase his toleration. He was a zealot, who, had he been less noble, and had more power, would have made an ideal persecutor; but he had ever been masterful, self-assertive, with a pride of opinion which could not conceive that any faith save his own could be of God. And yet he was generous to other churches, so be it they were of type evangelical. He was only illiberal to liberalism. He was the friend of temperance and education, one of the founders and trustees of Amherst College, when it was created as a bulwark for the defence of historic Orthodoxy. He built beside his home the Hillside Chapel, which for many years was the center of Orthodoxy for the region, furnishing it at large cost, establishing many of the features of the later institutional church, and making it one of the most tasteful and beautiful churches in New England. At the formation of the American Tract Society, he was elected its president, serving seventeen years with distinguished ability and success. He was its largest benefactor in its days of poverty.

His house was made notable among the country homes of Massachusetts. Furniture and curios brought from France adorned it, and to this home

Lafayette came in 1824, receiving a hospitality which was almost regal. His business activity did not cease. He reorganized the mills in which he had investments, made purchases of stock and land and removing to New York engaged in trade. But in 1841, his life long prosperity began to ebb and did not cease until the man of wealth was made poor. In his poverty, however, he was still the man of faith, repining not at his hard fortune, wishing back no gift that he had made, grateful for the mercies which had come to him in earlier years and the faith that taught him that life does not consist in the abundance of things one has. He died in Elizabeth, New Jersey, in 1865, and is there buried.

The religious enmities of his period have passed away. Beneath the elm bordered roads of Lancaster and Bolton, the neighbors dwell, holding their differing beliefs, but holding them in tolerant affection. The Hillside Chapel was burned long ago, and the curious traveler can only with difficulty, from the alien people who toil around it, learn its site. But somewhere in the life of the community which has run out to the ends of the earth have been lodged the gracious influences of the faith which was nurtured there.

Still stands on the Bolton road the old house of Sampson Wilder. It is christened "Rosenvec," and is the residence of J. Wyman Jones of New York, Its name is an anagram composed from the maiden name, Converse, of Mrs.

Jones. There are few finer examples of the colonial architecture in New England. Modernized, it yet keeps the old type. The additions are in keeping with the original, and all the new decorations repeat the faultless lines which exist in the unchanged portion. It has forty rooms, furnished with the richest furniture, yet colonial in style: a bedstead which once was in a French palace in the period of the Empire is in the room of Lafayette; and a taste intelligent and refined has kept the old form, while it has given to it the animation and spirit of the new and better age. The old clock, which has measured the flight of generations, swings its pendulum within the hall, and countless nooks and graces of architectural design tell how wise and resourceful were the old builders, who, two hundred years ago, erected the New England mansions. But changed as is the old house, there is the same landscape that was there when Lafayette came to be entertained by the prince of commerce, although the elms cast broader shadows and the forests have crept away from the meadows. Herds of nobler breed feed on the pasture slopes and within house and stable are luxuries which were inaccessible, even to wealth, in the long ago. But still the sunset paints the old-time colors on the western skies, and, rising in majesty, not far away, stands Wachusett, while, dimly outlined in the distance, rises Monadnock, the unchanging monarch of the New England mountains.

Roger Williams and the Plantations at Providence

By E. J. Carpenter

"A STATUE," says Addison, "lies hid in a block of marble, and the art of the statuary only clears away the superflous matter and removes the rubbish." About the life and name of Roger Williams, as they appear to the eye of the ordinary observer, is heaped a mass of debris, obscuring from sight the man himself, in his true proportions. Even history, as it is written to-day, sheds upon him a light, sometimes too roseate, sometimes too pale, as he stands upon the world's stage; and his contemporaries, too, come on in ghostly fashion, in form often distorted and misjudged.

It shall be my task to clear away, so far as may be possible, some of the rubbish which surrounds this man, and to turn upon him the true light of historical record.

Of the early life of Roger Williams, before his appearance in this country, we know but little. We do not even know the date of his birth; and what manner of man he was, in bodily presence, none can say. Tradition, always unreliable, has said that Wales was his native country. Recent genealogical researches in London by Mr. Henry F. Waters, in behalf of the New England Historic-Genealogical Society, lead to the belief, however, that he was born in that city; that his father, who died in September, 1620, was named John Williams; that his mother, who died in August, 1634, was named Alice; and that he had two brothers, Sydrach and Robert by name, and one sister, named Catharine, who was the wife of Ralph Wightman.

In a legal document, executed in 1679, Roger Williams records himself as "being now near to four-score years of age." It would appear, then, that he was born at the opening of the seventeenth century. He must, then, have been not far from thirty years of age, when he set sail from Bristol, England, in the ship Lyon, in the winter of 1630.

The records of the Charter House show that he was admitted a student June 25, 1621. He was matriculated a pensioner of Pembroke College, Oxford, in July, 1625, and he was graduated with the degree of Bachelor of Arts, in January, 1627. We know that in his youth he had attracted the attention of Edmund Coke, and it is probable that he was, in some measure, the protegé of that eminent man.

This brief record is all that we know, certainly, of the life of Roger Williams, until the ship Lyon, aforesaid, appeared off Nantasket, in February, 1631. His wife Mary is recorded as having been a passenger in the same ship. That she was then a bride is not improbable; for the first child of this couple, of whom we have any record, and who bore her mother's name,

Mary, was born at Plymouth, as Williams himself records, "ye first weeke in August, 1633."

We may be sure that Williams, before leaving England had been admitted to orders in the English church, or, at least, had been a student of theology; for Winthrop records his arrival as that of "a godly minister." It would appear, however, that, although he made his first home among the people of Massachusetts Bay, his sympathies were more in accord with the Pilgrims of Plymouth, than with the Puritans of the Bay.

It is well to remember that while the Plymouth colonists were Separatists, or "Brownists," the Puritans of the Bay colony were simply non-conformists. In this fact, and in the sympathy of Williams with the first named of these two classes, we may find the key to much, in the conduct of Williams, which is otherwise difficult to understand.

Even from the moment of his arrival, this extraordinary man displayed his unique personality. He was,—so he himself records in a letter to John Cotton, junior, in 1671,—offered the position of teacher of the First Church in Boston, as the successor of the Rev. John Wilson; but this invitation he refused. "Being unanimously chosen teacher at Boston," he writes to the younger Cotton, "(before your dear father came, divers years), I conscientiously refused and withdrew to Plymouth, because I durst not officiate to an unseparated people, as, upon examination and conference, I found them to be."

But we soon have evidence that, even among his Separatist friends in Plymouth, whither he soon removed, he exhibited evidences of erratic judg-ment. In his "History of the Plymouth Plantation," Governor Bradford makes this record:

"Mr. Roger Williams (a man godly and zealous, having many precious parts, but very unsettled in judgmente) came over first to ye Massachusetts, but upon some discontente left yt place and came hither, (wher he was friendly entertained, according to their poore abilitie,) and exercised his gift amongst them, and after some time was admitted a member of ye church, and his teaching well approved for ye benefite whereof I still blese God, and am thankful to him, even for his sharpest admonitions and reproufs, so farr as they agreed with truth. He this year (1633) begane to fall into some strang oppinions and from opinion to practise, which caused some controversie between ye church and him, and in ye end some discontente on his parte, by occasion whereof he left them something abruptly. But he soon fell into more things ther, both to their and ye governments troble and disturbance. I shall not need to name particulars, they are too well knowen now to all, though for a time ye church here wente under some hard censure by his occasion, from some that afterwards smarted themselves. But he is to be pitied and prayed for, and so I shall leave ye matter, and desire ye Lord to shew him his errors, and reduse him into ye way of truth, and give him a settled judgment and constancie in ye same; for I hope he belongs to ye Lord and yt he will shew him mercie."

For a time Williams remained at Plymouth as an assistant to Rev. Ralph Smith, and busied himself in the study of the language of the natives. His "Key to the Languages of America," published some years later in England, shows the results of this close and arduous study.

But, as Governor Bradford has already intimated to us, he found the Plymouth people not altogether congenial, and, near the close of the year 1633 we find him at Salem. Here he again began to promulgate the same, or other "strang oppinions," which had so disturbed the brethren of the Bay and of the Plymouth colony. First and chief of these was the opinion concerning separation. He was a young man, as we have seen, and his reproof of the Boston church, that they should still continue in fellowship in the church of England was, perhaps, not meekly received by such men as Winthrop, Bellingham and Haynes,—men accustomed to advise and direct others, and not to receive dictation and reproof from the mouth of a stripling. But to this "strang oppinion" he now added a second. He made a fierce onslaught upon the validity, from an ethical point of view, of the King's patent. He did not, perhaps, deny the legal right of the king to grant a patent to lands in America, the property of the English crown by right of discovery; for such a denial would, no doubt, have been regarded as open treason. But it was his contention, constantly and continuously made, at Plymouth, at Boston, and at Salem, that from the Indians alone could rightfully have been obtained a fee to the land upon which stood the homes of the settlers.

While at Plymouth, this was one of the chief of his "strang oppinions." He prepared an elaborate treatise which, as Winthrop records, disputed "their right to the lands they possessed here and concluded that, claiming by the King's grant, they could have no title, nor otherwise, except they compounded with the natives." It charged King James with lying and blasphemy and declared that all "lye under a sinne of unjust usurpation upon others possessions."

It would appear that the existence of this treatise was not known to the magistrates of the Bay until January, 1634. At all events, his teachings did not become actually obnoxious until that time, when the governor and assistants demanded the surrender of the paper. It does not appear that it was ever put into print and circulated among the people. But, nevertheless, Williams submitted to the court and offered his treatise to be burned. The magistrates were disposed to treat his offense with leniency and readily passed it over, with the understanding that it should not be repeated. The colony, just at this period, as we shall presently see, was passing through troublous times, and the magistrates, doubtless felt that they could not afford to allow any teachings which should present the slightest appearance of disloyalty to the English crown. But, notwithstanding this broad hint of the magistrates, Williams, still at Salem, soon recommenced with renewed vigor to promulgate his "strang oppinions." Now he vigorously urged the doctrines of the Separatists; now he inveighed furiously against the King's patent; now he created a theological ferment over the matter of the wearing of veils by women; now he insisted with equal fervency that one "should not pray nor commune with an unregenerate person, even though it be his own wife or child."

That Williams attained a considerable degree of popularity among the people of Salem is made certain from the fact that he was made an assistant to Rev. Samuel Skelton, although he declined to be formally inducted into the office of teacher.

In the winter of 1634, it again came

to the ears of the magistrates that the obnoxious political doctrines were still taught at Salem. Williams, they learned, had, in effect, retracted his submission to the authority of the court, was openly and violently attacking the validity of the King's patent and was declaring the English churches to be anti-Christian. When one recalls that the English Establishment and the British State were, as now, inextricably mingled, and that an attack upon the one was regarded by the home government as sedition as well as heresy, the anxiety of the magistrates of the Bay will be appreciated. John Cotton begged forbearance, believing that Williams's course arose from scruple of conscience, and not from seditious principle. And so it was resolved to bear yet a while longer with this contentious young man, with the hope that he would come into a better understanding.

Meanwhile the fear became general that, through the teachings of Williams and others of his way of thinking, a sentiment of disloyalty was slowly, but steadily, creeping in among the people. It was then that the practice of administering an oath of loyalty to the freemen of the colony was established. Here again Williams found food for his contentious disposition, and he violently attacked this new departure. "It is not lawful," he urged, and urged with vehemence, "that an oath should be administered to an unregenerate person."

Meanwhile Rev. Mr. Skelton, the minister of the church at Salem, had died, and in 1635 Williams had so far won over this people to his peculiar views, that it was proposed to ordain him as Mr. Skelton's successor. Then

it was that the magistrates of the Bay rose up in their indignation and wrath. Already it had been reported to the King's Council for New England that seditious teachings were not only tolerated, but encouraged, in the settlements, and the fate of the colony hung in the balance. A demand for the production of the charter had actually been made. The governor and magistrates, if ordered to appear before the council, would not be able to declare that such reports concerning their teachings were false. Endicott, always impulsive and intense, inspired by the teachings of Williams, had mutilated the English Standard by cutting out the cross—beyond question a treasonable act. His rash deed was, it is true, repudiated by the colony, for, on May 6, 1635, the records of the General Court contain this entry:

"The commissioners chosen to consider of the act of Mr. Endicott concerning the colrs att Salem did reporte to the court that they apprehend he had offended therein many wayes, in rashness, uncharitableness, indiscrecon, & exceeding. the lymitts of his calling; whereupon the court hath sensured him to be sadly admonished for his offense, wch accordingly hee was, & also disinabled for beareing any office in the comon wealth, for the space of a year next ensueing."

Williams, too, must be dealt with, and so, in July, 1635, formal charges were brought against him in the General Court. He was cited to appear and answer to these grave charges, and for the reason that, "being under question for divers dangerous opinions," he had "been called as teacher of the church in Salem, in contempt of authority."

The contentions of Williams, as recorded by himself in his pamphlet entitled "Mr. Cotton's Letter Examined and Answered," were these:

"1. That we have not our land by patent from the king, but that the natives are the true owners of it, and that we ought to repent of such a receiving it by patent.

"2. That it is not lawful to call a wicked person to swear, to pray, as being actions of God's worship.

"3. That it is not lawful to hear any of the ministers of the Parish Assemblies in England.

"4. That the civil magistrates' power extends only to the bodies and goods and outward state of men."

And Mr. Williams adds:

"I acknowledge the particulars were rightly summed up."

Williams appeared before the court and a long and earnest discussion was held, touching all the points at issue, but especially the first three—the question of the King's patent, the oath, and of separation. He was now not in the least disposed to submit to the authority or opinions of the magistrates, but remained firm in the positions which he had taken. Matters of minor importance were adhered to as rigidly as were those of greater import. It would appear to have been a serious defect in Mr. Williams's mental constitution, that he was unable to comprehend the relative importance of matters of his contention. He apparently regarded the question of the propriety of wearing veils, as of equal importance with that of the validity of the King's patent.

Despite the vigorous remonstrances of the magistrates, the church at Salem appeared to be upon the point of putting into execution its plan of formally inducting Mr. Williams into the position of pastor. Resort must be had to discipline and, that the church might feel the weight of the court's displeasure, a petition of the people of Salem regarding the establishment of their title to certain lands at Marblehead Neck was denied, or, at least was for the present held in abeyance.

Williams now assumed an aggressive position and, at his instance, a letter of remonstrance was addressed by the Salem church to the other churches of the colony, in which the latter were urged to administer discipline to such of the magistrates as were of their membership. The Salem church, that is, would have its sister churches force its magistrate members to take certain desired action, upon pain of church discipline for their refusal. Williams, in short, sought to use the ecclesiastical machinery to control the actions of the civil magistrates.

In brief, a full-fledged rebellion in the colony was hatched,—a rebellion which involved not only the ecclesiastical, but also the civil powers. The strong arm of the magistrates must put it down. The Salem church felt the weight of the hands of the magistrates and weakened. Williams attempted in vain to rally his supporters and finally renounced communion with them.

At the September session of the General Court, 1635, the matter was brought to issue. The records of the colony of Massachusetts Bay, under date of September 3, 1635, contain this entry:

"Whereas Mr. Roger Williams, one of the elders of the church at Salem, hath broached and dyvulged dyvers newe and dangerous opinions against the authoritie of magistrates as also writt lres (letters) of defamacon, both of the magistrates and churches here, and that before any conviccon, and yet maintaineth the same without retraccon, it is therefore or-

358 ROGER WILLIAMS AND THE PROVIDENCE PLANTATIONS

dered, that the said Mr. Williams shall dept out of this jurisdiccon within six weekes nowe nexte ensueing, wch if hee neglect to pforme, it shalbe lawfull for the Gouvr and two of the magistrates to send him to some place out of this jurisdiccon, not to returne any more without licence from the Court."

But Williams did not at once obey the order of the court. He lingered for a time and, later, was seized with illness, which we have no right to assume was not real and which prevented his departure. His sentence was not pressed, and the authorities decided among themselves that, since the winter was fast approaching, the sentence should be suspended until spring. But it will be readily understood that this clemency was extended upon the implied, if not upon the actually expressed, condition, that he should cease his contentious opposition to the established order of the colony. With this condition, however, Williams failed to comply; and when it became known that at secret gatherings, at his own house at Salem, he was still promulgating his views, and sowing dissensions among the people, it was resolved that the power delegated by the court to the governor and two of the magistrates should be forthwith exercised. It was determined to send him to England, by a ship that was about to sail. A constable was dispatched in a small sloop to Salem, to arrest him and bring him to Boston for deportation.

It was now January, 1636; but, notwithstanding the inclemency of the season Williams, when he was apprised of the approach of the officer, fled into the wilderness and thus avoided capture. To have consented to return to England would have been but to submit to the frustration of his plans of life. It was, without doubt, his in-

tention to become a missionary to the Indians. It is not to be supposed that his close study of the language of the natives was followed simply from love of philology. We have been accustomed to regard John Eliot as the great apostle of Christianity to the Indians, and his fame as such has obscured that of Williams, who was certainly his precursor. John Eliot translated the Scriptures into the Indian tongue, but doubtless in that literary effort he derived much assistance from Williams's "Key to the Native Languages of America," a volume, today, of the greatest antiquarian interest. "My sole desire," are Williams's own written words, "was to do the natives good." And to this end, he continues: "God was pleased to give me a painful, patient spirit, to lodge with them in their filthy, smoky holes, even while I lived at Plymouth and Salem, to gain their tongue."

To have submitted to be sent to England, would have been but to renounce his intention of and desire for missionary endeavor. Of his own free choice, therefore, he left the settlement, leaving behind him his wife Mary, and his daughters, Mary and Freeborne, the last an infant of two months. He fled into the wilderness and, in his own recorded words, it was "a sorrowful winter flight," for he was "severely tost for 14 weekes, not knowing what bread or bed did mean."

These weeks were, beyond doubt, passed among his friends, the Indians, still lodging in their "filthy, smoky holes." The few remarkable words just quoted are almost the entire record of these weeks of wandering. "I turned my course from Salem into these parts," he wrote, "wherein I may say Peniel, that is, I have seen the face of God." We only know with certainty that in the spring of 1636 he began "to build and plant" at Seekonk, within the limits of the present town of Rehoboth. He had hardly become settled here, in company with five friends, who had joined their fortunes with his, when he received a gentle intimation from the Plymouth colony, that he had settled within the territory covered by its patent. Unwilling to come into conflict with his Plymouth brethren, he resolved to migrate, and he consulted with Winthrop, who was ever his friend, concerning a place of settlement. The governor directed his attention to the head waters of Narragansett Bay, as a situation without the boundaries of both the Plymouth and the Bay colonies, and within the territory of Canonicus and Miantunnomi, the chieftains who had manifested a friendly disposition toward Williams. Therefore we find him in June, 1636, embarked, with his followers, in a canoe, paddling down the waters of the Seekonk.

Upon the bank at one point was a large rock of blue slate whereon stood a group of friendly Indians. These saluted the party as it passed with the cry "What cheer? Netop!" Williams acknowledged the friendly salutation and continued to drift down the bosom of the river to its mouth.

His voyage was short, and, with this exception, uneventful; but this incident served to supply the city of Providence, which was incorporated nearly two hundred years after, with its motto: "What Cheer!" which today it bears upon its seal.

Rounding the promontory, now bearing the names of Fox Point and India Point, and entering the northern estuary of Narrangansett Bay, Williams and his followers disembarked at the confluence of the Woonasquatucket and the Mooshaussic rivers, where was a great spring of sweet water. Here he made his settlement, which, in recognition of the Divine guidance which had brought him and his company safely to this haven of rest, he called Providence.

It was, doubtless, far from the intention of Roger Williams to found a new colony, when he departed from Massachusetts, or even when he settled at Providence. His intent, beyond doubt, was to found merely a missionary station. But, one by one, impelled by various considerations, others came to join his company, until the little settlement contained fully a dozen families. A large tract of land was given to Williams by the friendly sachems, in token of their kindly feelings toward him.

So large had the settlement now become that some form of government was necessary. And here we come to the narration of what must be regarded as the most important political event of the age in which it occurred,—the establishment of a commonwealth, the corner stone of which was a principle, now become the foundation of American political life. Here was founded a state, the basis of which was the idea of an entire separation of the religious and the civil powers. It was something new in political procedure; it was an experiment based wholly upon a theory. But it was an experiment, the success of which has been so broad and so grand that its feeble beginning at the head waters of the Narrangansett has well-nigh been forgotten. Very brief, yet strangely significant, are the words of the compact into which this handful of colonists entered:

"We whose names are hereunder desirous to inhabitt in ye towne of Providence, do promise to subject ourselves in active or passive obedience to all such orders or agreements as shall be made for publick good of our body in an orderly way, by the major consent of the present inhabitants maisters of families incorporated together into a towne fellowship and others whome they shall admitt unto them only in civill things."

It is not the purpose of this paper to trace the history of the Plantations at Providence through the turbulent years which followed. The colony was founded upon a political idea fully two hundred years in advance of its day; and the very liberality of its foundation was a temptation to anarchy. The colony, in later years, was refused admission to the New England confederacy upon the ground that it had no stable government of its own; and even after Roger Williams, in 1643, returned from England, bearing the charter of the colony, which he had solicited and obtained from the Long Parliament, it was difficult to control the various conflicting elements in this remarkable body politic.

Let us, however, pause here in the historic narrative and return to the discussion of Williams, his banishment and its causes, first considering the political status of the Bay colony, at the time of the advent of Williams, and during his career in the colony. This condition cannot be more fully understood than by consulting the remarkable record left us by John Winthrop. In his diary, known as his "History of New England," under date of 1633 we find this entry:

"By these ships (Mary and Jane) we understood that Sir Christopher Gardiner and Thomas Morton and Philip Ratcliffe (who had been punished here for their misdemeanors) had petitioned to the king and council against us, (being set on by Sir Ferdinando Gorges and Capt. Mason, who had begun a plantation at Pascataquack, and aimed at the general government of New England for their agent there, Capt. Neal.) The petition was of many sheets of paper, and contained many false accusations (and among them some truths misrepeated) accusing us to intend rebellion, to have cast off our allegiance and to be wholly separate from the church and laws of England; that our ministers and people did continually rail against the state, church and bishops there, etc."

Who were Sir Christopher Gardiner, and Thomas Morton, and Philip Ratcliffe? History has recorded the efforts of Sir Ferdinand to form settlements in New England, and of his humiliating failure.

Too great a digression would be necessary to follow the fortunes of Gorges and of his son Robert, and, afterward, of his son John, in their efforts to found settlements in the New World. All these efforts signally failed, and the ambition of Sir Ferdinando, who had fondly imagined himself the Governor General of a great and prosperous colony, or chain of colonies, fell into nothingness. When, therefore, the settlements of John White and his little company, at Cape Ann; of Roger Conant and John Endicott and their followers at Salem; and of John Winthrop and his friends at Charlestown, and later at Boston, bade fair to take firm root and to grow luxuriantly in American soil, what wonder that Gorges felt pangs of jealousy. When, too, King Charles chose to ignore the Council for New England, which his father had chartered nine years before, and granted a charter to the colony of Massachusetts Bay, empowering the colonists to settle within the limits of his grant, his anger was stirred within him. "The whole proceeding," writes Charles Francis Adams, "could not but have been extremely offensive to Gorges. * * * * In any case, from that time forward, however he might dissemble and by speech or letter pretend to seek its welfare, the infant colony had to count Sir Ferdinando Gorges as its most persistent and, as the result soon showed, its most dangerous enemy."

So much for Sir Ferdinand and his attitude toward the colony, still in its infancy. Sir Christopher Gardiner's was a character which made but little impress upon the life of the colony. He appeared suddenly, in New England, builded him a house upon the banks of the Neponset, not far from its mouth, and dwelt there in apparent inoffensiveness. Yet a female member of his household occupied an equivocal position, scandalizing the severe Puritan morality of the age and place; and advices from England proved that two wives had, in turn, been deserted by him. Moreover, he was believed, and no doubt with truth, to be an agent or spy in the pay of Gorges. The resolve of the magistrates of Massachusetts Bay, therefore, was that he must return to England and, accordingly, he was deported. Ample authority for this action was granted in the charter.

Of Thomas Morton of Merry Mount, history and romance have made a broader record. Every historian of Massachusetts has fully set forth the story of Morton, whose antics about the May pole of Merry Mount, in company with his "lassies in beaver coats," scandalized the Puritan brethren across the Bay. But the chief of his offences was his persistence in supplying the Indians with firearms and ammunition, to the great alarm of the colonists. When, therefore, he refused to be admonished and to turn from his evil courses, he too was deported and his dwelling burned.

Of Philip Ratcliffe, the last of this precious trio, the record says but little. We know him to have been a resident of Salem, who uttered "mallitious and scandalous speeches against the government and the church," and who thus came in violent contact with Endicott; a man irascible and hot-headed, and never noted for charitableness. Whatever may have been Ratcliffe's exact offence, which does not appear, he was sentenced to be whipped, to have his ears cropped, to pay a fine of forty pounds, and to be banished from the colony. He, too, was sent back to England; and so here we have three formidable enemies of the colony, embittered by what they regarded as personal ill-treatment, and led on by Gorges, whose life was now devoted to the disruption and disturbance of those who seemed about to succeed upon the ground where he had failed.

The efforts of these enemies of the colony came to naught. But they did not cease their exertions, with the first failure. A few months later, in February, 1634, a second complaint was entered, and an order was issued to Governor Craddock, by the Privy Council, for the production of the charter. Craddock, who was then in England, and who, in fact, never went to America, returned answer that the charter had been delivered to Mr. Endicott, and that it was then in New

England. He was instructed to communicate with Endicott and to direct him to send the charter to England. A month later, intelligence came to the magistrates and the people of the colony, that the king had appointed a high commission, consisting of two archbishops and ten others of the Privy Council to regulate all plantations, with power to call in patents, make laws, raise tithes and portions for ministers, remove and punish governors, hear and determine all causes and inflict punishments, even death.

In September, 1634, the General Court assembled, and to it the demand for the production of the charter was presented, as well as a copy of the commission. The alarm of the colonists was now undisguised. But the American spirit displayed itself, the same spirit that one hundred and forty years later, was fully aroused at Concord, and at Bunker Hill. Fortifications were thrown up at various points, and a beacon was erected upon the summit of the highest of the three peaks, within the limits of the settlement, by means of which an alarm might be given to the people of the surrounding country, in case of invasion. Hence we have today the name of Beacon Hill.

Winthrop, after recording the efforts of the colony's enemies, here recounted, adds: "The Lord frustrated their designs." Nevertheless, this was a critical period in the history of the colony. Its very existence was threatened. Enemies, bitter enemies, at court, were struggling hard for its overthrow, and the assertions upon which these enemies were founding their appeals to the crown, were not wholly without foundation. Winthrop

records, as we have seen, that their statements included "some truths misrepeated;" and also the assertion made that the ministers of the colony were, in effect, teaching sedition. In spirit we know that these charges were false; in word we know that they were true, for, as we have already seen, Roger Williams was busily and persistently engaged, in spite of repeated warnings and of strong opposition, in promulgating the very political doctrines, with the teaching of which the Boston clergy stood charged.

The settlers of Massachusetts Bay could not be possessed with another feeling than one of alarm, when they became aware of these efforts for their destruction. The effect of these efforts they could do but little to avert; but it did lie in their power to silence the intestine enemy, whose contentions gave excellent color to the charges of their enemies abroad. And hence, relying upon the permissive clause in their charter, which had already been made operative in the cases of Gardiner, Morton, Ratcliffe, and nearly a score of similar offenders, it was resolved to send Williams away.

Following thus closely the record of history we have failed to find color for the prevalent idea, that Roger Williams was banished from Masssachusetts Bay for the offense of preaching the doctrine of religious liberty. We have failed to find in him a martyr; and the words of Charles Francis Adams, in which the expulsion of Williams is compared to the dragging of Garrison about the streets of Boston, with a rope about his neck, for the offence of preaching the freedom of the slave, must be read with nothing less than amazement.

That astute historical student, Dr. Diman, has said: "To upbraid the Puritans as unrelenting persecutors, or to extol Roger Williams as a martyr to the cause of religious liberty, is equally wide of the real fact."

Search as closely as one may, the effort to find a record that this idea had been made prominent in his teachings, prior to his settlement at Providence, must result in failure. The Separatist idea was abhorred alike by churchman and Puritan. The attack upon the patent, the constitution of the colony itself, the very root and groundwork of its political and social fabric, as Professor Fisher explains, "opened the prospect of a collision with the English authorities, who would be ready enough to take notice of proofs of disloyalty in the Puritan colony." The opposition to the freeman's oath, as Diman insists, "cut at the roots of the theocratic system already firmly planted"; and this, adds Professor Fisher, "was at a time when the administration of this oath was deemed essential to the safety of the colony." "The judgment (the act of banishment) "was vindicated," says Bancroft, "not as a restraint on freedom of conscience, but because the application of the new doctrine to the construction of the patent, to the discipline of the churches, and to the 'oaths for making tryall of the fidelity of the people,' seemed about 'to subvert the fundamental state and government of the country.'"

Of the banishment of Williams, says Diman: "It was the ordinary method by which a corporate body would deal with those whose presence no longer seemed desirable. Conceiving themselves to be, by patent, the exclusive possessors of the soil, soil which they had purchased for the accomplishment of their personal and private ends, the colonists never doubted their competency to fix the terms on which others should be allowed to share in their undertaking."

But, although it cannot successfully be contended that Roger Williams was driven forth from the colony of Massachusetts Bay, for his advocacy of the cause of "soul liberty," that he subsequently became the great apostle of that idea cannot be successfully denied. John Cotton said of his removal from Massachusetts, that "it was not banishment but enlargement." "Had he remained in Massachusetts," says Diman, "he would only be remembered as a godly, but contentious, Puritan divine. Removed, for a time, from the heated atmosphere of controversy, he first saw, in its true proportions, the great principle which has shed enduring lustre on his name."

Williams had been, it is not to be doubted, somewhat under the Dutch influence and the doctrine of religious toleration there undoubtedly had its rise. But though Roger Williams may not have been the original discoverer of the idea of religious toleration, he so far improved upon it, that he was certainly entitled to claim it as his own. For Williams insisted upon far more than simple toleration. It was his contention, and upon this idea was his colony founded, that the right to prescribe the form of worship or the faith of the worshipper rests, in no sense, with the civil power; that the religious and the civil powers are utterly and wholly distinct and are in no manner interdependent. It was upon this broad foundation that the government of the

Plantations at Providence was builded. "For the first time in history," wrote Diman, "a form of government was adopted which drew a clear and unmistakable line between the temporal and the spiritual power; and a community came into being which was an anomaly among the nations."

In the year 1644 was published in London a treatise from the pen of Roger Williams, to which he gave the title: "The Bloudy Tenent of Persecution." Therein we read a sentiment differing in no essential degree from a similar utterance in the Virginia declaration of rights, adopted one hundred and thirty-two years after.

A little later, this opinion, broached by Roger Williams in 1644, and reiterated by Madison more than a century after, became the agreed opinion of the American colonies as expressed in their Declaration of Independence.

Roger Williams was, without doubt, erratic, and so, indeed, was Wendell Phillips, and so are nearly all great reformers. The character of Williams presents also in some degree, the element of inconsistency. While we find him vigorously and continuously inveighing against the validity of the king's patent, and, in effect, accusing his fellow-settlers of the theft of the land upon which their dwellings and farms stood, he himself was the owner of a dwelling and lot in the village of Salem. We know that this property he mortgaged to raise money with which to purchase gifts for his Indian friends; and the fee of the property was acquired, no one will deny, from a white settler, from whom he purchased it.

Governor Bradford has already been quoted as declaring Williams to be a man "unsettled in judgment." This characterization, perhaps, is the most just which students of his life and career will adopt. Whimsical, erratic. unwilling to submit to the guidance, or to listen to the advice of his elders, stubborn in the advocacy of his ideas. unable to distinguish clearly between the trivial and the important, we find him in the earlier years of his career. Later, we recognize in him qualities which stamp him, if not as the greatest, yet certainly as the most progressive statesman of the age in which he lived.

My Dream Garden

By Edith R. Blanchard

DEAR love, my love, though long since lost to me,
  Though by another's side you live the dreams
We dreamt we'd live together, long ago,
You are mine still, and I have made for you
A garden from whose gates you may not go.

Green walls of mem'ry keep you captive, love,
The trysting-tree you have forgot is there,
Old-fashioned roses by the pathway bloom
Unfading, since you loved them in the past,
And laden with a vaguely sweet perfume.

You are not lonely in your garden, love,
For every night, when dreary tasks are done,
I come to meet you in the same old place,
To hold you unresisting in my arms,
And feel your kiss of welcome on my face.

The moon, aswing amid the jasmine vine,
Smiles down upon you in your quaint white gown,
Till from your arms and breast the rose blush dies,
Melts to the silver of the lily's bloom.
Ah, love, the moonlight shining in your eyes!

The bold night breezes wanton in your hair,
They fling its maddening fragrance in my face,
Till I, from whom fate drew all love apart,
I fold you in these empty, longing arms
And crush you yielding to my lonely heart.

But ah, from that dear garden, yours and mine,
Harsh voices call me, cruel visions come,
Old shadows shut me from the joys inside.
Once more I lose you, as I lost you then,
Once more that other claims you as his bride.

So, when at last the great white stranger comes,
And midst the gloom I feel him press my hand,
This, as he bends above me, I shall say,
Dear Death, I care not for the courts of gold,
But lead me to my garden, there to stay.

The Pennsylvania Germans

By Lucy Forney Bittinger

THE ignorance concerning the Pennsylvania Germans on the part of English-speaking people is so deep and widespread that I have thought an account of them and how they came to emigrate to this country, so distant from their home and so alien to their language and government might result in a better understanding of an uncomprehended people.

The Pennsylvania Germans are the descendants of the German and Swiss emigrants to this country who came here between the time of the founding of Pennsylvania in 1683 and the Revolutionary war, and who formed a community homogeneous in blood, with language, customs, religion and habits of thought peculiar to itself and lasting unchanged for many years.

They were the only emigrants of any Continental nation, who came here in large numbers prior to the Revolution. The causes for so large an emigration from remote Germany naturally excite our inquiry. These causes were two-fold. First in point of time and importance, was a religious motive. The worldly condition of the German peasants and artisans, from which class the emigrants chiefly came, formed a secondary and later cause.

The religious motive of the emigrants is well stated by Prof. Oswald Seidensticker:

"Important as was the impetus which the political conditions of Germany gave to em-

igration, religious motives had a yet more powerful influence. For a man will put up with almost any injury sooner than an attack upon matters of religion. Indeed, the German emigration was in its causes, a parallel to that of the Quakers and the New England Puritans. In Germany, too, were sects, which lived at enmity with the recognized confessions and were bitterly persecuted. At the end of the seventeenth century there arose a reaction against the dead theology of the churches, which endeavored after a deeper comprehension of religious truth and a closer following of the commands of Christianity, and appeared, sometimes as Pietism, sometimes as hypercritical Mysticism. It manifested itself in all sorts of ascetic, "inspired," "awakened" conventicles, not without degenerating into fanaticism. For all these pious people, oppressed and maltreated, Pennsylvania was an asylum, a Pella, as Pastorius expresses it, where they could cultivate their particular form of belief and practice, without opposition. That it was the jewel of religious freedom, which lured the German emigrants by its glorious rays to Pennsylvania, we have express testimony. Let us hear what Christoph Saur, himself a so-called sectary, a Dunker, says about it: 'Pensilvanien is such a country as no one in the world ever heard or read of; many thousand people from Europe have gladly come hither just on account of the friendliness of the government and the freedom of conscience. This noble freedom is like a decoy-bird, which shall first bring people to Pensilvanien and when the good land gradually becomes too narrow, people will go from here to the neighboring English colonies and they will be settled by many emigrants from Germany, for Pensilvanien's sake.' "

And in Prof. Seidensticker's charming sketches, "Bilder aus der deutchpennsylvanischen Geschichte," he says:

"Three confessions only, the Catholic, the Lutherans and the Reformed, had obtained, thro' the peace of Westphalia, the right of existence in the German empire. Whoever felt driven by conscientious conviction to express his creed in a different form, to interpret the Bible differently, to clothe his worship of God in a different formula,—his life was made bitter by church and state. Such unchurchly Christians, who were violently opposed and unsparingly persecuted, were very numerous in Germany toward the end of the seventeenth century. The inoffensive Mennonites found only here and there a precarious toleration, the God-fearing Schwenkfelder were obliged to endure more revolting cruelty, even the Pietists, Spener's devout followers, who insisted only on a more ardent conception of and conscientious practice of religion in the Lutheran body, were regarded by the formal church with suspicion, grossly slandered, and denounced to the government as dangerous innovators. The Mystics who appeared in many forms among learned and unlearned alike, they would have liked to relegate to madhouses and jails."

The same writer, the highest authority on Pennsylvania-German history, thus describes with a rare union of accuracy and eloquence, the conditions of life in that part of Germany from which most of the emigrants came:

"The causes which at this particular time, the end of the seventeenth and beginning of the eighteenth centuries, gave a powerful impulse to the scarcely commenced emigration, are not far to seek. The Palatinate and other parts of western Germany had been for decades exposed to the plunderings and burnings of the French. Strasburg became their booty in 1681. With the year 1688 began a system of unexampled barbarity. Cities and villages, among them Heidelberg, Speier, Worms, Kreuznach and Mannheim, were laid in ashes, others ransomed by the extortion of considerable sums of money; there was endless misery and suffering; the dwellers in city or country found from their Fatherland no protection, from the uniformed robber-bands of Louis XIV. no mercy. And after Johann Wilhelm—bigotted and influenced by the Jesuits—came to the throne of the Palatinate in 1690, there was added religious intolerance. The Protestants were treated with unbearable contempt; the Huguenots and Waldenses, who had emigrated there under the Elector Karl, were forced to quit the country, and betook themselves, some to Prussia, some to America. But Johann Wilhelm was exceeded by his successor, Karl Philip, who made his Jesuit confessor, Father Seedorf, Conference-Minister; and in dissoluteness, pomp and extravagance, vied with the French court. Of course, his subjects must pay with their last penny for the costly fancies of their prince. Even when this ruler departed this life, times in the Palatinate were not improved, for the reign of Karl Theodor, which covered nearly all the remainder of the century, was, in the self-indulgence of the ruler, in bad government, and in impoverishment of the people, quite the most mischievous which the heavily-visited Palatinate ever had to bear. In other South-German principalities, things were not much better. The imitation of France, as contemptible as costly, when every prince took pride in being a follower of Louis XIV., pressed heavily on the subjects. This was particularly the case in Wurtemberg, from which as from the Palatinate, tho somewhat later, wholesale emigrations to America took place."

But you ask, how did these persecuted Christians, these oppressed peasants, come to know of the Pella beyond the seas. We answer,—through the founder of Pennsylvania, William Penn.

The Quaker apostle had made two "religious journeys" into Germany before he came into possession of his province of "Penn's woods." Among the Mennonites, the Moravians, the Pietists and the Mystics of the Rhine country, Penn thought he found a soil for the seed of Quakerism, and little communities of "Friends" were gathered in some places. Seidensticker has traced with the greatest care his journeyings through Holland and the Rheinland, now at an interview with a royal abbess or the Pfalz-graf, now "edifying the plain people of Krisheim in a barn." But his journey in its main aim was a failure. Quakerism in Germany was an exotic which took no root. Another result, undreamed of, is the one which lives to this day. Penn's journey made him acquainted with a group of sectaries in Frankfort —chiefly Pietists, men and women of culture and rank—who, when he published, in 1681, his "Account of the Province of Pennsylvania in America," translated into German in the same year as "Eine Nachricht von Pensilvanien," conceived the project of buying a tract of land there and emigrating in a body. But—strange are the devious ways by which any human enterprise proceeds to its accomplishment—not one of the Frankfort Company ever carried out their intention of emigrating to the "Landschaft Pensilvanien." Perhaps the many ties which bind cultivated people to the home and society in which they were born, were too strong to break. It was reserved to a little company of linen-weavers in Crefeld, mostly Mennonites, to be the path-finders for that immense following which in two generations made the province of Pennsylvania half German in population and left its impression on parts of it to this day, which has made the 16th of October an honored "Forefather's Day" to many German-Americans and the "Concord,"—peaceful name,—as well-omened as the English "Mayflower."

A good leader is half the battle in such an enterprise as the Crefelders had before them, and this indispensa-ble man they found in Franz Daniel Pastorius, the "Pennsylvania Pilgrim," whose sweet and sunny memory Whittier has rescued from the oblivion of two centuries. He was born in Sommerhausen in 1651. His family came from Erfurt, whence his grandfather, fleeing from the Swedes in the Thirty Years' War, was caught in hiding and so maltreated that he died. Pastorius's father was a lawyer of some local distinction in Windsheim. Franz Daniel, his eldest son, studied at the universities of Jena and Altdorf, travelled extensively, and then went to Frankfort to practise law. There he became acquainted with the Pietist circle of William Penn's friends who had formed the Frankfort Company and intended to emigrate to Pennsylvania in search of religious freedom. They persuaded Pastorius to become their agent and precede them by a little—as they thought—to their future home. But when the Crefeld Mennonites came instead, Pastorius assisted them, laid out their town for them, and took up his residence among them. His first impressions of the City of Brotherly Love were not very favorable. It consisted of a few temporary cabins. "The remainder," he says, "was forest and undergrowth, wherein I several times lost myself tho' at no great distance from the shore. What an impression such a city made upon me—who had seen London, Paris, Amsterdam and Ghent—I need not say." But he found kindly friends there. Lloyd, afterwards president of the Provincial Council, and William Penn received him with "loving friendliness," and Pastorius notes that his first meeting with the founder of Pennsylvania took place the day after his arrival, in "a tent

made of fir-tree and chestnut boughs."
His first residence in Philadelphia he
thus describes: "I had previously built
a little house in Philadelphia, thirty
feet long and fifteen wide, with windows which in the lack of glass I had
made out of oiled paper; above the
door I had written, 'Parva domus sed
amica bonis procul este profani,'
whereat our governor when he visited
me, burst out laughing and encouraged me to build further."

In a few weeks the emigrants arrived in the Concord. They chose their
land and began their settlement, aided
by Pastorius. In the town records of
Germantown he gave to posterity a
quaint and circumstantial account of
all their proceedings. Before beginning it, the spirit of prophecy descended upon the German pioneer, and in his
stately Latin he thus invokes posterity (I give Whittier's poetic trans-
lation):

Hail to posterity!
  Hail, future men of Germanopolis!
Let the young generations yet to be
  Look kindly upon this.
Think how your fathers left their native
    land—
  Dear German-land! O sacred hearths and
    homes!—
And where the wild beast roams,
  In patience planned
New forest homes beyond the mighty sea,
There undisturbed and free
To live as brothers of one family,
  What pains and cares befell,
  What trials and what fears,
Remember, and wherein we have done well
Follow our footsteps, men of coming years!
  Where we have failed to do
  Aright, or wisely live,
Be warned by us, the better way pursue,
And, knowing we were human, even as you,
  Pity us and forgive!
  Farewell, Posterity!
  Farewell, dear Germany!
  Forevermore farewell!

The history of "Germanopolis,"
while it was literally

"the German town
Where live High German people and Low
  Dutch
Whose trade in weaving Linnen cloth is
  much,"

is not eventful. The proverbial industry of the Germans soon enabled them
to live in comfort. They built little
houses, they planted cherry trees along
the streets in the fashion of the Fatherland, and to their great delight they
found that the grape-vine grew wild in
their new home, and they cultivated it.
They also planted flax, and soon built
up a thriving industry in knitting and
weaving. Their stockings were long
celebrated, and "Germantown" wool is
still a name well known in commerce.
To these elements of prosperity their
town-seal chosen by Pastorius himself,
"with *vinum linum et textrinum*"
wound," still testifies. There even
grew up some foreign commerce; they
sent furs, bartered from Indian hunt-
ers, to England; they exchanged cattle
with Barbadoes. The first paper-mill
in the colonies was erected in Germantown by Wilhelm Ruttinghuysen (Rittenhouse). He was a Hollander, but
most of the settlers of Germantown
were thorough Germans and German
was the language of the place.

From 1689 they had a corporate existence of their own. But the annals of
the government of Germanopolis are
exceedingly uneventful. It was difficult to find any one to accept the offices,
so Pastorius wrote in 1703 to William
Penn; but he hoped that the impend-
ing arrival of new emigrants would
help them out of their embarrassments.
It is hardly likely that there has ever
been a time since when it was neces-

sary to import office holders because the home product was insufficient. The chief concerns of the burgomaster and his council seem to have arisen from vagabond pigs and ill-kept fences. Sometimes there was no session of the court because there was no business to come before it; again they adjourned because the secretary had gone to Maryland.

Three years after the settlement was established, a small meeting-house was built by the Quakers. It soon became too small and was replaced by a larger one, but it must have been in this first "Kirchlein," as Pastorius calls it, that the protest against slavery was made by Pastorius and two other Friends, "the first association who ever protested against Negro slavery." We are probably right in ascribing the honor of the composition of this protest to Pastorius, who was the only man in the little settlement able to express himself so clearly in English, who did all the writing for the community, and who is known on the evidence of his poems to have held the same views on slavery and to have opposed it on the same grounds as are set forth in the memorial. But "the startled meeting" cautiously referred the protest to the Quarterly Meeting and that to the Yearly Meeting. This body was not less afraid of the simple deductions of the German Friends from the Golden Rule, and decorously smothered the anti-slavery movement thus: "It is not thought proper for the Meeting to decide this question." If Pastorius ever looked back over his life and its multifarious efforts for the good of his fellow-men to think of his unheeded protest, he must have thought it a complete and pitiful failure. He could not

foresee how at last that cause should triumph, though none should remember the simple "German Friends" who first of all on this continent, lifted their voices for the oppressed.

"And lo! the fulness of the time has come,
And over all the exile's Western home,
From sea to sea the flowers of freedom
　　bloom!
And joy-bells ring and silver trumpets
　　blow;
But not for thee, Pastorius! Even so
The world forgets, but the wise angels
　　know."

Every year the number of the settlers in Germantown was increased by new accessions, chiefly Mennonites fleeing out of Switzerland and Germany from the bitter persecution of centuries. In the eleventh year of the settlement, there arrived at Germantown about forty persons, men and women, the followers of Johann Kelpius, the "Philadelphian Society," the "Awakened," who had come to devote themselves to a life of solitude and celibacy in the forests of Pennsylvania.

Their leader, Kelpius, was so great a part of their life that we must first of all know him. He was the son of a pastor near Strasburg, educated at Altdorf, like Pastorius, and from his graduation, interested himself deeply in all sorts of mystical speculations. For a time he was under the influence of Dr. Fabricius of Helmstadt, the characteristic of whose opinions was a desire to bring about peace between the two warring Protestant confessions,—the Lutheran and the Reformed. More profitable than the speculations of Boehme or of Dr. Petersen, which he also took up, was the practical Pietism of Spener, in which he was interested. The "revelations" of the beautiful Rosamunde von

Asseburg, a ward of Petersen's, also attracted him.

Finally, with a company of like-minded souls, he resolved to go to Pennsylvania, which was then becoming a cave of Adullam for diverse people, from the patient Mennonite sufferers to these new emigrants—"maddest of good men." Going to London on their way to America, they fell in with English adherents of the Philadelphian Society, who had nothing in common with William Penn's "forest court" but were devoted to bringing all sects into a united body by means of the philosophy of Jacob Boehme. Their own account of their journey from England affords a vivid picture of the dangers of emigrants in those days. They were nearly shipwrecked, returned to Deal and awaited a convey. Being disappointed in this, they went to Plymouth and from thence, with the promise that several vessels going to Spain should accompany them for "200 Holland miles," they sailed. After their escort left them the two ships were attacked by as many French vessels. They defended themselves bravely, took a merchantman under the French vessels' convoy and after several false alarms, reached Philadelphia in safety.

In Germantown, Kelpius found the philosophy of Boehme little appreciated. He, however, obtained some land from an admirer,—tradition says Thomas Fairman, surveyor of the province,—and settled on the Wissahickon with his company. They built a log-house. cleared a field and planted corn. Then they gave themselves to the instruction of children. thinking there was no hope for a dissemination of their ideas. save with the rising generation. Tradition still remembers Kelpius as the "Hermit of the Wissahickon" and points out a spring which he is said to have walled up with his own hands. The company themselves called their settlement "the Woman in the Wilderness," in allusion to Rev. 12:6, and allegorized the name to their hearts' content. The hermit life must not be taken too strictly. Kelpius had considerable religious correspondence with various persons interested in his opinions, which though Chiliast in tone, did not permit him to fix a time for the millenium. "The matter will turn out quite different from what one or another, even J. L. (probably Jane Leade) imagines." He hoped for a union of all Christians; in a letter to his old teacher, Fabricius, he says: "I hope that God who saves men and cattle and has mercy upon all his works, will at length, as in the first Adam they all die, so in the other make them all alive," the opinion known as Restorationism. He wrote much religious poetry, full of a burning desire for the coming of Christ and a resumption into him in eternal love and bliss. These fiery longings early wore him out; he died in his fortieth year. We have this picture of his last days, which reminds us of the Morte d'Arthur, though nothing could have been far-ther from the thoughts of the narrator, Pastor Muhlenberg:

"Herr K. steadfastly believed, among other things, that he would not die nor his body see corruption. but would be changed, glorified, clothed upon, and he, like Elias, be taken hence. Now when his last hour drew nigh and forebodings, as with other children of Adam, announced dissolution and the separation of soul and body, Herr K. continued three days and nights before God, wrestling and beseeching that He should make no separation with him but leave body and soul together and take him up to heaven in glory. At length he ceased and said to his friend, 'My dear Daniel, I do not obtain what I believed, but the answer came to me, that I am dust and must return to dust; I shall die, as do other children of Adam.' Some days after this mortal conflict, Herr K. gave this friend Daniel a closely sealed box and commanded him solemnly to throw it forthwith into the river called Schulkil. Daniel went therewith to the water. But because he thought that this hidden treasure might perchance be useful to him and his fellow-men, he hid the box on the bank and did not throw it in. When he came back, Herr K. looked him keenly in the eyes and said: 'You have not thrown the box into the water but hidden it on the bank.' Whereat the honest Daniel, terrified, and believing that his friend's spirit must be in some measure omniscient, ran again to the water, and this time really threw in the box and saw and heard with astonishment that in the water the Arcanum, as he expressed it, thundered and lightened. After he came back Herr K. called to him, 'Now it is finished, what I gave you to do.' "

We have little knowledge of the ultimate fate of the "Woman in the Wilderness."

Some years before Kelpius's death, Pastorius resigned his agency of the Frankfort Company, and three other trustees were appointed, Kelpius (who took not the slightest notice of his appointment), Falckner, and Jawert of Germantown. Seven years after, Jawert received an offer for the Frankfort Company's land in Montgomery County from a speculator named Sprögel. Jawert rejected the offer as too low; Sprögel thereupon offered Jawert a *douceur* of £100 to sell him the land, which Jawert, an honorable man, indignantly refused. Shortly after, Falckner, the other agent, sold the land to Sprögel, without Jawert's knowl-

edge and to the latter's great anger. Falckner was indebted to Sprögel for a considerable sum of money. In a short time Sprögel terrified the industrious settlers of Germantown by attempting to eject them, by a legal process, from the homes which they had won from the wilderness six-and-twenty years before. The colonists in their extremity fled to their trusted friend Pastorius. He, going to Philadelphia to get legal advice, found that "alle lawyers gefeed waren," as he says, forgetting his German in his distress. I hasten to add that in those Arcadian days there were only four lawyers in the province of Pennsylvania. The Germantown people were too poor to bring legal help from New York, but Pastorius's old friend, the provincial statesman, James Logan, advised a petition to the Provincial Council. Jawert joined them in this. The Council pronounced Falckner's operations "an atrocious plot" and saved the inhabitants of Germantown from the loss of their all. But nothing could save the other property of the Frankfort Company, "and so we find that of the extensive possessions which the Frankforters had secured with such high expectations from William Penn, more than seven-eighths passed into the hands of a lucky speculator." The affair was a great grief to Pastorius and embittered his later years.

Kelpius had died before the Sprögel trouble. Pastorius survived the hermit of the Wissahickon ten useful years, employed in teaching a little school, in manifold labors for his fellow-men, in writing (he published four books "aus der in Pennsylvanien neulichst von mir in Grund angelegten und nun mit guten Success aufgehenden Stadt Germanopoli"), in filling 1,000 manu-script pages of his exquisite penman-ship with his "Rusca Apium"

"That with bees began
And through the gamut of creation ran,"

and, greatest joy of all, in cultivating his dearly loved garden. Of it he wrote poems; to its flowers he inscribed such as this, which happily shows his ming-led love of flowers and love of God:

"Ob ich Deiner schon vergiss
Und des rechten Wegs oft miss,
Auch versaüme meine Pflicht,
Lieber Gott, vergiss mein nicht.
Bring mich wieder auf die Bahn,
Nimm mich zu Genaden an;
Und, wenn mich der Feind anficht,
Lieber Gott, vergiss mein nicht.
Doch ich weiss, Dein Vaterherz
Neigt in Lieb' sich niederwärts,
Ist in Treu' auf mich gericht,
Und vergisst mein nimmer nicht."

The very date of Pastorius' death is uncertain; no man knoweth of his sepulchre unto this day. "That his re-mains rest in the old Quaker burying-ground in Germantown, is a conjecture with which one may unhesitatingly agree. Should it ever come to pass that a monument should be raised to the worthy man, the forerunner of mil-lions of German settlers in America, who, in a strange land, preserved his German integrity and strict conscien-tiousness unspotted, the words in which William Penn characterized him should be placed upon it: "Vir sobrius, probus, prudens et pius, spectatae inter omnes inculpataeque famae." (Sober, upright, wise and devout, a man re-spected by all and of unblemished fame.) No more perfect picture of Pastorius's land and time can be found than the "Pennsylvania Pilgrim" of Whittier. The student of its history is always astonished at the art concealing art with which the Quaker poet has combined historical exactness in the minutest details with the purest and sweetest strains of poetry. So let him portray a character in many ways so like his own:

"His forest home no hermit's cell he found,
Guests, motley-minded, drew his hearth around,
And held armed truce upon its neutral ground.

There Indian chiefs with battle-bows un-strung,
Strong, hero-limbed, like those whom Ho-mer sung,
Pastorius fancied, when the world was young,

Came with their tawny women, lithe and tall,
Like bronzes in his friend Von Rodeck's hall,
Comely, if black, and not unpleasing all.

There hungry folk in homespun drab and gray
Drew round his board on Monthly Meeting day,
Genial, half merry in their friendly way.

Or, haply, pilgrims from the Fatherland,
Weak, timid, homesick, slow to understand
The New World's promise, sought his help-ing hand.

Or painful Kelpius from his hermit den
By Wissahickon, maddest of good men,
Dreamed o'er the Chiliast dreams of Peter-sen.

Deep in the woods, where the small river slid
Snake-like in shade, the Helmstadt Mystic hid,
Weird as a wizard over arts forbid,

Reading the books of Daniel and of John,
And Behmen's Morning-Redness, through the Stone
Of Wisdom, vouchsafed to his eyes alone,

Whereby he read what man ne'er read before,
And saw the visions man shall see no more,
Till the great angel, striding sea and shore,

Shall bid all flesh await, on land or ships,
The warning trump of the Apocalypse,
Shattering the heavens before the dread eclipse.

Or meek-eyed Mennonist his bearded chin
Leaned o'er the gate; or Ranter, pure with·
in,
Aired his perfection in a world of sin.

Or, talking of old home scenes, Op den Graaf
Teasing the low back-log with his shodden staff,
Till the red embers broke into a laugh

And dance of flame, as if they fain would cheer
The rugged face, half tender, half austere,
Touched with the pathos of a homesick tear!

Haply, from Finland's birchen groves ex·
iled,
Manly in thought, in simple ways a child,
His white hair floating round his visage mild,

The Swedish pastor sought the Quaker's door,
Pleased from his neighbor's lips to hear once more
His long-disused and half-forgotten lore.

For both could baffle Babel's lingual curse,
And speak in Bion's Doric, and rehearse
Cleanthes' hymn or Virgil's sounding verse.

And oft Pastorius and the meek old man
Argued as Quaker and as Lutheran,
Ending in Christian love, as they began."

*   *   *   *   *   *   *

We come now to another period in the history of the Pennsylvania Germans. Prof. Seidensticker has well characterized it in his account of Christoph Saur, where he thus says:

"When he reached Germantown in the autumn of 1724 and settled among the Ger-

man-speaking inhabitants, the town had been founded almost a generation. There were many yet living who had seen the spot when it was an untrodden wilderness and could describe the cabin-building of the winter of 1683-4. The pioneer of German emigration, the learned Franz Daniel Pastorius, had died a few years before; but there still survived the Rittenhouse brothers, Johann Selig, the bosom-friend of Kelpius, and others. And yet the German immigration had long since entered upon a new stage. Not only had Germantown outgrown its idyllic childhood,—the rapidly increasing stream poured itself into the country districts of Skippack and Perkiomen, and further up the Schuylkill to Oley and other portions of the present Berks County. Other parts of the country which Germans and Swiss specially preferred, were the fruitful valleys of the Conestoga, the Pequae, and other tributaries of the Susquehanna in that part of Chester County which was organized in 1729 as Lancaster County."

It is impossible any longer to trace the progress of a single settlement like Germantown.

For twenty years after the weavers of Crefeld came to found Germantown, there was no large accession to their numbers at any one time. With the exception of Kelpius's little colony, no emigrants came in a body, though the settlers received constant accessions. But with the beginning of the new century a period of large emigration set in, lasting for more than a quarter of that century. It was largely a sectarian movement, and one of colonies. The first body to emigrate in large numbers was the sect of the Mennonites. Seidensticker says:

"The Mennonites, the meekest, most patient and peaceable of Christian men, had continually suffered the bitterest persecution. Menno Simons himself, after whom they are named, was outlawed and to the man who should kill him was promised not only pardon for all his crimes, but the reward of a 'Carlsgulden.' Sebastian Frank in his chronicle (1530) says of these Baptists, 'They laid hold of them in many places with the greatest tyranny, put them in prison and punished them with fire, sword, water and all kinds of imprisonment, so that in a few years many of them were killed in many places and it was estimated that more than 2,000 were killed in all parts of the country, and they suffered like martyrs, patiently and steadfastly.' "

It is true that Menno Simons first gathered the scattered Mennonites into a body, but they had existed long before. In fact they were but parts of that great movement of the Reformation times known (chiefly through its enemies) as Anabaptism. To most readers this name brings up images of Thomas Munzer, and the "Prophet" of Leyden, of community of goods and wives, and the bloody extinction of an abhorrent doctrine. But in truth the Anabaptism of Munster lasted but fifteen months, was embraced by only a few thousands of people and was a fanatical outburst reprobated by the leaders of the Baptists as much as by any one else.

It was a foregone conclusion that all the religious life of the Reformation would not run in the ecclesiastical channels provided by Luther and Zwingli. Those who believed in adult baptism, those who abhorred religious persecution, who found more in the Bible than in the confessions of faith promulgated by the churches, who required evidence of a moral change before admitting members to their churches, who pitied the peasants under their burdens of tax and tithe and corvee, who conscientiously refused to take an oath or bear arms, who opposed a paid ministry—these all were Anabaptists and foremost among them

were the Mennonites. Foremost too, in the persecution they bore. In Switzerland, under Zwingli's encouragement, they were pursued almost to extinction. Spreading over Germany, particularly along the Rhine, they found refuge and protection in Holland under William the Silent, and leadership under Menno Simons—a Catholic priest converted by the martyrdom of his brother to the latter's opinions. Menno died a peaceful death, after a persecuted life, in 1561. It was not till twenty years after, that his people found full toleration, even in Holland, the land of religious freedom. But from that time, Holland was the center whence help was sent the suffering brethren in Germany and Switzerland; a committee there offered assistance to those who wished to emigrate to Pennsylvania and were soon overwhelmed by German co-religionists, bent on escaping to the free land beyond the sea. In vain the committee implored and threatened. Their brethren came and, once in Holland, there was nothing to do but speed their emigration.

We have seen that the first comers in Germantown were principally Mennonites in faith. But they united themselves to the Quakers, with whom they had, religiously, much in common. In 1708, however, there were enough who remained Mennonites to build a meeting-house in the town. In the next year a colony of Swiss, descendants of men who had fled from their fatherland to Alsace a generation before, came with that flood of emigration from the Palatinate set in motion by Queen Anne's invitation to London. Thence they went to Pennsylvania and settled in Pequæ. Delighted with their new home, they sent back one of their number to induce others to join them. He was so successful that in 1711, and again six years after, emigrations en masse took place which have filled Lancaster County to this day, with "Mennists and Amish," whose careful farming has made it the Eden of Pennsylvania.

Before this time, the German emigrants were so commonly from the Palatinate that they were called not Germans but "Palatines." But about this time the people of Würtemberg, smarting under the oppressive rule of their Duke, followed the example of their neighbors and came over in large numbers.

The Germans were now spreading over Lancaster, Montgomery and Berks counties and the Provincial government, seeing this, fell into a panic, so utterly groundless as to be laughable. Governor Keith solemnly "observed to the Council, that great numbers of foreigners from Germany, strangers to our language and constitution, having lately been imported into this Province, daily dispersed themselves immediately after landing, without producing certificates from whence they came or what they are. . . . . That as this practice might be of very dangerous consequence, they were ordered to be registered and to take the oath of loyalty to the King of England," which they were perfectly willing to do.

For the previous history of the next body of sectaries who came to Pennsylvania, we need not go back as far as the Reformation. The Dunkers had arisen only a few years before their emigration, in 1709 at Schwarzenau, from which district they are sometimes called in Pennsylvania German, "Schwarzenau Taüfer"—at least a more respectful name than Dunker or its English corruption "Dunkard"— both derived from a colloquialism meaning "dipper," of course from their practice of immersion. They call themselves "Brüder" or Brethren and differ little from the Mennonites, save in insisting on immersion—the Mennonites sprinkle. The tiny principalities of Wittgenstein and Büdingen, where the Dunkers took their rise, were havens of refuge to all kinds of persecuted people, from Huguenots to Anabaptists and Moravians. The Counts of Wittgenstein were themselves Pietistically inclined, while Büdingen was a famous place for the publication of all manner of Separatist literature. The Dunker emigration was in comparison with others, an unimportant one; but three members of the sect attained to considerable prominence in the annals of the Pennsylvania Germans, though in very diverse ways; they were Conrad Beissel, the founder of the cloister at Ephrata; Christopher Saur, the first German-American publisher, and Conrad Weiser, the Indian interpreter.

In leaving the subject of the sectarian emigration, which was now drawing to a close, we should note two other sects which came somewhat later to Pennsylvania—the Schwenkfelder and the Moravians. Of the first, Seidensticker says:

"Their founder was Caspar Schwenkfeld von Ossing, a contemporary of Luther, and, like him, an opponent of the papacy. But his doctrine of the Lord's Supper and his teaching, almost approaching the Quaker doctrine, of the Inner Light, hindered a union with Luther and his followers. In Silesia and the Lausitz, the Schwenkfelder dragged out a precarious existence, disturbed by continual persecution. When they besought the Emperor Karl VI. for protection, they were 'once for all refused' and then finally given over to the Jesuits and the secular authorities. Most of them resolved on emigration in 1734."

The Moravians were encouraged by the British Parliament to settle in Georgia, but military service being required of them—at that time they were non-resistants—they betook themselves to the Quaker colony. There they first settled at Nazareth and with characteristic zeal for education, employed themselves in building a schoolhouse for negro children, under the care of the evangelist, Whitefield. But the next year they removed, and on Christmas Eve, 1741, was founded with appropriate ceremonies, Bethlehem, the "Herrnhut of America" and a center for the church's mission work among the Delawares. They had, at times, more than a dozen mission settlements of Christian Delawares.

The outskirts of civilization in those days were the banks of the Susquehanna. Into these western wilds had come in 1720, a strange sectary, one Conrad Beissel, loosely connected with the Dunkers who had settled thereabouts. He had been at one time a sort of pastor to the little flock at Pequae, but his extreme views on celibacy and the observation of the seventh day as the Sabbath had separated him from the other sectaries, who were plain, common-sense farmers with no special peculiarities in their religious views save in regard to immersion. He was a young baker, who thought himself to a certain extent inspired, and "had queer theosophic fancies." These led him to a hermit's life in the woods, in which he was presently joined by others like-minded. After nearly twenty years of asceticism in the wilderness Beissel began the buildings which grew into the future cloister of Ephrata, some of which still stand. And here for thirty years a monastic life grew and flourished in the Pennsylvania of Franklin and of the Stamp Act. Beissel or "Father Peaceful" (Friedsam) as he was known in religion, was the head. His followers erected buildings; they farmed, the brethren in their white Benedictine garb pulling the plough themselves at first, in the place of the oxen they were too poor to possess; they had paper mills and flouring mills, and a press from which issued the great "Martyr Book" of the Dunkers, a splendid specimen of book-making, 1500 folio pages, the largest book published during the eighteenth century in America. It was translated from the Dutch by Peter Miller, their learned and devout prior, and printed on paper manufactured by the brethren. Among other monastic arts, illumination flourished, and a peculiar and impressive sort of music, in which Beissel himself trained them. One of the brethren, Ludwig Hoecker, (Brother Obed) independently anticipated Robert Raikes by many years, and founded a Sabbath School, about 1740, which endured until near the time of the Revolutionary war.

Many of those who first or last felt the mysterious influence of Beissel were men of character and ability. By far the most learned was Peter Miller, afterward Beissel's successor as head of the community. A graduate of the University of Heidelberg, the Presbyterian minister, Andrews, wrote of him:

"He is an extraordinary person for sense and learning. We gave him a question to discuss about Justification, and he answered it, in a whole sheet of paper, in a very notable manner. He speaks Latin as readily as we do our natural tongue."

After his Presbyterian ordination, Miller was pastor at Tulpehocken for some years, where he fell under the influence of Beissel; he was baptized by him and entered the community of Ephrata as Brother Jaebez. Acrelius testifies to his linguistic and theological learning; he was a member of the American Philosophical Society in Philadelphia. The legend which tells how, during the Revolution, he procured the pardon of a deserter, his personal enemy, by his intercession with Washington, may have but little foundation, yet it testifies to the opinion held of his meek and noble character.

Another convert of Beissel's soon liberated himself from the glamour which this man, uneducated, fanatical, tedious in speech, and domineering, seemed to cast over all who knew him. This backslider was Conrad Weiser, the "Schoolmaster of Tulpehocken." He was one of those poor Palatines who came to England, fleeing from Louis XIV. and his devastations, at the invitation of Queen Anne; one-half of them perished of want and neglect, or returned to their desolated homes in despair, before the Queen's aid enabled the remnant to be settled in various parts of her empire. Weiser came with many others to the province of New York. But after nearly thirty years' experience of the faithlessness of the New York authorities, he, with many of his fellow colonists, fled again, this time to Pennsylvania. Settling at

Tulpehocken, he fell under Beissel's influence and he and Miller were baptized at the same time and together retired from the world. But in Conrad Weiser's case, it was only for a year. By the next year he had begun his long and useful career as a diplomatist among the Indians. Toward the end of his life he returned to Ephrata for a visit and was received with perfect friendliness.

The relations of Christoph Saur, another settler near Tulpehocken, with Beissel, were not so pleasant. He had known Beissel in Germany, and coming to Pennsylvania in 1724, he and his wife settled near the founder of Ephrata, and Saur's wife was persuaded to leave her husband and enter the community as Sister Marcella. Her husband quitted the place where his home had been thus broken up, and going to Germantown, began the business of a printer, being the first German publisher in the colonies. This was in 1739, when he published a German almanac, the prototype of the many almanacs still so dear to the heart of the Pennsylvania German. His first publication in book form, in the same year, was a collection of mystical hymns, printed for the brotherhood of Ephrata and bearing the characteristic title of "The Incense-mountain of Zion."

The strained relations which subsisted between Christoph Saur and Conrad Beissel, ever since the wife of the former had put herself under the spiritual guidance of the latter, are supposed to have come to a complete rupture during the printing of this book. The occasion of the quarrel was strange enough. In one of the hymns in the book a verse runs:

"Sehet, sehet, sehet an
Sehet, sehet an ben Mann
Der von Gott erhöhet ist,
Der ist unser Herr und Christ."

(Look, look, look, look, look at the man who is exalted by God, who is our Lord and Christ.)

Concerning this there arose a great excitement in the office. Saur asserted that Beissel meant himself by this and took the proof-reader to task about it. This man, a fanatical follower of Beissel, replied by the inquiry, whether he believed there was only one Christ? Saur lost his patience at this and in a letter reproached Beissel with such spiritual pride. The "Elder" replied by very cutting quotations, such as "Answer not a fool according to his folly," etc. This was too great a provocation to a man in possession of printers' ink and so a broadside appeared to prove that Beissel had gotten something from all the planets,—from Mars his severity, from Jupiter his friendliness, that Venus made all the women run after him, and Mercury taught him his acting; besides all this, Saur made known the astonishing discovery that in the name CONRADUS BEISSELIUS the number 666, the mark of the Apocalyptic beast, was concealed. No offence could be more deeply felt by a mystic than the imputation of this mysterious number, and the two men remained for many years at enmity. This quarrel very likely was the reason why the brethren at Ephrata set up their own press.

Saur possessed plenty of enterprise, for in this first year of the existence of his press, he also founded the first German newspaper, the Pennsylvanische Berichte ("Pennsylvanian News"), as he finally entitled it, for this reason:

"We had hoped to give nothing but true stories from the kingdoms of nature and the church. But we could not bring it to that. Therefore we have for some time done away with the title 'Historian' and instead have used 'News,' for afterwards it was discovered that sometimes this or that did not take place but was only a matter of news."

The "News" attained the, for those times, immense circulation of 4,000 copies.

There was yet a greater work before this pioneer of German-American publishers; the printing of the quarto "Germantown Bible," which is now a monument to his memory. Forty years later the first English Bible was printed in this English-speaking land, and its publisher had great misgivings about the undertaking. In the prospectus, which shows, as in a mirror, the devout, honest, simple character of Christoph Saur, he promised that the price of the Bible should not exceed fourteen shillings; "to the poor and needy," says the News, "there is no charge." It was published in 1743. Saur proudly sent a dozen copies to Germany, where, as the first Bible printed in any European language on the American continent, they are preserved in several collections.

Saur's other publications were numerous. On this point Seidensticker well says,

"People are too much inclined to consider the German immigrants of the last century to have been, universally, unlearned plebeians; sturdy farmers indeed, and industrious mechanics, but with heads entirely empty. Of course, they did not belong to the cultivated classes, and that Rascaldom had its representatives among them—as is the case in our own times—there is no doubt. But the German immigration was not a mass unleavened by culture, as is proved by the extension and the success of

Saur's publications, which embraced at least 150 titles—and indeed the new editions of books, if counted, would increase this by one-third. This is a very respectable showing which could hardly be surpassed by many publishing houses since then. By far the largest number of these writings were for purposes of devotion or edification. But where else could the plain man of the last century seek deliverance from the oppression and the sorrow of earth?"

The works of German mystics and Pietists, of course, were the most numerous; but Saur also printed translations of the "Pilgrim's Progress," the "Imitation of Christ," Whitefield's "Sermons," and Barclay's "Apology." His first English publication was the "Imitation of Christ." But he did not confine himself to religious works; English and German grammars, ready reckoners and one history were among the issues from the press of Germantown. Saur also wrote and published some political pamphlets, for he took much interest in governmental affairs and had immense influence among the Pennsylvania Germans. Naturally it was by the Separatists like himself, the non-resistants, that he was most respected and followed.

Nevertheless, the Sectarian, the Separatist, period of Pennsylvania-German history—a period so marked— was now drawing to a close. The "Church people," Lutherans and Reformed, were beginning to outnumber the earlier immigrants who had fled from persecution.

Two men had great influence in forming and organizing the "Church people;" one was Michael Schlatter, a Swiss-German, a native of St. Gall, that town from whose monastery Switzerland was evangelized—who was sent out in 1746 by the synod of

Holland as a sort of missionary superintendent, to organize the scattered members of the Reformed Church in Pennsylvania; the other was Henry Melchior Muhlenberg, the patriarch of Lutheranism in America, sent a few years earlier to do the same service for the Lutherans. These two missionaries found a sad state of things among their people. Muhlenberg reports in "Hallische Nachrichten," which is so valuable a source of Pennsylvania-German history, that the Lutheran ministers were largely "deposed preachers and schoolmasters who did not amount to much at home." He procured regularly ordained ministers through the Pietists of Halle, always active in good works, and it is no wonder that his memory is today reverenced as that of a second founder of their church, by the Lutherans of America.

Schlatter, as learned, pious and active, was not as fortunate. He was destined to end his life in poverty and obloquy, through his luckless and innocent connection with a schemer's plans. This was the project for the "German schools," engineered by the Rev. William Smith. Schlatter himself, in the year 1751, had collected in Europe a large fund to be used in the support of schools among the people of the Reformed church in Pennsylvania. But a year or two after, Mr. Smith took up the matter and turned it to a new purpose, that of teaching the Germans English. He addressed a memorial to the Society for the Propagation of the Gospel, setting forth the spiritual destitution of the Pennsylvania Germans, of whom he knew only by hearsay. It was a very poetical and classical production, picturing the utter lack of educational opportunities (as a matter of fact schools were everywhere founded with the churches, when possible) ; he threatened, too, that the Germans would become Catholics and unite with the French against the peace of the province—they who had been driven from their native land by the fire and sword of the "Most Catholic" king of France.

The memorial made an impression on the English public, proportionate to its lack of truth. In vain the Lutherans and the Reformed churches officially protested their unshaken loyalty and their unfaltering Protestantism. The schools were started in face of this protest of Saur's vigorous opposition. At first sight this seems mere contrariness in the publisher of Germantown. But events soon proved that he was right in his suspicions that the German schools were only part of a plan to rob the Germans of their cherished mother-tongue, to convert them to Episcopalianism and to detach them from the Quaker party in the province, to which the non-resistant sects naturally leaned. Smith now published a pamphlet, avowing these objects, accusing Saur of being a papist emissary, and proposing to make the use of the German language illegal, to forbid the publication of any book or paper in it, and, finally, he advised depriving the Germans of the franchise.

Naturally, these propositions raised a storm of indignation in the Teutonic element. Poor Schlatter's school project was confounded with Smith's intrigues, for he was the inspector of the new schools. He was forced to resign his pastorate in Philadelphia by the aroused feelings of his countrymen, and took a chaplaincy in the Royal American Regiment. It is not to be wondered at that the "Palatines" were not flattered at the portrait drawn of them or the plans made for them; as Seidensticker says,

"They awaited from the Germans the grateful reception of a benefit and at the same time denounced them as by way of being rebels and as inclined toward the French enemy. They were described as semi-barbarians, ignorant savages, and then people lamented that it was so difficult to reach them on account of the influence over them of their press. People desired to win them over and yet repelled them by the proposition to disfranchise them and to forbid the printing of German newspapers. They tried to undermine Saur's influence and, in order to do so, made use of a clumsy ·lander which nobody believed."

Saur's victory over the school project was a conflict, short, sharp and decisive ; his efforts in another field—the last battle of his stormy life—were not so successful. The wrong which aroused his latest endeavors was the outrageous treatment of German immigrants.

It was not until the German immigration had attained large proportions that we hear complaints of the ill-treatment of passengers. There then arose a class of men who lived by inducing simple Germans through glowing descriptions and lying promises, to emigrate to the New World, and who were spurred on to greater efforts by receiving a percentage on the recruits obtained. They were called "Neuländer" or less flatteringly, "Seelenverkaufer."*

They persuaded the emigrants to sign contracts which they did not understand, and lent them money for

* Goethe uses the latter word in "Wilhelm Meister.' He probably learned it in his Frankfort home, which was a center of emigration

their expenses, thus bringing them into the "Neuländer's" power. In concert with them worked the shipmasters, often cruel, inhuman, or careless; in any case, making the voyage almost equal to the horrors of the Slave Trade's middle passage. Caspar Wister, who came over in 1717, tells us:

"Sometimes the voyage is very hard. In the past year one of the ships was twenty-four weeks on the sea and of 150 persons who were on her, 100 miserably starved and died of hunger. . . . At last the remainder, half-starved, reached land, where after the endurance of much misery, they were put in arrest and were forced to pay the passage-money for the dead as well as for the living. This year, again, ten ships have arrived, bringing about 3,000 souls. One of these ships was seventeen weeks on the way and nearly sixty of the passengers died at sea. The remainder are all sick, feeble, and what is worse, poor and penniless."

Saur constantly published notices of the treatment of the emigrants; in 1745 he says:

"Another ship with Germans has arrived in Philadelphia; it is said there were 400 and not more than 50 are alive; they got their bread every two weeks and many ate in four, five or six days, what they should have eaten in fifteen. . . . Another man, who finished his bread in a week, begged the captain for a little bread, but got none, so he with his wife came humbly to the captain and begged he might throw him overboard, that he might not die a slow death, for it was yet long till bread-day; the captain would not do that either, so he brought the steersman his bag that he should put a little flour in it; but he had no money; the steersman went away and put sand and sea-coal into the bag and brought it to him; the man wept, lay down and died, he and his wife, a few days before the bread-day came."

And in 1750,

"For many years past, we have seen with

sorrow, that many German newcomers have had very bad voyages, that many died, most of them because they were not humanely treated; especially because they were packed too close, so that the sick must take one another's breath, and from the smell, dirt, and lack of provisions, that yellow fever, scurvy, flux and other contagious sicknesses often arose. Sometimes the ship was so full of merchandise, that there was not room enough for bread and water; many dared not cook what they themselves had with them. The wine was secretly drunken up by the sailors. Some of the provisions and clothing were loaded on other ships and came, long afterwards, so that many people were forced to beg and to 'serve' (verserven, a word invented by the Pennsylvania Germans to express the condition of those whom the English called Redemptioners) because they had not their possessions with them. Many must pay the passage for those who had died of hunger or thirst."

At this time efforts were made for the passage of a law regulating the transportation of emigrants. But Governor Morris refused to sign it, not without suspicion that he was influenced by the very men who made their gain from the poor passengers' sufferings. At this time Christoph Saur, ever the "unwearied friend of the emigrant," addressed several letters to the Governor, telling him of the abuses of the system. He begins,

"Thirty years ago I came to this province, from a country where no freedom of conscience existed, no motives of humanity had any weight with those who then ruled the land; where serfdom compelled the people to work for their masters three days a week with a horse, and three days with hoe, shovel and spade, or to send a laborer. When I arrived here and found the circumstances so altogether different from those at home, I wrote to my friends and acquaintances concerning the civil and religious freedom and other advantages which the country offered. My letters were printed and by frequent reprints, widely distributed; they induced many thousand people to come here, wherefore many are thankful to the Lord."

And in words that dimly remind us of those which Scott puts into the mouth of Jeanie Deans, he concludes:

"Honored Sir, I am old and feeble, draw nigh to the grave and shall soon be no more seen. I hope your Excellency will not take it ill of me, to have recommended the helpless to your protection. May the Lord keep us from all evil and every harm; we may the more hope for this, if we treat others so, who are in distress and danger. May the Lord bestow upon you wisdom and patience, that your administration may be a blessed one and when the time comes, give you the reward of a good and faithful servant."

Christoph Saur the elder was indeed near his end; he died in 1758 at Germantown, leaving to his son, the younger Christoph Saur, an honored name and a prosperous business.

It is sad to know that Saur's simple and noble appeal produced no effect. Things were to go from bad to worse, until, for very shame and pity, all hearts were roused and, four years after the elder Saur's death, the Deutsche Gesellschaft was formed, to give help to the immigrants. By its intelligent and concerted efforts, it succeeded in having laws passed through the legislature, which put an end to the worst oppressions of the "Palatines." The founding of this society—still in existence—was occasioned by more than ordinary distress among the Germans landed in Philadelphia in 1764. The system of allowing the emigrants to hire themselves out in order to pay the expenses of their voyage was, in itself, not a blameworthy one. In its earlier form, when each person "served' for his own passage-money,

it must have been a great boon to many poor but industrious people; but when, subsequently, the whole ship's company was made responsible for the passage-money of the whole list of passengers, it led, as may be imagined, to great injustice and hardships. Those who had paid their own fare must "serve" for those who had no money; they were held under English contracts, which they did not understand and which might contain any severe conditions; husband and wife, children and parents were separated, as in slavery; orphans or widows, left defenceless by the many deaths of the long voyage, were condemned to years and years of servitude; the old and the sick no one but the worst masters would take, or they were left paupers at the wharf. Says Muhlenberg:

"So the old people get free from the ship, are poor, naked and helpless, looking as tho they had come out of their graves, go begging in the city among the German inhabitants, for the English mostly shut the door in their faces, for fear of infection. One's heart bleeds at such things, when one sees and hears how the poor creatures, come to the New World from Christian countries, are some of them weeping, or crying, or lamenting, or striking their hands together over their heads at wretchedness and dispersion such as they had not imagined, and how others curse and call upon the elements and sacraments, the thunder and the wicked dwellers in Hell, that they should torture and tear into countless pieces the Neuländer, the Holland merchants, who have led them astray."

Sometimes these emigrants were educated men; the case was frequent enough for a thrifty Lutheran minister to form the plan which he thus expounds in the "Hallische Nachrichten":

"If I had twenty pounds, I would buy

the first German student who should land here in debt for his passage, set him in my upper room, begin a little Latin school, teach there in the morning myself and then let my servant teach, and by a small fee get myself.paid."

And indeed the benevolent pastor, in this way—no uncommon one at the time—came in possession of a certain college graduate, whom he educated for the ministry.   But few such men found so good a fate.

The system of serving lasted until the Revolutionary War, and, in some cases, later.

(To be continued.)

American Shrines IX   Mount Vernon

NEW ENGLAND MAGAZINE

NEW SERIES   JUNE   VOL. XXVI NO. 4

Famous Farm Houses in the Narragansett Country

By Harry Knowles

EVERY locality has its landmarks, and few regions have more which abound in historic interest than the famous Narragansett Country. Situated in the delightful region, the southern part of Rhode Island, traversed in "ye olden time" by travellers from New York to Boston over the "old post road," it was early settled by an aristocratic class who could well afford to spend time and money for hospitable homes, where were born many of those men and women whose names later became pre-eminent in American history. Now-a-days in these same localities there are attractive watering-places, where summer pleasure seekers enjoy those privileges and advantages which the early colonists fully appreciated. The historic interest, together with the beautiful scenery of the country, make an afternoon's drive to any of these houses a pleasure not easily forgotten.

Undoubtedly the only house in the Narragansett Country that can boast of a regal inhabitant, is situated in Charlestown, not over a mile from the shore. When the Puritans settled at Plymouth, they found all the Indian tribes of New England governed by one great sachem, Canonicus. His grandnephew, Canonchet, it will be remembered, ruled over the Narragansetts. This tribe was composed of several branches, one of them the Niantics, commonly, but inaccurately, spoken of as "Charlestown Indians." The leader of this division was named Ninigret He died a short time after King Philip's War, whereupon the crown descended to his eldest daughter, a child by his first wife. Upon her early death, her half brother, who was named for his father, inherited the throne.   Ninigret Second's reign was also short, and a son, Charles Augustus, succeeded him.   Upon his death, rather than let the crown fall to an infant son, the tribe chose his brother, George.   This monarch had three children, Thomas, Esther, and George.   The first, born in 1735, soon after his father's ascent to the throne, is said to have been slight in stature and sickly in appearance.

By the time "King Tom," as the English called him, had reached man-

THE KING TOM MANSION

hood, civilization was well advanced in Narragansett.   A few of the most artful Indians, including the King, imitated the white man, as best they could, and built more or less comfortable houses for their protection from the trying winds and weather.

Most structures that were built in Colonial times were from designs by Englishmen, and partake of the feudal architecture which is so effective. Though "King Tom's" house was intended for a king, it had none of the adornments of a palace, but was at-

tractive rather for its great simplicity. Originally square, it is of two and one-half stories, with a "barn," or "Canada," roof that has a "trap door" near the large chimney.   It fronts the west, and tall elm trees shade the porch while the forest primeval extends from its very yard in a southerly direction. The front door opens into a small hall-way, where slightly curving stairs wind upward at the right.   On the left, a massive oak door with brass catch and hinges admits to the parlor.   The wall on the east side of this room is panelled, and, on either side of the fire-place, are commodious cup-boards.   In the rear of the hall, and opening from the parlor, is a long and narrow living room.   This also has a fireplace, and is well lighted by two large windows at the south.   A door on the north of this room opens into the original kitchen, where the fireplace measures at least eight by fifteen feet.   This apartment is now used as a dining-hall and the "L" at its north has been built by the present owner.   The rooms are similarly arranged in the upper story, and throughout all, both upstairs and down, beams and corner posts invariably show.

It is sad to relate that "King Tom" lived but a short time after his home was completed.   Probably the modern methods of living proved ruinous to one accustomed to out-door life.   At any rate, like his ancestors, he early sickened and died, and the throne was next occupied by his sister Esther who, tradition says, was crowned upon a rock in his yard.

On the banks of the Pettaquamscutt, or, as it is now called, "Narrow" river and some distance above the upper-bridge, so designated, there is a house

THE HOME OF DR. McSPARRAN

that even the most casual observer will not fail to notice, as he rides along the road that follows the winding stream. Like so many other structures in Narragansett, it is shingled and has a gambrel roof. On the whole, however, it looks more commodious than ordinary country houses. A large barn on the opposite side of the road is evidence that the owner must have been in comfortable circumstances and must have had numerous domestics to perform the menial tasks. Then, again, its situation upon two terraces ("offsets" they are called in the Narragansett Country) gives it a dignified appearance. Great seclusion is afforded by tall lilac bushes which form a thick, continuous hedge around the edges of each terrace. It is in this quiet place that the famous Dr. McSparran lived when discharging the duties of rector to the first Episcopal church in New England.

About 1718 Mr. James McSparran emigrated from Dungiven, Ireland, to America as a licentiate of the Presbytery in Scotland, and finally drifted to Bristol, where he visited some friends. He was invited to supply the pulpit of the church at Bristol and later to remain as permanent pastor. Finding his ordination bitterly opposed by Cotton Mather he returned to Ireland to secure a ratification of his credentials. When he next visited America it was as a missionary of the Church of England to "Narragansett in New England, where he is to officiate as opportunity shall offer at Bristol, Freetown, Swansea, and Little Compton, at which places there are many people destitute of a minister." On his arrival he took up his abode in the home whose exterior we have just described.

The dwelling faces toward the east and fronts on the road that runs between it and the river, which is not over one hundred yards distant. The entrance is at the south-east corner and admits to a small hall; the case of winding stairs is hidden from view by a partition. Besides this hall there are on the first floor a large living room, with three chambers opening from it—two on the west and one on the north—and a kitchen of moderate size with an ample closet. The fireplaces in the kitchen and in other rooms are bricked up, thereby effacing one feature of primitive architecture. The second story is an exact duplicate of the first. Every room of the house has those evidences of antiquity invariably looked for in Colonial houses,— occasional beams running along the ceiling and four rigid cornerposts which appear to be guarding the plain walls. Other indications of age in this venerable mansion are the quaint figures on the wall paper (many of which peep out through rents in a covering of later design); the uneven floor; the brass latches (which, it is safe to say, have not been scoured for over a century); and the many paned window-sashes.

SAINT PAUL'S CHURCH

To the north of the house, there is a small orchard wherein are numerous fruit trees; chief among which are the apple, pear, and peach. The well is on the opposite side—or at the south. Attached to the rope that hangs from the long pole or "well-sweep" is a bottomless yet moss-covered bucket. Tall poplar trees cast a little shade over this spot; tiger lilies and sweet-briar rose bushes run wild in great profusion. A small locust or cherry tree can be seen here and there, while not far away is a bed of ripe asparagus. From this spot, the home of Mr. McSparran's father-in-law, as it stands near South Ferry upon the ridge between Narrow, or Pettaquamscutt, river and the ocean, is plainly visible. Hannah Gardiner, his wife, was the daughter of William Gardiner, an emigrant from England and one of the first settlers in Narragansett. Mr. Gardiner was a man of considerable wealth; the owner of extensive estates and master of numerous slaves.

On the death of Dr. McSparran his remains were interred beneath the floor under the communion table of Saint Paul's Church, of which he was the first rector. The church is still standing—the oldest episcopal edifice in New England—but not on its original site. As the population of Rhode Island increased, business slowly yet surely drew away from the favored Narragansett Country towards Providence and the northern part of the State. Thus it came about that there were not enough people to support the old Saint Paul's in its former situation. So, as an accommodation for the majority of its members, the church was moved to Wickford, in 1800, from the place where it had been built in 1707. For over half a century, Dr. McSparran's grave was unmarked.   In 1868 a monument was erected, upon the spot where his body now rests, by order of the diocese of Rhode Island.

On the east side of the road running north from the village of Kingston (formerly called Little Rest) there stands a large rock, built into a wall, upon which the following is painted in

THE MONUMENT TO DR. McSPARRAN

THE SITE OF THE JUDGE POTTER PLACE

red letters: "The ancient Judge Wm. Potter Place: Headquarters of the noted preacher Jemima Wilkinson (or "Universal Friend") for six years, from 1777 to 1783."

Jemima Wilkinson was the great-grand-daughter of the first Wilkinson who emigrated to this country (in 1645) and who had been a Lieutenant in Cromwell's army. Her own father lived in Cumberland, Rhode Island, where he was engaged in farming. Jemima, the eighth child, was born on the fifth day of the week, November 29, 1752. Since Mrs. Wilkinson died when Jemima was a mere child, the cares of the household early fell upon her shoulders. About the time she became eighteen years of age, a religious excitement prevailed in Providence County; the celebrated George Whitfield acting as preacher on many occasions. These meetings must have made a serious impression upon Jemima; for she soon cast off all her finery and from a vain, proud, selfish girl changed to a demure mistress. Her early education having been sadly neglected, she now tried to make up for this handicap by employing all her spare moments reading the bible; she determined to lead a religious life. She was stricken by a contagious fever, and her friends, when gathered around what was thought would be her death-bed one night, saw her enter into a trance. For hours the body was motionless, there being no perceptible heart beat or breathing. All at once Jemima spoke, telling those in the room that she had been reanimated and must now "raise her dead body." The watchers were startled but, fortunately, kept their senses. Her clothes were brought to her as quickly as requested, whereupon she arose, dressed herself, and fervently prayed for strength to carry out her mission. Then she said: "Jemima Wilkinson is no more. She has died; this" (touching her breast) "is her spirit henceforth to be known as the Universal Friend." Jemima's life thereafter was devoted to the preaching of a new religion, in which she adopted many of the teachings of the Quakers, but claimed to be the daughter of God and likened herself to Christ. One of her early converts was Judge William Potter of Narragansett, a noted Rhode Island lawyer, who built a large addition to his house for the accommodation of "the Universal Friend" and her followers. There they lived for six years, the mansion becoming known as the "Abbey." In 1784 Jemima and her proselytes removed to Yates County, New York, where they remained until her death in 1819, when the colony gradually dispersed.

Between the years 1746 and 1750 a number of Scotch gentlemen emigrated from Great Britain to the English Colonies. Some settled at Philadelphia, others at New York; but by far the major portion came to the southern part of Rhode Island, then known as the "Garden of America."

A prominent man in this colony was the celebrated Dr. Thomas Moffat, who settled upon a tract of land not far from the village of Wickford in what is now North Kingstown. It appears that Dr. Moffat was unfortunate in the choice of a home; for his gaudy dress and obsequious manners were so offensive to the plain habits of the Quakers who dwelt in this community that they refused to employ him. Consequently, Dr. Moffat began to look about for some other mode of "genteel subsistance."

Observing that large amounts of money were annually sent to Scotland in payment for the great quantity of snuff then imported each year, he designed to partially supply this demand by raising his own tobacco and then grinding it into the luxurious article of commerce. So, choosing some land at the head of the Pettaquamscutt River for his farm, he sent to Scotland for a mechanic who considered himself capable of constructing and managing a snuff mill. A certain Gilbert Stuart was secured, who married a daughter of one of Narragansett's most substantial planters soon after his arrival in America, and who settled in a house near the first snuff mill built in New England, of which he was the proprietor.

There is not a more picturesque or attractive farm house in the Narragansett Country than this one. Situated by the roadside, yet only half visible in the approach from either direction because of the drooping willow trees that partially hide it from view, this place has a particularly secluded appearance. As seen from the driveway, the structure is of two and one-half stories. But since it is built into a hill-side, the house appears to have only one story, besides the unfinished rooms under the wide-angled gambrel roof, when approached from the opposite direction. This is the front and, contrary to an old custom, it faces toward the north. Thick planks, under which the huge waterwheel can be heard turning whenever the dam-gate is lifted up, extend for a short distance (or about the width of a broad piazza) in front of the house. Beyond this, and still to the north, a beautiful sheet of water expands, reflecting the numerous trees that border upon its banks as well as the picturesque buildings at its foot. Is it any wonder that a person born among such delightful surroundings as these should be inspired to paint? The front door is not quite in the centre of the house—there being three windows toward the west and but one on the east side of it. The latter serves to light up the room where Gilbert Charles Stuart was born—for thus he was christened by the Rev. Dr. McSparran. However, his middle name —which betokens the Jacobite principles of his father—he dropped when a young man and, were it not for some letters written to his friend Waterhouse and the church records, we should have no evidence to prove that he was ever so named.

Not much of Gilbert Stuart's boyhood could have been spent in Narragansett, for he was early sent to the Newport Grammar School. His great talent first made itself manifest at the age of thirteen, when he began copying pictures in black lead. Some time after this, and during his sojourn in Newport, he made the acquaintance of Cosmo Alexander, a gentleman of

considerable means, who ostensibly made painting his profession while travelling in America though it is thought he was making the tour as a political spy. Stuart soon became Mr. Alexander's pupil, and it is to this gentleman that the famous portrait painter owes his rudimentary knowledge of the art in which he excelled. Mr. Alexander had become so attached to his apt scholar by the close of the summer that he requested Gilbert to accompany him on a tour through the southern states. Stuart accepted the invitation, and after travelling in Virginia, Carolina, and Georgia, they two journeyed to England where Mr. Alexander died shortly after they reached his home. Stuart next fell into the hands of Chambers, who also died a short time after adopting his protegée. Thence the young American artist returned to Newport in 1793.

About this time the conservative in-

terests of the Stuart family induced them to move to Nova Scotia. Being, as it were, left alone in the world, Gilbert again sailed for England (after a short visit in the colonies) for the purpose of studying under Benjamin West, the great historical painter of that day, and his subsequent career is too well known to need repetition here.

The snuff mill still stands. Nothing remains, however, to indicate the purpose for which it was originally built.

Christopher Raymond Perry, the father of two commodores, was born in Newport, and, after his marriage, settled upon a farm which borders on the road connecting the villages of Wakefield and Kingston or, as the latter was then called, Little Rest. The tall trees of an old orchard (which surrounds the house on the northern and western sides) make so dense a screen that the buildings are com-

393

pletely hidden when observed from the highway. The dwelling is a large square two and one-half story structure, having a "barn," or "Canada," roof. The front entrance, similar to that of many old-fashioned houses, is at the south over two flat granite-stone door-steps into a small hall that is scarcely four feet square. A curving stairway (partly hidden by a partition) leads to the upper story. Two spacious rooms, which are similarly situated on either side of the hall-way, each measure twenty feet square in size. Both of these are well lighted. Every window frame has thirty-two panes of glass, no pane measuring over six inches square. Huge beams, which have never been painted (hence the many knots and primal hewings can yet be plainly seen) run along the ceilings; while four stern corner-posts rigidly guard each room. In the rear

394

of the small hall and with an entrance from the rooms situated at either side of the hallway, is a poorly lighted apartment, probably measuring twelve by eighteen feet. A large fireplace running from floor to ceiling, covers over two-thirds of the southern side of this room, while its wide hearthstone extends fully half way across the floor. To the right, is a smaller opening (through which one can see a bricked floor) where the baking was done in "ye olden time," after heating the oven by means of red hot coals. This room was formerly employed as a kitchen, but is now used as a dining room by the more up-to-date inhabitants. The small "L" to the north is a mere shed where the vegetables and meats were kept in by-gone days, as is shown by the big oak staples run through the beams, upon which a whole ox was hung as soon as butchered.   The plan of the second story is almost an exact duplicate of the first; each room, however, being supplied with a fireplace.   From the windows of the southeast chamber one may have a panoramic view of exceptionally pretty scenery.   McSparran Hill rises up and extends toward the north; Tower Hill extends in the opposite direction.   The villages of Wakefield and Peace Dale lie serenely in the distant valley.   Here and there a little stream runs through barren pastures while, upon its banks, tall elm trees grow now and then.   And so the unequalled pastoral scenery continues, its beauty multiplying itself many times and making an ideal spot for the birthplace of a famous commodore.

Christopher Perry had five children, all of whom were boys.   The oldest of these, Oliver Hazard, was born in the house previously described.   Matthew Calbraith Perry was not born in the same house as Oliver.   It seems as if such a double honor would have been too much for one building.   His birthplace was upon a farm to the south of Wakefield in what is now known as Matumuck.   The entrance is off the old post-road and at a point where the ground rises just enough to command an unsurpassed view of the surrounding country.   Towards the east and across a beautiful sheet of water called "Great Salt Lake," Point Judith extends out into the bold Atlantic.   Still in this direction, but converging toward the north, is Narragansett Pier and just across the bay the merry city of Newport.   To the north, one has a view of hills, valleys, and villages while woodlands cut off a similar picture at the west.   The sandy shores of Matumuck wind along the

south, while opposite Block Island is vaguely visible.

But, if we follow a winding drive that leads through a small grove and thence into an open pasture, we shall finally arrive in front of a weather-beaten, one and one-half story gambrel roofed house, which is surrounded by a dilapidated picket fence and whose roof is covered with red waterproof paper in order to keep it from leaking.   The driveway continues toward the west to the barn, curving around an old orchard, where knotty pears and wormy apples hang in great

BIRTHPLACE OF OLIVER HAZARD PERRY

profusion upon the mossy branches. Clumps of blue larkspur and scarlet sage, evidences of the beautiful flower garden once existing there, have outgrown their limits and spread nearly all over the yard.   Bushes of japonica and syringa here and there take the place of the rotten fence or stand where it has fallen apart.

Like many other old buildings, the house faces south with a doorway in the middle of that front.   The hall is long and narrow and its monotony is broken only by a straight staircase that runs lengthwise along the eastern partition.   On the right of the en-

THE BIRTHPLACE OF MATTHEW CALBRAITH PERRY

trance is a room of moderate size, out of which a small bedroom extends toward the north. Back of the hall, with a doorway entering therefrom, stands the kitchen. It has but two small windows (both on the north side) which barely admit enough light to illumine the sooty fireplace opposite them. The latter is high enough for a man of average height to stand erect in. On the west is an "L" that is scarcely eight feet square, formerly used as a milk-room and closet combined, as its numerous shelves indicate. There is a small door on the south side of it that opens upon a terrace built up around the well-curb. The second story is quite similar to the first. Although uninhabited and allowed to go to ruin, this farm is the property (by purchase) of one of the Commodore's descendants.

Matthew Calbraith, the third son of Christopher Raymond and Sarah

Alexander Perry, was born here in 1794. His services to his country in the opening of Japan to the commerce of the world, although less brilliant, were no less distinguished than his brother's; and both form a part of the nation's history.

Perhaps there is no farm house in the entire Narragansett Country that has a more palatial appearance than the Robinson mansion, situated about a mile north of South Ferry or, as it was formerly called, Franklin's Ferry. The spaciousness and grandeur of this old Colonial home can not but impress one as he drives up and dismounts upon the stone horse-block that stands next to the road-side. Tall weeping willow trees cast a deep shade over the house and surrounding dooryard, while here and there is a clump of Boxwood which indicates the extent of the old-fashioned "posy garden." But nothing else, beyond a broken trellis or decayed rustic seat, now exists to suggest the gayety and high living that was formerly so customary here.

The house (including the slave quarters) was originally one hundred and ten feet long, as the stone underpinning, which still extends in easterly and northerly directions, indicates. But, at the present day, it measures only about sixty feet in length and is only about thirty feet wide. The structure is two stories high, above which there is a wide angled gambrel roof. Like all houses built over a century ago, it is covered with shingles which have never been painted, though the moss that has now grown upon them gives the building a dark green color. All the timber used in constructing this mansion was felled upon the farm; and the rugged rafters, which have not decayed or sagged an inch, are reminders of the famous trees that formerly grew in the forests of Old Narragansett.

The massive, weather-beaten door, on which hangs an unpolished brass knocker, admits to a small hallway. The black walnut stair-case, with its beautifully turned balustrade and unique drop ornaments, is magnificent. All the walls on the lower floor are wainscotted. In each of the rooms on either side of the hall (in both lower and upper stories) there is a fireplace which has blue and white Dutch tile, with allegoric pictures bordering around it. The west parlor is twenty feet square and has a most curious china cupboard on the north side. It is apse-shaped, and the top is beautifully carved in "sunbursts," while the shelves are either escalloped or serrated. There is a secret box on either side, while a door made of a single pane of glass served to keep the dust

off the beautiful china kept within. Below this and above a tier of drawers that extends to the floor, is a hidden shelf (not unlike a kneading board), that pulls out into the room, which was probably used for a writing desk. The space above the parlor is commonly known as the Lafayette chamber; for legend says that the General inhabited it for the space of one month during the Revolution. The numerous French signatures and monograms, supposedly inscribed upon the window panes by means of his diamond rings, would seem to justify this tradition. At the left of the hallway

THE HANNAH ROBINSON HOUSE

on the first floor, is a dining room that measures twenty by twenty-two feet in size. Above the large fireplace in it there is a dingy oil painting more crude than finished, which depicts a deer hunt that took place upon the premises while the house was building. The hunted animal is represented as leaping away toward the forest next to the shore with the sportsmen in hot pursuit. The riders appear to be standing up in their stirrups rather than sitting quietly upon those famous Narragansett pacers which they surely rode. The chamber above is still known as the "Unfortunate Hannah's Bed-room," it having been used by Mr. Robinson's beautiful daughter. The story of her life is a pathetic tale of misplaced love.

Rowland Robinson, her father, was a typical Narragansett planter—wealthy, proud, and irascible, yet kind at heart. His hospitality was great, and under his roof were given frequent entertainments and gay social functions. The beauty of his daughter Hannah was celebrated and brought her many suitors. No money had been spared on her education, but of all her accomplishments she was most devoted to dancing. In happened that a French Huguenot of aristocratic lineage had taken refuge in Newport, where he supported himself by giving lessons in dancing. A love affair between Hannah and Pierre Simond was the natural consequence, and it was accompanied by all those clandestine meetings and secret exchanges of missives which lend romance to such affair in the eyes of young people. Discovered by Hannah's mother, efforts were made to break off the affair, but in vain, and at last the mother was induced to lend her assistance to an elopement, by which the young people were finally united in marriage. Hannah was disowned by her father, and her lover, discovering that there was no hope of a reconciliation, out of which he might profit, deserted his bride, leaving her to sickness and despair. The reconciliation followed, but too late, for on the day following the unfortunate girl's return to her home the song of the whippoorwill was heard beneath the window, and when morning dawned she was dead. Her grave may be seen today in the old family lot on the homestead. Beside it bachelor's buttons and "Bouncing Bess" never blossoms, though heartsease blooms in great profusion as if to soothe the spirit of "Unfortunate Hannah Robinson."

Creating Character at the Lyman School for Boys, Westborough, Massachusetts

By Alfred S. Roe

"For I do not think that a measure costing an equal amount of money, care and attention could have been devised, that will in the end diminish to a greater extent vice, crime and suffering in the Commonwealth."*

THE annual average of erring boys whom the Bay State has sent to her Lyman School for juvenile delinquents may be reckoned from the fact that No. 1 was entered November 1, 1848, while No. 7784, in the latest volume of the great record books of the institution, represents a diminutive specimen of juvenile humanity, not many times larger than the volume itself, who at 10.30 A. M., March 4, 1902, was ushered into the Superintendent's office. The story which he told, in reply to leading questions, readily explains why he and very many of his associates are there. The youngest of seven children, he had just passed his eleventh birthday. To the best of his knowledge, he had a father somewhere in Boston, but he had no recollection of ever seeing him. His mother was dead. His latest home had been with a sister, his earliest, the town farm. The charge

*From Theodore Lyman's letter to the Commissioners, comunicating his willingness to donate the sum of $10,000 for the more effectual carrying out of the Act of the Legislature contemplating the establishment of the School.

of stubbornness, on which he was entered, like charity, covers a multitude of sins in the Lyman School. All offenses, not otherwise easily named, are lumped under this one head. This latest boy had repeatedly run away from his sister's home, impelled thereto, perhaps by the same inherited trait which in the lad's infancy had prompted the father to desert his family. Well may the Trustees, in one of their reports, make the pertinent query, *"How can a boy escape from his ancestors?"* Carefully kept in the vaults of the school, are nearly thirty volumes of records, telling when and why the boys appeared and, as far as possible, their subsequent careers. All sorts of histories are found therein. At least one lad passed out to a criminal manhood and finally expiated his capital offense upon the scaffold, while successful business men, college graduates, and devoted ministers of the gospel have dated their upward start in life to the help and encouragement given them here. Number 1 was sent from Lowell as "Idle and dissolute." He was fifteen years old; responding to the efforts made in his behalf, he learned the carpenter's trade and in 1851, went to California. There he became a farmer and in 1853, the last entry, he was in possession of a large and well-stocked farm. No. 2 came the 3d of November and in 1855 was at sea. No. 4 came on the 4th and he too went to sea, and was drowned. In 1876, No. 5 came back to visit the school. During the war he had been in the navy, and, an honest, reputable man, was then enjoying a pension from the Government on account of an eye lost in its defence. And so on.   .

In the care of over active boys, Massachusetts was a pioneer. In 1824, New York City had begun her institution for youthful delinquents on Randall's Island; in 1826, both Philadelphia and Boston followed with similar provisions for street waifs and juvenile offenders, but Massachusetts was the first state as an entire body politic to reform the young by an institution for punitive purposes. It was in the earlier days of the administration of Gov. Briggs, that the demand for such an institution as is at Westborough began to be heard. Too many boys of tender age were sent each year by the courts to the jails and state prison, there to become adepts in crime,* and there is little wonder that petitions for some action, obviating such procedure should pour in upon the Legislature. That body passed an act which the Governor signed, April 16, 1846, empowering him to appoint three Commissioners, who at an expense not to exceed $10,000, should purchase not less than fifty acres of land upon which the "State Manual Labor School" should be established. Governor Briggs appointed Alfred Dwight Foster of Worcester, who had only recently been

*In 1845, exclusive of Suffolk, Norfolk, Hampshire and Barnstable Counties, ninety-seven children, under sixteen years of age, had been arrested and sentenced to houses of correction in Massachusetts.

a member of the Executive Council, Robert Rantoul, the orator and statesman of Salem, and Samuel H. Walley, Jr., of Roxbury, a member of the Council, but better known among his contemporaries as Deacon of Boston's Old South Church. These gentlemen, after visits to the existing institutions of New York, Philadelphia and Boston, and a careful consideration of the proper location for the school, fixed upon the town of Westborough, as sufficiently near the center of population and they purchased on the shores of Chauncey Pond the 180-acre farm of Lovett Peters as their first decisive act.

It was at this time that there entered into their deliberations a man whose name has been for more than half a century a synonym for philanthrophy throughout the Commonwealth, though, and during his life, the fact that Theodore Lyman was the benefactor of Massachusetts boys was not known beyond the immediate circle actively interested. Scarcely had the Commissioners settled upon the location, when they received a letter, expressing the writer's warm sympathy with the project and indicating a willingness to give $10,000 towards the necessary outlay in securing the land, and a disposition to give an additional $5,000 or $10,000, provided the State would duplicate the sum, to help the boys to a start in life on their leaving the institution. The twenty letters between the Commissioners and Mr. Lyman, beautifully transcribed and in the finest bindings, form one of the most interesting possessions of the school. Theodore Lyman, whose name is forever associated with this heaven born effort to repair man's faults and crimes, was born in Boston, February 20, 1792, and died at his home in Brookline, July 18, 1849. Possessed of large wealth, he had the advantages of education at Harvard and of foreign travel in company with Edward Everett. Returning to Massachusetts, he studied law and entering the militia attained the rank of Brigadier-General. He was a member of both branches of the Legislature, was twice Mayor of Boston and, when serving his second term, at the risk of his own life, rescued Wm. Lloyd Garrison from the hands of an infuriated mob. As former president of the Boston Farm School, and dissatisfied with its management, he still may have gained there that appreciation of such attempts to make citizens out of waste material which prompted him to assume so large a part in the direction and maintenance of the, then so called, Reform School. Unhappily he did not live to see the beneficent results that followed his gifts, in all amounting to $72,500, the income of which was not to go into "bricks and mortar" but rather to the building and equipping of the boys themselves. Not till death had sealed the lips of the giver, did the authorities of the school reveal the name of its benefactor.

The Act appropriating $35,000 for buildings and $1,000 for stocking, improving and cultivating the farm was signed by Governor Briggs, April 9, 1847. As the first gift of Mr. Lyman had paid for the Peters farm, there was yet an unexpended sum of $10,000 to be applied with the above appropriation. By the same Act, the institution was established under the name of State Reform School. At first juvenile delinquents under sixteen years of

BUST OF THEODORE LYMAN

age could be sent, later the age was left discretionary with the courts. The management was placed in the hands of seven Trustees, to be appointed by the Governor. Including those first appointees of 1847, to date seventy-eight different men and women have served upon the Board. Naturally, they have come largely from the eastern portion of the State, as have the greater part of the boys themselves. In the list of Trustees are found the names of some of the most distinguished people in the Commonwealth. Among them may be recognized philanthropists of world wide fame, business men who have added to the prosperity of the State together with professional men and officers of high degree. The senior surviving Trustee is E. A. Goodnow of Worcester, now in his ninety-second year, who in 1864 received his first appointment from Governor Andrew and served till 1874.

MISS ELIZABETH C. PUTNAM

Eventually realizing that such philan-
thropy as this needed the refining influence of the gentler sex, in 1879,
Governor Talbot made Adelaide A.
Calkins of Springfield the first woman
member of the Board. To-day the
longest term of service stands to the
credit of Miss Elizabeth C. Putnam
who, appointed in 1880 by Governor
John D. Long, looks back upon nearly
a quarter of a century of devotion and
kindly labors. Westborough or some
other nearby town from the start has
had a representative, that immediate
conference in emergency may be held
with the Superintendent. In this way
the home town has had eight members
of the Board, to-day the resident Trustee being Melvin H. Walker, appointed
in 1884.

Supervising architects were selected,
plans were approved, and June 15,
1847, a contract for construction was
made for the sum of $52,000. April
15, 1848, the Legislature added $21,-
000 to the building appropriation, and
on the 25th of the same month gave

$10,000 to cover Theodore Lyman's
donation, to be expended at the discretion of the Trustees, and $8,000 for
farm buildings, stock, etc. The original edifice was evidently fashioned
largely on the then existing building
reared for the same purpose by New
York City on Randall's Island, and on
the congregate plan, for the advantages
of segregation had not, as yet, made
themselves evident. Boys for whom
there were supposed to be accommodations for three hundred, were admitted
before the structure was formally dedicated December 7, 1848.

However well appointed buildings
may be, they cannot make a school.
Much depends upon the man who directs. The first Superintendent was
Wm. R. Lincoln who served from
1847 until May 9, 1853. His successors
to date have been James M. Talcott,
now living after thirty years of reformatory work, aged eighty-five, in Elling-
ton, Conn. [1853-'51] ; Wm. E. Starr
[1857-'67], who at the age of ninety

MELVIN H. WALKER

years is living in Worcester, Actuary of the State Mutual Life Insurance Co., not only the oldest surviving Superintendent, but one of the oldest men in active employ in the Commonwealth; Joseph A. Allen [1861'67] and [1881-'85], who came to the school from Syracuse, N. Y., though Massachusetts born and bred; O. K. Hutchinson [1867-'68]; Benj. Evans [1868-'73]; Col. Allen G. Shepherd [1873-'78]; Luther H. Sheldon [1878-'80]; Edmund T. Dooley [1880-'81]; Henry E. Swan [1885-'88], and Theodore F. Chapin [1888], a native of New York State, who saw service during the War of the Rebellion, was graduated from Rochester University in 1870 and came to the Lyman School from a long and varied experience as a teacher in the Empire State. The Assistant Superintendent, Walter M. Day, is in his eleventh year of service. Very soon the edifice, large as it was, proved inadequate to the demands, and during 1852-3 an addition was made upon the eastern side almost doubling the original capacity of the school. November 3, 1853, the enlarged structure was again dedicated. Lest idle hands should get into mischief, it was neces-

sary to find something for them to do, and the problem of employment, from the beginning, has been one of the most difficult of solution. Very early, the boys were set to weaving cane seats for chairs and to making shoes under contract, but at no time did those in authority feel that this was the best form of work for their charges, and only resorted to it until something better could be devised. So long, however, as the congregate system prevailed, these forms of labor continued. Later years have revealed the possibilities and advantages of farm and skilled mechanical work. In 1853, Mary Lamb of Boston gave to the school one thousand dollars, the income from which should be devoted to the improvement of the library, a fund whose wide reaching utility it may be doubted if even the giver could have realized.

No incident in the history of the school is more thrilling than that of the first successful attempt to destroy the building by fire, August 13, 1859. One of the inmates, a boy of more than usual restlessness, with four associates, set fire to one of the wooden flues in the northwest corner of the edifice and in a short time three-fourths of the entire structure was destroyed. Officers had to think and act quickly. The 566 boys, considerably more than the building's real capacity, were immediately scattered in temporary quarters in Fitchburg, Concord and Westborough. In the latter 150 lads were housed in an old steam mill. The boys who set the fire were taken before the courts and the leader, No. 2298, was sentenced to Worcester House of Correction, where he died the next year. Using money from the Lyman Fund, the Trustees at once set about rebuilding, and in 1860, October 10, the renewed building was dedicated with an address by President Felton of Harvard College.

The Lyman School is an evolution. All interested felt the necessity of classification and were convinced that boys too old in years and experience were admitted. After the fire, efforts were made to obviate some defects. To begin with, fifty of the older boys were sent aboard the school ship "Massachusetts," and other reductions followed, so that at the dedication there were only 333 boys, the lowest number for many years. At this time, also, shoe making was given up and the reformative features of the institution began to be developed.

The strain through which the school had passed and the unruly nature of many of the inmates had necessitated forms of discipline to which open and determined exception was taken by very many citizens. Whether for good or evil, at this late day it would be idle to attempt a judgment though never, for one moment, could the integrity of the officers' intentions be questioned. Yielding to popular clamor, Governor Banks removed the entire Board of Trustees excepting Theodore Lyman,

the son of the liberal founder, and immediately appointed six new members. Upon these gentlemen came the responsibility of securing a new Superintendent and he was found in Joseph A. Allen whose reputation as a teacher was of the best. Of his ten years' stay in Westborough, his experience and conclusions in connection with the boys intrusted to his care, he has given us a most delightful account in a little book, the only one that has been printed concerning the school except the annual pamphlet reports of the Trustees. But even Supt. Allen's capacity, tact and devotion could not overcome the structural difficulties of the institution. There were still two radical faults: boys too old and vicious; and the congregate system, which permitted bad lessons to be imparted in the yard by the older to the younger lads. Although for some time a system of trust houses had been growing up outside, the yard was still within what were really prison walls, and the long lines of boys moved in close column to their cells at night to the refrain of clanging bolts. In 1873, the school ship boys came back and the conditions were even harder than ever. May 5th of this year, having secured duplicate keys, a break for liberty was made by one hundred lads, but so effectual was the effort to capture them, that all save four or five slept that night in the old quarters. It was no bed of roses for Col. Shepherd during his five years, and only his superb executive ability carried him through the trying period. May 31, 1881, a boy of thirteen attempted to fire the building, but with no such serious results as those of 1859.

As once before, the governor (Talbot) in 1879 removed the entire board of Trustees and appointed a new one. The yeast of development was beginning to work and neither authorities nor public were to be much longer satisfied with the old state of affairs. The first radical measure came when the Legislature voted to change the name of the institution from State Reform School to the present appellation in an Act, signed by Governor Robinson, June 3, 1884. As the present Superintendent remarked, "The name has long been a misnomer for it is a formative rather than a reformative place," in most cases a creation, rather than a reformation was necessary. The maximum age of commitment was reduced to fifteen, provisions were made for the securing of a new farm and during the year twenty-six of the worst boys were sent to sea. The old edifice on the shores of Chauncey Pond was given over to the Commonwealth for an insane hospital and entirely new quarters were sought on the most conspicuous elevation in the town a mile and over to the northwest of the village. This new location was historic ground, for the Bela J. Stone farm which was purchased, included the site of the first church erected in Westborough, the farm house is built over the cellar of the old first parsonage and the timbers of the old meeting house sheds formed a useful part of the farm-barn. Facing the main approach to the farm-house, now called Maple Cottage, is a large structure used in former days as a seminary and sanitarium, but now a part of the school, called Willow Cottage. At first it was leased, and in April, 1885, was occupied by the first installment from the old building. Next

MAPLE COTTAGE

THE WILLOWS

LYMAN HALL

THE GABLES

OAKS AND THE HILLSIDE

came the Hillside, then Lyman Hall, with a frontage of one hundred and four feet, the largest structure on the grounds. The report to October, 1886, says that the farm and buildings then in use, including the chapel, and introduction of water, steam heating and gas had cost $78,000, ten thousand of which had been taken from the Lyman Fund. The chapel, though mentioned, was not completed, but was to cost $3,500. It was dedicated June 3, of the following year. In February, 1887, the Willow Park Seminary was bought for $3,000, and the farm then consisted of 99 acres.

Owing to greater care in the commitment of boys and in the reduced age maximum, the number of inmates was smaller than it had been in more than a generation, but by October, 1887, crowding began again, one hundred and eighteen boys being quartered in space intended for ninety. The present convenient office and home of the Superintendent came in 1888 at a cost of $8,000, and the same year was purchased the Wilson farm to the westward, thereby securing more cottage space in the shape of the "Way-

side," one of the most attractive in the entire plant. Subsequent applications to the Legislature have resulted in appropriations for more cottages, till now there are nine with an average room for thirty boys each. The names assigned to these beginning with Wayside on the west are Bowlder, Oak, Hillside, Gables, Lyman, Chauncey, Maple and Willow. Lyman Hall, at first containing the residence and office of the Superintendent, is divided into two parts, the eastern part bearing the name of the early President of Harvard and of the nearby pond. The Gables is the made-over chapel, hallowed by the dedicatory words of Phillips Brooks, but thus altered when the opening of the new school building rendered a chapel no longer necessary. Careful counting reveals even more gables than those assigned to Hawthorne's famous house.

The latest of the many buildings clustered upon this hillside is the schoolhouse built especially for school and chapel purposes and opened March 1, 1900, in the presence of the school, the Trustees and many visitors. After the formal services

THE FARM BARNS

were over the boys were given free range of the edifice, and to their credit it should be added that in no way did they violate the confidence reposed in them. The main assembly hall is one of the finest proportioned and best lighted rooms in the Commonwealth. Nor is the building era ended, since increased population brings more boys and greater demands for quarters and the present Legislature is expected to authorize the erection of a tenth cottage. It should be stated that in the effort to separate and classify, in August, 1895, the Trustees bought in the town of Berlin, from seven or eight miles to the northward of the Lyman School, a farm of one hundred acres at a cost of $5,250, entering into possession in October and occupying in November, the total outlay for farm and improved buildings being about $9,000. Here are placed the smaller lads, those for whom homes are earliest sought in country towns, the theory being that good homes on the farm are the very best places for juveniles who have yielded to the temptations and allurements of city life.

In all this addition of buildings, one notable case of subtraction should be mentioned. August 26, 1900, after the great hay-barn had been well filled with provisions for winter, certain boys with incendiary proclivities and actuated by the desire to escape, set fire to the inflammable contents and the structure was entirely destroyed. For the sake of the other boys, it must be said that they turned to with a will and did all in their power to save the barn and contents. The firebugs were transferred to Concord and the barn was rebuilt in time for winter's use.

Here then is the plant of the Lyman School having in all 259¼ acres of land, valued at $22,500, with buildings large and small, rated at $205,970, besides personal property to the amount of $69,670, making a grand total of nearly three hundred thousand dollars. Is the game worth the candle? This is the query which is annually raised by some doubting Thomas who looks for a quick and visible return for money expended. To such, those who have given most time and attention to the school reply, "Yes, a thousand times yes." The most convincing evi-

407

SUPT. THEODORE F. CHAPIN

in charge. During the year, 292 had been received, 264 discharged, with an average presence of 303.89. For this period, the State paid out $70,803.96. Besides this cash outlay, there were the consumed products of the farm, fruit, vegetables, poultry, eggs, and milk to the amount of $8,177.

There is over the entire enterprise the spirit of continuity. Until the lamented death of Mr. H. C. Greeley, January 1, 1902, the seven members of the Board of Trustees represented eighty-nine years of consecutive service. Supt. T. F. Chapin is now in his fourteenth year; several of the teachers have been in their respective places many years. The Nestor of the school force is James W. Clark, engineer, who began his duties June 1, 1863, and saving one and a half years out, his stay has been continuous. Changes occur in the management of the cottages only at infrequent intervals, so that the ad-

dence is furnished by a visit to the institution itself. Even at this late day, there is abroad a notion that these lads are hemmed in by locks and bolts, that they sleep behind barred windows and that there are deep and dark as well as damp dungeons for boys who have transgressed the rules of the school. Were a total stranger to enter the plant at the "Willows" and to pursue his course to the "Wayside," he might marvel at the number of bright looking lads engaged in a great variety of occupations but not once would the thought arise that each and every boy is here for cause and sent here by due process of law. Should he behold them at their sports or farm work, or see them in their well appointed school rooms, he would simply wonder that so many boys should be gathered so far from a large town, and his natural conclusion would be that he had stumbled upon an unusually large and prosperous boarding school.

At the end of the school year, September 30, 1901, there were 327 boys

THE WORKSHOP

THE SCHOOLHOUSE

ministration is backed up by experienced help. Long since the punitive features of the school gave place to a heartfelt disposition to regard the boys as birds of passage, resting here for a time till their pinions are longer grown and their powers better developed. "The school's chief function is to surround the boy with influences which will foster a healthy development and all the

school has, beyond any other that I know of in this country, is that it undertakes, actually, to give efficient supervision and direction, thus insuring a realization upon the care bestowed when the youth was in the institution."

From the first there has been no lack of effort to instruct. Most excellent talent has been employed, but frequently teachers grew weary of their heavy

THE SCHOOL BAND

means and appliances should be subsidary to this, the idea of punishment and all thought or suggestion of it being absolutely banished from the question. It is quite enough that the boy is here against his will, however good his surroundings and care. Of course there is an element of compulsion, but the influences are not confined to a period here. The most critical period is the subsequent one of probation and the distinction that this

tasks and essayed their vocation in more congenial localities. There have been in past days uproars and confusion that come back to the witnesses with all the appalling force of a nightmare, but on the sunny slopes of the present plant, nothing of the kind now happens. At Chicago's Columbian Exposition the display of sloyd and other work from the Lyman School secured a silver medal and from the Atlanta Exhibition of 1895 a beauti-

THE CHAPEL

ful bronze is treasured as a well-earned trophy. While many remain a longer time, the average stay of the boys is eighteen months, in which time changes sufficient in boyish nature have been wrought to warrant the attempt for something higher. The State has no wish to restrain the lad a moment beyond the day when evidences are given of an ability and a disposition to help himself. As far as possible the boys are graded on entering and in no respect does their work differ from that of similar grades outside. In 1890, military drill was introduced and for four years was maintained, arms having been furnished by the State. Though the manual of arms was given up, the drill has continued as far as facings and marching are concerned. Each cottage has its company and officers who, wearing proper insignia, direct the concerted movements of their associates.

410

Manual training, beginning in 1888-9, has long been a feature of the institution, and perhaps no work pleases the lads so much as this. The results of their training may be seen on every hand as one goes about the premises. The large writing desk in the Superintendent's office is boy-made, and in the Gables may be found chairs, desks and chamber sets built and most exquisitely carved by these same youthful and now useful hands. On leaving the school nothing is more highly prized than the bric-a-brac which the youngster has here produced. Paper knives, card trays, photograph-holders, hat and umbrella racks, picture frames and tool chests, all are proofs of his own handiwork and he is proud of them. Many a brain has been reached through the fingers which had utterly failed to respond to every other method. No effort has been spared to di-

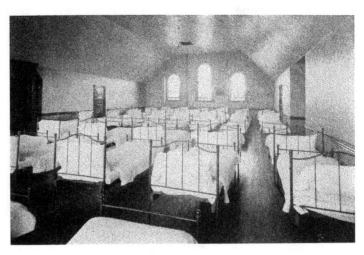

rect boyish energy into proper channels and evidence of this is readily discovered in the new school-house, half
of whose bricks, 750,000 in number,
were laid by the boys, and they did all
the rest of the work except slating and
plastering. The wood carving on the
interior must ever excite the admiration of all beholders. All the timber
and lumber were taken in the rough
and were planed and fashioned here.
The boys made all the doors and windows. At a moderate estimate, they
saved the State $15,000. Under com-
petent direction the lads built the
greenhouse, 100 x 28 feet, and remodeled the chapel, but did not rebuild the
barn simply because it was necessary
to have it completed in less time than
would be possible for juvenile strength.
Its burned predecessor was built entirely by the school. For the other
structures they did the excavating,
carried the mortar and nailed the

laths. As carpenters and bricklayers,
boys have found lucrative employment
immediately after leaving the school.
The culmination of manual training is
had in the workshop which is admirably equipped for labor on both wood
and iron. Work-bench, forge and anvil are all in evidence and the appren-
tice really gets what stands him well
in hand when he essays the journey-
man's task outside. The appliances in
this shop differ in extent only from
those found in first class technical
schools. In the basement is the laundry for the whole institution, and the
boys play the part of John Chinaman
with most commendable results.

The basement of the school-house
is given up to heating appliances and
to one of the largest and best appointed gymnasiums in the state. Here
from morn till night a competent instructor puts his charges through a
drill, never irksome, which straightens

backs, limbers joints and builds up structures which in many ways are lacking. While a large part of the time is given to calisthenics, a portion of each period is devoted to climbing, jumping and other sports dear to the boyish heart and hands. Every cottage has its own play ground and a well trodden diamond tells its own story of baseball. For more than thirty years there has been a brass band whose youthful tooters have given pleasure to themselves and others.

The latest report of the Board of Trustees gives a picture of the attempt to introduce, here, the system of self-government, so long in vogue at Freeville, N. Y., and called the George Junior Republic. The differences in conditions prevented that success in this school that its promoters hoped for. A radical difference in material and the constant changes in the personnel of the school compelled its discontin-

uance, though many beneficial effects are yet evident. There is still maintained a system of Lyman School money in which all exchanges on the grounds are conducted. It has an equivalent in U. S. Currency, but none of the latter is allowed in the hands of the boys. Every day's work has its pay credited and all that the boy eats or wears is debited and his accounts are as closely kept as though he were working for wages. Whatever remains over and above his necessary outlay will be redeemed by the Superintendent at the rate of one cent, U. S. money for every ten cents Lyman School currency. With this money the boys may do what they like, within reasonable limits. The savings bank of Westborough carries more than one hundred accounts of boys either in the school or out on probation, with an aggregate exceeding $5,000. Some of them are very old accounts, apparently

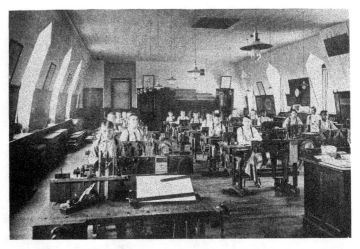

THE SLOYD ROOM

forgotten by the young men who opened them.

The cottages and the Superintendent's table are supplied from the same central source, for experience has taught the administration that one great kitchen is better than half a score of smaller ones. Each week the Superintendent makes out a bill of fare running through from Monday to Sunday and an inspection will convince the most incredulous that the boys have variety and plenty. While ice cream and escalloped oysters may not appear very often, the boys do not go hungry to work or to bed. The range of food is such that a high degree of health exists at all times in spite of the vicissitudes through which a large part of the inmates have passed. A physician, residing in the town, makes daily visits, but it may be doubted whether any equal number of people requires less attention.

The following schedule, varied according to the season, is a fair sample:

Bill of Fare, for week beginning March 24, 1902.

Mon. B. Oatmeal, sugar, milk.
D. Corn beef hash, cold slaw, bread pudding.
S. Bread, milk, molasses.

Tues. B. Combination soup, bread.
D. Hamburg loaf, string beans, potatoes, rice pudding.
S. Bread, milk, prune sauce.

Wed. B. Indian meal, molasses.
D. Beef stew, dumplings, prune surprise.
S. Bread, milk.

Thurs. B. Pea soup, bread, milk.
D. Stewed beans, brown bread, prune roll, syrup.
S. Bread, milk, cheese.

Fri. B. Lentil puree, bread, milk.
D. Fish or clam chowder, brown betty.
S. Bread, milk, peach sauce.

Sat. B. Bean soup, bread.
D. Roast beef, onions, potatoes, blanc mange.
S. Bread, milk, raisin loaf.

413

AT BREAKFAST

Sun. B. Tomato soup, bread.
       D. Baked beans, tomato pickles, prune dessert.
       S. Bread, milk, peach sauce.

The boys are clad in a uniform in which blue predominates. It is warm and serviceable and no lad appears to suffer from the cold though he is out at all times and in all seasons. When he goes away he is furnished with an appropriate suit for which he has been measured. The shoes are made by the boys on the premises. The long line of cow-stables is policed by the boys and they do all the milking. No more pleasant sight greets the visitor than that of the barn-brigade starting out on its very useful round of duties. The boys, under proper guidance, do all the farm work. They plow, harrow, plant, sow, hoe and reap. They cut the corn stalks which are run through the machine for the silo. They pile the great bay full of sweet smelling hay and all this must be done in the forenoon, for the after dinner hours are given to regular school work.

Regularity and constancy are rules of the institution and unless some entertainment in the large hall keeps them up, they are all in bed before nine. In the large hall the boys have lectures, concerts, magic lantern exhibitions and the same round of diversions which come to lads of the same age elsewhere. Sundays they gather here for a short service, in which they participate in the singing, and then listen to a brief address by some one invited for the purpose. Those who desire, can have the ministrations of their own particular denomination and the Catholic priest of Westborough includes the boys of his religion in the school as a portion of his particular charge. While there is a large and well supplied library maintained from the Mary Lamb Fund, each cottage has its own reading matter, so that no boy need lack for literary diversion. The school has its own monthly paper, *The Lyman School Enterprise,* wholly prepared and printed on the premises. While there is some selected matter, in the main the contents are of local and personal interest. The weekly programmes for the Sunday services are here produced and the young printers are learning the art preservative in a way which admirably fits them for similar labor beyond the confines of the Lyman School.

At the first glance, the word cottage hardly seems applicable to the stately piles of brick and mortar which have space and entertainment for thirty or more boys, but the name came when the buildings were smaller and doubtless will ever cling. Here, too, continuity prevails and unless the head of a household departs to assume the direction of an institution elsewhere, as has happened many times, the chances are that he will remain a long while. The boys are prompted to a proper pride in themselves and their own cottage.

In each dormitory there are small rooms, the occupation of which comes as a reward for long-continued good conduct.   Soon after a boy's arrival the workings of a system of merits and demerits are explained to him and he is shown that in order to be even considered by the Trustees as a candidate for release or ticket-of-leave he must attain the maximum.   If careful and well disposed, he can secure this required number within one year, but even then there may be circumstances which render his longer detention desirable.   As all commitments are for

minority, even if he does go out he is still under the constant supervision of the Board of Visitors who have had long experience in this work. If they find that he is not doing well he is returned to the school or even sent to Concord. But it is a satisfaction to report that in the large majority of cases no such punishment is necessary. Where boys run away, known in school parlance as "eloping," they are, if caught, as they usually are, returned to school with the loss of all credits and for a given period assigned to a place of detention generally called "The Inn," an easterly extension of "The Wayside," where certain privileges are withdrawn and a range of duties including the breaking of stone is imposed. Corporal punishment may be inflicted only in the presence of the superintendent. It is impossible to over-estimate the value of the probationary system. Under it the boy has from the start the very strongest incentive to do his best.

Now as to the final results. Carefully tabulated records of fifty years have been kept to show the future of boys leaving the school. Of course some on release go quickly and irretrievably to the bad; others turn out so well that they are ashamed to have it known that they were ever in the custody of the courts, and so change their names and are also lost sight of. But of the larger number who are perfectly willing to have it understood that their beginnings of true manhood were found here, from sixty to seventy per cent. are known to have turned out well. Naturally many boys of the adventurous nature received here go to sea and little subsequent knowledge of them can be had except as they render

MEDALS AWARDED THE SCHOOL

it. These are the boys, too, who in a love of adventure readily essay the soldier's part. During the Civil War twenty-six boys enlisted directly from the school and of the 2,500 who had been in the school before 1861, 629 wore the blue either in the army or navy. There was no regiment from the Bay State that did not have representatives from the Lyman School, and not always in the ranks. These boys, then grown men, fought in every battle of the Army of the Potomac, they followed Sherman from Atlanta to the Sea and, behind the iron or wooden walls of the navy were with Farragut on the Mississippi and at Mobile; they helped man the fleet which battered down the defences of Wilmington and at least one of them was on the "Kearsarge" when she sent the "Alabama" to the bottom. In later days the boys tried hard for a chance to fight beneath the flag in Cuba, Porto Rico and the Philippines. No sure data of their numbers are at present accessible, but of the boys out of school and under the direction of visitors and who are still less than twenty-one, for-

416

ty are known to be in the army and thirty-three in the navy.

Without doubt there is a seamy side to the picture. The thirty or forty per cent. not included in the roll of honor could tell stories of sorrow, degradation, misery, sin and crime, but is this number of persistently erring much larger than the average, if all walks of life are included? Is it not small when the origin of these boys and men is considered? No boys are sent to the school on account of excessive goodness. On the contrary there are charges against every lad, large or small, who in his suit of blue walks these paths. In drawing conclusions this should be constantly borne in mind. When that vital spark, manhood, supposed to exist in every breast can be touched we may expect growth and development, but when it is dull or incased and securely locked in the hard shell of generations of vicious heredity, Solomon himself could not reach it. That the lost are not more numerous is a lasting tribute to the men and women who have wrought here for the uplifting of their kind.

A Public School Garden

By Henry Lincoln Clapp

THE interest in school gardens in this country has grown until many, including the writer, have visited Europe to see the progress made there along the same lines. So far as is known the kitchen garden on the grounds of the George Putnam Grammar School in Boston is the only one in New England directly connected with a public school. The success of this pioneer undertaking is therefore worth observing.*

On May 12, 1900, sixty-six square feet of land situated south of the building, covered with a tough turf, was ploughed and left in the rough. Volunteers from two classes of the seventh grade were called for to convert the plot into a kitchen garden where they would be allowed to raise and enjoy such vegetables and flowers as each chose to introduce. So far as possible the difficulties of the undertaking, as well as the pleasures, were carefully explained so that the children would not be easily discouraged and abandon their work at the very outset. They could not help seeing that the land was rough and full of sods from which the earth must be shaken and saved and the useless remainder disposed of, and they understood that ploughed land would soil shoes and

hands and entail much hard work before it could be brought into the condition required for an orderly garden. They were asked to bring seeds, plants and tools for the prosecution of their work, and, in the preparation of the soil, to mix in some well-rotted stable manure which had been put in a convenient place during the preceding winter. The older boys being stronger and more skilful in the handling of tools were advised to assist the girls in preparing the soil and making the beds. They could use the spading forks in extracting or turning under sods and the iron rakes in leveling beds and raking off stones and coarse useless material. The girls could turn under the lighter sods and use the smaller garden tools, many of which they already owned.

An examination of the ground showed that it was possible to make eighty-four beds ten feet long and three and one-half feet wide with a fourteen inch path running around every bed and a centre path two feet wide running entirely through the garden, in one direction. Laid out in this manner and with beds of this width the pupil could reach every part of his plot with his hands. The children were asked to bring rules, stakes and long stout strings to lay out the arrangement with surveyor-like accuracy, insuring his full share of land to each gardener. The nature of the proposed work having been fully ex-

---

*Since this article was written a school garden has been established in connection with the Rice Training and Boston Normal Schools by the Twentieth Century Club of Boston; and another in Hartford, Conn.

417

plained to the class, those who desired to make and take care of a bed, agreeing not to neglect it, were asked to raise their hands. The number wishing to undertake the labor was greater than could be accommodated and so the teachers had an opportunity to use discrimination in selection. The number of thirty was chosen as more manageable for one teacher to properly oversee and direct, and accordingly the work was begun by thirty children full of enthusiasm on the afternoon of May 21.

There was no lack of vigorous effort on the part of either girl or boy, but various degrees of skill were manifested from the beginning; some pupils were as methodical as experienced gardeners and others as helpless as infants, but in two hours three-eighths of the ploughed land was laid out with commendable accuracy in accordance

with the plan agreed upon, and the satisfaction of the young people in thus changing the appearance of the plot to such a noticeable degree in so short a time was manifest. No system of indoor gymnastics could have done so much for the health and strength and enthusiastic pleasure of the children in so short a time as did this work. The boys had ample opportunity to show their skill, strength and helpfulness, and even the girls, after a two hours' tussle with refractory sods, seemed in no way weary or discouraged.

Following this work simple instruction in planting various kinds of seeds was given in the class rooms. The children were advised to restrict corn and pole-beans to outside beds so as not to hide from view low growing vegetables and flowers. They were recommended to plant the seeds of lettuce, radish, turnip, cabbage, parsnip, carrot, beet, onion and peas while tomato and potato plants were also suggested together with a great variety of flower seeds. Some were to be planted in drills and some in hills and others singly at regular intervals. They were shown that the last method would do for vegetable roots and tomato plants; that small seeds were to be covered with soil lightly, larger ones more deeply in proportion to their size, and that then the beds were to be watered.

May 24 the thirty beds already made were planted according to instructions, and twenty new ones were started by as many new gardeners assisted by those who had had their three hours' experience. Improvement in disposing of the sods was made so that it was not necessary to cart them away They were stamped down into the depres-

sions in the rough surface and covered with loose soil scraped out of the paths. In this way the beds occupied a higher level than the paths and were more readily distinguished and protected. The desire for building high often resulted in making the beds too short or narrow and the paths too wide, but strings were carefully applied and the soil was finally leveled down to the prescribed limits. The children were shown that low beds were preferable to high because they held moisture more easily and so produced better plants.

June 7 seven boys made the eighty-fourth bed in a very short time and in one end planted a beet, a round turnip and a French turnip to see how vegetable roots flower, seed and then die in the manner of biennial plants.

The desire to work in the garden out of school hours became so general that

it seemed best to place some restriction on the hours and number of pupils who without a director could obtain such permission. Tickets were issued for early morning, late afternoon and for the Saturday half holiday. It was, of course, impossible to foresee or guard against what the children would do that would have to be later undone but no serious complication was encountered. Wherever the seeds were planted too thickly the young radishes, turnips, beets and parsnips were too crowded to thrive and that fact was noticed by the children themselves when they saw the plants which they had given plenty of room grow quickly and large. They thus learned the need of thinning and transplanting. Surplus plants were given away to those who did not have that kind, and finally order came out of chaos.

The development of the young plants, each species in its own peculiar manner, excited the curiosity of the children. When they examined the corn they could not help seeing the long. tough, spreading, fibrous roots,

420

sometimes in a double row, which hold up the stalks in spite of wind and storm like so many underground guy ropes. The storage of plant food in the tap roots of the radishes, turnips and beets was called to their attention. Many singular phenomena of plant growth like, for instance, the bean's habit of coming out of the ground with the skin of the bean perched on the leaf; or the marked difference between the seed leaves and the first pair of ordinary leaves interested them and sharpened their powers of observation. Comparisons as to who had the best bed, who had shown the most skill in planting, who had the most appropriate tablets, whose name was clearest painted thereon, and so on, led to constant friendly rivalry.

In many cases the transplanting was not successful, the children not knowing how carefully young plants must be treated to live and thrive. They were told plants resembled babies and could no more than they be pulled out of their warm beds, deprived of their supply of food, or exposed to the hot

sun, without harm. They were taught to lift them carefully from the ground with as little disturbance of the roots as possible. They were shown how the trowel, fork or shovel was to be thrust under the plant so as to leave a mass of earth clinging to the roots, none of which should be broken. The plant should be protected from the sun by a covering of some kind and watered later in the day. Such instructions, however, did not make half the impression that their failures did. When the children saw their plants wilt, grow pale and sickly and actually disappear from the beds, they had an object lesson worth hours of lecture. Experience as usual was the best teacher, and practice surpassed precept. Many an early June afternoon was spent in weeding; for ragweed, pigweed and cudweed were abundant, and oats and grass from the old sods added to the variety of intruders. The children were taught the characteristic feature of both seedling plants and weeds, and they in turn were asked to point them out to others, until at last all learned to distinguish young beets by their red leaved stems, radishes by their peculiar first pair of leaves reniform in shape and blue green in color, turnips by their crumpled and wrinkled leaves, lettuce by its yellow green shade and so on through a long list. This was a most practical and useful lesson in observation and a sample of many that the garden furnished before the last work was done in November.

When the school closed on June 21 and many of the young gardeners left to spend their vacations in the country the beds were quite free from weeds. The summer was remarkably warm and dry, but these conditions had been anticipated and an attempt to keep the garden in good order had been made by the appointment of a committee of nine to meet once a week and attend, meanwhile, to weeding and watering. The committee found it difficult to live up

to their good resolutions. Water had to be brought from the children's homes, when not far distant, or from the main school building, two hundred feet away and only occasionally opened; so that although some of the beds were carefully tended all through the twelve weeks' vacation many of them when the school opened, September 12, were so overgrown with weeds that the economic plants made a poor showing. Some of the owners of the former had cropped their beds a number of times during the summer. Radishes, lettuce, corn, kohl-rabi and other vegetables were carried home for the table as well as flowers of many kinds.

When work was taken up again September 17 on account of change of city residence and promotion fully half of the beds changed hands. The gardeners who were in grade seven before the summer vacation were now in grades eight and nine, and pupils of the former grade take *their* manual training in the schools of carpentry

and cooking. The beds of such were given to children who had been promoted from grade six to seven and, again, the number was not equal to the demand. The most pressing business was weeding and was begun by thirty pupils, some of whom were novices in the work and could not distinguish the wheat from the tares. Under the tutelage of the experienced, whose beds served as models, the tussle began. But knowing how is quite as applicable to this as to any other art. They had to be taught not to clutch a handful of weed tops, jerk and break off half of the stalk leaving the roots in the ground, the beds merely disheveled, and the work to be done over again. The most abundant weed and the most difficult to eradicate on account of its numerous tough and spreading roots was the common plantain. Individual pupils after skirmishing with one or two heads hesitated to openly attack an enemy so stoutly entrenched. Strategy

was resorted to by the teacher to encourage quick work, and a certain number of girls were pitted against as many boys to see which group could first clean out the weeds from an entire bed. That many hands make light work was never better illustrated. Victory perched first on one banner then on the other but whichever side won the contest was strenuous and eminently successful from the point of view of the manager. The roots were so nearly removed as to encourage the owner of the bed to dig them out completely, and the gardeners learned that to pull up one weed at a time was the most successful if the slowest way.

Reports of the out-door doings came to the knowledge of the children in the school rooms and they envied their young friends at work in the clear air and the beautiful sunshine of these October afternoons. Indeed, an observer of similar scenes in France on seeing the pictures made by these children could hardly help recalling Jules Breton and Normandy, Millet and Barbizon.

The work of weeding and digging up the beds was completed by the end of October, but the accession of forty inexperienced hands was the cause of irregularities in line and level. November 1 seventy-six children went to work straightening the paths, which had been made too wide in some cases and too narrow in others, reducing the beds to a general level, some having been made too high, others too low, and widening them to the prescribed limit. Once more the more experienced boys showed their knowledge of rudimentary surveying and reconstruction by stretching long strings along the edges of the beds. Words were unnecessary, the defects were obvious and soon remedied with hoe, rake and broom. On this occasion forty pupils of the science

class in the Boston Normal School made their third visit to the garden to see the children work and to talk with them about the vegetables and flowers which they had raised. Certainly here was an opportunity for striking out a spark to set on fire the true spirit of observation in many a class for many a year.

The methods of cultivating the soil in Germany were explained to the children, especially the custom of fall ploughing and keeping the soil open to the influences of the atmosphere, four-fifths of which is nitrogen, that most important element for plants which in the United States is generally supplied by means of fertilizers, natural and manufactured. Certainly, the Germans raise remarkable crops with comparatively little fertilizing material directly applied. Reliance is placed on stirring the soil and the nitrogen in the atmosphere does the rest.

There was another purpose in view in putting the beds in good order at this

time. After the children had planted in the previous spring they were obliged to wait till the middle of June before any considerable number of blossoms appeared. That seemed a long time to wait so they were encouraged with assurance that they might have beautiful flowers very early in the spring if they would take the trouble to put their beds in order in the fall and plant the bulbs of tulips, crocuses, hyacinths and narcissi. Accordingly, the beds were prepared for bulbs and there was a lively demand for catalogues which were looked over with great interest. The selections having been made, the names of the desired bulbs were written on a slip of paper which with the price, varying from ten to thirty-five cents for each pupil, was given to the director, who made the purchases for the children and returned to each his package fully labelled.

It was not easy for the children to wait for November 13, the day appointed for the planting. Careful instructions having been given in regard to using sand, depth of planting, making holes with large round pegs, distance of holes apart, etc., the children went out with their packages, strings and pegs and set in their bulbs by hundreds. This ended the season's work. It will go on for as many seasons as the land is not otherwise occupied; and Boston should see than digging in the dirt or sand; and when to this natural interest in the soil is added the great amount of useful information that may be obtained from the care and study of vegetables and flowers, it seems as if gardening should be one of the first forms of manual training to be put into an ideal course of study. In Europe it is so considered by the most distinguished

to it that the school garden is made a permanent institution and a pattern for similar ones where the purpose is to educate children in a broad and beautiful way.

The reasons for putting garden work into the course of study for elementary schools are numerous and cogent. Children are fond of doing something with their hands, and it is a matter of common observation that hardly anything is more fascinating educators. Kellner, school councillor in Trèves, says, "I recommend, above all things, horticulture in all its branches to the teachers of rural schools." "The advantages of even the smallest garden are so many and so great that no school should be without one." (Demeter.) "A school without a garden is like a stag without water." (Dr. Georgeus.) "School gardens are a fountain for the knowledge of nature and its consequent

pleasure, and an excellent means of training." (Professor Schwab.) "Not trees, shrubs, herbs and grasses alone are what we offer the children in the school garden, but love of nature, labor and home." (F. Languerres.) "No public school should be without a garden; every community that resolves to connect a garden with its school is laying up capital whose interest it enjoys in the prosperity of its future members." (Jablonzy.) E. Gang, of Thuringia, Germany, says, "School gardens are of paramount economic significance. Franz Langaner, of Vienna, makes the best characterization by calling them the pioneers of agricultural progress. As elementary schools lay the foundation of all subsequent education, so all beginnings of civilization and all progress in industry proceed from them. The impetus and the

progress that are observed in agriculture in several countries are mainly the result of school gardens. Many a village is indebted to school gardens for its outward attractions."

In 1898 in Austria-Hungary there were over 18,000 school gardens, covering an area of thousands of acres. For twenty years the question has been a live one in Switzerland and model school gardens now exist at the normal schools of Schwyz, Berne, Küssnacht, Zurich and Chur, and at many elementary schools. In Belgium the study of horticulture is compulsory, and every school must have a garden at least thirty-nine and a half square rods in area, to be used in connection with botany, horticulture and agriculture. In 1894 Sweden had 4,670 school gardens. In 1895 two hundred and fifty-seven elementary schools in southern

Russia cultivated 296 acres of land. In Germany there is a central school garden of five acres in each of the cities of Breslau, Cologne, Dortmund, Mannheim; Leipsic and Altona each has one of three acres, Karlsruhe two acres, Gera and Pössneck each three-fourths of an acre, and many other towns have those of less area. France, too, has thousands of school gardens. In 1898 Russia had 7,521 school gardens. At the Nizshni-Novgorod fair in 1896 a model school garden containing 1,225 square yards was established in the educational section.

The value of a thorough introduction of the idea into this country would be as great as it has been and is in Europe to-day, and any school system that would lay claim to the first rank must include school gardens among its educational means. It may be worth while to raise the question whether beating the empty and close air of a school room with or without gymnastic implements can favorably compare with cultivating plants of economic and æsthetic value in the open air, or, indeed, whether with the latter work the former is at all necessary. Productive energy should be worth more than non-productive.

Something should be done in rural schools, at least, to prevent young people from such districts from making city life and workshops the goal of their ambition. The pleasures and advantages of country life should receive adequate consideration, and some of the detractions from city life might also be considered with profit. More should be done to create respect for labor and to discover the pleasures in it. The importance of agriculture to the prosperity of our nation should be better understood and appreciated by teachers as well as scholars. There is no industry more important. Abundant crops bring prosperity and stimulate inland and outland commerce. They increase activity in mill, mine and workshop. So important a subject should therefore receive its due attention.

Moreover, children do not have to be taught to love to work in a garden. People who ask "Will it pay?" generally refer to money values. Contentment is better than wealth. A hundred-dollar garden may yield more happiness than a hundred thousand dollar house. Elizabeth in her delightful German out-door book says, "What a happy woman I am, living in a garden, with books, babies, birds and flowers! Yet my town acquaintances look upon it as imprisonment and burying. Sometimes I feel as if I were blest above all my fellows in being able to find my happiness so easily. The garden is the place I go to for refuge and shelter, not the house. In the house are duties and annoyances, servants to exhort and admonish, furniture and meals; but out there blessings crowd around me at every step * * * * and every flower and weed is a friend and every tree a lover. * * * * It is not graceful and it makes one hot, but it is a blessed sort of work, and if Eve had had a spade in Paradise and known what to do with it, we should not have had all that sad business of the apple." It will pay to give children opportunity to tend living plants, to learn lessons from them and to work in the open air, to the end that they may enjoy country life and respect manual labor.

At Harvard Class Day

By Elsie Carmichael

IT was a mild, damp day in the February thaw. The snow and slush lay deep all over the Yard, and the low afternoon sun felt warm on Monteith's back as he strolled aimlessly towards his rooms. It was one of those days that takes away a man's energy and leaves him "dopy," as the college boys say. He had come across from the Law School with nothing particular to do, and was feeling too lazy even to go to the library and read, when he found himself in front of Stoughton, and decided to go in and see Pomeroy, a senior, whom he knew very well, but whose rooms he had never seen. He remembered that Pomeroy had promised to show him some curios that he had picked up in Egypt. Pomeroy was out, the solitary occu-

pant of the room said, but he would be back in a moment, and Monteith had better come in. Partly because he had nothing else to do, and partly because the room attracted him he strolled in, sat down in the wide window seat, and lighted his pipe, while the other went on busily writing.

The room was low studded, and a cheerful fire was blazing on the hearth. There were book cases running all around the walls, and one or two fine casts, and all the available space was covered with pictures and souvenirs of many trips abroad.

Monteith's eyes wandered from one interesting bit of decoration to another, until they suddenly stopped at the desk, and he sat up. Looking straight at him out of a silver frame was a very beautiful girl's face, with eyes that looked straight into one's own—eyes one trusted. Monteith drew a quick breath. It was a photograph of Edith Somers.

A great wave of recollection swept over him, and he closed his eyes for a moment. There was a confusion of golden sunsets and a still green lake and mountains beyond mountains reaching to the horizon line. Then one picture stood out clearly in his mind. He and Edith had been driving all the soft September afternoon over those glorious mountain roads. Here and there a scarlet maple branch flamed out, and the sumach and purple asters and golden-rod made great patches of brilliant color. At sunset time they had reached the top of the mountain. Off to the northwest, the Catskills lay blue and misty. The Rondout valley below was all ablaze with gold and purple, while behind them, on the other side of the range, the Wallkill valley was sombre in the twilight, and over the mountains beyond the Hudson rose the full moon.

It was a time for silence—that twilight time, when the day was dying. Edith had turned a little away from him and was looking off into the sea of color in the west, with dreaming eyes. Her pure profile was silhouetted against the gold of the sky, and her face was radiant. He remembered how he had looked away from her and crushed down the torrent of passionate words that rushed to his lips. It would not be right, he felt, to speak to her then, when he had nothing to offer her. He was very old-fashioned in his ideas; he felt it would not be honorable. They were both silent as they drove home in the cold twilight, with

the fire still burning low in the west, and the pale moon-light shining through the trees.

Ah, how lonely he had been since that September sunset two years ago! He had never quite realized before what he had missed out of his life, in not having a home or a mother or sisters. All the love he would have given to those home-makers had been crushed in his heart. Now all that he had ever meant, when he thought of home, lay in one girl's eyes. He was through the Law School, ready to go out to battle with the world and succeed. He felt he should not fail, if he had some one to buckle on his armor and bid him God-speed. He looked across into Edith Somer's trusting eyes.

"Dear heart," he whispered to her, "I have waited so long for you—all my life I had dreamed of you, before I ever saw you. With you, little comrade-heart, I could fight forever. You must help me—you must! I shall *make* you love me somehow. It couldn't be that you would not come, when I have waited so long for you."

He sank back in the shadow of the curtains on the broad window seat and looked at the picture through a haze of smoke.

Several fellows strolled in to see Pomeroy, but he did not notice them, until Garth threw himself down in the Morris chair, and tossed a pillow at him.

"Say, you old duffer, why so solemn over there in the corner," he cried. "Heard the news? Jim says Pomeroy is going to announce his engagement on Class-Day."

"Who's the girl?" asked Monteith, lazily, only half listening. His eyes were still fixed on the eyes of the picture, that looked straight back into his.

"Why, Miss Somers, of course," returned Gartha. "He has been devoted to her for the last year. There is a picture of her over here somewhere."

There came a sudden exclamation from the window seat. Gartha turned.

"What a shame, old man," he said, "You've broken that amber mouthpiece. How did you do it? I should think it would make you swearing mad."

Monteith was white to the lips and rose unsteadily and went out. Once he stumbled, as he passed the desk. Then he shut the door without a word, pulled his hat down over his eyes, and disappeared in the wind and twilight.

Everyone noticed the change in Monteith, as the end of the year came; he was pale and thin, and had a stoop he had never had before. He seemed old, like a man who had struggled long and failed.

He had grown quite used to the thought, that if he could not have love in his life, he would at least make the most of what he did have. He pictured the long evenings by his open fire, with his dog for company and his pipe and his books. Then he would sigh. He could not crush out of his thoughts the other picture he used to keep in his heart of that same fire-side, with a radiant, beautiful little comrade beside him, who would sit with dreaming eyes looking into the flames while their hearts spoke to each other—they two all alone in the world. Or he, with his pipe, would lie at her feet on the hearth-rug, while she read to him in her dear voice the poems they both loved. Then with a groan he would open his books and bury himself for

hours, or he would dash away in the wind and rain for a long cross-country tramp.

The fellows had tried to get him to enter into their plans for those last, half-sad, half-happy days of college life, but he shut himself up like a hermit and refused all invitations for Class-Day spreads. Pomeroy told him to be sure to drop in at his rooms after the Statue exercises and meet some very particular friends of his, and Monteith half promised, though he knew he would not have the nerve to do it when the time came.

Class-Day was such a day of blue skies and soft breezes as sometimes comes at the end of June. The grand old trees in the Yard were swaying gently against the bluest of skies and casting cool shadows over the grass, when Monteith started for a long paddle on the Charles, before the crowds poured out from Boston. He had made up his mind to escape and not return until it was all over, but an irresistible impulse drew him back in the late afternoon; he *must* see her once more before he went out into the world alone.

It was twilight and the sunset was still burning low in the west, when he reached the Yard, and the long strings of gayly colored lanterns were being lighted. He tried to go to his room, but instead, he found himself pushing through the strolling crowds, which were growing denser as evening came on. The sombre black of the seniors' gowns was relieved by the bright-colored dresses of the hundreds of pretty girls and women who were fluttering about like a flock of brilliant butterflies. The two bands were playing alternately at either end of the Yard.

All was gayety, music, laughter, and the sound of women's voices. The grass was covered with confetti, and many a dignified unconscious senior was decorated with it. The soft orange and red lights shone through the trees. Over at Holworthy a string of electric lights festooned the front of the building, and transparencies with the score of the baseball game of the day before and many legends hung from the trees and buildings.

But Monteith was hardly conscious of the gay scene. His heart ached for one look or word from Edith, and his eyes were fixed on the brightly lighted windows in Stoughton, where he knew that the only person in the world who really existed, was receiving the good wishes of all their friends—hers and Pomeroy's.

Then he found himself opposite those low ground-floor windows. The room was softly lighted by lamps with rose-colored shades. There were girls and men talking gayly and eating salads and ices. Sitting a little apart from the others in the window seat behind the curtains where he had lounged that day that seemed to have been the end of his life, sat Edith. The light shone on her face, and he saw that it was strangely sad, framed in her black plumed hat. There was a glint of gold in her hair, where the light fell on it. Her eyes were faraway and wistful as she gazed out into the gay crowd, without seeing Monteith, who drew back into the shadow. He longed so to take her in his arms and comfort her, she was so adorably pathetic and childlike.

Then, as he watched, he saw Pomeroy come over to her and bring her an ice. She looked up, smiled her thanks,

and began to talk in an animated way. Monteith clenched his hands and turned away into the darkness outside the gates.

About nine o'clock he came back after a long stroll out Brattle street. There was a tense look on his pale face. The Glee Club was singing over on the steps of Mathews, and it made him blue. "Fair Harvard" floated over to him, and he was pushing his way through the crowd quickly, to get away from the sound, when suddenly he felt his arm clutched in a tight grip, and he swung round to find Pomeroy and a crowd of his friends. The only face he really saw was Edith's. When he looked into her glad welcoming eyes for a moment the old thought of home came back to him.

"Just the one we were looking for," cried Pomeroy joyfully. "Here come and take Miss Somers over to the Gym for the dancing—we are one man short and have been looking for you all evening. Why didn't you drop in and have some feed, you old hermit?"

Before he had recovered from his surprise, he found himself strolling through the Yard towards the Gymnasium, with Edith looking up at him with her bright frank eyes, and the color coming and going in her cheeks as she talked. He hardly knew what she was saying, and he did not realize at all that he had not said one word, had only looked, and looked, he was so starved for a sight of her.

He thought he had persuaded himself that at least his life was the better and richer for having known her, and it was something to know that she existed—that he was living in the same world with her. He had believed that his love was great and unselfish enough to be glad that she was happy, even with another man. But now that he was with her he forgot everything, except the one great fact, that no one else existed in the world but they two. Over at the Gymnasium the crowd was more dense than in the Yard. They waltzed once about the great room, and then stopped breathless near an open door. through which a fresh night breeze floated in. It looked quiet and cool out there on the lawn dimly lighted with lanterns, and Edith made a little motion towards the door.

"Let us go out there," she said. She looked white as the crowd of dancers brushed by her.

Monteith had never realized before how adorably little she was. The crazy thought dashed through his brain that it would be so easy to pick her up in his arms and run away with her—away from all those people to the other end of the world, if necessary.

"That is quite as bad as the old Tree," she said, laughing, as they went down the steps. "I wonder the Faculty has not abolished it. It's what my small brother calls a regular rough-house."

Monteith was looking down at her absently. He was thinking so hard, that he was not paying much attention to what she said.

The night wind blew fresh and cool after the heat of the day as they strolled about the grass where only a few solitary couples wandered in the soft light of the lanterns while dreamy waltz music floated out.

"We were sorry not to see you this afternoon," she said, looking up into his sad face, and wondering why he had changed so from the gay fellow she used to know. Her heart ached for him; she longed so to help and comfort him. She wished so—a flood of color swept over her face as she watched him. A little mist came before her eyes.

"Why didn't you come?" she said, softly. "We looked for you all afternoon; Jack had something to tell you. Perhaps you know already?" She smiled archly up at him.

He stooped to pick up her scarf, and put it gently around her shoulders.

"Yes, I had heard," he said. I wanted very much to congratulate Jack,"

She wished he would not look at her like that; it made her want to cry.

"I think Jack was very good to give me this chance to see you," he said, after a pause. "It is unselfish of him. I have wanted to see you very, very often in the last two years."

"You have not forgotten that summer in the mountains?" she asked in a low tone.

"Forgotten?" he cried, passionately. "I remember every moment of the time. Over and over again have I lived those days, that were the happiest in my life. It was the only summer time I ever knew. Forgotten?"

She trembled and drew a little away from him, and then he remembered.

"Ah, they were jolly old days, weren't they?" he said in such a different tone, that she looked up at him in surprise. "Do you remember those paddles on the lake and how we explored the mountain, and best of all how we used to go and read under the pines on the cliff above the lake, with the waves beating against the rocks far below us?"

"Ah, yes, yes," she cried, eagerly.

"How steep that cliff was! Sometimes it made me shudder to look down, it was such a sheer drop to the water. Do you remember the day we read Sidney Lanier up there, beautiful musical Sidney Lanier, and Mr. Rogers and Annette and two or three others drifted by in the canoes in the shadow of the cliff and played on their mandolins and guitars, and then Annette sang Schubert's Serenade? It was all so beautiful there, in the soft summer afternoon, with the pines murmuring overhead and that spicy smell of the needles."

She had seated herself on one of the little benches at the far end of the lawn. Monteith stood above her leaning against the tree trunk, and watched her, as she clasped her hands on her knee, and bent forward eagerly, with a faraway look in her eyes.

"Oh, it was all so beautiful—that mountain top," she went on, softly. "Do you remember how the lights and shadows used to play across the valley? Sometimes it would be all in shadow and, then a bright beam of light would flit across, like a smile. Just the way a smile will sometimes come to the lips of a little sleeping child when it dreams it is back in heaven, playing with the little angels."

"You darling," Monteith said, under his breath. It almost seemed as tho' she had forgotten him, as she went on talking half to herself.

"Then one day after a long hard rain the sun came out, and we went for a walk, just riotously happy, after being shut up so long in the hotel. I felt like a little child. Do you remember how we ran down a steep needle-covered path through the dear wet woods, while the wind blew away the clouds.

The air was divinely fresh and laden with the perfume of pine and birch and wet leaves. You sprang up on a high boulder, with the wind beating against you, and quoted, "O the wild joys of living!" It was as though nature were playing joyously that morning and had taken us right into the game, and it was so much more fun than the game of people."

She rested her chin on her hand, her elbow on her knee, and looked straight ahead of her, all unconscious of everything but her memories. The music throbbed on the air, rising and falling on the breeze—a sad, dreamy waltz, that seemed to contain all the heartache of all the lovers in the world. Around them floated the perfumes from the June gardens of Cambridge.

There was a long silence, then Monteith said a little huskily, "I have never forgotten any of those days, Miss Somers, and I shall keep them locked up in my heart as the dearest memories of my life. When I go away next week from you all, I shall like to think that you, too, have not forgotten—that they were happy days for you, as well as for me."

"Going away?" she said, startled. She sat up and looked at him, with wide, troubled eyes. "Where are you going?"

He looked away from her. Oh! if she only would not torture him this way! She looked then for a moment, as though she really cared. He felt he could not stand this much longer—he must go away from those soft brown eyes.

"I think I shall go to the Far West," he said, slowly. "Sometimes I want to break with the whole thing. I have unhappy associations—there are some things I would like to forget—but I cannot."

His voice was low and tense.

"Ah," she said, slowly, "I am sorry. So you want to go away. And I had hoped that now I should see more of you, that you would be good friends with me. I hoped to see more of Jack's friends, of whom I have heard so much."

He clenched his hands.

"It was good of Jack," he said, somewhat stiffly, "to let me have this little talk with you. It will be another memory to add to those others."

"Good of Jack?" she repeated, surprised. "He was only anxious to be rid of me. It was you who were good to come to the rescue. It is not pleasant to be third party, you know, especially in a case like this."

"Third party?" he queried.

"Aren't you well enough acquainted with engaged men," she said, laughing, "to know that they don't want another girl around when the *regina orbis terrarum* is there?"

"I don't understand," he said, slowly. "If Jack is engaged to you, I don't see how he could bear to give you up for all this time to me."

"I—engaged to Jack?" she cried. Oh, what a joke! I'm not engaged—it is my sister. Didn't you know? Oh——"

Then she stopped and looked confused. Monteith dropped on the seat beside her and seized her hands, crushing them against his breast.

"Edith, oh Edith," he cried, with a great light on his face. "And I have been in torment all these weeks because I thought you were lost to me. I had waited so long, so long, to tell you how I loved you. There has never been a moment in these two years when you have not been with me—when you have not been my guiding star. Ah, don't tell me that I must lose you again——"

There were tears in the eyes lifted to his face as she whispered:

"Dear, there has never been any one else but you."

Rev. Elijah Kellogg–Author and Preacher

By Isabel T. Ray

THERE died Sunday, March 17, 1901, in a humble home at North Harpswell on the Maine coast, a man who for many years has delighted the youth of the land with his stories; and not only the young people, who have been charmed by his books, but older ones as well, who have known him as an earnest preacher exhibiting rare origi-nality and above all a sturdy common sense, mourn his loss.

Elijah Kellogg was born in Port-land, Maine, May 20, 1813, in a house on Congress street. He was the son of Rev. Elijah Kellogg and Eunice McLellan.

The father, Elijah Kellogg, was born in South Hadley, Mass., August 17, 1761. Early in 1775 he was a drummer boy in the minute men and helped with the wounded at the Battle of Bunker Hill.   He also served at the siege of Dorchester as a member of Colonel Dike's regiment.   January 1, 1777, he enlisted for the term of three years in the regiment of Colonel Charles Thomas Marshall and marched to Fort Ticonderago.   He doubtless was an interested witness to the scene of Burgoyne's surrender, and was also at Valley Forge during the dark days of that memorable winter of 1777-78, as he fought in the Battle of Monmouth and came back to the Hudson River, where his term of elistment was finished.

After his discharge he entered Dartmouth college, where he was graduated at the age of twenty-five years and was made a Congregational minister, being settled over the Second Parish Congregational church of Portland, Maine, as its first pastor in 1788.   The church then stood on the corner of Middle and Deer streets. He remained with this church twenty-five years, for those were the days when ministers were not changed every new moon. During the latter part of his ministry Rev. Edward Payson was associated with him as colleague.   After his retirement from the Second Parish he became pastor of the third Parish Chapel Society and later a missionary in the eastern part of Maine for seventeen years. He was one of those quaint old parsons who graced the pulpits of an earlier generation, but, alas, whose like is never seen now. He died March 9, 1842, at the age of eighty years.

The first of the Kellogg family known in Massachusetts was Joseph Kellogg, a weaver by trade, who removed from Farmington, Connecticut, to Boston in 1659 and from there to Hadley about 1662.   His first wife, the ancestress of the subject of this sketch, was named Joanna.   Joseph was the father of twenty-five children. He was a landed proprietor in 1663 as well as sergeant in the militia, ensign in 1678, and lieutenant in 1679.   He took part in the Indian skirmish called the "Falls Fight" in 1676, and at that time was the ferryman at Hadley; which business was kept in the family for one hundred years.   Joseph frequently served as selectman. He must have been well to do, for in 1673 his second wife was before the court for not dressing in silk attire according to the prescribed custom of her station. She was acquitted of any misdemeanor, however.   John, next in line, son of Joseph, was born in 1656.   He married Sarah Moody in 1680 and died before 1728.   His son, Joseph, born in 1685, went to South Hadley in 1711 and married Abigail Smith.   Their son, Joseph, Jr., born in 1724, married Dorothy Taylor.   He was on a committee of correspondence and inspection at South Hadley in the Revolution and died in 1810.   His son Elijah, born in 1761, was the father of Elijah Kellogg of Harpswell.

Eunice McLellan, the mother of the subject of this sketch, was the daughter of Joseph and Mary McLellan of Portland, Maine, and was born January 1, 1770.   Her father's house stood on Congress street nearly opposite Casco.   It is of his maternal ancestors Mr. Kellogg treats in his first book, "Good Old Times." Joseph McLellan was the son of Bryce and Jane McLellan, who came from Antrim in the North of Ireland.   Joseph McLellan died in 1820, aged eighty-eight years.   He was a sea-captain and was at the siege of Quebec when General Wolfe was killed. He was also a commissary and a captain in the army of the Revolution.

When Portland was burned by Mowatt on October 18, 1775, Captain Joseph McLellan arrived off the port, but in order to save his vessel put in at Harpswell harbor.   His wife, Mary McLellan, was in the Congress street house, and when the notice was given that the town was to be burned, she sent off her furniture to Gorham. She also prudently took out the windows of the house.

THE OLD HUGH MCLELLAN HOUSE

Thinking of others as well as herself she sent her son with their horse and chaise to remove the aged and infirm to a place of safety.   The boy rode all night doing this.   This chaise, by the way, was a rare thing in town and was much thought of. In 1778 the Provincial Congress voted seven pounds to Joseph McLellan for damage done to this same chaise by the Penobscot Indian chiefs when on their way to Cambridge in 1775.

Mrs. McLellan having aided those not able to help themselves started her children for the most likely place of safety, the home of their grandparents, Hugh and Elizabeth McLellan of Gorham, for Joseph McLellan had married a relative.   Elijah Kellogg's mother was one of that little band of children, and although but ten years old she went the whole distance of the ten miles on foot.

Mrs. McLellan staid by the Congress street house, in which was stored a quantity of salt, then very valuable. A shell from the bombarding vessels in the harbor fell in the garden; the fearless women immediately ran out,

and, heaping damp earth over it, put out the fuse, thus preventing an explosion.   A round shot came into one of the rooms as she was passing through it, but nothing daunted she still remained in the house to protect her property.   People came in to help her, ostensibly, but in reality they were after plunder and stole a considerable quantity of her precious salt despite her vigilance.

After the burning of the town— nearly two hundred and eighty dwelling-houses, and other buildings bringing the list up to four hundred, were burned—those left standing were occupied by the army.   The McLellan house was used as a commissary store and barracks.   The ell of the house is still standing, having been moved from its original site. Mrs. McLellan spent the next winter in Gorham. Such was the ancestry of "Parson Kellogg," as his Harpswell people loved to call him.   Could we ask for a braver lineage?   A knowledge of it gives a better understanding into the life and lifework of this man, remarkable in so many ways.

THE FIRST BRICK HOUSE IN CUMBERLAND COUNTY

Mr. Kellogg entered Bowdoin College in 1836. Small of stature, sharp-eyed, lean and wiry he comes before us on that day, momentous to him at least, for he says: "With humility I requested an inhabitant of the village to point out the President of the college. I gazed upon him with anxiety and solicitude inspired by the belief that my fate lay in the great man's clutches."

Although he was the son of a city minister Elijah Kellogg had not lived all the twenty-three years of his life in a city. Much of the time had been spent on the farm of an uncle in Gorham, where he learned all kinds of farm work, the knowledge of which meant much to him in after life. It is said his mother kept him from the sea as much as possible, knowing his fondness for it; in fact, before entering college he had spent six years as a sailor. This, a reader of his books can readily see—there being that in some of them which could not have come from one

438

not cognizant of Ocean's varying moods, or who had not exulted in a struggle with the elements and felt the salt spray on his cheek.

Many were the punishments he received as a boy for having stolen away to the wharves to listen to the sailors' yarns. Several anecdotes are told of these escapades.

One Sunday morning his father did not see him at church. When the boy returned from the wharves he was met by an indignant parent who demanded where he had been.

"To the Methodist church," was the reply.

"Give the text," the father demanded.

This was glibly given. An outline of the sermon was next asked for. Nothing daunted he started in, but, well versed as he was in Congregationalism, he soon got into deep water in Methodism, for these were the days of doctrinal sermons. He was sternly interrupted by a (by no means gentle) box on the ear and ordered to stop lying, for "no Methodist minister ever preached such doctrine as that."

Associated with Elijah Kellogg at Bowdoin college and graduating with him in 1840, were Ezra Abbott, assistant librarian at Harvard and Professor of New Testament Criticism; Edward, Robie, D. D.; Rev. Dr. James Partelow Weston, President of Lombard University of Illinois and also Principal at two different times of Westbrook Seminary and Female College, Deering District, Portland, Maine.

A very full and complete life of Elijah Kellogg under the editorship of Professor W. B. Mitchell, of Bowdoin College, assisted by General Joshua L. Chamberlain and others is now in active preparation and will be published within a year by Lee & Shepard, of Boston.

Young Kellogg was a popular man in college, always good-tempered, fluent and exceedingly interesting in talk. One characteristic was his strong personal affection toward his classmates. Many are the pranks told of him while at Brunswick. Some are wholly without foundation, yet enough are doubtless true to establish his reputation as a practical joker. He was ever fertile in expedients in getting out of scrapes —as resourceful when he gave as an excuse for being late at school, when a boy, that the frogs screamed "K'logg, K'logg!" at him and he turned back to see what they wanted, as he was when a young man in Bowdoin. A sign had been stolen and the men in Kellogg's dormintory were suspected. Now, according to the regulations, a tutor was not allowed to enter a student's room during devotions; in this instance, so

tradition has it, when the sign was almost consumed in Kellogg's fireplace a tutor came to the door. Receiving no response to his knock he listened and heard these words from sacred writ: "And he answered and said unto them, 'an evil and adulterous generation seeketh after a sign and there shall no sign be given to it.'"

Although full of fun Kellogg had underneath a serious purpose. In his studies he by no means stood at the foot of his class, as shown by his being appointed to take part in the junior and senior exhibitions, which appointments are made on a basis of rank.

While at college he went frequently to Harpswell to preach to the people, and a strong friendship grew up between the young man and the fisherfarmer community. He was asked if after his graduation he would come and settle there, to which he replied that he would do so on condition that they build him a church.

Time went by and he was nearly ready to graduate from the Andover Theological Seminary, when one day a committee waited upon him and asked if he intended to keep his promise. To which he made answer, "If you keep yours."

He was then informed that the lumber was on the ground for the building of the edifice. To this he is said to have unhesitatingly answered, "Then I am with you." He had not really thought they would build the church and had already received an offer from a Massachusetts society at a larger salary.

The church was built and dedicated September 28, 1843, his salary being three hundred dollars; and from that day to the day of his death his connection with the society was never broken, although in 1854 for lack of support he went to Boston and became connected with the Seamen's Friend Society as chaplain, still preaching at Harpswell during the summer season.

In 1855 he married Hannah Pomeroy, a daughter of Rev. Thaddeus Pomeroy, who was for some years settled over the Congregational church in Gorham, Maine. Two children were born to them, Frank Gilman Kellogg and Mary Catherine, wife of Mr. Harry Bachelder, both living at Melrose Highlands, Mass.

As has been said a portion of Mr. Kellogg's early days were spent in Gorham, Maine; in the historic Gorham Academy he fitted for Bowdoin. In those boyhood days he displayed great mental ability, and when a student there was always ready to take his full share, as in later years, in all that pertained to educational interests. One who remembers him distinctly tells the following incident.

Sixty or more years ago it was the custom of the village during the winter months to hold public meetings to discuss important matters that interested the people. One of these questions was the claims of the colonization society in opposition to the promoters of the cause for the immediate abolition of slavery. One evening an invitation was given Mr. Kellogg, then a young man of perhaps twenty years, to address the people on this exciting question which had been debated over by the citizens of the place for many weeks. One who was present says: "Kellogg took the colonization side in a forcible and eloquent manner, defending it against what then seemed to be the wild ideas of the anti-slavery

abolitionists of the day. So convincing was his eloquence that, when the vote was taken on the main question, colonization was almost universally supported."

Mr. Kellogg had a great love for Gorham. He visited the village as frequently as possible and oftentimes supplied the pulpit of the Congregational church. He delivered an address on the one hundred and fiftieth anniversary of the settlement of Gorham which was received with much admiration. It is printed in the pamphlet gotten out in commemoration of the occasion and is a most faithful picture of the times and people.

He followed the political opinions of his relatives and was in early life a pronounced Democrat. He was a great lover of his country and an ardent patriot, loyal to every demand for liberty. In his later life he became identified with the principles of the Republican party.

While chaplain of the Seaman's Friend Society in Boston Mr. Kellogg began the literary work that was to make him famous. His object in writing these stories was to increase his income, but he received little for them. His first book, "Good Old Times," the scene of which is laid in Gorham, Maine, is, by some, considered his best. It is largely a tale of what actually took place in the pioneer life of his ancestors. It was written for the Magazine "Young Folks," and I have heard it stated, on how good authority I cannot say, that he received five hundred dollars for it.

While "Good Old Times" is a story, the true story of the pioneer life of Elijah Kellogg's great grand-parents, it is history as well and gives in a most graphic manner the life of the age, showing the emigrant's love for land. We of America can little realize the passion for land these people possessed, having lived for generations under conditions not to be compared with those of our own land. It is not strange that Elizabeth McLellan was willing, as she said, to "risk her scalp for land." The story of their struggles to take land from the forest and bring it into tillage is most entertainingly set forth.

From the first they were friendly with the Indians, and, although so poor themselves, they often found chance to exercise hospitality. Elizabeth often treated them to a drink of milk, although by so doing she sometimes pinched herself; or gave them food or a small piece of tobacco; or spun for the squaws a little thread which they prized highly, as it was much better than deer sinews for stringing their beads in working moccasins. When the family first went to Gorham the door was never fastened. and it was not an uncommon thing to find in the morning an Indian sleeping beside the fire. The Indians were not backward in returning these favors. They taught her to tap the maple trees and boil the sap down to sugar, of which they were very fond. A haunch of venison or a fine salmon was not an uncommon present, and the white children played with the Indian children. But this security was rudely disturbed by an Indian war. The most thrilling chapters in the booκ are perhaps those describing the war, the block house and the life in garrison.

A most interesting chapter is devoted to a description of mast hauling, which the early settlers found most

GORHAM ACADEMY

lucrative. In those days when the states were colonies of Great Britain, the Royal Commissioner of Forests employed surveyors, who went through the woods and marked with a broad arrow every sound and straight pine over thirty-six inches in diameter. These were reserved for the King's ships, and the owner of the land where they grew could not cut or sell them. But the government would pay him liberally to cut and haul them to the landing. They were tremendous trees, some more than four feet through. The stump of one from which Hugh McLellan and his son William cut a mast, stood for many years; on this stump a yoke of oxen six feet in girth were turned around without stepping off. To fell these masts and haul them through the woods with the cattle of the period was an enterprise that might well seem insurmountable. How this was done affords most entertaining reading.

The last chapter in the book gives a rather amusing account of the courtship and marriage of Mr. Kellogg's maternal grandparents.

James and Joseph, sons of Bryce McLellan of Portland, both fell in love with Abigail, the eldest daughter of Hugh and Elizabeth of Gorham. James was a cooper, plain but pious, Joseph was a shipmaster younger, handsomer, and rather wild in his youthful days. Elizabeth, like many a modern mother, considered it her duty to find husbands for her daughters. Now James was all right, Joseph might be, but there was always the chance of his not being so. As Kellogg says: "Joseph and Abigail went blueberrying; he broke a gold ring in two, gave half to Abigail and she hid it in her bosom. The next day he went to sea. Elizabeth sent for James. When he came she asked her daughter how she liked the man she had chosen to be her husband."

"I don't like him at all," said Abigail; "he's old and he's ugly. I won't have him."

"Tell me you won't have the man I have selected for you? Which knows best? You shall have him!" and she boxed her ears.

Joseph came home, found Abigail married, and reproached Elizabeth in no measured terms. He then said, "I will have Mary, she's younger and she's handsomer."

"You cannot have Mary," was the reply; "I have destined her for another man."

"I will have her," said Joseph, and turning to Mary he then and there asked her if she would marry him. She replied "Yes."

Elizabeth yielded, perhaps because she knew Mary was too much like her mother.

So, while war was going on, Elizabeth was busy marrying her children. After they were all settled in life a new house began to be thought about. The McLellans planned this, as they did everything else, within themselves. It was the first brick house erected in Cumberland County and is standing to-day, although it has passed out of the McLellan family. In 1858 the old roof was taken off and a modern one substituted, as will be seen by a comparison of the pictures.

The McLellans hewed all the timber, made of shingles, moulded the bricks, tempered the clay, and set up the kiln. They were four years in building it. A brick in the wall marked by the fingers of Elizabeth records the date of the erection—1773.

Elizabeth lived to the great age of ninety-six years, leaving two hundred and thirty-four living descendents. After reading the book we are fain to agree with the author that those were indeed "Good Old Times."

Elijah Kellogg's books in all number about thirty. They were divided into series—the Forest Glen, the Elm Island, the Pleasant Grove, and the Whispering Pine series. In the last named a glimpse is given into the lives of the students in the early days, and many Bowdoin customs are told. He pictures in vivid colors the early Commencement. One can see the long line of carriages, the barns and sheds filled with horses, every house filled to overflowing with people, the dignified officials, sober matrons, gay belles and beaux of the time, also horse jockeys, gamblers, venders of every sort. The college yard, not campus then, dotted with booths where ginger-bread, pies, egg-nog, cigars, and beers were sold.

In his "Sophomores of Radcliff" Mr. Kellogg tells of the Society of Olympian Jove, whose customs are parly the wild imaginings of the author and partly his own experience. But perhaps the most interesting of the Bowdoin customs he describes is the "Osbequies of Calculus." This practice was in vogue many years, and a head stone is still to be seen upon the campus, marking the spot where are buried the hated ashes. Besides the books of the above mentioned series there is a volume called "Norman Cline."

The opening scene of "A Strong Arm and a Mother's Blessing" is laid in the town of Fryeburg, Maine, and the book tells the story of the historic Indian fight of Lovewell's Pond, which took place in May, 1725. It adheres very closely to the actual facts of history and gives much historic information. The scene at times changes to places, in and around Portland and we find pen pictures of ancient places and dwellings now passed away. While perhaps not great from a literary standpoint, this is a most readable book. "The Unseen Hand" was Kellogg's last story.

While Elijah Kellogg's books are most entertaining, amusing, if you like, that was not altogether his chief intention. He had a purpose in every book that left his hand. His idea was to write something that would make boys more genuine, more manly. He taught the value and dignity of labor—manual labor. "The essence of hoe handle, if persistently taken two hours a day," would, he averred, cure many diseases of mind and heart. This was the object lesson he wished to teach—not mental equipment alone, but manual as well, fits a man for the battle of life.

These books are as much in demand today as they were when first written, and not in Maine alone. I am told that librarians in the New England, Middle Atlantic, and even the Western states are forced to keep more than one copy of several of the books, so sustained is the demand.

Mr. Kellogg liked to talk with his friends concerning his "brain children," and would relate many amusing anecdotes as to the letters he had received asking about localities and names. He would frequently receive letters from people bearing the same name as one of his characters, striving to claim relationship, and bitterly were some of his correspondents disappointed when told that the people so real to them existed only in the imagination of the story writer.

As he became famous this correspondence became really a burden to him. So when he wrote "John Godsoe's Legacy" he cast about for a name that had never been heard of. But he was not to escape. The book had been out only a short time when he received a letter from a woman who stated her name was Godsoe and made minute inquiries as to the details of the story.

One prominent characteristic of Elijah Kellogg was his interest in and love for young men. It was a great delight to him to know he had helped one young man either by written words or personal effort.

For some years Bowdoin College had the custom of sending young men who were "rusticated" (to use a college term) to stay with Mr. Kellogg.

One young fellow whom the college sent to him was especially sullen and unapproachable, in fact inclined to sulk. On July Fourth there was to be a celebration in Portland. The boy wished, but did not expect to go. "Well," Mr. Kellogg said, when the celebration was spoken of, "I am afraid you can't go. I have no authority to let you go; but, then, I really want to attend that celebration myself, and I can't be expected to leave you at home alone." When July Fourth dawned the preacher and the student both attended the celebration.

While Elijah Kellogg was intensely interested, as has been said, in all young men, he came especially near to the Bowdoin students. They saw him in many lights, driving into Brunswick in the chaise—of which in surprise, when someone called it old, he said, "Why, no, I only bought it forty years ago"—sometimes with a load of potatoes, sometimes driving a yoke of oxen with the rack loaded with hay. They saw him as he farmed and fished; they saw him in his beloved pulpit, when on Sunday afternoon they walked down to hear him preach. They talked with him, and they one and all came to see in this retiring, quaint, unconventional, eloquent man no ordinary preacher. They saw a man who, through a life much longer than that of the average man, had kept his spirit young, his heart free from guile.

Perhaps nothing better illustrates how Bowdoin men regarded him than when his Alma Mater celebrated her 100th birthday, and from the Atlantic to the Pacific her children gathered to do her honor. One after another, men who were known through the world in Art, Medicine, Law, Theol-

ELIJAH KELLOGG'S CHAISE

ogy, and Science arose and spoke, to reveive generous applause, but to the man of small frame, but large soul, to this farmer preacher of Harpswell, was accorded a tumultuous applause not given to her other sons.

Elijah Kellogg perhaps best expressed his own attitude to the college when he said in 1890, looking back for half a century; "I stand here today like an old tree among younger growth, from whose trunk the bark and limbs have fallen, and whose roots are dying in the soil; but there is no decrepitude of the spirit. Moons may wax and wane, flowers may bloom and wither, but the associations that link a student to his intellectual birthplace are eternal."

Not a few churches were blessed by his labors at different intervals during the years he was settled at Harpswell. In Portland he was greatly beloved. The Second Parish, his father's old church, at one time extended him a call, as did also the Congregational church at New Bedford, Massachusetts, both of which he refused.

He preached for a time in the Warren Congregational Church, at Cumberland Mills, Westbrook, Maine;

also at Wellesley, Rockport, and Pigeon Cove, and New Bedford, Massachusetts. He also preached at Topsham, Maine. But he was ever true to his Harpswell parish. These people were his first and last love. He came to them a young man, he had married many of them and buried not a few in his pastorate of fifty-seven years. He was content and satisfied to have their love and devotion and with his dying breath to speak his last loving benediction upon them every one.

He gave himself unsparingly to his people, not only in things spiritual but temporal as well. It was his habit to keep, as he phrased it, "a purse for the Lord." Into this he put one tenth of whatever he earned. He was generous to a fault, and, it is said, often seriously embarrassed himself thereby.

PULPIT IN THE OLD HARPSWELL CHURCH

His services as a preacher were in constant demand. He had large congregations during the summer months, and it was not uncommon, after the service, for as many as twenty boys to gather around him, wishing to shake the hand of the man whose stories had given them so much wholesome enjoyment.

The last sermon preached by Rev. Elijah Kellogg, away from his own little sea-side church, was delivered in the First Parish Congregational church at Yarmouth, Maine, Sunday evening, August 4, 1900, during Old Home week, All other religious services in the town were given up, and the several churches united to do honor to the venerable man. The house was filled to overflowing. The words of his text were: "Which hope we have as an anchor of the soul, both sure and steadfast, and which entereth into that within the veil."

He said in substance that hope in Christ is to the soul what an anchor is

THE HARPSWELL CONGREGATIONAL CHURCH

to the ship, and he described a storm at sea, the use of an anchor in case of an emergency, his words reminding his hearers of some of the passages in his books. Then he continued: "My friends, life is like the sea; the soul is the vessel; the rich experiences of the soul, the cargo; and Heaven is the harbor for which we are bound. The temptations of life are the tempests. It is a strong sea and a wintry passage. You will need a good anchor and a good holding ground. Have you such?" Later in the sermon he said: "I am like an old and decayed tree among the young growth in the forest, but there is no age in my spirit. Time has not caused me to care any the less for the welfare of the younger people to whose fathers and grandfathers I have preached."

The house at North Harpswell which Elijah Kellogg built in 1848

and in which he lived for more than half a century is as retired as one could wish. It is perhaps 50 rods from the main road with front toward the sea he loved so well. Hemmed in by trees, the approach is toward the rear, with a weather beaten barn on the right. There are no very near neighbors and the farm contains about seventy acres. The field he cultivated did not contain more than twenty acres, and this was all he attempted to care for except his horse and cow. Here he lived, the days passing all too quickly with his reading, his preparation to preach twice each Sunday, and his farm cares.

While Elijah Kellogg was famous as a writer and eloquent preacher he was hardly less well known as a writer of declamations. He composed several of these, which have found their way into nearly every collection of recitations of the better sort, and which are

THE HOME OF ELIJAH KELLOGG

still deservedly popular in schools and colleges througout the country. The two best know are "Spartacus to the Gladiators" and "Regulus to the Carthaginians." To a party of friends over a Yarmouth breakfast table Mr. Kellogg told in his own inimitable way how he came to write the former.

In 1842, when he was a student at Andover, rhetorical exercises were always a part of the seminary program, and a committee was appointed to act as critics. It was the custom for the criticisms to be so severe that the students looked forward to a declamation as an ordeal.

"At last I made up my mind," said Mr. Kellogg, " that I would try to get something so unusual and so interesting that it would hold attention too closely for the committee to think of criticism." He thought over the matter for several weeks, and "Spartacus" was the result.

The day for the speaking arrived and a large audience was present with Professor A. F. Parks presiding. At last came Kellogg's turn. "When I began," he stated, "it worked just as I expected. You could have heard a pin drop as I said 'Ye call me chief, and You do well to call him chief, who for twelve long years has met upon the arena every shape of man or beast the broad empire of Rome could furnish, and never yet lowered his arm,'—and on to the end. The critics were so taken by surprise they didn't recover until after I had finished.

"Then,when Professor Parks turned to the students and inquired "what criticisms have you to offer, young gentlemen?' there wasn't one of them had a word to say."

The unusual performance had so astonished them that all criticism was silenced. Professor Parks then spoke, "Young gentlemen," he said, "it is customary, as you know, to dismiss the audience before remarks are made by the president. I shall violate that rule to-day. This is a rhetorical exercise. We don't want old sermons rehashed; we don't want anything stale and yellow with age; we want rhetoric, and gentlemen, that is rhetoric."

Among those present who heard Kellogg speak were the members of his Sunday school class made up of students in Phillips Academy. One of the boys, named Masters, afterward entered Harvard and received an appointment for the Boylston prize declamations. Remembering "Spartacus" he went from Boston to Harpswell to try to get it. He easily found his former Sunday school teacher and introducing himself told his errand. "Well," said Mr. Kellogg, in reply, "I haven't the piece in writing and cannot give it to you at once, but if you will stop with me over night I will think it out and write it off for you."

Of course Masters staid, and, equally of course, Mr. Kellogg did as he said. Back to Harvard went Masters, and on the day of the contest delivered the declamation destined to become so famous, and obtained the Boylston prize.

One of the judges to award the prize was Epes Sargent, a publisher of popular speakers and readers of that time. Mr. Sargent was so delighted with "Spartacus to the Gladiators" that he secured it for publication; and thus was given to the world one of the masterpieces of literature with the name of Elijah Kellogg as its author.

To the funeral of this man who held life as a sacred trust from God and whose conscientious purpose was never in the least guided by selfish aims, came those who loved him as a lifelong friend, as the author of the stories all have read. The old and the young, the man of affairs, the professional man, the clergyman, those well known, those unknown, the rich, the poor—all were there in the historic Second Parish church, of which the dead man's father was the first pastor, to pay the last tribute of respect to this aged man of God.

In the Western cemetery he lies at rest by the side of his wife, who died in 1891. It is but fitting that the town of his birth should be the sepulchre of one who leaves to her the heritage of a pure and well spent life together with no small measure of what the world called fame.

A Cinderella of the Blackberry Patch

By William MacLeod Raine

THE westering sun was sinking below the horizon at the close of a sultry Arkansas day, and the panting of the parched earth beneath the tury of the untempered heat was abating. Along the roads and cleared places the languorous air was heavy with the odor of the rank dogfennel which bordered the highways.

Out of the dense brake behind the Lyndon place a young man crept painfully to the broken rail fence which surrounded the neglected, untilled cotton field. He climbed the fence wearily, as one who has almost reached the limit of endurance, and limped slowly across the long rows of dead cotton stalks to the wild blackberry patch beyond. His uniform of blue was hopelessly stained and torn from contact with the moist earth and brambly bushes of the slough where he had spent the past few days in hiding. Long ago the chills and fevers of the swamp had got into his blood and left him the sallow complexion which comes to the dweller in the river bottoms. Unwashed, unshaven, and unkempt, he appeared a wretched rag of humanity, an ill-looking specimen of the living flotsam which the tide of war was leaving stranded all over the South.

To the girl picking blackberries in the tangled fence corner the crackling of dry cotton stalks gave warning of his approach. Her startled eyes fell on the hated uniform of blue, took in at one swift glance the squalid desperation of the man, and turned instinctively to seek a way of escape. Of that, however, there was no chance, for the rank growth of bushes rose thick between her and the fence, and the Northern soldier barred the road in front. Though her heart beat like a trip-hammer, she tried resolutely to drive the fear out of her eyes; and even while she awaited inevitable discovery noted with relief the dragging limp and the faded chevrons, which told her he was a wounded officer.

Abruptly he came to a halt at sight of her, standing there with dilated eyes, a picture of suspended animation. For an instant he stood looking at her with parted lips, then his hand travelled quickly to his forage cap in a salute. The curly brown hair tumbled over his forehead as he lifted his cap, and she saw with instant reassurance that he was little more than a boy.

They looked at each other in a long silence, from which he was the first to recover.

"I beg your pardon," he began frankly. "I'm afraid I was about to poach on your private preserves. It would not be the first time, and I did not know you were here," he explained.

She was a thorough young Southron, and she hated "Yankees" with an exceeding bitter hatred; but something in this ragged youth's evil plight and in

449

a faint resemblance which she thought he had to her own brother, lying captive in a military prison somewhere in the North, stirred in her the maternal pity which is dormant in every woman.

"If it is the berries you mean, there are enough for us both. Anyhow, I am through," she told him.

"Thanks. You are quite sure I am not driving you away," he said politely.

"Oh, yes, my bucket is full, you see."

But though she repeated that she must be going, she did not leave at once, but moved away some yards, ostensibly still picking berries, but really watching him curiously out of her sloe-black eyes. She had never before seen a union soldier off duty, and the study of him fascinated her. Somehow she did not feel the repulsion she had expected.

Though he was not apparently looking at her as he devoured the wild fruit, he seemed to see every detail of her person: the dark hair and the flashing eyes, the straight nose, the fruit-stained lips, the cotton dress neatly patched here, there, and everywhere, the little shoes in woeful disrepair. He knew at once that this charming little Cinderella of the fields was the daughter of a gentleman, and that her threadbare dress was typical of the ruined South which still fought on despairingly to make a lost cause good. Presently he ventured to call out to her.

"You will not give me up to them?" he asked.

"No, I wont," she answered indignantly. "But I don't see why I should not. There is every reason why I should." The facts spoke for themselves, but the girl emphasized them with a defiant assertion which was also a question. "You are a Yank," she said, with the slow sweet drawl of the Southland.

Despite his forlorn condition a whimsical smile twitched the corners of his mouth.

"The evidence is writ too plain to deny," he admitted.

"I shouldn't blame you for denying it if you could," she flung back at him.

He smiled again, this time without any attempt at repression. She was so childish in her girlish defiance, so slight, and withal so full of indignant fire, that he forgave the anger in appreciation of the effect as a whole. She caught the amused smile, and turning on her heel went off indignantly with her head in the air.

The young soldier watched the slim figure take its way along the dusty road to the big house in the grove with a regret that was almost sadness. She was the first girl he had spoken to in— he hardly dared to think how long— and the memory of buggy rides in the long afternoons, far away in the distant North, came back to mock him in this alien land where he was a hated intruder. He was a victim of malaria, weary for want of sleep and good food, and racked with a wound that would not heal so long as he kept on his feet; and because he was only a boy, after all, in spite of the epaulets, he hungered for the touch of his mother's encircling arms and wanted to sob aloud with sheer homesickness. But he remembered that he was an officer of the United States army, and he forebore. Yet he sighed deeply as he trudged back on his aching ankle to the lonely hut down in the slough where he had been staying for the past few days.

Three hours later young Culver

appointed himself a committee of one to forage provisions from the enemy. The full, moon lighted the way more brightly than was necessary as he cut across the cotton field, with its occasional girdled leafless trees soughing uncannily in the wind, to the walnut grove in which the house was placed.

Before the war, he could not have got within fifty yards of the house without his presence being detected by some of the half-score dogs that belong to a Southern home, but as the war continued the dearth of provisions had brought famine to the hounds, which had much diminished their numbers. Culver made his way directly to the smoke house, into which he forced his entrance through a back window. He selected a ham from the scant supply, and slipping through the window again, dropped to the ground. As he turned to pick up his booty, someone hurled himself upon him and bore him down.

"Yeou ornery, shif'less nigger, I'm a-goin' tuh hide yer till yer plum cayn't stand," a voice drawled above him. "I'm fixin' tuh give you all the bud good and plenty, fo' suah. I be'n a-honin' tuh do hit fer a right smart time. Consequence is—Well, I'm derned!" The man had dragged his prisoner to his feet, and as the moonlight fell upon the shining buttons of the blue uniform his lank jaw dropped in grotesque surprise. "By gum, ef hit aint a Yank. No, sirree, yeou don't. Keep still, will yeou, dad burn your hide? You all air a-coming right along uv me."

Culver confronted a gaunt, immobile-faced renter in homespun, one whose muscles were of iron, whose grip of steel held the weak and wounded young man as in a vise. (His captor was Joe Snellings, orderly to Captain Lyndon, home on a furlough on account of disabilities received at Chickamauga.) The prisoner was marched ignominiously around to the front of the house, and now that he was captured he realized that he did not care. Anything was better than the misery of the past week.

Captain Lyndon and his daughter Apthia sat on the porch to catch the breath of evening wind that cooled the air. The time was not far distant when the Captain had been the most jovial of men; his hearty jest and infectious laugh had been the life of the country side; the war years had brought him nothing but sorrow, and were turning him into an old man before his time. Just as the war began his wife died, and in the fierce fighting his sons Jeff and Homer had fallen at Shiloh and Seven Oaks. His only remaining son, a brave bright-faced lad named Will, had been captured a month before in the same battle at which his father had been wounded. Since then Captain Lyndon, still debarred from active service by reason of his wound, had been much given to sitting on the porch in sombre silence, with his head sunk on his breast. He needed action to take him out of the past, which oppressed him. It hurt Apthia to look into his eyes so full of sad memories, and, though she dreaded it, yet she longed for the time when he would be able once more to join in the stress of battle.

"Found the derned Yank stealing a ham from the smoke-house," explained Snellings triumphantly. "'Lowed when he seed me he'd light a shuck, 'lowed it were time ter be a puttin' out, fer true; but hit mightily struck me that since I had met up with him he mout as well stay—fer a spell. Leastways, ef the Yanks can spare him, though I hate turrible tur inconvenience him."

The man who rose with his arm in a sling to meet Culver was dressed in a nondescript suit of jeans, a pair of worse than ragged shoes, and a felt slouch hat that would never again celebrate its fourth birthday. But he looked every inch the gentleman in spite of his ridiculous clothing. It was not only that he was handsome, though he was that in the large, generous Southern way, nor that his face was frank and his blue eyes singularly winning, but also that he had the subtle distinction of manner which is not to be defined. He bowed to the young officer in the old-school way, the trick of which had been lost to the present generation.

The young man explained that he had been left on the field, wounded in a skirmish some days before, and that he had escaped observation by crawling into the bushes. Since then he had been hiding by day and travelling by night in an effort to make his way across country to the Federal lines at Helena, but that for the past few days he had found himself quite unable to travel and had availed himself of a soldier's privilege to forage from the country of the enemy. He stood very erect as he spoke, his chin tilted high in boyish defiance. Apthia, looking at the deadly pallor of his face, emphasized by the black hollows under the deep-sunk eyes, felt again the surge of pity sweep over her.

The face of Captain Lyndon wore a puzzled frown. In his present state of mind he frankly disliked "Yankees," though he was too much a man of the world to be, like his daughter, unreasonably intolerant of them. At any rate, he did not care to assist any of the enemies of Dixie to escape, nor, on the other hand, did he propose to give up this boy to the authorities. It was an awkward predicament any way he looked at it, for he could not disguise from himself that to let the wounded and fever-stricken lad go back into the miasma-laden Cache bottom was to consign him to death. The Confederate officer thought of his own boy in the distant, unfriendly North, possibly as much in need of a friend as this blue-coated youth, and vowed impulsively to help his prisoner safely to his destination.

"By God, I'll see him through for Will's sake," he told himself in swift decision. Then aloud, "Apthia, you better take Lieutenant Culver in for some supper and then tell Mammy to make Will's room ready for him to-night. Perhaps to-morrow you may be able to ride to Helena, Lieutenant."

"What's that? What's that you say?" asked Culver wildly. "I don't seem to hear you right. You can't mean that—that——"

"I've got a boy of my own," the Captain explained gravely.

"But—but—" Robert Culver swayed unsteadily to and fro, then pitched forward in a faint.

"Well, I'm derned," ejaculated Snellings, not unkindly, and, stooping, he took the young officer in his arms. "Where yeou want me to tote him, Captain?"

"Better take him up to Will's room, Snellings, and undress him. What that young man needs is good food and nursing. He's starved; that's what's the matter with him."

In the week that followed, the last stray chicken on the plantation went into the pot to make broth for the delirious stranger within the Lyndon gates. Nothing was too good for him, and no trouble too much to take. Had he been Will Lyndon himself, better care could not have been given him. Snellings looted the neighborhood for luxuries, and Mammy spent hours concocting delicacies for "the "Linkum man." That he might have the nourishment he needed, the rest of the household fared ill.

For a time he lay in the balance between life and death, but unremitting nursing won him slowly back to health. Captain Lyndon found balm to his wounded soul in caring for this young enemy, for in some unexplainable way it seemed to him that he was doing it for his son and making his lot lighter. Apthia too nursed him with an unremitting devotion. At first she had found it hard to reconcile her great liking for him with her loyalty to the South, but presently, woman-like, she gave up the attempt. Her heart went out to him, and logic was a matter of no importance.

Culver would wake from troubled sleep to find the bearded, grave-eyed Captain fanning him or to see Apthia flitting about the room like bright sunshine. His eyes followed her with deep satisfaction. He was like a child that is very tired, content to rest peacefully, in the surety that he will be taken care of without effort on his part. The lithe grace of the girl, the harmonious colors of the darkened room, the fine white spotless linen, all soothed his

jarred nerves with the sense of home after long wandering in camp and field. Both he and his hosts came to understand more clearly through sympathy for each other, developed in long talks, the abyss of misunderstanding which had brought the country into the horrors of a civil war.

One day Apthia Lyndon was arranging roses in a vase, the while the young officer watched her intently out of half-closed eyes. He noted how everything she did was done with a grace that charmed him.

"Why do you take so much trouble over me? I'm only a 'Yank'," he asked at last.

She started, having supposed him asleep.

"So long as you are ill it does not matter what you are," she answered.

"But when I am well again——?"

The girl made no answer. Her deft fingers were busy with the roses.

"You will hate me then, I suppose?"

The color began to surge into her face. "No, I shall—not hate you."

"Indifferent?"

"Always I shall be glad to hear of you." The color of the flowers was not more beautiful than the tint in her cheeks now.

He knew himself cruel when he pressed her further.

"As you are always glad to hear of Snellings' welfare——Is that the way you will care?"

She flashed one look of appeal at him and fled. It begged of him to let their relations rest unfixed, at least until the war was over. He understood that she could never promise herself in words to a man fighting against the cause she loved, and he respected her feeling.

When Robert Culver rode away to Helena on the war horse of the Confederate Captain he carried with him many pleasant memories of the plantation, but none so persistent and so enduring as those which had to do with the slim, black-eyed little rebel whose womanly heart had surrendered at discretion to the "Yank" officer.

Since he was a practical lover, Culver busied himself in finding the whereabouts of Will Lyndon, that he might begin to wipe out the debt that had accumulated against him. It chanced that Culver had a cousin who was a Congressman, and by means of legislative and military influence, he succeeded in securing an exchange for the young man.

And so it came to pass that when Will went South, to make glad the hearts of his anxious kindred, he carried with him a letter to his sister from Robert Culver. Beyond doubt common gratitude demanded an answer, but something more than perfunctory duty must have stimulated the correspondence which followed, for it is a matter of record that long after the war had ended Lieutenant Culver, now a civilian, followed one of his letters into the Southwest, and took to wife his Cinderella of the blackberry patch.

Similitude

By E. Carl Litsey

DIDST ever stand, my love, at night, when winds were low,
    Beside a silent pool, where, mirrored soft, did glow
        The eyes of night?
So far above they were; so fair and pure they seemed;
But lo! beneath thy feet their magic beauty gleamed.
        It seemed you might
With outstretched hand glean one by one each gem,
Celestial lamps, watched o'er by seraphim!

And so, my love, whene'er I gaze upon thy face,
I see reflected there a light which has its place
        About God's throne.
And as a star is set within the heavens there,
To turn the thoughts of men to God and prayer,
        Thou, thou alone,
Art set on earth to bless my weary life,
And in thy love my soul finds rest from strife!

THE EMPEROR OF KOREA

Korea, the Pigmy Empire

By W. E. Griffis

WHAT was the part played by Korea in the old Chinese world of sun and satellites? Then there were hermit nations. The ocean separated mankind. China, the Middle Kingdom, claiming the sovereignty of the earth and immediate legation from Heaven, was surrounded by pupil nations, and the outlying islands were the tassels pendant to her robe's fringe. The inhabitants of distant countries were barbarians.

What is Korea's role in these days of the New Pacific and the changed world? Now the ocean unites nations and fleets make ferries with no dependence on wind or tide. The once pupil nations are independent. China, herself no longer free, is on inquest, and if paralyzed by too much "indemnity" is likely to be partitioned. Japan is the recognized equal with the nations of Christendom. The pivot of history is no longer in the Mediterranean or the Atlantic. The United States, Russia, Great Britain, France, Germany, Italy and the Netherlands have possessions in that once lonely ocean, now the highway of all peoples.

Geographers reckon that in round numbers there are about eighty thousand square miles in Korea. Looking from the west her shape is that of a headless butterfly. She hovers between what seems to be the great Japanese silk worm, spinning out of its head and mouth at Kiushiu a long thread of islands ending in Formosa and bordering on the possessions of the United States, and China, the rampant monster ready to devour, with its maw in Liao Tung and its paw at Shantung. All along the northern wing-edge lies the Imperial province of Shing-king, while at the northeastern tip is Russia. The most striking landmark on this northern frontier is the Ever-White mountain, which holds, sparkling on its breast, the lake called the Dragon's Pool. Over the brim of this crater fall the streamlets which, reinforced all along the mountain slopes, form rivers flowing east and west to the sea, making Korea a true island, with water boundaries on all sides. The Ever-White peaked mountain, named less from its "eternal" snows than from its white rock and earth, is the central seat of Manchiu legend on its northern side, and of Korean fairy lore on the south.

Orographically, Korea consists of a great mountain spine which gives the eastern side of the country an abrupt slope to the sea, with for a hundred miles a great cliff wall, where there are no harbors. Speaking roughly, all the rest of the country, particularly its western side, is one prolonged slope. Rivers which have their cradles in the mountain tops, run to the sea, forming rich alluvial plains, making also a sea coast having many islands and fine harbors, but most dangerous to navi-

gation because of its sudden and high tides, which, receding leave enormous areas of mud exposed which are malarious and dangerous.

Facing Japan and a shallow sea, the rocky and abrupt coast, though sinuous, shows no gateway or efficient harbor from the Russian line down to Gensan on Broughton's Bay. There, on the flat land and adjacent hills has risen a smart settlement. It is located on the great high road which skirts the sea from the far north to the capital, throwing off also a branch roadway which further follows the coast down through the thinly inhabited region to Fusan. At this latter seaport, which was for three hundred years a Japanese trading station and is still substantially a part of Japan, we find again a main road coming from the capital, while the surveys for a railway from Seoul to Fusan have already been made by Japanese engi-

A STREET SCENE IN KOREA

neers, even as it promises to be built and equipped by Japanese capital.

We find what is exceptional on the east coast,—a great alluvial plain drained by "the river," and forming for the most part the province Kyong-Sang, warm, rich and fertile, where in the Middle Ages, the famous kingdom of Shinra, to which came the Arabs to trade and settle, had its domain, and in 1122 Chinese fleets from Ningpo steered by the mariner's compass. Of both of these facts there is clear record. Ginseng, deerhorn, aloes, camphor, saddles, porcelain and satin were sent from the Korean to Arabian land. A greased magnetic needle thrust through a ball of pitch or cork, and laid to float in a bowl of water formed the "south pointing chariot," brought to Shinra.

The southern tip of Korea has a frontage of hundreds of isles and out in the sea is the largest of Korean islands, rich in bulls, beef and ruffianly people, with vast store of mythology and folk-lore—the potter's field of Korean romance and chronology. On the western coast, between mountain and sea, lie the three provinces, Kyong, Ki-ung and Cholla, so often overrun by Japanese and Chinese armies, and again and again devoured by them. Just north of the capital there is the province, Whang Hai, rich in history, in Buddhist and mediæval remains and monuments, and in fisheries which provide both food and pearls. The northwestern province, Phyong An, borders on China and for centuries contained at Wi-ju, near the Green Duck river's mouth, the western and only gateway into the kingdom. It confronted also that "neutral strip," which once nominally dividing queues from topknots, became during our century the home of outlaws, until Li Hung Chang, with more generosity to China than justice to Korea, sent a fleet of gun boats up the river and a force of soldiers into the land, thus annexing the whole strip. To-day the "walls of stakes," or lines of palisades, hundreds of miles long, which once fenced in the Imperial domain, with its sacred city of Mukden, have vanished and should have no place upon the maps.

All over Northern Korea, in the mountain region, even far below the 38th parallel, the tiger, alert, hungry and daring, is the chief ruler of certain districts. The old Chinese sarcasm that "The Koreans hunt the tigers six months in the year (in summer) and the tigers hunt the Koreans the other six months," (in winter) had a large basis of truth. In these days when its superb robe is in such demand abroad, and the mountaineers are beginning to use Remington repeaters, the tiger is less the king of beasts, human and otherwise, than formerly. Besides pelts, these northern provinces produce gold. Already an American syndicate has men and machinery at work, testing (with satisfaction and abundant revenue) the question whether the rocks of Korea are yet to disturb the monetary equilibrium of the world. The main source of revenue to the country is obtained from ginseng, rice and beans. Hides, bones and oxen are exported also. The possibilities of making "the peninsula" produce the beef supply for the lands adjacent are excellent.

As yet there is but one railway from Chemulpo to Seoul; that is from the main seaport to the capital, with an electric tramway in Seoul. The Japanese line from Fusan to Seoul and the possible iron road, to be built thence to the Chinese frontier by the French, to connect with the great Russian continental line, will make Korea more accessible to Europe. As yet, however, the means of communication by hoof or vehicle are of the crudest, the most general and efficient being the human back. Man is still the chief beast of burden. The apparatus of porterage is a wooden frame or saddle set to the back and strapped over the shoulder. This work is controlled by a guild, with despotic rules forming a mighty power with which even the nobles and the government have to reckon.

A WOMAN IN STREET ATTIRE

BOAT BUILDING

Next after man, the bull and the horse divide the honors of toil. Strange to say, the pony, usually small, stunted and suggesting, especially in the north, a big dog rather than a small horse, has a bad character, while the bull glories in a noble reputation and is the friend of the family. For kicking, biting, squealing and making himself a general nuisance, the Korean pony may be warmly commended. He is vicious, untrustworthy and needs much development to bring him up to our ideas of even the average horse. He lives, when decently treated, in a stable and is usually fed on boiled beans, or roots and hay.

The bull, from the moment of his birth, is the pet of the household, and the children's companion during most of his lifetime. He does not love foreigners, but he is very sociably inclined toward Korean human beings. With a ring in his nose and usually made next to invisible under his load of bundles of brushwood for fuel, he can be seen in considerable numbers in the capital and is welcomed as a friend all over the country. Korea cannot expect to be either rich or civilized, while her roads and vehicles are what they are at present. Her "palace car," used much for ladies, is still the palanquin. Beside the rude ox cart, heavy and clumsy to the last degree, there used to be much in use in the capital and yet survives occasionally, the monocycle which is used only by natives of much importance. This vehicle is something like a sedan chair, perched on two supports above a single wheel. Out from the base of the chair

459

A FAMILY GROUP

run two poles to the front and rear, across either end of which is set a cross-bar. Three men propel the vehicle,—two behind the front cross-bar run along pulling, while one in the rear, holding the two bars, merrily guides and pushes the machine along. This desire for height above common folks is also to be observed in official gentlemen, who are swathed in bright robes of silk or crepe, and wear hats that, in a gale of wind, must be found dangerously large, notwithstanding that they are held on with a throat-lash of huge yellow and red beads. On a saddle, high and lifted up above the back of his tiny stallion, the rider strives to maintain on his perilous seat what passes for equilibrium and dignity. Alongside of him are usually half a dozen servants, who are ready to act as shores and guys when the master seems about to capsize.

The Korean dress is white, even the lowest classes wearing what was once so, and always professes to be. It is

astonishing how snowy-hued and glossy the gentlemen's robes are and in most cases, the outer garments, at least, of the people. Cotton is the great textile, though silk and hemp are also much used. There is no land on earth, perhaps, where the women work harder with the especial purpose in view of keeping the men looking dapper. Although soap is not used, the results of laundry and lye are wonderful. When the Koreans begin to emigrate to our country, they may drive the Chinese out of business. The women boil the clothes three times, clean them with lye, wash them in running water and then, after drying, begin that tedious process which requires them to toil during the long hours of the night. The characteristic sound which one hears while traveling through the unlighted streets of a Korean town, is the beating of the clothes on a flat board with a wooden ruler. A gloss

DANCING GIRLS

which is almost like silk results from this long castigation and lasts for some days.

Hard, indeed, is the lot of a Korean woman; generally speaking, she is anonymous. She is somebody's daughter, or sister, or wife, or mother —for the most part a cipher attached to some male integer. In general, the dress of women in Korea resembles that among us much more than does the female garb of China and Japan. The palace attendants have an enormous and elaborate head dress, behind which are stuck two colossal hairpins. The other women with some variety in coiffure, gather their hair in a knot held by pins made of brass or other material, or, in the case of the young girl, it is worn in a braid down the back.

The stranger in Korea is often puzzled in deciding upon the sex of the youthful and often rosy-cheeked creatures that wear a braid, but show no fullness in the chest, and soon learns that in the land of top-knots all males until they are married are looked upon as children only, without anything to say in company and with few rights which adults are bound to respect. Let the minor, old or young, marry and the world changes its attitude towards him. He can then pile up his hair on his scalp, or imprison it in a cage of horsehair, and exult in all the privileges of manhood, which seem chiefly to be that of squatting instead of sitting down properly, and of holding between the teeth, occasionally supported by the hand, three or four feet of tobacco pipe. The Korean is an inveterate smoker, but he usually puts between "the fool and the fire" a yard stick in the form of a bamboo cane.

In winter the summer's thin white

461

clothes of cotton or hemp give way to padded and baggy arrangements of the same color, so that whether in frost or heat Korea at night looks like the land of ghosts, and by day suggests a huge sleeping chamber with the occupants just out of bed. The great horsehair caps and big varnished hats, the conical wicker head dress and four-sided matting covers which the mourners wear, using also a little flag or fan-shaped device to shield their faces, are additional peculiar features of the Korean costume.

As the Korean footgear is midway in development between that of China and Japan, so also in type is the house in this Cyprus-like land, which historically is the link between the Asian Egypt, China, and the far-Oriental Greece, Japan. In general, the Korean

HULLING RICE

dwelling, whether hut or palace, is a one storied affair. It rests on a platform of masonry enclosing earth, through which runs a network of flues. To obtain warmth, the fires are built at one end and the chimney at the other, so that all caloric is utilized. When the heat is well regulated, the stone or brick floor makes the abode very comfortable. The houses of the nobles contain usually parlor, dining and bed rooms, with tiger skin screens, cabinets and bedding and toilet articles. In the average house, however, and especially among the poor, the cracks in the floor allow the smoke to escape, irritating the eyes of the occupants, and making the atmosphere exceedingly uncomfortable to the traveller. If staying at an inn, he will usually be disturbed further by the near noise of the horses and quarrels of the hostlers.

Yet a Korean house with its substantial frame, strong tiled roof and windows made with shutters much like ours, lends itself more admirably than either the Chinese or Japanese dwelling to the needs and uses of the American. One curious phase of life in Korea is the utilization of the roofs of the houses in the country for the growing of vines, melons and other fruit ripening in the sunshine at the top. Another phase of life is the skill of the burglar, who becomes a sapper and miner, often removing without noise the foundation stones and getting up through the flue into the house. Indeed, in the Korean romances, as well as in actual life, the lover obtains his surreptitious interviews in this way, and the widow or the unprotected woman suffers from this source of danger.

AN ANCIENT PAGODA

Despite their low estate in general, the native women have played a great part not only in religion but in politics. In our own day the strongest character in Korean history, after the Regent "of stone heart and iron bowels," was the able queen Ming, who long thwarted, not only the plots of the king's father against herself and her clan, but also nullified both the machinations attempted and the reforms inaugurated by the Mikado's envoys. She was in every sense a queen, but was at last brutally assassinated, her body being cremated in the raid made upon the palace by Japanese ruffians in 1896. It has cost the nation millions of dollars to get her remains properly buried and built over, and further removal and rebuilding must take place in 1902.

The native historians persistently claim Kishi, one of the ancestors of Confucius, as the founder of their civilization. After the fall of the Shang Dynasty of China, 1122 B. C., he moved towards the East, making his capital at Ping Yang, where the decisive battle of September, 1894, was fought. It is certain that there are many alleged relics of this famous man, who, if not actually the founder of Korea, has furnished in his name a convenient centre around which traditions have arranged themselves. He named the new land Cho-sen, or Morning Radiance, a term which mirrors either the tranquility and promise, as of early morn, which the exile sage sought and found; or, as is more probable, it refers to that benignant favor of the Dragon Countenance so desired by vassals and servants of the Chinese Emperor, who gives audience at auroral hours and sometimes as early as two o'clock in the morning. Kishi and his descendants ruled until the end of the third century, B. C., when they were dethroned by a Chinese refugee. The new state thus formed existed, with occasional lapses of revolt and renewals of vassalage and tribute, until 108 B. C., when Cho-sen was annexed to the Chinese Empire. This ancient Cho-sen of the native histories lay mainly in what is now Russianized China or Liao Tung.

Within the boundaries of the Korea known since the tenth century, we have historic phenomena much like those on the island of Great Britain. About the beginning of the Christian era three kingdoms began to form themselves, and have through a thousand years worked out a history characterized by peaceful development, but of-

IN THE OLD PALACE

ten interrupted by border wars and alternating invasions from or alliances with China and Japan. The various tribes became slowly consolidated into one people, who borrowed the civilization of China and assimilated it so thoroughly that they were able to become the teachers of the Japanese. It was mainly through Korea and not from China directly, that Dai Nippon received from India and China her letters, arts, philosophy and religious ethics. Mainly in the north and east was the kingdom of Korai, in the south and east Shinra, and in the central west Hiaksi. In the year 352, Buddhism was introduced and by the tenth century was widely disseminated.

During this time and until A. D. 1600, frequent colonies of skilled workmen, artists, teachers and mis-

sionaries, both men and women, crossed to Japan, enriching the civilization of the Japanese. Not only do the mythology, early legends and traditions of the Japanese point toward Korea, but many a pathetic story of love, valor and sacrifice is told of the Korean scholar, soldier, nun and monk in Japan. Classic literature is rich in allusion to the Jewel Land over the Western Sea, the Treasure House of Untold Blessing.

In the Japanese nursery, Cho-sen is the realm of fairy and ogre, the theatre of the strenuous valor of the Mikado's soldiers, the land of the tiger and the home of wonders and mysteries. The enthusiastic lads who landed in 1894, with Murata rifles, to annihilate the Chinese army at Ping Yang, on the old camp-ground of their own generals, Kasiwadé and Kato, must have felt as

CELEBRATION OF THE KING'S BIRTHDAY

an American child would if transported to Bluebeard's country.

To-day Korea looks to the many travellers, who all agree in their report, like a despoiled land, scraped and wasted by old wars. Its art is languishing. It has the general look of a poverty-stricken country. Yet all the old testimony, as abundant as it is sound, goes to show that Korea's past is to be measured by contrast, her ancient grandeur with the poverty of to-day. During the era of the Three Kingdoms, A. D., 9-966, Korean Buddhism was in its missionary activity. From 960 A. D. to 1392 was its golden age. This meant more wealth and a landscape richer in human interest than that seen to-day. The evidences from language and the study of place names, the ruined cities, the colossal Buddhist sculptures, now found in the forests and remote from town and highway, the journals of the Japanese officers during their great invasion, 1592-1597, as well as the native chronicles, testify to a degree of civilization marked by wealth, art, architecture and literature, which the tourist at this time would never imagine to have existed. Their absence demonstrates how devastating was the Japanese invasion. The "art-besotted" Japanese generals scooped Korea clean of the art treasures which they did not destroy. Along with hundreds of artists and thousands of slaves, they carried home fleet loads of treasure and relics with which they decorated their houses and temples.

Often the Buddhist remains are *in situ*, colossal sculptures on mountain spurs cut out of the native rock. Because of their substance of white gran-

TORTOISE AND COLUMN CARVED OUT OF ROCK

ite, at a distance they have been mistaken by naval travelers for light houses. Sometimes these *miryeks* stand in pairs, representing the male and female principles that rule the universe. These monoliths are chiseled according to the degree of art possessed in their locality. In quality of conception and workmanship, the Buddhist art works vary from the exquisite marble bas-reliefs of the pagoda in Seoul to colossal stone columns which, now bearded with the lichens and moss of centuries, seem little better than the hideous wooden posts set up on the wayside as village gods or as distance markers.

It was Wu-wang who in 960 A. D. gave political unity to the country by blotting out the rival states, and proclaiming anew the ancient name which had prevailed in the northeastern states, Korai. He fixed his capital at Sunto, some miles north of Seoul, where to-day are ruins in granite and vast ginseng fields. He borrowed from China the centralized system of government, with boards or ministries, sending out provincial governors from the capital. Under this regime the old feudalism was greatly modified, though never extinguished. To this day the internal politics of the Pygmy Empire take their trend, color and movement from forces surviving from ancient, almost prehistoric feudalism. Nominally the throne is above all, but the various clan-factions, as they are up or down, victorious or defeated, direct Korean policy. During this time of nearly four hundred years of Buddhist supremacy, albeit of luxury and corruption, Chinese civilization, especially those phases of it most prominent under the Sung (A. D., 960-1126) as before under the Tang dynasty (A. D., 618-905) was studied in detail and applied by the Koreans. This eagerness to absorb Chinese culture, continued with redoubled vigor under the dynasty now in power, has produced a phase of Confucianism which is distinctly different from that of either China or Japan. While in the former it has produced a detailed system of ethics, which gives material for philosophy and serves the purpose of a religion, and has created the Chinese literatus, who is a civilian pure and simple, in Japan it has become the code of conduct in the round of daily life, nourishing the Samurai, who is a soldier *and* a scholar, and mightily reinforcing the fundamental duty of loyalty to the Emperor. In Korea, Confucianism is, in its main force, etiquette, the rule of social life, making but slight application of its precepts to business or trade.

Toward the end of the fourteenth century, the Mongol dynasty in China was overthrown by the Mings. In Korea a revolution was started which overthrew the old dynasty that had patronized Buddhism, now corrupt and degraded, and set up the Li family which, beginning in 1392, has held the throne over five hundred years. Buddhism was disestablished and the priests, forbidden to enter walled cities, were allowed only to live in their monasteries among the mountains and in the government fortresses. There, despite their professedly peaceful calling, they still form the chief garrisons and a sort of clerical militia. Nevertheless, Buddhism is the popular religion in Korea, for all the women and most of the men seek salvation by this path to the Infinite.

Confucianism, the cult of the court, became rampant, and all things Chinese were cultivated with fresh ardor. Sunto was dismantled and its streets became fields. The royal residence, Han Yang, on the Seoul, was fixed on the Han River. The eight provinces were organized as to names, boundaries, and administrations, as we know them on modern maps. For the most part the boundaries are those furnished by nature, river, sea and mountain. Speaking roughly, each province is a river basin or drainage area, with a name made up from the first syllable of the chief city's name with the word sea, mountain, river or some other natural feature joined to the word *do* or circuit.

LIBRARY IN THE OLD PALACE

From 1392 until 1866, with the exception of the great Japanese invasion of 1592-1597, the story of the people within the "passive peninsula" is that of a hermit or sleeping nation. Then followed failure of royal heits, adoption and the regime of the Tai Wen Kun or regent; the outbreak of persecution against the Christians; the slaughter of the French priests; the destructive raids of the General Sherman, the French and American chastising expeditions; the Japanese treaty of 1876, succeeded by the American treaty and others; the anti-foreign reactions and riots; the turbulent and murderous attempts of Korean stalwarts who had been abroad to introduce "civilization" within twenty-four hours; the storming of the Japanese legation, the fighting between the soldiers of China and Japan; the Li-Ito convention, and finally the Chino-Japanese war of 1894.

Then Korea was independent—though hating her deliverers. The Chinese gateway near Seoul, at which the kings of Korea had for centuries done obeisance to China's ambassador, was torn down and a handsome modern structure erected named Independence Arch. Korea, no longer a vassal, but a free state between two empires, took another step in imitation of the greatness and claims of the various "sons of Heaven" and "world-powers" around her.

Not to be outdone by the people or the rulers of other countries in manifestation of nationalism or imperialism, the newly formed Independence Club held patriotic meetings at the arch and discussed the abolition of slavery, moral reforms and Korea's true policy, while the king assumed the title of emperor. This ceremony was performed on October 12, 1898, before the great altar dedicated to the Spirits of the Land, with all the spectacular show and accessories of solemnity once peculiar to Korea, but now vanishing away.

Russian influence was powerful in this same year. During a twelvemonth, Colonel Putiati with three officers and ten drill sergeants, tried to remodel the Korean army. This body, so vast on paper, and efficient in the depletion of the treasury, is pitifully small in actual numbers. Jealous Japan looked on, but could do nothing in Seoul or Peking to stop Russia from putting her nominee in charge of the Seoul treasury also. When, however, the double-headed eagle shadowed all northern China and secured an ice-free port and railway terminal at Port Arthur, Korea fell below par in Russian appraisement and the Czar with-

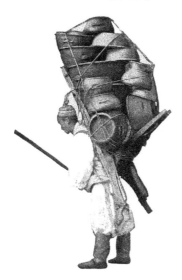

A Street Vender

drew his agents. The little country suddenly became once more a vacuum of diplomacy; that is, in all probability the dead calm at the centre of a rising typhoon.

The pivot of history is now in the Pacific. Down at the bottom of the outer ferment is the control of the Chinese market. Who shall have it? Russia or Japan? Before this question can be answered, must come the settling of the possession, or at least the disposal, of Korea. Each nation, like a new Archimedes or Atlas, wishes to lift the commercial world of Asia and walk off with it. Each needs Korea as a fulcrum for his lever. Japan has swept away feudalism and knighthood, and the day of the mill hand, the manufacturer and the merchant has come. To make money is the aim of men in this new nation of shopkeepers

that will fight for the markets of Asia. But Russia wants these also and has the land base of supplies, a railway and an army. In 1894 Japan, like a falcon, struck the fat goose China to the earth, but the double-headed eagle drove off the victor and appropriated the prey. Now, Japan with a mighty fleet of transports, cruisers, battle ships, torpedo boats and the ability to throw 250,000 men into Korea within a month, waits and hopes for peace. Meanwhile Korea cowers in weakness at the opening of a new century, believing that her weakness is her only strength.

The question naturally arises, why have the Japanese and not the Koreans been able to modernize themselves, to be a "self-reformed hermit nation?" What is the difference between the islanders and the continentals? One fact is patent. In Japan there is the samurai—the gentleman-soldier, civilian and war man in one—a character wholly absent in China or in Korea. The samurai or shizoku form a large body of educated men, who for a thousand years have enjoyed culture, and have had the same body of traditions and opinions. These men and their families form a full tenth of the population, and through their unifying sentiment of loyalty to the Emperor have been enabled to swing the whole country out of the rut of Asiatic conservatism into the path of modern progress.

In China, between the Emperor and the people, or rather between the Imperial Clan and the body of 6,000,000 Manchius who govern nearly 400,000,-000 Chinese, there is no middle term, or large body of intelligent patriots, but only a few mandarins, who are, for the most part steeped in a hoary system of corruption.

In Korea anything like patriotism in our sense of the word is unknown. The feudalism of many warring clans prevents anything like unity. Selfishness, greed and the instincts of clanship are as yet too powerful to lift the nation out of the morass of immorality into patriotic virtue. Outside of the new Korea, as yet scarcely as big as a man's hand, which is forming under the influence of Christian teachers, it is difficult to see where there is any force for the regeneration of this once hermit nation, forced into the world's market place and still too much dazed to know exactly what is going on.

Nevertheless a new Korea is forming.

Sisters

By Helen M. Richardson

ONE opened her eyes in the meadow,
 Way down 'mid the grasses, tall;
She heard the chirp of the crickets,
 The lilt of the robin's call;
And trimming her new spring bonnet,
 She worked by the glow-worm's light,
And danced to the tinkling music
 Of a brooklet, clear and bright.
A delicate hot-house darling
 Looked out where the breezes played
At hide-and-seek, in the sunshine,
 With this little meadow maid;
She longed for the daisy's freedom,
 And she thought her fair and sweet,
But she did not know they were sisters,
 For they called *her* Marguerite.

Marie Adelaide of Orleans

By Mary Stuart Smith

EVERY one knows the loving gratitude that has been manifested by all patriotic Americans to the French in general and Lafayette with his comrades in particular who shared personally in the hardships and glory of our Revolutionary War. How strange does it seem, then, that in this connection the name which heads this sketch is hardly known to the closest students of that stormy but never-to-be forgotten period of our history.

Although a great-granddaughter of Louis XIV., wife of a man who, for a while was heir-apparent to the throne of France, and one day to become the mother of the King of the French, Marie Adelaide, Duchesse de Chartres, the richest, wittiest and most beautiful woman of her nation, from the very beginning, was an ardent sympathizer with the American colonies in their struggle for liberty and aided them incalculably by most generous contributions of money and munitions of war, beside using her great social influence in their behalf. Her salon was ever open to the representatives of the youthful republic, and her purse responsive to every appeal for its many imperative needs.

Doubtless one reason why no acknowledgement was ever made by the American people of the gratitude due her was that her benefactions were dispensed in the most unostentatious and modest manner.

Inheriting three immense estates at the early age of eighteen, she had been wedded to Joseph Louis Philippe, Duc de Chartres, and the warm, romantic attachment existing between this young couple, in the early days of their union, was very different from the general idea entertained concerning French marriages. This duke is the only Bourbon who seems to have been born with a love of liberty for the people as well as for himself, so that when in 1786 he became, in the natural order of succession, Duke of Orleans, he dropped his title and henceforth desired to be known only as the *Citizen Philippe Egalité*.

But the Parisian populace could not forget that he was of the blood royal, and ever mistrusted his sincerity, so that when "the Mountain" obtained supremacy, his comradeship with republicans of many hues was speedily forgotten; he was arrested as a royalist and sent to prison, whence the short step to the guillotine followed as a matter of course.

His fate was the more surprising as his lovely wife, during all those hideous days of famine, blood and strife, had spent nearly all of her time and a large share of her income in bestowing aid wherever needed, irrespective of class or condition, so that even the *sans culottes* looked up to her, as an angel of mercy, with reverence and love. What love, though, could quench the insatiable thirst for blood that ran riot in Paris at that time? But this is to anticipate.

The lively interest in American affairs taken by this high-born couple had its source in the warm friendship that subsisted between them and the naval hero, John Paul Jones, which began in the heyday of their youth and prosperity. The Duc de Chartres, young as he was, had been nominated High Admiral of France, and preparatory to filling this exalted station, had been sent out upon a cruise of instruction, as it was called, under the tuition of his predecessor in the admiralty, and in the course of this cruise, they crossed the Atlantic in a splendid new frigate *"La Terpsichore,"* and anchored in the harbor of Norfolk, Virginia.

John Paul Jones, who was at that time, a Virginian landed proprietor, no sooner heard of the presence of this vessel at Hampton Roads, and the quality of its officers, than he waited upon them, and conveyed to them large stores of the dainties and delicacies for which that region is famed, and which must have been so grateful after a long voyage.

But this was in 1775, when already men of discerning minds like Paul Jones, foresaw clearly that war with England was imminent. Hence his visit to the French frigate was not a mere idle social call, but a visit fraught with momentous consequences. The hospitable, intelligent planter, soon obtaining the favor of the ship's commanders, was permitted to closely inspect the vessel and its armament, taking its dimensions so exactly that he was enabled to direct the construction of a man-of-war modelled precisely after the *Terpsichore;* as soon as Congress decided upon having a navy built.

In 1778, when, in response to earnest pleading, Paul Jones was permitted to carry the war into European waters, after his victory over *"The Drake,"* when he came, with his prizes, into the French harbor of Brest, he was most hospitably received and entertained by the Duc and Duchesse de Chartres in their cottage-palace by the sea, and immediately there sprang up between the lady and hero that remarkable friendship, of which her eldest son, Louis Philippe, long afterwards remarked, when an exile and guest of the Morris family in New Jersey:

"In all my checkered life, I have never known so beautiful a relation between woman and man as that of my mother and Paul Jones."

But these royal hosts did not confine themselves to feasting and flattering the commander of the victorious *"Ranger."* The officers and common sailors shared their attentions, and the good Duchess supplied them with sorely needed changes of raiment and whatever other comforts they lacked, at her own expense, knowing full well that the United States Commissioners were utterly unable to raise the funds necessary to provide for the requirements of these gallant fellows.

Again and again during the war she did the like, and when Commodore Jones would demur she would peremptorily silence him by exclaiming:

"Commodore, I command you! This is not charity; it is not even gratuity. It is my offering to the great cause of which you are by far the ablest and bravest champion on the sea."

Marie Adelaide had a lively imagination, and was in the habit of play-

PAUL JONES

fully applying descriptive epithets to persons whom she particularly admired. Washington she styled: "His Uncrowned Majesty," that is to say, *"Sa Majesté Sans Couronne."* Jefferson was "The Clever," viz: *"Monsieur l'habile"* and Paul Jones had several soubriquets, such as "The Untitled Knight of the Sea," "The Wrathful Achilles of the Ocean," and "The Bayard Afloat."

The princely pair went so far in their complaisance as to insist that the young hero take up his abode in the palace, while he remained at Brest, which was such a condescension as court etiquette pronounced perfectly inadmissible, and much censure was incurred. Louis Philippe years afterwards said that he accounted it one of the greatest privileges of his life to have had association with Paul Jones, when a boy, under the auspices of his gracious mother.

It was this friendship which procured for the Scottish-American hero of low birth, but lofty soul, introduction to the most select society of Paris, and never had the Duchess to blush for her *protégé*.   He not only sustained himself, but was considered to add *éclat* to every assembly that he attended.   The King Louis XVI. himself conversed with him freely as friend with friend, and in the end ennobled him and bestowed favors upon him never before accorded to a foreigner and a plebeian.

• Full as was Marie Adelaide of exalted patriotism, she was especially devoted to the memory of her grandfather, the Count of Toulouse, High Admiral of France, who had achieved the feat, so rarely accomplished by a French naval officer, of wresting a victory from the English.   At the great battle of Malaga, in 1704, he had done more than any other officer to win the day.   And yet, like all other great warriors he had his critics, and, at a dinner given by the Duke and Duchess at Brest, where Paul Jones was one of the guests, conversation fell upon the conduct of that famous seafight, and a leading courtier presumed to animadvert upon the admiral's orders.   Hereupon Jones responded so spiritedly and took the part of the Count de Toulouse so ably, that his critic was confounded, the Duchess charmed, and all at table wonderstruck by the knowledge of his-

tory and naval warfare displayed by one who had, comparatively speaking, had so little opportunity of storing up such an amount of practical information.   Calling to a trusted servant, while the dinner was still going on, the Duchess had brought to her a fine watch of unique workmanship that had belonged to the Commodore, and begged him to keep it as a memento of that gallant ancestor of her's whom he had so eloquently defended.

No one could have been more amazed than was Jones, at receiving such unlooked for recognition of his honest tribute to real merit, yet he mastered his embarrassment, and accepted the priceless gift as gracefully as it had been tendered.   After thanking the lady reverentially, he said: "May it please your Royal Highness, if fortune should favor me at sea, I shall some day lay an English frigate at your feet."

To the tactful persuasions of Marie Adelaide alone did Louis XVI. yield when he made a present to the United States of the frigate *"Le Bon Homme Richard,"* which, old and crazy as it was, enabled John Paul Jones to win the most memorable sea-fight of modern times, at once raising the government under which he fought to the rank of a maritime power.

Ordinarily calm and undemonstrative, when the news of this glorious victory reached Paris, the Duchesse de Chartres was rapturous in her joy, causing her palace to be illuminated and assembling a large company to do honor to the occasion.   Well might she rejoice in the fruit of her own modest but effective intercessions!

In April, 1780, Paul Jones chanced to visit Paris on business, and was again handsomely entertained by his steadfast friends, the Duc and Duchesse de Chartres. In her journal, the lady herself records what happened at supper. When a suitable pause between the courses allowed the opportunity, Chevalier Paul Jones asked her Royal Highness if she deigned to remember his promise, made two years before, that he would lay a frigate at her feet. She bowed assent. Then Jones sent an attendant to bring from his apartment in the palace a leather case. When the messenger returned, Jones took from the case a sword and said:

"Your Royal Highness perceives the impossibility of keeping my promise in kind. The English frigate proved to be a forty-four on two decks, and she is now at l'Orient, with French colors flying. The best I can do towards keeping my word of two years ago is to place in your dainty hands the sword of the brave officer who commanded the English forty-four. I have the honor to surrender to the loveliest of women the sword surrendered to me by one of the bravest of men—the sword of Captain, the Honorable Richard Pearson of His Britannic Majesty's late ship the Serapis."

Elsewhere in her journal the Duchess says:

"Although the company at table was most distinguished, Commodore Jones, fresh from his marvelous victories, was easily the centre of attraction to all.

"I said to him that all the world had read the account of his exploits, and the more we read the more we marvelled. And I asked him what thought, what impulse, what inspiration could have sustained him to persevere when his ship was on fire and sinking under his feet, and his men almost all in the throes of death about him. To this he replied with a profound bow and the greatest solemnity: 'May it please your Royal Highness, I could not be the first to strike the flag that I had been first to exhibit in Europe; and besides, surrender must have postponed the rapture of greeting you again!' Then I could only reply as I did: 'Ah, my dear Commodore, not Chevalier Bayard nor Charles the Bold himself could have laid his helmet at a lady's feet with such knightly grace.'"

But the time of feasting and playful dalliance was soon to be over for Marie Adelaide.

Although during the Reign of Terror she was the only one of the royal family allowed to remain in France, how could her generous soul enjoy an exemption in which no dear one had a share. After the execution of her husband and the exile of her sons, even Paris had no attraction for her, and she took refuge in Spain, where she resided until 1814, when the era of the Restoration lured her back to her beloved country. Napoleon also honored himself by extending more than one invitation that she should return to Paris, thus acknowledging her as a public benefactress. Moreover, during Napoleon's hundred days' reign after his return from banishment to Elba, he had settled upon the widowed Duchesse d'Orleans an annuity of 200,000 francs, at the instance of the ever generous Hortense, Queen of Holland.

From 1814 to 1821, when Marie Adelaide died from the effects of a sad accident, her home was in Paris, but we cannot imagine her life to have been otherwise than dark, so fraught was every scene with painful memories. If even goodness cannot bring happiness, at least her existence must have been filled with the calm peacefulness that results from a quiet conscience.

An Early Coronation Sermon

By George H. Davenport

ON the 9th of August, 1727, the first Sunday after the proclaiming of George II. King of England, the Reverend Benjamin Colman, minister of the Brattle Street Church in Boston, preached a powerful and interesting sermon from the text I Chron. XII.18. Its subject was "Fidelity to the Protestant Succession in the Illustrious House of Hanover." At the request of his parishioners it was printed, and the pamphlet bears this inscription:

"Boston in New England"
"Printed by T. Fleet for T. Hancock,
at the Bible and Three Crowns
Near the Town Dock.
1727."

In 1689 William succeeded to the throne of England, and in 1701 gave his consent to an act of settlement which secured the succession of the crown to the House of Hanover, to the exclusion of all Roman Catholic claimants. On March 8th, 1702, William ·was thrown from his horse and killed, and Queen Anne came to the throne. In 1708 a purely whig ministry was formed, and in 1714, on the death of Anne, the whigs proclaimed the Elector of Hanover king, as George I. In 1727 George I. died and George II. came to the throne.

The New England colony of faithful subjects was interested in all that pertained to Old England, and especially, of course, to who was to be their king and ruler; and their clergymen kept in touch with the religious and civil life across the sea, as is everywhere evident in the records and writings of the time.

The introduction to this special sermon is so quaintly and seriously written, and sets forth so forcibly the feelings for the Mother Country prevalent in the New England colonies, that it is worth giving it in full.

To The
"Loyal Protestant Reader."
"If I had not been persuaded that the Text and this short Discourse upon it here presented to thee, breathes the heart and soul of the Churches in New England, both Pastors and People, I should not have brought the one into the pulpit on the present occasion, nor have permitted the other to go into the press at the desire of those who heard it. But as I am conscious of no motive in the choice of the Subject, but I trust a sincere and fervent zeal for the Religion of Christ and the Protestant Succession in the Royal Family; so I am confident that the Gentlemen who have asked this copy of what they heard, did it on no other motive. And if it may in any measure help to confirm and increase a dutiful and loyal affection to Christ, his truths and spiritual worship; and to our rightful King as the Defender of them; I shall not repent the making so minute an offering at the Temple on so great an Occasion."

"The name of the great King William was ever dear to these his loyal New English Colonies, and that beyond expression; but there is no one thing by which his Immortal Memory is more endeared to us, than the wise and just provision by Him

The Reverend Benjamin Colman D.D.

made for the Succession of the Crown in the Protestant Line."

"When we saw it take place in a manner so peaceful, after so much reason to fear the contrary, our mouths were filled with laughter and our tongues with singing. Our Churches rang with the high praises of God, and with continued prayers for the Life of the King and of his Son. We trusted in God that he was building a Sure House for the Protestant cause, and speaking of it for a great while to come in the Person of His Royal Highness and his numerous illustrious offspring; as the Lord gave to David a lamp in Jerusalem, to set up his Son after him and to establish his people."

"But we were soon struck with horror and just detestation at the hellish plots and

enemies more than ours. The meanwhile it was their humble trust in the mercy of God, that while his Majesty was asserting the rights of conscience, and restoring to God his Throne in the soul of man, God would not fail to defend his Servant on the British Throne. God answered the faith and prayer of his people, and returned the wickedness of the King's enemies on their own head."

"This was the language of the Addresses from the Ministers of the Province at their annual conventions; and I have presumed to transcribe a paragraph or two of them, for an abiding testimony of their fervent loyalty to Christ and the Protestant Royal Family."

"Thanks be to God the Protestant Succession lives in his present Majesty, King George II; and accordingly the tide of joy has run as high among us in the happy Succession of the Son, as it did on the Accession of the great King his Father."

"May the Clemencies of his Majesty's Government extend always to these American Churches, which know not of one single person in their Communion that is not loyally affected to Him and to his House. May he shine long at the head of the Protestant interest, its powerful Friend and Protector; and reign always in the hearts of his protestant subjects, being ever to them as the light of the morning, and as the breath of their nostrils. BENJAMIN COLMAN.

Boston, N. E., August 16, 1727."

rebellions, formed by the restless party in the Nation, whom no oaths could bind, nor clemency conquer, nor the rebukes of a righteous Providence deter: Nor were we from time to time less affected with a sincere and dutiful joy, to show how God brought their wicked devices to light, and covered the abetters of them with infamy; while at the same time the fame of the felicity of the Nation under the King's wise administration reached us, and of the vast influence of his Majesty's Counsels and power upon the grand affairs of Europe."

"When some of the Clergy, doubly sworn to the King and the Faith he defended, appeared to head the vile attempts to disturb a Protestant Reign, we readily took the occasion given us to declare our astonishment at the abhorrence of the perfidy and impiety. For what were those Englishmen and Protestants, falsely so called, plotting to introduce, but the two transcendent plagues of popery and slavery upon the Nations? With amazement and disdain, the protestant Dissenters beheld the villainy, and cried to the God of Heaven against the men, his

Then follows the sermon, in which he sets forth the truth that "Our faithful zeal for and adherence to the Protestant Succession in the House of Hanover is our Fidelity to Christ and His Holy Religion."

The Rev. Benjamin Colman was quite a remarkable man. Born in Boston October 19, 1673, he entered Harvard College in 1688, and under the Presidency of Dr. Increase Mather, received in 1692 his A. B., and in 1695 his A. M. Three weeks thereafter he sailed for England, then in the heat of the King William war with the French

THE BRATTLE STREET CHURCH

From Drake's "Old Landmarks and Historic Personages of Boston," published by Little, Brown & Co.

King.   At the end of seven weeks of storm and trial, a French Privateer sighted them, gave chase, and captured them, and he was carried to France, subsequently released, and after many trials reached England.

In July, 1699, the Brattle Street Church in Boston sent for him to become their minister; this call was signed by Thomas Brattle, Benjamin Davis, Thomas Cooper, John Leverett, and others.   He accepted the call, and sailed for home August 20th, 1699, arriving in Boston November 1st.   On the 24th of December of that year the newly built Brattle Street Church was opened to public worship, Mr. Colman choosing for his text II. Chron. VI. 8.

For forty-eight years he ministered to this people.   On November 18, 1724, upon the decease of Hon. John Leverett, President, he was chosen by the corporation of Harvard College, his successor, but declined the honor, submitting to the desire of his church and people, that he remain; but for many years, however, he was a fellow of the corporation and an overseer until his death.   In November, 1731, the University of Glasgow conferred on him the degree of Doctor of Divinity.   He died in Boston, August 29, 1747, in his seventy-fourth year, honored and beloved by all New England.

The Brattle Street Church, over which he ministered for almost half a century, was built in 1699, of wood, and was called the Manifesto Church being the first to adopt the rule that the choice of the minister should not be confined to communicants, but enjoyed by everyone who belonged to the society.   This edifice was in use for seventy-three years. In 1773 the new brick church was consecrated, and was occupied by the congregation until its demolition in 1872. To the building of this new church in 1773, Governor Hancock donated one thousand pounds, and gave the bell on which was inscribed,—"I to the church the living call, and to the grave I summon all."

On March 16, 1775, a twenty-four pound shot, from our guns at Cambridge, struck the tower. This cannon ball was picked up, and 1824 was imbedded in the masonry, where it remained until the work of tearing down began in 1872.

An array of clerical talent unsurpassed in any Boston pulpit stands as the record of this church.

Benjamin Colman, 1699 to 1747.
William Cooper, 1716 to 1743.
Samuel Cooper, 1746 to 1783.
Peter Thatcher, 1785 to 1802.
J. S. Buckminster, 1805 to 1812.
Edward Everett, 1814 to 1815.
John G. Palfrey, 1818 to 1830.
S. K. Lothrop, 1834 to 1876.

One hundred and seventy-five years have passed since Benjamin Colman said to his congregation in the Brattle Street Church, "The name of the great King William was ever dear to this his loyal New English Colonies, and that beyond expression." Another King is to be proclaimed on June 26th of this year, and what the good minister was thankful for,—the Protestant Succession—has been maintained in England up to this time. But the English Colony is no more. A great Nation has arisen, and if Benjamin Colman should come forth from his tomb in Kings Chapel burying ground, and revisit the scenes of his ministry, instead of the thirteen churches within its borders, he would now find two hundred and eighty-nine of every sect and name under the sun; instead of a city containing 17,500 inhabitants, he would find a city of 560,892. He would be able to find the Common, and many of the old streets and lanes, the Old State House, the Old Corner Book Store, and Faneuil Hall, but of the churches, only five remain on the same sites and substantially as he left them when he died in 1747:—The Old South, West Church, Kings Chapel, Christ Church, and the New North Church. But, of these, only the last three are used for services at the present time.

With the Protestant Succession still maintained in a large proportion of these Boston churches, and in the great country at large, Mr. Colman could return again to his quiet resting place under the Kings Chapel trees for another one hundred and seventy-five years, in peace and contentment.

The Professor's Commencement

By Willa Sibert Cather

THE professor sat at his library table at six o'clock in the morning. He had risen with the sun, which is up betimes in June. An uncut volume of "Huxley's Life and Letters" lay open on the table before him, but he tapped the pages absently with his paper-knife and his eyes were fixed unseeingly on the St. Gaudens medallion of Stevenson on the opposite wall. The professor's library testified to the superior quality of his taste in art as well as to his wide and varied scholarship. Only by a miracle of taste could so unpretentious a room have been made so attractive; it was as dainty as a boudoir and as original in color scheme as a painter's studio. The walls were hung with photographs of the works of the best modern painters,—Burne-Jones, Rossetti, Corot, and a dozen others. Above the mantel were delicate reproductions in color of some of Fra Angelica's most beautiful paintings. The rugs were exquisite in pattern and color, pieces of weaving that the Professor had picked up himself in his wanderings in the Orient. On close inspection, however, the contents of the book-shelves formed the most remarkable feature of the library. The shelves were almost equally apportioned to the accommodation of works on literature and science, suggesting a form of bigamy rarely encountered in society. The collection of works of pure literature was wide enough to include nearly all the major languages of modern Europe, besides the Greek and Roman classics.

To an interpretive observer nearly everything that was to be found in the Professor's library was represented in his personality. Occasionally, when he read Hawthorne's "Great Stone Face" with his classes, some clear sighted student wondered whether the man ever realized how completely he illustrated the allegory in himself. The Professor was truly a part of all that he had met, and he had managed to meet most of the good things that the mind of man had desired. In his face there was much of the laborious precision of the scientist and not a little of Fra Angelico and of the lyric poets whose influence had prolonged his youth well into the fifties. His pupils always remembered the Professor's face long after they had forgotten the things he had endeavored to teach them. He had the bold, prominent nose and chin of the oldest and most beloved of American actors, and the high, broad forehead which Nature loves to build about her finely adjusted minds. The grave, large outlines of his face were softened by an infinite kindness of mouth and eye. His mouth, indeed, was as sensitive and mobile as that of a young man, and, given certain passages from "Tristram and Isolde" or certain lines from Heine, his eyes would flash out at you like wet corn-flowers after a

481

spring shower. His hair was very thick, straight, and silver white. This, with his clear skin, gave him a somewhat actor-like appearance. He was slight of build and exceedingly frail, with delicate, sensitive hands curving back at the finger ends, with dark purple veins showing prominently on the back. They were exceedingly small, white as a girl's, and well kept as a pianist's.

As the Professor sat caressing his Huxley, a lady entered.

"It is half past six, Emerson, and breakfast will be served at seven." Anyone would have recognized her as the Professor's older sister, for she was a sort of simplified and expurgated edition of himself, the more alert and masculine character of the two, and the scholar's protecting angel. She wore a white lace cap on her head and a knitted shawl about her shoulders. Though she had been a widow for twenty-five years and more, she was always called Miss Agatha Graves. She scanned her brother critically and having satisfied herself that his linen was immaculate and his white tie a fresh one, she remarked, "You were up early this morning, even for you."

"The roses never have the fragrance that they have in the first sun, they give out their best then," said her brother nodding toward the window where the garden roses thrust their pink heads close to the screen as though they would not be kept outside. "And I have something on my mind, Agatha," he continued, nervously fingering the sandalwood papercutter, "I feel distraught and weary. You know how I shrink from changes of any sort, and this—why this is the

most alarming thing that has ever confronted me. It is absolutely cutting my life off at the stalk, and who knows whether it will bud again?"

Miss Agatha turned sharply about from the window where she had been standing, and gravely studied her brother's drooping shoulders and dejected figure.

"There you go at your old tricks, Em," she remonstrated. "I have heard many kinds of ability attributed to you, but to my mind no one has ever put his finger on the right spot. Your real gift is for getting all the possible pain out of life, and extracting needless annoyance from commonplace and trivial things. Here you have buried yourself for the best part of your life in that High School, for motives Quixotic to an absurdity. If you had chosen a University I should not complain, but in that place all your best tools have rusted. Granted that you have done your work a little better than the people about you, it's no great place in which to excel,—a city high school where failures in every trade drift to teach the business they cannot make a living by. Now it is time that you do something to justify the faith your friends have always had in you. You owe something to them and to your own name."

"I have builded myself a monument more lasting than brass," quoted the Professor softly, balancing the tips of his slender fingers together.

"Nonsense, Emerson!" said Miss Agatha impatiently. "You are a sentimentalist and your vanity is that of a child. As for those slovenly persons with offensive manners whom you call your colleagues, do you fancy they appreciate you? They are as envious as green gourds and their mouths pucker when they pay you compliments. I hope you are not so unsophisticated as to believe all the sentimental twaddle of your old students. When they want recommendations to some school board, or run for a city office and want your vote, they come here and say that you have been the inspiration of their lives, and I believe in my heart that you are goose enough to accept it all."

"As for my *confrères*," said the Professor smiling, "I have no doubt that each one receives in the bosom of his family exactly the same advice that you are giving me. If there dwell an appreciated man on earth I have never met him. As for the students, I believe I have, to some at least, in a measure supplied a vital element that their environment failed to give them. Whether they realize this or not is of slight importance; it is in the very nature of youth to forget its sources, physical and mental alike. If one labors at all in the garden of youth, it must be free from the passion of seeing things grow, from an innate love of watching the strange processes of the brain under varying influences and limitations. He gets no more thanks than the novelist gets from the character he creates, nor does he deserve them. He has the whole human comedy before him in embryo, the beginning of all passions and all achievements. As I have often told you, this city is a disputed strategic point. It controls a vast manufacturing region given over to sordid and materialistic ideals. Any work that has been done here for æsthetics cannot be lost. I suppose we shall win in the end, but the reign of Mammon has been long and oppressive. You remember when

I was a boy working in the fields how we used to read Bunyan's "Holy War" at night? Well, I have always felt very much as though I were keeping the Ear Gate of the town of Mansoul, and I know not whether the Captains, who succeed me be trusty or no."

Miss Agatha was visibly moved, but she shook her head. "Well, I wish you had gone into the church, Emerson. I respect your motives, but there are more tares than wheat in your crop, I suspect."

"My dear girl," said the Professor, his eye brightening, "that is the very reason for the sowing. There is a picture by Vedder of the Enemy Sowing Tares at the foot of the cross, and his seeds are golden coins. That is the call to arms; the other side never sleeps; in the theatres, in the newspapers, in the mills and offices and coal fields, by day and by night the enemy sows tares."

As the Professor slowly climbed the hill to the High School that morning, he indulged in his favorite fancy, that the old grey stone building was a fortress set upon the dominant acclivity of that great manufacturing city, a stronghold of knowledge in the heart of Mammon's kingdom, a Pharos to all those drifting, storm-driven lives in the valley below, where mills and factories thronged, blackening the winding shores of the river, which was dotted with coal barges and frantic, puffing little tugs. The High School commanded the heart of the city, which was like that of any other manufacturing town—a scene of bleakness and naked ugliness and of that remorseless desolation which follows upon the fiercest lust of man. The beautiful valley, where long ago two limpid rivers met at the foot of wooded heights, had become a scorched and blackened waste. The river banks were lined with bellowing mills which broke the silence of the night with periodic crashes of sound, filled the valley with heavy carboniferous smoke, and sent the chilled products of their red forges to all parts of the known world,—to fashion railways in Siberia, bridges in Australia, and to tear the virgin soil of Africa. To the west, across the river, rose the steep bluffs, faintly etched through the brown smoke, rising five hundred feet, almost as sheer as a precipice, traversed by cranes and inclines and checkered by winding yellow paths like sheep trails which lead to the wretched habitations clinging to the face of the cliff, the lairs of the vicious and the poor, miserable rodents of civilization. In the middle of the stream, among the tugs and barges, were the dredging boats, hoisting muck and filth from the clogged channel. It was difficult to believe that this was the shining river which tumbles down the steep hills of the lumbering district, odorous of wet spruce logs and echoing the ring of axes and the song of the raftsmen, come to this black ugliness at last, with not one throb of its woodland passion and bright vehemence left.

For thirty years the Professor's class-room had overlooked this scene which caused him unceasing admiration and regret. For thirty years he had cried out against the image set up there as the Hebrew prophets cried out against the pride and blind prosperity of Tyre. Nominally he was a professor of English Literature, but his real work had been to try to secure for youth the rights of youth;

the right to be generous, to dream, to enjoy; to feel a little the seduction of the old Romance, and to yield a little. His students were boys and girls from the factories and offices, destined to return thither, and hypnotized by the glitter of yellow metal. They were practical, provident, unimaginative, and mercenary at sixteen. Often, when some lad was reading aloud in the class-room, the puffing of the engines in the switch yard at the foot of the hill would drown the verse and the young voice entirely, and the Professor would murmur sadly to himself: "Not even this respite is left to us; even here the voice of youth is drowned by the voice of the taskmaster that waits for them all impatiently enough."

Never had his duty seemed to call him so urgently as on this morning when he was to lay down his arms. As he entered the building he met the boys carrying palms up into the chapel for class-day exercises, and it occurred to him for the first time that this was his last commencement, a commencement without congratulations and without flowers. When he went into the chapel to drill the seniors on their commencement orations, he was unable to fix his mind upon his work. For thirty years he had heard youth say exactly the same thing in the same place; had heard young men swear fealty to the truth, pay honor to the pursuit of noble pleasures, and pledge themselves "to follow knowledge like a sinking star beyond the utmost bound of human thought." How many, he asked himself, had kept their vows? He could remember the occasion of his own commencement in that same chapel; the story that every senior class still told the juniors, of the Professor's humiliation and disgrace when, in attempting to recite "Horatius at the Bridge," he had been unable to recall one word of the poem following

"Then out spake bold Horatius
The Captain of the gate;"

and after some moments of agonizing silence he had shame-facedly left the platform.   Even the least receptive of the Professor's students realized that he had risen to a much higher plane of scholarship than any of his colleagues, and they delighted to tell this story of the frail, exquisite, little man whom generations of students had called "the bold Horatius."

All the morning the Professor was busy putting his desk and bookcases in order, impeded by the painful consciousness that he was doing it for the last time.   He made many trips to the window and often lapsed into periods of idleness.   The room had been connected in one way and another with most of his intellectual passions, and was as full of sentimental associations for him as the haunts of his courtship   days are to a lover.   At   two   o'clock he   met his last class, which was just finishing "Sohrab and Rustum," and he was forced to ask one of the boys to read and interpret the majestic closing lines on the "shorn and parceled oxus." What the boy's comment was the Professor never knew, he felt so close a kinship to that wearied river that he sat stupefied, with his hand shading his eyes and his fingers twitching.   When the bell rang announcing the end of the hour; he felt a sudden pain clutch his heart; he had a vague hope that the students would gather around his desk to discuss some point that youth

loves to discuss, as they often did, but their work was over and they hurried out, eager for their freedom, while the professor sat helplessly watching them.

That evening a banquet was given to the retiring professor in the chapel, but Miss Agatha had to exert all her native power of command to induce him to go.   He had come home so melancholy and unnerved that after laying out his dress clothes she literally had to put them on him.   When he was in his shirt sleeves and Miss Agatha had carefully brushed his beautiful white hair and arranged his tie, she wheeled him sharply about and retreated to a chair.

"Now Emerson, say your piece," she commanded.

Plucking up his shirt sleeves and making sure of his cuffs, the Professor began valiantly:

"Lars Porsena of Clusium
By the nine gods he swore,"

It was all Miss Agatha's idea. After the invitations to the banquet were out and she discovered that half-a-dozen of the Professor's own classmates and many of his old students were to be present, she divined that it would be a tearful and depressing occasion.   Emerson, she knew, was an indifferent speaker when his heart was touched, so she had decided that after a silence of thirty-five years Horatius should be heard from.   The idea of correcting his youthful failure in his old age had rather pleased the Professor on the whole, and he had set to work to memorize Lord Macaulay's lay, rehearsing in private to Miss Agatha, who had drilled him for that fatal exploit of his commencement night.

After this dress rehearsal the Professor's spirits rose, and during the carriage ride he even made several feeble efforts to joke with his sister.   But later in the evening when he sat down at the end of the long table in the dusky chapel, green with palms for commencement week, he fell into deep depression.   The guests chattered and boasted and gossiped, but the guest of honor sat silent, staring at the candles. Beside him sat old Fairbrother, of the Greek department, who had come into the faculty in the fifth year of Graves's professorship, and had married a pretty senior girl who had rejected Graves's timid suit. She had been dead this many a year; since his bereavement lonely old Fairbrother had clung to Graves, and now the Professor felt a singular sense of support in his presence.

The Professor tried to tell himself that now his holiday time had come, and that he had earned it; that now he could take up the work he had looked forward to and prepared for for years, his History of Modern Painting, the Italian section of which was already practically complete.   But his heart told him that he had no longer the strength to take up independent work. Now that the current of young life had cut away from him and into a new channel, he felt like a ruin of some extinct civilization, like a harbor from which the sea has receded.   He realized that he had been living by external stimulation from the warm young blood about him, and now that it had left him, all his decrepitude was horribly exposed.   All those hundreds of thirsty young lives had drunk him dry. He compared himself to one of those granite colossi of antique lands, from which each traveller has chipped a bit

of stone until only a mutilated torso is left.

He looked reflectively down the long table, picking out the faces of his colleagues here and there, souls that had toiled and wrought and thought with him, that simple, unworldly sect of people he loved.   They were still discussing the difficulties of the third conjugation, as they had done there for twenty years.   They were cases of arrested development, most of them. Always in contact with immature minds, they had kept the simplicity and many of the callow enthusiasms of youth. Those facts and formulae which interest the rest of the world for but a few years at most, were still the vital facts of life for them.   They believed quite sincerely in the supreme importance of quadratic equations, and the rule for the special verbs that govern the dative was a part of their decalogue.   And he himself—what had he done with the youth, the strength, the enthusiasm and splendid equipment he had brought there from Harvard thirty years ago? He had come to stay but a little while —five years at the most, until he could save money enough to defray the expense of a course in some German university.   But then the battle had claimed him; the desire had come upon him to bring some message of repose and peace to the youth of this work-driven, joyless people, to cry the name of beauty so loud that the roar of the mills could not drown it.   Then the reward of his first labors had come in the person of his one and only genius; his restless, incorrigible pupil with the gentle eyes and manner of a girl, at once timid and utterly reckless, who had seen even as Graves saw; who had suffered a little, sung a little, struck the true lyric note, and died wretchedly at three-and-twenty in his master's arms, the victim of a tragedy as old as the world and as grim as Samson, the Israelite's.

He looked about at his comrades and wondered what they had done with their lives. Doubtless they had deceived themselves as he had done. With youth always about them, they had believed themselves of it. Like the monk in the legend they had wandered a little way into the wood to hear the bird's song—the magical song of youth so engrossing and so treacherous, and they had come back to their cloister to find themselves old men—spent warriors who could only chatter on the wall, like grass-hoppers and sigh at the beauty of Helen as she passed.

The toasts were nearly over, but the Professor had heard none of the appreciative and enthusiastic things that his students and colleagues had said of him. He read a deeper meaning into this parting than they had done and his thoughts stopped his ears. He heard Miss Agatha clear her throat and caught her meaning glance. Realizing that everyone was waiting for him, he, blinked his eyes like a man heavy with sleep and arose.

"How handsome he looks," murmured the woman looking at his fine old face and silver hair. The Professor's remarks were as vague as they were brief. After expressing his thanks for the honor done him, he stated that he had still some work to finish among them, which had been too long incomplete. Then with as much of his school-boy attitude as he could remember, and a smile on his gentle lips, he began his

*"Lars Porsena of Clusium, by the Nine Gods he swore
That the proud house of Tarquin should suffer wrong no more."*

A murmur of laughter ran up and down the long table, and Dr. Maitland, the great theeologian, who had vainly tried to prompt his stage-struck fellow graduate thirty-five years ago, laughed until his nose glasses fell off and dangled across his black waistcoat. Miss Agatha was highly elated over the success of her idea, but the Professor had no heart in what he was doing, and the merriment rather hurt him. Surely this was a time for silence and reflection, if ever such time was. Memories crowded upon him faster than the lines he spoke, and the warm eyes turned upon him, full of pride and affection for their scholar and their "great man," moved him almost beyond endurance.

*"——the Consul's brow was sad
And the Consul's speech was low,"*

he read, and suited the action marvellously to the word. His eyes wandered to the chapel rostrum. Thirty-five years ago he had stood there repeating those same lines, a young man, resolute and gifted, with the strength of Ulysses and the courage of Hector, with the kingdoms of the earth and the treasures of the ages at his feet, and the singing rose in his heart; a spasm of emotion contracted the old man's vocal cords.

*"Outspake the bold Horatius,
The Captain of the gate."*

he faltered;——his white hand nervously sought his collar, then the hook on his breast where his glasses usually hung, and at last tremulously for his handkerchief; then with a gesture of utter defeat, the Professor sat down. There was a tearful silence; white handkerchiefs fluttered down the table as from a magician's wand, and Miss Agatha was sobbing. Dr. Maitland arose to his feet, his face distorted between laughter and tears. "I ask you all," he cried, "whether Horatius has any need to speak, for has he not kept the bridge these thirty years? God bless him!"

"It's all right, so don't worry about it, Emerson," said Miss Agatha as they got into the carriage. "At least they were appreciative, which is more than I would have believed."

"Ah, Agatha," said the Professor, wiping his face wearily with his crumpled handkerchief, "I am a hopeless dunce, and you ought to have known better. If you could make nothing of me at twenty, you showed poor judgment to undertake it at fifty-five. I was not made to shine, for they put a woman's heart in me."

Washington-Greene Correspondence

A large collection of original letters written by General Washington and General Greene has come into the editor's possession. It is our intention to reproduce in fac-simile those of the letters which present the most interesting details and side lights on the great events of the period covered, even though some of the letters may have been previously published.

The reproduction of these letters in chronological order will be continued through the following two issues. A printed copy of the letter herewith appears on page 493.—EDITOR.

Mount Vernon 16th Novem: 1781

Dear Sir

I wrote you so fully & freely by Lieut Colo.
Lee, who left me about the 29th ulto, that I have at this
time but little else to say, than to acknowledge the receipt
of your Letter of the 25th ulto, which came to hand two
Days ago, and by which I am surprized to find that
you have received nothing from me later than the 28th
of Septem:

Since my last, the American troops destined
to the Northward, except the 2d N York Reg't who march with
the prisoners by Land, have all embarked with their stores &
are I presume by this time arrived at the head of Elk.
Those under the command of Maj'r Gen'l St Clair, who are ordered to join your Army, began their march on the 5th
and I hope are well advanced. — — The French fleet
left the Bay, as I am informed, about the 6th or 7th and from
the best Accounts I have been able to obtain of the British
who were last seen standing Southerly on the N Carolina
coast, there is but a possible chance of the two fleets meeting. — — Ld Cornwallis, with the British officer going
to N York & Europe, fell down the River York on the 4th
                                                        The

the Prisoners who are to remain in the Country, are all marched to Winchester & Fort Frederick, except such sick as remain too bad to remove — of these there are still a considerable Number —

I am thus far myself on my Way to the Northward — I shall remain but a few days here, & shall proceed to Philadelphia, where I shall attempt to stimulate Congress to the best Improvement of our late success, by taking the most vigorous & effectual Measures, to be ready for an early & decisive Campaign the next Year — My greatest fear is, that Congress viewing this stroke in too important a point of Light, may think our Work too nearly closed, & will fall into a state of Languor & Relaxation — to prevent this ~~that I employ every means in my power~~ and if unhappily we sink into that ~~unhappy~~ total mistake, no part of the Blame shall be mine —

Whatever may be the Winter politics of European courts, it is clearly my Opinion, that our grand Object is to be prepared in every point for War — not that we wish its continuance, but that we may be in the best situation to meet every event —

I am anxious to know whether the British fleet drops a Reinforcement at Charlestown — before this arrives, you will be informed from my last that a chain of Expresses will be established from Philadelphia to S° Carolina, by which means I hope to have a

a more frequent Communication of Intelligence
than has hitherto been experienced with your Army
With very great Regard & Esteem
I am
C2
Dear Sir
Your most obedient and
most humble Servant
G: Washington
Hon. Major Genl. Greene

DEAR SIR,
I wrote
have at this Time
which came to hand
from me later than
Since my last,
march with the pris
at the head of El
army, began their
am informed, about
who were last seen
fleets meeting.—L
York on the 4th. T
Frederick, except
I am thus far m
ceed to Philadelphia
cess, by tak'g the
next Year.—My gre
think our Work too
I shall employ every
Blame shall be mine
Whatever may
Object, is to be prep
the best Situation to
I am anxious t
arrives, you will be
to So. Carolina, by
hitherto been experi
With very great

Hon. Major Genl. G

Gen. Washington to Gen. Greene

DEAR SIR,

    I wrote you so fully and freely by Lieut. Colo. Lee, who left me about the 29th ulto. that I have at this Time but little else to say, than to acknowledge the Receipt of your Letter of the 25th ulto. which came to hand two Days ago, and by which I am surprized to find that you have received nothing from me later than the 28th of Septem'r.

    Since my last, the American Troops destined to the Northward, except the 2d N. York Reg't, who march with the prisoners by Land, have all embarked, with their stores, & are I fancy by this Time arrived at the head of Elk—Those under the Command of Maj'r Gen'l St. Clair, who are ordered to join your army, began their march on the 5th and I hope are well advanced.—The French fleet left the Bay, as I am informed, about the 6th or 7th—and from the last accounts I have been able to obtain of the British, who were last seen stand'g Southerly on the N. Carolina coast, there is but a possible Chance of the two fleets meeting.—L'd Cornwallis, with the British Officers going to N. York & Europe, fell down the River York on the 4th. The Prisoners who are to remain in the Country are all marched to Winchester & Fort Frederick, except such sick as remain too bad to remove—of these there are still a considerable Number.—

    I am thus far myself on my Way to the Northward—I shall remain but a few Days here, & shall proceed to Philadelphia, where I shall attempt to stimulate Congress to the best Improvement of our late Success, by tak'g the most vigorous & effectual Measures, to be ready for an early & decisive Campaign the next Year.—My greatest Fear is, that Congress viewing this stroke in too important a point of Light, may think our Work too nearly closed, & will fall into a State of Languor & Relaxation—to prevent this Error, I shall employ every Means in my Power—and if unhappily we sink into that fatal mistake, no part of the Blame shall be mine—

    Whatever may be the Winter politics of European Courts, it is clearly my opinion, that our Grand Object, is to be prepared in every point for War—not that we wish its Continuance, but that we may be in the best Situation to meet every Event.—

    I am anxious to know whether the British fleet drops a Reinforcement at Charlestown—before this arrives, you will be informed from my last that a chain of Expresses will be established from Philadelphia to So. Carolina, by which means I hope to hand a more frequent Communication of Intelligence than has hitherto been experienced with your Army.

    With very great Regard & Esteem,

                        I am,
                              Dear Sir,
                                  Your most obedient and
                                      most humble Servant,
                                          G. WASHINGTON.

Hon. Major Genl. Greene.

The Don Who Loved a Donna

By Will M. Clemens

THIS is the Story of a Brave Man, who some years ago was known to the hundred or more persons composing the population of San Juan, a mining camp in Arizona. He was a Mexican, this brave man, named Don Juan Cubebico, and he was without question the ugliest "greaser" who ever stole a horse or ate a *tamale*. He was short and thin, blackhaired and pockmarked, garlic scented and tobacco-stained, and in the making of his pure white soul bleaching powder must have been freely used.

The Don claimed to be of Spanish blood, but my instinct taught me to trace his lineage through an Apache on his mother's side and a horse thief at the fraternal end of his genealogy. He once boldly declared before a well-filled bar room that he was heir to the Spanish throne, and it is easily remembered how, for a brief moment, he was in danger of falling heir to a rope dangling from the limb of a cottonwood tree. That brief moment and the noble bearing of the Don saved his funeral expenses.

His noble bearing was the secret of his bravery; he related stories of how he had slaughtered Gringos in the early days and accompanied his recital by whetting his hunting knife on a pair of boots that he had stolen from the camp at Red Creek three years before. When he could borrow tobacco, he would nimbly roll it in corn-husks and smoke

cigarettes with great gusto. I have often thought how it would have pleased the soul of a Madrid cavalier to observe the Don blow smoke through his nose—always with that same outward indication of nobility. He was ever a brave man—in telling of deeds of the past, and of the hosts of men he had killed "too dead for smelling."

Of the hundred men in San Juan, including of course the four Chinese and the six women, there were others almost as brave and self-assuring as Don Juan Cubebico. It could not have been otherwise in that typical town of a typical state of a typical nation. There was Patrick Farrelly, for example, another brave man, who died not from a want of nobility of character, but merely from a lack of common sense. In an evil moment, Mr. Farrelly conceived the idea that a little powder thrown upon some green hemlock would facilitate its burning. Thereupon he directed a small stream from his powder keg upon the burning wood, but, not possessing a hand and a presence of mind quick enough to cut off the stream of powder at the proper moment, he was blown into a thousand fragments; whereupon, Judge Barton, himself a brave man, who was also coroner, was called upon to render a verdict, which he delivered with great gravity as follows: "Patrick's death can't be called suicide, 'cause he didn't mean to kill

494

himself. It wasn't a visitation of God, 'cause he wasn't struck by lightning. He didn't die for want of breath, for he hadn't anything to breathe with. It is very plain he didn't know what he was about, so I will bring in a verdict that the deceased died for want of common sense."

Shorty French was another brave man, who in his day was the champion cow-puncher of Rhubarb Creek. Soon after his arrival amongst us at San Juan he proposed the formation of a Society for the Preservation of Sanitary Measures, and for two weeks he didn't dare lay down his gun, for fear some one would "get the drop on him." After the excitement had somewhat abated, Mr. French, who was a born organizer, suggested the formation of an Olive-branch Benevolent Association, with meetings to be held monthly in Murphy's saloon. At the first monthly meeting three members were killed and four others badly knifed. For a long time it was thought that the president, Pete Riley, could not recover, for his skull was badly mashed by a billiard cue as a result of his decision on a point of order. The billiard cue was turned over to the sheriff as evidence in case Pete did not recover. Well, he did not die, and the sheriff retained the billiard cue waiting for Pete to die a natural death. The sheriff was always looking forward for the impossible to happen.

Out of the four Chinese in San Juan only one could be called a brave man. He was Lee Chung, aggressive and consequently successful. When there was war in the Chinese end of the town and the air was filled with Hong Kong swear words Lee Chung was nearly always the victor in the dis-

putes. On a certain occasion, when Lee landed "a good one" on Ah Wong's nose with a flat iron, the whole camp acknowledged Lee's bravery, for Ah Wong was not able to smell for a month.

Recalling the six women in San Juan, the less said the better. Two, however, were undoubtedly brave to the extent of a brief mention. Rose Jenkins was a white woman who won the bitter enmity of the Chinese because she was in the habit of taking home washing. She was a lame girl and far from beautiful, but she was brave, else she would have never consented to marry Bill Badger. The entire town admired her for this, and when the marriage ceremony took place at the water-tank she was the recipient of many beautiful presents, including a pair of brass knuckles and a hog-ringer. The new preacher performed the ceremony. They called him Parson Brown. I understand he was allowed to remain in town under one condition: he was handy with the fiddle and thus helped out on festival occasion. Well, he married Bill and Rose at the water-tank, and every one in camp turned out to make the event a complete success. Rose had attired herself gaily for the occasion, having smuggled into the camp, a yachting cap and a new pair of overalls. After her marriage Rose, at her husband's request, continued to take in washing.

The other brave woman was a half-breed from the Sioux tribe across the range. One day in early spring she drifted into camp with her aged father, along with the first robins, so we called her Princess Birdie. It was a hard life for her and all the worse after she met with a serious accident, losing her right foot by falling between two cattle cars. After that she was forced to earn her living as best she could. For an entire season she made money by giving music lessons on a police whistle which was a present from the sheriff. Birdie's great failing was the weakness displayed by women everywhere: all the money she earned she spent on dresses. In the dug-out, half a mile from town, where she and her father lived, she hoarded her possessions—all sorts of things, from rubber boots to army overcoats. Birdie would bloom out every now and then in a hoop-skirt or a plug hat, while her poor old father would sit around the dugout waiting for night to come, when he could paint his trembling legs with pitch, in order to slide into town after dark and get a supply of chewing tobacco.

But of all these brave ones in San Juan, the "greaser," Don Cubebico, was the bravest of the brave. He had one fault and only one—with all his bravery he was brutal. He loved to see his fellow man suffer pain and sorrow; his heart was hard and his brutality always seemed to assert itself. Doubtless the horse-thief blood in his paternal ancestry had much to do with this peculiar trait in his character. The little burro upon which he rode in and out of camp was a patient beast, and it stirred one's blood to see him choke the animal with his infernal Spanish bit, or to observe the way he dug his ugly spurs into the burro's scarred and battered flank.

The sweetheart of Don Cubebico—wherever you find the "greaser" you also find a sweetheart—lived across the *arroyo*, where she raised red pepper in a bit of a garden patch. The dusky Donna Bettina occupied a small adobe house with her old mother, who was very, very old, very wrinkled, and very blind. In many ways the Donna was a counterfeit presentment of Don Cubebico, but inasmuch as the Don loved her devotedly she differed from him in this one respect, for she was inconstant. She deceived him and toyed with his heart in a manner that boded her nothing but evil, and the result of her folly was sure to come sooner or later. Would that we had had a poet in San Juan better able to tell this sad, strange tale of Gringo love, for

When the Don had gaily gone,
    Marauding in the valleys,
His donna fed some other Don,
    Frijoles and *tamales.*

Sufficient to the night is the danger thereof, and there must come an end to all deception and to wronged love. Women cannot play with the hearts of men forever and forever; there must come a day of retribution.

One evening late in the month of October, there was a tragedy in San Juan. Just as the moon was peeping over the Cuyamaca Range and the tarantulas were closing the front doors of their dew-covered nests and the coyotes were slinking out from the mountains, Don Cubebico rode in from the far south mounted on a stolen horse. He brought with him a phenomenal appetite for supper, as he had had a hard day's ride. Across the *arroyo* he rode, a cigarette clinched between his teeth. In the garden of red peppers he found his Donna at the gate bidding *adios* to a stranger—a Gringo he had never seen before.

It was all over in a moment. The Don alighted from his stolen horse, crept stealthily as the wild cat upon the two at the garden gate, and then with the grunt of a Sioux he plunged his knife into the back of his rival, who dropped at his feet without a murmur. The scream of fright and agony that the Donna essayed to utter was stifled before it could be given birth, for Cubebico, true to his race and birthright, choked her to death with his long and sinewy fingers.

The Don stood there a moment in the presence of the two dead ones, and then, calmly rolling a fresh cigarette and lighting it, he wiped the blood from his hunting knife on the pampas grass at the side of the garden gate, and, remounting his stolen horse, he again crossed the *arroyo* on a gallop to the town. At the stage-house he broke down the door, robbed the till of the gold he found there, added a new blanket and a Colt's revolver to the pommel of his saddle, and, remounting, dug his spurs deeply, and flew away like the wind to the mountains beyond the plain.

The other brave man in San Juan buried the Donna and her lover side by side with their feet to the south. It required no special reasoning to couple the murder with the burglary at the stage-house, and Don Cubebico from that time was a marked man, a much-wanted man. I believe the sheriff of San Juan is looking for him even to this day. But when the Bravest Man in San Juan left the camp he left it never to return, and now only the memory of his daring lingers like a dream among the miners.

Homesickness

By Ethelwyn Wetherald

A T twilight on this unfamiliar street,
  With its affronts to aching ear and eye,
    I think of restful ease in fields that lie
Untrodden by a myriad fevered feet.
  O green and dew and stillness! O retreat
Thick-leaved and squirrel-haunted! By and by
I too shall follow all the thoughts that fly
  Bird-like to you, and find you, ah, how sweet!

Not yet—not yet! To-night it almost seems
  That I am speeding up the hemlock lane,
    Up to the door, the lamp, the face that pales,
And warms with sudden joy. But these are dreams.
  I lean on Memory's breast, and she is fain
    To soothe my yearnings with her tender tales.

The Pennsylvania Germans

By Lucy Forney Bittinger

(Continued from May number).

WE have now reached another, in many ways a new, period in the annals of the Pennsylvania Germans; the Province was being settled up; the frontier had passed the Susquehanna; "the Mountains" were now the new country, whence came tales of Indian invasion. In this settlement the Germans had taken the lead and it was only later that the Scotch-Irish gained a place at their side.

The Pennsylvania Germans were not only settling up the State which has given them its name, but Virginia and North Carolina had many emigrants from Pennsylvania. In 1746 Shenandoah and Rockingham Counties, in Virginia, were being settled by them. A letter from Lawrence Washington, about 1750, speaks of his endeavors to get "Pennsylvania Dutch" settlers for the lands of the Ohio Company, in which he and his brother George were so much interested. Another like project was more successful; Col. Shepherd (his name had been Schaeffer and he was himself a Pennsylvania German) induced many colonists of his own race to settle in Virginia and so Shepherdstown was founded, in 1742. Six years later, we hear of Germans at Redstone (now Brownsville on the Monongahela) a famous point of departure, for the "great West" of pre-Revolutionary days.

"What Pennsylvania owes to her German farmers has been freely acknowledged. Indeed the farm of a German or Pennsylvania German, betrays at the first glance, that intelligent management and honest labor have gone hand in hand to make a fruitful and beautiful property. Their superiority in the tillage of the ground, the breeding of fine cattle, the building of suitable stables and barns, as well as their unpretending, suitable and simple style of living, induced the well-known Doctor Benjamin Rush to make them the subject of an ethnological study, which he published in 1789 in the Columbian Magazine, not only to do them justice, but to spur on others to imitate them. The Germans in Pennsylvania had gained an honorable reputation in many kinds of manufacturing. * * * German millers, brewers, tanners, sugar-refiners, merchants, innkeepers, butchers and bakers were proportionately as numerous as now. The Pennsylvania Germans particularly distinguished themselves as iron-masters. Ten years after the first forge was begun in Pennsylvania, we find the furnace of the German Mennonite Kurtz in Octarara in Lancaster County. In Berks County, which was early the center of the iron manufacture, most of the iron-masters were Germans. The Oley Smithy was erected in 1745 by two Germans and an Englishman."

In the Indian wars which desolated the once peaceful frontiers of Penn's colony during the long struggle between France and England for the possession of America, the Pennsylvania Germans bore an active part. Their leader, in war and diplomacy, was Conrad Weiser, whom we last saw falling under the influence of the mystic Beissel; but this was only a passing phase of the stirring career of Weiser. He had been brought up among the Indians of New York and adopted into the Six Nations; he was at all events known and trusted by them. The Province of Pennsylvania employed him again and again to negotiate with his "Indian brothers" until the plottings of the French made all negotiations useless, and Braddock's defeat brought down clouds of confident Indian warriors upon the frontier settlements. Among the pioneers killed or taken as prisoners were many Germans; it is estimated that in the Indian attacks of the next eight years, three hundred fell victims. There were massacres at Tulpehocken (Weiser's home) and at Gnadenhütten, the Moravian town of Christian Indians. There is no evidence that these Indians took part in the atrocities of their heathen kinsmen. But the white men suspected them, the Indians hated them, and a wandering band of Munseys fell upon the settlement, set fire to the houses, and murdered missionaries and converts alike, as they sought to escape. The counties of Lancaster, Berks and Northampton were invaded. Then Weiser took up arms with such a host of other Germans that the provincial legislature ordered that all officers of its militia should be chosen among those able to speak German. A chain of forts was established along the line of the Kittatiny mountains; the Moravian bishop at Bethlehem put his town in a state of defence which commanded the admiration of the authorities, and the savage tide was held back, but only for a time. Treaties and conferences, destruction of Indian towns and building of frontier forts alternated with massacres and plunder, scalping and

capture, for eight years. Weiser died in the midst of this misery, and was buried in the graveyard of Womelsdorf.

Weiser's mantle, as a negotiator trusted by white men and Indians alike, fell upon another German Christian, Frederic Post. Let us hear for him and his fellow-missionaries of the Moravian church, the witness of the historian Parkman—not prepossessed in favor of Pennsylvania Germans or missionaries to the Indians:

"He had been sent at the instance of Forbes as an envoy to the hostile tribes from the Governor and Council of Pennsylvania. He spoke the Delaware language, knew the Indians well, had lived among them, had married a converted squaw, and by his simplicity of character, directness and perfect honesty, gained their full confidence. He now accepted his terrible mission and calmly prepared to place himself in the clutches of the tiger. He was a plain German, upheld by a sense of duty and a single-hearted trust in God; alone, with no great disciplined organization to impel and support him, and no visions and illusions, such as kindled and sustained the splendid heroism of the early Jesuit martyrs. Yet his errand was no whit less perilous. And here we may notice the contrast between the mission settlements of the Moravians in Pennsylvania and those which the later Jesuits and the Sulpitians had established. . . . The Moravians were apostles of peace, and they succeeded to a surprising degree in weaning their converts from their ferocious instincts and warlike habits; while the Mission Indians of Canada retained all their native fierceness, and were systematically impelled to use their tomahawks against the enemies of the Church."

Post's first journey was successful, amid perils that rival those enumerated by the apostle Paul. He and his companions lost their way, they lost each other; they came upon scalps, "one with long white hair," hung to dry upon a bush; when he reached the Indian town the young warriors rushed at him to kill him, pressing their knives against his undaunted breast; war parties hung in the dark skirts of the forest to take his scalp if he ventured from the friendly radiance of the camp-fire. Yet from all these dangers he brought back an answer of peace. The "Great Council" of Easton called to all the tribes on the Ohio to stand neutral, while Forbes moved against Fort Duquesne. Post was chosen to bear this message and plunged again into a wilderness in which the soldiers who escorted him part of the way were murdered by lurking Indians as soon as they left him, where "wolves made a terrible noise" at night, and Indians "were possessed by a murdering spirit and with bloody vengeance were thirsty and drunk." The message was received; the tribes sat quiet, and Forbes was left to descend on Fort Duquesne, unmolested by the Indians who had hitherto been the most dreaded auxiliaries of the French.

In 1761, Post built a block-house and established a mission to the Indians in what is now the State of Ohio. But the Indians were suspicious, even of Post; then begrudged him the little piece of garden-ground which was all he asked; and in the next year Post returned, while Heckewelder, his young assistant (at the time of his first missionary journey but nineteen years old) left the block-house in Stark County and went to assist Zeisberger, "the apostle of the Delawares." in his work. The mission was thus abandoned, but the block-house, of which a few remains still exist, was the first habitation of civilized man in the present State of Ohio.

Another of these "plain German" heroes deserves more than the passing mention I can give him; this was David Zeisberger. Born in Bohemia and taken thence when a little child, on his parents' flight to the protection of Count Zinzendorf, he grew up in an atmosphere of hardship and self-sacrifice. He early consecrated himself to work among the Indians, but always, through his long life, refused any salary, preferring to serve "without any view of a reward other than such as his Lord and Master might deign to bestow upon him." He studied their language in Pyrlaeus' school for Indian missionaries, at Bethlehem; then went to Onondaga, the capital of the Six Nations, to perfect himself in their tongue. Here he was adopted into the Iroquois clan of the Turtle, and was made "Keeper of the Wampum" (or records of treaties) to the confederacy. His life is the history of the Moravian mission among the Delawares—a history "full of sadness, of faithfulness and of discouragement." The little flock which he had gathered fell under suspicion resulting from the acts of their heathen kinsman in Pontiac's conspiracy; they were requested to come to Philadelphia, that the provincial government might better protect them. Arrived there, a howling mob pressed upon them and their faithful Zeisberger, who had accompanied them, and threatened their lives. Presently they were exiled to New York, but the authorities of that province refused to receive them. They came back, dragging wearily through the snow, for it was now December. Their missionaries remained with them through an epidemic of small-pox and an imprisonment of more than a year; then the poor creatures, only half of whom survived, were permitted to go, but not to their homes. They sought a new asylum, farther from the white man, on the Susquehanna, and gave it the pathetic name of "Frieden-shütten, "the Tents of Peace." And it was the abode of peace for a few years.

It was not till the French were finally driven from Fort Duquesne and Pontiac's conspiracy crushed, that there was any security from scalping-knife and tomahawk for the pioneers of Pennsylvania; and this was chiefly accomplished by Colonel Bouquet and his regiment, the "Royal Americans," largely recruited among the Pennsylvania Germans. This regiment's part in the "Old French War" is today forgotten in the land which they helped to save for England; but it was none the less a brave part. Raised the year after Braddock's defeat, when two years old and become the 60th of the Line, it helped to take Louisburg in the north, and, under Forbes and Bouquet, drove the French from Fort Duquesne and made it Fort Pitt, thus breaking that chain of French forts erected and maintained with such proud dreams and deep-laid plans by the men of New France. In that same year it was their desperate valor that hurled itself against Montcalm's abatis at Ticonderoga, where their gallant foe wondered, as they attacked him six successive times—"masses of infuriated men who could not go forward and would not go back; straining for an enemy they could not reach, and firing on an enemy they could not see; caught in the entanglements of fallen trees, tripped by briers, stumbling over logs, tearing through boughs; shout-

ing, yelling, cursing, and pelted all the while with bullets that killed them by scores, stretched them on the ground, or hung them on jagged branches in strange attitudes of death." (Parkman.) In the following year, they were with Wolfe at Quebec; it was their imprudent gallantry which was beaten back in the assault at Montmorenci; but afterward came that sad, triumphant day when Wolfe and Montcalm died—the one in his victory, the other murmuring in defeat and death, praises of the steadiness of his English foe. No wonder that "the 60th of the Line" still bears proudly the motto "granted for distinguished conduct and bravery under Wolfe"— *Celer et Audax*. The Royal Americans helped to garrison their conquest during the bitter winter of 1760 and to hold it when its fate trembled in the balance as the French tried to retake it. It was their colonel who received the surrender of Canada, when Montreal, the last stronghold of France, dipped the lilies to St. George's cross.

Again, it was the Royal Americans who garrisoned the little forts throughout the wilderness on which fell the horrors of Indian massacre in Pontiac's conspiracy. Perhaps men more experienced in Indian treachery would have been able to cope with the deceitful savages successfully; the men of the 60th fell helpless victims in many cases, though not without gallant, unavailing resistance; and many of them died bravely, horrible deaths of murder and torture. One of their battalions had been in the army that took Martinique and Havana. Returning, much broken, from their tropical campaign, they found yet harder work

before them.   Pontiac's plot had set
the whole frontier ablaze and one of
the two forts which held out, was their
own conquest, Fort Pitt.   Colonel
Bouquet ventured to lead an expedition for its relief.   Plunging into the
woods which had entrapped Braddock,
with a little handful of his Royal
Americans, a few invalided soldiers just
from Havana, and some provincials,
he was surrounded by a mob of "howling and yelping" savages, a few miles
from Fort Pitt.   For two days his men
fought against a foe they could not
see and who simply disappeared when
attacked.   The second day a pretended
retreat was devised, and the joyous
savages, pursuing their prey, were
drawn into an ambush and destroyed.
"The behavior of the troops, on this
occasion," wrote Bouquet, "speaks for
itself so strongly, that for me to attempt their eulogism, would but detract from their merit."   Five days
after, the distressed and exhausted
garrison of Fort Pitt were relieved and
Pennsylvania's frontiers saved from
farther Indian warfare.   Bouquet and
his men remained at Fort Pitt a year,
during which time he marched into the
wilds of Ohio and at the Muskingum,
made a treaty with the now humble
conspirators of Pontiac and forced
them to restore all the captives taken
during the last eight years of savage
warfare.

Among the prisoners a young German girl was recovered and brought
to Carlisle.   Her mother had come
with the hope of finding her daughter,
but was unable to recognize her, after
the years of separation.   Telling her
trouble to Colonel Bouquet, he asked
if there was nothing by which her child
might remember her.   Recalling a

hymn she used to sing, at his advice
she sang:

Einsam, und doch nicht ganz alleine
bin ich in meiner Einsamkeit,
Denn wann ich gleich verlassen scheine,
Vertreibt mir Jesus selbst die Zeit:
Ich bin bei Ihm und Er bei mir,
So kommt mir gar nichts einsam für."
(Alone, yet not alone am I, tho' in this
solitude so drear. I feel my Jesus always
nigh; He comes, my dreary hours to cheer.
I am with him and He with me; I cannot
solitary be.)

As the old mother finished this hymn
of the wilderness the girl threw herself into the singer's arms.

The authority and the machinations
of France in the Western wilderness
alike were ended.   The Royal Americans were reduced to a peace footing;
and many of the officers and men, leaving the service, settled in the colonies
they had defended—a body of German
soldiery which England had enlisted
and trained—for what?   When the
Revolution came, they knew; and perhaps England knew also.

In the time of peace between the
close of the old French War, and the
approach of the Revolution, the Germans of Pennsylvania seem to have
given themselves especially to the development of what was to be the great
iron industry of their State.   John
Pott, the founder of Pottstown, made
stoves there in 1749 which he decorated with Scripture scenes, and designs of pots of flowers, in punning
allusion to the English meaning of his
name, and with such verses as this:

"Wer daruber nur will lachen,
Der soll es besser machen.
Tadeln konnen ja sehr viel,
Aber besser machen ist das rechte Spiel."

But the bright particular star in this
field—call him rather a comet—was

"Baron" Stiegel; whence he came, no one knows. In 1763 he bought a quantity of land in Lancaster County and purchased Charming Forge, which dated back to the beginning of Potts' iron manufactures, and also another German forge, the Elizabeth, started in 1750 and renowned for remaining in blast for a hundred years. Stiegel built two "castles" on his extensive property, which are said to have been decorated with enamelled tiles and tapestry,—wonders in those days. A cannon was fired to announce the coming of the "Baron," his workmen left the forge and took up musical instruments to welcome him. But the inhabitants called one of the mansions "Stiegel's Folly," and prophesied a ruin, which was not long in coming. Stiegel is said to have cast on his stoves the boast,

> "Baron Stiegel ist der Mann
> Der die Oefen machen kann."

It is certain that he was the first to make flint-glass in Pennsylvania, and that he founded the pretty town of Manheim in Lancaster County, in connection with his works. The outbreak of the Revolution, combined with his visionary extravagances, ruined him.

Christopher Saur the younger, who inherited his father's business, made paper, printer's ink, and lampblack, and was the first type-founder of America; the excellence of his types was attested by the Provincial Convention of 1775, which advised patriots to use them in preference to imported types. He is said to have been also the originator of the stoves which were afterward developed by Benjamin Franklin and bore the latter's name.

When the Stamp Act drew from the merchants of the colonies the decision not to buy any English wares, among the names signed to the Philadelphia declaration of such intentions, are those of many prominent German merchants. Their paper, the "Staatsbote," was so rejoiced at the appeal of the Act, that it "dropped into poetry" and headed its jubilant "extra" announcing the fact, with

> "Den Herren lobt und benedyt,
> Der von der Stempel-Act uns hat befreit."
> (The Lord be praised, who has freed us from the Stamp Act.)

"The Germans," says Bancroft, "who formed a great part of the inhabitants of Pennsylvania, were all on the side of Freedom." High praise, but borne out by no less an authority than Dr. Franklin, who, when examined before a committee of Parliament as to the American dissatisfaction, was asked, "How many Germans are there in Pennsylvania?" "Perhaps," said Franklin with characteristic caution, "a third of the whole population, but I cannot say certainly." "Have any part of them served in European armies?" inquired the British, anxious to estimate the strength of their opponents. "Yes," said Franklin, "many of them," probably in allusion to the Royal American regiment. "Are they as dissatisfied with the Stamp Act as the natives?" "Yes," responded Franklin, "even more so."

When the British measures against Boston showed that war could not be far off, all over the country the Committees of Safety and Committees of Correspondence sprung up and addressed themselves to the task of organizing resistance to the British with that energy and fertility of resource which we have now learned to call American. Whoever takes the trouble to look through archives and county histories of Revolutionary times will find the Pennsylvania Germans well represented on all these Committees; to give the names which prove it would be tedious, but in this, which might be called the civic part of the resistance to England, they bore their full share. A document, important for the light it throws on the feelings of the Germans of Philadelphia, was sent out by the German churches and the Deutsche Gesellschaft in that city. It was addressed to the Germans settled in New York and North Carolina, and its spirit, as well as its expressions, are interesting. It shows a confidence in the reasonableness of the whole body of patriots, that appeals such as these—argumentative, grave, unimpassioned—were relied on, instead of the frothy rhetoric which characterized the French Revolution, ten years later.

"We have from time to time been daily witnesses, how the people of Pennsylvania, both rich and poor, approve the resolution of Congress; especially the Germans of Pennsylvania, far and near, have distinguished themselves and not only raised militia, but formed select corps of Yaegers who are in readiness to march wherever they are ordered; and those among the Germans, who cannot serve themselves, are thoroughly willing to contribute for the common good, according to their means. Therefore we have been sorry to learn, that Congress had received news that different German people in Trion County, and some few in other parts of the colony of New York, have shown themselves unfriendly to the common cause and that many Germans in North Carolina are of the same way of thinking. But one can easily excuse the people of Trion County; they live too far from those great cities and ports, where one

can, week by week and often day by day, read and hear reliable intelligence of all that happens in England and the colonies;"

and the letter proceeds, on the dignified assumption that information is all that is wanting to those lukewarm Germans, to give a short account of the causes of the rebellion, of Lexington, "where the first blood was split in this unnatural war," of the "yet greater blood-bath" of Bunker Hill, and of the burning of Charlestown.

The Staatsbote was, in those times, a trumpet giving no uncertain sound: "Think," it said, "and tell your families of this, how you came to America with the greatest hardships and toil, to escape from servitude and to enjoy the blessings of freedom. Remember, that the English statesmen and Parliament would have America in the same case and perhaps worse off." Miller, the publisher of the Staatsbote, was the printer to Congress; and Steiner and Cist, a German firm of booksellers, published translations of Paine's "Crisis" and his "Common Sense."

Another German who served his adopted country, was Michael Hillegas, who was chosen treasurer of the United Colonies; he remained for some time "the Spinner of the Revolution." The manufacturers of powder for the war were chiefly Germans, to judge by their names. Ludwig Farmer was, in later Revolutionary times, the Commissioner-General of the Continental forces; and the sturdy "Baker-General," Christoph Ludwig, deserves more than a passing mention.

Born in the little university town of Giessen in 1720, he had a life full of adventure behind him when, in 1754, he settled in Philadelphia. He had fought the Turks, he had served the great Frederick, he had been to India and sailed the seas for seven years, before he was a baker in Pennsylvania. He was an imposing soldierly man and people called him jestingly "the Governor of Letitia Court." When the Revolution broke out, he was a man of more than fifty, but he gave himself to the cause of freedom with youthful ardor. He was a member of many conventions and committees; when resistance was resolved upon and the Convention hesitated at the cost of the proposed army, the old soldier rose and said, "Mr. President, I am only a poor ginger-bread baker, but put me down for two hundred pounds." The shamed Convention at once resolved to appropriate the money needed. In spite of his age, he served in the militia, but refused pay or rations. When some of his fellow-soldiers, disheartened at the hardships which they had to endure, were about to quit the camp, the old man threw himself on his knees before them and pleading with the deserters, shamed them into return to duty. "Comrades," he said, "when there is an alarm of fire, how we all run to put it out and save our own homes. Now save Philadelphia from a worse fire, the British army." It is said that he went in the character of a would-be deserter to the Hessian camp on Staten Island and "drew so enchanting a picture of the life of the Pennsylvania Germans that thousands, filled with longing for the flesh-pots of Pennsylvania and the blessings of freedom, embraced the first opportunity to desert." And Ludwig served the country, also, in the exercise of his calling. In 1777 he was appointed Inspector General of Bakers for the army. His predecessors had contracted to deliver 100 pounds of bread to every 100 pounds of flour, not taking into account the weight of the water in the bread. The same contract was offered to the new baker. "No," answered the honest old man, "Christoph Ludwig will not grow rich by the war. From 100 pounds of flour one bakes 135 pounds of bread and that will I give, no less." Small wonder that Washington, made acquainted with this unique specimen of an army contractor, entitled him his "honest friend." The baker was often invited to the General's table, frequently consulted in matters pertaining to his department, and became a great favorite with the officers. A certificate given him by Washington, testifying to the General's respect and good will for him, was carefully framed and formed one of the veteran's most cherished possessions. He lived to fourscore, a sturdy, cheery figure on the streets of Germantown, known to the inhabitants in affectionate jest as "our General." A table gravestone in the churchyard there, and the Ludwick Institute, a school which he endowed, perpetuate his name, but the story of Washington's "honest friend" and baker is wellnigh unknown to modern Americans.

Mere chronological mention of the battles of the Revolution in which the Pennsylvania Germans took part may give some idea of their patriotic efforts for the freedom of the land which had given them refuge from the grinding oppression of their Fatherland.

Among the first troops from outside of New England which hastened to join Washington's army before Boston in 1775, were a company from York County, Pennsylvania, commanded by Captain Michael Doudel.

It is said that so many wished to 'join it that the captain chalked the outline of a nose upon a barn-door at some distance and ordered the volunteers to fire at it. Only those who hit the mark were permitted to enlist. "General Gage, take care of *your* nose !" commented the provincial papers. A German company went from Cumberland County, under the command of Captain William Hendricks on the ill-fated expedition to Quebec in the same year, and their commander was shot down at the side of General Montgomery, just at the moment of what might have been victory. Hendricks was "tall, of a mild and beautiful countenance, his soul animated by a genuine spark of heroism." He was buried as he fell, beside his general, and the British officers marked their funerals with every honor which a soldier can show to a gallant and fallen foe.

The luckless regiment of Col. Miles's which was cut to pieces on Long Island in 1776, had many Germans in it, as the list of losses testifies. At Fort Washington the Germans in the "Flying Camp" suffered severely, being captured and subjected to the barbarities exercised upon "rebel" prisoners in the British prisons of New York.

On the same day that the Declaration of Independence was signed, the Pennsylvania German Associators" of Lancaster County were meeting at Lancaster, choosing their officers and passing rules for their association, for they made their Revolution "decently and in order." The participation of so many Lancaster County Germans in these war measures is the more remarkable in that a large part of the population of this county were, as they still are, Mennonites, Dunkers and

other non-resistants. Christoph Saur the younger, the son of the publisher of Germantown, who was himself an ardent non-resistant, a Dunker, laments that "whole companies of Mennonites are formed in Lancaster County and Quakers are drilling."

So marked was the patriotism of the Pennsylvania Germans that Congress, in 1776, resolved to form a German Regiment. It was to consist of eight companies, four from Pensylvania and the same number from Maryland ; but so many offered from Pennsylvania that a fifth company was enlisted under the command of David Wölpper. This man was a good specimen of the class from which came the best fighting material of the Revolution, the bushranging soldiers of the "Old French War." He had served in Germany under the great Frederick, had made several campaigns with Washington before Braddock's expedition, was well known and valued by him and through him recommended to Congress. A German nobleman, Baron v. Arendt, was its first active colonel, succeeded by Ludwig Weltner. The German regiment took part in the retreat across the Jerseys ; it shared the dramatic success which closed that gloomy year, the daring surprise of Trenton ; it fought at Princeton and Brandywine, and, attached to the German brigades commanded by Muhlenberg and Weedon. it nearly defeated the British,—indeed, would have done so, had not the American army retreated in a panic, "frightened at their own success," and left the two brigades unsupported. It shared the hardships of Valley Forge, and the next year made a campaign in the "Indian Country."

During the occupation of Philadelphia by the British troops, while the Continentals were freezing and starving at Valley Forge, their sympathizers in the city were made to have their share of suffering. The Deutsche Gesellschaft has already been mentioned as sending out addresses to the Germans in America to inspire them with some portion of its own Revolutionary ardor; in this it was joined by the principal men of the Philadelphia German churches, so the attention of the British was drawn to these patriots. The Deutsche Gesellschaft had just given out the contract for the building of a hall for the society; the materials were already deposited on the site, and the society had "resolved that the work be begun to-morrow," when the British occupation interrupted it. The English troops took the building materials to construct stables for their horses. They wrecked the printing office of Heinrich Miller, the printer to Congress, plundered the house of the sturdy patriot-baker, Christoph Ludwig, broke into the German Zion's-church and turned it and the Reformed church into hospitals. The pastor of Zion's-church, Ernest Henry Muhlenberg, took refuge in the country, where he employed his exile in the study of botany to such purpose that he became one of the first of American botanists, in point of time and attainments. His brother, Frederick A. Muhlenberg, had already fled from his pastorate in New York, on account of his dangerously outspoken patriotism. Pastor Schmidt of Germantown was another of these refugee patriots; while the preachers of the Reformed church, Schlatter and Weyberg, were imprisoned, Schlatter's house sacked and a reward was offered for the apprehension of a third rev-

erend rebel, Pastor Nevelling. The sugar-refinery of the Schaeffers was demolished, probably because they were connected by marriage with the patriotic Muhlenbergs.

It was not only the patriots who suffered at this time; the fortunes of war brought ruin on a man as honorable, an enterprise as well founded and widely known as any among the Pennsylvania Germans,—Christoph Saur the younger, and his printing office. The elder bearer of that name had died twenty years before; his business had been carried on by his son of the same name, a fact which has been a source of endless confusion to the few English writers who have alluded to the Saurs and their publications. The younger Christoph Saur was brought up in Germantown under his father's care; his mother, as has been previously mentioned, had entered Beissel's cloister at Ephrata as Sister Marcella. Her son was a devoted Dunker and became a minister in this body of non-resistant Baptists, of which Beissel's flock was an eccentric offshoot. On his father's death, the son took up the publishing business which the former had made so successful, saying, however: "I indeed would rather earn my bread by the book-binder's trade as heretofore, and be spared the burden of the printing-office, which would be much easier; but so long as there is no one here to whom I can entrust the printing-office, I find myself compelled by my duty to God and my neighbor, to carry it on until it may please Providence to give me a helper who will not let himself be moved by gold or flattery to print anything opposed to the glory of God and the welfare of the country; for to the welfare of the country and the glory of God, this printing-house is dedicated and I shall always seek to maintain this aim." Among many other publications, he brought out the second and third editions of the "Germantown Bible," as it is called by collectors; and as one of these editions was a source of considerable profit to him, he felt it his duty to share these profits with his customers and so printed and distributed (gratis) for two years the monthly publication called the "Geistliche Magazien," the first religious periodical which appeared in America.

A nobly conscientious man in everything, he was a determined opponent of slavery; that some Pennsylvania Germans now held slaves, was a grief and a reproach to Saur. A certain master advertised in Saur's paper his runaway slave, who had departed "barefoot, with a white shirt, an old hat, old linen small-clothes," etc., whereupon Saur printed, in larger type, beneath the notice these observations: "It is a wonder, that the above-mentioned negro was so foolish, and went off barefoot and in nothing but old clothes; he ought to have put on new ones (if he had any.) If masters oftener did what is right and just to their servants, and remembered that they also have a Master in heaven, many would not think of running away. But the love of money is the root of all evil."

The younger Saur was one of the founders of the still existent "Germantown Academy,"—in short he was an unselfish, courageous sympathizer with all good things,—all, at least, but the Revolution, which he, as a non-resistant, regarded as an unchristian taking-up of carnal weapons. When Germantown was filled with troops, he left

their hated neighborhood and took refuge with his sons in Philadelphia. Returning to Germantown in the next year, he was arrested by the Continentals, shamefully maltreated and finally, when delivered by the interposition of "the noble Gen. Muhlenberg," as Saur calls him, ordered to reside in the little village of Metuchen so long as the British were in the city. During his absence, he was declared a traitor, and when he came back to his home, he was put under arrest, his house, types, presses, etc., confiscated, and, with all his property, sold by the Commissioner of Confiscated Estates. Saur was completely ruined. He might have saved his property, had he been willing to take the oath of loyalty or appeal to the courts for justice, but these things being against his religious principles, he submitted without a word; though the reproach of being declared a traitor he deeply felt. The few remaining years of his life were spent in the house of a friend who gave him shelter, and in the exercise of his office as one of the unordained and unpaid ministers of his peaceful sect, for whose doctrines he had literally suffered "the loss of all things."

In these disastrous years of the Revolution many suffered besides patriots in captured cities, conscientious men like Christoph Saur, and shivering soldiers at Valley Forge. On the frontier were Indian attacks or massacres, instigated by the British at the western posts, often by means of such renegades as Simon Girty, the "White Savage," whose name was one of terror and execration all along the border. It was he who led the attack on Wheeling, then Fort Henry, and defended by Colonel Shepherd and but forty-two men and boys. More than half of these were cut off in an ambush early in the fight. Girty had with him about four hundred Indians, and taking post at one of the cabins outside the fort, —deserted at the first alarm,—he called to the garrison to surrender and go over to the British, as he had done; but Col. Shepherd answered that they would neither desert nor yield, and the unequal fight went on through the whole of a "warm, bright September day." The next morning, a body of militia relieved the fort and chased off the discomfited Indians. Many ot these border fighters showed so merci less a spirit, when chance gave them an opportunity to take vengeance on their savage enemies, that it is a pleasure to record of Col. Shepherd that, three years later, when with a party under Gen. Brodhead, making a foray into the "Indian country," his fellow-soldiers planned the massacre of the Christian Indians of the Muskingum, the defender of Wheeling dissuaded the rest from the attack and saved the Moravian mission, for the time.

The history of these missions belongs to the story of the Germans of Pennsylvania, for their most devoted workers were Germans, Zeisberger and Heckewelder. The latter was a most self-sacrificing man, a man who once rode three days and two nights to prevent an Indian outbreak, and succeeded; who escaped perils of savage ambush, and wild animals; who was the friend and associate of Washington and of Rufus Putnam; the author of valuable philological works on the language of his "brown sheep," the Delawares—a useful, cheerful man, simple and transparent in his character, who closed a long life at Bethlehem

and was buried there among the Indian converts.

Of Zeisberger's early life and labors we have before spoken. After many dangers and discouragements, he had led his converts again westward and had founded Gnadenhütten. This was the golden age of the mission. For ten years they had peace; several other villages were founded in the neighborhood. The first Protestant sermon preached in the state of Ohio was preached at one of these mission stations, in 1771; the first church and the first schoolhouse in the state were built by these German missionaries; the first white child of Ohio was the daughter of Heckewelder, born at Schönbrunn in 1773. Thus these Moravians were pioneers, and pioneers of the best type, nearly a score of years before the settlement of Marietta.

But when the Revolutionary war was nearly at its close, a band of Wyandots, instigated by the British, burst upon the settlement, drove away the converts and burned the houses and the church. Zeisberger was taken to Detroit; some of his Indians, starving, stole back to gather their harvests, when a band of militia,—white men, Christians, Americans—fell upon them, penned them in two cabins to which they gave the appropriate name of "slaughter-houses," and killed them, many of them women and children. The converts had given themselves to prayer and singing, when they found their death resolved upon, and so they died. For fourteen years the little remnant that escaped wandered about with their faithful pastor—to Michigan, to Canada, and back to the shores of Lake Erie. Then the Government offered them the site of their old home, when they went back, to the overgrown fields and blackened ruins. But Zeisberger was old, many of the converts were dead, the faith of many had failed among their trials and wanderings. The new home was but a feeble echo of the old, and when Zeisberger, nearly ninety years old, died, the settlement perished with him. A remnant of Christian Delawares, who have joined their brethren in Kansas, are all that now remains to tell of a work as self-sacrificing as Christianity can show, a destruction as cruel as history ever told.

We must return from this sad incident of the war, to the services of other Germans in the patriot armies. At the battle of Monmouth, fell Col. Rudolf Bonner of the Third Pennsylvania regiment,—distinguished by his gallantry in the fight. This regiment, and the Second, Fifth, Sixth and Eighth Pennsylvania, were filled and officered by Pennsylvanian or foreign Germans. The First Pennsylvania was the second regiment to enlist under Washington. It was more than half made up of Pennsylvania Germans, being recruited in Reading. Its colonel was Philip de Haas, an old soldier of Bouquet's of the French and Indian war. He was subsequently in command of a brigade. The adjutant, David Ziegler had fought in Russia against the Turks, then emigrated and, when the Revolution broke out, entered its army. Later he fought the Indians on the western frontier, and died as the first mayor of Cincinnati, in 1811.

A Reading family of Pennsylvania Germans, the Hiesters, deserves mention for the number of its members who entered the Continental service. One of them had already aided in defending his town against Indian invasion at the time of Pontiac's conspiracy. Four sons of the family were Revolutionary officers: Col. Daniel Hiester, Majors John and Gabriel, and Captain William Hiester. Daniel and John became Major-generals of militia, and a cousin, Joseph, was in the "Flying Camp," was captured at Long Island and became a colonel and later a major-general of militia.

In the early part of the war, a Saxon nobleman, Baron von Ottendorf, came to this country with Kosciusko. He had served under Frederick the Great and his services were gladly accepted by Washington. He was directed to raise an independent corps, which, filled in Pennsylvania, became a dragoon regiment and subsequently served as a nucleus for various unattached commands composed of, or officered by, Germans. It was merged into Armand's "Legion." After the heroic death of Pulaski, his command, which contained many Pennsylvania Germans, was united with the Legion. Another of the Great Frederick's soldiers, Capt. Schott, had recruited a company of dragoons among the same folk, and after Schott was captured (at Short Hills, in 1777), the remnant of his command was likewise incorporated in the all-embracing Legion. After Schott's release he resumed command of his company, which meanwhile had made a campaign on the frontier with the "German regiment" of Col. Weltner.

Another organization which consisted largely of Pennsylvania Germans, was Washington's provost guard, dragoons commanded by Major von Heer, also a pupil of Frederick II. The Prussian king's indirect services to the cause of American liberty in training officers for its army have been overlooked even by his determined panegyrist, Mr. Carlyle.

One of the "mountain men" who drove the British from the South by their brilliant border fight of King's Mountain was a Pennsylvania German, Hambright, a colonel of militia, who was wounded in the action but kept on fighting and helped to gain that victory of the Rear-guard of the Revolution.

The most distinguished officer among the Teutonic soldiers of the Revolution was a Pennsylvania German, Gen. Peter Muhlenberg. He was born in Montgomery County, Pennsylvania, and was the son of that patriarch of the Lutheran Church to whose labors I have already alluded. The three sons of the venerable clergyman were destined for the church, but Peter, who was lively, fond of hunting, and a general favorite, seemed little inclined by nature to this profession. He was educated, partially in Germany, where he ran away and enlisted as a soldier, earning among his comrades the nickname of "Peter the Devil." But on his return home, he settled down, was ordained, threw himself with characteristic ardor into ministerial work, and became the pastor of a church in the Shenandoah Valley colony of Pennsylvania Germans. Here he made the acquaintance of Patrick Henry, and often hunted with Washington. When the first stirrings of resistance to Great Britain were felt, the Rev. Peter Muhlenberg was made the chairman of the Committee of Safety for his county, and it was his eloquence and the votes of the German delegates from the "valley" that turned the scale in Virginia when measures of armed resistance were first discussed. Muhlenberg, still pastor of the Woodstock church, was made colonel of one of the regiments raised at this time. Then occurred that thrilling moment which is perpetuated in the statue of the patriot in the Capitol. I quote Seidensticker's description:

"The intelligence that Col. Muhlenberg would preach his farewell sermon drew together an extraordinarily large audience; not only the Woodstock church, but the surrounding church-yard was filled with people. In the most impressive manner, the speaker referred to the duties which their country and its good cause laid upon all, and concluded with the ringing words: 'There is a time to preach and pray, but also a time to fight; and the time to fight is come.' Then he pronounced the benediction. His career as a preacher was closed. There followed a scene, unique of its kind. He threw off the Genevan gown which he wore and stood before them in the full uniform of a soldier. Then he descended the pulpit and ordered the drums to be beaten. The enthusiasm burst into flame; many of his hearers enlisted in his regiment; old men brought their sons, women their husbands, as fellow-combatants with him for freedom. Nearly three hundred men from Woodstock and its neighborhood placed themselves under Muhlenberg's banner that day."

To tell of his services to his country would almost be to write the history of the war. He was fortunate in being almost always in active service and was exceptional among the officers of the Revolution by remaining in the army until the close of the war. At first in Virginia he was soon attached to Washington's army; the deeds of his men at Brandywine and Germantown have been described, their sufferings at Valley Forge and their valor at Monmouth. A characteristic scene occurred at Brandywine, where the Germans under Muhlenberg and Weedon held back the victorious advance of the whole British force and gave the shattered remants of the Continentals time to escape; again and again they drove back the English with the bayonet, when some Hessian officers, seeing their tall, fiery leader at the head of these stubborn defenders, cried out in sudden recognition, "There's Peter the Devil." When the South became the theatre of war, Muhlenberg was sent to Virginia to organize an army out of discouragement, apathy and poverty, and succeeded in performing the impossible so far as to furnish Gen. Greene with a respectable body of provincials. He was present at the concluding scene of the war at Yorktown. His Germans of Steuben's division were allowed to storm one of the redoubts, and being frontiers-men, accustomed to help themselves, they did not wait to have the abatis removed in regular military style, but tore it away with their hands and scrambled over, carrying the redoubt at the point of the bayonet; while the French at the other redoubt waited under a withering fire, until their abatis was properly removed by their pioneers. In five minutes more, both redoubts were carried, and Washington, looking on, summed up the War for Independence in the grave words, "The work is done, and well done."

(To be concluded.)

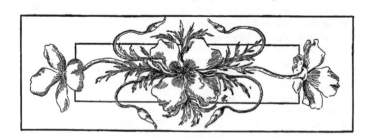

Photograph by Cassill

American Shrines X

Dorchester Heights

" Dorchester Heights witnessed that 'more than victory' commemorated in the first medal of our minted history, with its proud motto, *Hostibus primo fugitas:* the first rout of the enemy."

EDWARD EVERETT HALE.

NEW ENGLAND MAGAZINE

NEW SERIES   JULY   VOL. XXVI No. 5

Whale Oil and Spermaceti

By Mary E. Starbuck

"I know an Isle clasped in the Sea's strong
    arms,
Sport of his rage, and sharer of his dreams;
A barren spot to alien eyes it seems,
But for its own it wears unfading charms."
           EMILY SHAW FORMAN.

LOYALTY, with the islander, is rather an instinct than a principle. With the Nantucketer it is a passion. And this is hardly to be wondered at, for from that far-off day when the Indian deity, Man-shope, after eating his whale roasted over the volcanic fires of Gay Head, carefully knocked the ashes from his after-dinner pipe into the sparkling waters of the Sound and called the arid little heap "Nantucket,"* this low-lying island has been, nevertheless, a conspicuous object on the horizon of the New World.

---

*Nantucket signifies "it is heard" or "it is sounding," referring probably to the booming of the surf—or possibly to the hissing of the hot ashes as they fell into the sea.

The story has been told many times of how, less than forty years after the landing of the *Mayflower*, the island was bought and settled by a sturdy little company of Englishmen led by Thomas Macy and Edward Starbuck who, with the boy Thomas Coleman, spent here the first winter, testing the physical hardships differing only in degree from those of the mainland, rejoicing in the freedom from petty official tyranny which had driven them hither, and learning to know the friendly Indians—first inheritors of the pipe-ashes—whose hour was soon to strike.

As the tale unfolds we learn that upon these wave-washed, wind-swept sands, life is not only sustained and en-

515

dured, but in spite of drawbacks and disadvantages, becomes vigorous enough in course of time to pour out streams of colonial energy southward and westward, meanwhile maintaining a home city of some nine or ten thousand inhabitants, carrying on countless industries, sending ships to every known port and to the hitherto undiscovered countries of the islands of the Pacific; and at last, in its special business of the whale-fishery, leading the world.

Then the tide turned. Within ten years the "Great Fire," the decline of whaling, owing both to the necessarily longer and more expensive voyages and to the introduction of petroleum, and lastly the discovery of gold in California, combined to sweep away Nantucket's wealth and population, and brought her low before her rivals.

During the ebb of the tide, the civil War claimed the last generation of the men who, too young for participants, had been at least eye-witnesses of the prosperity, picturesqueness, and intellectual productiveness of the whaling days.

Then it was that many a brave and well-known Nantucket ship "made a good end," as she obediently sank by order of Government, to block the entrance to Charleston harbor. Since that time, Nantucket is no longer a force to be reckoned with, but a dear thing to be loved and cherished by her own. Her part is no longer to lead but only to remember. And it is this sentiment of pride and tenderness, so strong among the few surviving islanders at home and the many more "abroad," that has led to the organization of the Historical Association. And

if with the islander's loyalty there exists also a keen perception and enjoyment of his island's idiosyncrasies, let no presuming "stranger" think that he may freely share such enjoyment—it is for the elect alone.

Hospitality has its limits, and the old insular pride flames even more fiercely now than when, in the cosmopolitan days of the island's ascendancy and power, her children making their way all over the globe, hailing from a home port whose name was the open sesame to all harbors, could afford a hearty give-and-take with aliens whom in their island hearts they despised.

But the days of gay badinage are over. These are new times, and new people are coming in who do not know, who may not understand. With these new-comers we do not discuss our island home, though to the reverent and receptive mind often found among them, we may, when the mood takes us, reveal some of the reasons for our love and pride. And so we gather the symbols of the old life— and a motley collection it is.

There are household utensils from the days when wants were few and shops were none, and the necessity of the hour was manufactured and in use before the hour was up. Those were the times when, whatever might be the quality or qualification of a man's brain, his hands must be trained to some practical use; when a surveyor was also a tailor, a school teacher was a day laborer in other men's fields; when blacksmithing and coopering attained the importance and dignity of the learned professions in this almost

OLD MEETING HOUSE

ideal community where everybody was related to everybody else, with only twenty grandfathers among them, whose names were repeated over and over again on the outmost curve of the fan shaped family charts.

Of a later date, there are more beautiful articles brought, however, from foreign lands, for the time came when the well-to-do housewife sent directly to St. Petersburg for her six-yard damask tablecloths and "long towels," to Navarino or Leghorn for her big poke bonnets, to Lyons for her velvet capes and satin pelerines, to Callao and Talcahuana for exquisite embroidery and drawn-work.

Her messenger, the gallant captain of a gallant ship of which he was perhaps part owner, would order in Yokahama or Canton the long sets of fine china, dropping in at England, may be, on the way home, for the decoration of monogram, or coat-of-arms to which there was legitimate claim.

518

However, to the true Nantucketer domestic manufactures are always the most interesting, and in truth the islander could turn his hand to anything, from harpooning a whale to discovering a comet—having first invented the telescope that made this latter feat a possibility.

In these early days of home production, when, for instance, George Swain's wife needed a pricker for the appetizing biscuits baked in the covered kettle over the coals—and under too, since the cover with the turned up rim was filled with hot embers—it was George himself who deftly whittled out two thin discs of wood, pierced one with sharp pointed, handmade shingle nails, tacked the second disc firmly over their clumsy heads, and in the centre of the bristling nail points fastened the carved initials "G. S.," which thus proclaimed both ownership and skill.

From the same little Swain house at

Polpis—until its total collapse, a few years ago, the "oldest house on the island"—on the south side of the lovely harbor, came this cradle which rocked the first white child born on the island, little Mary Starbuck, daughter of the "Great Mary" whose influence, according to history, seems to have been equally powerful in spiritual and secular affairs.

Near the cradle stands a home-made loom, for weaving tape, holding still a bit of the stout web. Among the house furnishings, besides the ordinary lamp stands and ladder-backed, rush-bottomed chairs, we see also handsome three-cornered arm-chairs made at home for an island bride, a "swift" for winding her yarn, and even the embroidered satin slippers worn at her wedding; samplers and "mourning pieces" which can hardly be said to have "adorned" her walls, though the latter are exquisite specimens of silk tapestry work, beautiful

in color if not wholly satisfactory in composition.

Of course one finds in this museum a complete line of whaling-irons, compasses, signals, models of ships, and all the various odds and ends connected with shipping, for at one time Nantucket not only built ships but fitted them in every detail from stem to stern, from keel to truck.

Fascinating, too, for a rainy morning are the log-books recording the voyages of these said ships and holding between their stained leather or canvas covers most thrilling tales told simply in outline by the day's jottings.

As a rule the first mate kept the log and usually followed time-honored precedent in beginning with the direction of the wind, then stating the course of the ship, events, if any, like the raising of a sail on the horizon, a "gam," or the boarding of a derelict, the pursuit and capture or loss of a blackfish or a whale, the position of the ship as to latitude and longitude, and winding up with the familiar "so ends," whose full form, sometimes wholly written out, reads: "So ends the day by the grace of God."

The margins of these journals are enlivened with silhouettes of whales printed with a wooden die about two inches long; in case of capture the entire figure is given, with a square white space left in the centre, in which is written the number of barrels of oil obtained; in case of failure the flukes only are printed by one end of the same die.

Occasionally the illustrations of these old logs are done free-hand, and to the whales are added outline sketches of islands or carefully drawn miniature portraits of the ships that were met. We use the word portrait advisedly, for a ship comes to have in time a personality almost human. It gives one a curious sensation to come across a package tied up in a yellow newspaper of 1809 and carefully marked, "Papers belonging to the late ship Thomas"— lost on the "west coast" (of South America, of course).

On the other hand, the consideration shown to the human individuality of the crew as "crew" may have left something to be desired either in degree or mode of manifestation, probably both. Like the rigging, the crew belonged to the ship and were used with the same disregard of consequences, and in case of damage or loss were replaced with the same impersonal spirit. Outgoing short-handed ships often stopped at the Azores to recruit with Western Islanders, and the following entries, taken verbatim from a log-book are full of suggestion to the initiate who understands that the three entities at sea in order of importance are captain, ship, mate; everything and everybody else having merely a relative significance.

"Sunday, Aug. 2nd,

First part strong winds and squally from N. W. Lying off and on the north side of Flores. Boats on shore for recruits. At 6½ p. m. boats came on board and take our departure, steering S. S. E. under moderate sail. Thick weather.

Middle part steer S. E. by S. Make all sail.

Latter part steer S. S. E. to S. Saw breeches. Fayal in sight bearing E. S. E. 30 miles distant. At noon strong winds from N. N. W."

"Monday, Aug. 3rd.

First part strong winds, thick weather from N. N. W. Steer S. to S. S. W. by compass 2 points variation. Furl mainsail, fore and miz-topgallant sail and jib.

Saw killers.* Middle part strong winds, latter part much the same.

Overhaul recruits, etc. Lat. 36.00 north. Long. 28.52 at 4 p. m."

An imaginative mind, especially if it be feminine and more familiar with the absolute ways of a ship with a man than with the animus of the denizens of the "far-off, flashing, bright Azore," naturally wonders if the new recruits feel no regrets when they find themselves on board ship in rough weather, about to undergo the operation plus the "etc." thus briefly referred to above.

Visions of the night are often found in the logs, carefully marked for historical verification on arrival home, for the annals of the whaling days contain enough accounts of remarkable coincidences and mysterious happenings to keep any number of psychological so-

---

*A species of Orca. Cosmopolitan, carnivorous, living on marine mammals, often attacking the Right whale. Sometimes called the "wolves of the sea."

cieties in a pleasant state of excitement for an indefinite time.

Just one more log-book item, and we will leave the library for another day.

"Remarks on board ship Washington, 184. Nine months out.—25bbls. sperm oil.—Oh, dear!"

But think not that the momentary feeling of discouragement was anything more than that. The Nantucket captain was made of sterner stuff. Defeat was rarely encountered and never recognized. Tradition tells us that one of these captains, returning from a three years' cruise with an empty hold, met the pilot's hail of "What luck?" with the cheerful announcement, "Haven't got any oil, but I've had a mighty good sail!" The Historical Association does not happen to possess the documentary evidence of the truth of this statement, moreover it is a matter of history that never an empty hold was brought back to the bar by Nantucket captain;—but we all believe the essential truth of the story, revealing as it does the undaunted spirit of the man whom we all know.

Perhaps one of the most interesting of these collections is the string of lanterns extending quite across the room, just under the gallery—a portion remaining of the second floor where were taught the girls of the Quaker school, the boys being on the ground floor. This was the original purpose of the building which was later used as a Meeting House, the gallery enclosed with movable partitions serving for the business meetings of the women Friends.

From the lanterns, pathetically empty and wickless as they are, pale rays of light still slant backwards on the island life. For the seeing eye, their power of illumination has not quite vanished with the oil and spermaceti that fed them.

The perforated tin deck-lantern near the middle blinked its countless eyelids at the salt spray through some of those early and dangerous experimental voyages; though with a light behind them of literally one candlepower, as it swayed in the rigging in the night's darkness, it could hardly have given light enough to show more than its good intentions.

Rebecca Sims carried the next lantern at the right, on her merchant voyages about 1850, and the handsome brass mountings and chains of the middle lantern once brightened even the gloom of daylight in the cabin of a Macy whaler.

Third from the brass chains, and belonging to the period of fine houses and lavish entertainments, is suspended a hall lantern containing an elaborately fluted sperm oil lamp, while on its left might hang the very lantern of Dogberry and Verges, for it is truly made of horn, scraped to the pearly translucence of the Nantucket fog. It really does not date from Shakespeare's time, being but a modern affair, not more than fifty or sixty years old. It was made by the last elder or overseer of the "Fair St. Meeting;" a man of genius and of Quaker sanctity as well, who, one stormy First Day a few years ago, held, together with one woman Friend, the last service in the old meeting-house where his lantern now hangs.

Alone he sat on the men's side of the elder's raised bench facing the meeting, and after a few minutes of silence he was moved to ask Friend H., alone on her side in the body of the house, to come up and sit on the elder's bench, but she refused, feeling that she was not "worthy." So for the hour these two sat in the stillness. At last the Elder rose and came down the steps and with a grave hand-shake the meeting "broke up" and the two old worshippers, the last of their sect, passed out into the storm never more to meet in the beautiful silent communion of the Friends.

But this is a digression. Let us to our lanterns again. The Nantucket ship *Rose* carried the fourth lantern from the left on both whaling and merchant voyages. Artists seem to agree that this is the most beautiful of all the lanterns, on account of its proportions and of the exquisite openwork design of the copper mountings.

The tiny lantern, fifth on the right, is nothing more than a glass chimney with bottom and cover of metal, but it was a great improvement upon the tin lanterns, and its first owner, arriving late at his own wife's tea-party, gave as his excuse that his new lantern, being so much brighter than the moon, had bewildered him so that he had lost his way among the sand dunes of the cliff.

In the corner of the big fire-places of long ago, there used to hang a slender iron rod, and from a hook at the end there was suspended a little tin lamp like the third in the row, holding no more than a gill of sperm oil, and by the light of this "coffee-pot" lamp the wonderful old embroidery was done, as well as the coarser household sewing. A larger sized lamp and also a more elaborate one of the same style was used aboard ship. The latter had four tubes, each with a cotton wick which fed the

oil too freely for entire combustion, so the surplus trickled over into the little troughs under each tube and ran down into the lower compartment of the lamp. This method was thrifty and clean, even if odoriferous, but in the atmosphere of the fo'castle or the blubber-room, one smell more or less was probably a matter of no importance.

The big lantern, Number 9, used to swing aloft, "long in the forties," at the bow of a hand fire-engine, not differing greatly from some still in use on the island. One of these ancient "tubs" lately condemned by the town is now anchored fast to the old Meeting House. This machine is painted shrimp pink, its brass balls and bells are kept beautifully polished, its age is respected, and it is also carefully protected by a capacious tarpaulin for nights and wet days.

From the lanterns, one naturally drifts to the lamps, to which an entire case is devoted. This pewter lamp hung with a swivel was in constant use and perpetual motion for forty years in the cabin of the South Shoal lightship, forty miles off Nantucket to the south, whose mast-head lanterns are the last seen and first sighted by the outgoing and incoming European steamers.

The tiny pewter lamp in the foreground of the first group was the prophecy of the double-flounced "petticoat" lamp in the second group. And the pear-shaped ground glass lamp in the latter illustration is one of a pair still holding the molasses-colored whale oil with which it was filled by one of the famous Folgers some "thirty odd" years ago. It must not be inferred, however, that it has burned steadily ever since that time.

Among the first group mentioned

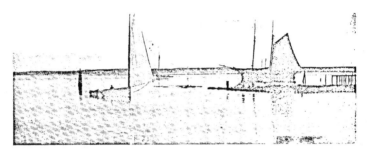

IN THE HARBOR

above are two rather unusual designs —the 200 year old pewter lamp with thick bull's eye reflectors, and the one of gaudily painted tin, with a flat wick and a tin shade, one of the last patented for sperm oil.

Between the two is a lamp-picker for raising the wick, made on board ship, the standard and handle shaped from a bit of whale's tooth; in the foreground is another, with the steel picker alongside.

The candlestick in whose covered saucer is contained flint, steel, and tinder and also home-made matches of shavings dipped in melted sulphur, is doubtless a familiar object to all New Englanders at least, and the snuffers are not at all uncommon in the East. The glass "dolphin" candlesticks belonged to the last resident member of the orthodox Wilerite Friends who owned the Meeting House. The lamp next the "petticoat," white glass with blue dots, is of interest as being the first kerosene oil lamp used in a private house in Nan-

tucket, probably in the year 1853, though previous to that a public exhibition had been given at the Ocean House of the new discovery for illumination. It was not sufficiently satisfactory, however, to convince the Nantucketer, who preferred the aromatic atmosphere to which he was accustomed, until the time came when the odor, smoke, and danger of kerosene had been greatly modified.

Between whale-oil and kerosene there was a short and exciting period of "fluid" which was nothing more nor less than a preparation of alcohol. An elaborate lamp of this time is at the left of the "petticoat."

We must not, as we leave the lamps pass the corner devoted to foot-stoves and fire-dogs without a brief glance at the pair of Dutch smokers once the property—whence acquired, who shall say?—of that Quaker importer and financier, Miriam Coffin. In a little case near by is her husband's bookplate, the cause of almost as much anxiety, when he brought from England

523

this significant bit of worldly vanity, as was aroused when Miriam built their ostentatious house in town. From that house came her thousand-legged table, and just above it hangs the blue-edged platter on which she served the much-prized calf's head dinner. There is on the wall a faded ambrotype of this famous woman, copied doubtless from an oil painting. The firm, strong features, the direct gaze, the expression of power and determination make us wonder to what extent her remarkable business ability was held in check by the ribbon strings of that dainty Quaker cap.

The portraits would require a day by themselves. Just a moment before the row of life-size silhouettes, all descendants of Ruth Gardner, who heads the procession.

True Nantucket faces all, of a vanishing type never to be reproduced. This early race served its turn in the one great scheme and the world is stronger because of it.

The old Nantucket is a thing of the past, along with the useless lanterns and the empty lamps, the folded hands and the closed eyes. A new Nantucket is being evolved, but what shall be its character no prophet may yet foretell.

Shepherd

By Stephen Tracy Livingston

SWEET word from old Judæan time,
　And Arcady of gentle ways,
What part hast thou in this our grime
　And haste and roar of modern days?

No peaceful swain with trebling reed
　Pipes to his flock by sunny rills;
Our sheep no guardian watcher need,
　To fold them on the starlit hills.

And yet, oh name forever blest,
　Thou still art ours to keep and love,—
While mothers guide small feet to rest,
　And God doth shelter us above.

BRIDGE IN PEASLEE MEADOWS

The King's Highway, Known as the Common Road From Swan's Ferry to Back River Mill

By Charles W. Mann

IN these days of modern road building, of Town, County, and State Highways (and even private ways) built of gravel and stone with the aid of heavy machinery under the control and management of able and specially educated men, and with large and increasing expenditure of public money for the construction and maintenance of our thoroughfares; when all are interested in and many are studying the subject of good roads; when everybody travels with all kinds of vehicles, from the twenty ton steam roller to the twenty pound bicycle; and all unite in desiring perfection in their highways (even if not reaching that point in all their ways), it will, perhaps, be of interest to look back into the very early history of our town and study the ways of our forefathers.

Our good old town of Methuen, Essex County, Massachusetts, lying between the Merrimac River and the New Hampshire line, and reaching from Haverhill to Dracut, was incorporated in 1725 because of the great difficulties under which the inhabitants

GAGE'S TAVERN, METHUEN

labored on account of "their remote-
ness from the place of Publick Worship."

The first public building, if it may
be called so, was the pound on Powder
House Hill, built the same year (1725),
one wall of which is still standing.

The first board of selectmen laid out
a road from Hawkes's meadow brook
to James How's well, which probably
extended from near the mouth of the
brook, where Elder Runels had his
farm in later years, connecting with
the path from Richard Messers' Ferry,
established two years before and later
known as Gage's Ferry, and continuing up over the hill by the old road.
This road, now long neglected and almost forsaken, is one of the most beau-

tiful of the many "woodsy" drives in
the vicinity. With a small expenditure
of money, it might be made safe for
pleasure travel, and would add one
more to the many attractions that our
town now possesses. Following on
through Currier Street, where are the
ruins of several very old houses,
around past Tozier's Corner (the corner of How and Hampstead Streets)
to the How Farm, where the highway
connected with the path running westerly, to the south of what was later
called World's End Pond, and now
known as Stillwater, it continued to
Mistake meadows and beyond, and
was known as the Dracut Path.

One other public way might be called
a main line of travel at this time. This

was the path leading from Haverhill to Spicket Meadows above Salem Village, as we now call it, though at that time a part of Methuen and called the Spicket Path, first laid out in 1659 and relocated in 1685, as it had become somewhat doubtful where the line was at that time. The Spicket Path is probably now known as North Broadway. Other paths or trails there were though few if any that could be called roads. Travel at that time was on foot, on horseback, or with ox-teams, and thirty years later we find only one two-wheeled chaise and nine calashes in Haverhill, and probably not one four-wheeled carriage.

The next year, 1726, after much discussion, the church was begun and the frame raised on land across the path from the pound. Now in those days the centre of the town was where the church stood, for there all the people met for their business with each other as a town, as well as to worship God, and it soon became necessary to have a public way, instead of a path over private property, to the place of "Publick Worship."

It had been the custom in Haverhill to lay out a path for owners of outlying meadow or timber land by appointing two men at a town meeting to lay the bounds, and they often had to appoint committees to rediscover and readjust them, they were so numerous. Roads from one town to another were thus laid out, the road "from Andiver to Haverell" being laid by John Osgood and Thomas Hale in 1647, the road to Salisbury in 1651, and to Rowley in 1686, showing Haverhill and Andover to be well connected with the lower part of the county, but with no roads inland or northward.

THE SWIMMING HOLE ON THE ROAD TO MESSERS' FERRY

Of course there was much discussion of the new road to the church, and it would seem that it became so warm that the old methods of laying out by the selectmen or a committee would not satisfy, and an appeal was taken to "his Majestis Court of Generall Sessions of the Peace" to summon a jury of twelve good and lawful men to lay out the road, and from the action of the court comes "The King's Highway," the first road in our town laid by an authority greater than that of the town meeting, and the first road of any great importance in our history.

Among the "Barker Papers" given to our Historical Society by Deacon Foster of Milford, N. H., we find the "Return of the Jury," which is as follows:

Essex ss. Anno Regni Regis Georgii nunc Magna Britania,
Françesca & Hibernia Deccimo Tertio.
At his Majesties Court of Generall Sessions of the Peace begun & held at Salem for & within the County of Essex on the last Tuesday of December being the twenty seventh day of said month annoque Domini 1726.

On Reading the Return of the Jury who were Summoned to lay out a high way or Common Road from Swan's ferry so called through the Town of Methuen and part of Haverhill up to Londonderry and the sheriffs Return of the warrant Directed to him for summoning of them which is as follows vizt.:

Essex ss. Decem. 3, 1726.
In obedience to the within warrant I have Summoned Jeremiah Stephens, Lieut. Thomas Hoyt, Lieut. Orlando Bagley, Jun., Ensign Daniel Morrel, Ensign Jacob Sargent, Jarvis Ring Jun., Ephraim Brown, John Bagley, Benjamin Currier, Sam'l. Reynolds, John Harvey & Nathaniel Fitts a jury of Twelve good & lawfull men to lay out the high way or Common Road in the within written Warrant mentioned to appear at Haverhill on the fifth day of December

Currant, who accordingly Appeared and were Sworn before John White Esqr. one of his majesties Justice of the Peace for the County of Essex to lay out the Said high way According to law & their best Skill and Judgment, who upon the Sixth day of this instant December went upon the Spot & viewing the Same have laid out Said high way or Common Road from Swan's Ferry so Called to a pitch pine Tree marked H Standing near Back River mill, and have Also Estimated the Damages that Particular Persons have Sustained by the same as by their Return under their hands & seal hereunto Annexed may at large Appear Mr. Swan has paid the Justice, the Jury & my fees. In witness of all above written I have hereunto Set my hand the 7th day of Decemb. 1726.

BENJ. MARSTON, SHERIFF.

We the Subscribers being Appointed and Sworn a Jury to lay out the high way or Road within mentioned According to our best Skill an' Judgment and Agreeable to law having met on the Spot on the Sixth day of Decemb. 1726 id lay out the Said way as follows, vizt.:

To begin at Swan's ferry so Called and to Run four rods wide as the path now goes untill you Come to the meeting house frame and so Along by the west End of the Said frame to the path at Jonathan Emmersons land and so through Said Emmersons land about fifty Six rods to a small Black oak marked Standing on the East Side of the Road so long about One Hundred and Twenty rods as the line now Runs between land of Kimball & others & Thomas Silver laying four rods wide in upon the Said land of Kimball and Others & So upon a Straight line to a Town highway & through the said way to a large white oak markd and from thence to a Black oak markd and from thence on a Straight line to Muddy Brook Bridge so Called. thence through Sam'l. Clarks land to his house by Severall markd Trees then through Thomas Eatons land About Thirty Six rods by Two black oak Trees markd thence to Run between the land of Said Eaton & Ephraim Clarks two rods wide in upon each of their lands then through Said Clarks land about Forty rods bounded by Two white oaks markd then

about fifty rods thro Saml. Curriers land bounded by a Walnut tree markd a great rock & a black oak stump all being on the west side of the way & so to Run between the Said Samuel Currier & John Baileys land About Twenty Two rods and to be Two rods wide in upon Each of their lands.

Then to Turn Northeasterly round the said Bayley's land till you Come to a white oak tree markd Standing by a Brook upon Evan Jones land and so thro' the Said Jones land to an heap of Rocks by the Town high way and so by the said way to Spicket River. then over Said River through Joseph Peaslee meadow then through Nathaniel Peaslee land along by Severall markd trees to the Bridge by Peaslee mill so Called. so over Said Bridge through the Said Peaslee land by marked trees till you Come to the End of Said Peaslees land then through land of the Proprietors of Haverhill by markd Trees till you Come (to) a pitch pine tree markd H. near the Back River mill where we Ended the work.

The markd Trees Referred to in the Above written Stand on the Westerly side of the road & the Said Road is to be understood to Keep Four rods wedth throughout the whole way from Swan's Ferry to Back River mill before mentioned.

In laying out of the Above said way we have had Regard to the Committee Return and the Conveniency of the Publick And have as little Prejudiced Particular Persons as was Possible. But some Persons being unavoidably damaged We Estimate their Damage thus To Samuel Clark for Running through his land Ten pounds and to Evan Jones for Damage to him Ten pounds and to Joseph Peaslee for crossing his meadow four pounds and as for the Other lands through which the Afore mentioned Road or highway Passes We are of Opinion that the Respective Owners thereof are Rather benefitted than damnified by the same. In witness whereof We have hereunto Set our hands & Seals the Seventh day of December 1726.

JEREMIAH STEVENS
DANL. MORREL.
EPHM. BROWN.
SAML. RUNNELS.
THOMAS HOYT.
JACOB SARGENT.
JOHN BAGLEY.
JOHN HARVEY.
ORLANDO BAGLEY, JR.
JARVIS RING, JR.
BENJ. CURRIER.
NATH FITTS.

What an interesting old document

THE EATON HOUSE

we have here! As we study it we gain
a great deal of information from it.
We find that this King George, whose
"Court of Generall Sessions of the
Peace" issued it, was the first George,
King of Great Britain, France, and
Ireland, a German unable to speak
English, and the grandfather of the
George III. who, fifty years later,
brought on the war of the American
Revolution and was defeated by
George Washington. From all of
which we begin to realize that this
"King's Highway" is a very old way
indeed.

Even the date of this old paper is of
interest, for some of the great nations
of the world as we know them now
were but in their feeble infancy at the
time. It was in the thirteenth year of
the reign of Frederick William of
Prussia, the father of Frederick the

Great, the famous general who brought
his country to a commanding position
among the nations of Europe, and
ruled for forty-seven years. (One of
his last public acts was the conclusion
of a commercial treaty with the United
States of America, then in their fifth
year of freedom from England.) It
was scarce a year after the death of
the greatest of all Russians, Peter the
Great, who, like Frederick, was the
"Father of his Country," and who
founded and built the city of St. Petersburg only twenty years before.
Again, when we realize that James
Watt, who watched the tea kettle and
invented the steam engine, did not see
daylight till ten years later, we surely have right to claim that this road
was laid out in an age remote from
our day.

Coming again to our own local history, we find that the year before a scouting party was in service during September and October as a defense against the Indians who were lurking among these same old black and white oaks, and the firing of guns was heard, to distress and annoy the settlers. Only after four years more was it thought safe to remove the fort from around the Haverhill parsonage; and but ten years previously five full grown wolves were killed in Haverhill. A year later occurred the great fall of snow, driving the deer from the woods, followed by the wolves that killed many of them. Thus, with dangers from Indians and wild beasts hardly past and keenly remembered, we see that the laying out of a road eight miles or more in length, and much of it through an unbroken forest of old growth timber, was no small undertaking and required a great deal of that courage and push for which our forefathers were so noted. These virtues have descended in some degree at least to the present generation, who in that vicinity are still pushing for new and better roads, and getting them too, just as they did one hundred and seventy years ago.

Let us now trace the line of this King's Highway which was "understood to Keep Four rods wedth throughout the whole way," but today has been so encroached upon that it varies from forty feet to little over fifty feet, and so never has become the broad thoroughfare that its projectors desired. It is perhaps of interest to note that previous to this the road in Haverhill from Holt's rocks to Sander's Hill was laid twelve rods wide, and in 1754 cut down to four rods, while in 1744 what is now Merrimac Street was laid only forty feet wide.

THE JOEL PORTER PLACE

THE GREAT ROCK

The King's Highway begins at Swan's Ferry (which crossed the Merrimac from Andover, now North Andover, to Methuen) at a point near what is now the Lawrence city farm, and followed the path "untill you Come to the meeting house frame." This part of it is still known as Ferry Street in Lawrence, but is at present called Prospect Street in Methuen, though commonly termed the How Road for many years. Then, following Prospect Street to Marston Corner it becomes How Street to the corner of Hampstead Street, whence it follows the latter to the Salem line, where we lose our interest in it without tracing it to the "pitch pine marked H near the Back River mill."

It seems that this road was not for local convenience only, but was a part of the road to Londonderry, which place had been incorporated four years before, although settled three years earlier still by sixteen families of Scotch-Irish under the name of Nutfield. These people brought the potato with them, and Wm. White of Haverhill raised the first ones. Having a crop of four bushels he greatly overstocked the market. This also may have been a part of the road from Haverhill to Pennacook (now Concord, N. H.), which was settled by Haverhill men the year before, one condition of the grant being that a road should be cut through from Haverhill.

Of the metes and bounds described we recognize but three in what is now Methuen; the two brooks and the great rock, the former apparently "going on forever" while the latter seems to have "forever stood." It should forever stand as an ancient landmark, with a proper inscription and date showing its history. "Muddy Brook so called" is the one near the corner of the Slough Road at the Worthen place, and the great rock is near the house of Charles

Merrill, while the brook upon Evan Jones's land is at the foot of the hill a short distance beyond.

It cannot be claimed surely that there is even one house now standing that was built before the laying out of this road, though the old house on Ferry Street toward the river from East Haverhill Street dates well back

Weed Eastman as pastor of the First Church. The Eaton house next above "Grovesnors Corner" still stands on land once belonging to the Thomas Eaton mentioned in the Jury return, and descending in his family to the father of one now living, Mrs. Emily Eaton Davis, who may claim as direct descent from the original settlers of

HASTINGS ELM

toward that time, and was once occupied by old "Master Isaac Swan" who was related to Asie Swan, one of the first selectmen of the town, and lived near by. "Gage's Tavern," for many years past occupied by Eben Whittier, is one of the old mansions, though probably not reaching back quite to the times before the road. Eighty-two years ago a council of twelve churches met there to settle the Rev. Jacob

Methuen and the dwellers upon the King's Highway as any one. The old Hastings house near "Muddy Brook Bridge" must have been built long ago, though perhaps not the first house built at that place. We can locate the sites of some of the old houses by the cellars and wells found along the line. The old well on Powder House Hill in land belonging to Mr. Edward F. Searles marks the spot where Phineas

Messer lived, who was born in 1750 and died in 1836, being for many years the leading musician of the town and the head of the musical society then in existence. The house on the Marston place is the fourth one built on the same site, the first one being a house of refuge built of heavy plank, with loopholes for defense against the assaults of Indians, and probably standing by the path (the Indian trail of a few years previous) before the road was laid out.

The cross roads at the Marston place now goes by the name of "Marston Corner," as shown by a suitable stone monument in memory of the Marston family whose home was there for more than a hundred years, and whose lives and fortunes are closely identified with the early history of our country and our town. To this family we are forever indebted for the courage, ability, and usefulness they displayed in their

day and generation, which preserved much that we enjoy in ours. This family was represented in the army, in the Indian wars, at the siege of Louisburg, and through the battles of the Revolution, and the war of 1812. Some of its members are pioneer settlers in many towns in New England, and some went farther west and south. At this corner stood the old blacksmith shop, one of the first in the town, for half a century or more, and on the opposite side of the road was the old red school house of our childhood days.

Among the names of the abutters mentioned in the document we find six who soon after became members of the First Church, four of them at its formation in 1729, one in 1731, and one in 1734. They were Thomas Silver, Samuel Clark, John Bailey, Thomas Eaton, Samuel Currier, and Evan Jones. James How lived on that part of it which had been laid out the year previous, and was chosen a deacon in 1732. Of these men we know but little. We find their names on the church roll and most of them on the early tax lists of the town among the well-to-do citizens of the time. Thomas Eaton was one of the first schoolmasters of the town, besides owning one of the best farms, it being taxed one shilling and eight pence, while his personal property tax was only four pence less. His father witnessed the will of Rev. John Ward, the first minister of Haverhill, in 1692, was selectman of Haverhill in 1675, was killed by the Indians in 1697. The How Farm was evidently then as now the best on the road, as James How paid the heaviest real estate tax, being assessed two shillings; but while rich in land he was not so blessed with personal property, which was taxed only one shilling. The one resident of the "King's Highway" at this time bearing the family name of any of those mentioned in the return. is Isaiah How, a descendant of Deacon James How.

Richard Currier, being one of a family of fifteen, removed from Haverhill in 1735, only nine years after the laying out of the road, to land on or near the road. He was a neighbor to Thomas Eaton, and the same land has descended in the family to its present owner Stephen Currier; but we can hardly trace it back nine years more to Samuel Currier, whose land was crossed by the new road. In repairing the road at the How Farm a few years ago, at the brook, we found three stone culverts built one above another, as the grade was raised from time to time.

About thirty-five years after the laying out of the road Robert Hastings watched his father set a small elm tree by the roadside near his house just north of Muddy Brook Bridge. When Robert was a small boy he at times amused himself by climbing the little tree and swinging down as the boys often do now upon the birches. Robert Hastings was born in 1750, lived four score and six years, and was gathered to his fathers; the little elm still stood to shelter and protect his household, and now, after three score years more have passed away, there stands the noblest elm of the country round, the most interesting landmark of the King's Highway, a noble monument of the love and care of one of the early settlers who planted not for himself. but for the blessing of many generations yet to come.

The Fruit of His Bravery

By D. H. Talmadge

THE Pacific Overland was due to leave the Union Station at 8:24. At 7:00, Express Messenger Tom Wilson closed the front door of the modest dwelling in which he lived. He did not slam the door as some men would have done; he latched it gently, thus displaying a fine sense of consideration for the nerves of those within. Once or twice before reaching the avenue which led direct to the station, he stopped and looked back, as if hoping that some one might call to him. But the door remained closed and no one called. He went on to the long night's work.

He had eaten supper that evening, as was his custom when at the home end of the run, in company with his wife and his wife's mother, and he had not enjoyed the meal keenly for the reason that he and the elder lady were not congenial. They jarred upon each other. There was between them a lack of that respect which is so essential to pleasant relations among all animals.

The conversation that evening had turned upon the subject of foreign travel, Mrs. Wilson having mentioned in a purely incidental way that a friend of hers was on the verge of a trip to Europe.

"I think it is just lovely," she said. "I told Grace I'd give anything if I could take such a trip."

"Grace married a successful man," said her mother, casting a significant glance at Tom. "Your father and I visited Europe in the fall of '81, and I had hoped that you would be able some day to do the same, but"—concentrating her gaze upon Tom, who was looking steadfastly at his plate— "I'm afraid you never will."

She gave vent to a dismal sigh, and Tom shuffled his feet uneasily but said nothing. He was used to such things. Scarcely a day passed that some reflection was not made upon his failure to provide as much money for his wife's disposal as she had been provided with in her girlhood. True, her father had failed at last. Nothing remained of the former vast estate but the cottage, in which they lived. He had carried a small insurance on his life—not enough to suport his widow in comfort; and when he had died Tom and his wife, who was an only

child, had sacrificed the greater portion of their honeymoon, foregoing their dream of happiness unalloyed, and had taken up their abode with the old lady, who had declared that she positively could not live alone.

"It is my duty, dear," Mrs. Wilson had said to her husband. "I must take care of mamma."

"Why of course," Tom had assented, although he felt certain misgivings. "One of us may be old and alone some time. We'll move in at once, my love."

And move in they did. Tom did not like it, but he never said so. When the fact was made much of that the shoes he bought for his wife were poor, cheap things compared with those she thought she had to have when she was a girl, he flushed and swelled a bit under the ears but held his peace. When the husband of one of his wife's friends was promoted for conspicuous gallantry in the Spanish war to a lucrative position in the War Department, he listened to a series of acrid comments, directed squarely at his own face beyond possibility of error, and curbed the desire to answer back. And so it went on for many weeks and months.

The strain told upon him somewhat. More than once the plethora of his suppressed temper was visited upon his wife, for whom he had no sentiment in his breast but love. Such demonstration was unjust, but it was really necessary for the preservation of peace. He took it for granted that she would understand, and he was pained because she did not seem to do so. Gradually the honey oozed out of their life and only the comb was left.

Perhaps it would have been better had he asserted himself more forcibly. There were moments during the nights when he was alone in the express car that he worked himself into a state of indignation quite tremendous, resolving with many frowns and clutchings of the hands to adopt a different and less pacific policy. But he had never done so. His nature forbade, not because he was afraid but because he was not afraid. And it came to pass that the wisdom of his course was proven good.

His thoughts were dwelling upon the matter that night, long after the Pacific Overland had left the Union Station. The rush of work was over, and he was sitting in front of the express safe, his chin upon his breast, his hands in his pockets, his legs outstretched. Suddenly the train came to a standstill, and he aroused himself wondering what was wrong, for they were far from a station in a rough country.

Caution prevented him from opening the door or looking from the barred windows. So he waited, hearing the sound of voices faintly, feeling the jar as the car was uncoupled from the rest of the train, nervously handling his two pistols. He had not long to wait. The car was drawn forward possibly a mile, then stopped, and the door was pounded upon.

"Open up here or we'll blow you to pieces!" called a voice.

Tom gave no reply nor made a movement to obey the demand.

"Hurry!" called the voice with an oath.

Two minutes later the car rocked from the force of an explosion, and the door was splintered.

"Come out!" called the voice. "Come out or we'll dynamite you!"

Then for the first time Tom spoke.

"Dynamite and be d—d!" he said, discharging his pistols, one in either hand, at the doorway.

One of the robbers uttered a yelp of pain, and for a moment there was silence. Then a fusilade of rifle shots penetrated the wall of the car. Tom sprawled upon the floor, not failing for an instant to cover the doorway with his pistols, and was not hit. Again an attempt was made to enter the car, and again the attempt failed. Tom was upon his feet now by the side of the safe upon which he had placed his ammunition. The pistols were hot to the touch. The atmosphere reeked with powder fumes. He was wet with sweat.

A dynamite bomb with a sizzling fuse attached was thrown in at the doorway and rolled almost to his feet. He picked it up and threw it back with scarcely a wink of time to spare before it burst.

The concussion was followed by a chorus of howls and groans. The battle was over.

Presently the engineer's face appeared in the doorway. He grinned grotesquely, holding up his thumbs.

"The devils have gone, taking their wounded with them, Tom," he announced, "and the whole fruit of their labors amounts to just fifty cents, being thirty cents handed over at a gun's point by the fireman and two dimes that I coughed up myself under the same influence. My God, boy, you've earned your salary this night!"

"I believe you," said Tom, quietly, drawing his sleeve across his grimy face.

Then they returned for the balance of the train and went on again, two hours late.

The story was in the papers the next day under great black headlines. Tom was the hero of the hour. Crowds cheered him at many stations by which the train passed. His passage through the streets at the home end of the run amounted to a continuous ovation. At the door of his home—the door which he had closed so gently the night before—his wife welcomed him with open arms, and sobbed upon his shoulder.

Supper was steaming upon the table, and they had seated themselves in their accustomed places, before the old lady appeared. Her face wore the severe expression habitual to it. She greeted Tom in the same even tone of condescension that had characterized it in the past. But she was less talkative than had been her wont.

She listened without show of emotion or especial interest as Tom answered the questions his wife asked. Yet when she raised a teaspoon to her lips it might have been observed that her hand trembled. It was evident also that she had contracted a cold, for she cleared her throat many times and coughed frequently, one paroxysm being so severe that tears started from her eyes.

"Mary," said she to her daughter when napkins were being folded, "I wish you'd run upstairs and get my crocheted shawl. 'Tis on my bed, I think."

Mrs. Wilson departed obediently, and Tom drew an evening paper from his pocket, half turning his back to the old lady, and began to read. But the sheet was struck to the floor at his feet in that instant, and two old knees were upon it, and two old hands were upon his hands.

"O, Tom!" cried his wife's mother, her voice shaking miserably, "I thought you were a man of no spirit, and—and—you were only a gentleman! Forgive me, Tom! Will you forgive me?"

"Why, of course," said Tom bewilderedly. "Good Lord! Of course! Please get up!"

She glanced apprehensively at the doorway through which her daughter must come, and arose to her feet.

"And Tom," she whispered rapidly, "won't you please talk back when I say things you don't like? Won't you p-l-e-a-s-e, Tom? I can't—I can't be meek before Mary. I'm her mother, and—and—I've just got to keep up. You won't mind, will you, now that you understand?"

"Not a bit," said Tom, "not a bit."

He was gasping from astonishment, and the fingers which a few hours before had pressed the triggers of great grim weapons hung limp at his sides.

When his wife returned he was still in that attitude, and there was a damp spot upon his forehead where two old lips had dabbed a kiss.

The Stars and Stripes a Boston Idea

By George J. Varney

THE troops of which General Washington took command, standing under the great elm in Cambridge, Massachusetts, in July, 1775, were a motley aggregation of hastily formed militia regiments or companies, undisciplined and undrilled, variously and insufficiently armed, and imperfect in all sorts of equipment. Scarcely were the companies in a single regiment in similar uniform; for the picturesque and elegant military costume known as the "Continental" had not then come into use.

In flags, the deficiency in number was more than compensated by variety of design. The most acceptable standard among the Massachusetts men was a red or, sometimes, a white flag bearing the figure of a pine tree. The cross of St. George had continued in use on

Massachusetts vessels, but it was banished from the camp of the besiegers; though possibly a newly arrived Maine or New Hampshire company may have borne a St. George's cross with a yellow or gilt crown at the center, and the king's monogram below it in black—banners which their predecessors had borne in the French and Indian wars or in the glorious campaign against Louisburg.

The first Connecticut regiment paraded that Colony's insignia of a vine having beneath it the pious and courageous motto *"Qui transtulit sustinet,"* on a white field; while the banners of the other two (one green, the other red) had to be made and sent after them. When, after the evacuation of Boston by the British, Washington transferred his headquarters to New York, the hostility had become too deeply fixed for patriots to march willingly under any British banner. Some New Yorkers displayed a flag of Dutch origin; but by the time Americans found it necessary to retreat across New Jersey and into Pennsylvania, still another flag had become quite popular. It bore the words "Liberty or Death" on a white field, over a sword crossed with a staff bearing a liberty cap. This was the principal standard at the battle of White Plains.

At least two of the flags carried by American Patriots in the first and part of the second year of the war were the same as those chiefly used by the British army and navy about Boston. Evidently the Americans had no common visible standard around which to rally; and companies sometimes found themselves in awkward and dubious positions. Naturally this diversity in standards tended to disorder, jealousy,

and insubordination. The matter certainly gave Washington some concern; for two of his correspondents in the Congress received from him letters dated at Cambridge, October 20, 1775, each containing the request, "Please fix on some particular flag, and a signal by which our vessels may know one another." To this was added the question, "What do you think of a flag with a white ground, a tree in the middle, with the motto, 'An Appeal to Heaven?'" Evidently Washington had no strong predilection for his own ensign armorial as the standard for the people who, he hoped, would form themselves into a nation. The cruisers fitted out by the Continental Congress sailed during the autumn and most of the following winter under flags of nearly this description; and in the spring the Massachusetts Council adopted this form for the Colony's vessels—making the tree a pine. Had northern and southern troops been massed at this time, the rattlesnake, crescent, and other banners of the latter section would have "made confusion worse confounded."

That Congress appreciated some of the difficulties of the situation in this respect is shown by the fact that the committee of their own number sent by that body to confer with General Washington in regard to the reorganization of the army, were instructed also to devise a flag for the United Colonies. The committee consisted of Dr. Benjamin Franklin of Pennsylvania, Colonel Thomas Lynch of Carolina, and Hon. Benjamin Harrison of Virginia. A letter of General Greene, then in command at Prospect Hill, Somerville, says, under date of October 16, 1775, that the committee arrived "last evening; and I had the honor to be introduced to that very great man, Dr. Franklin."

The journals of Congress show that this service of the committee caused an absence of six weeks from their seats. Belknap writes of a conference on the plan of campaign, in which Judge Nathaniel Wales of Connecticut participated; that Lynch, Harrison, and Wales wanted to give Boston to the flames, so as to expel the British,—to which plan Hancock had previously given his consent; but Washington found a better way.

The journal of a Cambridge lady, who was the hostess of the committee during a portion of their sojourn, says that they arrived on December 13— which may have been a return from a trip to other colonies, or, merely a removal to her residence. The only detailed account which we have of the proceedings at Cambridge in regard to the flag is in her memoranda—which were added to and completed in 1777, at the request of Dr. Franklin, then in Paris. This lady's husband was a highly respected citizen, and his house was deemed the most secure place for the discussions which must occur in the conferences; wherefore Washington was desirous that the committee should lodge there. Two of them therefore took the only spare room, while Dr. Franklin shared another room with an old professor of the college, then staying with the family. The Doctor's room-mate was a firm patriot of extensive information and philosophic mind. It is mentioned that an utterance of his which had become familiar to many of his acquaintances was, "We demand no more (of England) than our just due; we will

accept and be satisfied with nothing less than we demand."

The professor and their host were invited by the committee to become their associates in designing an American standard. The professor then proved himself one of the earliest advocates of woman's equality by proposing to the visiting statesmen that the graceful sex be represented on the flag committee by their hostess. These Congressmen promptly adopted the suggestion, and carried it out fully by appointing the professor and the lady a special committee to furnish a design. When at evening the party came together again, the design was presented. It consisted of alternate red and white stripes, thirteen in number, for the field; with the union jack in a white ground in the upper staff-corner, as a union. Other insignia had been suggested and discussed. The stripes corresponded to the bars with stars, so familiar to Washington in his family escutcheon; and those very fitting emblems could scarcely have failed of respectful consideration.

In placing the design before the committee, the professor made a somewhat formal address in its explanation and advocacy, the main points of which—much condensed—were the following:

"We are now self-acknowledged Colonies, —dependencies of Great Britain; which government we, as loyal subjects, humbly sue for justice. These demands will, of course, in the future as in the past, be neglected or denied. Yet we must not alienate our companions; but our justice-demanding and freedom-loving countrymen will soon learn that there is no hope for us as British Colonists, and that we can secure the rights we contend for only as the loyal and united citizens of a free and independent American nation. The flag which we now offer must testify in its design to our present loyalty as English subjects, and yet have a form to be easily modified, so as to announce and represent the new nation that is rapidly forming. . . . The field of our flag must, therefore, be an entirely new one,—because it will represent a new nation; second, the field must be one hitherto unused as a national flag,—because it will represent a nation with an entirely new principle in its government,—the equal rights of man as man."

It was then explained that the thirteen longitudinal and horizontal stripes would be readily understood to represent the thirteen existing Colonies; and that their equal width typified the equal rank, rights, and responsibilities of the several Colonies; and the union of the stripes in the field of the flag would announce the unity of interests and the co-operative union of efforts which the Colonies recognize and put forth in their common cause. The white stripes will signify that we consider our demands just and reasonable, and that we seek to secure our rights through peaceable, intelligent, and statesmanlike means, if possible; and the red stripes at the top and bottom of the flag will declare that first and last and always we have the determination, the enthusiasm, and the power to use force whenever we deem force necessary. The alternation of the red and white stripes will suggest that our reasons for all demands will be intelligent and forcible, and that our force in securing our rights will be just and reasonable. He said further:

"There are other reasons for making this the field of our flag; but it will be time enough to consider them, when, in the near future, we, or our successors, are considering—not a temporary flag for associated and dependent colonies, but a permanent standard for a united and independent nation."

No doubt the conversation previously held on the subject, including suggestions of General Washington, furnished the basis of this discourse; yet there is a terse strength in its passages which the reader will scarcely fail to note—as well as the clearness with which the professor sets forth the fitness of the emblems to represent harmoniously abstract principles and existing conditions. The design presented a progressive flag, one that would not offend American citizens who were slower to apprehend the inevitable trend of events, and yet one that could be fully developed by a slight change in the canton—such as the substitution of a constellation of the heavens* for the union jack.

This new American flag was not, however, the first banner that bore alternate red and white stripes; for they constituted the figure on the standard presented to the Philadelphia Light Horse, in the autumn of 1775, by Captain Abraham Markoe, a well-known merchant and ship-owner of that city. The field of both flags was doubtless suggested by that used by the British East India Company, half a century before,—then still remembered by some in both ports. The flag with stripes alone had only a commercial meaning to the world until the Americans flung it out with thirteen of the stripes—the number in the other flags not exceeding ten.

The diminutive model prepared by the professor and their hostess proved satisfactory to the committee, and was formally adopted by them. As quickly

* There is elsewhere evidence tending to support the belief that the constellation Lyra was mentioned, but it is not conclusive.

as possible, full-size garrison flags were made in exact accordance with the design presented.

Now comes a conflict in dates. A memorial stone set up on Prospect Hill, Somerville, a few years ago by the local historical society, bears the inscription, "On this hill the Union Flag with its thirteen stripes, the emblem of the United Colonies, first bade defiance to an enemy, January 1, 1776." This date is doubtless taken from Frothingham's "Siege of Boston," whose authority appears to have been the letter of a Lieutenant Carter, who was with the British on Charlestown Heights when the new flag was run up. Writing under date of January 26, 1776, Lieutenant Carter says:

"The king's speech was sent by flag to them (the Americans) on the first instant. In a short time after they received it, they hoisted a union flag (above the Continental with thirteen stripes) at Mt. Pisgah (the name by which Prospect Hill was known to the British); their citadel fired thirteen guns, and gave the like number of cheers."

The account by the Cambridge hostess places the first raising of this flag on the second day of the month, and also mentions the salute—which was fired on Prospect Hill. A letter of General Washington, however, will generally be regarded as settling this doubt. Writing under date of January 4, 1776, to Colonel Joseph Reed, the General says:

"We are at length favored with the sight of his Majesty's most gracious speech, breathing sentiments of tenderness and compassion for his deluded American subjects; the speech I send you (a volume of them was sent out by the Boston gentry, the British officers and the Tories); and farcical enough—we gave great joy to them without knowing or intending it; for it was on that day (the 2nd) which gave being to our new army (the reorganization of the hitherto heterogeneous force having just been completed); but before the proclamation came to hand we hoisted the (new) union flag in compliment to the United Colonies. But, behold! it was received at Boston as a token of the deep impression the speech made upon us, and as a signal of submission. By this time I presume they begin to think it strange that we have not made a formal surrender."*

As a matter of fact the troops tore up the copies of the speech and made little bonfires of them.

The account by the lady afore-mentioned says that the flag was raised by the hands of Washington himself, with appropriate ceremonies, in which the military participated, "the commissioners"—perhaps from Connecticut, Rhode Island and New Hampshire—being present. The staff, according to the same account, was a towering pine-tree liberty pole, specially erected for the purpose. Another letter of Washington says "soon after the flag-raising at headquarters, we marched to the citadel on Prospect Hill, and participated in the ceremonies there." On March 4, 1776, there was issued to the army from headquarters, the following order:

"The flag on Prospect Hill and that at Laboratory on Cambridge Common are ordered to be hoisted only upon a general alarm."

By this it appears that while headquarters and the chief citadel had each a union flag, we may fairly infer that other points were still without them, after two months had passed. The fact is, that the troops still looked to their own Colonies to prescribe their colors.

There is no record of any action by

* American Archives, 4th series, Vol. III, p. 1126.

Congress upon a report of this Cambridge Committee; but the flag was used thereafter to some extent by the army, and it was flown by the belated portion of the fleet of Commodore Hopkins, which did not sail from the Delaware until February 17th.* Hon. John Jay, in a letter dated in July, 1776, expressly states that Congress, up to that date, had made no order "concerning Continental colors, and that captains of armed vessels had followed their own fancies" in respect to standards. It is well-known that previous to the summer of 1777, all vessels, especially privateers, generally bore the colors of their ports or of the colony which chartered them, sometimes with devices peculiar to their mercantile or to their family connection.

Scanning these various flags the philosophic eye can now see that the people at large were gradually putting aside old forms and attachments, and developing by degrees, through one phase of sentiment after another—not always noble—better conceptions of popular liberty and loftier national ideals.

According to the records and recollections of the family of Mrs. Elizabeth Ross (the worthy maker of a great number of American flags for the army and navy) and of Mrs. Wilson, her niece, who succeeded to her business, it was in June, 1776, that General Washington, together with Colonel George Ross and Hon. Robert Morris, brought to Mrs. Ross the rough design of a flag with thirteen red and white stripes, bearing a union with thirteen stars, from which

* Scharf and Westcott's Hist. of Philadelphia, Vol. I, p. 303.

she was directed to make a flag. Mrs. Ross, it appears, pointed out the unusual number of six points in the stars in the drawing, which Washington, at her suggestion, at once changed to five. The tradition is believed to be trustworthy.

From the same source we learn that the exact form of the canton, or "union," in this particular flag was a blue field bearing a spread eagle with thirteen stars in a circle of rays surrounding its head. Was this the way the eagle got into the American insignia, and came early to be regarded as a sacred bird, the killing of which was an omen of ill?

It can scarcely be doubted that a union of stars, as in our present flag, was proposed at Cambridge, but considered premature—for reasons given by the professor for the temporary use of the union jack—and was at this time carried out by General Washington.

Various historical publications state that General Washington was summoned to Philadelphia, in May of 1776, to confer with Congress on the conduct of the war. These absences of Washington from headquarters were without jeopardy, as there were no British troops in any of the thirteen colonies from the day of the evacuation of Boston until almost the date of the adoption of the Declaration of Independence.

It would be no suddenness in conduct for Washington to put forth a design for the flag of a new nation at this time; for it was known by his associates that as early as January 1, 1776, he confidently expected and desired independence to be avowed at an early day. Neither would the display of such a flag at this time forestall the action of Congress; for John Adams had on the 6th of May previous offered the resolution which was passed on the 10th; the preamble to which, presented subsequently and adopted on the 15th, plainly declares the purpose of independence—as Adams himself remarks in a letter to his wife, under date of May 17, 1776.* It would seem as though the Commander-in-Chief should have been too much in earnest to wait longer for a standard about which *all* his troops would rally, even if Dr. Franklin did not suggest to him that it was time a proper flag was ready for Congress to authorize.

One writer on the flag (whom a few others seem inclined to follow) contends that the Ross date is erroneous, and that Washington's visit was not until the following year; but in 1777 the enemy was giving the Commander-in-Chief all he could attend to and more—in New York and New Jersey, so that he had no time to travel to Philadelphia for the manufacture of flags. Indeed I do not think that Washington was once in Philadelphia from early spring until the 23d of August, in that year,—on which day he marched his army through the city on the way to Wilmington, with the British forces following quickly on his movements. The year 1777, instead of 1776, appears to have been fixed upon by the afore-mentioned writer, mainly because it was in that year that the design of the flag was formally adopted by Congress.

Were one of these early flags, made by Betsy Ross under the direction of Washington, now in existence, it would be worth its weight in gold—staff and all. But these interesting emblems of the new republic, pierced by the shot of many a battle-held, stained by the sulphurous smoke, soaked by the rains, stiffened in the freezing sleet, buffeted by many winds, were torn into ribbons and shreds long before that terrible seven years of war were over and the independence they signified nobly won. There is one flag still existing—not hitherto so noted in its origin as that first one of Mrs. Ross —which, probably, is the only ensign made under Washington's supervision that living eyes have ever seen. It is the "Paul Jones starry flag" worn by the *Bon Homme Richard*—the first stars and stripes ever flown upon the sea.

Admiral Preble in his history of our country's flags says that the official documents place the identity of this flag beyond a doubt. He further says: "It was made in Philadelphia by Misses Mary and Sarah Austin, under the supervision of General Washington and Captain John Brown" (of the informal navy department), "the design being mostly from General Washington's family escutcheon." * The principal authority for this detailed statement is Mrs. Patrick Hayes, niece of the Sarah Ross just named,—who was subsequently the wife of Commodore John Barry, of the Revolutionary and United States Navies.

The flag was presented by the makers to John Paul Jones, who placed it on a small vessel and sailed up and down the Schuylkill to show to sailors and to maritime people on the wharves the future ensign of the nation.

---

* Familiar letters of John Adams and Abigail Adams, p. 173.

* Preble's History of the Flag of the United States, p. 281.

This brilliant naval warrior had, at the last of December, 1775, as senior first lieutenant of the frigate *Alfred*, the flag-ship of Commodore Hopkins' fleet, run up to the masthead of that vessel the first flag which had any distinct recognition from the general government, though the Massachusetts flag bearing a pine tree and the motto, "An Appeal to Heaven," may have shared the approval of the Naval Committee. This banner was of yellow silk, and bore the figure of a pine tree with a rattlesnake coiled at its root, underneath which was the motto, "Don't tread on me."

The resolution adopting the stars and stripes was passed by Congress on June 14, 1777; and on the same day this body appointed Captain Paul Jones to the command of the ship *Ranger*, "upon which he soon after hoisted the new flag at Portsmouth, New Hampshire. He did not, however, get to sea until the first of November." * Victories had in the meantime been won under this flag on land; and it is inconceivable that this remarkable cruise could have been conducted under any other standard. On the way over to the coast of France, the *Ranger* captured two prizes, and was chased by a British man-of-war of the largest class. About the middle of the following February, Captain Jones, then in a French port, wrote the American Commissioners in Paris as follows:

"I am happy to have it in my power to congratulate you on my having seen the *American flag for the first time recognized* in the fullest and completest manner by the flag of France. I was off this bay on the

13th inst. (February, 1778) and sent my boat in the next day to know if the Admiral would return my salute. He answered that he would return to me as the senior American Continental officer in Europe the same salute as he was authorized to return to an admiral of Holland, or any other republic,— which was four guns less than the salute given. I hesitated at this, for I demanded gun for gun. Wherefore I anchored in the entrance to the bay at some distance from the French fleet; but after a very particular inquiry, on the 14th, finding that he really told the truth, I was induced to accept his offer; the more as it was an acknowledgement of American independence. The wind being contrary and blowing hard, it was after sunset when the *Ranger* was near enough to salute *Le Motte Piquet* with thirteen guns,—which he returned with nine. However, to put the matter beyond doubt, I did not suffer the *Independence* (another vessel of Jones' fleet) to salute until the next morning, when I sent word to the admiral that I would sail through his fleet in the brig (the *Independence*), and would salute him in the open day. He was exceedingly pleasant, and returned the compliment also with nine guns."*

An American ensign was recognized by Johannes de Graef, Governor of the Dutch Island of St. Eustachius, in the West Indies, on November 16, 1776; but this was a flag of stripes without the stars; so that the "Paul Jones starry flag" is undoubtedly the veritable piece of bunting first saluted by a foreign power as the colors of the United States of America.

The testimony in the case of the *Bon Homme Richard* leaves no room for doubt that she not merely wore the stars and stripes, but flew the identical flag presented to Paul Jones by the Misses Austin. During the hard-fought battle by which Jones made the British ship-of-war *Serapis* his prize, this flag, which floated at the masthead

* B. F. Prescott (Secretary of State of New Hampshire, 1875) in "The Stars and Stripes: The Flag of the United States of America."

* Maclay's History of the United States Navy, Vol. I, p. 73.

of the *Bon Homme Richard,* was shot away and fell into the sea; when James Bayard Stafford, a lieutenant on that vessel, instantly plunged into the water, recovered the flag, and nailed it to the mast.

After the war the flag was presented by the Naval Committee of Congress to Lieutenant Stafford; from whom it has come by gift and inheritance to its present possessor.

Miss Sarah Smith Stafford, daughter of Lieutenant Stafford, and possessor of the flag for many years, has described it as follows:

"This flag is six feet wide, less five inches, —and was originally about fifteen feet long; but has been so long at the mercy of the patriotic relic-hunters that it has lost two yards of its length."

The flag is of English bunting, sewed with flax thread. It is now barely two and a half yards long and two yards wide. It contains twelve stars in a blue union, and the thirteen stripes, alternately red and white. The stars are placed in four horizontal lines, with three stars in each line.

"Paul Jones' starry flag," the reader will note, is not so elaborate and well-developed as the one made by Mrs. Ross, of which we have the special account, and it may have been an earlier essay. In design, it is more like the Washington coat of arms, which has three stars in a line above three bars, or stripes.

Another point in the flag itself approximately fixes its date. As stated, this flag bears but twelve stars; and the explanation has come down to us that the number was limited to twelve because Georgia, the thirteenth colony to enter the union, had, at the time, vacated her membership. This action

of the colony was on account of the emission of bills of credit by Congress to the amount of 3,000,000 Spanish milled dollars, to defray the expenses of the war. Georgia refused to be responsible for her part, and the whole sum was apportioned to the other twelve.* From how many flags the star of Georgia was omitted cannot be known; but her defection occurred in 1775. This repudiation having become known to the British they thought it a favorable omen for their recovery of the colony; consequently an army and fleet were dispatched against her; and Georgia became again a subject of Britain. The forces of our General Greene drove her conquerors out of Georgia territory, and the name of the colony took its place with the other twelve on the next apportionment list.

On June 14th, 1777, Congress passed the following resolution:

"Resolved, that the flag of the thirteen United States be thirteen stripes alternate red and white; that the union be thirteen stars, white in a blue field, representing a new constellation." (See stanza near the close of this article).

The inattentive habit of Congress in regard to what seemed minor matters is further seen in the fact that the official adoption of the flag of stars and stripes as the national ensign was not formally announced until eighty-one days later, that is, on September 3d, following; and even the newspapers did not mention the matter for six or eight weeks.†‡

* Holmes' Annals of North America (ed. of 1829) Vol 2, pp. 212, 336.
+ Campbell ("Our Flag") p. 56; Boston Gazette and Country Journal, Sept. 15. 1777.
‡ Preble states that a thorough examination under the direction of the Librarian of Congress shows that the foregoing resolution, found in the Journal of Congress, is the first record of Congressional action for the establishment of a national flag for the United States of America.

It must be surprising to those unfamiliar with the methods of the period, that Congress should have adopted, as it did, a resolution fixing the design of a flag for its armies and navies, without modification, debate, or objection; but this appears to be what was done. It seems therefore a necessary inference that a flag of this design was familiar to the members, and that it had long been a subject of approving conversation among them. Says Preble:

"Beyond a doubt the thirteen stars and thirteen stripes were unfurled at the Battle of Brandywine (September 11th), eight days after the official promulgation of them at Philadelphia."

But the first conflict waged under them on land, after their direct authorization, is known to have been at Fort Stanwix (subsequently re-named Fort Schuyler), in Rome, New York. The fort was invested by the British on the 2d of August,—at which time the garrison was without the authorized standard; but they had a description of the design, and soon formed a flag from materials in the fort. Victory perched upon their rude and hastily constructed banner; and in one sortie made by the Americans they captured five of the enemy's standards.

By an order of Congress, approved by the President January 13, 1794, the flag was changed on the first day of May, ensuing, so as to consist of fifteen stripes and the same number of stars. This continued to be the design of our flag until the year 1818, when the Union embraced twenty states. On the 25th of March, in that year, on the motion of Hon. Peter H. Wendover, of New York, Congress passed an act entitled "An act to establish the Flag of the United States." It read as follows:

"Section I. *Be it enacted, etc.,* that from and after the Fourth day of July next, the flag of the United States be thirteen horizontal stripes alternate red and white; that the Union have twenty stars, white in a blue field.

Section II. *And be it further enacted,* that on the admission of every new state to the Union, one star be added to the Union of the flag; and that such addition shall take effect on the Fourth of July next succeeding such admission. Approved, April 4, 1818."

The flags of the United States have since continued to be of this construction; so that, whatever their variations to indicate the branch of the government service to which a special flag belongs, every one shows by its red and white stripes the number of Colonies which originally formed the nation, while its white stars in a blue ground will tell the number of States now embraced in our local Union.

The earliest recorded suggestion of stars as a device for an American ensign—even before Washington's—is to be found in an issue of the "Massachusetts Spy," published in Boston, March 10, 1774. It is in a song (author unknown), of which the lines referring to the device are as follows:

"As a ray of bright glory now beams from afar,
The American ensign now sparkles, a star
Which shall shortly flame wide through the skies."

This brief stanza is good evidence that by one group, at least, of our countrymen, the future American nation had been forecasted, and that there had been a thought of stars as a most suitable emblem for a nation then unique in its form, character, and ideals

The Things That Were

By Agnes Louise Provost

McADAMS leaned against one of the plain, square pillars of his veranda and stared out toward the horizon at a distant speck there which might ultimately resolve itself into humanity. The wide sweep of his own range lay before and around him as far as he could see,—hundreds upon hundreds of acres stretching away in gentle undulations, innocent of human habitation save for this ranch house and the few shanty-like buildings back of it, and desolate indeed save for the scattered herds of horned beasts which roamed this wide pasture-land at will, and the handful of rough men who worked for McAdams and belonged here when they were home at all.

All day the sun had beaten down out of a brazen sky, unmarked by so much as the slow sweep of a vulture. McAdams had just come in from a long ride of inspection over his range, and he was hot and tired, but a fresh horse stood saddled near him, ready to go out again.

"I wonder if they will come?" McAdams speculated to himself. "It will seem queer to have her here. Three years ago she was to have come as mistress, and now she comes as another man's wife—rich chap, travelling in the Southwest for his health. That sounds like lungs—that's what they always come out here for. Dimmick said in his letter that 'Mr. Thatcher contemplates taking a well-

equipped ranch and settling out here if it agrees with him. It must be lungs, and it must be recent. I don't believe she'd ever have married a half dead man."

The distant speck grew, and became two specks, flat and broad, which meant wagons. These must be strangers of some sort, travellers of course, since plains people would have been on horseback. McAdams watched the two specks with growing interest, feeling uneasy, now that it seemed possible that his invited guests were on their way.

"That looks like them—one rig for them and one for a lot of cumbersome luggage, which no plainsman would bother with for two minutes. I suppose she thinks this is a God-forsaken country, where gently bred people have to travel like that. It would be a grim sort of justice if she had to live out here after all. Shouldn't exactly call it a punishment, I suppose, since she hasn't committed any crime—just been a little cruel. It's queer how people can hurt you and grind your life into little bits, and still keep the decalogue and the law of the land unbroken. Perhaps she never cared— as I cared. Anyway, I'm glad Dimmick wrote. So long as they are passing this way, I'm glad of the chance to offer them the hospitality of my quarters on the way, and show them, her at least, that I'm still man enough to pick up the pieces of my old life and make a fairly decent new one out of them. Thatcher must have been surprised at my friendliness, since he never knew me at all, but he'll probably like the chance of talking ranch with a ranchman, and in these days, husbands seem to take rejected suitors rather as a matter of course, sort of a walking credential as to the super-excellence of their own choice."

McAdams stopped, smiling bitterly, and looked out again toward the distant travellers, little bobbing blots now, which only the trained eye of the plainsman could translate into horses and men.

* * * *

"And this is your home?" Mrs. Thatcher paused on the veranda and looked out over the billowing plains by which they had come, a wide, monotonous ocean of grass lands and mesquite, cupped by a limitless arch of sky. When she turned toward the house again, it was with a bright grace which seemed to glorify the long, plain building. Mrs. Thatcher was gifted with a radiant presence.

"Yes, this is where I hang out." McAdams's practical reply and frank hospitality did not suggest his thoughts as he busied himself in attending to the comfort of his guests. Had it occurred to her that this was the house he had built expressly for her occupancy, that he had toiled for in a country where building materials are scarce and high, that much of it had been the work of his own hands, in those dear, tense, hard-slaving days? One end of it was still rough inside, just as he had dropped his tools when her letter came three years ago, and just a month before the day they were to have been married. That was

long enough ago, and she was another man's wife now, but a queer sort of breathlessness had come over him as he had met her, and his fingers had tingled as they had closed over hers. Three years ago he might have lifted her bodily from the wagon here at his own door—her door, too—and held her to him, close and tight, but that was Thatcher's place. Poor Thatcher—he was past lifting people bodily without ruing it. McAdams looked at him with the wondering compassion which a strong man bestows on a sick one.

"It seems a good sort of country for worn-out city men to toughen up in, doesn't it?" Thatcher said thoughtfully, after his wife had retired with her maid—unprecedented luxury on the plains—to remove the dust of travel. He looked from his stalwart, browned host to the free sweep of prairie, and something remotely like a sigh of envy trailed off from his last word. He was weary and haggard, and the hollows in his cheeks and at his temples told their own tale. Two years ago he had not dreamed of such a thing as this, but the down grade had been steep, once started. McAdams felt vaguely sorry for him, and all possible hint of bitterness toward a successful rival faded before the sight of this tired, stricken man. He caught himself wondering if Marion were used to it, or if the sight of this creeping disease were not a horror to her.

"It is that," McAdams answered heartily. "Why, I've four times the strength and endurance I had when I was a city man. I suppose it's the open air life and primitive habits. Civilization takes an awful toll on our systems."

"Yes, the inevitable law of compensation. I was thinking of taking a ranch myself, just a small one, you know, more for recreation than profit. This is pretty large, isn't it?"

"Oh, no, it isn't a large holding as they go here, about forty-five hundred acres. Part of it is Government land, free range, you know, which left me more money to invest in a superior breed of cattle. I began on borrowed money and had to go slow, but I've made it back now, and feel like branching out. You can get a small holding right easily."

Whereupon McAdams proceeded patiently to explain the problems of cattle-ranching to this pathetically incapable invalid, who didn't know a Hereford from a Durham, and couldn't ride ten miles on horseback without being laid up the next day. But in the midst of these things there was the rustle of a womanly presence behind them, and Marion Thatcher came out and stood before them both, with the light of the plains sunset slanting like a glory across her hair. She dropped her fingers lightly on her husband's shoulder in passing—had McAdams been super-sensitive, he might have construed it into a tactful reminder to him that these were not the days that had been—smiled brightly upon them both, and the subject of ranch holdings was tacitly dropped.

*   *   *   *

The quiet grass lands lay bathed in the white radiance of a perfect moonlight, silence was upon them, a stillness as breathless as the night before resurrection, and silence was back in the ranch house, and the low buildings clustered near it. There was one hint of human presence, a smell of tobacco stealing out from the veranda where McAdams sat alone, the veranda he had built for her to sit on, to watch for him as he came in from a long day out on the range. He liked the silence tonight, and the loneliness, because in it he seemed like another man. The last two days had been disturbing.

Thatcher was in bed, done up by his ride over the range that morning. Poor Thatcher, what a pitiful madness to think that he could do anything on a ranch but sit huddled in an easy chair and watch himself die. The man ought never to be beyond five minutes' call of a physician. He could not be good for more than six months, or a year at most. McAdams wanted to get away from that thought. Was he sorry—or glad?

"Oh, you are here?"

A murmur of smiling surprise from the doorway where Marion Thatcher stood like a spirit woman in the silver light, gowned all in white, a clinging creation with which she had graced their evening meal as meals had never been graced in that house before. And she had been so frank, so sunny, so altogether friendly.

"I may come out also, if I do not intrude? It is so glorious, I could not sleep if I tried."

Marion's questions were always mere suggestions with a rising inflection. The effect was odd at first, but singularly pleasant.

McAdams made place for her promptly, but felt that the atmosphere had become suddenly charged. Politely he would have laid aside his beloved pipe, but she raised her hand in a pretty deprecating gesture.

"You will continue to smoke?" she

suggested. "If I am to disturb your quiet comfort, I shall feel that I must go in, and I do want to enjoy a few breaths of this wonderful night. My husband must miss this," she added regretfully after a pause, during which McAdams had returned to his pipe, feeling more comfortable behind that non-committal refuge. "The ride tired him so, although he wished to take it."

"Mr. Thatcher seems to be interested in ranching," commented McAdams, looking at her thoughtfully. She sat near him on a low chair, her hands clasped negligently before her, and the white folds of her gown seeming to melt into the white moonlight. She was not a real woman to-night; rather the visible memory of a remote, dear dream.

"Yes, we may be neighbors some day, if the interest continues. At least, I hope he can buy near enough to call ourselves neighbors. It is so much nicer to feel that some one you know is near."

"You will be lonely," he suggested. He had no formulated intention of being cruel, but he could not forget that this woman had dropped him from heaven to the nethermost pit one day, because at the eleventh hour, when all things were ready, she could not face the isolation of the life she had promised to share with him. Before she answered she arose with slow grace and stood before him, with no apparent preconsidered motive but to lean lightly against one of the unpainted pillars of the veranda and look thoughtfully out at the wide sweep of sky and plain, with the brilliant silver light upon them.

"I shall not mind. It is a loneliness which has a weird fascination of its own. It is mysterious, almost haunting. I never dreamed it was like this."

Inferentially, this was waking an' echo of the past, which had received its mourning and deep burial three years back. McAdams wished she would sit down, where he could not see her standing against that limitless background. He wondered uneasily whether it were her pure good-will in the present, or a love of the old power which would assert its sway, which made her add softly:

"And we shall be friends then, is it not so?"

"I have never been your enemy," McAdams answered bluntly, still shy of committing himself, but unfitted by nature to conduct a dangerous conversation along the trails of ambiguous allusion. "You certainly need have no fear that I would make myself unpleasant because of—of the way things used to be."

"Ah, please!" She made a little gesture of protest, and he remembered with shame that he was her host, and had been rude. "I did not mean that, Dick. I knew you would never be that. What I meant was something very different. Why, I knew when you wrote that you had left that far behind you, as I had. It isn't that we would belittle the things that were, but that we have outgrown them. We learn differently, is it not so?"

"Oh yes," assented McAdams practically. "It isn't in nature to stand still in one spot. It takes a lot of experiences to make up a lifetime, and I suppose they all have their peculiar value in shaping us out."

"To be sure. And it is just because we have both taken experience at its just value, and have developed accordingly, that I would prefer your neighborly friendship here to that of others I might meet. I need it; Wilfred needs it. I am his wife, but I could not entirely fill the place of men friends to him when we are out here. Why,"—she threw out her hands and laughed aloud, not mockingly, but as though filled with a delicious humor which he must share—"how ridiculous it would be, Dick, if, after three years, we should sit and sulk and glower at each other, just because we made a mistake once. Just as though we could not both afford to smile at that now! How beautifully our tiny problems work out. To-day, I have my husband, and you——"

She paused again, with the faintest of upward inflections. McAdams finished the sentence for her.

"And I am not without ambitions of my own."

"So? Is it—oh, do tell me! Is it a girl, Dick?"

"Yes."

McAdams's eyes were looking out over the prairie again, and did not meet hers as he answered her half teasing question. It would never be for him to know whether his answer was a generous gratification or a dull pain, a proved suspicion or a shock. Neither was it for him to understand whether her coming here had been a joy, an annoyance, or a dread, nor what comparison her mind and heart might make between her husband and him. She would hold her dignity in any case; of that he might be sure.

"You will tell me about her?" she said gently.

"Well—if you wish. There isn't much to tell, for it is only an ambition after all. She is a plains girl, raised from childhood at the army post which affords my nearest glimpse of civilized society, and she is also the daughter of one of the finest old officers that ever breathed. I'd be proud to have him call me his son. She loves the plains as I do, because they're home to her, and have been always, except when she was East at school and college, and she is a gentlewoman in heart and breeding. I'm not good at describing, you see, but I've done my best."

In truth, McAdams looked sorely uncomfortable as he blundered out his description. Her request had taken him unawares. Mrs. Thatcher was not yet satisfied.

"I know, but somehow, you've left out the most important part. Those are the surroundings, the incidents. And she, Dick?"

"Oh, now you are pinning me down. Well, she's awfully bright, you know, reads books that give me the shivers to look at, but never rubs it in. And she sings some, and rides horseback like a breeze, and has a laugh that warms you right up, and she's earnest and cordial and, m'm—sort of saucy, sometimes, but gentle too. There, I've made a beastly mess of it, but it's the hardest thing on earth to describe a woman."

"Behold an honest man! I knew not that they ever confessed it. But I thank you, Dick. Perhaps—I shall meet her sometime, if we come out here, and I shall like her, because an old friend of mine likes her too. I fear I must go in now, fascinating as this outlook is to-night. If Wilfred awakens, I should not like to be away. He may wish something. Good-night, and good fortune in your wooing."

There might have been a pin-prick in that, had it not been for the cordial hand she held out to McAdams. He took it, forgetting to rise as he held it for an instant and looked from it to her with thoughts which were obviously abstracted. It was a frail little hand. How easy it would be to pull her down to him as he sat there, to hold her close, with the silence of the plains around them, and the maddening white moonlight upon them both!

But McAdams did nothing so foolish He merely said, "Thank you," smiling in a half embarrassed way, and rose tardily to his feet as she turned away and went into the house, pausing by the door for a light farewell gesture of her hand, the one he had held.

When she had gone, McAdams returned to his chair and pondered these and other things. With a side glance at the door he took from his pocket a worn leather case. Opening, it showed a woman's face within, and as McAdams looked at it he saw her as she had been on the day they had parted at her home, she to wait for him, years, if need be, he to go forth, buoyant and determined, to recoup his shattered fortunes in the far Southwest, biding hopefully the time when she should come out to him and share the best that love and labor could give. She had given him that picture then, sturdily protected in leather to withstand the roughness of his new life, and he had carried it ever since, even after her letter had come, a year and a half later, and after he had heard of her marriage to Thatcher.

With sudden resolution he carefully pried the picture out, brushed his fingers across it with a curious regretful gentleness, because it had been his companion for so long, and striking a match, held it deliberately to one corner until the cardboard broke into flame. So he held the little picture until it had burned almost to his fingers, wondering why it did not hurt him to see the little creeping flames writhe over her face, and when only a corner was left he ground out the last spark under his heel and arose to lean against one of the posts of his veranda —as it happened, the one at which she had stood—and to stare thoughtfully across the moon-drenched plains.

He had lied. There was no other girl. At least, there had not been up to that night. To be sure, so far as flesh and blood existence and proximity went, she was real enough, and she was all that he had said, and more, but he knew that it was not merely this which he had intended to convey.

What sudden instinct of pride or resentment had impelled him to speak so, he could not tell; he was thinking now of the discoveries he had made. The touch of Marion Thatcher's hand had thrilled him, the sight of her standing in the moonlight had made mad notions flicker through his mind, but they were unrealities, born of his memories of the past. They were the lingering echoes of what she had been to him, rather than what she was now, or could ever be. He knew that he had appeared sulky and stupid and not altogther polite, and he was sorry; he would make amends in the morning.

Years ago he had thrust his love roughly into the hidden recesses of his soul and had grimly held it there, while it burned and smarted. To-night she had come and lightly stretched forth her hand to that hidden spot, and lo, there were but dead white ashes, where he had thought a treacherous volcano slumbered.

"Perhaps she wanted to probe me," he thought resentfully, "to put her finger on a raw spot and see if I winced. I didn't think she would do that. It's such a needless sort of a hurt. I suppose it's just the love of power that people can't seem to let go of."

He thought again of the girl who was sweet and merry and wholesouled and strong, whom he had met but a few times at the army post which had provided his only glimpses of social life for nearly five years. He liked her, so far as he knew her, but it had taken the shadow of what he had lost to quicken his pulses at the thought of what he yet might gain. McAdams was slowly awakening, and his drowsy soul still rubbed its eyes and lingered between dreams and action.

"It's worth a try!" he said suddenly, and felt unaccountably foolish at the sound of his own voice.

The next day the Thatchers left. They were going up to Pasadena. Thatcher said, explaining their sudden change of plans. He and Mrs. Thatcher had talked it over together.

and had decided that perhaps it would be best to winter there, but they had enjoyed McAdams's hospitality immensely, and would remember his good advice if they decided to settle out here.

*   *   *   *

A year later, when Marion Thatcher received McAdams's wedding announcements, she was in the East again, in sweeping widow's weeds. There were many who said that she had never looked so fair as in this sorrowful garb, with the dignity of grief sweetening and subduing her charming vivacity of manner. She let the announcement lie in her lap for some time after she had read it, unheedful of the rest of her morning's mail, and she smiled, a trifle wearily, as she took it up again and put it in its envelope.

Her husband's picture was on her writing table, and behind it, a little locked drawer. Letters were there as she opened it, a tiny trinket or two, and a photograph showing its edge from beneath. She placed the announcement with these things, brushing her fingers over them with lingering touch, locked the drawer again, and turned slowly back to the unopened letters awaiting her.

Dancing Flowers and Flower Dances

By Alice Morse Earle

"When as tradition teaches
Young Ashes pirouetted down
Coquetting with young Beeches,

"The Linden broke her ranks and rent
The Woodbine wreaths that bind her
And down the middle, buzz! she went
With all her bees behind her."
Alfred Tennyson.

THERE has ever been a close kinship in my mind of flowers with dancing, nearly as close as music and dancing—"that married pair," as Lucien calls them. This association is more vivid to me than to some blind souls because, when a child, I knew that blossoms were not constantly attached to their stems and roots; they had feet, and perhaps wings, and could fly and walk and dance of their own power and volition. I felt sure that by dusky twilight and brave moonshine, flowers danced away from their restraining leaves and stems and branches, that they visited and talked with each other, and played games, and gave flower-balls, and danced together gayly. I used to look at the sly things hanging their heads demurely in the noonday sunlight, but blowing back and forth in the breezes, as if taking little dance steps, and plainly longing to be whirling away.

Trees dancing after the pipes of Amphion have been oft sung of the poets, and though I never saw trees dancing (as I did often flowers in my childhood) I find much spirited suggestion and action in Tennyson's tree dance, "when legs of trees were limber."

556

Flowers are like people: some are much better dancers than others; some have a certain carriage of the head and gesture like pretty, vain women; others have a bold expression; some look unkempt, untidy; others are precise and formal to a degree; others show extreme refinement; some are awkward; long pendant racemes, such as the wistaria or locust or laburnum, linger heavily and move slowly, and clusters of bloom like the lilac stand stiffly upright. Flower heads like hollyhocks or foxgloves are too crowded to dance well; but all disc-shaped blooms or single flowers on long stems dance bravely. Single flowers dance better than double ones, who wear too many petticoats. A certain purple clematis and its starry white sister used to take many pretty short steps all day long; waving, sidling, peeping in our windows, until at night the great flowers all vanished to the sound of fairy music, to join the dance. I was told that the morning-glory led many a jolly country-dance in the small hours of the morning Scarlet poppies made gay Spanish dancers, strewing their silken ruffles and petticoats by the wayside. Single dahlias and sunflowers danced the reel. Dora and William Wordsworth both noted the dancing daffodils as they pirouetted in the wind in English meadows.

He wrote:

"A host of golden Daffodils
Fluttering and dancing in the breeze.
Ten thousand saw I at a glance,
Tossing their heads in sprightly dance."

Her description of them is far more poetical: "They grew among the mossy stones; some rested their heads on those stones as on a pillow, the rest tossed and reeled and danced, and seemed as if they verily laughed with the wind, they looked so gay and glancing." It is such word-painting as this that makes me convinced of the great debt William Wordsworth's poetry owes to Dora Wordsworth.

I don't know what fanciful association in my childish mind made the columbine to me ever the gay jester of the garden. It was certainly long before I saw a ballet of harlequins and columbines, because it seemed to me perfectly natural to find these dancers in the Christmas pantomime garbed in yellow and green peaked caps, and gay scarlet-pointed petticoats, with golden bells, just like the flowers in our garden. Look at columbines the next time you see them in the ledges of a rocky field or in a garden. What bright and happy things they are! Pierrot and Pierrette! Listen, you hear their jingling bells, their castanets, as they laugh and dance, such cheerful merry flowers! it is good to see them.

Columbines are, according to Parkinson, "flowers of that respect as that no gardener would willingly be without them that could tell how to have them." These English aquilegias were not, however, our own dashing scarlet columbines, but the duller colored English ones, who are more clumsy dancers.

Emerson had a fine comprehension of the columbine's nature, and named a rock-loving columbine as a "salve for his worst wounds." How many Worcester flower-lovers can recall the special magnificence of the rock-loving columbines which grew in the rich woods near the Tatnuck Cascade! And a picture of my childhood, as vivid as if of yesterday's sight, as vivid as the color of the flowers, is of an old quarry left untouched by man's hand for years, but which had never remotely approached being field or pasture—not even one of our New England pastures of rocks and stones. It was simply a shallow hollow of broken stone, filled scantly with dead leaves and wind-blown earth, and grown round about with cedars; but it was hung in gorgeous color with oriental gold and scarlet, in flowering columbine. I was with my father; we had driven to Rochdale, a little village near our Worcester home, and I can recall his delight as he saw the rough stones, so scant of earth, so rich of fluttering, dancing, brilliant blossoms.

This columbine quarry thereafter became one of the regular haunts of my father and mother, visited yearly as were scores of other fields and forests, upland pastures, meadows, and swamps, by this flower-loving twain. They had their own cherished spots where they greeted their beloved flower friends and gathered for scores of successive years trailing arbutus, hepatica, bloodroot, anemone. polygala, twin-flower, azalea, the varied lady's-slippers and violets, orchids, Arethusa, calopogon, lady's-tresses, pitcher-plant, grass of Parnassus, fringed gentian, and many, many others. All the flowers of field and forest knew these their human friends, as did the flowers of their garden, and all gave to them freely and gladly of perfume and beauty.

Many years ago, a little child ran out into the June gloaming and brought into the house an apron half full of the blossoms of a sulphur-yellow rose, which had large blooms that were scarcely double, and were much prized by her mother, who had received this rare rose from an author who knew as much of roses as of American history, George Bancroft. The child was sharply reproved for picking these stemless roses, but was sent to bed in far deeper disgrace for asserting that "the roses picked themselves," adding, what her mother deemed a specious invention of Satan, that the roses were dancing on the grass. But to this day the child *knows* she saw those yellow roses dancing.

The dances of all primitive peoples, were associated with flowers; many tied dancing garlands. A modern Egyptian dance called "The Bee" is acted in pantomime by the dancer, who appears to be stung while gathering flowers. The nightly moon-dances of eastern Africa are the most beautiful and graceful of measures, in which the dancers, garlanded with wreaths, circle round the opening night flowers.

Among many savage races in New Mexico, South America, and Ceylon, a man takes part in formal dances dressed in green branches, like the English "Jack in the Green." A charming dancing petticoat is made for the male dancers of Torres Straits; the pale yellow green sprouting leaves of the cocoanut palm are arranged in rows of fringes, and the man wears gorgeous flowers in his hair; others personify the beautiful red and black pigeons of that country. The ancient Greeks and Romans had special flower dances; one, the Anthema, had a flower chorus with special steps indicative of flower gathering, and these dancers sung:

"Where's my lovely parsley, say,
  My violets, roses, where are they?
  My parsley, roses, violets fair,
  Where are my flowers? Tell me where?"

All dances were originally a part of religious worship and the Maypole Dance was foreshadowed in the Cult of the Tree; in arid countries to-day the tree is revered as an emblem of endurance and fertility. Christian missionaries in Thibet and other countries found it wise to adapt themselves to many local religious customs, especially in tree worship. In Goa, in 1650, a dance of converts to Jesuitism was held around a huge tulip-shaped flower which opened and showed the figures of the Virgin and Child.

Dancing and flowers have been associated in English life since Chaucer's day, when "knights and ladies daunced upon the greene grass; and the which being ended, they all kneeled downe and did honor to the daisie—some to the flower, some to the leafe." The Mayday dances of old England, with Morrismen, and scores of characters dressed in "green, yellow, and other wanton color," formed a festival of importance. Parts of the mummery and dancing still survive in Lancashire and Cheshire. The Mayday dancers wear knee-breeches and ribbons, and carry stick swords, and wear garlands on their straw hats. The garland or nosegay was ever imperative; without it the dancer was "unmorrissed." Originally the nosegay was of the herb *thrift,* then called "Our Lady's Cushion." The old dance music which was used, "Staines-Morris," is very cheerful and catchy.

Sweet was the music and sweet the names, even of the simplest dances. "The Milkmaid's Delight," "Cheshire Round," "Nonesuch," "I loved thee once, I love no more," "The Beginning of the World," "John, kiss me now," and the famous "Greensleeves":

"Greensleeves was all my Joy,
    Greensleeves was my delight,
Greensleeves was my Heart of Gold,
    Who but Ladie Greensleeves!"

A kiss was the established fee for a partner. King Henry VIII. says, "Sweetheart! I were unmannerly to take you out and not to kiss you." A custom still exists among country fiddlers in England, when tired of fiddling, they close with two squeaking notes which all rustics understand thus, "Kiss her!" Even the poet Wordsworth noted this:

"They hear when every dance is done,
    When every whirling bout is o'er,
The fiddles *squeak*—that call to bliss
    Ever followed by a kiss."

The first of May was scarcely the time in New England for open-air dancing around a Maypole, unless with vigor, in order to keep warm; yet several Maypoles were erected in colonial towns in early days. They were promptly destroyed.

In New England it has ever been the custom of children, not to demand gifts, as did English children, but to give them, of May baskets. But the closest approach to any Mayday celebration was the annual gathering of

the exquisite blooms of the trailing arbutus. Gay parties of young people went on these excursions together, but any thought of dancing would have been frowned upon. The more watchful among our parents did not favor these Maying parties, as we were prone to sit down upon logs and stones, and in New England, April and May are ill suited for such loiterings. To one rough field, just beyond Tatnuck, full of vast boulders, tree stumps, and brushwood, I went each year with my father to gather the pinkest Mayflowers. I remember the exact scent of that field under the spring sun, and the intense heat among the bushes. And there we always saw a huge black snake, the same snake every year, I do believe. And there, when fourteen years old, I took cold, and had the only severe illness of my life, and was never permitted to go Maying again. The beautiful blossoms thus gathered were tied in tight little bunches with an encircling edge of ground pine, and were deemed the choicest of gifts for a friend, or to carry to school to our teacher. Some thrifty boys made these knots for sale, at a penny each; and displayed them in baskets upon beds of green moss with partridge berry vines, in most attractive fashion.

Dancing was in ancient times a classic endowment, a stately accomplishment, but little short of a fine art, as was the arranging of significant garlands, and the wreathing of the head with flowers. Even so profound a thinker as Sir Francis Bacon could write of dancing as "a thing of great state and pleasure." The fair and daring maid who now tries to wear a garland must have classic beauty and bearing, and even then is usually a guy. Not less venturesome is she who attempts any formal art of dancing. We have now on our stage the skirt dance, a pretty but monotonous series of poses which are hardly dancing steps, in which many yards of material are gracefully whirled about, and the attraction seems not in the dancing but in the skirt, a pretty diaphanous material of artistic tints, which, with carefully thrown lights and clever mirrors, supply the charms of skirt dancing. There be those who long for a real ballet, such as the delightful Butterfly Ball, which, some years ago, we saw with gratitude danced in New York after each opera performance. It wasn't danced very well, but people enjoyed it nevertheless. The weary hours of spectacular plays have been endured for the sake of the few minutes of ballet. How eagerly we gaze on some nervously agile little dancer, beating her tiny feet and her heart out in a few graceful and delightful steps, in some vaudeville show. I think had we good dancers, we should have dance enthusiasts and lovers as of yore. Read of the craze over Taglioni and Fanny Ellsler; elderly folk raved till the day of their death over the charms of those dancers of their youth. In America Fanny Ellsler was adored; clergymen saw and admired her grace, purity, and goodness, and vied with each other in offering her pew seats for her Sunday church-going. Whole families attended her performances, and gazed on her in edification as well as delight. It is told on somewhat vague authority, that Ralph Waldo Emerson and Margaret Fuller sat entranced through one of her *pas seules*. "Margaret," said he, as the vision vanished from the stage, *"this is Love."* "Nay, Waldo," she answered with solemnity, "it is more than Love, it is *Religion.*" The dancer wore rather long, scant, and clinging petticoats. A wreath of flowers rested on her coal-black hair which was drawn over her ears in the primmest fashion ever known to woman; usually she danced with a garland.

Flowers no longer dance for me. They grow firmly and properly on their stems, and die where they are born, like quiet, dull, stay-at-home citizens. I don't know why they should dance when no one else does; but I am glad they did dance when I was young.

Sea-Born

By Virna Sheard

AFAR in the turbulent city,
In a hive where men make gold,
He stood at his loom from dawn to dark,
While the passing years were told.

And when he knew it was summer-time
By the gray dust on the street,
By the lingering hours of daylight,
And the sultry noon-tide heat—

Oh! he longed as a captive sea-bird
To leave his cage and be free,
For his heart like a shell kept singing
The old, old song of the sea.

And amid the noise and confusion
Of wheels that were never still,
He heard the wind through the scented pines
On a rough, storm-beaten hill;

While, beyond a maze of painted threads
Where his tireless shuttle flew,
In fancy he saw the sunlit waves
Beckon him out to the blue.

An Historic Town in Connecticut

By Clifton Johnson

With illustrations by the author.

MY acquaintance with Say-
brook began rather unpro-
pitiously at its one hotel.
This was a shapeless, yel-
low structure, evidently an old residence remodelled and enlarged. Its
busiest portion was the bar-room
adorned with a heavy cherry counter
and an imposing array of bottles on
the shelves behind. When I entered
the adjoining office several men were
in the bar-room running over their vo-
cabularies of swear-words in a high-
voiced dispute, while in the office itself
sat two young fellows drowsing in
drunken stupor. The whole place was

permeated with the odors of liquor
and with tobacco fumes, both recent
and of unknown antiquity.

But if the aspect of local life as seen
at the hotel was depressing, the village,
the evening I arrived, was, to my eyes,
quite entrancing. In the mild May
twilight I walked from end to end of
the long main street. The birds were
singing, and from the seaward
marshes came the piping of the frogs
and the purring monotone of the
toads; lines of great elms and sugar
maples shadowed the walks, and the
latter had blossomed so that every
little twig had its tassels of delicate

yellow-green, and a gentle fragrance filled the air. Among other trees, a trifle retired, were many pleasant houses of the plain but handsome and substantial type in vogue about a century ago. In short, the place furnished an admirable example of the old New England country town and imparted a delightful sense of repose and comfort.

The most incongruous feature of the village was an abnormal modern schoolhouse that in its decorative trickery matched nothing else on the street. From this it was a relief to turn to the white, square-towered old church near by, which gave itself no airs and cut no capers with architectural frills and fixings. On its front was a bronze plate informing the reader that here was

The First Church of Christ
in Saybrook
organized
in "the Great Hall" of the fort in the summer of 1646.

Thus it was one of the earliest founded churches in the commonwealth.

An odd thing about the town was that it seemed the greatest place for bicycles I have ever visited. Everyone rode—old and young, male and female. Pedestrianism had apparently gone out of fashion, and I got the idea that the children learned to ride a wheel before they began to walk.

Another odd thing was that the village looked neither agricultural nor suburban. It is in truth the dwelling-place of a country aristocracy possessed of a good deal of wealth, and labor is not very strenuous. The people are content if they have sufficient capital safely invested to return

them a comfortable living and save them the necessity for undue exertion. Yet, to quote a native, "They are nothing like as rich as they were fifty years ago."

Much money has been lost in one way and another. The decrease, however, is particularly due to removals and to the division of large individual properties among several heirs. But whatever the ups and downs of fortune, the town apparently changes slowly and the inhabitants cling to the customs of their forefathers. This I thought was evidenced by the retention of miles and miles of unnecessary fences about the dwellings, some of them of close boards, suggestive of monastic seclusiveness.

The oldest house in the town and one that still presents in the main its original aspect, dates back to 1665. It is painted a dingy yellow and has a high front, from which the rear roof takes a long slant downward until the eaves are within easy reach and you have to stoop to go in at the back door. The windows have the tiny panes of the time when the dwelling was erected. The rooms all have warped floors, and low ceilings crossed by great beams, and the heavy vertical timbers assert themselves in the corners. The upper story has only two apartments finished. As was usual in houses of this kind the rest was left simply garret space bare to the rafters. In the heart of the structure is an enormous chimney that, on the ground floor, takes up the space of a small room. There are fireplaces on three sides, but their days of service are past, though they never have been closed except with fireboards.

At the rear of the house under an

apple-tree were two vinegar barrels, each of which had an inverted
bottle in the bunghole. The contents
of the barrels in their cider state had
been allowed to freeze and then were
drained off. A highly concentrated
beverage, much esteemed by the well-
seasoned cider-lover, was in this
manner obtained. I was offered a
chance to make the acquaintance of
the liquor, yet not without warning
that, as it was almost pure alcohol,
there was some danger of overdoing
the matter.

To the north of the town one does
not follow the highways far without
encountering country that, with all the
years passed since the settlement of
the region, is still only half tamed.
Here are rocky hills, brushy pastures,
and rude stone walls overgrown with
poison ivy. The work is carried on in
a primitive fashion. Many of the
homes are ancient and dilapidated and
the premises strewn with careless
litter. A landowner of this district
with whom I talked affirmed that
farming did not pay, and the reason
he gave was the competition of the
West—it had knocked the bottom out
of prices.

I wondered if there were not other
reasons. He was furrowing out a
half-acre patch on which he intended
to plant potatoes. His hired man was
leading the horse while he himself
held the plough-handles. It seemed
to me his patch was not large enough
to work economically with a view to
profit, and that the profit was also
being dissipated by having two men
do work that might be done by one.
Down the slope was a long stretch of
marshes that swept away to the sea
with a muddy-banked creek wander-

ing through the level. On the
marshes the man said he would cut salt
hay later in the year, and as the soil
was too boggy to bear the weight of a
horse, not only would the mowing
have to be done by hand, but he and
his helper would be obliged to carry
the hay to firm land between them
on poles. Here again it was not easy
to discern much chance for profit.
The process was too laborious where
the product was of so little value.
Then, at the man's house, I noted that
the stable manure lay unprotected by
any roof, leeching in the sun and rain,
that the mowing-machine and other
tools were scattered about the yard,
accumulating rust, and that things in
general looked careless and easy-going. I did not wonder that he took a
pessimistic view of farming.

The places of many of his neighbors
were akin to his, and as a whole this
outlying district had an air decidedly
old-fashioned—an air that was emphasized by the presence of an occasional
slow ox-team toiling in the fields, and
now and then an antiquated well-
sweep in a dooryard.

A well-sweep was an adjunct of one
house in the town itself—a gray,
square little house far gone in decay. Lights were missing from the
windows, clapboards were dropping
off, blinds were dilapidated or gone
altogether, and the out-buildings
either had fallen and been used
for stovewood or were on the
verge of ruin. The shed used as a hen
house leaned at a perilous slant. Near
it was a scanty pile of wood and a saw-
horse made by nailing a couple of
sticks crosswise on the end of a box
so that the tops projected above the
box-level and formed a crotch. Along

ON THE WALK

AT WORK IN THE GARDEN

the street-walk staggered a decrepit picket fence with a sagging gate. The yard was a chaos of weeds and riotous briers and the place looked mysterious —as if it had a history.

A tiny path led around to the back door, so little trodden I was at first in doubt whether the house was inhabited or not until I saw a bent old woman coming from the grass field at the rear of the premises. On her head she wore a sunbonnet of ancient type and over her shoulders a faded shawl. She was hobbling slowly along with the help of a cane and bore on her arm a basket with a few dandelion greens in the bottom. I stood leaning on the fence hoping chance would give me an opportunity to know more about this strange home; and, to avoid an appearance of staring, I now looked the other way. But my loitering had attracted the woman's attention and, instead of going into

the house, she set her basket on the back doorstep and came feebly down the path and spoke to me. She was a mild-eyed, kindly old soul, and in the chat which followed I learned that she was eighty years old and that her brother, aged seventy-six, the only other member of the household, was a "joiner." Presently I asked about some of the garden flowers which had survived in their neglected struggle with weeds and brambles.

"They need the old woman," she said, " but I'm most past such work now. My lameness is getting worse. I have it every winter and it doesn't leave me until warm weather comes. I shall have to get my brother to hoe some here. He isn't much for taking care of flowers, but he likes 'em as well as anyone, and if he's going to make a call he'll pick a bunch to carry along. I used to have more kinds and I'd keep some of 'em in the house through the

AT THE WELL

SPRING WORK

winter, but w...
see the fire d...
got too hard f...
"What are...
spreading all...
quired.
"Those are...
Want one?"
My reply w...
invited into th...
tle blossom a...
"You can ha...
"Thank yo...
are these li...
"Those are...
first plants of...
in Tolland Co...
"Yes, I bel...
"Take some...
"No. I'd ra...
Here are some...
What are the...
"Those are...
have a ro...
you can ca...
Thus our...

FURROWING FOR POTATOES

winter, but when I did that I had to see the fire didn't go out nights and it got too hard for me."

"What are those white flowers spreading all through the grass?" I inquired.

"Those are myrtle—white myrtle. Want one?"

My reply was affirmative and I was invited into the yard. I picked a myrtle blossom and the old woman said, "You can have more just as well."

"Thank you, one will do; and what are these little flowers at my feet?"

"Those are bluebottles. I got the first plants of them at my cousin's up in Tolland County. Want one?"

"Yes, I believe I would like one."

"Take some more if you care to."

"No, I'd rather have just the one. Here are some pink flowers in a bunch. What are they?"

"Those are polyanthus. You can have a root to take home with you if you can carry it."

Thus our talk rambled on while we considered double violets, "daffies," bloodroot, mandrakes, "chiny asters," tiger lilies, "pineys," tulips, hyacinths, etc. The garden had formerly been very tidy and I could trace its decorative arrangement of beds and paths. The borders of the beds were outlined with rows of big "winkle" shells which the brother had brought up from the seashore a mile or two distant, where he sometimes went "clamming and oystering."

Close about the house were blue and yellow lilies, bunches of ferns, and a good deal of shrubbery, including roses, a "honeysuckle" bush, and a tall "li-lack." This last carried its blossoms so high they were far beyond the woman's reach as she stood on the ground, and she only picked such as she could reach from an upper window. Near the back door was a big butternut tree and a grapevine overrunning a shaky trellis. Here too was the well-sweep with its rickety curb and its oaken bucket.

I was made welcome to step inside the house and see the old dwelling, but I did not find it especially interesting. The barren, cluttered rooms with their suggestion of extreme poverty were depressing. In the parlor, which was used as a sort of storeroom, were a number of antiquated pictures on the walls, most of them in heavy frames that the woman had contrived herself —some of cones, some of shells stuck in putty. The cones and shells varied much in size and kind and the patterns were intricate and ingenious. Then there was a specimen of hair work, dusty and moth-eaten, which she took out of its frame that I might inspect it closer. "I used to be quite a hand at these sort of things," she explained, "but now I don't have the time. It's all I can do to get enough to eat."

I came away wondering what the trouble was that the brother and sister were so poorly provided for in their old age, and when I inquired about it I was told that the brother was "one of the smartest men in Connecticut," an architect and builder of great ability, but "he had looked through the bottom of a glass too often."

The most historic portion of Saybrook is what is known as "The Point," a seaward-reaching projection a half mile across, connected with the mainland by a narrow neck. Here the first settlers established themselves in 1635. The leaders of the expedition had in October of that year reached Boston from across the sea. There they collected twenty men and hired a small vessel in which they sailed about the middle of November for the mouth of the Connecticut. They brought with them materials for the erection of homes to accommodate both themselves and others who were to follow; and they were prepared to construct a fort, in part to prevent the Dutch, who aspired to control the river, from accomplishing their purpose, and in part to defend themselves against the Indians.

They arrived none too soon; for a few days after they landed, a vessel from New Amsterdam appeared off shore with intent to take possession of the region and build fortifications. Luckily the English had mounted a couple of cannon, and the Dutch thought best to return peaceably whence they had come. Winter soon set in, and the settlers could do little beforehand save to provide themselves with shelters of the most primitive kind. In the spring, work was taken up in earnest, and other settlers came; but for a long time the colony grew very slowly, and the earliest years were years of annual struggle with the stubborn earth and the hard winters. One of the first tasks of the pioneers was to build a wooden fort and to set up a line of palisades twelve feet high across the neck of the peninsula. Like all the early towns Saybrook suffered at the hands of the Indians. A number of its inhabitants were slain in the immediate vicinity and the cows sometimes returned from pasture with arrows sticking in their sides.

By 1647, while the population was still less than one hundred, a church was erected. Up to that time the meetings had been held in what the records speak of as "the great hall" of the fort. The church stood at one end of a public square called "The Green."

To assemble the people for service a drum was beaten, and it was voted that at the front door of the church should be "a gard of 8 men every Sabbath and Lecture-day compleat in their arms." A sentinel, too, was stationed on a turret, or platform, built on the meeting-house roof. The necessity of this protection against savage assault is seen when one remembers that an average of over four score English are estimated to have been slain yearly by the Indians during the first half century of Connecticut's settlement. This seems distressing enough, but from the Indian viewpoint the slaughter was far worse; for twenty of their number were killed to one of the white.

A second meeting-house was completed in 1681 near the site of the first. Of this structure it is known that the seats in the body of the house were plain wooden benches assigned to members of the congregation according to age, rank, office, and estate. Several leading men were given permission to build square pews against the walls of the audience room, and the minister's family had a square pew at the right of the pulpit. The pulpit itself was a high, angular construction furnished with a Geneva Bible, a Bay Psalm Book, and an hour-glass with which to time the service. The two deacons faced the congregation sitting on a seat at the base of the pulpit, and the tithing man with his fox-tail rod of office took his position where he could best oversee the behavior of the worshippers.

The original settlement of Saybrook Point about the fort gradually overflowed to the mainland, until presently the center of population and the chief village were a mile or two from the earlier hamlet. Thus, when the third

571

ON THE OUTSKIRTS

church was built in 1726 at a cost of $1,600 a new and more generally convenient location was chosen.

Until near the end of the century this edifice had neither steeple nor bell. After these were added it was customary, down to 1840, to ring the bell every noon to announce to the people the arrival of the dinner hour. The bell was also rung during the winter at nine in the evening as a notification it was bedtime. Neither of the previous churches were ever warmed, nor was this for more than one hundred years.

The chief feature of the church interior was the high pulpit overhung by a huge sounding-board, both much elaborated with panels and mouldings. On Sunday the pulpit stairs were filled by small boys who were always eager to get the upper step, for this position gave the occupant the honor of opening the pulpit door to the minister when he ascended to his place. The pews were square with seats on three sides so that a portion of the worshippers sat with sides or backs to the preacher. A wide, heavy gallery extended clear around the room except on the north, where rose the pulpit Its east wing was exclusively for women, the west for men. The front tier of seats was reserved for the singers. Behind them on the south side were four box pews regarded by many as most desirable sittings. Some of the young people of both sexes found these especially attractive, though more because the seclusion was adapted for social purposes than because of any religious ardor. Finally, in each of the remote rear corners of the gallery was still another box pew for the occupancy of the colored people, who were not allowed to sit elsewhere.

Perhaps Saybrook's strongest appeal to fame is the fact that the town was the first domicile of Yale University. It was characteristic of the settlers of New England that no sooner had they set up their homes on the soil than they began to make provision for the education of their children. Not content with establishing primary schools, they founded Harvard College within seven years of the settlement of

Boston. Connecticut, in proportion to its population and means, bore its full share in Harvard's support; but after the lapse of some fifty years the people of the colony began to feel a need of having a collegiate school of its own. The idea took definite form at a meeting of Connecticut pastors in September, 1701, when each one present made a gift of books to the proposed college.

The infant institution which, subsequently, in honor of a generous benefactor, took the name of Yale, was thus started, and shortly a citizen of Saybrook gave it the use of a house and lot. This house was quite sufficient, for during the first six months the college community consisted of the president and a single student, and only fifty-five young men were graduated in fifteen years. The trustees were far from unanimous in locating

the College at Saybrook, and its affairs continued in an unsettled state until 1716, when it was transferred to New Haven. The change was not accomplished without turmoil, a curious account of which is found in the Rev. Samuel Peters's *General History of Connecticut,* published in 1781. He says:

"A vote passed at Hartford, to remove the College to Weathersfield; and another at Newhaven, that it should be removed to that town. Hertford, in order to carry its vote into execution, prepared teams, boats, and a mob, and privately set off for Saybrook, and seized upon the college apparatus, library, and students, and carried all to Weathersfield. This redoubled the jealousy of the saints at Newhaven, who thereupon determined to fulfill their vote: and accordingly having collected a mob sufficient for the enterprise, they sat out for Weathersfield, where they seized by surprise the students, library, etc., etc. But on the road to New Haven, they were over-

A SEAWARD LOOK ACROSS THE MARSHES

taken by the Hertford mob, who, however, after an unhappy battle, were obliged to retire with only a part of the library and part of the students. The quarrel increased daily, everybody expecting a war; and no doubt such would have been the case had not the peacemakers of Massachusetts-Bay interposed with their usual friendship, and advised their dear friends of Hertford to give up the College to Newhaven. This was accordingly done to the great joy of the crafty Massachusetts, who always greedily seek their own prosperity, though it ruin their best neighbors.

"The College being thus fixed forty miles further west from Boston than it was before, tended greatly to the interest of Harvard College; for Saybrook and Hertford, out of pure grief, sent their sons to Harvard, instead of the College at Newhaven."

The Resurrection of a Minister

By Edith Copeman

LIKE millions of diamonds, against a background of deepest blue, the stars were gleaming. Among the leaves of great oak trees on the campus, the wind whispered softly; and beneath the branches two figures paced slowly back and forth.

"It's hard to realize," Dr. Halstead was saying, "that six years have passed since we walked here together and talked of our future on Commencement night. Six years! You have 'Reverend' prefixed to your name, I 'M. D.' added to mine. Truly a wonderful six years! Philip, I can only wish for that young brother of mine, for whose sake we have come so far, a future as bright as ours seems to-night; for yours will be bright in spite of this year's enforced idleness."

Silence for a moment,—then

"Perhaps it was not 'enforced' idleness," the other answered; "and concerning my future, Fred, it's as dark as that sky, and there is no light to brighten it. Shall we sit down here? Smoke, if you like, as you did the last time we sat here, six years ago. And now—I'm lame—"

"Not very," the Doctor interrupted; "and you have your work, and Marion——"

"Don't!" broke in his companion sharply. "Fred, I have nothing: not Marion—*not* my work."

The Doctor's hand dropped, and the cigar fell unnoticed to the ground.

"You don't mean—" he said, amazement in every syllable, "that Marion, to whom you have been engaged—always, it seems——"

"Declined to marry me," the other finished, his voice vibrating with pain. "You know that my horse threw me a year ago, and you know that I shall always be lame. I never dreamed it could make a difference to Marion; but one day, more to hear her tell me that it did not matter to her than for anything else, I asked her if it would hurt her to walk through life with a man who limped. She answered, evasively, that of course I'd recover, and we would wait." The voice faltered then.

The Doctor's hand was on his shoulder. "Don't tell me now," he said; "some other time if you care to."

But Philip recovered himself in a moment.

"I'll tell you now," he said steadily. "I've seen you only once, you know, during those six years. Perhaps as many more will slip by before we meet again, and I want you to know. I could not recover, and I knew it; and the next day I offered to release Marion. She cried, of course, as women all do—doubtless—when they are crushing a man's heart and wrecking his life; but she said, 'it must be for the best.' Can you understand that? *Her* 'best,' no doubt; but for me—. That's all," he added in a moment, "except, as I told you, I have no work; for I gave it up."

"Surely not your ministry, Phil," exclaimed the Doctor.

"My ministry and my church," came the answer in hard tones. "Do you remember the day I was ordained three years ago? You came five hundred miles to see me then, and we stood together near the altar after the services that night. You held out your hand and grasped mine. 'Keep the faith, old man,' you said. 'I'll keep the faith,' I answered. But I have not kept it. The faith of my boyhood and manhood is gone. Called to preach? No! I left my church a year ago,— not as you thought, and as others thought, because I needed a long time in which to regain my strength,—but because I'll never preach a gospel of love and peace and good-will, when with all the power of my being I rebel and protest against the midnight darkness that has come to me."

Dr. Halstead's outstretched hand and warm grasp voiced the sympathy his lips refused to express; and the two men left the seat under the oaks and walked slowly towards the college buildings.

"But surely you have something in mind," the Doctor said. "What next, Philip?"

"Europe for the next few months: then I'm going to look after my father's interests in Jacksonville. That will take but a few days, however. I have no plans beyond that. I wish you were going with me."

"So do I," answered the Doctor heartily; "but I can't, not even to Jacksonville. That's a temptation, however, for my cousin lives just across the river from there. She was Margaret Leslie: you remember her, do you not?"

"Perfectly," Philip answered, "a slender slip of a girl with wonderful hair and eyes, who attended our College Commencement."

"Yes," Dr. Halstead replied, a strange expression stealing over his features. "Margaret isn't Margaret Leslie, Phil. She is Margaret Hammond; and the 'slender slip of a girl' whom you knew has disappeared. You will find her changed—much changed: but go to see her. Promise."

"I shall be most happy to go," Philip responded, wondering at the Doctor's earnestness. And as, side by side, these two men walked up the steps of the College chapel, the Doctor said to himself,

"He must see Margaret. Margaret will help him as no one else can."

Months passed: and the Easter lilies were blooming when Philip Douglass, having reached Jacksonville the day before, left his hotel and stood at the river's edge looking for some one to row him across.

"Massa Douglass, sah?" a voice called, accompanied by a vigorous splashing of oars. "Gwine to cross, sah? Miss Margaret say be sho' to look fo' yo'," and a woolly head was bared, and two strong hands steadied the boat as Philip climbed in, understanding at once that Dr. Halstead, whom he had seen a week before, had written his cousin of his coming.

"How did you know me?" Philip asked curiously as they glided away.

"Miss Marg'ret 'scribe Massa," came the answer; " 'Massa Douglass look like dat, Ben,' Miss Marg'ret say, 'less he much changed—an' he come from dat hotel.' "

Swiftly the man rowed; and they neared the green bluffs of the opposite shore. Then the long strokes sent the boat up one of the creeks, and soon the rower turned his head.

"Dat's de house, sah," he said, "an' dat's Miss Marg'ret up dar."

Far back from the water Philip saw the rambling many-windowed house, sheltered on all sides by cypress and pine trees. Near the water's edge, great trees stood in stately beauty— their branches bearing proudly their burdens of heavy moss, which hung over the water. Beyond the house stretched acres of woodland, and over all the blue arch of the heavens reflected itself in the water, over which the light boat flew. Hundreds of the fair white lilies of the Southland

nodded their pure heads between the water's edge and the two women standing halfway up the gently sloping bank, and the air was heavy with the perfume of the flowers.

The girl had disappeared; and the figure on' the bank was that of gracious, well-rounded womanhood. The softly waving brown hair was unchanged, but the wonderful eyes— dark as midnight—held in them, not the light of the stars as of old, but a certain indefinable something that made the tears spring unbidden to one's eyes, only to be checked as one became conscious of the rare strength and sweetness of the softly curved lips.

Beside her stood a woman with skin like brown satin, with eyes full of adoration and love. She said something to her mistress as the little boat came near, and a smile lighted up the face.

Philip glanced at his companion. The negro's head was bare, and his features twitched.

"Your mistress is very beautiful," the passenger said, half to himself, when Ben had pulled past the two and towards the landing a little way up the stream.

"She's de kin' wot de Lawd lub bes', sah," the man answered.

"Why?" queried Philip in surprise.

"Cos she lub His will," came the answer reverently. "O, Massa, many's de time I's seed her standin' dar wen I's rowed Massa Hammon' ober; an' she wave her han', an' smile, an' her lubly eyes dey sparkle like de sunshine on de watah. O, Miss Marg'ret— honey——"

"And he died!" Philip said under his breath.

Ben nodded.

"He ketched de scarlet feber up No'th, sah," he said. "Miss Marg'ret she take car ob him—get it too; Massa die, an' Miss Marg'ret get well, but——"

He hesitated, then went on, his voice almost a whisper: "Ob cose de gen-'leman know, ebber since den Miss Marg'ret blin'.'"

"Blind!" Then he understood the note of pain that had crept in the Doctor's voice when he spoke of his cousin.

He left the boat, and a moment later walked along the path to where a white-robed figure advanced with out-stretched hand to meet him.

"You are very welcome, Mr. Douglass,' his hostess said; "Dr. Halstead wrote that you were coming to Jacksonville yesterday, and would come over here to-day. And you have so lately seen the Doctor, whom I have not seen for over three years. Will you tell me all about him?"

They were walking towards the house; and Philip understood perfectly that Mrs. Hammond was talking in order to give him time to recover from the shock he felt at the change that had come to her.

He was quite himself when they reached the house; and he told her—and few could tell as well—of the Doctor's work, his new home and his charming young wife.

"You make me *see* it all," Margaret said softly. "I knew he would succeed—that the world needed him—but we did not dream that success would come as soon as it has. He deserves it."

"He does," responded her guest emphatically; "more perhaps than others, because he thinks less of success than of his work."

Not a word that day of himself, not a word of the change that had come in her life; but before he was rowed back across the St. Johns he knew he would not leave Jacksonville in six days as he had planned.

Day after day he crossed the river, conscious—in a strange, vague way—that hope and help lay in Margaret Hammond's hands; and each day he wondered what *that* day would bring.

Two weeks slipped by. He was rowing across in the white moonlight, and Mrs. Hammond was sitting on her porch, with Nellie a few yards away.

The splash of the oars made music, far-reaching and sweet, and across the still night air it stole and reached her ears. Her lips parted and a low sobbing breath came from them.

"Nellie, do you hear that?" she asked, almost in a whisper.

The woman came close to her chair.

"Yes, Miss Margaret," she answered.

"Is it moonlight, Nellie, bright moonlight?" came from the white lips.

"Yes, Miss Marg'ret. O honey, don't listen!"

But her mistress did not hear her. She rose from her low chair and walked to the edge of the veranda. From head to foot she trembled.

"Oh!" she whispered. The sound of the rowing, then the footsteps, the bright moonlight and the scent of the lilies—— "O Nellie, Nellie, take me in."

Silently the woman led her into the house and to a softly-cushioned chair. She knelt beside her, the tears falling over the dark face: full well she knew the memory it brought to her mistress.

On moonlight nights her lover had rowed himself across the silvery river, and the girl on the porch had waited with love-lit eyes and smiling lips while the voice of the water had told her of his coming.

Since Mr. Hammond's death no one had rowed to that landing at night, for a little way down the stream was another, where by tacit understanding they moored their boats.

Steps came up the porch—not the eager, springing ones of old, but the halting steps of a lame man. Directly Philip Douglass was announced, and, in spite of Nellie's tearful protest, Margaret rose, her face as white as the moonlight without, and left the room to receive her guest on the veranda, which was also a most delightful sitting-room.

"I came over to say good-bye," Philip said, after the first greetings. "I am going on to-morrow."

"On to New Orleans, or back to your work?"

"To New Orleans," he answered quickly. "I have no work, Mrs. Hammond. Did not the Doctor tell you?"

"Yes," she said quietly. "He told me of your sorrow and—all he knew. But you have your work nevertheless."

"I think not," he replied.

"Pardon me," she said, as she turned towards him. "You may not accept it; you may cast it aside and let it go undone forever—for your work no one else can do: but it *is* yours, and you are not doing it."

"I was ordained a minister, Mrs. Hammond, as you are aware," he responded, "and that part of me is dead."

"The dead shall live," she answered, only half aloud; and her face was

turned towards the spot across the river where *her* dead lay sleeping.

"Mr. Douglass, will you let me speak very plainly to you? Because I have suffered, because I too have seen all that was best and dearest pass out of my life, will you let me touch this wound of yours? Listen! You can see, I cannot—but I know just how the leaves of the trees are waving softly out there. I know well how the white moonlight is playing through them, and how it is gleaming on the water beyond, making it look from here like one mass of moving silver. One night, a night like this three years ago, when they had laid my husband across the river there, and when I knew that I must live all my life in the dark, I slipped away from the house when I thought no one knew, and I walked down there to the edge of the water. You call the taking of one's physical life sin, do you not? I did not care then. I only knew that the sunshine and the daytime had become darkness and midnight. I had turned to stone: I did not hate or love. My love was buried in the grave with my husband, and only one thought filled me—to leave it, all the misery and suffering and horror—and I hoped that, turning my back on this life, God would give me in another world a glimpse of light."

She shivered and paused, living over again the night of which she told him.

"I walked out in the stream," she went on, her voice hardly above a whisper. "When the water reached my waist I let myself fall, and felt it close over me. Then two strong arms were around me, and some one half dragged, half carried me back to the shore. Then I was picked up bodily and carried into the house, where I lay unconscious for hours. They said the fever had not left me, that I was not responsible; but Nellie knew better—Nellie, who had dragged me out of the water. 'Miss Marg'ret,' she said to me, 'de Lawd sen' fo' yo' wen He want yo' up dar. Spec' He's got lots ob wuk fo' yo' 'mong de common folks down heah.' And then I knew I was a coward."

He could hear her quick breathing in the silence that followed. Then—

"Do you know why I have told you this?" she asked. "Because I want you to know that I learned, or am learning, that our lives are *not* our own to use as we choose. Mr. Douglass, will you go back to your work?"

"Not to that work."

"Why? Are you willing to lose your opportunity?"

"I do not see it."

"Do you not?" she asked quickly: and he felt the depth of earnestness in her voice. "Oh, do you not see that if you accepted this sorrow bravely and manfully you would be worthy to preach? But you were not worthy when, at the first burden laid upon you, you faltered and turned back. How could you disappoint God so when He had trusted you? You told your people of Divine strength and power and goodness: but when darkness came in your sky, you said there was neither sun nor moon nor stars! Think! You, a man, God-made and God-endowed, to have looked only for happiness, only for self, when perhaps hundreds of people are waiting for the help you can bring them!"

Then the voice faltered. A lash could not have stung more than the words she had spoken, backed as they were by the scorn and pain in her voice.

The man's face was white. He rose and stood beside her chair.

"You think me a coward!" he said.

A moment's intense silence.

"Yes," she said, quietly, "I think you a—coward."

"I am," he responded: "good night."

To which she replied,

"Will you come over again in the morning?"

"Yes," he said: "good night."

She heard the halting footsteps die away. He had gone—not down to the water's edge where his boat was fastened—but had turned aside and taken the path through the pines, towards the lower landing, intending—Margaret thought—to get Ben to row him across from there.

There was a moss-covered rock in the shadow of the trees; and hardly knowing where he went, he found himself half kneeling, half lying against it, and there in the stillness Philip Douglass came face to face with himself. All that was best and noblest in the man's nature arose and stood a merciless judge over all that was weak and small and selfish.

Like a panorama, scenes of his life passed before him, and always—everywhere—was Marion. He looked back to his school-days, and Marion walked beside him and he carried her books; back to the days when he had planned his future, and Marion had begged, with eyes shining, "Be something *great*, Philip. Be someone in the world who 'counts.'"

Through his college days, Marion's letters and Marion's self had stood like a shield between him and evil: for her he had overcome temptation, that he might look in her eyes unshamed. He heard again her answer on the wonderful white day when he had told her what she had always known, and she had answered as he had always known she would. And during his theological course, and during the time he preached, Marion had been the bright light in which he walked, the faith by which he lived, and the gift of which he tried to be worthy.

And then—in the stillness of the night he breathed hard and fast at the remembrance of the day when he had known that over and above all else towered the *pride* of the girl who had promised to be his wife—a pride that left no room for sacrifice in one whose life had been all sunshine.

He had taken a certain melancholy satisfaction in the belief that life for him was over. But to-night Margaret Hammond had torn the veil from his eyes, and he stood forth as he was.

"You have called yourself a servant of God," his stern judge said, "and you have been serving self. You called on your people to worship a living, real Father, and you set up for yourself an idol of clay and worshipped it. You taught men to be brave, and told women to endure: but *you* proved traitor and coward at the first test."

Dimly there came to him the thought of One who long ago for the sins of others endured the darkness of Gethsemane, One to whom angels ministered. To this man, seeing his own sin and hating himself, would an angel of hope draw near?

He never knew how long he stayed there. He knew it was hours: and then, like one hopeless, he slowly left the still woods and rowed back across the river. And he never knew that the faint splash of his oars reached Margaret's ears and made her start up suddenly in her sleep.

No rest came to him that night; but in the early morning he fell into a heavy dreamless sleep from which he did not awaken until nearly noon. He would have to take the night train, or else break his promise to see Mrs. Hammond again, which was quite impossible.

Early in the afternoon he rowed over. Half-way across he met Ben. He saw the man start at sight of his white hopeless face; and to avoid the question he knew was trembling on the old man's lips, he asked,

"Is Mrs. Hammond at the house, Ben?"

"No, sah; Miss Marg'ret up to ol' Susie's cabin. Susie's lil boy dead. I's gwine across fo' de pa'son, sah."

Then Ben rowed on, and Philip pulled on towards the other side, and up the creek past the landing.

Under the spreading branches of the trees he laid his oars down and let the boat float. He was unwilling to go up to the house until Margaret returned, or to join her in the negro's cabin. He had heard of Susie's little child. Margaret had gone every day to help care for it, and two days before had told him of its death.

An hour passed. Through the trees he could see little groups of people going towards Susie's cabin. Then he saw Ben come back alone. Vaguely he wondered what Ben would say if he knew he had once been a minister. He would be, he knew—even in the eyes of this ignorant black man— an object of scorn and pity: and in the depth of his self-loathing, he almost wished the old man did know. He was puzzled that Ben should have returned without the minister; and after all, he thought he might as well go up to the cabin and walk back with Mrs. Hammond.

The room was full when he entered it, ten minutes later. Margaret stood near the sobbing mother and father, and made room for him when Ben, who had caught sight of him, whispered his name.

"It's very sad," Margaret said in a low tone. "Their minister could not come. He fell this morning and was hurt, and Susie did not receive the message he sent."

"Is there no one else—your own minister, for instance?" Philip asked quickly.

"He is away," Margaret answered sadly. "He would come if he were here. I will sing for them, and old Ben will talk to them."

Then in another minute the full, rich contralto filled the room.

Philip looked about him. On every side his eyes met dark wet faces, and sobs that they vainly tried to check because "Miss Marg'ret" was singing—broke from those who had loved the tiny boy lying so quietly there. He looked towards the white flower-covered casket, and needed no one to tell him it had been Margaret's gift. Beside it stood a small wooden table covered with a white cloth, and on it an open Bible. He could touch it if he reached out his hand. "Nearer, My God to Thee," he heard the voice sing, and it seemed far off. He forgot his shameful fall—the agony of the night before—all the years of his life; and all his world was the space bounded by the walls of the cabin.

The voice of the singer died away. Then in the hush that followed, Margaret felt some one pass her. Old Ben rose slowly; but a tall figure stood before the table, and white hands turned the leaves of the Bible.

"Massa Douglass gwine to read from de scripters," Ben whispered to Margaret.

And she answered as softly: "Mr. Douglass is a minister, Ben. Tell Susie."

"Bress de Lawd!" exclaimed Ben: and soon everyone in the room knew that a white man and a minister was conducting the funeral service of the little negro baby.

Verse after verse he read—the low-toned, perfectly modulated voice speaking comfort to the sore hearts; but Margaret knew that the words held in them for him no life or hope. Then a strange tone crept into his voice.

"'I am the Resurrection and the Life,'" he read: "'he that believeth in me, though he were dead, yet shall he live.'"

The sobbing was hushed. Not the sound of a breath broke the silence that fell. Margaret Hammond's hand was pressed over her heart as if to still its wild throbbing; and she wondered what the Voice speaking to him in this lowliest of places had said. She understood a moment later: for—

"'I am the Resurrection and the Life,'" he repeated, faith and confidence in his tones. "'He that believeth in me, though he were dead, yet shall he live.'" And the voice rang with triumph over death itself, conquered.

Softly, slowly, reverently, he closed the Book and reached out his hands.

"My friends," he said, "let us pray."

*   *   *   *

Margaret Hammond was a guest in Dr. Halstead's home a year later, and he stood beside her with an open letter in his hand.

"From Philip Douglass," he said. "You hear from him, I know, and know of his work; but I wish you could talk to him and know his people."

"Tell me about him," she said: "he writes of his church—of his people—nothing of himself."

The doctor seated himself beside her.

"You know of the church to which he was called," he said "a month ago I heard him preach there. Margaret, a power not of earth fills him , and he stands before a congregation as cultured and intellectual as any in his city, and he holds them spellbound—not because of rare eloquence—not because of anything one can understand; but he speaks straight from his heart to the hearts of his people, and they drink in his words like thirsty ones drinking pure water. 'You should work among the needy,' I said to him after church. 'I do,' he said quickly, 'they *are* needy—the rich.' But the poor belong to him too: and that afternoon I went with him to the homes of those in depths of poverty and sin, and heard him tell hopeless ones of hope, and broken-hearted ones of Divine peace and love. How they love him! They say he's killing himself with work, and I told him so too. Margaret, his face was wonderful when he turned to me, full of earnestness, full of faith and courage. 'I'm not killing myself,' he said: 'I'm living. And to live is what I'm trying to teach others.'"

Then silence reigned, for Margaret heard again the sobs in the negro cabin, the rustling leaves of the Bible, and the wonderful ring in the voice that read, and then repeated, " 'I am the Resurrection and the Life'."

The Quest

By Charlotte Becker

I SEARCHED the world in quest of happiness,—
Through crowded places, and through ways apart,
Unsatisfied—nor knew till your caress,
    It waited, hidden safe, in my own heart!

Washington-Greene Correspondence

A large collection of original letters written by General Washington and General Greene has come into the editor's possession. It is our intention to reproduce in fac-simile those of the letters which present the most interesting details and side lights on the great events of the period covered, even though some of the letters may have been previously published.

The reproduction of these letters in chronological order will be continued in the following issue. A printed copy of the letter herewith appears on page 587.—EDITOR.

Phil.ᵃ Dec.ᵣ 15ᵗʰ 1781.

My dear Sir,

Your private letter of
the 22ᵈ ult.ᵒ came to my hands
the day before yesterday, —
and giving fresh assurances
of your attachment & regard
for me was received with gratitude and affection. — As I
feel myself interested in
every thing which concerns
you it is with unfeigned plea
sure I hear the plaudits
which are bestowed on your
conduct by men of all de-
scriptions — public & private
— and I communicate them to
you with heart felt pleasure
——— there is no Man that does
not acknowledge your emi
nent services, nor is there
                              any

any one that does not allow
that you have done great
things with little means

I wish the detachment
commanded by Genl St Clair
may not be much reduced
before it reaches you — from
what I have heard this is
much to be feared. —

Mrs Greene is now in
this city on her way to So
Carolina — she is in perfect
health and in good spirits
—and thinking no difficulty
too great not to be encoun=
tered in the performance of
this visit, it shall be my en
deavor to strew the way over
"with flowers" —— Poor Mrs
Washington who has met
with a most severe stroke in
the loss of her amiable son &
only.

only child Mr. Custis, is here
with me, and joins me most
cordially in every wish that
tends to your happiness and
glory.— Most sincerely
& affectionately
I am — D Sir
Yr. most obed Ser
G Washington

Majr. Genl. Greene.

My dear Sir,

giving fresh a...
As I feel myself
plaudits which ar...
nicate them to...
services, nor is th...

I wish the d...
—from what I h...

Mrs. Greene
spirits—and thi...
my endeavor to...
severe stroke in...
cordially in every...

Maj'r. Genl Greene

Gen. Washington to Gen. Greene

PHILA., Dec'r 15th, 1781.

MY DEAR SIR.

     Your private letter of the 22d ulto. came to my hands the day before yesterday,—and giving fresh assurances of your attachment & regard for me was received with gratitude and affection.—As I feel myself interested in everything which concerns you it is with unfeigned pleasure I hear the plaudits which are bestowed on your conduct by men of all description—public & private—and I communicate them to you with heartfelt pleasure—There is no man that does not acknowledge your eminent services, nor is there any one that does not allow that you have done great things with little means.

     I wish the detachment commanded by Genl. St. Clair may not be much reduced before it reaches you—from what I have heard this is much to be feared.—

     Mrs. Greene is now in this City on her way to So. Carolina—She is in perfect health and in good spirits—and thinking no difficulty too great not to be encountered in the performance of this visit, it shall be my endeavor to "strew the way over with flowers"—Poor Mrs. Washington who has met with a most severe stroke in the loss of her amiable son & only child Mr. Custis, is here with me, and joins me most cordially in every wish that tends to your happiness and glory.—Most sincerely and affectionately

     I am—Dr Sir,

          Yr. most obed Ser.,

            G. WASHINGTON.

Maj'r. Genl. Greene.

ROWAYTON HARBOR

Norwalk, Connecticut

By Angeline Scott

NORWALK, the only town save one in Connecticut which bears its original Indian name, claims its rank among New England's oldest towns, having celebrated the 250th anniversary of its recognition as a township on September 11, 1901. It is undistinguished in history by Indian massacres, persecutions, battles, or literary associations; and its people seem to be blessed because they have no history in the annals of Connecticut, as read by the world in general, save in a bare mention of Norwalk as one of the coast towns burned by General Tryon during the Revolution. But a little research, stimulated in these days by patriotic and historical societies, brings to light quaint reminiscences of the forefathers'days, typical of every Connecticut town 200 years ago. The first settlement was begun in 1650 after the planters had

purchased rights from Roger Ludlow and signed an agreement "to set upon the plantinge of the sayed Norwalke with all convenient speed." The names mentioned in this document are those of Nathaniel Eli, Rithard Olmstead, Rithard Webb, Nathaniel Rithards, Matthew Marvin, Rithard Seamer, Thomas Spencer, Thomas Hales, Nathaniel Ruskoe, Isacke Graves, Ralph Keeler, John Holloway, Edward Church, John Ruskoe associated with others not named, constituting thirty in all. The little company came from Hartford in the spring of 1651, having been preceded by a few of the hardiest spirits in the previous autumn. They made a camp one night on Blue Mountain, in the northern part of the town, where they must have looked eagerly upon the lovely landscape of their promised land, with the bright blue waters of Long Island Sound sparkling in the distance. The site of the

588

earliest settlement is in East Norwalk, very near the present railroad station. In 1894 the Norwalk Chapter Daughters of the American Revolution marked the place with a block of native granite suitably inscribed. Roger Ludlow was led to purchase Norwalk from the Indians in 1640 by the beauty of its situation and diversified hills and valleys "butting on the sea," intending probably to plant another colony as he had previously done at Fairfield. He at first reserved two lots for his sons in Norwalk, but finally relinquished all title to Norwalk lands before his sudden departure from Connecticut with his family in 1654. Roger Ludlow is nevertheless claimed as the Founder of Norwalk, and a handsome monument of Quincy granite, adorned with a bas-relief in bronze representing Ludlow treating with the Indians, was dedicated to him a few years ago, bearing this inscription: "This stone, erected December, 1895, commemorates the purchase from the aboriginal inhabitants, made February 26, 1640, by Roger Ludlow, deputy governor of the colony of Connecticut, framer of its first code of laws and founder of Norwalk, of all the lands, meadows, pasturings, trees, whatsoever there is, and grounds between two rivers, the one called Norwalk and the other Soaketuck, to the middle of sayed rivers, from the sea, a day's walke into the country."

The settlers shortly afterward purchased a tract on the west side of the Norwalk River from Capt. Daniel Partrick, "as far as the brook Pampaskeshanke" (now known as Roton Brook) which is the present western boundary of the city of South Norwalk. The Norwalk Islands and the

part of the town now called Rowayton were purchased from the Indian Sachems Runckinheage, Piamikin, Magise, Townetom, Winnepucke, and others, in 1708-9. Within the first year of occupation Norwalk was recognized by the Connecticut Court in a decree dated September 11, 1651, "ORDERED, that Norwalke shall bee a Towne, and that they provide an inhabitant, according to order, who shall seasonably be tendered to take the oath of a constable." And, in the following month the first tax was laid. The settlers had their hardships; a wilderness cannot become available for crops until trees have been hewn, swamps drained, and prodigious effort expended in subduing the soil; and they had, in addition, the task of building their dwellings from the trees of a virgin forest, thatching them with the grass of the marshes. All of their implements and provisions other than fish and game

OLD TOWN HOUSE

were necessarily brought from Hartford until the first crop was harvested. There were no difficulties with the Indians to harrass the pioneers. The Norwalk forefathers peaceably treated with the few sachems round about and found them honorable in keeping their word. The rights of the townsmen and of the Indians were well defined, and strict account was kept of boundaries. When "bad coats" were inadvertently given to Mamachimon in payment for land, the wrong was redressed on his complaint. There was sometimes a little friction occasioned by complaints of the "arrowes, gunnes, and dogges" of the red men, but nothing which could not be adjusted by the town officials.

Winnipauke, an Indian sachem deeded lands to the Rev. Thomas Hanford, calling him his "beloved friend." There were wolves in the forest, and a bounty for killing them is an item in town accounts for a number of years. When the log-cabins had become comfortable homes and the meeting-house was built and the training band organized, a period of typical New England town life ensued. All the men were obliged to attend town-meeting under

the penalty of a fine of a shilling for absence. All meetings, both religious and secular, were summoned by beating the "drumb," and one drummer was "rewarded for his Service with the drumb." Later a bell was hung in the meeting-house "for to be wrung ther for the probation of the goodness of the bell." When it became a permanent acquisition the bell was ordered "to be rung by Zerubabell Hoyt at nine of ye clock every night." A law had previously been made that no public transaction should take place after nine at night. Thomas Lupton was chosen, in July, 1668, "to look after the young people in the meeting-house on the Lord's day and to doe his best endeavor to keep them from playing and unsivill behavior in time of public worship." Thomas Barnum undertook the same task in 1681, "to keep good decorum amongst the youth in times of exercise on the Sabbath and other publique meetings; and the Towne doe impower him, if he see any disorderly for to keep a small stick to correct such with, only he is desired to do it with clemency."

Questions of boundaries and high-

A REVOLUTIONARY HOUSE

OLD HOUSE IN WINNEPUCKE

ways required grave and judicious committees. Stamford was very quarrelsome over bounds and the question was carried finally to the Court, and there was a similar difficulty with Fairfield. The site of the meeting-house was changed three times from 1651 to the Revolution; carrying with it the center of population away from its original place. Each time the change was proposed strenuous objections were made, but the movement northward began with the building of the bridge at the "Point of Rocks near the mill" (now the heart of the city of Norwalk), and the progressive spirits carried the day. Later generations sometimes wish they had not, for, after the N. Y., N. H. & H. Railroad was built a new community grew up about the station, resulting in two centers of population divided by a mile of residential district, resulting finally in two municipalities in one township of 20,-000 population; while, if the first settlers had remained at East Norwalk the town would have grown larger in a compact way. Before building each meeting-house the two parties were so evenly divided that it became necessary to submit the question to arbitration committees from outside who

could give impartial judgment on the matter, "the honored deputy Governor, the honored Major Goold with the Rev. Elder Buckingham" served on one committee, and the resolution appointing them reads, "the town ingages to sit down satisfied with there determination as to the place of its standing." In 1718 "Major Peter Burr, Major Samuel Ealls and Mr. Jonathan Law, Esq.," served on a similar committee. Norwalk's first minister, the Rev. Thomas Hanford, was tutored by Dr. Charles Chauncey, second president of Harvard. He was the typical Puritan clergyman of his day, a gentleman and scholar, possessing, too, a turn for practical affairs, since he is rated in 1671 as the possesser of £300, the second largest estate on the list of tax-payers. His ministry covered a period of 41 years; and, in 1686, when he was growing old, the town passed a resolution desiring "Mr. Hanford to proceed in the work of the ministry, and therein to continue in the sayd work, until the Lord by his providence shall dispose of him otherwise; —promising to indeavor to our ability for to give him due incouragement." His salary at first (1656) was "three score pounds allowed for the yere in-

OLD HOUSE, NORWALK

1. FIRST CONGREGATIONAL CHURCH. 2. METHODIST, NORWALK. 3. TRINITY, EPISCOPAL, SOUTH NORWALK.
4.   . 5. CONGREGATIONAL, SOUTH NORWALK. 6. FIRST METHODIST,
SOUTH NORWALK. 7. ST. MARY'S, ROMAN CATHOLIC. 8. ST. PAUL'S, EPISCOPAL

suing, to be paid as followeth—30 pounds in wheat pease and barley at the prices—4 shillings per bushel for wheat and barley, and for pease 3 shillings per bushel, the other 30 pounds to be payed, 8 pounds in (obliterated) and the other 22 pounds is to be payed in beefe and pork at the common currint prise that it brings, when it is dew."

The common school was early established, of course. In 1678 the town-meeting "voted and agreed to hier a scole master to teach all the childring in the towne to lern to reade and write, and that Mr. Cornish shall be hired for that cervice and the townsmen are to hire him upon as reasonable terms as they can." While the schoolmasters were engaged by the town, it appears in 1701 that the parents of the children had to pay at a certain rate for their tuition. "All children from the age of five years old to the age of twelve years, shall all pay an equall proportion; excepting the feamale; all that doe not goe to school, and all youths above the age of twelve yeares as goe in the day shall pay equally with the others above sayed; and all night schollers shall pay a third part so much as the day schoolers; and the schoolers to pay fifteen pounds; and the remainder of the charge of the schoole masters sallary shall be paid by the towne according to their list of estate in the publique list of the Collonie." We have a glimpse of Norwalk in 1704 in the diary of Madame Knight, who made the difficult journey from Boston to New York and return on horseback in the inclement season of the year. She came into Norwalk by the old Stamford Path, which was the highway between Stamford and Fairfield

UNITED BANK BUILDING

250 years ago, "marked by barked trees, heaps of stones and staddle patches." Madame Knight says, "About nine at night we came to Norwalk, having crept over a timber of a Broken Bridge about thirty foot long and fifty to ye water. I was exceedingly tired out and cold when we came to our Inn, and could get nothing there but poor entertainment and the impertinant Bable of one of the worst of men, among many others of which our Host made one, who had he bin one degree Impundenter, would have outdone his Grandfather, and this I think is the most perplexed night I have yet had. From hence, Saturday, December 23, a very cold and windy day, after an intolerable night's lodgings, wee hasted forward, only observing in our way the Town to be situated on a Navigable River, with indifferent Buildings, and people more refined than in some of the Country towns wee had

GRUMMAN'S HILL

passed, tho vicious enough, the church and Tavern being next neighbors." The Rev. Stephen Buckingham was the minister from 1697 to 1727, a man of exceptional culture, possessing a library of a thousand volumes. These books were destroyed fifty years after his death, when the British burned the town. His wife was a grand-daughter of the Rev. Thomas Hooker, and it was said of her "she was the most accomplished lady that ever came to Norwalk." Mrs. Buckingham's mother was the daughter of Capt. Thomas Willett, first mayor of New York City, and her grave in the old "Down Town" cemetery has been suitably marked by her Hooker descendants. All of the early generations of Norwalk are buried in this cemetery at East Norwalk, which has been so ineffectually guarded that many old graves have been encroached upon by modern burials. It is proposed, however, by the Historical Association, to protect those that remain, and a plan has been started to build a wall about the grounds with a memorial arch at

594

the entrance composed of blocks of stone inscribed with the names of the founders of the town, contributed by their descendants.

When one begins a search into Norwalk history the most interesting relics and traditions seem to relate to the burning of the town by British invaders on July 12, 1779. To follow the course of the enemy through the town on that day of terror one should start at Fitch's Point, where the troops landed on the evening before and encamped for the night. The place has been marked with a metal tablet mounted on a wayside stone by the Norwalk Chapter D. A. R. Uncertain of the strength of the Americans, Gen. Tryon divided his forces, one wing commanded by Gen. Garth crossing to the west side of the river, and landing at Old Well (South Norwalk), while the main body under Tryon himself marched up the east side to the heart of the town, taking Grumman's Hill for headquarters. The chair in which Tryon sat that day, watching the flames kindled by his soldiers' torches spreading from farm to farm, is now the property of the Rev. C. M. Selleck, author of "Norwalk," a very complete history of the town, published in 1896. Only a small number of men were available for the defence of the town, so many were enlisted in the war. Capt. Stephen Betts, who commanded the patriots, in an affidavit made by him July 26, 1779, says he had "less than fifty Continental regulars and some militia with which to resist a superior force." They seemed to hold their own for five hours, yet were driven slowly toward "the Rocks" on France Street, where from ten o'clock till noon they resisted the enemy. Two Americans were killed and one wounded, while the British loss, reported by Tryon, was twenty killed, ninety-six wounded, and thirty-two unaccounted for. The burning was accomplished as the British retreated, and the loss in this way was 135 houses, eighty-nine barns, twenty-five shops, five vessels in the harbor, and four mills. None of the houses off the line of march were burned. The detachment under Gen. Garth lost three men in a sharp skirmish on Flax Hill. From there they marched up West Avenue to join Tryon at the northern end of the town. On the way it is said, they came to grief at the home of Deacon Thomas Benedict, who had placed wine and cider on his porch for the refreshment of the patriots who had watched during the previous night. The British soldiers drank of the liquor too freely and, the deacon used to say when he told the story, "a drunken person is as harmless as a corpse." Owing to this delay the Americans from Flax Hill joined their comrades at "the Rocks" before

FLAX HILL REVOLUTIONARY BOULDER

Garth's men reached the place. The Norwalk Chapter D. A. R. has marked the scene of the battle with a granite boulder. The taxable property in Norwalk at the time of the Revolution amounted to three hundred thousand pounds, and the amount of damages allowed by the assembly was about one hundred and sixty thousand dollars, paid in grants of land in the Connecticut Western Reserve in Ohio, known as "sufferer's lands." The inventory of the claim of Fountain Smith's estate shows what a typical house of the times contained. This yellow time-stained document was found, not long since, in a secret compartment of an old chest in the attic of one of his descendants.

Fountain Smith's Loss By Burning of Norwalk. July ye 11, 1779.

One house 28 by 26 one story and a half well finished below......L65.0.0.
One Shop 20 feeat by 18 wide finished ....L5.0.0.
Two Load of Good English hay two ton.......................L4.10.0.
One Chest of Curld Maple draws..L2.0.0.
Two Square Table one Wallnut and one White Wood..........L1.0.0.
Eight Black Chears part Worn....L0.10.0.
One Large Pott Iron about 4 Gallons ....L0.12.0.

COMMEMORATING THE "BATTLE OF THE ROCKS."

One Brass Cittle of 30 We........L.1.10.0.
One Larg Iron Cittle about 2 gal-
lons ....L.0.6.0.
One pair of Styllards...........L.0.3.0.
One Frying pan.................L.0.6.0.
One Small Looking Glass.......L.0.10.0.
Two good Duck Whealls at 15 pr
peas ....L1.10.0.
One Reall......................L.0.4.0.
One Large Wheall..............L.0.6.0.
Two Bedsteads and 2 cords at 10..L.1.0.0.
One Large Duftail Chist with a
lock ....L.0.12.0.
Two puter plates and 2 porringers.L.0.4.0.
One Dozen of Spoons...........L.0.2.0.
Two woden beads...............L.0.12.0.
Two Good Pillows filed with feth-
ers ....L.0.8.0.
One Iron Ladel................L.0.3.0.
One Brass Skinner..............L.0.4.0.
Six Butter Tubs at 3/ pr peace....L.0.18.0.
One Hundred Weight of fish......L.0.19.0.
Three Pork Barrell at...........L.0.12.0.
One Barrell of Tobacco About 60
We ....L.1.10.0.
Two Good Sedar Tubs...........L.0.10.0.
Seventy-five flour casks at 1/6/2....L.5.12.6.
Eight sets of barrells Trushpops..L.1.4.0.
Twenty Two Flax Seeads Cacks at
3/ pr P.......................L.3.6.0.

Six Hundred White Oak staves and
heading ....L.1.10.0.
One Thousand black oac sheaves..L.1.0.0.
Three sinter stocks..............L.4.0.9.
Four hundred black oak staves for fox
Seed Casks at 5/ pr hundred......L.1.0.0.
Two Shaving horses.............L.0.6.0.
One hundred hoop poales.........L.0.4.0.
One Sedar Tub Half Barrell......L.0.4.0.
One Churn at 4/ per...........L.0.4.0.
One half Dozen of round bottles..L.0.2.0.
Three Athorn pals 1 Gallon Each..L.0.3.0.
Six Wooden boles 2 Quarts Each..L.0.6.0.
One Bread Tray................L.0.30.
One Long Salt Morter...........L.0.60.
One Weaned Calf...............L.1.0.0.
Fifteen Geas at 1/6 p. p.........L.1.1.0.
Two Iron Candlesticks...........L.0.30.
Fifteen Pounds of Soape Grees....L.0.3.0.
One Half Barrel of Soape.......L.0.10.0.
Six pounds Tallow at 6/.........L.0.3.0.
One Hundred of Chestnut Rayls...L.1.0.0.
Thirty weight of Good Flower....L.0.5.6.
Three Large Bee hives at 1/6......L.0.3.6.
One half hogshead Tub.........L.0.3.6.
One half Barrell Cask L
Vinegar Barrell and all.........L.0.18.0.
One Box Iron..................L.0.30.
Two wooden Bottles of /3.......L.0.6.0.
Two outside Jackets half worn both
wooling ....L.0.15.0.
Six pair of Good pillow-bears at 3
pr pair.......................L.0.18.0.
One large Earthen platter.......L.0.1.6.
One Cradel White Wood.........L.0.16.0.
One pair of hand Bellows........L.0.30.
Three Crows Stocks for hogsheads.
And 2 barrell Crows at Stocks 1/6..L.0.7.6.

Fountain Smith was taken prisoner when the town was burned, and died of hardship in one of the wretched British prisons in New York. He was a cooper by trade, and the inventory includes his stock as well as household furnishings. Late in the eighteenth century there was an important carrying-trade between Norwalk and the West Indies. Horses, hoops, staves, flour, hams, butter, and earthenware were exported in ex-

change for sugar, molasses, and liquors. There is no evidence to show that Norwalk contained any stately mansions in Colonial days; the houses of the wealthiest and best born families seem to have differed from the humbler ones only in size. They were all of the farmhouse type of architecture. The description of the Esaias Bouton house on Wilson's Cove accurately given by W. S. Bouton, a local antiquarian of twenty years ago, is probably typical of the houses of the Revolutionary period. "It was a two-storied frame structure with a long roof sloping to the rear, the main timbers were of oak, fourteen inches square and covered with chestnut shingles, with the butts fourteen inches to the weather. The chimney was situated in the center of the building, constructed of rough stone, plastered with lime made of clam and oyster shells found at Naramake, now Wilson's Point. The windows were few and small." This particular home had a Tory owner, and the fire on its wide hearth, facing the front windows, was used as a beacon to British foraging parties from Long Island, only eight miles away across the Sound, on which the house faced. When the building was torn down a workman found in the wall an order signed by General Tryon, which read, "Deliver the beef, grain, and vegetables, previously ordered to my commissary. Send them to the usual place of shipment." The chimney of the Bouton house, drawn by William Hamilton Gibson, appears in "Picturesque America," published about twenty-five years ago. For years it served as a landmark for fishermen and surveyors of the oyster beds, but is no longer in existence. Naramake, the Indian village mentioned above, was occupied before the settlement of Norwalk by a tribe of Mohegans. Traces of it were long visible, and heaps of shells, graves, and arrow-heads were abundant. A doctor of two generations ago discovered an Indian herb garden there, which, he declared, contained a remedy for

SURF, ROTON POINT

every ill to which flesh is heir. That
has disappeared, but the botanist finds
all the flora of this region in the Wilson Point woods, and the pink mallows
in the marshes are one of the glories
of the place. The Knob Outing Club
controls the beach and a wooded knoll
at Wilson Point, with private bath-
houses, boat-houses, and casino, where
the families and visitors of the club
find recreation and social pastimes for
eight months in the year. The Norwalk Yacht Club has an attractive
boat-house at Hickory Bluff on Wilson's Cove, which is another rallying-
point for Norwalk society people in
the summer time. Bell Island, near
by, is a summer colony of cottages
whose occupants come from New
York or inland Connecticut to enjoy
the sea breezes on its rocky cliffs and
beautiful beaches. Following the
coast line we come next to Roton
Point, a pleasure resort for all sorts
and conditions of men from everywhere. Two iron steam-boats from

New York bring daily excursion parties from the city to the hotel, groves,
and magnificent beaches of Roton; and
all the seaside pastimes are provided
for them. Rowayton is a village at
the mouth of Five Mile River, whose
chief industrial interest is oyster growing. Artists find it very paintable,
with its wharves and water craft and
picturesque location. John Kensett
painted some of his best pictures at
Contentment Island, near Rowayton,
and one often sees the easel and umbrella or the sketch-book in the hands
of summer visitors.

Adrian Block discovered the Norwalk Islands in 1614, styling them
"the Archipelago." Rocky and cedar-
grown they are a picturesque feature
of the harbor. Sheffield or Smith's
Island, one of the largest, is distinguished by a lighthouse, which is soon
to be superseded by a new light further out on Green's Reef, for which
Congress has appropriated $60,000.
At night Eaton's Neck light on Long
Island, directly opposite, winks across
the water at its neighbor light in Con-

. ROTON POINT

OAK HILL, NORWALK

RESIDENCE OF HENRY LOCKWOOD

RESIDENCE OF HON. J. H. FERRIS

RESIDENCE OF T. H. VANDERHOEF

THE G. B. ST. JOHN HOUSE, NORWALK

RESIDENCE OF T. J. RAYMOND

MOUTH OF FIVE MILE RIVER

necticut. Long Island is always visible by day, a blue mass on the horizon with white sand banks flashing in the sun. An old saw runs,

"When Long Island goes to sea,
   Then fair weather there will be.
When Long Island comes ashore,
   Then the storm will surely roar."

From the Knob at Wilson's Point one sees Keyser's Island, on which is a monastery known as Manresas Institute, a retreat for Roman Catholic priests. The island was purchased about forty years ago by John H. Keyser, a New York business man and philanthropist, who spent thousands of dollars in building a road across the marsh connecting it with the mainland and converting the rocky island into a park with rare trees and shrubs, greenhouses and orchards surrounding a fine house. About twelve years ago it was sold to its present owners. Tav-

ern Island is the home of Norwalk's oldest pilot, Joseph Merrill, who is saluted daily by the New York steamboat in its passage out of the harbor. Two picturesque red cottages perch on its rocky bluffs belonging to summer residents. Norwalk harbor is a difficult one to enter on account of the islands and reefs at the mouth of the Norwalk River; and, when Tryon's fleet brought the invaders from Long Island in 1779, he had to find a Norwalk Tory to serve as pilot. Gregory's Point, nearly opposite Keyser's Island, is another favorite resort in the summer. A good hotel furnishing shore dinners and excellent bathing facilities are the attractions of the place. In 1878 the steamboat *Adelphi*, which had just started from its wharf for New York, was blown up by a boiler explosion off Gregory's Point, and about 30 persons were killed and

OPENING OYSTERS

CURLING ROOM IN HAT FACTORY

many injured. Another fearful accident which gave Norwalk notoriety for
years afterward among people who
had never heard of it otherwise, occurred in 1853, when an express train
plunged into an open draw, and 45
passengers were killed and many more
injured, the engineer having failed to
notice the signal. Such a thing could
not happen to-day with the modern
system of signals, in addition to
which the railroad has further provided an automatic switch which

place. Its industries are numerous.
Hats, locks, shoes, air and gas com-
pressors, and cigars are some of the
products, and the firms are known
throughout the country. The bustling
little city is about forty years old, and
it may be said to have been brought
into existence by the New York, New
Haven & Hartford Railroad; for, when
the first train went through, Old Well
was a hamlet, and it has to-day about
7,000 inhabitants. South Norwalk is
proud of its municipal electric plant,

SMITH ISLAND LIGHT HOUSE

would derail the locomotive if, by any
chance, the engineer should disregard
the signals. At the wharfs in South
Norwalk one may count a dozen oyster
steamers on Sunday, when they are
not at work on the oyster beds of the
Sound. It was a South Norwalk man,
Captain Peter Decker, who first applied steam to oyster dredging in 1872,
by fitting up the sloop *Early Bird* with
an engine and tackle for the purpose.
From the deck of a steamboat entering
the harbor one gets a general view of
South Norwalk as a manufacturing

which is a model of its kind, and frequently visited by committees from
other cities. Strangers are always
puzzled to find two cities in the township of Norwalk, for a mile separates
South Norwalk from the City of Norwalk, which is the older section of the
town, and an earlier center of population. As a background to the business
portion of South Norwalk, is a ridge
of high land with many beautiful
streets on which are some of the pleas-
antest homes commanding an outlook
on Long Island Sound. West Avenue,

which is the principal highway between Norwalk and South Norwalk, is lined with beautiful homes surrounded by lawns and shade trees. The handsomest residence in Norwalk is "Elmenworth," on West Avenue, which was built about thirty years ago, by Legrand Lockwood, at a cost of a million dollars. The house is of granite, and situated in a beautiful park. It is owned at present by Mrs. C. D. Matthews of New York, who uses it

Norwalk is full of houses of local historical interest, and its streets have an air of olden times which is most attractive. Passing through its business portion and climbing up Mill Hill past the picturesque Town House, surrounded by an ancient burial ground, we find ourselves on "The Green," shaded by noble elms. Norwalk used to be famous for its great elm trees, but the finest specimens succumbed to the ravages of the beetles a few years

PILOT'S COTTAGE, TAVERN ISLAND

for her summer home. In South Norwalk a soldiers' monument and three churches are on this avenue. In front of the Armory, between the two cities, is a memorial drinking fountain, after a design by McKim, Mead and White, erected by the Norwalk Chapter, D. A. R., in honor of Nathan Hale. The Connecticut hero obtained a disguise in Norwalk and embarked for Long Island on his fatal errand from its shores, so that Norwalk claims an especial interest in him. The City of

ago, and only the younger trees remain. The old First Church and St. Paul's Episcopal Church, the edifices of the oldest religious bodies in town, face the Green, and also the First Baptist Church, founded in 1837. The South Norwalk churches are offshoots of those in Norwalk, though they are of equal size and importance. In the case of the Methodist churches the case is reversed, and the First M. E. Church, founded in 1790, is in South Norwalk. The Roman Catholics have

CONNECTICUT MILITARY ACADEMY

HILLSIDE—MRS. MEAD'S SCHOOL

FRANKLIN SCHOOL, SOUTH NORWALK

two churches in Norwalk, housed in expensive buildings, and a club-house on West Avenue. On East Avenue, near Grumman's Hill, is the University School, which occupies the building formerly used by the Selleck School, founded by Rev. C. M. Selleck, A. M. Mrs. M. E. Mead's School sends many fair girls to Vassar and other colleges, and Miss Baird's School for girls has been in successful existence for twenty years. Of public schools there are ten graded schools, four of which have high-school departments, and a number of district schools in the outlying suburbs. A well-appointed hospital occupies a site on a hill with a beautiful outlook. There are picturesque drives in every direction around Norwalk, and the electric cars afford delightful trips to all the towns and resorts along the Sound, since it is possible now to travel from New Haven to New York by tramway, and the scenery is pretty all of the way. When one tires of the sea it is possible to drive to the hills of New Canaan. Ridgefield, and Weston, about ten miles into the country. The latter place, quite away from all rail-

RESIDENCE OF E. BEARD

roads, and thinly populated, reminds one of nooks in the Catskill Mountains, especially in the vicinity of the Forge, where the falls of the Sangatuck River dash over great boulders beside an ever-green forest. Or, if one searches for human touches in a quiet country landscape, West Norwalk will reward him with glimpses of old New England homes, some of which have stood unchanged for over a hundred years, their shingles silvered by the weather, with porches draped in vines, and door yards a mass of shrubbery. All of the country roads are rich in flora and bird-life, and nature lovers need not go far to find these things. The shallow reaches of the Norwalk River, running over a bed strewn with boulders, its banks embowered in a wealth of shrubbery and moisture-loving plants, delight botanist, bird-lover, and artist alike; while the Camera Club of Norwalk found subjects for a year's work in the variety of scenes afforded by the river through the country, from the city to the salt waters of the Sound.

Close at hand, for an afternoon drive, are Gregory's Point, Fitch's Point, and Calf Pasture Beach, where the carriages drive to the brink of the waters of Long Island Sound. Calf Pasture is unspoiled by "improvements," and its crescent-shaped beach of white sand affords a lovely view of sea and sky and rocky islands just off shore. One reaches it by the Pine Hill road, near the Ludlow Monument, crossing the Marvin lands on the ridge, which have descended directly to their present owners from the first generation of Norwalk settlers. The ridge commands one of the loveliest views imaginable, showing the mouth of the river, and Long Island Sound for miles to the south and east, with South Norwalk below its green hill on the west.

Danbury, New Canaan, Wilton, Westport, and Ridgefield are all in some sense daughter towns of Norwalk, being largely settled by Norwalk families. The list of illustrious men of Norwalk ancestry is a long one, including two presidents of Yale, Rev. James Lockwood and Timothy Dwight, 2d; the three famous Perrys, Commodore Christopher Raymond Perry, Commodore Oliver Hazzard Perry, of Lake Erie fame, and Commodore Matthew C. Perry, who opened the ports of Japan to commerce; Rev. Elizur Goodrich, D. D.,

"ELMENWORTH"

and Right Rev. Abraham Jarvis, Henry J. Raymond, who founded the New York *Times;* A. H. Byington, war correspondent of the *Tribune,* and American Consul at Naples, as well as editor of the old Norwalk *Gazette;* Capt. Moses Rogers, commander of the first steamship which crossed the Atlantic; the two famous brothers, Hon. John Sherman and Gen. W. T. Sherman; Gen. Rufus King, Briga-dier-General E. F. Bullard, and Col. Wolsey R. Hopkins, U. S. A.; S. T.

unique honor upon Norwalk by hav-ing both branches of the legislature presided over by Norwalk men, Lieu-tenant-Governor E. O. Keeler and Speaker John H. Light. General Rus-sell Frost, of the State Militia, is also a Norwalk man. Hon. E. J. Hill, of Norwalk, is serving a second term as member of Congress for the Thir-teenth district, and is a member of the financial committees of the House of Representatives. Norwalk of to-day and the future differs from the Nor-

NORWALK HOSPITAL

Goodrich, "Peter Parley"; Horatio Seymour, L.L. D., Judge O. S. Sey-mour of the Superior Court, and ex-Governor T. H. Seymour; Chancellor James Kent, "the Blackstone of America"; ex-Governors P. C. Louns-bury and George Lounsbury; the three Warren brothers, who founded Troy, N. Y.; Nehemiah Rogers, founder of St. John, New Brunswick; these are only a few of the eminent men who have Norwalk blood in their veins. Hon. Clark Bissell, of Norwalk, was Governor of the State in 1846-49. In 1901 Connecticut conferred a

walk of the first two centuries of its history. The colonists were English-men, the two generations succeeding the Revolution were Americans; but fifty years ago new elements came in, and a new type of citizen is making. First came the Irishman, and he and his children are already assimilated; then came the German, and he is one of us; the children of the first Italians are taking their place in public affairs; the Scandinavian, the Hungarian, and the Russian Jew have followed, and all these are to influence the future of the good old Town of Norwalk.

Thomas Jefferson and Higher Education

By George Frederick Mellen

THE many-sided Franklin had his counterpart in the many-sided Jefferson. From whatever point of view the latter may be scanned, he is found almost equally as interesting as Franklin, if not always so original. His activities, bestowed upon widely diverse fields and questions, were marked by surprising thoroughness; his achievements were the results of clear vision and cautious experiment. Though known to fame as statesman and diplomatist, the work done and the influence exerted by him in the cause of education are becoming better known as educational movements and problems are more carefully studied. More than any other American, Franklin not excepted, he was instrumental in interesting foreign scholarship in America and in inducing foreign educators to make this country the scene of their labors. In thus doing he affected vitally educational ideals and changed radically some of the current educational practices. The contribution made by him, directly and incidentally, to the educational forces of America through men and influences from across the Atlantic Ocean must always command grateful interest and recognition.

It will be remembered that religious persecutions and political revolutions, from the outset, have been the great feeders for the intellectual life of America. Liberty, civil and religious, has been the inspiration and the watchword guiding the movements of colonists and the consciences of individuals. In Jefferson, victims of unjust oppression found always a ready sympathizer and ardent advocate. Especially was this true in the case of men of the highest intellectual gifts. From the dawn of his intellectual life to its serene setting, he was dominated most by men of foreign birth or education and by the literature and science emanating from European sources. In this there was a singular breadth of vision instead of a narrow provincialism. To him civil liberty and individual freedom found their most congenial atmosphere and exercise in America; but the highest forms of learning and the truest expositions of philosophy had their seat in the Old World. The combination of these upon American soil in richest measure and under the guidance of leading scientists and scholars was the task set for a lifetime, and it was followed with unwavering purpose.

This preference for foreign educators and this attitude towards foreign learning are easily explainable from early training and environment and from subsequent official position. Jefferson's first teacher, who introduced him to the study of Latin, Greek, and French, was a scholarly Scotchman. His second teacher, of considerable reputation in the province of Virginia, was a highly educated English clergyman. The man whom he credited with fixing his destinies for life was Dr. William Small, his professor of mathematics and philosophy in William and Mary College, a native of Scotland and a graduate of Edinburgh University. Williamsburgh, the seat of the College, in manners and customs, in history and traditions, and in culture and society, was a miniature reproduction of London. The first men of Virginia were educated almost wholly by teachers imported from Scotland, England, and Ireland. Madison, Monroe, and Marshall were the trained products of such men. This was none the less true of the post-Revolutionary era, when Henry Clay, Winfield Scott, and Edgar Allan Poe were thus schooled; and it continued so until the foreign schoolmaster was displaced by the New Englander with his diploma from Harvard, Yale, or some other New England college. As an occupation or means of livelihood teaching was not looked upon with favor by the average Virginian.

In 1779, appointed Governor of Virginia, Jefferson was made a visitor to William and Mary College. Influenced no doubt by the alliance made the year before with France, he revolutionized the course of study in the college and introduced a distinct chair of modern languages. By this step he infused a new element into educational practice and became the first champion of modern language studies in an American college curriculum. In 1784, made joint commissioner with Adams and Franklin to negotiate treaties of commerce with foreign nations, he took up his residence in Paris.

Soon he was appointed Minister to France. In this station and in Paris, the intellectual capital of the world, his zeal and activity in familiarizing himself with the best institutions and methods of instruction were commensurate with his opportunities for study and observation. Association with distinguished scientists and scholars, and diligent investigations into those institutions offering the greatest advantages, were utilized for the benefit and information of inquiring students and officers of instruction and discipline at home. To J. Bannister, Jr., asking information concerning "the best seminary for the education of youth in Europe," he answered, after weighing their respective merits, Geneva and Rome; to President Stiles of Yale College he wrote giving accounts of the latest movements and discoveries in science, the results of the researches of astronomers, chemists, and physicists; to President Willard of Harvard College he wrote advising him as to recent publications in science, language, and history, and citing the questions at the time absorbing the attention of European scientists. While living in Paris he became a subscriber to the dazzling scheme of Chevalier Quesnay to found at Richmond, in Virginia, an academy of arts and sciences for the United States of America. Projected as a memorial of the friendly relations between America and France and as a bond of future amity, in the magnitude of its scope and aim it surpassed the wildest dreams of any educational promoter or enthusiast in the New World. That the movement, conceived the year of the French alliance, revived after the declaration of peace, and prosecuted with vigor up to the outbreak of

the French Revolution, should have received such strong countenance as the names of the subscribers indicate and such financial support as to enable the founder to erect a building in which to begin operations, bespeaks the enthusiasm of its originators for the higher education and their confidence in the possibilities of the higher culture in America.

Having shown the historical basis of Jefferson's admiration and preference for European scholarship, there remains to be seen how his successive and long-continued efforts led to the final achievement of his purposes to transplant some of its best representatives to American soil. This determination increased the farther in years he was removed from his European sojourn. When hopes for realization seemed bright and he hastened to unfold his plans to fellow Virginians, he was met with indifference, discouragement, or opposition. The picture of this great man working persistently and waiting patiently for the fruition of his desires is one of the inspiring and instructive lessons of educational history. In his last years, seizing on the hopes inspired by the younger generation of educated Virginians, he brought them into hearty sympathy with his efforts and used them for the accomplishment of his great aims.

Returning to America Jefferson was urged by Washington to become Secretary of State in his cabinet. He reluctantly yielded, protesting that it meant the abandonment of a purpose to retire to private life and give himself over to studies congenial to his tastes. While in this office he was called upon for information touching foreign universities, and gave it as his settled conviction that Edinburgh and Geneva were the best in Europe. When, therefore, in 1794 the faculty of the latter, at variance with the tyrannical aristocracy recently come into control of the Genevan Republic, proposed through their representative D'Ivernois to transfer the university to Virginia, it was the prospective gratification of his hopes and aims. Taking up the proposition with lively interest and bent on trying its practicability, he laid it privately before influential members of the State Legislature, intending with encouragement to push the measure. Though received with some warmth, it was deemed too expensive and impracticable.   Not disheartened by this refusal to consider overtures or ways and means he pressed the matter upon the attention of Washington, who was now impressed with the need of a national university. Washington had expressed his purpose to make a liberal donation to this end, and Jefferson hoped to divert it into this new channel.   At the same time he appealed to the patriotism and state pride of the President, urging that he give it for an institution to be located in Virginia and within easy reach of the Federal capital.   Washington refused to consider the offer of the Genevan professors, and that with reasons so cogent as to make Jefferson's enthusiasm appear trivial and his espousal ill-advised. While deeply impressed with the importance of the higher education and the necessity of immediate organized action for its promotion, the views of these distinguished men appear in striking contrast.   Both were agreed in objections to sending young men to Europe to be educated, Washington's objections being chiefly political, Jefferson's

moral.   The ideas of the former were practical and national, investing the whole country with a proprietary interest in a university, while those of the latter were sentimental and sectional, the proposed institution benefitting Virginia chiefly and the nation incidentally.   Washington dying at sixty-seven years of age, it cannot now be conjectured what he might have accomplished towards the realization of his plans and ideals, had he lived to the age of Jefferson, who was eighty-two years old before he saw the University of Virginia, the ripened product of his brain and genius, opened for the reception of students.

Jefferson readily acquiesced in these judgments, and frankly wrote the Swiss professors the decision reached. With this scheme abandoned, he is found next planning new measures for Virginia's educational welfare and turning to English sources for information and advice.   In 1792 one of the periodic attempts made for parliamentary reform in England was renewed, given impetus by the French Revolution. The drastic measures employed by the government to suppress the growing sentiment, and the unfriendly attitude of its partisans towards all dissenters, drove to America some men distinguished in letters and science.   Among these Jefferson was brought into confidential relations with Joseph Priestley, scientist and theologian, Thomas Cooper, scientist and jurist, and Henry Toulmin, a man of great learning. Their political and religious views were in harmony with his own, all being staunch republicans and Unitarians.   He expressed a feeling of regret that Priestley and Cooper settled in Pennsylvania, intimating that a wider and more needy field was offered in Virginia. He sent Toulmin to Kentucky with strong letters of endorsement, which put him into the presidency of Transylvania Seminary, the germ of Transylvania University.

In framing the educational system of Virginia Jefferson, in the spirit of loyalty and gratitude to William and Mary College, which had proved itself a school of statesmen, intended to make that institution the capstone of the structure. However, conscious of its charter limitations and local disadvantages, he entertained little hope of carrying out the scheme. By the opening of the new century all currents, commercial, political, social, and religious, had turned adverse to the venerable seat of learning. His practical wisdom and prophetic sense saw Virginia's need to be an institution which should attract by the learning of its faculty, by the adequacy of its equipment, and by the favorableness of its location. While dictating the creed and policy of a new party he found time to plan for a new institution at the very dawn of a new century. He began to correspond and to converse with distinguished scientists personally familiar with European universities, trusting from their combined wisdom to formulate a plan suited to a new country and to new conditions; at the opportune time he hoped to receive the support of the State Legislature in carrying it out. In the request for plans he invariably sought to impress the idea that the institution was to be liberal in policy and modern in ideas. In 1800, in a letter to, Dr. Priestley, he indicated the source whence he intended to draw his professorial material thus: "We should propose to draw from Europe the first characters in science by considerable temptations.
* * * From some splendid characters I have received offers most perfectly reasonable and practicable." The same year the French economist, Dupont de Nemours, landed in the United States, a political exile, and visited Jefferson while Vice-President in Philadelphia. From so eminent an authority views were eagerly sought, and out of them was evolved an elaborate treatise on a complete system of education for North America, from the common school to the university. Three years later, after he had become President, Jefferson wrote to Professor Pictet, of the Genevan faculty, a letter practically of the same tenor as that addressed to Priestley. For little more than ten years the interests were held in abeyance, crowded out by the cares of state and by international complications. With the burdens of the Presidency removed and the War of 1812 virtually ended he resumed the task with a firmer grasp and a wider outlook.

Albemarle Academy, practically the germ of Jefferson's "pet institution," was coincident in inception with his conviction that Europe should be the resort for teachers. To note how the one kept a sluggish pace with the other it will be necessary to retrace our steps somewhat. In 1783 he was requested to find a principal for a proposed grammar school in his home county, Albemarle. After unsuccessfully appealing to President Witherspoon of Princeton College, and trying in vain to find in Philadelphia an Irish gentleman of satisfactory habits and qualifications, he finally deemed it would be necessary to secure a teacher from

Scotland, feeling well assured of the sobriety and attentiveness of one from that quarter. Albemarle Academy was chartered in 1803, but only nominally existed until 1814, when Jefferson was placed on its board of trustees. The University of Virginia opened its doors in 1825. The history of the intervening years is one of masterful purpose and orderly progression. There was no wavering, no faltering. The temporary obstacles met served but to give time for the gathering of fresh strength with which to make a more vigorous advance. There was at times a change of base or tactics; but always the same end was kept in view. Virginia was to have a real university, manned, in the main, by European specialists.

Immediately upon the acceptance of the trusteeship Jefferson, with wonted energy, applied himself to the endowment and organization of the academy, intending it as the crowning act and service of his last years. Thomas Cooper, the eminent scientist, was selected as chief adviser, and Joseph C. Cabell, the young scholar in politics, was his chosen representative in the State Legislature. Cooper, who was a graduate of Oxford, England, had been twenty years in America, had sat on the bench, and was professor of chemistry in Dickinson College. In science Jefferson esteemed him the ablest man in America, and had profound regard for his legal knowledge. The propriety of taking one of the several professorships in the contemplated institution had been suggested to him. Cabell, after graduating at William and Mary College and three years of study and travel in Europe, where he attended famed universities in France and Italy, had chosen a professional career, and was just beginning to consecrate his culture and talents to the service of the state. With financial aid from the State and from private sources, Jefferson counted confidently upon establishing "the best seminary of the United States." This was not an empty claim. College education in America had not advanced beyond the grammar school of England. The standard north and south was practically the same; in 1811 A. B. Longstreet, author of the inimitable sketches, "Georgia Scenes," and George McDuffie, the fiery orator and statesman of South Carolina, left the academy of Moses Waddell, the former to enter the Junior class in Yale College, the latter the same class in South Carolina College. For his professorships he declared that he had in hand three of the ablest characters in the world, surpassing in scholarship any three professors in any European university. These were Jean Baptiste Say, one of the world's celebrated economists, Thomas Cooper, and possibly, in the opinion of the late Professor Herbert B. Adams, the historian of the beginnings of the University of Virginia, Destutt de Tracy, the noted metaphysician,—two Frenchmen and one Englishman.

Fortunately for the coming university the Legislature was not brought over to all the demands made upon it. In the course of the next three years it changed the name of the institution to Central College, reorganized the board of visitors, and granted substantial privileges. In 1817 matters had progressed so far as to encourage the beginning of faculty organization. There is also, on the part of the guiding spirit, a change of point of view concerning the source of supply for professorial material. Instead of employing only educated Europeans, with a decided preference for Frenchmen, men of European training are preferred and New Englanders are invited to hold chairs. The first choice of the board fell on Rev. Samuel Knox, a Maryland educator presiding over Baltimore College. Many interesting and significant factors entered into the selection. He was a native of Ireland and a graduate of Glasgow University, a Presbyterian minister of the strictest order, who had preached and published a sermon condemning the views of Dr. Priestley. In advocacy of Jefferson for the Presidency he had vindicated his religious conduct and principles before the American public, and was the author of a treatise on education supposed to have influenced Jefferson in planning his university. The nomination of Knox never reached him. More than a year had passed when Knox heard incidentally that Jefferson desired to have him in the new college. He wrote instantly and applied for a position. Jefferson's reply gave no encouragement, and put him aside on the plea that plans were immature, and that he had given them over to other hands. Jefferson's action would appear inexcusable and inexplicable, were it not known that at the time he was greatly distressed by the storm which had broken over his head. Rescinding its action in electing Knox, the board had chosen Cooper, a Unitarian, professor of natural science and law. Though irreproachable in life and character, his religious views were so obnoxious to orthodoxy in Virginia as to outweigh all considerations of

preëminent scholarship and distinguished reputation. Indignant protest was made; charges were rife that the institution was to be committed to irreligion. The pressure brought to bear forced Cooper's resignation. This was a sore disappointment to Jefferson, and for a brief season dampened his ardor. The comfort he took to himself was in the possibility of bringing "from Europe, equivalents in science" to take Cooper's place, whom he followed with good wishes and patronage to South Carolina College.

In casting about for a faculty Jefferson was not averse to the employment of New England men whose qualifications complied with his requirements. In 1815 George Ticknor had visited him at Monticello previous to going to Germany for study and travel. From this intercourse mutual admiration and sincere affection developed. The intimacy, in subsequent years, bore fruit in the broadening and liberalizing of the work at Harvard College. The Harvard professorship of French and Spanish Literature tendered to Ticknor while abroad was accepted before his return. Despite this fact, from time to time, Jefferson continued to write pressing upon his attention Virginia's coming institution and the hope indulged of having him in its faculty. By formal action of the board of visitors, one year after Ticknor had entered upon his work in Harvard, he was called to the chair of languages in what was now, 1820, the University of Virginia. At the same time Nathaniel Bowditch, another New Englander, a noted mathematician, was invited to accept the chair of mathematics. These offers, declined by both, discredit an unfathered story which has appeared in print. Jefferson, it is said, when it was suggested to him that he could find able professors for his chairs in New England colleges, replied that he could not think of depriving those colleges of their professors, but privately said that he did not desire to have any "Connecticut Latin" in the University of Virginia. In this connection, it is interesting to note that it was while returning from a visit to Jefferson that Ticknor sought out two scholarly young German refugees in Philadelphia, who, disappointed in their efforts to find congenial employment, were in the act of engaging themselves as farm hands in the interior of Pennsylvania. Impressed by their scholarship and other qualifications, Ticknor induced them to accompany him to Massachusetts, where, in time, both became professors of distinction in Harvard College. These were Dr. Charles Beck in the chair of Latin, and Dr. Charles Follen in that of German.

The successive failures to secure professors worked in the end to the advantage of the new university. The following four years were eventful in preparation and consolidation. Increasing appropriations were made by the legislature; popular prejudice was minimized or overcome; religious sects were won over; the various sections of the State were united in support of the young institution, and buildings were erected which Ticknor praised, describing them as "a mass of buildings more beautiful than anything architectural in New England, and more appropriate to a university than can, perhaps, be found in the world." Some years before Jefferson had felt that it would be necessary to send an agent to Europe to find suitable men with whom to fill the chairs, and wished Cabell to undertake the mission. Writing to Ticknor he suggested that these would likely be selected from Edinburgh. From under the French spell, he had become convinced that the best results were to be secured only from professors who could communicate their instruction to students in the latter's language. A kinship of race and language carried with it a knowledge of customs and manners, and a guarantee of better understanding and readier approach. Cabell declined to go, when Francis W. Gilmer was selected for the delicate task. Though not educated abroad, he was accredited by Jefferson as "the best-educated subject we have raised since the Revolution." In 1824, bearing letters to Richard Rush, minister to England, and to John Cartwright, English politician and reformer, he set out on his momentous errand. Oxford, Cambridge, and Edinburgh were the objective points, with London as a base. At this time, from the practice of favoritism in the bestowment of professorships, Edinburgh occupied a very different rank in Jefferson's esteem from that held when he wrote to Ticknor saying that this seat of learning would be largely drawn on for material. The man who declined to consider his own kinsman, universally held to be fully qualified, in connection with a chair in the university, could not tolerate nepotism even in an institution which he had venerated and praised a generation before as one of "the two eyes of Europe."

At this late day Jefferson's expressed dread of the average testimonials of scholarship and character, and his cautious measures to evade the presentation of such make interesting reading. By this time he had grown too wise to suppose that he could draw from Europe "their first characters in science," as twenty years before he had written to Priestley. Men whose reputations and positions were secure he did not hope to entice to the outposts of civilization by any consijerations, pecuniary or otherwise. His hope now was to attract ambitious young scholars who, in teaching power and scholarly research, were treading eagerly in the footsteps of older professors, crowding them too closely for comfort, and showing themselves abundantly able to take their places. The comprehension of this sound principle in university supply and administration proved all the more the practical wisdom of the man and his supreme fitness for the work he was setting on foot.

Gilmer did his work thoroughly and satisfactorily. In the chair of ancient languages the selection fell on George Long, a graduate of Trinity College, Cambridge; in mathematics, on Thomas Key, a graduate of the same college; in modern languages and Anglo Saxon, on George Blaettermann, a native of Germany then living in London ; in natural philosophy and astronomy, on Charles Bonnycastle, a graduate of the Royal Military Academy at Woolwich ; in medicine, on Robley Dunglison, an Englishman and a graduate of Erlangen University in Germany. For patriotic reasons the chairs of law and of ethics and political economy were reserved by Jefferson for Americans, or rather for Virginians. The standards set by these men were high and rigidly maintained, and

conformed to the pronounced wishes and ideas of the founder.

The infusion of new ideas and methods and the large liberty hitherto unknown in American college life were unappreciated and misunderstood by a large and influential element of the student body. These gave unceasing trouble, becoming so untractable as to cause the professors to contemplate seriously the resignation of their positions. It may have been that they were not so far removed from the war of 1812 as to forget the bitter wranglings and struggles with Great Britain, and resented the wholesale introduction of English educators. A student insurrection was the occasion of one of the most dramatic incidents in Jefferson's life. So violent in outbreak and ungovernable in disposition had the students become that the board of visitors felt it necessary to intervene. In a body, the aged rector at their head, they adjourned from Monticello to the University, four miles distant, to summon the students before them. There sat Jefferson, Madison, Cabell, Chapman Johnson, and others. In the hush and suspense of the throng Jefferson arose and declared that he confronted the most painful event of his life. Then, overcome with emotion and unable to proceed, he yielded the floor to Johnson requesting him to give expression to what he felt. The speech of Johnson, supported by the dramatic act and distressed feelings of Jefferson and marked by impassioned outbursts of oratory, by bitter denunciation and stirring appeal, so swayed the students as to bring about the instant reformation of the culprits and good discipline afterwards. Only a few months elapsed before Jefferson passed away. In the meantime he witnessed the pleasing spectacle of harmonious relations between faculty and students, and of steady devotion to scholarly work. Among his last declarations was the high estimate placed upon the quality of the work done, and approval of the conduct of the students.

The terms of service of these educators were comparatively brief. Long, after three years, accepted a call to the University of London, leaving a record no less enduring from the beneficent results of his labors than the fame achieved in England; Key returned after two years, became a professor in the same university and a philologist of reputation; Dunglison, after eight years, was attracted to the University of Maryland, and thence to Jefferson College in Philadelphia; Blaettermann was removed in 1840 from his chair, and Bonnycastle died the same year—a year otherwise memorable in the history of the institution, inasmuch as Professor Davis, chairman of the faculty, was murdered by one of the students. Jefferson's intention that "the first set" of professors should not only give reputation to the institution, but also prepare "fit successors" was fulfilled in a measure.

The foundations, however, had been well laid and the general policy definitely fixed. Degrees based upon broad scholarship and certificates of graduation or proficiency based upon narrow specialization, as honors to be obtained and conferred, became the options opened to students. In permitting freedom of teaching and of learning, in adopting a scheme of independent or coördinate schools, in eliminating the idea of sectarian control or interference, and in establishing the honor system of discipline, the institution exhibited the rich mature fruit of real university life and experience, and pointed to the consummate flowering of true university ideals. In the years that have passed, the high hopes of Jefferson have been to a large extent realized, his unselfish toil has been generously rewarded; as the years flow on, the significance of that portion of the inscription on his monument, "Father of the University of Virginia," widens and deepens. In the outcome of his laborious efforts and multifarious plans to give Virginia a complete system of education, the introduction of the foreign educator stands a lasting credit to his prescience and wisdom, a permanent monument to his fame and genius. From the university he founded and fashioned an influence went forth which was soon felt in the East and throughout the South.

The Pennsylvania Germans

By Lucy Forney Bittinger

(Continued from June number.)

THE Revolutionary War being over, the Indian invasions, stimulated so largely by the British, ceased on the frontier. This, and the activity which had been aroused by the war and was now turned into peaceful channels, encouraged Western emigration, and in this movement the Pennsylvania Germans had their part. There had long been a German settlement on Dunkard's Creek, in what is now Fayette County, and from this region, the headwaters of the Monongahela River, commerce took its rise. In 1782 Jacob Yoder set out from "Redstone Old Fort" (Brownsville) with a flatboat loaded with goods, and floated down to New Orleans to trade. When Michael Fink arrived, in the same year, the French officials had never heard of Pittsburg, their starting-place. These two men seem to have been the pioneers of the keelboatmen who subsequently made such a figure in the development of the West.

Ten years later, a German, George Anschütz, made the first iron ever made in the "Iron City," in a little furnace where is now Shadyside.

Many of the Western pioneers were Pennsylvania Germans, though they often emigrated directly from the Valley of Virginia or from Maryland, both of which had received their German settlers from Pennsylvania. Some were daring guides or Indian fighters, some, simple frontiersmen. One is glad, for the honor of the Pennsylvania Germans, to say that there were few among them of the type of pitiless and bloodthirsty borderers represented by Lewis, or Ludwig, Wetzel. His father had been killed by Indians at Wheeling, sacrificing his own life to save his comrades, and Ludwig, then a young man, vowed eternal vengeance on the whole red race. He had four brothers who were inspired by the same hatred; one of them sunk his tomahawk in the head of an Indian chief who came under a safe-conduct to treat with Gen. Brodhead. Ludwig did the same in Harmar's expedition in 1790, was promptly arrested, but had to be released, as the excitement of his comrades, who intensely admired him, was so great. He was indescribably fearless and daring; would hunt alone a hundred miles in the depths of the "Indian Country," with numberless hair-breadth escapes from his enemies, as savage and merciless as himself. He took more scalps than did the two armies of Braddock and St. Clair; and with all this ferocity, he was something of a dandy and was proud of his long hair, which, when he unloosed it, hung like a mane to his knees. He often served as a guide and guard to parties "coming out," as the phrase was, and his name was a tower of strength. He

617

died in Texas and is buried on the banks of the Brazos.

It is strange to turn from this wild and bizarre character to the peaceful life of German settlements in eastern Pennsylvania. Here the toils and dangers of pioneer life were over; the Pennsylvania Germans had, as has been shown, borne their part bravely in the struggle which had made the scattered colonies a nation, and men's minds were now occupied with questions of government, of science, of commerce, of education. In all these, the leading men among the Pennsylvania Germans distinguished themselves.

One of the first scientific men of the United States was David Rittenhouse, the astronomer of Germantown. He was the great grandson of that Wilhelm Rittenhouse, who, in 1690, erected in Germantown the first papermill in America. David Rittenhouse was born in Germantown in 1732, and was brought up a farmer, but showed an astonishing genius for mathematics. When he had made, without any help, a wooden clock, it was concluded that he should give up farming for clockmaking. While working at his new trade by day, he used to give his nights to the study of the higher mathematics; early in life, he had made, independently, the discovery of fluxions, and thought it, for some years, a knowledge peculiar to himself. Presently he constructed an orrery, which seems to have excited among the philosophers of the province much the same quality of wonder which the wooden clock had among his simpler friends. He came to the notice of the provincial authorities, who employed him to survey their south-

ern boundary, which had been many years in dispute. Rittenhouse had no instruments, save those of his own manufacture, and must have been largely self-taught, but when the surveyors, Mason and Dixon, who have given their names at the once famous "Line," came to review his work, they found it faultless, and used it as the basis of their work. Rittenhouse was afterwards employed in settling the other boundaries of his State, south, east, and west, and his labors extended over many years, before and after the Revolution. He was for a time Treasurer of Pennsylvania; he succeeded Franklin as President of the American Philosophical Society, having introduced himself to their notice by a communication on the transit of Venus in 1769, which he viewed in an extemporized observatory of his own; so interested was he, that at the moment of contact he fainted from excitement, but recovered and made some valuable observations. He was the first Director of the United States Mint, holding the office until almost the time of his death, in 1796.

Two Pennsylvania Germans did themselves honor in the beginnings of our government, in what Fiske has well called "the critical period of American history;" these were Gen. Peter Muhlenberg and his brother, Frederick Augustus. After the war, Gen. Muhlenberg's old congregation wished him to return to their pulpit, but he refused, probably feeling himself better fitted for civil life; and indeed he had in this sphere a long and honorable record. His brother, Frederick, we last saw banished from his New York pulpit by the Tories on account of his patriotic sentiments, and his fearless declaration of them. Since that time, he had served in the Continental Congress, been Speaker of the Pennsylvania Legislature, and President of the "Council of Censors," a venerable institution of which the State of Pennsylvania made a short trial in the governmental chaos succeeding the Revolution. When this was to be ended, he and his brother, the general (who had been the acting Governor of the State), threw all their influence on the side of the new constitution, and its adoption by Pennsylvania was secured. One or the other of these brothers, and sometimes both, sat in the First, Second, Third, and Fourth Congresses. Frederick was chosen Speaker of the Third Congress. It was his casting vote which decided the acceptance of the Jay treaty and averted a war with France. Gen. Muhlenberg was also elected to the United States Senate in 1801, but soon resigned to take the office of collector of the port of Philadelphia, in the incumbency of which he died.

A third of this remarkable brotherhood found his distinction in a very different sphere. Henry Ernest Muhlenberg was, like his brothers, educated for the church, but, unlike them, continued in the ministry through life. His faithful labors in his vocation did not procure him the celebrity which was won by his scientific accomplishments. It was during his patriotic exile from his pulpit in Philadelphia that his attention was first called to botanical study. Afterwards becoming pastor of a church in Lancaster, he published there, in 1813, one of the earliest botanical catalogues of Pennsylvania. He corresponded with the Hessian surgeon and botanist, Schöpf, and gener-

ously allowed him to use the scientific materials he had collected. He exchanged specimens with European botanists and was a member of various Continental societies, as well as the American Philosophical Society, of which his fellow-countryman Rittenhouse was the president. The botanist Engelmann gave his name to a North American oak, the Quercus Muhlenbergii, more familiarly known as the "Yellow Chestnut Oak."

Botany seems to have been peculiarly attractive to such Pennsylvania Germans as had scientific tastes. Indeed the first American professor of botany was Kuhn, of Philadelphia, a pupil of Linnæus, but he did little for the science. A little later than Muhlenberg, lived Lewis David de Schweinitz, a Moravian clergyman, a great-grandson of Count Zinzendorf and the author of several botanical works, the most important of which was published in 1823. He particularly devoted himself to the abstruse department of cryptogamic botany and is said to have added twelve hundred species of American fungi to those already known.

The mention of this Moravian botanist naturally brings up the subject of education among the Pennsylvania Germans. Prof. Seidensticker's remarks on their intelligence, apropos of Saur's publications, will be remembered. The early efforts of the hermits of the Wissahickon, Brother Obed's Sunday-school at Ephrata, and the title of Conrad Weiser, "the schoolmaster of Tulpehocken," have been mentioned. Many schools had been established in connection with churches. Immigrants frequently brought their schoolmasters with them; indeed the schoolmaster often conducted services when there was no minister and, conversely, the pastor often taught in the schools. And the ministers of German Pennsylvania, in the latter half of the eighteenth century were, many of them, well educated—university men who compelled the admiration of the Harvard professors for their learning and their Latinity. One enthusiastic historian has said that, owing to the clergymen's supervision, the schools were, in early times, often better in the German districts of the State than in the English ones; but this is probably a hasty generalization. Whoever has read Judge Pennypacker's delightful account of the old schoolmaster, Christopher Dock, must think that the children who were taught by that Pennsylvania-German Pestalozzi, were highly favored in their educational advantages. The Moravians, in particular, gave great attention to education, and had early established several excellent schools, as had Lutheran pastors in Philadelphia in their congregations.

In spite of these efforts and of Provost Smith's unlucky project of the "German schools," there was doubtless much truth in Pastor Kunze's description:

"The Germans consist for the most part of such Palatines, Würtembergers, and Alsatians as in their native land were oppressed by the greatest poverty, and lived in the meanest fashion. There are hundreds and thousands of these (I heard last week of a ship on which there were 1,500 Germans, of whom 1,100 died at sea;) packed like herrings on shipboard, and, when they arrived, sold as slaves for a certain time. When they are free, they naturally want to grow rich; and there are those who have done so; but the fundamentals of education concern rich and poor alike. The Germans here, taking them altogether, are not very desirous to gain knowledge, chiefly because they see little opportunity to get outward advantage thereby; besides, they have little comprehension of real learning. And the English here judge all Germany by them."

Almost all the early educational efforts perished in the storms of the Revolution. In the last years of the war the University of Pennsylvania had a large and flourishing German department; but its prosperity was short. It is now impossible to understand why this department, which for a few years had a greater number of students than the English section, should have declined and perished so suddenly. Perhaps the departure of the energetic and learned Kunze had something to do with it; he went, in 1784, to New York, where he was the first to introduce the study of Hebrew and Oriental languages into the United States. Another cause for the failure may have been the competition of the Lancaster High School, founded in 1787 by the State Legislature, and under the auspices of the botanist Muhlenberg, as a reward to the Pennsylvania Germans· for their services to the cause of Independence. This institution, after very various fortunes, became a part of the present Franklin and Marshall College of the German Reformed Church.

In this connection, it must not be forgotten that the founder of the public school system of Pennsylvania was a Pennsylvania German, Gov. Wolf, who established it in 1832, in the face of opposition, of penuriousness and sectarianism. He well deserves the memorial arch raised by the school children of his state to his honor.

Many of the governors of Pennsylvania have been of its German race. That Gov. Ritner of whom Whittier writes—"The fact redounds to the credit and serves to perpetuate the memory of the independent farmer and high-souled statesman, that he alone of all the Governors of the Union in 1836 met the insulting demands and menaces of the South in a manner becoming a freeman and hater of Slavery, in his message to the Legislature of Pennsylvania"—was a Pennsylvania German.   To this the poet alludes, in his "Ritner";

"And that bold-hearted yeomanry, honest and true,
Who, haters of fraud, give to labor its due;
Whose fathers, of old, sang in concert with thine,
On the banks of Swatara, the songs of the Rhine,
The German-born pilgrims, who first dared to brave
The scorn of the proud in the cause of the slave;
Will the sons of such men yield the lords of the south
One brow for the brand, for the padlock one mouth?
They cater to tyrants? They rivet the chain,
Which their fathers smote off, on the negro again?"

How widely the Pennsylvania German race is scattered and what share of influence it has contributed to the development of the country, is difficult to decide and impossible to tabulate. The practice of changing German names to English ones, easier to spell or pronounce, is responsible for much of this obscurity, and also the traditional opinion of the Pennsylvania Germans as a stolid, unprogressive race makes their descendants some-times ashamed to confess and glad to conceal the tie.

The most obvious field in which to seek the influence of the Pennsylvania Germans is afforded by the State's record in the Civil War; and it is certainly not a record of which to be ashamed—rather one of which to be proud.

It is impossible to treat the share of the Pennsylvania Germans in the Civil War as we have treated their part in the Revolution—to discriminate from the rest, German organizations. They served in all the regiments that their native State sent to the field; and it was the largest contribuion given by any State to the suppression of the Rebellion.   From a carefully taken average of the Pennsylvania German names on the rosters of the two hundred and fifteen regiments given in Bates's five portly volumes, "History of the Pennsylvania Volunteers," I draw the conclusion that more than one-fifth of Pennsylvania's soldiers bore undoubtedly Pennsylvania-German names and hence were of this race.   Some regiments, raised in the southeastern counties, contained twice as high a percentage.   This calculation purposely excludes all with such names as would indicate foreign-born Germans; and necessarily counts out, as well, men who were allied to this people only on their mothers' side.   Neither does it include such names as "Long," "Miller," etc., which might be English as well as anglicized German.

Of the regiments which Rosengarten, in his "German Soldier in the Wars of the United States," gives as Teutonic, many were composed principally from the Pennsylvanian branch of the race.

The "First Defenders"—the five companies of Pennsylvanians who reached Washington at the very outset of the rebellion and by their presence prevented the capital from falling into the hands of the insurgents—were preponderantly of this race. Their services were not brilliant, but they were very important; none knows how timely was their arrival, and at their discharge, they received the rare compliment of a vote of thanks from Congress, as follows:

"Resolved, That the thanks of this House are due, and are hereby tendered to the five hundred and thirty soldiers from Pennsylvania, who passed through the mob of Baltimore, and reached Washington on the eighteenth of April last, for the defence of the National Capital."

Nearly a quarter of a century later they received gold medals from the Government as a testimonial of its gratitude and an heirloom to show their children that the Pennsylvania Germans were first in defence of the country, the capital, and the flag of the Union.

A large proportion of the "three months men" were Pennsylvania Germans; and many of them afterwards, when the magnitude of the task of repressing the Rebellion had dawned upon our peaceful people, re-enlisted for the three years service; one of these regiments, the Eleventh Pennsylvania, being permitted, as a special mark of favor for its soldierly qualities, to retain its old number.

The fifteen regiments of the Reserves—"the largest organized force, indeed the only division, sent by one State to the field," contained many of these Germans.

The Forty-eighth Pennsylvania—which contained many of the "First Defenders" from Schuylkill County, was largely composed of miners, who turned their craft to account in the construction and explosion of the famous mine at Petersburg.

The Fiftieth's gallant colonel, Brennholz, killed in the Vicksburg campaign, was a Berks County man; his Pennsylvania German regiment was the one chosen, on the recommendation of Gen. Grant, to represent the infantry at the dedication of the National Monument at Gettysburg, in 1865.

The Fifty-first, under Hartranft—afterwards a general, then governor of his native State and organizer of its present admirable National Guard—fought with distinction through the whole war, the carrying by assault of the bridge at Antietam being one of their most gallant exploits.

The Fifty-sixth Pennsylvania was the first regiment to fire at Gettysburg. Its division commander says, "That battle on the soil of Pennsylvania was opened by her own sons; and it is just that it should become a matter of history."

The Seventy-ninth, a Lancaster regiment, whose colonel bore the name of the Revolutionary soldier, Hambright, fought in the West and marched with Sherman to the sea.

The Ninety-seventh "gained credit with and for" Pennypacker.

The Sixty-fifth (Seventh cavalry) and the One Hundred and Thirteenth (Twelfth Cavalry) had many Pennsylvania Germans in their ranks; and the same was true of the notably well-drilled One Hundred and Fifty-second (Third Artillery); from its ranks "all the field and nearly all the line officers of the One Hundred and Eighty-eighth were promoted and the excellent discipline and soldierly bearing of the command was the frequent subject of remark and commendation by its superior officers." (Bates.)

Largely Pennsylvania German in their composition were the One Hundred and Thirtieth and the One Hundred and Thirty-first, which fought so bravely and suffered so heavily at Antietam and at Fredericksburg. So was the One Hundred and Fifty-third, which withstood the terrific charge of the "Louisiana Tigers" at Gettysburg. In parting from these "nine months men" its brigade commander, Col. von Gilsa, said:

"I am an old soldier, but never did I know soldiers, who, with greater alacrity and more good-will, endeavored to fulfill their duties. In the battle of Chancellorsville you, like veterans, stood your ground against fearful odds. In the three days' battle at Gettysburg, your behavior put many an old soldier to the blush, and you are justly entitled to a great share of the glory which my brigade has won for itself. In the name of your comrades of the First Brigade, and myself, I now bid you farewell."

No Pennsylvanian German soldier of the Civil War was so picturesque and interesting a figure as the Revolutionary general, Muhlenberg; but among the soldiers who did themselves and their race honor may be mentioned such men as Zinn of the One Hundred and Thirtieth, killed at Fredericksburg while exhorting his men, "Stick to your standard, boys," and Heintzelman, who was born in Lancaster County in 1805. He was a West Point graduate, "was promoted and brevetted for his gallantry in the Mexican War and at the outbreak of the Re-

bellion became colonel of the Seventeenth U. S. Infantry. At Bull Run he was wounded; on the Peninsula he commanded a corps, and throughout the war he was always on duty."

The services and honors of Hartranft, "the hero of Fort Stedman," have already been mentioned; not so those of Bohlen, the son of a Philadelphia merchant, whose strong bent for the military life found its consummation and honor in raising—at his own expense—the Seventy-fifth Pennsylvania; he died at their head, leading his men to the attack. Seidensticker fitly closes his sketch of him with the couplet, from a song of his German regiment:

"Und opferst du dich auch, wohlan.
Vergebens stirbt kein Ehrenmann."

Gen. Herman Haupt, a West Point graduate, served in the Civil War, and has since distinguished himself in trans-continental railway building.

Nearly twenty per cent. of President Lincoln's body-guard were of this race, as the names testify; and one of the treasures of the company was an autograph letter of his, in which he said: "Capt. Derrickson and his company, are very agreeable to me; and while it is deemed proper for any guard to remain, none would be more satisfactory to me."

There were many families among the Pennsylvania Germans who rivalled, in the Civil War, the records of the Hiesters and Graybills of the Revolution. The wide-spread family of the Pennypackers gave eighty-nine of its members to the Union army. The most distinguished scion of this old German stock was that Gen. Pennypacker of whom Rosengarten says:

"At the age of eighteen, after he had begun life as a printer, young Pennypacker became a member of a local volunteer company, and marched with it to Harrisburg on the first summons for troops in 1861, serving with it in the Ninth regiment. He soon became captain and then major of the reorganized regiment in the three years' service, the Ninety-seventh, and bravely fought his way through the war, became colonel of the regiment, was soon put in command of a brigade, won his star as a brigadier-general for his gallantry at the capture of Fort Fisher, at twenty-two was the youngest general officer in the war, and was brevetted a major-general. He was the youngest colonel in the regular army, and finally retired in 1883 at an age when with most men a career of distinction such as his is usually just beginning."

Gen. Pennypacker's sufferings from the terrible wound received at Fort Fisher and for which he has unavailingly sought relief from the surgeons of Europe and America, are probably the cause of his premature retirement from active life.

Col. Schall of the Fifty-first Pennsylvania, was one of eight brothers in the army. "The Wisters," says the author of the "German Soldier," "who served in the war by the half a score, were all of that good old German stock whose representatives are so well and honorably known in every walk of life." And the Vezins and Muhlenbergs may be added to this roll of honor.

Surely these facts—a few only, selected from the ignored annals of the Pennsylvania Germans—show that it is not a race to be ashamed of. A recent American writer has called them stolid and ignorant. But is that race ignorant which printed the first Bible in any European tongue, on this continent; which, in the person of Kunze, introduced to America the learning of the Orient; which gave us scientists like Melsheimer, "the Father of American Entomology," and Muhlenberg and De Schweinitz; philologists like Zeisberger; forest diplomatists like Post and Weiser; which, in the persons of the Moravians, founded some of our oldest schools, and in Gov. Wolf gave their State its school system, as another Pennsylvania German, Gov. Hartranft, created her National Guard; and which, with humble "Brother Obed," founded a Sunday-school before Robert Raikes founded his?

Is that race stolid—intent only on money-getting, on sleek cattle and good farming—which was the first to raise its voice, with Pastorius, for the freedom of the slave? It has fought, as well as spoken, for liberty. It helped to break France's power at Fort Duquesne; to withstand the circling savages at Bushy Run; it fought from the siege of Boston to that of Yorktown; it retreated through the Jerseys, suffered at Valley Forge, and starved in the prison-ships and "the Sugarhouse." It all but saved the day at Germantown and did save the wrecked army at Brandywine. In the later conflict for freedom, it was the first to defend the capital and there was no battle in which Pennsylvania's soldiers fought, where Pennsylvania Germans did not have their share. It took the bridge at Antietam and held Cemetery Ridge at Gettysburg, stormed Fort Fisher and Fort Stedman, was at Vicksburg and went with Sherman to the sea.

Such a race is not stolid, though they may be deliberate and slow to rouse; but they have done much for their country in time of peace and in her hour of need have never been found lacking.

Hazel

By Mary Teprell

HAZEL toyed idly with her fan.

"Who is that young woman?" she asked.

"The Princess Las Casas, Mademoiselle," answered the maid deferentially. "She it is that is contracted to Monsieur the Earl of Darnwood. He arrives to-day. Quite rich, they say, and handsome — ah!" Hazel sighed and twisted the corner of her white silken shawl between her fingers. Monte Carlo somehow lost its charm when viewed exclusively from a Bath chair.

"He must be brought to me, Sophie, for inspection!" said she with a languid smile. "I believe a good, old-fashioned flirtation would almost make me well again—I'm so bored! And I'm sure the Princess has plenty of admirers — has she not?" Sophie shrugged her shoulders. "Mademoiselle sees!" said she.

The Princess was coming down the path toward them—a tall, handsome woman with rather large features but fine eyes and an exquisite, cream-tinted complexion, through which the the rich red surged now and again as she talked with the gentlemen on either side of her. The man on the Princess's right was the handsomest Hazel had ever seen. He was over six feet tall, with a fine head, light curling hair, and frank gray eyes. He had evidently just arrived, for he was in travelling suit, and a servant followed closely behind carrying his portmanteau.

"If that is the Earl," said Hazel when they had passed, "he isn't bad. She must be rather fond of him."

* * * * * *

Three weeks later, one July evening, while soft strains of music floated out from the ball-room of the Casino and died away amid the roses and orange blossoms of that wonderful garden, while the moon was rising over the summer sea, Hazel, robed in white and with a single rose in her auburn hair, was sitting in a summer-house a little to one side of the loggia. Beside her, looking into her face as if held by a charm, was the nobleman with the curling hair and the frank gray eyes. He held one of her hands in his.

"I love you, Hazel," he said. "Will you marry me?" Hazel gave a little laugh and tried to withdraw her hand.

"But the Princess?" she said.

"I have thought of her, dear," said Darnwood. "She is one of the finest women I have ever known. I became betrothed to her because I thought I never could love anyone and I wanted to please my mother. But, Hazel, since I have seen you I have known what love is and even if I were unselfish—which I am not—I could not offer the Princess less than I would ask of her in return—all my heart,— and that is yours, dearest, dearest Hazel."

"Do you love me so much?" Hazel almost whispered.

"More than I ever thought that I could love anyone," said he. "Oh be kind to me, Hazel!" He bent over and kissed her hand and his golden locks brushed her sleeve.

"You are nothing but a boy at heart," said Hazel softly, and she laid her hand on his shoulder as he knelt there—"a big, handsome boy. You ought not to be thinking of engagements and marrying yet. But I'm proud that you love me, Darnwood,—indeed I am! It is a great honor to me. No, I cannot tell you to-night," she added, in response to the appealing look in his eyes. "I'll tell you to-morrow. You must go now. The music has stopped and Mrs. Allen will come for me here."

He went out, brushing through the masses of jessamine and honeysuckle that perfumed the night air, and Hazel settled herself comfortably, her head on her hand, looking out upon the calm, dark slumber of that southern ocean. A light step sounded on the threshhold. Hazel looked up. A radiant vision in softest pink, with a garland of roses gleaming like stars in her dark hair, stood before her—the tall figure of the Princess Las Casas.

"Mademoiselle," she said, in the saddest, most melodious voice that Hazel had ever heard, "may I talk with you for a few minutes?"

*   *   *   *   *

"What did you tell him?" asked Mrs. Allen excitedly. She and Hazel were sitting on the after-deck of La 'Bretagne watching the stars as the ship ploughed steadily through the water on its way back to the land where there are no earls and no princesses.

"I told him," said Hazel quietly, "that it had been merely a flirtation on my part—that I had wanted to see whether I could get him. It was humiliating but I said it."

"Poor boy!" said the older woman. "You treated him badly, Hazel." Hazel looked out toward the very farthest line of the horizon and there was a suggestion of hardness in her light laugh.

"I know you began it as a mere flirtation, Hazel," pursued Mrs. Allen, "but did it end so? What did the Princess say to you that night in the garden?"

"That must be our secret, dear Mrs. Allen," said Hazel with one of her sweet smiles. As she spoke she choked back something very like a sob in her throat and added, "Let's talk about something else!"

Beautiful Death

By S. H. M. Byers

BEAUTIFUL death—that is what it is;
   And that very day I had told you so,
When you stooped to give me a one last kiss,
   And your eyes filled up; oh, you did not know
How sweet and sudden a dream was mine,
   Without a pain or a pang, at the last,
One single sip of the nectared wine,
   And out of the there to the here I passed.

Still for a little the clouds were cleft,
   And there behind me I still could see
The flowers, the room, and the friends I left,
   And the beautiful body God gave to me.
And just a moment I waved my hand
   From the rosy heights of the newer dawn,
To tell you, dear, did you understand,
   That I was not dead, but was living on.

Now there is nothing of pain or pride;
   Rapturous beings are everywhere,
And the dear, dear dead who have never died,
   They are just the same as they were back there.
The very mountains and lakes you see,
   Oh, all that gladdens your mortal eyes
Are a thousand fold in their joy to me,
   For I see them, dearest, in Paradise.

In the scented grove when the night is near,
   And the pine trees murmur a low sweet song,
It is I that speak—do you sometimes hear?
   That you stand so still, and you stand so long?
What do I tell you? Oh, this, no more:
   Beautiful Death, it is sweet, so sweet,
Not the death that we thought before,
   But the miracle death that is life complete.

Out on the lawn when the rose is red,
   And its breath an odorous ecstacy,
It is not the rose—it is I instead—
   When you kiss the rose you are kissing me.
Oh, I often speak in the voice of things
   That move your soul, and you know not why;
In the evening flute, and the sound of strings,
   And the radiant isles of a summer sky.

When the nightingale on the hedge-row sings,
   Till the very trees in the woods rejoice,
And a nameless rapture around you clings,
   It is I that speak in the sweet bird's voice.
Oh, could you hear me; oh, could you know;
   Oh, could you breathe of this joyous land,
You would long for the beautiful death, and go
   So glad, so glad, could you understand.

Boston Schools One Hundred Years Ago

By George H. Martin

ONE hundred years ago Boston was a town of about twenty-five thousand people. There were some who called it an old-fashioned town. These were persons who had come in contact, during the war or after it, with the freer living and freer thinking people of the Southern and Middle States. Some of them had become acquainted with French officers and soldiers, had followed with interest the tragic fortunes of France, and had learned to talk more or less openly of liberty, equality, and fraternity.

The sympathies of these people were sufficiently outspoken to awaken alarm in the minds of the more conservative, that is, of most of the substantial classes,—ministers, lawyers, judges, and merchants.

The first families were intensely conservative. These were in reality second families, as most of the first families of provincial days had been loyalists, and had gone with Lord Howe to Halifax on the evacuation. The new comers had formed the social aristocracy of the smaller towns, and in their new home were maintaining those social distinctions which had been as marked in New England as in old England. They had brought with them considerable wealth, to which the African trade in rum and slaves had contributed not a little, and they were adding to it

by the new commerce which flourished between the close of the war and the embargo. They lived well, had fine furniture and plate, rode in their coaches, and gave grand entertainments. To these people, living their life in the main on the old lines, worshipping in the old churches under the old creeds, feeling some contempt for the poor, and some distrust of the lower classes, all suggestions of change brought a vague feeling of uneasiness which caused them to range themselves in open hostility. They inveighed against the "spirit of innovation," which seemed to threaten the stability of the established order. They saw in the excesses of the French Revolution omens of disaster at home. This made them Federalists in politics. There must be a strong government to restrain the people and to maintain the old social institutions intact. Against this seawall of conservatism,—social, political, and religious, the rising tide of nineteenth century thought beat for a generation.

On the side of public education the first break was made in 1790. During the colonial and provincial periods schooling had been simple. For seventy years the first grammar school had held the field alone, teaching Latin for its chief work. Early in the eighteenth century another Latin school was established, and three Writing schools, where boys whose parents had no social ambitions could learn the simple arts of writing and arithmetic. Children learned to read at home, or at the private schools that flourished through the period.

But if the formal education was scanty and narrow during the pre-Revolutionary period, that dynamic education which comes through the experiences of life was broad and liberal. The children were always in close touch with men and things, and novel and instructive events were following each other in rapid succession.

In the early part of the period they had the experiences of the wilderness, and throughout they were close and interested observers of the rapidly changing life. Natural objects and processes were all about them. They lived a rural life by the side of the sea, a most happy combination of conditions. Each house had its garden, and the wealthy had outlying farms in Brookline and Braintree. Market days were early established when the people from neighboring towns brought in their produce. Trade by sea began early, and from the time when Gov. Winthrop built the *Blessings of the Bay*, vessels in increasing numbers were coming and going—some to England and the West Indies, and others, before the navigation laws were strictly enforced, to the ports of Southern Europe.

The children saw the first log-houses built and they saw these give way to frame buildings and later to those of brick and stone. All industries were in sight. When Franklin's father wanted to keep Benjamin from the sea he took him about the town and showed him all kinds of mechanics at work, hoping to find among them one that would attract the boy.

Religious influence was strong and constant. The schoolmasters were ministers or theologians. "He taught us Lilly and he gospel taught," wrote Cotton Mather of Master Cheever. Religious observances were strict,—Sundays, Fasts, and Thanksgivings. The catechism was learned by all.

Civil life was carried on in the open. There were town meetings in the First Meeting-house, in Faneuil Hall, and in the Old South Meeting-house, and the Provincial Legislature met in the old State House. Public functionaries were coming and going, with more or less of parade. The jail was next to the school house, and the stocks, the pillory, and the whipping posts were in the most public places. Hangings were a public spectacle. There was always more or less of military life,—the early train-bands, the later minutemen—and news of wars with Indians and the French. The town was so small and so compact that everything happened within sight and sound of everybody. The children grew up in the midst of this bustling, vigorous, healthy social and public life. They entered it early, but they were prepared for it. They were educated by it.

In 1789 the Legislature framed a school law more complete than any that had preceded it. It embodied the ancient principles and gave authoritative sanction to new practices which had grown up in the towns. Its most significant feature was the broadening of the work of the common schools by the mandatory study of English in the form of grammar and spelling. It marks the beginning of modern in distinction from the renaissance ideas in education. For three hundred years in Europe and America so complete had been the domination of classical learning that a grammar school everywhere meant a Latin school. The most conspicuous change wrought by the nineteenth century in all the countries of Europe as well as in our own has been the enthronement of the vernacular as the chief means of culture for the masses.

In 1790 a town-meeting was held in Boston to consider a petition from numerous "respectable" citizens for a revision of the system of public instruction. In this petition these respectable citizens asked that provision should be made for "youth of both sexes." That the town should be asked to admit girls to the public schools showed that the "spirit of innovation" was abroad, and having come to possess "respectable" citizens, must be reckoned with.

Samuel Adams, then Lieutenant-Governor, was a member of the committee appointed to consider the subject. He was not afraid of innovation, and the committee in their report gave the girls a chance, or rather, half a chance, for they recommended that girls be allowed to attend the schools from the twentieth of April to the twentieth of October.

The new scheme which the committee recommended and which the town adopted provided for one Latin school, three Writing schools, and three new schools called Reading schools. There were, for the first time, certain structural elements of a system, in that conditions of admission and a leaving age were fixed. Boys might enter the Latin school when ten years old and

might remain four years. They must have studied English grammar before entering. Boys and girls might enter the other schools at seven and remain until they were fourteen. But they could not enter unless they had previously received "the instruction usual in women's schools." This proviso was the root of much subsequent trouble. Children must be taught to read at home or in private schools. The children of the illiterate poor who needed school most were wholly deprived of it.

The Reading and Writing schools were established as distinct and independent institutions, occupying, at first, separate buildings. The pupils were the same in both, spending a half day in each by alternation. When the boys were in the Reading school the girls were in the Writing school. In the winter, when the girls were not present, the upper and lower classes of boys alternated in a similar way.

This unique arrangement, called later "the double-headed system," was the result of a compromise. One purpose of reorganizing the schools was to secure a higher grade of teachers than the old writing-masters had been, who had been chosen chiefly for their beautiful chirography. They had too little education to carry on the new work, but they had been too long in the service to be easily displaced. So they were allowed to continue to do their old work in their old way, while college graduates were selected for the new schools.

School-keeping and school-going were meant to be serious business a hundred years ago. The daily sessions were seven hours long until 1802, when they were reduced to six. The holidays and vacations were only those in which the public shared, so closely were the schools and their interests identified with the social life of the time. There was no school on Thursday and Saturday afternoons, nor on Fast and Thanksgiving Days, April 1, June 1, Christmas, and the Fourth of July. For vacations there were the four afternoons of Artillery training, six days in Election week, the four last days in Commencement week, and general training days.

The merit of these occasions for vacation purposes lay in the fact that they furnished for the children not only freedom but entertainment and occupation, things sadly missed in the modern, more extended holiday periods.

The work prescribed for the Writing schools was the same that they had always done—writing and arithmetic. In all the early records of New England towns by a "ritin skule" was meant a winter school kept by a man who taught writing and arithmetic chiefly to boys and young men. In the Boston schools the children were not to begin arithmetic until they were eleven years old. Then they were to study in order Numeration, Addition, Subtraction, Multiplication, Division; Compound Addition, Subtraction, Multiplication, and Division; Reduction, the Simple Rule of Three (direct), Pratice (including Tare and Trett), Interest, Fellowship and Exchange, Vulgar and Decimal Fractions.

The Reading schools which represented the advanced thought of the day in education were expected to teach spelling, accent, and reading, English grammar, and, to the upper classes, epistolary writing, and compositiou. The masters might introduce, when expedient, geography and newspapers, occasionally.

It is interesting to note that the fault-finding about an overloaded curriculum began at once when boys were required to study spelling and grammar. Only two years after the new plan went into operation there was a petition from some parents praying that their boys might be excused from attending the Reading school and give all their time in the last year to arithmetic. Their idea of a practical education was expressed by the New England farmer—"The Bible and figgers is all I want my boys to know."

The prescribed books were few. For reading there were the Bible and a small book by Noah Webster called "American Selections for Reading and Speaking." For spelling, "Webster's Spelling Book" was designated, and for grammar, Caleb Bingham's "Young Ladies' Accidence," a small book of sixty pages, simple and sensible, and much better than the bulky volumes which succeeded it. No text book was prescribed in arithmetic until Daboll's was introduced in 1819. School life began with attendance upon the dame schools, kept mostly in their own homes by women who found it a respectable way to earn a livelihood. Some of the teachers were gentlewomen who had known better days, to whom their old friends sent children out of kindness. Others were by no means gentle, and children in their hands were victims of what Richter in his "Levana" calls "the sour malevolence of antiquated virginity." Some were like the English dame who said to an inspector, "It's but little they pays me and but little I learns 'em.' The "instruction usual at women's schools," the pre-requisite for admission to the public schools, was meagre at its best. All that was attempted was to teach the alphabet, the meaningless syllables a-b, ab, and the rest, and to read easy words of one syllable. To this was added much memorizing of Bible verses.

General Henry K. Oliver has left some interesting pictures of his own early school-days. He went first to a dame school kept on Hanover Street by a man. "The old gentleman holding an old book in his old hand and pointing with an old pin to the old letters on the old page, and making each one of us chicks repeat their several names till we could tell them at sight, though we did not know what it was all for."

He went next to Madame Tileston's, where he was taught reading and spelling. Each child had about twenty minutes of instruction each half day— "forty minutes worth of teaching and three hundred and twenty minutes worth of sitting still." This scanty ratio of learning time to sitting still time is by no means confined to "a hundred years ago." A very few years ago a visitor to a country school saw the little ones called forward to spell out their little lesson at the teacher's knee. Two or three minutes for each, fifteen minutes for all sufficed, and they were sent to their seats. The visitors mildly inquired what other work they would have that afternoon. He was told, "Nothing." What did they do this forenoon? "The same." Then he rashly ventured the question, "What is the use of keeping them? Why not let them go out and play?" The teacher replied with great decision and some contempt, "It learns 'em to set up!"

Having reached the age of seven, the children were allowed to enter the public school. Here they found themselves in a great bare room, lighted on three sides and holding from two hundred and fifty to three hundred children. There were no separate class rooms and no cloak rooms. The outer garments of the children were hung on hooks about the room. Mrs. Mary A. Livermore has told us how ·in her day, much less than a hundred years ago, the streams from the wet clothing ran along the floor, and made fun for the girls, as they tried to keep their feet above the water. There were no shades to the windows, no blackboards, no maps or pictures. The seats were narrow and without backs.

The schools were divided into four classes. The two lower, comprising the larger part of the school, were taught by an usher, the two upper, by the master. In the Reading school the younger children in the two lower classes spent their time in reading, spelling, playing, and being whipped. The last two exercises were also a regular part of the Writing school routine.

Each read one verse from the Bible or a sentence from "Webster's Spelling Book," called sometimes "Webster's First Part." This contained long lists of "easy" words of one, two, three, and four syllables, grouped according to accent. Then followed some short pieces for reading, Bible verses, fables, and easy dialogues; after this came the harder spelling— words of "learned length and thundering sound."

At the end of the list of so-called easy words there was a note which said: "If the instructor should think it useful to let his pupils read some of the easy lessons before they have finished spelling he may divide their studies, let them spell one part of the day, and read the other." So the teacher might keep the children studying spelling without reading, until they had spelled through the book.

The second class had, for new work, to commit the grammar to memory, taking lessons of six lines or more at a time and going over the whole book three or four times. The first class applied the knowledge so acquired to parsing. This class also read occasionally in the geography.

The difference between a course of study on paper and the same in practice, a difference even now familiar to all school people, was illustrated early in the matter of composition. When these schools were established the upper classes were to be instructed in "epistolary writing and composition." William B. Fowle, who received all his early education in these schools, from dame school to Latin school, avers that he was never required to write a sentence or a word of English. He says that for twenty years there was not a word written in any school in Boston. In the Writing schools the work of the children between the ages of seven and eleven was writing, and learning and saying arithmetical tables. The "cipherers," about one-third of the school, spend the first hour of the school session in writing, and the other two in ciphering. The copies were set by the master. While he mended pens the children brought up their exercises for inspection. During this writing hour the lower classes were studying their tables, usually aloud, and reciting them in concert. It was not uncommon for the tables to be sung to some familiar tune, as "Yankee Doodle."

For the cipherers the "sums" were set in a manuscript book from the master's own manuscript book. This practice was universal before the introduction of text-books in arithmetic.

The scholars worked on their sums until they were right. The Connecticut artist, Jonathan Trumbull, who spent a short time when a boy at one of these Boston schools, is said to have spent three weeks on a sum in long division. These sums were no trifles. Examples in multiplication exist having as many as fifteen figures in each factor, and in long division quintillions were divided by billions.

This work offered two advantages. It furnished to the pupils occasions to learn by practice "patient continuance," and it gave to the master some assurance that he had provided sufficient "busywork" to keep his pupils out of mischief.

There was one interesting feature of this early arithmetic work. It made little demand on the reasoning powers of the pupils. The work on the processes with simple and compound numbers was done by rules easily learned and applied. The same was true of the Rule of Three, with its cabalistic phrase, "If more requires more or less requires less." Fractions were studied last, and by many children, perhaps by most children, were not studied at all. Nearly all the work consisted in applying the rules directly to examples constructed for the purpose of illustration.

With the introduction of text-books came "problems" testing the ingenuity of scholars. At first these were few, but they increased in number and complexity with each new book and with each new edition, until they came to be considered the supreme test of intellectual ability. In its tax upon the mental power of children the arithmetic work a hundred years ago was play compared with the modern requirements.

The work in all the schools consisted chiefly of memorizing words. In the Reading and Writing schools there was nothing during the first three or four years of school life but oral spelling, writing, and arithmetic tables. It is not to be wondered at that the schools are said to have been characterized by "listlessness, idleness, and disorder."

General Oliver, in writing of his experience in these schools, says: "I do not remember that my powers of perception or observation were ever awakened or drawn out or cultivated. I do not remember that my attention was ever called to the consideration of any object great or small in the great world into which I had been born, or in the little world by which I was surrounded." Mrs. Livermore says that she never heard, except from one teacher, any explanation or definition of rules or difficult passages.

The work in the Latin school was no different. On entering at ten years of age (afterwards at nine) boys were set to learning "Adams' Grammar" by heart. Oliver speaks of "month after month, forenoons and afternoons of dreary monotony." "This grim and melancholy work was only relieved by an occasional lesson in spelling * * * or a weekly exercise in declamation."

Of the later work in Latin he says: "Translating, parsing, and scanning, with unmitigated drill but with no more knowledge imparted of Roman history, Roman life and manners, and the genius of the Latin language than was imparted to me of the manners and customs and language of the Choctaws."

The work in Greek was similar. It began with committing to memory the Greek Grammar. "Nine dreary and weary months of tedious memorizing did I spend at this fearful and exhausting job, hating Greek, with no love for those who taught it with a book in one hand and a cowhide in the other."

Rev. James Freeman Clarke, speaking once of his experience in the Latin school, said: "I can repeat passages from the Latin grammar which I learned fifty years ago and which I have never had occasion to use from that day to this." Hon. William M. Evarts, speaking on a similar occasion, said: "I certainly was taught to say in the most perfect manner the longest list of Latin names and prepositions, became intimately acquainted in their whole pedigree and relation with large nouns and words that I never expected to meet in my subsequent life at all." One of the masters of the Latin school says of the work that the boys were required to learn "much that they did not understand, as an exercise of the memory and to accustom them to labor." This kind of work served scholars and teachers in good stead when the school committee came to make the annual examination.

The school committee was one of the new features that came in with the reorganization in 1790. Before that the selectmen had been the guardians of the public interests in school affairs as in most others that belonged to the "prudentials" of the town. Beginning with 1790 the town annually chose twelve men of professional and business standing, who, with the selectmen, formed a permanent body of officials. The first committee consisted of three ministers, three doctors, three judges, two senators and one rising young lawyer, who afterward became Governor of the State. They attended faithfully to the duties imposed upon them. They chose teachers, fixed salaries, selected books, made regulations, heard complaints, and established new schools. Sub-committees made quarterly visits to the schools to inquire into their condition and needs.

The annual visitation of the boys' schools in July or August and of the girls' schools in November was a solemn affair. The selectmen, the school committee, and such specially invited guests as they delighted to honor went in imposing procession to all the schools. The time allotted to each school was brief, but the masters knew they were coming and had everything ready to show when they appeared. Thirty minutes were allowed for a Writing school, fifty for a Reading school, and from fifty to sixty for the Latin school. The visitors inspected the copy-books, and the "special pieces," which had been prepared under a formal vote of the Board, allowing them to be presented as "beneficial to the spirit of emulation." Later they found themselves obliged to restrict the number of pieces to be presented by any one pupil to two. Evidently the chirographic artists had been laying themselves out in this sort of work.

Each year when the masters were notified of the date of the intended visit they were requested to confer together as to the pieces to be read, "to avoid needless repetition." The girls were forbidden to read dialognes. Perhaps such reading suggested the theatre, one of the innovations not yet fully domesticated. At the Latin school the same kind of work was shown. One who was there says: "A very few pages of the book we were to be exercised in were marked off and regularly drilled into us day after day." "No one could doubt an instant of the exact passage he would be called on to show off before the fathers of the town." A boy who had been drilled on the declension of *duo* was called on by mistake for *tres.* "That's not my word, sir!" The mistake was promptly corrected and he went through *duo* in triumph.

The exercises closed with a Latin oration. From this the dignitaries marched to Faneuil Hall, where they recuperated themselves with a dinner at the public expense. In "Dwight's Travels," when speaking of amusements in Boston, the writer says, "A considerable amusement is also furnished by the examinations and exhibitions of the superior schools." Certainly the most rigid Puritan could have found no fault with an amusement so mild and so innocent.

These annual official visitations had a value as a recognition of education as a public function and of the schools as public schools and as an expression of public interest in their success. As such they furnished an incentive to teachers and scholars. But by the encouragement they gave to show work, to exercises of the verbal memory, they fastened on the schools narrow and mechanical notions of education. They set up false standards which generations have not outgrown.

To such work as has been described the pupils, from the dame school to the Latin school, were held by sheer force. The school dame wielded a long rod, with which from her chair of state she could reach the most distant child. This interesting functionary always sat. She was a veritable "Madonna of the chair." In all other schools flogging was universal and perpetual. It had been so from the colonial days and continued to be so until a much later period. Indeed the practice was one "wherof the memory of man runneth not to the contrary." If at any time during the first two hundred years Boston boys had thought of complaining of their treatment, they would have been silenced by the sanctions of Scripture and the examples of history. Had not Solomon said, "Foolishness is bound in the heart of a child: the rod of correction shall drive it far from him"? Had he not also said, "Spare the rod and spoil the child," and "Chasten thy son while there is hope and spare not for his crying"? The old schoolmasters heeded well this injunction.

General Oliver says: "Of the eight different teachers before I went to college, but one possessed any bowels of mercy." Mrs. Livermore remembers to have seen a master in her day rattan in turn fifty-two girls standing in a row that reached across the schoolroom. Of the school experience of Robert Treat Paine there is an account in the Historical Sketch of the Boston Latin School.

"Before going to the Latin School Mr. Paine went to Mr. J. Snelling to learn to write. This was in Court Square. The scene there was a perfect farce of teaching. There was no sort of instruction. J. S. told the whole school when school began to write four lines. If, in looking round, he found anyone had written his lines before the time was over, he thrashed him for writing too fast. If he had written none he whipped him for laziness. But this was only with beginners, for more experienced youngsters wrote two lines and then began their fun—which was unlimited and almost unrestricted—and the next two at the close of the exercise. When the copies were done they all passed in procession with them through a narrow gangway—quite equivalent to running the gauntlet, as J. S. stood ready with a blow with a word. Paine was there six or eight weeks to write a little."

Of the masters of the Latin school there is abundant evidence that they too did not spare the rod. Of the best of them it has been said, "he swayed even the ferule, which he rarely used, with singular dignity and grace." "Good master Gould used to flog us in a noble way, but it was over very soon." Of the worst some graphic accounts exist.

"One of them was a wholesale dealer in tortuous leather and torturing blows, whose image is that of a stalwart man of six feet in his stockings, with the sweet poet of Mantua in his left hand, and a twisted thong in the other, striding across the floor of the Boston Latin School to give some luckless blunderer over back or shoulder-blade sundry savage wales from fearful sweeps of his tremendous right arm."

This man was profuse in his epithets, —"idler," "blockhead," "dolt," "blunderhead." A boy has committed some indiscretion, and the rattan rushing through the air descends on his shoulders. "I won't be struck for nothing!" screams the urchin. "Then I'll strike you for something!" and the rattan whizzes again about his ears.

Another scene:—"Bangs, what is an active verb?" Bangs hesitates and looks imploringly to his neighbors, who cannot or will not help him out of his difficulty. "Well, muttonhead, what does an active verb express? I'll tell you what it expresses," bringing down the stick upon the boy with emphasis; "it expresses *action,* and necessarily supposes an *agent* (cane descends again), and an *object acted on.* As *castigo te,* I chastise thee. Do you understand now?"

This man had an odd habit of dropping into rhyme:

"If you'll be good I'll thank you,
If not, I'll spank you."
"If I see anybody catching flies
I'll whip him till he cries
And make the tears run out of his eyes."

Of all this work it has been said "The highest motive and the one most prominently held out, with its portentous instruments kept in full sight, was to be the best scholar under fear of punishment."

During the early part of the century the records of the school committee refer to frequent complaints by parents of excessive punishments by masters or ushers. The complaints were signs that the "spirit of innovation" was becoming dangerously active. Hearings were common and the details of floggings are recorded in full. School whippings produced less impression then than now from the severity and publicity of all civil penalties. There were three whipping posts, one on Queen Street, another on the Common, and still another on State Street. A writer speaks of seeing from his schoolhouse windows women brought in an iron cage, stripped to the waist and punished with thirty or forty lashes, their screams only partly drowned by the jeers of the mob. The pillory, too, was in sight of the school. In this frequently could be seen poor wretches confined by heads and hands, and pelted by the unfeeling crowd with rotten eggs and all manner of garbage.

When we hear people sighing for a return of the good old-fashioned New England education we should know that it consisted chiefly of memory tasks, mostly meaningless, to which children were driven by fear of the rod. The work and the rod always went together. This point needs to be especially emphasized just now when from many quarters are heard complaints of modern theories and practices in education. There is talk of "soft pedagogics," of a lack of robustness in the modern training, of a disposition to turn work into play. There is a fear that school life is being made too pleasant, and that students brought up in modern ways will lack disposition and power to grapple with the difficulties of life.

That it is possible for children to learn and to exert themselves to the utmost in learning, and to do it *con amore,* many people cannot understand and will not believe. But this state of mind is not new. When Horace Mann made his urgent appeals for less severity in school-keeping, the weight of great names were used to overbear his arguments. They quoted Augustine, "Discipline is needful to overcome our puerile sloth," "From the ferules of masters to the trials of martyrs the wholesome severities may be traced." Melancthon wrote, "I had a master who was an excellent grammarian. He compelled me to the study; he made me write Greek, and give the rules in twenty or thirty verses of the Mantuan. He suffered me to omit nothing, and whenever I made a blunder he whipped me soundly, and yet, with proper moderation, he made me a grammarian." Dr. Johnson explained his own excellence as a Latin scholar by saying, "My master whipped me very well; without that, sir, I should have done nothing." One of the clerical pamphleteers in the Mann controversy wrote: "Knowledge may be compared to a garden full of delicious fruits and flowers, but surrounded with a thorny fence. We must break through with painful scratches before we can sit under the comfort of its shades or hear its waterfalls break upon the ear." "The incipient stages of education never can be made delightful."

In all these discussions there is never an intimation that the kind of work that went by the name of education could be dissociated from youthful repugnance, nor that that repugnance could be overcome in any other way than by corporal punishment. If we were to return to the grind of a hundred years ago, we should need to bring out the old instruments of torture, and resurrect the old-fashioned school-masters.

Although the people of Massachusetts appreciated fully the value of popular education, and expressed their feeling eloquently in all their public utterances, the more influential classes, especially in the commercial towns, were very unwilling to make such education universal. They believed in educated leaders, and their loyalty to the Latin school never flagged, but it required an act of the General Court in 1683 to induce the selectmen of Bos-

ton to open writing schools for the boys of less distinguished social position. The bickerings, sometimes breaking out in open hostilities, between the Latin school boys from School Street and Master Carter's Writing school boys from Scollay Square, reflected something of the feeling of their elders. A childish doggerel serves to indicate the prevailing sentiment:

"Carter's boys shut up in a pen,
They can't get out but now and then;
And when they get out they dance about,
For fear of Latin School gentlemen."

Boston was the last town to admit girls to the schools, and it kept them on short allowance of schooling longer than any other. The narrowness and illiberal spirit of the social aristocracy of the capital is shown in its dealing with three classes,—young children, girls, and children of African descent. Only after the most persistent efforts, continued in the case of African children more than fifty years, and in the case of girls more than half that time, was equality of opportunity secured.

In 1800 there were in Boston 1,174 persons of African descent. Many of these were children of the slaves of pre-Revolutionary times. Others had escaped from the South during the war. Some had come from the West Indies. They were generally poor, shiftless, and ignorant. There were, however, some among them who had aspirations, and these had started by subscription a school in a private house. This was in 1798. A gleam of light upon the sanitary condition of the town is thrown by the fact that the school was dispersed by the prevalence of *yellow fever*.

In 1801 the school was revived, largely through the influence of President Kirkland of Harvard College, who secured the co-operation of philanthropic people. After fourteen years of struggles with poverty a small contribution was secured from the town, and in 1815 the town assumed the whole support and placed the school in charge of the school committee.

The general character of the African population and the indifference of the white people had withheld the opportunity for education so long, that it was found impossible to break up the habits of vagrancy and idleness which the children had acquired. There was no law to compel attendance, and no gospel of winning it by making the place and the work attractive. So the school was always a "thorn in the flesh" to the committee.

A special report on the school describes the accommodations (in the basement of a colored Baptist church) as very inferior. The distinction between the condition of the colored and white children was pronounced "invidious and unjust." The signers declared that if either were to be less favored it should be the white children. The city council was asked to build a school house, but refused. In 1835 a building was erected with money left for the purpose by Abiel Smith, and the school was named the Smith School. It early became a bone of contention between the anti-slavery people of Boston and their opponents. Efforts were made to abolish the school and to admit the pupils to the schools for whites. The fiery eloquence of Wendell Phillips was enlisted in support of this change. But all efforts to give equal opportunity to the colored children with the whites failed until

the Legislature, in 1855, enacted a general law forbidding the exclusion of children from public schools on account of race, color, or religion.

The metropolis was far behind the rest of the State in making public provision for the beginning of education of those whom the old English deeds of foundation quaintly called "petties and incipients." The country towns, some of them for a hundred years, had paid for the tuition of children by school dames.

Boston, serene in the contemplation of its great school-houses, and impressed by the showy exhibitions of copybooks and Latin orations, was blind to the fact that hundreds of children were growing up in illiteracy, because their parents were too poor or too negligent to patronize the private schools, and too ignorant to give even the elementary instruction demanded for admission to the public schools.

When the facts had been discovered they failed to make much impression on the social leaders. It required the strenuous efforts of philanthropists to secure equal opportunities for the poor, as it did to secure the same for children of color. Even by those who were influential in starting them, primary schools were intended for the lower classes. When early in the century children had been gathered into Sunday schools, by the Society for the Moral and Religious Instruction of the Poor, the good people were surprised to find that in Boston there were some who could not read, and did not even know their letters. That this had been the case in New York was not to be wondered at, but in Boston—

The town was asked to do something about it. The school committee and

Selectmen made a thorough canvass of the situation and found several hundren children not attending any school. They reported eleven public schools with 2,365 pupils and 162 private schools with 4,132 pupils. They found 283 children between four and seven years of age, and 243 above seven, not in any school. In the face of these facts they advised against any action, alleging a variety of reasons. The schools were already a great expense. They were in a flourishing condition. The school committee was wise and good and might be depended on to do all that was really necessary. The number of children out of school was not very large. The older ones might go if they wanted to. The younger children, now at private schools, furnished employment and support to a very useful and respectable class of citizens of both sexes. It was good for the parents who could afford it to pay something, and the overseers would pay for the poor. New schools would have to be numerous and expensive. Most of the parents had time enough, and Boston parents were intelligent enough to teach children their letters. The office of instruction belonged properly to parents, and the retirement of domestic life was the most fitting place.

The final argument is a felicitous expression of that narrow view of the scope of public education characteristic of social aristocracy everywhere.

"It is not to be expected that free schools should be furnished with so many instructors and be conducted on so liberal principles as to embrace the circle of a polite and finished education. They have reference to a limited degree of improvement."

The advocates of the new schools, not impressed by the multiplicity of excuses for inaction appealed directly to the town in a special meeting, and in spite of the arguments of the respected Harrison Gray Otis and Peter Thacher, whose services had been enlisted by the selectmen, the voters expressed their approval of the new movement by an overwhelming majority. So public primary schools came into being in 1818. Under the fostering care of a special committee they soon began to rival the older schools in loading the memory with meaningless symbols. The school held up by the committee as a model presented on the examination day a child of six years of age who repeated all the rules for spelling and pronunciation in the prescribed book—fifty or sixty in number. Another repeated all the reading parts of the book. Rules for "stops and marks," for the use of capitals, long lists of words pronounced alike but spelled differently, several pages of "vulgarisms," as "vinegar, not winegar," "vessel, not wessel," and a multitude of abbreviations, these were given by different children, though learned by all as a condition of promotion to the first class. As we read the enthusiastic report of the visiting committee we cannot help thinking of Dr. John Brown's highland minister—commending the parish school as a "most aixlent cemetery of aedication."

In striking contrast with this was the primary school attended by Mrs. Livermore, where the children used to amuse themselves by rocking back and forth on the high and narrow benches until they fell in a delightful tumult of confusion into the laps of the row behind them. When the mistress was asleep they threw their spelling cards out of the window, and then protested that they had not had any, and every forenoon they went to the neighboring store for the teacher's morning dram.

We may place all other schools between these two extremes. They continued for many years to be thought of as somewhat eleemosynary in their character, and as being justified by the beneficent results in improving the morals of the lower classes. When they were finally merged in the general system in 1855 (only by legislative interference), it was declared to have been their object "to extend the blessings of education to the children of poverty and ignorance, and by this means to qualify the children of poor emigrants for intellectual citizenship."

As evidence of the good they had done it was said within a few years of their starting:

"The character of the lower classes has been effectually reached and elevated by this important improvement in the free education of their families.   *   *   *   The numbers of begging children have sensibly diminished, and there has been great improvement in neatness of dress and propriety of manners."

When we compare the schools of a hundred years ago with those of to-day we see that the most important change is not the superficial one that first attracts us. The great aggregations of children and the lavish expenditure for physical convenience and comfort are not peculiar to the schools. They are characteristic of modern social life in all departments. Slowly through the century there has been developed in the public mind a new idea of education as a process, of the conditions necessary for its successful progress, and of its scope as a function of society. When the nineteenth century

began, that education was a process of imparting and receiving knowledge had been an immemorial and a universal belief. "A good scholar," said the Talmud, "is like a well-plastered cistern that lets no drop escape."

The business of the teacher was to set lessons to be learned. The business of the pupil was to learn them; this was study. The next business of the teacher was to examine to see if they had been learned; this was recitation. Failure to study and learn was rebellion against constituted authority and must be punished as such. The teacher was judge and executioner. The whole process was simple in conception, the relation of the parties to each other obvious, and their mutual obligations unmistakable.

For the purpose of this education all knowledge had been formulated. It was expressed in definitions, rules, and exact propositions, in catechisms and grammars. These were the same for all, for truth was one and all were alike in their natural ignorance and natural sin. Now and then a voice had made itself heard in question of the theory and of the practice, and in doubt whether education were so simple a matter. But the voices had died away and left no impression on the prevailing thought. Not until the nineteenth century was well under way, and then not widely until the doctrine of Evolution had gained ascendancy, did the modern theory of education get itself expressed in schools.

Now education is seen to be the most complex process in the universe. It is deemed to be not something done *to* a child but something done *by* him and *in* him. It is thought to be from within, so that there is no education but self-education. Its instruments are not the old ones, a book and a stick, but a world of people and things. With the prevalence of this new notion, the old figures of rhetoric have lost their meaning. Those familiar metaphors which did duty at school functions for so many generations,—the teacher an artist, the child a block of marble to be hammered into a form of beauty, or a mass of clay to be molded into one, have been laid aside. The new figures suggest life-processes. Froebel ventured to call his school a *garden* of children (kindergarten), and this idea underlies all modern educational theory from kindergarten to college. The essential conditions are seen to be similar to those demanded by every living and growing organism. There must be suitable mental and moral food, and social warmth and sunshine. It is these elements that differentiate a good school of to-day from the schools of a hundred years ago. Nor is it expected that all will need the same food in kind or quantity. A new meaning has been read into the old injunction, "Train up a child in the way he should go." Now the emphasis is on the *he,* implying that there is for every child a way which is peculiarly his way, in which he should be taught to go; and that only as that way is found and followed is the education successful. And the public has come to see that it cannot afford to neglect any class of its members. Social safety is seen to lie in the most complete development of every member of the social whole. So, means of education are multiplied in number and variety to meet the needs of all classes and all ages as fast as those needs are discovered. The new education is scientific in its ground and rational in its methods. It is everywhere defensible in general, even when it is vulnerable in particulars.

CHARLES RIVER FROM THE CHARLESBANK

New England Magazine

New Series   AUGUST   Vol. XXVI No. 6

The Charles River Valley

By Augusta W. Kellogg

AUTHORITIES agree that this land was once covered by an ice-sheet from one to two thousand feet in thickness. In grinding its way to the sea, everything that impeded its course was torn up by the roots. Valleys were raised, mountains brought low, boulders loosened and swept far from their moorings. Sometimes these rocks fell apart and showed exactly corresponding cleavages. A single one has furnished building material for a factory, the walls of which are thirty by sixty feet and two stories high, besides the underpinning and steps of a church. The small stones and *névé* swirled about in the tumultuous waters, scooped out deep kettle-holes, or carved the shallow basins that were the beginnings of the numberless reedy marshes of the neighborhood. Moving sheets of successive glacial periods thus played havoc till, the ice-age, removed far back beyond all save the scientific memory, the present fair configuration emerged from chaos. Then nations came and went. The Norseman may have moored his galleys, built stone dams and fortifications, and laid his hearthstones in no mean city. He passed away. Bretons succeeded—perhaps, and passed also. Indians roved over the country—and, passing, their heritage has become ours.

On the southwestern border of Middlesex County, in Massachusetts, is the town of Hopkinton, among the hills of which, within a radius of half a mile, rise three rivers: the Sudbury, an outlet of Lake Whitehall, flows northward, till, mingling with the

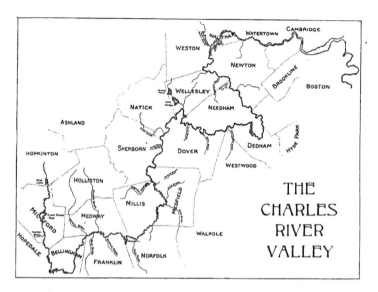

THE
CHARLES
RIVER
VALLEY

Concord, it joins the Merrimac at Lowell; another takes a fairly direct southerly course from North Pond to Long Island Sound, uniting itself meanwhile with the Blackstone on its way to swell the Pawtucket River; and, lastly, the Charles, bubbling to the surface of the same marshy tract, begins its winding way to the Atlantic Ocean. The pre-historic drift imposes characteristic conditions, which add greatly to the picturesqueness of the river. Following the line of least resistance it tumbles down sharp declivities, broadens over shallows, seeks the bosom of convenient ponds from which it runs to join forces with a score of brooks, curls under the cliff and circles in closest convolutions, till, its frolicsomeness spent in thus doubling upon itself, at a distance of more than eighty-five miles, and with a descent of four hundred and thirty-two

feet from its highland source, it lapses into the waters of Boston Harbor.

In many of the munificent land-grants bestowed by royal charter, the Charles was named as boundary line, and, in sooth, its crookedness served well for that purpose from any point of the compass. Stimson, in his delightful "King Noanett," makes the jolly Irishman exclaim: "The river is like its master, our good King Charles of sainted memory; it promises overmuch, but gets you nowhere."

The vastness of the Colonial possessions bred prodigality, and an indefinite tract "north of the Charles," or a wilderness to the "south of the same" stretching more or fewer leagues made little difference to the royal grantor. The Indians had called this river the Quinobequin, but Professor Horsford satisfied himself that its earliest name was the Norumbega. Be that as it

THE SOURCE OF THE CHARLES RIVER

may, when Captain John Smith betook himself to England in 1614, he carried the map he had so laboriously drawn "from point to point, isle to isle, harbor to harbor, soundings, sand, rocks and landmarks." This he laid before the King, with the request that his young son, the Prince Charles, would rechristen the localities. Smith supposed, naturally enough, that the Indian names were designations merely, without special significance, but, in reality, they were in the aboriginal splendidly descriptive, and in euphonic charm much exceeded the commonplaceness of the Prince's selection. To the river Quinobequin, or Norumbega, he gave his own name; to Cape Ann on the coast, that of his mother; while Elizabeth and Plymouth are among the few others that still exist. But commonplace as it is, our associations have endeared this terminology, and in truth "the Charles" himself "writes

the last letter of his name" so often in his meadows, that we almost feel that he perforce really named himself.

The Charles was early described as "one of the most beautiful rivers in the world," but without waxing so enthusiastic as that, it is safe to say there is no more picturesque water course in New England, nor one that runs through more historic ground.

No account has come down to us of any exploration of the valley during the first decade after the establishment of the Bay Colony, but it was early in our history that the several falls invited industries for which the pressure from the Mother Country made the necessity imperative. Several men from Winthrop's party pushed three leagues up the river in 1631 and established themselves at Watertown, Roxbury, and Newtowne. Using the waterway for a road and the canoe for vehicle, the hardy pioneers gradually penetrated farther and farther inland. If we follow their footsteps in the reverse order, *i. e.*, from the source to the mouth of the Charles, we must begin with the town of Hopkinton, which has a history unique in our annals.

A London merchant, Edward Hopkins, came to this country in 1637, settled in Hartford, Connecticut, of which state he was governor for many years. He returned to England, where he died twenty years later. Of his New England estate he willed five hundred pounds "for the upholding and promoting the kingdom of the Lord Jesus Christ in those parts of the earth." After the death of his widow in 1699, the legacy was paid, but the executor and the residuary legatee both being dead, a suit was brought in the Court of Chancery, which resulted in a decree, that, with the consent of the Society for Propagating Christianity, the original amount with accrued interest should be laid out in lands, the rental of which should go to Harvard College and Cambridge High School. The trustees of the "Donation Fund" petitioned the General Court for license to purchase from the Natick Indians "a tract of waste land known as Magunkaquog." Six hundred pounds were paid in bills of credit, and a deed of warranty was executed by the Indians. Thus eight thousand acres lying between Sherburn, Mendon, the Province Lands, and Sudbury became the property of the trustees. To this territory twenty-five thousand acres were added, and all called, in honor of the donor, Hopkinton. From the first, and until 1742, an annual rental of a penny per acre was paid; later the price was advanced to threepence

"from that time forward forever," an arrangement however that was terminated by mutual consent nine years later, when the commonwealth paid eight, and the tenants two thousand pounds, for which sums the trustees gave full release to the tenants.

Joseph Young, father of Brigham, the Mormon leader, was a native of Hopkinton, as was also Patrick Shays, whose misguided son conducted the Rebellion in the attempt to coerce the courts of the state.

Closely associated with this region is the honored name of John Eliot, that "morning star of missionary enterprise," as Bancroft called him. This good man held, in common with many another, that the North American savage was the descendant of the ten lost tribes of Israel. Coming from England in 1631, he applied himself so diligently that in twenty years he was able to translate the Bible, or, as Mrs. Stowe wrote: "the harsh, guttural Indian language in the fervent alembic of his loving study was melted into a written language." Winthrop said of this stupendous achievement, that "no more marvelous monument of literary work in the service of either God or man, can be found upon the earth. Allibone calls it "the monolith of a race that has passed." This Bible, the first to be translated into a savage tongue, was the first of any kind to be printed in America. It bears the imprint of Cambridge 1661-3. It went through two editions of two thousand copies each. The first edition was inscribed to the English Parliament, and the second to Charles II. Several of these copies are still in existence. One in perfect condition, save for a missing title page, was presented to

Wellesley College by Dr. Bonar of Glasgow, Scotland, in whose possession it had been since 1840. The Lenox Library of New York has a copy ot each edition, and Mr. Trumbull of Hartford, Conn., has one in his valuable collection of books. South Natick also possesses one. The title of the New Testament is Wuskuwuttestermentum, and words of twenty even thirty-five letters were not uncommon. The present market price is quite one thousand dollars.

John Eliot began his mission in 1646, when forty-two years of age. When his little company of converts begged to be organized into a religious body, they represented that they "were trying to observe the ordinances of God, in observation whereof we see the goodly Englishmen walk.". Such organization was deemed inexpedient till the petitioners should acquire more civilized habits. When they applied for a form of civil government, Eliot referred them to Jethro's advice to Moses: "Moreover thou shalt provide out of all the people, able men, such as fear God; men of truth, hating covetousness, and place such over them to be rulers of thousands and rulers of hundreds, and rulers of fifties and rulers of tens." This was done, and the historian remarks that "the titles remained fairer than those of any belted Earl." The slope of Magunco Hill in the easterly part of Hopkinton was chosen as a suitable place for this settlement. The deed of sale was signed by the two chiefs, Waban and Pegan.

The rude wigwams of these "Praying Indians" gave way a century later, to a handsome country-seat owned by Sir Charles Henry Frankland, Collector of the Port of Boston. This scion of nobility bore in his veins the blood of the Earl of Chesterfield, Horace Walpole, and Oliver Cromwell. He was young, handsome, and selfish. With his beautiful but unfortunate mistress, Agnes Surriage, he lived on his lordly estate of four hundred and eighty-two acres the life of a Southern planter or English nobleman. He planted extensive orchards and pleasant gardens, imported trees, shrubs, fine furniture, and the choicest wines to fill his ample cellars. The romantic tale has been too often told in verse and story to require more than the merest mention here. When Sir Henry took his mistress to England, his family refused to recognize the connection. His affairs called him to Portugal, where, in the terrible earthquake of 1755, he was buried in the débris of falling buildings in the streets of Lisbon. Agnes Surriage had the happiness to arrive upon the scene of horror before life was extinct, and by her efforts her lover was rescued. As soon as he recovered from his injuries they were married, and lived happily until his death in 1768. Lady Frankland returned to America, where she witnessed the battle of Bunker Hill from a window in her town house on Garden Court Street corner of Ball Alley, now Prince Street. Naturally she was regarded with suspicion by the Patriots, and she returned to England, where she contracted a second marriage with a wealthy banker of Chichester. The Frankland mansion was destroyed by fire first in 1856 and again in 1902. As Upton and Ashland have been set off from Hopkinton, the Frankland estate is now (in more senses than one) in Ashland. The few remaining magnificent elms shading the box paths of the terraced lawn, are within gunshot of the buzzing trolley as it nears Hopkinton.

A long and pleasant street with its own post office, called Haydon Row, leads out of Hopkinton, and carries the Charles River directly from its birth spring through a culvert into a sloping field, where, under its first

bridge it makes its way into Echo Lake, whence, emerging over Willow dam it becomes a full-fledged river. It then enters Milford in Norfolk County and, parallel to the Pawtucket River, flows with great dignity the length of the town from north to south, over the straightest part of its entire course. The whilom beautiful Cedar Swamp Pond is merely the broadened river. Milford, like most New England towns, has been so cut up into smaller ones that to separate histories is not an easy matter. It was originally the Neck Hill of Mendon, but was set off as an independent township late in the eighteenth century. Today it is a busy, clattering little village: water, steam, and horse power are employed to turn wheels for

the manufacture of a score of useful articles,—cabinet and tinware, straw goods, varnish, wagon-irons, whips, curried leather, clinching screws, and shoe heels.

These industries are the outgrowth of a few dozen hand-made shoes, peddled by their maker from house to house. Milford also possesses fine rose granite quarries, the quality of which commends the material for building purposes. Whoever has enjoyed the faint flush of the Boston Public Library *façade* on bright days or at sunset may readily conclude that no richer suffusion of color can well be given out from gray granite.

From the very first the Milfordians proved themselves both thrifty and shrewd. It was decreed that "all such persons who should transport themselves into the Province of New Jersey within time limited by said concession, should be entitled to grants or patents under seal of the Province for certain acres for said concessions expressed, paying therefor yearly the rent of a half penny sterling money, for every acre to be so granted." Another decree was: "that all lands should be purchased by Governor or Council from Indians, as there should be occasion, in the name of the Lord Proprietor, every person to pay his proportion of purchase money and charges." This was intended as a just protection to Indian rights. It was conceded that they should receive compensation for their lands, and therefore must both sell and buy through responsible persons, viz., the proprietors. They also offered a bounty of seventy-five dollars for the importation of each able slave. This was in compliment to the Duke of York, who was a patron of

THE DAM AT SOUTH MEDWAY

the Slave Trade and President of the African Company.

The early annals of New England villages are little more than records of church and parish organizations. In 1841 Milford church as the result of a schism, was divided against itself, and one division, led by the Rev. Adin Ballou, founded the Hopedale Community. It was situated on Mill River, and had about thirty zealous but poor persons enrolled upon its books. Their object was "to establish a state of society governed by divine moral principles with as little as possible of mere human constraint, in which while the members may be sufficiently free to associate or separate their secular interests according to inclination or congeniality, no individual shall suffer the evils of oppression, poverty, ignorance, or vice through the influence or neglect of others." The Community was a joint stock company, having its savings bank, lyceum, and an "Industrial Army" which corresponded to our Village Improvement societies. "The streets, squares, and cemeteries were to be beautified, by combined labor and pleasure, usefulness and recreation, friendship and public spirit, that the Community may become a dear home for all its inhabitants." This declaration has been summed up as an enlightened, practical, Christian aim to regenerate the world.

It happened that in the "Dale" on the Jones farm there was standing an old house built entirely by one man's hands. This, with barns, and two hundred and fifty-eight acres of land, the Company purchased for four thousand dollars. In 1850 the number of families was thirty-four, consisting of one hundred and seventy-five souls, living on five hundred acres. Fourteen years after its establishment there were fifty families and three hundred individuals. This attempt to set up the Kingdom of God on earth, came to an end in 1856, when the Hopedale Parish, as its heir and assign, inherited the property.

The Roman Catholic St. Mary's Church inherited an ancient bell of exceedingly rich tone cast in Ireland and weighing four thousand pounds. In 1878 the same parish bought the organ of the Old South Church of Boston.

At South Milford the Charles enters Bellingham, also in Norfolk County, and at the center of the town makes a broad northward curve. Bellingham, named for Sir Richard Bellingham, was an unimportant part of Dedham until 1719. It never had a corporate charter, but came into existence solely on the proviso that a learned minister should be settled within three years. The land was drawn by numbered lots, and many conditions were attached to the quality of persons participating in the lottery. The town warned away all persons likely to become public charges in these words: "To the Constable of the town of Bellingham—Greeting. In his Majesty's name you are required forthwith to warn ——, his wife and children out of our town within fourteen days, as the law directs, and make return of this warrant unto the Selectmen." And further to sift the town of persons with undesirable habits, the records show that in 1777 it was voted that "all persons were forbidden to have the small-pox, and in the houses of Daniel or Silas Penniman, except said Silas now sick, if

any person in either of the two houses be so presumptuous as to have the small-pox, shall forfeit to the town £10 to be recovered by the treasurer." Discussion for and against inoculation became very heated. In 1722 a sermon had been preached from the text, "So Satan went forth from the presence of the Lord, and smote Job with sore boils from the sole of his foot to the crown of his head," and it was argued that the devil was the first inoculator and Job his first patient.

"We're told by one of the black robes
The Devil inoculated Job,
Suppose 'tis true, what he does tell,
Pray, neighbors, did not Job do well?"

Men patrolled the streets with halters in search of Dr. Zabdial Boylston, who had taken the suggestion of inoculation from Cotton Mather. He was hidden in his own house for fourteen days, only his wife knowing his whereabouts. Hand-grenades were thrown in at the windows. He treated his own child and two servants, for which he was cited before the Boston authorities. Of the one hundred and eighty-six persons inoculated that year, only six died. Dr. Boylston was the first American made Fellow of the Royal Society of England. Inoculation was succeeded by vaccination and practised by Dr. Waterhouse of Cambridge and Dr. Aspinwall of Brookline. The system of the patient was prepared by medical treatment, the skin scarified, and virus applied under a nut-shell.

When the General Court made its first call for a member in 1755 Bellingham refused to send one and was fined for contumacy. In 1757 and again in '61 the same thing occurred.

Beaver Brook is the outlet of Beaver Pond, which unites with the Charles and leaves Bellingham at the extreme northeast corner of the town, forming a boundary line between the adjacent towns of Franklin and Medway. It does not touch Holliston, but receives so many affluents from that town that it may, properly enough, be considered a part of the valley. Hopping and Chicken brooks both rise there and find the Charles at Medway.

The town was named for Sir Thomas Hollis and began its history in 1724. Someone has said that in New England "the town was the church acting in secular concerns, and the church was the town acting in religious concerns." The civil and ecclesiastical bodies were so closely united that only members of the church were voters, or freemen of the town. Hoyt thought, "the making of piety and church communion a qualification for civil offices, a premium offered to hypocrisy." And can less be said of the curiously undemocratic custom, which obtained in many if not all of the river towns, namely that of "Dignifying the Pews" by joint action of deacons and selectmen? This meant "to assign to families and to individuals their places in the house of God, in reference to their dignity, rank, standing, or worth, but at the same time taking due care that no person be humiliated or degraded"! This would seem to be a work requiring superhuman wisdom, and the heartburnings in the back pews must have been out of harmony with the spirit of worship. The schedule was drawn up with great care and discrimination, yet there were found five men who protested against the custom "as not according to Law and Reason."

The dissenter from the dominant principles of pure Congregationalism was a heretic and a political alien. The meeting-house served its religious purpose on Sunday, but was used as a town-house on Monday, thus occupying the place of a "true communal core." When it was decided that no parish was under obligation to provide a town meeting-house, the separation between it and the religious meeting-house took place. A "Great sickness" carried off an eighth of the population in 1754 and was regarded as a direct punishment of God for certain litigation in the town.

BRIDGE BETWEEN FRANKLIN AND MEDWAY

Franklin, separated from Medway by the Charles, became an independent township in 1778. The territory belonged to the Proprietors as a Company, in which each held shares in proportion to his property valuation. The

MEDWAY VILLAGE

ratio was one Common right per each £8 of estate. Five sheep counted as one cow. Each owned such a share of this land, or so many common cow rights, as one eighth of his property valuation might express in units.

Benjamin Franklin, in whose honor the town received its name, sent in acknowledgement one hundred and sixteen volumes, instead of a bell, hoping, as he explained, "that they would prefer sense to sound." There is a beautiful group of lakes and rivers between Franklin and Norfolk, viz., Lake Wollomonopoag, King Philip's Pond, Populatic Pond, Uncas, Beaver, and Mill rivers. The region was a favorite resort of Massasoit, and later, of his son King Philip of unfortunate memory.

KING PHILIP'S BRIDGE

The Rev. Nathaniel Emmons was pastor from the dedication to the demolition of the meeting-house. In the pulpit he was grave and dignified, but out of it, his witty repartee and fund of anecdote have left an abiding memory. When the building was torn down, the old sounding-board settled on a well-house in Ashland, and the breast-work of the pulpit found its way to the Chicago Theological Seminary. The bell had received a coat of paint whereby the *ring* was virtually destroyed. It was disposed of in Paxton, before the expedient of removing the paint was suggested in the town.

Horace Mann was born in 1796 in a house on an adjoining Plain, bearing his family name. When the Franklin land was allotted, an old squaw begged to exchange her portion for Wollomonopoag Farm. This became in 1673 the town of Wrentham, but in 1870 received the name of Norfolk. Its subdivisions are Pondville, Stony Brook, City Mills, and Highland Lake. In King Philip's War every house but two was burned, and those two were spared because persons ill of the smallpox—of which the savages were mortally afraid—were in them. Norfolk is a farming as well as a manufacturing place. The Populatic Pond covers seventy-four acres, and is another of those shining river breadths, spreading over the low lands.

Chief Chickatawbet was said to have sold, in 1651, certain lands between the Charles and the Neponset rivers to William Pynchon. If any deed of transfer passed, no record has ever been found of it, but the Chief's grandson entered a claim, which was recognized by the payment of a small sum of money. On these meadows and uplands north of the Charles and west of Boggastow Brook a pretty hamlet of small houses with high, narrow gables was built, and called Medfield. King Philip himself inhabited adjoining land. In an early morning in February, 1675, with a party of two or three hundred painted Narragansett warriors, he swooped down upon his neighbors, burning fifty houses and killing eighteen men.

A bridge called King Philip's and another named Dwight's here span the river. The rock foundation is largely gneiss and granite, the soil a clayey loam. This town was the birthplace of Mr. Lowell Mason, and also of the Mr. Dowse whose name is associated with the foundation of the Cambridgeport Public Library and the Franklin Memorial at Mt. Auburn, as well as with the nucleus of a library left to the town of Sherborn.

From Medfield the new and pleasant town of Millis receives the fine chirographical Charles as it winds and turns in curious convolutions bounding the entire eastern and part of the southern front. Boggastow Brook enters Millis at the northeast, and forms two ponds and three oxbows, uniting with the Charles at the northwest. At South End Pond are remains of the fortifications thrown up in King Philip's time. Millis was a part of Medfield until 1885. It has thriving industries, brush and broom, carriage and wagon factories being prominent among them.

The peculiar institution of Sherborn is the Woman's Prison. opened to criminals in 1877. For some years and until her death Ellen Cheney Johnson was matron. Her life and

OLD FARM BRIDGE BETWEEN SHERBORN AND DOVER

qualities are worthy a public memorial.

As the bird flies, Sherborn is fourteen miles from Dover, but thirty-eight and a half by the river which bounds it on both the north and the west. Trout, Clay, and Noanett brooks join it here, affording delightful riparian variety. The Dingle Hole Narrows and Nimrod's Rocks, with five hills from three to five hundred feet high, present very delightful scenery. Dover was set off from Dedham —that mother of much progeny—in 1729, and is one of the very few agricultural towns of the valley.

The next town on the Charles is Natick, with division of South Natick, which, in the Indian vernacular means Place of Hills. Nobscott's Height, Hopkinton, Wachuset, with Monadnock in New Hampshire are clearly visible. Its first settlement was made in 1651 by John Eliot's "Praying Indians," for, said that good man, "The Lord did discover that there it was his pleasure we should begin this work. When grasse was fit to cut, I sent In-

dians to mow and others to make hay, because we must oft ride hither in the autumn and in the spring before any grasse is come." A round fort was built against Pegan Hill, an outpost palisaded with trees was established, and a footbridge in the form of an arch, the foundations of which were seamed in stone, was thrown across the rapids. To each family was accorded a house lot, and one was also set apart for the missionary. This was surrounded by "trees of friendship" whose girth well above the ground is today twenty-one feet. A strenuous attempt was made to instill methodical habits of life and work. The Indians felled trees, and made clapboards and shingles, evincing genuine interest in the project. The troubles encountered did not come from the red men, but from the white man in the neighboring town of Dedham. Eliot was obliged to protest that these professing pious Dedhamites "do take away the railles prepared to fence our corne fields, and on another side they have taken away our lands and sold them to others, to the trouble and wonderment of the Indians." The missionary efforts for the aborigines continued till the breaking out of King Philip's War, when it was deemed prudent to confine their residence to five out of the seven settlements they had made, and to forbid them to roam more than a mile away. This arrangement put an effectual veto on their fishing and hunting habits, and they were soon taken under guard to The Pines, now the Arsenal, at Watertown, and finally deported to Deer Island. Some escaped to the woods *en route,* returned to their people, and sometimes served as spies. They never returned except as occasional stragglers. In twenty years all had passed away, and in 1745 the Natick plantation had become a parish.

The Charles covers a hundred acres in Natick, and its picturesque rapids, with Sawin's and Bacon's brooks, and Lake Cochichuate, combine to furnish lovely views. Just here too the vaga-

ries of the Charles are as fanciful as anywhere in its course. It enters Wellesley, where the land falls to the southwest and to the northeast towards different parts of the river. The beautiful country-seat of Mr. H. Hunnewell occupies over four hundred acres, and the river flows along its entire eastern front and a short distance on the southwestern curve.

Wellesley was a part of Dedham at first, and later of Needham. When incorporated as an independent township it was named for the Welles family. It is already subdivided into Wellesley Hills (originally Grantville), Wellesley Farms, Rice's Crossing, and Riverside. Wellesley College site was the Cunningham Pasture bordering the lake named for Chief Waban. Henry Fowle Durant was the donor of the four hundred and fifty acres designed as a memorial to his only child. The college was opened in 1875 with three hundred students and thirty professors and instructors.

WELLESLEY COLLEGE AND LAKE WABAN

POWDER HOUSE ROCK, DEDHAM

Great stress is laid upon the recognition of the Bible as the basis of all learning and of all true philosophy, and it is a required study throughout the course.

Wellesley has hosiery, shoddy, and paper mills, shoe, paint, and chemical factories within its limits. The discoverer of ether as an anæsthetic, Dr. W. G. T. Morton, was a native of the town.

The whole southern line of Needham is washed by the Charles, which here has quirks and capers innumerable. It almost cuts an island out of Dedham, an attempt encouraged by man in the ditch across the narrow connecting link of land. This ditch affords a saving of labor to many a canoeist whose aim is to "get there" rather than to loaf around the bends at all points of the compass. Needham was named from Nehoiden, a chief

who had adopted William for a given name. This was a friendly custom with the Indian tribes living at peace with the settlers, as witness Alexander and Philip, Massasoit's sons. Its annals are complicated with those of Charles River Village, which separates the town proper from Dover. The town of Dedham originally contained Norwood, Walpole, Norfolk, Wrentham, Franklin, Bellingham, Medfield, Dover, Needham, parts of Natick and Hyde Park. The word Dedham is said to be synonymous with Contentment. It was settled as a plantation by a population of about nine thousand in 1635.

The digging of Mother Brook Channel was a great design and permanently beneficial in its consequences. About a third of the water of the Charles continues its natural course, while the other two-thirds runs in a

direct line through the meadows and around the highlands by the town to Neponset River.

Newton has a water front of seventeen miles, being surrounded on three sides—south, west, and north—by the winding Charles whose course is a continuous curving line for fifteen miles. A boulder in the river, called County Rock, marks the abutting corners of Norfolk and Middlesex Counties, and also the towns of Newton, Wellesley, and Weston. Baptist Pond covers thirty-two acres and sends its outletting stream southward to the Charles. Hammond's Pond is connected with Ballou Ponds, which join the Charles at Watertown. It has several hills: Waban, Oak, Sylvan Heights, Nonatum, and Institution, where is situated the Baptist Theological Seminary. Newton was cut off from Cambridge when the common lands were divided in 1662; another division took place two years later, when one Edward Jackson re-

ceived four hundred acres, which, at his death, were bequeathed to Harvard College. Among his assets were two male slaves valued at five pounds each. As Cambridge was unwilling to forego the educational and bridge taxes derived from Newtowne, the final separation of the towns was not effected till 1776, after thirty-two years of constant petitioning. Where the ground descends from Nonantum Hill in Newton near to the limits of Brighton the Indians had a settlement with Waban their chief. He listened to Eliot's first sermon in the Indian language. It was three hours long and the text was from Ezekiel 37:9. "Come from the four winds, O breath, and breathe upon these slain that they may live." Curiously enough the Indian word for breath, or wind, was Waban, and all unconsciously the preacher had tickled the vanity of his Chieftainship, who, as may be guessed, lent a willing ear to a doctrine drawn from a book in which he was mentioned by name. Roger

ECHO BRIDGE, NEWTON UPPER FALLS

Sherman, a signer of the Declaration of Independence was born in Newton, as was also Ephraim Williams, founder of Williams College.

Smelt Brook joins the Charles on the south, while the Sudbury River conduit pipe crosses it at Newton Upper Falls, upon Echo Bridge. The total length of this bridge is five hundred feet, and its main span one hundred and thirty feet long and seventy feet high was, at the time it was built—1876-7—the second largest on the continent. Here is that most lovely bit of scenery, Hemlock Gorge, the steep rocky sides of which are clothed with fine evergreen. The conglomerate bedrock makes a natural dam with a perpendicular fall of twenty feet, and, in the next half mile a drop of thirty-five. Unfortunately, but inevitably, such material advantages could not be ignored, and the whirr of ma-

chinery from snuff, grist, saw, cotton, iron, and cut-nails mills and factories has long been heard. A fine silk industry has also been established, the yarn for which comes from every silk-producing country in the world: China, Japan, Italy, and France. As early as 1704, two dams utilizing sixteen and six feet falls of water respectively, were placed at Newton Lower Falls, two miles beyond the Upper Falls. Iron works, paper, silk, hosiery, and cloth mills have thus desolated the scene. The Middlesex Canal was chartered in 1793 and was navigable from the Charles to the Merrimac in 1803. The subdivisions of Newton are Newton Centre, Upper and Lower Falls, Chestnut Hill, Highlands, West Newton, Thompsonville, Newtonville, and Auburndale.

At Riverside, where a branch of the Boston and Albany Railroad crosses

THE WILLOWS, NEWTON LOWER FALLS

the river, is one of the noblest of pleasure grounds open to the public, with proper restrictions. Mr. Charles W. Hubbard began to lay out a scheme for it in 1896, and his ideas enlarged and improved by experiment till there are now 54,000 square feet of floor space in the various buildings, and his floats cover 13,500 square feet. There are forty acres of land, a quarter mile cinder track, seven tennis courts, and fully equipped base and foot ball fields.

Thousands of canoes are stored here, with lockers for cushions and paddles. The proximity of the Newton Boat Club, the Boston Athletic Association, and several smaller organizations, turn out numberless canoes on summer evenings. The Saturday night band concerts are delightful. Then the basin is often a solid mass of canoes, long strings of gay lanterns rise to the apex of the boat house flagstaff, and as one lolls back in the cushioned canoe both sight and hearing are entertained. The shores are under the control of the Metropolitan Park Commission, and policemen have patrol boats to ensure safety.

Waltham, Watertown, and Weston were three military districts. At Waltham the river is twenty feet above sea level, and from Prospect hill-top, four hundred and sixty feet in height, five miles from Boston, a view of the State House and sea can be obtained. Half way between Waltham and Wa-

662

tertown Cheesecake Brook joins the Charles. Beaver Brook runs across the lower end of Waltham Plain, where it receives Chester Brook and takes it with itself into the Charles.

Waltham is a centre of canoe building. Here, too, are many mills: Chocolate, snuff, grist, saw, cotton, woolen, hosiery, and coarse wrapping paper; also crayon, watch and clock factories; and watch machine works. Waltham watches are a triumph of automatic accuracy. At Watertown was the first inland settlement. Roger Clapp from Winthrop's party was there in 1636. It was itself cut off from Newton, only in its turn to be sliced up so effectually as to be at present one of the smallest townships in the State. It is separated from Boston and Newton by the Charles, which here is about eight rods wide. Stony Brook, originating in Sandy Pond, and increased by the Stower, or Hobb's Brook, is one of the largest tributaries. Cherry Brook also contributes a mite, but far the largest change in the river is caused by the tides, which affect it at this distance of twelve miles from the sea. It is navigable for small vessels, and unobservant persons have been known to think it "only an arm of the sea." Bishop Brooks was of the opinion that John Eliot preached here five years earlier than at Natick.

Weston is a farming town, being one of the several cut out of Watertown. The settlers "built their homes on the gentle slopes rising from the two brooks that flow each side of the village street," and the historian says that "the pleasant springs, like rivers through its body," drew them to Weston. A drum called the worshippers to meeting, instead of the "bells which now knoll to church"; and tithing men or constables kept the congregation in order with wand, a hare's foot on one end and hare's tail on the other. Children were not allowed to sit with their parents. It was voted "unseemly to turn ye back towards the minister, to gaze abroad, or to lay down ye head upon ye arms—in a sleepy posture, in time of public worship." The mention of Weston introduces the theory, advanced and well-defended by Professor Eben C. Horsford of Harvard College, of the early settlement of the Northmen in New England. It was his opinion that at the junction of Stony Brook with the Charles (or Norumbega) River, there stood, in 1543, a fine city called Norvega. David Ingram described it as "having buildings with crystal and silver pillars, golden chairs and peeks of pearls." The word Norumbega may apply to any bay from the bottom of

which rises a narrow tongue (Norum), and this involves a sheet of water with a peculiarly escalloped shore. The only one on the Charles is between Riverside, the Boston and Albany Railway, and Waltham, two miles north. Professor Horsford said: "If I am correct every tributary of the river will be found to have, or to have had, a dam and a pond, or their equivalent at or near its mouth or along its course." There are rare groupings of moraines for some distance above and below Stony Brook. Even as far as Millis, and beyond in Holliston the Professor found verification of his theory. A stone dam was discovered, made of such boulders as were used in the construction of churches in Weston, Watertown, and Wellesley; these were not squared, nor split, nor hewn. It is at head of tide water, and only once, in 1858, when Minot's Ledge Light was swept away, has the water risen higher than this dam. It was certainly there before 1631, five years before the Winthrop party's settlement of the region. There are remains of wharves, docks, dams, walls, canals, forts, terraces, and pavements, all believed by the enthusiastic scholar to be the work of Northmen seven to nine centuries ago.

To commemorate the event Prof. Horsford had built the stone Tower shown on the following page. A part of the tablet reads thus:

River
The Charles
Discovered by Lief Erikson 1000 A. D.
Explored by Thorwald, Lief's brother, 1003.
Colonized by Thorfinn Karlsfinn 1007.
First Bishop Erik Gunpson 1121.
Industries for 350 years,
Masurwood (burrs), Fish, Furs.
Latest Norse ship returned to Iceland 1347.

The neighborhood around the Tower is said to have been occupied in the 15th, 16th, and 17th centuries by Breton French, although nothing very accurate is known about the tradition.

The next town is Brighton, which has developed from a Cattle Fair Hotel Corporation. The establishment of a market for the sale of cattle is coëval with the Revolution, originating in the demand for ampler supplies for the Army. In 1870 the General Court of Massachusetts endorsed the incorporation of an association, with a capital of $200,000 for bringing under one general management the business of slaughtering cattle, sheep, and other animals, and that of rendering fat, offal, etc. Sixty acres of dry and sandy soil were chosen, with a frontage of a thousand feet on the River, and an Abattoir established, which in some respects is an improvement on the best in England and France. Some one has said: "The skill and industry shown in the manner of conducting the business here, if it do not make slaughtering a fine art, will at least place it high above its earlier position." The great slaughter-houses of the West are, of course, on a far larger and more modern scale. The raising of fruit and flowers are thriving industries.

The Brighton Bridge, leading to Cambridge, was built in 1660, and is interesting from the fact that it is the one over which Lord Percy marched his nine hundred troops on April 19, 1775, *en route* to Lexington.

The beautiful cemetery of Mt. Auburn is folded in the embrace of the
"River that stealeth with such silent pace
Around the city of the dead."
The natural beauties of the ground were so many that it was long the resort of pleasure parties, but eventually was sold to the Massachusetts Horticultural Society for six thousand dollars, and in 1831 was formally dedicated to its present use.

History records that "wherever a navigable river or creek swept past a gentle slope of the glacial drift, a settlement of the colonists was made. The creeks were the first roads, the marshes the first hayfields. Cambridge and Watertown were thus settled." The former has two tidal rivers with broad estuaries, the Charles and the Mystic. Within a radius of four miles there are the municipalities of Old, North, East Cambridges and Cambridgeport, so that after New York, it has a larger aggregation of population about her ocean port than any on this continent. Cambridge was projected as a city of refuge from the Indians, and pieced out from bits of Brighton, Brookline, Roxbury, and

Waltham. Its early annals are like those of other towns, first a meeting-house, a parish, a school, a town—differing only that this received the crown of a university. John Harvard's bequest, the acorn for this sheltering oak, amounted to only £779.-17.2.

Rowing on the river became an earnest sport at Harvard about 1844, when the class of '46 bought a six-oared boat and christened it Oneida. It was "thirty-seven feet long, lapstreak built, heavy, quite low in water, with no shear and with straight stem. The Heron, Halcyon, Ariel, and Iris followed directly and a Boathouse was put up in '46. The first intercollegiate race took place on Lake Winnepissaukee at Cedar Harbor, the Oneida vs. the Yale Shawmut. Harvard won. Since those days the athletic course may be said to be included in the college curriculum. The noble gift of Major Henry L. Higginson to Har-

vard students of the "Soldiers' Field" goes far to make athletics not the least atractive feature of a liberal education. Cambridge has a life distinct from that of the University, as her many industries witness: namely, glass, lumber, boxes, bricks, rubber, biscuits, furniture, scientific instruments, pianos, pork, tanneries, printeries, and distilleries.

In the line of Cambridge and just beyond, lies Charlestown. Webcowit deeded a part of the land in 1632, but the portion known as Somerville since 1637, was purchased from the Squaw Sachem, widow of King Nanapashamet, or, translated, the New Moon. Thirty-six shillings, twenty-one coats, nineteen fathoms wampum, and three bushels of corn was the price paid. The market is higher now. It was here that General Putnam unfurled the new Union flag of the Colonies in 1776.

The history of Charlestown is so

linked with Bunker Hill, that it needs no repetition here. But it is at this point that the Charles sweeps its gathered stream by its namesake city, unites with the Mystic and mingles with the sea in Boston Harbor. We have followed "its vagrancy of motion" from source to mouth, and as far as space permits, from the time (to quote Mrs. Stowe) "when the hard, rocky, sterile New England was a sort of half-Hebrew theocracy, half-ultra democratic republic of little villages."

Our river has had its poets, Lowell, Longfellow, and Holmes, all of whom lived upon its banks. Its lovers and friends are the great body of youth who fill our halls and schools from every quarter of America.

The Story of Jess Dawson

By Imogen Clark

IT was the popular verdict in Straitsmouth that Dick Hawley and Jess Dawson would be man and wife one day, but to my thinking the two were born comrades—nothing more. They were about the same age and kept pace in everything, even to growing, Dick only at the last shooting up a bit above the girl, who was unusually tall for her sex, so's he could tease her by making her look up to him. I never could abide your great giants of women, being smallish myself, thank God, and grudging even the amount of material it takes to make a gown for one of my inches; still, there was something about the way Jess carried her height that made you almost forgive it (especially when you didn't have to consider her clothes) and you got a feeling of strength from her you wouldn't have had from one of lesser stature. Why, her hands were as strong as a man's—what a heft they could lift!—yet they were gentle too, when it was needful. That was the woman in her! She was awkward and unlike other girls, but put her in a boat, or set her at some task she'd learned along with Dick, and she was as easy as a fish in water. They were well-favored too, though there again Dick had the advantage. Brown-haired, brown-skinned, brown-eyed, both of them; but the lad's eyes were warm with laughter, while the girl's were full of an unsatisfied yearning that made your heart ache.

When Steven Dawson died his daughter Jess, who'd just turned fourteen, was left without kith or kin saving only me her cousin three times removed. I'd had little cause to care for Steve—he'd stepped between me and his brother (a man long since

dead, God rest his soul!) but I'd always been drawn to the child because
of the resemblance she bore her uncle,
so I took her to live with me and glad
enough was the poor thing of a home.
She'd never known the meaning of
one before. Having her in my house
I'd plenty of chances to see. as time
went on, how matters really stood between her and Dick, and that's why I
always maintained they were just
friends like David and Jonathan.
There are tricks and signs to point the
way of love to an outsider—blushes
and giggles and all the other little
foolishnesses—and I never surprised
any of them between the boy and girl.

Dick went on a longish cruise when
Jess was nineteen and it seemed to me
then that, if she really loved him, her
true feelings would crop out somehow.
separation showing up what's in a person's heart as a light shows hidden
places. But she went about her work
as if nothing had happened. It wore
on my nerves to see her so uncon-
cerned. and once, being driven to the
end of my patience. for I like to see a
woman a woman (though not too partial to tears except on their rightful
occasions), I let fall something about
the dangers of the sea. Jess only
laughed; she hadn't the trick of much
laughter. but when it came to her 't was
a mellow. twinkling sound that was
good to hear.

"Oh! the sea doesn't keep all that
go out faring on it." she said. "it only
keeps its fee. What if some do lie
down in its bed deep in the dark!
There are lots that come back to love
and life. and Dick's one of them.
They'll put him away at the last beneath the grass where the sun will
shine all day and the birds and flowers

will come in their season. and he'll
rest easy. He's safe enough, so I
don't fret. Where's the use?" She
stopped and laughed again, then she
went on after a moment, peering out
beyond her with great hungry eyes as
if seeing something.

"Yes he'll lie in the sun. but I—I
shall be out there. That's what the
waves say. Why, I know it. as true as
my name's Jess Dawson, and I ain't
afraid—Heaven isn't any farther from
the sea than it is from the land. It
may be many a year before the call of
the waters comes to pass—many and
many a year—but I'm marked for the
sea one day and every little laughing wave chatters of it to its fellow.
The sea don't take more than its toll—
be sure of that—but what belongs to
it. it will take and keep."

"You wouldn't?—" I gasped.

"No, I wouldn't." she answered.
quick to understand my meaning.
Sometimes her womanishness surprised me. cropping out when 'twas
least expected. "No. I wouldn't.
When the sea claims its dues I've got
to go, but please God that won't be
yet. The sun is warm and life is
good even if you have to toil and moil.
Oh! it mustn't be yet—I'm only nineteen, cousin Lyddy."

And that was the girl I'd taken to
companion me in my solitude the girl
all Straitsmouth was talking about as
a possible bride! It was the first time
I'd had so much as a peep into her
heart. and the next moment she'd
drawn the curtain again. but I'd
caught no sight of Dick there: I'd only
seen that she loved life. as we all
start out by doing. so I said "amen" to
her "please God" and make a prayer of
my own—I couldn't bear the thought

of the hungry sea, that had been no friend to me and mine, seizing its toll of her.

Dick came back unharmed, and the old comradeship was resumed with never a trace of love on either side. The following March he went away again, but this time back in the country; he'd bought a lottery ticket and the drawing falling due, his was the lucky number. He took the notion to go for the prize himself; he simply had to go, he was as powerless to resist fate as a straw, caught in the swirl of the waters, is to resist the current and guide itself. He meant to return in a week, but I was full of misgivings. I said no word, however, to Jess, and she kept her own counsel; she was never much of a talker. It was clear though that she was under a strain, as if she, who could trust him to the wind and waves and feel secure, seemed fearful of the land and its unknown ways.

The week passed, bringing no sign of the boy; then the days went on and still he didn't come. Folks began to think it queer—we were like one big family in Straitsmouth—and I, watching, could see Jess's face sharpen with anxiety, though she said nothing. Presently she received a letter written in an unfamiliar hand that gave the clue to Dick's absence. He'd fallen ill and the folks who were caring for him sent us word; there'd never been any danger and he was mending rapidly and in a little while would be home again. We felt our heart go out to the woman who signed herself Ida Bennet, and curiosity for a time ran pretty high in the village concerning her, but other things coming up, Dick and his benefactors were crowded out of mind.

Jess was the only one to remember, and then I discovered she'd cared for him all along, unknown to herself. She was hungering for the sight of his face, the sound of his voice, the touch of his hand—and only a woman knows the misery of such longing.

April slipped into May and the country about our doors showed the beauty of new life in bursting blade and blossom; even the sea seemed to feel the change, for it took on a young look, and for days its murmurs were like the voices of happy children at play. News came about this time that Dick was coming back—and not alone. He was bringing home his bride. We didn't need to be told that she was Ida Bennet, we'd suspected something all along, yet our first feeling was one of resentment that he should marry out of the village. We were a clannish people, and besides there were too many girls of marriageable age among us for our young men to go far a-field in selecting their mates. But the feeling passed quickly, so curious were we to meet the stranger, and making the best of matters, Straitsmouth prepared to welcome the bride.

Jess and I put the simple home in order, Dick had no women-folks to do for him, and the house was just a step beyond mine—a little, low buff cottage clinging like a limpet to the rocks with a tangle of bayberry bushes about its doors. It was a pleasant place where the sun loved to linger. When all was in readiness and we'd closed the door for the night, knowing that on the morrow it would be opened by its owner's hand, we passed down to our home in silence. At the threshold Jess paused and glanced back.

"What will it be like to see the two

together?" she demanded with a fierce sort of suddenness. She'd never said much of Ida Bennet, but with the news of Dick's marriage she'd grown strangely quiet, and I'd respected her mood. She repeated the question.

"Why," I answered, " 'twill be a fair sight for my old eyes and most folks will agree with me. You've been closest to Dick, and 'twill seem strange at first to have him prefer another to you; like as not you'll resent it—that's human nature—but you'll get over it—"

She uttered a sound that was half cry, half sob, and caught my arm with her hands.

"But if a girl has had other thoughts—" her voice shook and her face flamed with her shame. "Tell me what then?" she finished huskily.

"I don't know as I can," I said all in a flutter, "nobody can. 'Twill be like looking on at a feast that's spread beyond your reach and you starving, 'twill be like seeing water in a dry land where you can never touch a drop and you dying of thirst, 'twill be as if Heaven's door was open and you'd a glimpse of its beauty and yet must stand forever without. By and by you'll get used to it, but even then life'll seem a long twilight and you'll go shivering to the end."

She stood still for a long minute, holding my arm with a grasp that eat into the bone; beyond and around us came the sound of the sea with its persistent calling. She lifted her head suddenly and glanced out at it stretching away to the horizon line where the purple shadows were creeping up; there were flecks of red on the near-by surface beneath some rosy clouds. She seemed to be listening to its voice, and

I, choked with fear, found myself listening too, trying to fit words to its unceasing murmur. Presently she dropped her hands, and setting back her shoulders as if to readjust some unseen weight that galled her, she entered the house. I waited a moment. I had no fear of the sea at that time, but there was no word of comfort that I could give. Do you know what it is to see past all barriers into another's soul—to see it in its utter nakedness? It leaves you dumb.

The summer wore away and Straitsmouth, that had been so sure of the marriage of Dick and Jess, now proclaimed the new match Heaven-ordained. From the first the stranger won all hearts. She was a little, young thing with hair like crinkled gold and eyes as blue as the speedwell at our doors. Dick had the air of a man living in a dream—mystified, so to speak, with his happiness; and there was no doubting her love for him—it was clear even to the blindest—and which feeling was the prettiest to watch was a question. Straitsmouth found the sight a fair one, as I'd prophesied, and, satisfied, it turned away from the little buff cottage, leaving it with a sense of security.

But something else turned too. I'd come to know that happiness paints itself with soberer colors as the days pass—life teaches us that!—yet somehow, perhaps because I was getting old, I'd hoped the first brightness would last a long while with Dick and Ida—they were so young. But something happened to mar it. Why was it? Had the woman's love, worth all of earth and heaven to the man in the beginning, palled so soon? For Dick was the first to change, he took up his old pursuits, and Ida was left alone. Long days she'd sit in my low room—she couldn't bear to be by herself—and I, knowing that those two lives might drift so far apart they'd never really join again if this first estrangement continued, encouraged her to talk of Dick and made her promise to take interest in what pleased him. I suspected that was the real trouble. She took what I said kindly enough and things mended for a time, then they slipped back again and I grew accustomed to have her with me constantly; we were near neighbors, the village lying at some distance, and the rough weather had set in.

One day I woke to the fact that Jess had never been with us in all the time we'd sat and sewed and gossiped together; to tell the truth I hadn't missed her, so engrossed was I in Ida and her affairs. From the first Jess had held aloof from the newcomer, refusing all her pretty offers of friendship, and I ought to have remembered my poor girl's sufferings. On a sudden her absence filled me with a thousand vague fears; the night set in and Ida left me, going back to her own home; I tried to busy myself, but the fears began to take on form, to move before me, upbraiding me with my negligence, and just then Jess entered the house bringing in the savor of the sea in her clothes. Her hair, roughened by the wind, lay in a dark mass far down her shoulders and drops of moisture caught in its meshes glittered like jewels, her cheeks were crimson and her eyes brilliant as stars. It was as if a light had been kindled within her, its shining lending her a strange, unearthly beauty. Her presence filled the room, dwarfing everything, yet there was somthing tremulous and uncertain about her, as if she were looking on at some beautiful, hidden thing that, with the least jar, would vanish into air. Suddenly I seemed to see with her eyes. She was looking at happiness, but radiant as it was to her sight, in mine it was the abomination of abominations.

"Where've you been?" I demanded.

"Out there—miles and miles at sea."

"Were you alone?"

She glanced down at me and laughed that pretty, unusual laugh of hers.

"Dick was with you," I cried, "I don't need your words. Have you forgotten Ida? Why have you gone off day after day, ignoring her? Why haven't you taken her with you?"

She laughed again, and this time it was an ugly sound to hear. "That—woman—" her voice broke. "What do we want of her? We took her once; she came whimpering like a child, begging to go, and Dick was willing—I'd no say in the matter. But she never wanted to go again. 'Twasn't over and above rough that day either, though we shipped water some—I managed we should to scare her—the baby—and she crying all the while. My!—how Dick swore. She kept on whining about drowning till finally I told her pretty sharp to keep still, if the boat upset she could cling to the keel. And what do you think? That precious landlubber came lurching over to me, screaming out, 'Where's the keel, Jess—for love of heaven, where's the keel?' I'd no words for the poor fool, and no more had Dick. He just turned the boat and headed her home—we came back in silence save for Ida's crying. No, we haven't taken her with us since."

"You sinful girl," I sobbed, "you must give Dick up—"

"Why must I? Haven't I loved him my whole life long? He didn't know how much he needed me, Cousin Lyddy, for I was always here and—and—he'd never thought of me in that way, till it was too late. Am I to blame for his waking?"

"But her happiness—"

"But my happiness—Isn't it as much to me, as hers is to her?"

"Listen—she's his wife—you've no call to come between now because there's been some little falling-out. Shame on you, Jess! You can't help your love for him—that's part of your very being—but you can make it a thing to be respected. Many a woman has lived her life by the light of a hopeless passion, and no one has suffered because of her, and many another has thought only of self and the love that was so holy in the beginning has been trailed in the mire. 'Tis for you to choose. But I tell you he belongs to her, and besides"—I pushed my work across the table—"Take it up," I said softly.

She obeyed in silence, utterly bewildered; her large brown hands looked larger and browner in contrast with the white material, and trembled for all their strength over the little garment I'd been making. Suddenly her face blanched and her eyes, half frightened, sought mine in a mute question.

"Yes, it's for their child—the baby that's coming with the new year, please God."

She stood still, white, haggard, and old, all in a moment, and the silence went on till it became intolerable. Then I, looking at her dumb grief, saw the color leap up in her face like a flame, devouring the ghastly pallor with a rush; her hands tightened their hold, there was the singing sound of rent muslin in the room, and, before I could interfere, she had torn the little garment from neck to hem with her powerful fingers. The next moment she gathered the sundered pieces to her lips kissing them again and again as if demanding pardon.

"My poor Jess," I cried, "my poor Jess."

She didn't heed me, but fell on her knees by the table, her face hidden in the baby's dress, sobbing piteously. I moved nearer and as I did so I caught the words, "Thank God—" and then I knew she'd made her choice.

There was no sign during the years that followed that Jess ever regretted the choice she made that night. In some ways, as if realizing I understood her sorrow though 'twas never mentioned between us, she clung to me, if one can use such a word about so strong a nature. Silent she always was, but she grew more companionable—her silence being that large, tolerant kind that is often as satisfying as speech—and she was with me more than formerly, helping about the house. Nor was that helpfulness confined to me alone; she served Ida with untiring devotion. It was as if she laid herself and her time at the other's feet in atonement for a sin that, mercifully, had been averted. Ida took all service without question. If she read the girl's secret, if she had any idea how near shipwrecked her own happiness had trembled in the grasp of a guilty love, she was mute on her part.

Dick's sudden infatuation for his old friend had had a speedy termination, but I never knew how matters righted themselves between them; it was enough for me that the clouds had lifted and, with the coming of the child, husband and wife were one again. Nor was that all. Strange how much power lies in a baby's hands! It was little Dick who crowded that other image from Jess's heart; every thought of hers was consecrated to him. He was a big, heavy infant, and Ida gladly relinquished most of the care to Jess. Many a time have my eyes filled with tears to see the way she'd clasp the little fellow in her strong arms—those arms that I knew would never fold a child of her own to her breast. She had her reward for her tireless, loving service; as the boy grew she was the one he singled out from all the others, happiest with her, and when he could toddle about it would seem as if his feet were only made to follow her.

The spring little Dick was three years old an uncle of Ida's died, leaving her the bulk of his property on condition that she should make her home on the old farm. She welcomed the idea of the change gladly, she had never cared for Straitsmouth—the air was too strong for her—and her dread of the sea had obliged Dick to find what employment he could on land. Their circumstances were in a bad way when this good fortune befell them, and they were both like children in their eagerness to begin a new life elsewhere. When Jess heard the news she went white as snow and gathered the child in her arms, looking over his head with wide, defiant eyes. Poor arms! how powerless they were to hold him! I think she must have realized that all of a sudden, for she put him down on the floor and ran from the room and he, not understanding, cluttered after. We could hear his little feet going up the stairs and his cries at her door till she opened it to him— she could refuse him nothing.

The preparations went forward briskly—a woman's heartache won't stay the inevitable—and time, with its tale of weeks and days, fulfilled itself. Jess offered no protest. What right had she? She grew white and gaunt and crept listlessly about her work; mornings she was up with the dawn and over at the buff cottage—the first to greet the waking child—staying there far into the night, fashioning little clothes for him and going a hundred times to the room where he lay asleep. Even in the midst of the approaching desolation there were blessed intervals of joy—those evenings when Ida and Dick were in the village at some frolic made in their honor—and she remained alone with the child, crooning over him, watching him, fancying him her own for those few hours' space. Dick laughed at her devotion, but there was no sting in his ridicule; with Ida it was different. Sometimes the remarks she let fall had a hidden twist that cut Jess to the quick. Perhaps in that way Ida paid her back for winning the full wealth of the baby's love— she was only human after all, and besides she'd the littleness of a little nature in many things. To her had come great blessings and she flaunted the purple of her possessions continually in the face of the other's rags; still Jess, I think, would have felt no envy had it not been for the child.

The last night of the Hawleys' stay in Straitsmouth we three—Ida, Dick, and I—came home together from a merry-making in the village; the young people were staying with me, as the little cottage had been utterly dismantled. I opened the door and we entered the house, which seemed strangely dark and silent after the glare and noise we'd recently quitted; there was a low light in the living-room, but Jess was nowhere to be seen. I think we had all expected to find her waiting up for us.

"I s'pose she's got Baby," Ida said fretfully—she was very tired—"please see if he's all right, Cousin Lyddy."

"Cousin Lyddy's worn out," Dick interposed, "Don't bother her, the kid's safe enough."

But Ida persisted. She was not a fanciful woman, nor one given to worrying about her child, yet several times on the homeward walk she had burst forth with some unusual question concerning his welfare. I had set her anxiety down to fatigue, but it had filled me with unaccountable forebodings. Without a word I lighted a candle and went up to the girl's room; her door was closed, and as I set it wide a rush of damp air from the open window—it was a raw murky night—caused the flame to flicker and almost go out. I shielded it with my hand and passed quickly to the bed, throwing the gleam down to rest on the two sleepers lying there. But the light, cast it as I would, did not reveal that sight to me. The bed was empty—undisturbed! I seemed to turn to stone as I stood there—I couldn't move—I couldn't speak—I couldn't breathe. From the lower room came the mother's cry: "Is he all right, Cousin Lyddy, is he all right?" It was like a far-away echo, almost drowned by the moaning of the sullen, desperate sea without, that grew and grew until it deafened me with its thunders. Then suddenly from the vanished years some words sounded in my hearing: "When the sea claims its due I've got to go." The candle dropped from my hand to the floor, but the darkness around me was not so dark as my life was at that moment; in terror of it I fled from the room, my ears whirling with the bedlam voices of the mighty waters, and so running, stumbling down the stairs, I joined the father and mother where they stood waiting for me.

It seemed as if we were searching for eternities after that in every little nook and corner of both houses, and the sea mocked our cries, the rising wind gave them back, the rocks laughed with them. I kept my thoughts hidden from my companions, I wouldn't let them see the hideous fear I carried in my breast, but every moment it grew into a deeper certainty. Jess had received her summons—and she had not gone alone. Finally we came back to my cheerless house to wait for the little time that must pass before the dawn. I made Ida lie down on the settle. and very soon, spent with grief and fatigue, she sank into a deep sleep, I sitting close, holding her little hands. In my care of her I hadn't noticed Dick's absence. but presently he joined us again, and the moment I saw his face I knew he knew the truth. "Her boat is gone," he whispered. That was all, but I needed no words to convince me that he was familiar with the strange fancies Jess had about the sea.

We sat in silence; all search seemed so impossible—so unavailing. Where could we go on the trackless waste— north, south, or out to meet the morning? How could we tell? And what reason had we to think that a girl's hand had guided the boat with its precious freight safe through the darkness of mist and murk? I could speak no comfort to the strong man in his agony, and mercifully his wife slept, unconscious of everything, while the clock ticked off the age-long minutes—and the voice of the sea went on calling— calling—calling.

Dawn came at last chill and grey. I got up and turned out the lamp and Dick started to his feet; the hopelessness of his quest made him seem like an old man. The furniture grew from dim shapes into familiar lines; fingers of light touched the curtains at the windows as if to draw them aside. I moved and let in the day, and Ida awoke, crying with her sense of loss. Then along the path outside we heard stumbling, uncertain steps coming nearer and nearer. We waited with held breath. Some one tried the door, it yielded to the touch and swung slowly in disclosing a glimpse of the waking world, then that was blotted from our sight by a tall, dark figure.

It was Jess who stood there on the threshold, and in her arms, his face lifted high against her own, was little Dick. For a moment she stared back at us without a sound, while only the laughing, gleeful child broke the stillness; then she came unfalteringly into the room. We were dumb in our turn. What could we say? Slowly,

tenderly she unloosened the little fists from her hair, took down the clinging arms that threw themselves rapturously about her neck again and again, silenced the noisy mouth with a kiss of renunciation, then, stooping, she placed the child on his mother's breast.

"I couldn't do it," she said brokenly, "I—I—wanted to keep him with me always—you won't understand— but I—couldn't do it."

Ida covered the baby's face with passionate kisses and Dick stood close, the great tears raining down his cheeks. I, too, was speechless, glad in their gladness and glad also for what they didn't see—the triumph of a woman's soul. Once I had watched the home-coming of a ship after a heavy gale; everywhere there were marks of her struggle with wind and wave in broken spar and trailing canvas, but she made port proudly. The little picture came swiftly between me and Jess, and I recognized the likeness between them—she, too, had weathered the storm! She turned and stumbled toward the stairs. Half-way there Dick caught her by the arm.

"God bless you, Jess Dawson," he cried hoarsely.

Her face softened at his comprehension, she hesitated, fighting with herself, then she looked bravely at the mother and the little one. Ida met the gaze unwaveringly, her own face set like stone. It was an anxious moment. The day grew clearer, the child laughed, from somewhere outside there came the thrill of a bird's song. Then Ida said very softly: "God bless Jess, say it, baby."

"Dod bless Jessy," crowed little Dick.

The School Garden as an Educational Factor

By Lydia Southard

WE are living today in an age of object lessons. Close observation of the manifold delights of a beautiful world is coming more and more to precede the study of books. The child is attracted by the brilliant flowers on the teacher's desk, or by some bright-eyed squirrel waving a bushy tail outside the school-room window. So much the better if the flowers are of the child's own gathering, and the animal his own discovery. Then the teacher leads him to talk about these fascinating objects, giving no information till the pupil feels the need of it. He comes to that need unurged.

For the last few years educators have discussed at length the pros and cons of industrial training in the public schools. That it has been tried with excellent results is certainly true. That it may sometimes fail to do quite all the good intended by its advocates is undeniable. It is chiefly to those who feel that industrial training makes for a broader life, a better citizenship, that the suggestion of a school garden usually appeals. Such persons are most apt to see in it an admirable opportunity to teach the child by object lessons; while at the same time giving it at least two branches of industrial training—gardening and working.

The school garden is no new idea, but it has been tried surprisingly little in America. Our German cousins across the sea have led the way. Those who have visited the German district schools will remember the small lot of cultivated land usually attached to each. In general, this is used by the teacher solely for his own benefit. Exceptions exist, however. In the Rhine province, especially, the educational value of such a plot is realized, and is made the basis of a wide range of instruction.

In our own land the highly congested state of the cities is bringing its natural reaction. Philanthropists and economists alike hope for a day when the trend will be away from the over-populated centers, back to the region of pure air and lower rents. The wealthy appreciate suburban life, and are adopting it more and more. The poor and struggling who most need the changed conditions, will not seek the country to any great extent until they are trained to cultivate successfully that most natural source of livelihood, the soil. It is to the public school that we must look, very largely, for the stimulation of a taste for country life and its employments. We need professional men, we need artisans, and we need intelligent and successful tillers of the ground. There are many boys in city and country schools today who might, if they realized it, find better openings a few years hence in suburban truck-farming than in the overcrowded occupations of the city. Our argument for the school garden is that it will show wide-awake boys and girls how they may become producers, on a large or on a small scale, and will create or foster a taste for country life.

What should be the size and what the location of the school garden is in many cases a grave question. In the country, the matter is comparatively simple, but in the city, serious difficulties sometimes arise. Several public schools in Boston have solved the problem by means of joint ownership. Possibly this might be done with success in other places; that school which has the largest play-ground giving up a certain number of square feet to the cultivation of vegetables and flowers for the profit and enjoyment of children in more than one district. Naturally the ideal place for a school garden is in country or suburb where there is plenty of room for each child to have plants of his own.

The choice of soil for the garden is something which the wise teacher will have the pupils understand. Why loam is preferred to gravel or sand, for example, is an interesting question for the beginning of the work. Without knowing it the child will master a simple lesson in geology and plant biology.

As regards the seeds or slips to be planted, two things must be borne in mind, beauty and utility. While almost everything that grows can be made attractive to the normal child, there are certain forms and colors which fill him with special delight. The bright-faced pansies, the gay nas-

turtiums, for instance, are always favorites; and if room can be made they should have a place. They teach, in their way, lessons as useful as the more sombre vegetables. In general, it is of course most satisfactory to raise such plants as shall fulfil their particular mission, that of bearing blossoms or fruit, before the end of the summer term.

Around the care of the garden centers much that is of keenest interest to the child. It is well to let him do with his own hands just as much of the preparation of the soil, the planting and the subsequent tending of beds, as possible. It will add to his education and enjoyment if he is allowed to keep the same set of tools throughout the season. Whether owned by the pupil himself or by the school, responsibility for their proper use is beneficial. It may perhaps be found feasible to teach the evolution of the farming implement. In such cases let the pupil begin work with the rudest tools imaginable. He will soon feel his limitations and be encouraged to devise improvements. Thus, step by step, he will be led, under the general supervision of the teacher, to reinvent in a crude way, the later developments in farming implements. General principles are thus impressed upon the mind, and training is given in thinking something out connectedly. It will be found possible, by enthusiastic teachers, to correlate garden work with lessons in history, literature, and drawing.

The study of elementary botany immediately suggests itself on the mention of a school garden. The child has·close at hand, not any plant from any field or wood, but a specimen of his own raising, and doubly wonderful on that account. He can follow its entire life history. A general study of the seed will probably be made. The teacher will doubtless open some of these and show the embryo, if the latter is large enough, as in the bean, to be seen by the naked eye. Enough seeds of one kind will be planted so that a few young plants may be taken out of the ground before maturity. These should illustrate different stages in development. The cotyledons and plumule will be observed, as well as the stem, leaves, and root of older growth. In the mature plant the child will enjoy a study of the textures of the different parts. Some of the pupils will be old enough to take an intelligent interest in the veining of leaves, and in the hair-like tubes which compose the stem. The capillary attraction by which water from the soil is conveyed to different parts of the plant, gives opportunity for correlation with physics.

It is to be hoped that at least one flourishing tree will exist on the school ground. If so, the spring-dressmaking done in that establishment will furnish fascinating lessons which may be combined or associated with those in the garden. The teacher will find great help in drawing comparisons between these two sources of interest. The tree has the advantage of remaining in position all winter; so that studies in buds, closely packed and varnished to protect young leaves from cold, and the swelling buds of early spring, will make a good foundation for lessons on the school garden.

The relation of perfume to color in flowers will prove suggestive to some teachers. The striking sunflowers, the brilliant nasturtiums, have their peculiar odors, but lack the attractive sweetness of the modest white violet and heliotrope. The biological reason for this may well occupy the children's thought. The law of compensation, recognizable in every form of life, is rarely impressed too early.

It cannot be out of place to call the attention of children to the color schemes of nature. It does not require an accomplished artist to show the young the softening effect of a background of green for example, and the perfect harmony found in the individual flowers.

There are children in every school who inherit no artistic instinct, and who will be more acceptable members of society all their lives for a few early lessons in aesthetics. The school building will be at certain times decorated with flowers. Blossoms may be arranged daily for the instructor's desk. If the children be allowed to do this themselves, under the teacher's guidance, it may prove a valuable part of their education. One useful lesson to be learned in this way is the best method of preserving cut flowers. For instance, the proper temperature at which to keep them fresh, and the principle of recutting stems under water to prevent the passage of air up the tiny open tubes, are points easily grasped.

The day for the old-fashioned "bouquet," often a compact bundle of all the different kinds of flowers within a certain radius, is past. Children can learn that blossoms are selected and combined with special reference to their form and color, and that they must be held in receptacles appropriate in shape and harmonious in tone.

The garnishing of food with leaves or flowers often interests children, and is a pleasing adjunct to a cooking lesson. Even young pupils can sometimes be taught to do this tastefully.

The school garden will of course attract to itself various insects and possibly some birds. A study of the appearance and habits of these will come most naturally into the work in nature-study. Children will quickly learn the names of some of the more common living things, and a few striking facts concerning them. It will increase the pupil's powers of observation. Someone has said that "The child should learn to listen with his eyes."

To return to the industrial side of the question, the materials furnished by the garden for cooking classes are important. Lessons on the proper preparation of roots, tubers, and legumes should have great value for the child as he grows older. Probably in most schools the instruction in cooking is confined to girls. This is perfectly natural, but the experience of at least one prominent educator goes to prove that cooking lessons are of equal interest and value to some boys.

In these days, when cooking is studied by sanitarians, and the proper feeding of the human body is considered worthy the attention of all intelligent people, it would be well for school children to know something of the relative value of foods. Most of them come from homes supported on limited incomes. They, in turn, will have to nourish their children on moderate sums of money. Most of these pupils will have no "higher education." It is clearly for the good of the race, however, that they should be taught which foods yield the best return of body tissue or of energy, at the least cost. If such lessons can be brought home to classes in cooking and in gardening, it will be possible to correlate the work of the school garden with physiology, hygiene, and economics.

In the minds of those who have given industrial lessons to children, the moral education of the pupil stands out as an important factor of the work. There are few better opportunities to encourage fair play and generosity. In the case of the school garden a number of children will work in the same enclosure. They will see how necessary it is to respect the rights and material possessions of others. The practical application of the Golden Rule alone will settle their childish disputes. The boy who is generous, the girl who is kind, will find that thought for others yields a good return in pleasant feeling. The laying out of the ground and the distribution of seeds and slips will, if rightly managed, cultivate a sense of justice.

The child learns other lessons. Without tools he can do nothing, so they must not be broken through carelessness nor neglected at night. He will see the fitness of laying out his plot of ground with due regard to order. Rivalry will spur him on to make his lines straight and his groupings intelligent. He will see that if he is ever to gather his tiny harvest or have it good to look at as it stands, he must be faithful in his work. He must fight the bad and cultivate the good with a hand that is strong against the one and gentle with the other. He must show in miniature the promise of the coming man.

Old York, a Forgotten Seaport

By Pauline Carrington Bouvé

Illustrated from Photographs by W. N Gough, and others

THERE is a picturesque and romantic element surrounding the earlier settlements along the Maine coast that is quite distinct from that which invests other places in New England with historic interest. Here religious zeal was not so primarily the keynote, as in the rising scale of progress in the Massachusetts Bay Colony, nor did social prestige continue so long a dominant factor as among the Cavaliers of Virginia. Nevertheless, religious predilection and social ambition were the motive springs that brought into existence that aristocratic little Episcopal settlement of Gorgeana, now York, in the Province of Maine, on the Atlantic seaboard. latitude 43° 10′ north, longitude 70° 40′ west.

Although the first settlement in Maine was at Kittery in 1623, the ancient town of Gorgeana has a more important claim upon the interest of the student of American history, a claim, indeed, which envelopes old-fashioned York with a dignity that cannot be shared by any other town, for an English city charter—the first grant of incorporation for city ever given in America—was made over to York by his Majesty King Charles I. in 1640. This fact establishes for York a priority right to some measure of national as well as local fame.

But there are hints of fair-faced foreigners along this rugged coast before the Spanish, French, Dutch, English came. Five hundred years before Columbus set sail to find a new world, the prows of Scandinavian vessels had breasted these tides, if one may believe the records of Thorlack of Iceland, in which are chronicles of Norse voyagers gale-driven to the coast of Labrador, who cruised southward, reaching the New England coast. In these records one reads the story of Gudrida, wife of a bold Northman navigator, who bore a fair-haired child on the new world's shores. How much of the romance of the Saga has crept into these ancient Icelandic chronicles, it is not easy to say, but certainly Sir Humphrey Gilbert and Captain Gosnold and Martin Pring and doughty Captain John Smith sailed along the coast in the vicinity of York, a long time before the town was in existence.

In the year 1622 the Plymouth Council granted a tract of land lying within the Province of Maine to two gentlemen. Sir Ferdinando Gorges and Captain John Mason. Some years later, in 1629, the two divided their interests, Captain Mason taking the part that lay north of the Piscataqua River and Sir Ferdinando, that which lay south of it.   In 1635 the Plymouth Council gave up the old patent and took out a new one, under which the land comprised was divided into twelve portions.   The third and fourth divisions which lay between the Kennebec and Piscataqua rivers and extended one hundred and twenty miles from the sea, were granted to Gorges.   The charter to the Council was afterwards revoked, but Charles I. gave on the third of April, 1639, the same territory to Sir Ferdinando Gorges, whom he invested with almost royal authority and to whom he entrusted the establishment of Episcopal worship in a region where the power of Puritan dissent was already becoming more than ever obnoxious to the haughty Stuarts.   Sir Ferdinando, who had been a British naval officer and had held the important office of Governor of Plymouth, England, belonged to an ancient family whose fortunes had fallen from them, so he eagerly embraced the opportunity that

now seemed to be within his grasp, to better his worldly condition and restore the prestige of wealth to his name.

The colonies in America seemed to be an asylum for religious belief, a stage for the play of political ambition, and an Eldorado where destitute scions of noble houses might retrieve their fortunes, as the needs in each case might be. Such diverse elements made up one of the strangest social and political eras that the world has ever seen—an era in which sombre fanaticism, daring adventure, rapacious greed, and sinister intrigue mingled in a wild pageant.

Sir Ferdinando, who was past middle life, dreamed of founding on this strip of Maine coast a great seaport city from whose wharves armed vessels and ships of commerce should sail to all parts of the world, bearing the victorious arms of the King and bringing back merchandise of every description.   So it came about that the King gave his ambitious emissary, in 1640, the first English charter for a city that was ever issued in America, and so, with the dream of a Cathedral City in his brain, where the power

YORK HARBOR

YORK VILLAGE

of stole and mitre should be second only to that of crown and sceptre, Sir Ferdinando ordered a "Church Chapel" or "oratory," and "Governor's palace" to be built, and sent his young kinsman, William Gorges, as his deputy until he should come.

In 1639 he had sent to the "plantations" a band of skilled workmen with all of the necessary implements of toil, and the tools and machinery in use at that time for the building of houses and ships, together with oxen and the requisites for agriculture.

A year later, when his "cosen," nephew, or grandson (severally described by different histories), Thomas arrived from England with the deputy Lord Proprietor, William Gorges, he found the "Governor's palace" in dilapidation and everything in a state of demoralization. Yet despite this condition of affairs. Sir Ferdinando persevered in the project and secured the city charter, dated March 1, 1640,

The territory incorporated comprised twenty-one square miles, and the first city in America was named Gorgeana.

The citizens had authority to elect a mayor and eight aldermen each year, and could hold estate to any amount. Thomas Gorges was the first mayor, and the aldermen were, Bartholomew Barnett, Roger Garde, George Puddington, Edward Godfrey, Arthur Bragdon, Henry Simpson, Edward Johnson, and John Rogers. Roger Garde was also the recorder. The mayor and eight aldermen were *ex-officio* justices, and annually appointed four sergeants, whose badges of office were white rods.

In 1643. Thomas Gorges returned to England, leaving Roger Garde as mayor, and in 1647 the ambitious Sir Ferdinando. without ever having seen the embryo city of his dreams —for the great warship which was to convey him to the colonies was wrecked when she was launched—

OLD YORK GAOL

died in prison at the age of seventy-five, discouraged but not yet quite hopeless of the ultimate future of Gorgeana. Two years later, 1649, unhappy Charles I. laid his head upon the block. Meantime, after the proprietor's death, the people of Gorgeana, Kittery, Wells, and the Isles of Shoals (which latter were included in Sir Ferdinando's grant) met together and after much squabbling and turmoil formed themselves into a Confederacy for administration and protection.

After the King's execution, the rivalry that had always existed between the two colonies, Massachusetts and the Province of Maine, was no longer held in abeyance, and in 1652 the stronger colony of Massachusetts

made good her claim to the ownership of her weaker sister and assumed control of her. The city' charter was revoked, a town charter was granted, and the name of Gorgeana was changed to that of York. At the same time, Roundhead influences were immediately set in motion to suppress the Royalist feeling that was very strong in the Episcopal settlement.

One of the first acts of the new rulers was the erection of the Gaol, which was in accordance with the act passed in 1647 that "Each County shall have a house of correction," and these persons committed to such houses of correction or prisons "shall first be whipped not exceeding ten stripes." There is a bit of genuine Puritanical spirit in this enactment, and in 1653

the famous old York Gaol was built, to stand, perhaps, as a silent menace to those who might be secretly in sympathy with the cause of young Charles Stuart, the exiled and fugitive heir to the throne of Great Britain.

The Civil War in England that raged between Charles I. and the British Parliament from 1641 to 1649 was a period of great inquietude to the inhabitants of York, who were at heart loyal to the Stuarts, and who detested Cromwell and their Roundhead neighbors, the "Bostonians," as the Massachusetts Colonists were now called by the French settlers in Canada. It was during the first year of this war that Cromwell gained a victory over a body of Scotch troops fighting under the Royal Standard in the north of England. In this engagement a number of Scotch royalists were taken prisoners, and among them were the Donalds or Donnells, the Maxwells and the McIntyres, all of whom were destined to play no inconsiderable part

in the history of loyal little York across the wide Atlantic.

Cromwell's officer ordered that the Scotch prisoners should be ranged in a row and that every tenth man should be shot and that the rest should be deported to the American Colonies. Micum McIntyre, one of the prisoners, counted and discovering that he was *a tenth man*, with one superhuman effort broke his bonds and attempted an escape. The daring of the venture pleased his captors, and though he was recaptured they commuted his sentence to exile. Packing all that was left of his individual belongings in a small oaken box, McIntyre with his fellow prisoners, the Maxwells and Donalds, set forth upon the voyage to New England. It was natural that upon hearing of Sir Ferdinando Gorges' Settlement at York, these young soldiers should make their way thither, and they took up their abode in what is now known as the second parish, a little settlement

683

which still bears the name of Scotland. But Micum McIntyre, "Gentleman," the most destitute one of the penniless Scotch troopers, met good luck in the

MIGUM McINTYRE'S BOX

New World. His story was told the writer by his lineal descendant, Mr. John McIntyre, the richest man in York County today. "Micum had a neighbor, a sort of Scotch cousin, who was in failing health and who had taken a great liking to the young fellow. One day this man sent for him and said, 'Kinsman, I am dying, and I am grieved to have my wife alone without protection in this wild country. 'Tis no fit place for a woman without husband, father, or brother, so I will bequeath her and all my land and property to you, Kinsman, if you will take them both and do fairly by each. What say you?' And Micum agreed to the arrangement, so before many months passed he was the inheritor of an estate and a wife!"

It was this same Micum who built the old McIntyre Garrison House on York River, which is within a few rods of Mr. John McIntyre's dwelling. This landmark of a fearsome and tempestuous period is the only one left of the many block houses that were built by the early settlers of the region, and it is still in a state of comparatively good preservation. Like all such of that section, it faces south, for that way runs York River, down whose waters came the canoes of the hostile Indians. As frequent and sudden incursions of their savage neighbors might always be expected, it was of the greatest importance to have a clear river view. The old house with its rough-hewn timbers dove-tailed and trunnelled together, its caulked seams, and its loopholes for musketry, is one of the most interesting relics of the colonial period in New England. Up in the loft where the flooring is still intact there are "draws" from which watch could be

THE BEST ROOM

kept on an approaching enemy, while in the juttings of the second story that projects over the first all around, there are openings from which missiles could be thrown upon the heads of the invaders, or from which water might be poured if the enemy should set fire to the house. The stout wooden bar that was held in place across the heavy oaken door by another of like dimensions, the latter one being propped against it and made fast by the first step of the stairway, did good service two hundred and sixty years ago, before the day of locks in York.

Up at the new McIntyre mansion, the daughter of the house shows visitors a smooth, round stone that is known in the neighborhood as the "pound stone." When Micum's "inherited wife," Hannah Pierce, was preparing to emigrate to the Colonies, she was walking along the shore one day, and picked it up. "This, perchance, weighs about a pound," she said as she balanced it in her palm. "I'll see if it does," and finding that it really did, and exactly to a dot, the thrifty housewife put it in her pocket and brought it all the way across the broad ocean. "For," said she, "it may chance there be no such thing as

THE POUND STONE

scales and weights for the fair measure of cheese and butter in those savage lands."

Here, too, young Malcolm McIn-

TABLE CHAIR IN THE GARRISON HOUSE

tyre, after a good deal of persuasion, arrayed himself in an ancestor's suit of clothes, and, holding an old sword taken from the Junkin Garrison in his hand, posed for an illustration of "Ye olden time." There was a bit of inspiration in the boyish freak, for his family's arms show a hand holding a drawn sword, with the prophetic motto, *"Through Difficulties."*

From the time of its earliest settlement, the location of Maine made it an easy prey to the incursions of the savage tribes that roamed from its boundaries northward to the French settlements of Acadia and Canada. Acadia, as the French understood it, consisted of Nova Scotia, New Brunswick, and a very large part of Maine. In these wilds, the Abenakis, who were converts to Romanism and strong allies of France, hunted, fished, and harassed the English trading settlements of Maine. In 1689 they entirely destroyed the outpost of Pemaquid.   In 1690 they and their French friends had made so many attacks upon the New England ports and villages that nothing was left on the eastern side of the Piscataqua River except the towns of Wells, York, and Kittery. Sir William Phips's easy conquest of Port Royal had, however, somewhat changed the attitude of the Abenakis toward the English settlers, whom they began to fear and whose trade was attractive. Five chiefs of the nation signed a truce with the Massachusetts commissioners which filled the French with alarm.   If these Abenakis made terms with the "Bostonians," the settlements on the St. Lawrence would be in danger of attack, a thing not to be feared so long as the savages remained loyal to France.   It was French policy, therefore, to arouse the antagonism of the Abenakis against the English.   Some of the tribes had no part in the truce and were still thirsty for English blood. To them the French addressed themselves to such effect that the village of York was attacked and almost destroyed by a band of savages led by French, on the night of February 5, 1692.   The enemy had made their way along the frozen streams and trackless forests on snow-shoes, journeying for nearly a month toward hapless little York. Arriving at Mount Agamenticus on the afternoon of the fourth, they could see plainly from its summit the group of scattered houses of the settlement along the banks of the Agamenticus or York River. The attack was successful and before dawn one hundred and fifty of the inhabitants had been killed or taken captive, and every house on the northeast side of the river burned, with the exception

of the garrison house, the meeting-house, and the old gaol.   Among the captives was a child of four, whose sturdy efforts to get away so amused his captors that he was allowed to escape.   This was the first Indian adventure of Jeremiah Moulton, whose name afterwards became a terror to the red man, who was a distinguished officer in the French War, holding the rank of Colonel at the capture of Louisburg and marching all the way from York to Quebec with a company of soldiers.   He was also an official resident of the Gaol years afterwards, while serving as sheriff of the Province of Maine.   His son, Jeremiah junior, was an officer in the Revolutionary War and died of "army fever" in 1777, while his grandson, Jotham, was commissioned Brigadier-General February 8, 1776.   The three daughters of the second Colonel Jeremiah, Abegail, Hannah, and Lucy, were married to Dr. Job Lyman, Captain Samuel Sewall, and Mr. Storer Sewall, respectively, and the ancestral home of the Moultons and of the original Colonel Jeremiah is now the residence of Judge Putnam, who inherited it from his mother, a daughter of Captain Samuel Sewall and Hannah (Moulton) Sewall.

Although Sir Ferdinando Gorges had dreamed of establishing an Episcopal form of worship in York, there was no clergyman there during his government.   In 1660, one Burdet had, indeed, gathered a congregation about him, but he was found guilty of improper conduct by the civil authority and soon after gave up the rôle of teacher and preacher.   Due, perhaps, to this lack of spiritual instruction, one may read an extraordinary record

PUTNAM COAT OF ARMS

of "an humble petition to the Court" presented by Richard Cutts and John Cutting, stating "that contrary to the act or order of the court which says 'no woman shall live on the Isle of Shoals' John Reynolds has brought his wife thither, also a stock of goats and swine. . . . Your Petitioners therefore pray that the act of court may be put in execution of the removal of all women, also the goats and swine." The Court had the obnoxious swine removed, but Goodie Revnolds was allowed to enjoy the company of her husband "if no further complaint come against her." Two decades later, however, the order of things was changed, for at a court held Dec. 24, 1665, "Joane Ford of the Isles of Shoals was sentenced to receive" nine stripes at the post for "calling the Constable a horn-headed and cow-headed rogue."

After the death of Charles I. the Episcopal element seems to have been eliminated almost utterly from the town of York, and the stricter re-

ligious principles of the Puritans began to thrive on that soil that was intended to nurture Episcopacy.

The restoration of royal government in England brought unpleasant changes to the people in the Province of Maine, who had found under the administration of Cromwell's Protectorate more freedom of thought and action than they had before enjoyed, for dissolute Charles II. was growing jealous of the Colonies. In 1676 he confirmed the rights of the heirs of Sir Ferdinando Gorges "both as to soil and government." All of these rights and titles to the Province of Maine the people relinquished to Massachusetts in 1676 for the sum of one thousand two hundred and fifty pounds. This proceeding the king bitterly resented. Massachusetts declined to give up what she had bought and at once assumed absolute jurisdiction.

Sir William Phips, the hero of Port

SEWALL COAT OF ARMS

Royal, and the new Royal Governor, brought the William and Mary charter from England. This was dated October 7, 1691, and went into effect May 14, 1692. As Parkman remarks, two giant intellects within two invalid bodies were now struggling for supremacy in Acadia—the genius of Richelieu and the genius of William of Orange—and the Province of Maine was the scene of many conflicts.

It was the June following the terrible massacre at York that the French and Abenakis crossed Penobscot Bay and marched upon Wells, one of the villages of the early York Confederacy. This village had been, during the winter, crowded with refugees from pillaged farmhouses, but famine and misery had driven most of them beyond the Piscataqua, and the few left had taken refuge in the five fortified houses. Of these that belonging to Joseph Storer was the largest and safest, as it was surrounded by a palisade. It was occupied by fifteen armed men under a militia officer, Captain Convers. Two sloops and a sail boat ran up the neighboring creek, bringing fourteen more men and food for the half starved garrison. This was fortunate, for the next morning one of Storer's men, John Diamond, while on his way from the garrison house to the sloops was seized by the Indians "and dragged off by the hair." With yells and warwhoops some of the Indians rushed upon the garrison, demanding their surrender, while others attacked the sloops, but were repulsed by the handful of men on board. The ebbing tide had stranded the vessels and the Canadians constructed a shield of planks which they fastened to a cart

and attempted to shove toward the sloops in the mud; then the tide began to rise, and, the chief of the attacking party being killed, the rest broke and ran, many falling under the fire of the sailors. Then the whole body, nearly four hundred in all, fell upon the garrison house. The disparity in numbers was appalling. An Englishman suggested surrender. "If you say that again," answered Convers, "you are a dead man." "Had the allies made a bold assault," remarks Parkman, "he and his followers must have been overpowered; but this mode of attack was contrary to Indian maxims." When the assailants offered terms brave Convers replied, "I want nothing but men to fight with!" The women in the garrison passed ammunition to the men, and sometimes they fired themselves upon the enemy. Thirty resolute men had withstood four hundred and foiled one of the fiercest and most formidable bands that ever attacked the settlers in Acadia. Poor John Diamond, the prisoner, was tortured to death. There is an archaic simplicity, an antique heroism, an imperishable glory in this story of Captain Convers and his dauntless band of thirty!

The William and Mary Charter embraced the whole territory of the State of Maine, in two divisions: that extending from the Piscataqua to the Kennebec was called the Province of Maine; that between the Kennebec and St. Croix River was called Sagadahoc. Legislative power was vested in two branches. The Council, or Board of Assistants, consisted of twenty-eight members, and formed the upper house, while the other was called the House of Representatives.

COL. JEREMIAH MOULTON'S WAISTCOAT AND
TANKARD

The ecclesiastical history of York dates from the organization of the first Congregational Church by the Reverend Shubael Dummer, about 1662. This man of God, who was a native of Newbury, Massachusetts, a graduate of Harvard, and greatly respected, was killed by the Indians in the York massacre. He married a daughter of the celebrated Edward R. Rishworth, the first chosen "recorder of writts." Six years later a remarkable man, also from Newbury, came to York, where he preached until his ordination in 1700. This was the eccentric Samuel, familiarly known as "Father" Moody, who declined a stipulated salary and chose to live upon the voluntary contributions of the people. This does not appear to have been an altogether successful arrangement, for more than once his family came very near to starvation. In fact, Mr. Moody had to appeal to the General Court of Massachusetts for "such allowance as your wisdom and justice shall see fit." The Court "saw fit" to allow twelve pounds sterling. Father Moody appears to have exercised the privilege of making personal remarks from the vantage ground of his pulpit with appalling frankness. It was the Sunday after Judge Sewall's marriage, that that stately gentleman in small-clothes, silver shoe buckles, powder and ruffles, repaired to the house of worship accompanied by his bride in her wedding slippers and arrayed in one of her bridal gowns. Father Moody paused in his discourse, and pointing to the pair said rebukingly, *"Here comes Judge Sewall with his lady and his ungodly strut."* How the poor bride must have felt! The memory of her gracious and dignified bearing is still cherished in York where they point out the old Sewall Mansion to strangers with pride, and those historic wedding slippers are

kept under a glass case in the loan collection of local curios.

For half a century York's leading man was David Sewall. He was graduated from Harvard in 1755, and was classmate and life-long friend of John Adams. Admitted an attorney in 1760 he was for sixty-four years identified with the town's history. It was during Washington's administration that the beautiful and stately residence now known as Coventry Hall, the summer home of Rev. Frank Sewall of Washington, was built. Here Judge Sewall entertained President Monroe on

his "progress" eastward, horses for the President's private coach being furnished along the road, and the officers of the York County Regiment of Militia acting as mounted escort from the Maine line.

David Sewall's stone in the Old Burying Ground bears the following well deserved inscription:

"Concecrated to the memory of the Hon. David Sewall, L. L. D. An elevated benevolence was happily directed by an enlightened intellect. Conscientious in duty he was ever faithful in its discharge. Piety with patriarchal simplicity of manners conspired to secure him universal esteem.

"Having occupied the Bench of the Supreme Court of the State and District Court of the U. States with dignified uprightness for forty years without one failure of attendance, he retired from public life in 1818 and died Oct. 22, 1825, aged XC years.

Death but entombs the body,
Life the Soul."

It was during the ministry of Father

Moody that the "Parish Society" of York was organized under a warrant issued by William Pepperell, dated March 5, 1731. It was also during his pastorate, in 1747, that the old meeting-house was burned and the present one was erected, such of the timbers as were sound of the old building being incorporated in the new. Father Moody married Hannah Sewall, and left a son and daughter, The Reverend Joseph Moody and Mrs. Emerson of Malden, great aunt of Ralph Waldo Emerson.

The son's life story makes one of the strangest, saddest pages of York history. Born in 1700, he graduated from Harvard at eighteen and soon afterwards was made Register of Deeds of York County. In 1730 he was Judge of the County Court. Father Moody, however, was anxious to have his son enter the ministry, and with filial obedience but poor judgment, Joseph resigned his civil office

HANNAH SEWALL MOODY

and was ordained pastor of the Congregational Church of the Second Parish of York in 1732, his father assisting in the ceremony.   The eccentric disposition of the father was accentuated in the sensitive, dreamy, morbid temperament of the son. Perhaps the young minister regretted having given up a profession which promised a brilliant career.   Perhaps overwork destroyed the equilibrium of a peculiarly delicately balanced brain, or it may have been that the morbid New England conscience made him brood overmuch upon the unfortunate accident of his boyhood when he had accidentally shot his hunting companion, young Preble, when they were out together one day.   At all events, the brilliant young minister's mind became impaired.   He resigned his pastorate, declaring that the weight of an unpardonable sin was upon his guilty soul and that he was unfit to enjoy the fellowship of men.   Retiring from the society of friend and neighbor, he cov-

ered his face with a black handkerchief.   This he never removed, and he became known far and near as "Handke. chief Moody."   One can imagine the awe of the villagers, the fear of the children as they scudded down lanes and around corners, the hush of feminine chatter when that ghost-like figure with the veiled face was seen about the streets of the quaint old town—a figure of mystery and tragedy.   The old moth-eaten table upon which he took his solitary meals is one of the most interesting relics preserved in the Gaol, now used as a museum.

One day the black-veiled minister, who had not for many years lifted his beautiful voice in song, suddenly began to sing. Through the closed door of his room came in clear melodious notes, the hymn,

"Oh for an overcoming faith
To cheer my dying hours!"

The next morning they found him dead in his bed. Let us hope that the "overwhelming faith" was given to cheer the lonely end of a lonelier life.

There were other strange personages who used to wander about old York. The mysterious St. Aspinquid, the In-

, HANDKERCHIEF MOODY'S TABLE

dian missionary whose grave lies on the heights of Mount Agamenticus, was once a familiar figure in the vicinity. Tradition says he was a native of York, England, who came to Maine, and dwelt among the Indians, who grew to know and love him, and to whom he was somewhat a father as well as a teacher. None knew his name. From the date of his advent in York it might very reasonably be assumed that he was one of the English Jesuit priests, exiled by the destruction of the monasteries by Cromwell's Puritans, and that as was the fashion of that Order, he adopted the dress and manner of life of the savages he came to Christianize. How else could the title St. Aspinquid have originated? It would have been natural for the children of the forest to have learned stories of angel, martyr and saint from his life and to have called their benefactor by that name he had taught them to revere. At his death his faithful followers brought a sacrifice of six thousand five hundred and eleven votive animals.

"Old Tricky," a piratical fisherman who lived at Bra'boat Harbor, was very much feared along the coast as a malevolent creature who "laid curses" on

those he disliked. These curses, however, could not take effect until he had bound a certain amount of sand with a rope. According to tradition, before a storm he used to be heard muttering, "More rope, more rope," and even now superstitious folk say the figure of an old man with shaggy locks flying in the wind and bearing a bag of sand on his back may be seen hurrying along the gray sands, and between the sobbing of the wind and sea, the cry "more rope, more rope," may be heard now and

then. His bible, which is supposed to be haunted, is one of York's most cherished treasures.

Still later, before 1832, Mistress Betty Potter and her familiar friend, Mistress Esther Brooks, were awe-inspiring citizens of York. These spinsters lived on the dividing line between York and Kittery, by which device they escaped paying taxes in either town. When, however, President Jackson had the nation's "surplus revenue" divided among the inhabitants of the United States, Betty and Esther, not living in either place, were the only people in America who failed to receive their respective shares, the just reward of iniquity!

Mrs. Emma L. Paul, the great-granddaughter of Elder John Brad-

OLD BRADBURY HOUSE

bury, who was a staunch adherent of the King, owns and resides in the old Bradbury house in York. Elder John was a grandson of Thomas Bradbury who came to York in 1639 as the agent of Sir Ferdinando Gorges, and who afterwards settled in Salisbury, Massachusetts. It was Mary Perkins, the wife of this Thomas Bradbury, who at the age of ninety years was tried and condemned for "witchcraft." The good lady's escape is a strange story, belonging to Salisbury rather than to York history.

The loan collection of curios in the Gaol Museum owes its existence to the energy and good judgment of the ladies of York village, who three years ago saved the historic old building from the ravages of time, rats, and tramps. The suggestion came from William Dean Howells, the novelist,

who, passing the dilapidated house one day and observing the door swinging open over the rotting sills, remarked: "Why can't you save the old house? It is worth saving." This was the seed of the idea. Not only the old Gaol was preserved, but colonial relics, some of much more than local interest and value, were collected by the ladies of the town, who established a museum of York antiquities within the walls that once grimly guarded evil doers. Mrs. Newton Perkins, who owns the ancient Pell House, just above Sewall's Bridge, gave a lawn party to inaugurate "doing something to get funds for the project." Thomas Nelson Page, John Fox, and Mr. Howells read on the occasion. The idea was popular and the "Village Historical and Improvement Society" began its work of preservation and rejuvenation.

The Pell house stands not far from the famous old "Sewall's Bridge," said to be the first pile bridge in the United States, built in 1761 by Major Samuel Sewall, a great architect in his day. He was engaged soon after to build a similar bridge between Boston and

of old laces and brocade still hanging about it—aristocratic York with its legends, its traditions, its historic associations—is no longer isolated and remote; although it is in truth a forgotten seaport, for its wharves are almost deserted and sea-traffic has passed it by, it has become a Mecca for artists, literary folk, and summer visitors.

The first summer hotel was built early in the seventies and when the steam railroad came in 1887, to take the place of the dusty stage coach

THE PELL HOUSE

THE BARRELL MANSION

Charlestown. The Pell house, which is supposed from its architecture to have been contemporary with the Gaol, possesses the dignity of antiquity and the charm of modern comfort, and makes an ideal country home. Almost all of the distinguished old Colonial families that helped to make York honored of old are represented in name and in blood today,—Moulton, Bradbury, Sewall, McIntyre, Dennett, Moody, Barrell, Varrell, Donnell, Bragdon, Dummer, Stacey, Jenkins, and many others of note.

But this old town with the fragrance

from Portsmouth, hotels and boarding houses grew in number and improved in quality and handsome cottages for summer residents began to dot the shores. The growth of the town as a summer resort has been very fast during the last few years and has developed within its limits four quite distinct summer villages,—York

Harbor, York Beach, York Cliffs, and Long Beach. Even York Village, always the town's centre for business and public and church affairs, gains by the summer invasion so that frequently the resident population of about three thousand becomes between the months of June and September a community of ten thousand, and much has been done to make life pleasant for the strangers and those who come back to their birth-

SEWALL'S BRIDGE

GOLF CLUB

place. The handsome new Golf Club House is a good example.

The historic houses of this quaint town draw visitors from the surround-

THOMAS NELSON PAGE'S COTTAGE

ing neighborhoods, and the witch's grave in the old burying ground, where the dead of many generations sleep, arouses a great deal of speculation. As witches, by an unwritten law, were almost never married, and as they were usually buried either at low-water mark or at the junction of three roads, this grave of "Mary Nason, wife of Samuel Nason, died August 28, 1772, aged 29 years," does not seem to fit the requirements of a *bona fide* witch. In spite, however, of these discrepancies, this wide tablet slab lying between two upright head and foot-stones possesses a weird interest to those who are inclined to superstition.

Stage Neck, where the Marshall House stands, is the historic ground where the people from the Isles of Shoals were ordered to remove during the Revolution. The view from here is one of the finest in the neighborhood, surpassed only perhaps by that from Mount Agamenticus, the highest point along this part of the Maine coast. Northward stretches the rocky coast with a background of woodland, while to the east lies the blue ocean with Boon Island Lighthouse clearly visible nine miles away. One of the early lighthouse keepers, Captain Eliphalet Grover, spent his time in making bass viols, one of which he presented to the first Congregational Church in York,

June 4, 1834. His successor was also a musician and played upon it for many years.

The old town celebrates, this summer, its two-hundred-and-fiftieth birthday since Massachusetts bought out the right of the Province of Maine in 1652, and it will wear holiday garb during the pageant: but to enjoy the unique charm of the place, one must visit it when the hush of a drowsy summer afternoon lies over the town; when the shady streets are quiet and the grim old Gaol, the haunted witch's house, and the ancient head-stones in the cemetery are bathed in the sunshine and, like the land of the Lotos Eaters, it seems a place where it is "always afternoon."

Then indeed the magic thrall of history, poetry, and tradition falls upon the visitor, and invests with a halo of romance this quaint old York—a forgotten seaport.

THE WITCH'S GRAVE

The Hill Stream

By Alice D'Alcho

HIGH on the hillside, here I sit and dream—
And, far below me, see bright waters gleam;
Now dancing onward, wreathed with rainbow spray,
Now winding gently among the boulders gray;
Hid for a moment 'neath the o'erhanging shade,
Then to the glory of the moon displayed.
Yet ever lovely—ever giving grace—
Some light reflecting, e'en in darkest place.

Say, O my soul, shall this be said of thee—
Thy light withdrawn, and dark adversity
O'ershading all; thy chiefest friend grown cold;
Yet thou wert fair, as in the days of old?
Those days of old—when all Earth's joys were thine,
When thou didst quaff life's richest, rarest wine;
When it was sweet to live—thy way to trace;
Say, canst thou shine, e'en in the shadowed place?

Washington-Greene
Correspondence

A large collection of original letters written by General Washington and General Greene has come into the editor's possession. It is our intention to reproduce in fac-simile those of the letters which present the most interesting details and side lights on the great events of the period covered, even though some of the letters may have been previously published. A printed copy of the letters herewith appears on pages 702 and 703.—EDITOR.

Philadelphia 19th December 1781.

My dear Sir

    The president informs me that you have been furnished with the Resolves of the 10th instant, requiring the several States to complete the deficiencies of their respective quotas by the 1st of March next — He also informs me it is expected that I should myself call for and transmit the necessary returns. But as this would occasion an immense delay and loss of time, I must require you in the first instance to furnish the Executives of Delaware — Maryland — Virginia — North Carolina — South Carolina and Georgia with the state of their several lines, and give them Credit for any Men they may have serving in those Legionary Corps or Artillery under your command. You will be kind enough to transmit duplicates to me. The Returns of the pennsylvania Line may be sent to me and I will present them myself.

    That the Adjutant General may more easily digest the whole into one general Return, he has made out a form and forwarded it to the several posts. One set of them you have enclosed,

by

by which you will be pleased to direct your Deputy
Adjutant General to guide himself.

Inclosed you have the Copy of a letter which
I have written to the States from whence your Troops
are drawn, apologizing for not transmitting the
Returns myself—pressing a compliance with the
requisition, and pointing out the only mode of preventing the importation of unfit Men upon the
Army.

The European Fleet consisting of upwards
of one hundred Vessels sailed from New York the 15th
I can yet hear of no preparations for the embarkation
of any troops from thence; which makes me conclude
that they do not think at present of giving any
reinforcement to the Southward.

I am with the greatest esteem
My dear Sir
Your most obedient and humble Servant
G Washington

Majr. Genl. Greene.

Head Quarters
St Pauls Parish
January 24th 1782

Sir

Since I wrote your Excell-
cy on the 9th of December I have been favored
with your dispatches of the 15th & 17th & 19th & and
19th of December. My letter to Congress of
this date a copy of which I inclose will inform your Excellency of the arrival of
General St Clair with the Pensylvania
and Maryland troops. The Virginians protested against marching until they got their
pay, and are still in Virginia. Your
Excellencys apprehensions were very
right respecting the diminution of Gen
St Clairs command. The Virginia line left
us at the same time the other came which
which leaves us little stronger than we
were before. Some reinforcements have
arrived lately from York. It is said near
400 Men. Through a good channel

of intelligence I got information of troops on
both from Cork and New York. I was so
alarmed at it that I sent off Capt Ragsdale
to Virginia and Lt Col Stewart to North
Carolina to try to hasten on support, and
wrote to Count Rochambeau for a
1000 men of his command but if more
convenient and consistent with the plan
you & he has concerted it would still be
more agreeable for him to move with
his whole force this way. Since I sent
off those dispatches the Cork fleet arrived with
out troops except about 500 artillery men.
I am still under great apprehension of those
coming from York notwithstanding the
flattering accounts your Excellency gives
me. We are in a poor situation to con
tend with every superior force. our men
are almost naked for want of over alls
and shirts, and the greater part of the
army bare foot. We have no rum or

prospect of any. Here neither four hundred miles
spur and little or none provision in Virginia; and
if there was ever so much there, the difficulty
of transportation would prevent our getting it
or we were four weeks without ammunition
from we have been in the lower country
and a plenty of this article at Charlotte waiting
for the means of transportation. Had the enemy
got knowledge and availed themselves of our
situation they might have ruined us.

  I shall agreeable to your Excellencys
directions transmit to the respective States
an exact return of their troops, and I wish
your representation may have the desired
effect. But the States here become so lengthy as to
regard representations little more than an
idle dream in Eastern tale. Nor have I the
least hopes of our difficulties ceasing on
this head until the powers of Congress are more
interposed and the faith and interest of the States
better acknowledged. When any State can be
made to feel an inconvenience from its
obliging or acquiescence of Congress then and not

til then can we hope our measures will
have vigor and a combination of our force
take place. We may wait until we are
blessed and the local policy of the States in perfect security will coalesce our wishes.
From this, very few source I apprehend it
almost impossible to establish matters upon
upon such footing as to answer the public demand. If each of the States or refused or neglected to comply with the Congressional requisition,
were deprived of the liberty of trade either foreign or domestic out of their own State it
might serve to pass little skegoleon to
effect a compliance.

I cheerfully agree with your
Excellency that we should improve every
moment of the winter, to be in readiness to
open the campaign to advantage. To be
well prepared for war is the most likely
way of procuring a peace. I have recommended to this State to raise four black Regiments. To fill up these Regiments without
is impracticable and to get reinforcements
from the Northward precarious and at best
difficult from the prejudices respecting

704

the climate. Some are for it but the greater part of the people are opposed to it. The Assembly are now sitting at Jacksonburgh four Miles from our Camp on the other side of the Edisto.

I am with great respect
Your Excellencys Most
Obedt humble Sr

N Greene

To General Washington
January 1782

His Excellency
General Washington

Gen. Washington to Gen Greene

PHILADELPHIA, 19th December, 1781.

MY DEAR SIR,

The president informs me that you have been furnished with the Resolves of the 10th instant, requiring the several States to compleat the deficiencies of their respective quotas by the 1st of March next—He also informs me it is expected that I should myself call for and transmit the necessary returns. But as this would occasion an immense delay and loss of time, I must request you in the first instance to furnish the Executives of Delaware—Maryland—Virginia—North Carolina—South Carolina and Georgia with the state of their several lines, and give them Credit for any men they may have serving in those Legionary Corps or Artillery under your command. You will be kind enough to transmit duplicates to me. The returns of the Pennsylvania Line may be sent to me and I will present them myself.

That the Adjutant General may more easily digest the whole into one general Return, he has made out a form and forwarded it to the several posts. One set of them you have inclosed, by which you will be pleased to direct your Deputy Adjutant General to guide himself.

Inclosed you have the Copy of a letter which I have written to the States from whence your Troops are drawn, apologizing for not transmitting the Returns myself—pressing a compliance with the requisition, and pointing out the only mode of preventing the imposition of improper men upon the Army.

The European Fleet consisting of upwards of one hundred vessels sailed from New York the 15th. I can yet hear of no preparations for the embarkation of any troops from thence, which makes me conclude that they do not think at present of giving any reinforcement to the Southward.

I am with the greatest esteem,
my dear Sir,
Your most ob't and h'ble Ser't,
G. WASHINGTON.

Maj'r. Gen'l. Greene.

Gen. Greene to Gen. Washington

SIR,

Since I wrote your Excellency on the 9th of December I have been favor'd with your despatches of the 15th and 19th of December. My letter to Congress of this date, a copy of which I enclose, will inform your Excellency of the arrival of General St. Clair with the Pennsylvania and Maryland troops. The Virginian officers protested against marching until they got their pay, and are still in Virginia. Your Excellency's aprehensions were very right respecting the diminution of Gen. St. Clair's command. The Virginia line left us at the same time the other came up which leaves us little stronger than we were before. Some reinforcements have arrived lately from York. It is said near 400 men. Through a good channel of intelligence I got information of troops expected both from Cork and New York. I was so alarmed at it that I sent off Capt. Rosedale to Virginia and Lt. Col. Stewart to North Carolina to try to hasten on support and wrote to Count Rochambeau for a 1000 men of his command, but if more convenient and consistent with the plan you & he had concerted it would still be more agreeable for him to move with his whole force this way. Since I sent off those despatches the Cork fleet arriv'd without troops except about 60 artillery men. I am still under great apprehensions of troops coming from York notwithstanding the flattering accounts your Excellency gives me. We are in a poor situation to contend with a very superior force. Our men are almost naked for want of overalls and shirts, and the greater part of the army bare-foot. We have no rum or prospect of any. None within four hundred miles of us and little or none providing in Virginia; and if there was ever so much there, the difficulty of transportation would prevent our getting it as we were four weeks without ammunition since we have been in the lower country and a plenty of this article at Charlotte waiting for the means of transportation. Had the enemy got knowledge and availed themselves of our situation they might have ruined us.

I shall agreeable to your Excellency's direction transmit to the respective States an exact return of their troops; and I wish your representation may have the desired effect. But the States have become so tardy as to regard representations little more than an idle dream or Eastern tale. Nor have I the least hopes of our difficulties lessening on this head until the powers of Congress are more extensive and the subordination of the States better acknowledged. When any State can be made to feel an inconvenience from disobeying a requisition of Congress then and not till then can we hope our measures will have vigor and a combination of our force take place. We may write until we are blind & the local policy of the States in perfect security will counteract our wishes. From the very same source I apprehend it almost impossible to establish matters of finance upon such a footing as to answer the public demands. If such of the States as refused or neglected to comply with the Congressional requisitions were deprived of the liberty of trade either foreign or domestic out of their own State it might serve to fix a little obligation to effect a compliance.

I perfectly agree with your Excellency that we should improve every moment this winter, to be in readiness to open the campaign to advantage. To be well prepar'd for war is certainly the most likely way of procuring peace. I have recommended to this State to raise some black Regiments. To fill up their Regiments with whites is impracticable and to get reinforcements from the Northward precarious and at best difficult from the prejudices respecting the climate. Some are for it but the greater part of the people are opposed to it. The Assembly are now sitting at Jacksonborough four miles from our camp on the other side of the Edisto.

I am with great respect,
Your Excellency's most
obedt humble Ser,
N. GREENE.

His Excellency
General Washington.

A Fair Exchange—An Old-Home-Week Romance

By Emma Gary Wallace

MRS. CROMPTON was in a flutter of excitement. Besides being one of the Reception Delegation, a Patroness of the Grand Ball, and Convener of the Old-Home-Week Committee of Hospitality, she was to entertain the Honorable Josiah Hilton, who was to come all the way from Texas to be the orator of the week's festivities.

She sighed as she wondered if he had changed, and she could not refrain from a glance at her mirror to satisfy herself of the permanency of her own charms. It was a handsome face that looked back at her: the face of a woman in the prime of a perfectly matured womanhood.

She had placed two rooms of her finely appointed home at the service of loyal Vermonters, and it was with no small degree of satisfaction to her that the honorable gentleman and his nephew had fallen to her lot. She was pleased to renew the acquaintance with the uncle, and secretly hopeful that the nephew might interest Sadie. It would take her mind off that unfortunate school-girl love affair which had so disturbed their summer's peace. Mrs. Crompton smiled complacently as she thought how cleverly she had nipped that *affaire d'amour* in the bud; for she well knew her niece to be as willful as she was pretty. As that young lady's guardian she had pointed out to

her the undesirability of such an entanglement. Sadie argued with the fluency of a second Portia. Then, losing her temper, Mrs. Crompton scolded. Sadie wept, but was still obdurate. Finally a prompt discontinuance of all communication was ordered. The letters ceased to come, and it was presumable that they ceased to go also. In place of spending her mornings scribbling, Sadie took long horse-back rides on "Kentucky Belle."

The rides were doing her good, Mrs. Crompton reflected. Only that morning her niece had gone out pale and heavy eyed, and returned from her gallop across the hills with sparkling eyes and rosy cheeks. Clearly she was learning to forget the University student, who had no fortune but his own indomitable courage (Mrs. Crompton mentally designated it "cheek"). Some day Sadie would rise up and call her blessed for preventing such a *mésalliance*. It was a relief to have the affair over, and she paused to listen to her niece's clear sweet voice singing blithely as she busied herself among the decorations. Her deft fingers banked flowers and trailed vines until the house was a bower of fragrant beauty.

"Do you suppose the Honorable Mr. Hilton will appreciate all this, Aunt Sarah?" Sadie inquired, with a wave of her hand as she sank wearily into a chair to watch her aunt draw on her gloves preparatory to departing to meet her guests.

"Of course he will, child, and if he should not, I do," and she leaned over and fondly kissed the fair young girl, "go and rest, dear, until we return."

* * * * * *

It was with mingled emotions that Mrs. Crompton welcomed the Honorable Josiah Hilton.

"Why—why, Sarah, how handsome you are still, and as young as ever," and he shook her hand as only a man can shake it who has not seen home and home people for nearly twenty years. "Allow me to present my nephew, Mr. Charles Hamilton. He is an out and out Texan, but when he heard that I was coming, nothing would do but he must come too, to see his father's old home. Well—well, how good it is to be back again among the old familiar scenes."

"And such a pleasure for us to have our friends come back to see us. Is it not a delightful idea—this yearly 'At Home,' to renew old acquaintances and form new ones?" and Mrs. Crompton turned to Mr. Hamilton with a charming smile. She saw a tall athletic fellow, with a wholesome complexion, frank blue eyes, and wavy chestnut hair. "Just as Joe looked before we quarrelled," she thought, "why could not Sadie fall in love with some well-connected fellow like that?"

"Any children, Sarah?" asked the Honorable Josiah as he seated himself in the carriage.

"None of my own, but my niece lives with me. Otherwise, since Mr. Crompton died I should have been quite alone."

Both sighed, and involuntarily looked over at the old elm-tree on the hill-side where their own lover's quarrel had taken place—the quarrel which sent him headlong into a new country and her to a marriage of pique.

"And you, Josiah?" she said timidly.

"I never married," he answered slowly, "I was true to my love's young dream," and he looked at her searchingly.

Mrs. Crompton crimsoned and then grew deadly pale. Young Hamilton saw nothing. He was drinking in the pure mountain air, and feasting his eyes on misty highlands and verdant intervales. He did not notice the long pause and the renewal of commonplaces, until he was brought back to his immediate surroundings by the voice of his hostess.

"Here we are at 'The Crest.' Welcome, in this your first home-coming to the dear old Mother State, and may this be the precursor of many happy reunions."

Mr. Hilton hastily drew his hand across his eyes. They were suspiciously moist, and he coughed with unnecessary violence to clear his throat. On the broad piazza before him he saw a vision of girlish loveliness. "Just as Sarah looked before I went to Texas," he thought, "why couldn't Charley fall in love with some sweet country-girl like that?"

In another moment the introductions were over, and Sadie had cordially greeted the Honorable Josiah, and rather coldly shaken hands with the nephew. She quite ignored him at luncheon, and studiously avoided him all the afternoon. Mrs. Crompton was disappointed and annoyed. She felt it her duty to expostulate with her niece, but the opportunity did not occur until the ladies retired to make their evening toilets.

"He is such a perfect gentleman, Sadie," she remonstrated, "that I can see no occasion for this Arctic frigidity."

"Why, Auntie dear, I thought I had been perfectly lovely to him. He is such a dear old soul that I fell in love with him at first sight."

"I do not mean Mr. Hilton, child, but the nephew."

"Mr. Hamilton? Oh, he is too young, altogether too young; besides young men nowadays do not amount to much anyway."

The words sounded suspiciously familiar to Mrs. Crompton, and she turned sharply to Sadie, but that young lady was gazing out of the window with child-like innocence.

"Now, girlie, don't be naughty, be nice to them both; they are my guests, and, as an especial favor to me, I ask you to try to like Mr. Hamilton. Remember it is to be only for a few days, dear."

Sadie's face was a study. There was a flicker of a smile in the big brown eyes and an expression of positive pain about the rosebud mouth. Mrs Crompton thought her on the verge of relenting, but a moving shadow in the rose-garden below, hardened her heart.

"Very well, Auntie, for your sake I'll try to be nice to Mr. Hamilton, but I cannot help thinking his uncle perfectly sweet, can I?"

Mrs. Crompton bit her lip with vexation. What if Josiah should take a fancy to this slip of a girl?

The shadowy figure below moved impatiently.

"I will be good, Auntie, indeed I will, and the very next time I see this much abused swain I promise to make peace with him. It is growing late; bye-bye! I must run down and get a rose for my hair." And with a snatch of song upon her lips, she ran lightly down the broad stairway, across the garden, under the vine-covered arbor, and straight into the arms of the detested Mr. Hamilton.

"I thought you would never come, Sweetheart."

"And I thought I should never get the chance. Oh, Charley, I feel that I am such an arch-deceiver. Aunt Sarah has just been lecturing me on my treatment of you."

"And Uncle Josiah threatens to send me home at once if I do not proceed to bow down and worship at your shrine."

They both laughed in the joyousness of youth and love.

"I have discovered another secret besides our own, Charley. This morning I went over to take some flowers to old Mrs. Bettis who has been bedridden for years. The Old-Home-Week celebrations made her reminiscent, and she told me that long ago, Aunt Sarah and Mr. Hilton were lovers, and only through a foolish quarrel were separated."

Charley gave a long low whistle.

"So that is why Uncle Joe was so eager to join the Old-Home pilgrimage. You ought to have seen how excited he was. Then I found out where he was coming and suggested that I join him."

"And Aunt Sarah never once suspected our medium of communication in the little post-office among the hills at Greenville."

"None but the brave deserve the fair,
It takes them both to do and dare."

laughed Sadie, as she plucked a rose
and gave it to her lover.

"I must go now, or Aunt Sarah will
think I am lost, so good-bye, and I
intend to be a little more civil, for her
sake, you know."

*   *   *   *   *

The ball was a grand success from
the opening strains of "Home Sweet
Home," to the moment when they all
joined hands in one big old-time circle
and, to the rhythmic motion of clasped
hands, sang Auld Lang Syne.

Someway it brought back to Sarah
Crompton another ball of many years
ago, when Joe Hilton had asked her to
be his bride. She remembered that
she had worn a simple muslin gown
with blue ribbons, and to-night she
was radiant in heliotrope satin and
diamonds.

And once more the Honorable Josiah Hilton's eyes grew moist as he too
thought of that other ball, and all that
life had promised and all that he had
lost.

Together they walked out of the ball
room.

"Sarah," he began with manly directness, "years have come and gone
since that other ball when we two
plighted our troth. Then you were
a simple country maid, but a sweeter
never lived, and I was plain Joe Hilton. Now you are a stately matron
with wealth and position, and the
world accredits me with having rightfully won a place on its ladder of
fame. Sarah, I love you still. Can
you find it in your heart to plight our
troth anew? To me, Sarah, you were
Vermont, the old home, everything.
I have travelled far to hear your answer from your own lips. What is it
to be, Sarah?"

"The same as on that night so
many years ago, Josiah, for you have
not travelled in vain," his companion
responded softly. "I will try to make
the sun-set years of your life richer
for what the noonday has lost."

He bowed reverently and kissed
her hand.

"You have made me a happy man
to-night, Sarah—and a proud one—
the proudest man in all the old Green
Mountain State. How surprised the
youngsters will be!"

"I am so sorry they do not seem to
like each other," Mrs. Crompton remarked in a troubled tone.

"Well—Charley is still bothering
his head about a chit of a college girl,
but I put my foot on that."

"And I have had a similar experience with Sadie, but the dear child
submitted to my judgment most gracefully. It will be less embarrassing to
tell them our relationship at once,
Josiah. Why, here they come now."

The pair started guiltily as they met
their seniors face to face.

"Charlie—Sadie—" began Mr. Hilton, "we may as well tell you that a
wedding is to be one of the results of
this Home-Week reunion, I——"

"Why, how did you find out, Mr.
Hilton," interrupted Sadie, "we have
not told a soul, have we, Charley?"

Mrs. Crompton and Mr. Hilton
looked at each other in amazement.

"We thought," said Charley, "that
if you, sir, could become acquainted
with Sadie, and Mrs. Crompton could
know me things might possibly be different."

"I do not think you understand,
children," Mr. Hilton said with dig-

nity," Mrs. Crompton and I have renewed an old engagement, and hope
soon to be married."

"And Miss Crompton and I entertain the same hope, sir," added Charley.

"Sadie," expostulated her Aunt,
"and you have known Mr. Hamilton
less than a day."

"No, Auntie dear, Charley is that
dreadful University student. I'll forgive Mr. Hilton for taking you away
from me, if you both consent to my
marrying Charley."

"A fair exchange, Sarah, a fair
exchange," laughed the Honorable
Josiah.

"A fair exchange in more ways
than one," echoed Charley looking
fondly at the sweet girl by his side.

And so it was amicably decided that
the Honorable Mr. Hilton should remain at "The Crest," while Sadie
should go to Texas as Mrs. Charles
Hamilton, and thus both the Lone
Star and the Green Mountain States,
were richer in happy hearts for the
good Old-Home-Week.

The Pond

By Mary Clarke Huntington

SHUT in by length of verdant bank
      And tree growth, rising rank on rank,
Its surface, 'neath the slanting shine
Of summer sun in its decline,
Invites the wand'ring dragon-fly
To hover o'er the water grass;
Down lures the swallows as they fly
To dip their plumage ere they pass;
And tempts the ever loit'ring feet
Of one who loves a fair retreat
In Nature's labyrinth, to while
Yet longer at the roadside stile—
Where this o'er-bending sycamore
Shuts in a gnarled and leafy frame,
Such vista as must put to shame
All canvas ever artist set
On world famed easel. So forget

That life is of a world of chance,
With power to try us as before;
Just watch those midges as they dance
Above that clinging water sedge
But yonder at the bank's green edge;
See how the dropping sun ball burns
Its track across the pond, and turns
To limpid gold the whole expanse!
Life's sad defeats, its pains, its care
Lie now behind us. Everywhere
The balm of Nature's grand repose
Smiles like the substance of a prayer,—
Fills mellow sky and mellow air
With grand yet subtle harmonies
Which reach the soul through gazing eyes.
And soothes as mothers soothe to rest
The babe close held to loving breast.
The day's soft benediction flows
Through all our senses as we lean
A dream—and dwell upon the scene.
But hark! a tinkle faint and far
Tells how o'er yonder pasture land
The cows file to the farmyard bar
And there await the milker's hand.
Faint, fainter yet the cow bell rings,
And o'er our head a robin sings
For vespers. Yet the swallows dip
To preen their plumage dry again;
A dragon fly o'er hovers still
The water grasses, and our glance
Shows all the midges at their dance
'Mong sedge where length'ning shadows slip.
But we, oh, loit'ring heart! must go—
(Sweet, sweet the robin sings, and low!)
Go back to busy haunts of men
And join once more the world of chance.

Wee Jamie's Cab

By Margaret W. Beardsley

"YE mustna touch him, Ritchie, but see, if yill aff wi' that smutty cap I'll hold him sae ye can get a kiss onyway."

Ritchie Mackentyre had donned his miner's suit with some reluctance that morning. Any other miner at Glen Jean would have considered the putting on of clean clothes at rising and the changing again before going to the mine, a rare waste of time; but the satisfaction of feeling wee Jamie's weight in his arms for the smallest fragment of time, with the liberty to cuddle and caress at will, easily recompensed Ritchie for the trouble.

It was quite wonderful how the bairn adapted himself to circumstances. He had such an instinct for early rising that he was generally ready to be taken up by the time Ritchie had the fire well going, and there was the comfort of holding him all the while Janet prepared the meal.

It was a disappointment then, that the laddie should so long over sleep on this particular morning that his father was starting for the mine when his first peep was heard. Janet had run in, bringing him out all pink and blinking with sleep, to hold him up with the exclamation quoted above; and Ritchie had held his hands stiffly at his sides and craned his neck well out that no part of his attire might so much as brush the small white "goony."

714

Janet's admonition was not wholly responsible for this extreme care. Ritchie would as soon have thought of going to the meeting in his bank clothes on a "Sawbath," as to touch wee Jamie with soiled hands; for it must be understood that this small monarch of the Mackentyre was no ordinary bairn. Sent, as he had been, full ten years after the firstborn had opened his eyes only to close them in far-away Scotland, to Ritchie's mind he was as much God-given as the infant Samuel, and he mingled with the father-love a tender reverence beautiful to see.

"Ah, I doot feyther's wee mannie is getting a bit of a sluggard;" reproached Ritchie fondly, and Jamie put out his pink fists and caught at his father's face as it went from him.

"He is wanting tae gang tae thee, Ritchie! Na, na, laddie, feyther's ower dirty. Mither'll hold ye for anither kiss. Eh, the great lad! Dinna ye think, Ritchie, we may hae Gibson send for his cab come pay-day?"

For all the question appeared thrown in quite carelessly, the note of anxiety in Janet's tone betrayed the irrelevancy to be more of speech than thought; and Ritchie's face became grave.

"I doot, Janet, we canna manage it this month;" he said, hesitatingly. "I hae been thinking on it considerable, an' I dinna see oor way clear. By the time we hae oor rent paid, an' sent

the mither her bit money, there'll hardly be enuch beyond what wull carry
us over anither month."

"An' if we did run short, is it sic a
matter for us tae get a scrip-book ainee
as the ithers do?' '

"Na, na, Janet," said Ritchie, almost sternly; "You and I hae never
held wi' the notion o' spending money
afore it were earned. Now we
hae oor lad, we mustna be getting in-
tae habits we wadna like him tae follow. By anither month we may manage."

" 'By anither month,' " echoed Janet,
in dismay. "There's your very words
o' last! Make it anither year, when
he'll get no good o' it. An' him get-
tin' sic a weight tae carry aboot, as far
as the meeting particular."

"I did think mysel we would make
it afore this, but there was things
came unexpectit. The insurance for
accidents now, I didna think o' that.
But as for carrying him—Why Janet,
I just love to feel o' him in my arms.
It seems I could carry him always, an'
gladly."

"Ay l and you dinna care hoo his
claes gets wi' the doing o' it. I declare
I hae been pit aboot afore now, he
was that crumpled, and ithers taking
their bairns oot o' their cabs at the
kirk door wi' never a wrinkle in their
frocks!"

"But wi' all the crumpling there's
nane whase claes look hafe sae white
an' beautiful as Jamie's ain," declared Ritchie. "Your a master hand
at making an' doing up, Janet."

It was not in nature to be displeas-
ed with such appreciative words.
Janet smiled while she still insisted:

"But Ritchie, wi' ten days left o'
the month ye might yet hae money

enuch coming. There's some they say
get oot their eight car a day, and in
Scotland they ca'ed you the best miner
in the pits."

"Weel, I canna be as fast here as
some then. If I get oot six loads its
a good day, an' wi a' the props tae be
pit in I canna count on more than five
for an average."

"Props!" cried Janet sharply; "it
dis seem, Ritchie, ye spend good hafe
yir time wi' props an' sic like thing
that disna count!"

Ritchie looked at her with opening
eyes. "Why, Janet, I didna think ye
wad count blame o' me for taking or-
dinair precaution. The mine is nane
sae safe at best, an' I wadna like the
little lad tae gang orphanted."

It was the knowledge of wrong in
Janet's heart that gave an added bitterness to her next words:

"There's little danger o' that wi'
all the fine care ye gie yirsel. Weel if
ye dinna want puir Jamie tae hae the
cab, then he must juist do wi'oot, an'
there's nae use tae waste words wi'
it," and Janet whirled about into the
house.

Ritchie stopped a full minute on the
step before it was clear to his mind
that Janet had made use of such a
taunt, and then all the way to the mine
presented arguments to convince himself that he was mistaken. Harsh
words were not so common between
the pair as to cause no thought or hurt.
Ritchie and Janet, with none to divide
their affections, had grown more outspoken in their regard for each other
than was usual or indeed was thought
proper in their native village, some declaring: "The Lord kens that folks sae
daft wi' each ither, cud no' be trusted
wi' the raisin' o' bairns." That this

child of their prayers should be the cause of ill-words made the sting none the less keen.

Unthinkingly Ritchie tapped the ceiling of his room as he entered, in accordance with his usual custom; but when a place gave back a hollow ring, he hesitated, recalling Janet's words before fetching a prop and placing it with his usual care.

At the home Janet was still sore with the disappointment over the enjoined waiting for the cab. It was surprising what a matter its possession had come to be to her. She would have been content with a rude cart for her firstborn had he lived to require it, but upholstered baby-cabs were unknown in the little Scotch mining town. Here, even the babes of the poorest rode, as Janet said, "like kings in their chariots," and surely Jamie was as deserving as any.

One knowing Janet, however, would feel no surprise that her anger had long spent itself before the noon hour, and that a dish especially to her good man's liking awaited his coming. And Ritchie ate, and praised to her satisfaction, but he went back to the mine full ten minutes earlier than his wont. He had calculated that much time had been consumed in the placing of the prop.

In the days following Ritchie took to earlier rising, and it was seldom Jamie got his kiss even at the door.

Pay-day at the Glen Jean mine came on the Saturday that ended or immediately followed the close of the month. The office was not open for payments until four in the afternoon. This gave the men an opportunity to put in nearly a full day at the mine, though it was known that only a handful of men ever went to work after the noon hour.

The Mackentyre house was one of the nearest to the company's store and office buildings. On the pay-day following Janet's plea for the baby-cab she watched the men from her window as they went in to have their car-checks verified and to receive the balance due after the deduction of their scrip-book account.

Outside the entrance, leaning on the railing of the small porch, were several men whose store clothes and white shirts distinguished them from the miners. They kept an eye on the doorway, and first one and then another of them stepped forward and spoke to the miner as he passed out from the cashier's office. This was kept up scarcely without exception during the afternoon. The miner got some sort of a coin out of his pocket, and handed it over to the person who addressed him, who thereupon fell back to the railing and went on watching the door. Occasionally the coin appeared unsatisfactory, and an animated though subdued conversation went on; resulting sometimes in the production of another coin, and sometimes in an evident warning delivered by the store-clothes-man. One out of the secret would have found this a puzzling feature of the day, but the familiar knew these men to be agents for organs, sewing-machines, plush-rockers, enlarged pictures—and, possibly, baby-cabs—who had sold their wares on time, but who were shrewd enough to be on hand for the monthly installment.

There was another thing that appealed to the curious. The village lay entirely to the west of the office buildings, the Mackentyre house being on its east side. There was little lingering at the door after coming from the office, but not one man in ten crossed the filled-in ravine to his home. In groups and pairs and singly they struck into the road leading down the valley. A cluster of women hung about the door of the store; and just as the store-clothes-men had come forward singly, so one and another of the women timidly approached the side of the road as the miners passed. A few were rewarded as had been the men on the steps, but others went back disconsolate and empty-handed, while their husbands continued their way down the road. Everyone knew where that way led. There was no saloon at Glen Jean, but Starr, a few miles below, boasted of both a saloon and a jail!

Janet caught Jamie to her with sudden feeling when this had been many times repeated.

"Eh mannie," she exclaimed, "if ye never get a cab in all yir days, ye onyway hae a feyther that always hes heid enuch tae carry ye. Some o' the bairn's feythers willna be able tae carry theirsels come evenin'."

Ritchie would not be coming until shortly before his usual time. He had never seen the necessity of laying off half a day, because his month's wage was to be paid. It would be just before the sounding of the whistle that Ritchie would appear at the office to be welcomed by the cashier with:

"Here comes Mackentyre, last as usual, but he'll carry away the weightiest envelope."

Something a little out of the ordinary in the culinary line, by way of celebration of the day, so occupied Janet, that the whistle caught her unawares.

"Hoots, Jamie lad," she exclaimed, "that's the whistle, an' here's nither with the supper no' din. It's a wonder feyther's no' here a'ready."

She lifted the babe from the cradle as she spoke and went to the window. As she looked, a boy, evidently from the tipple, ran up the office steps and went in. Gibson, the book-keeper, and Bristol, the cashier, came out at once, looked anxiously toward the mine, and then straight across to the Mackentyre house.

Janet went to the door.

"Has Richard come in tonight, Mrs. Mackentyre?" called Bristol.

"Is he no' at the affice?" called back Janet.

Bristol turned without reply and spoke a few words with the book-keeper. The boy who stood on the steps with them was evidently given some direction, and he started on a run down the road toward Starr. Gibson left the porch and went at a rapid pace up the hill to the tipple; while Bristol, after locking the office door, came across the causeway to the village. He turned the corner without coming as far as the house; and Janet, who had waited, went back into the house, shut the door, and sat down. She held Jamie close to her. He was a hardy little fellow, and did not cry, though the pressing kept the color back from his soft little cheek.

Presently one of the neighbor women came in through the back door. Bristol had been a shrewd man when he sent Mrs. Lukin. She came over to Janet's chair.

"Why, yer a-holdin' that baby too tight. Yere, let me hev him. Come ter aunty, little man. La, I b'lieve somethin's burnin'. You'll spoil yer man's supper, Mis' Mackentyre, if you don't look to it."

And then Janet relaxed her hold on Jamie, with a great sob. Mrs. Lukin took Jamie in one arm, and patted Janet's shoulder with her free hand.

"There," she said gently, "you'd better cry some. There hev been a cave-in to the mine, but taint mebbe nothin' serious. It hev blocked the way to your man's room but it mightn't hev caught him. I would try to feel he was safe, leastwise till ye knowed better."

Bristol came in some time later. All the miners at the camp had been set to digging, and it was hoped a large force would be got in from the other mines. Unfortunately, pay-day was uniform throughout the valley, and there were few miners of the Ritchie Mackentyre stamp. Almost no responses of help came in from the other mines, while the Glen Jean's own men at Starr were found incapable of service. It was, moreover, unfortunate that the manager and his bank-boss had been ordered before a meeting of the company's directors for a report on the condition of the mine.

It was impossible to keep the state of affairs from Janet, who watched from the window all coming and going at the mine, even after the shadow of the opposite mountain had long turned everything to blackness. Something after nine the twinkling bobbing lights of the miner's caps were seen descending the hill.

"They're coomin' awa'," cried Janet. "Dae ye think——"

"Set still," commanded Mrs. Lukin, "whilst I bring ye word."

It appeared that the digging, entirely in slate, was so heavy that the men had been compelled to abandon it for the time through utter weariness. They would return after a few hours' rest, and it was hoped by that time other help might be got in. The knowledge that rescue work had been stopped, even for the time, threw Janet into despair.

"They dinna care," she moaned. "If only Meester Murray or the bank-boss were at home it wadna be sae."

"It aint Mr. Murray as could make men work when they're dead tired," said Mrs. Lukin somewhat sharply, for her own man was of the party; "but as for the bank-boss it mightn't hev happened if he'd been yere ter see 'at the props was right— Land, Mis' Mackentyre, hev you turned faint?"

"I think I wull lie doon," said Janet feebly.

"Shall I put the babe down beside ye," asked Mrs. Lukin when Janet was on the lounge. "There's an amazin' heap o' comfort in his small body?"

"Na, na," cried Janet, "I dinna want him. I dinna want tae see him at a'!" she continued passionately. "I wad like"—a moment later—"if ye wad gang tae bed wi' him in the room yonner."

"Well now," thought the good neighbor, as she complied with the request; "folks is surely curious whenst they hev trouble."

Alone, Janet turned to the wall in a desolation that shut out from her heart even the bairn of her own flesh. The hardness of the words over the cab had haunted her through the long evening; but its peculiar significance in relation to the accident had not before confronted her. It seemed probable, nay certain, that Ritchie had taken her at her word, and had risked a long life for the saving of minutes.

Always with the hope that the crush of slate had not reached him, the awful dreariness to Ritchie, shut away from help and light, came to her, filling her heart with a pity that made her own misery less evident. Many times had Ritchie spoken of the depressing loneliness of those dark holes in the earth to one in solitude.

Janet sat up suddenly, thanking God who had directed her thoughts in these channels. It had been only a short time since Ritchie had spoken of being startled, almost alarmed at first, by hearing some one singing when he was at work. Investigation showed that a room had been worked in from another passage until the two had come near meeting. For the sake of strength, the bank-boss had directed a change of direction; "But I can hear him yet when he gets tae loading," Ritchie had said. "He a'ways sings, an' it's quite heartening. Baily wad be a real good fellow if it werena for the drink."

She was familiar with the workings of the mine, and Ritchie had made a sketch on the back of the almanac to show her how the unusual occurrence had come about. She brought the almanac to the light, and examined it carefully, and then put it away in her dress.

The loud breathing of Mrs. Lukin in the adjoining room had long told her that she watched alone. She took the light and went cautiously into the shed. Ritchie had always an extra cap and oil about. When she had found what she wanted she extinguished the light and went out from the back.

Janet always insisted that the Lord had led her, quite as surely as He had the Israelites with the pillar of fire by night, through the labyrinth of windings to drunken Hank Baily's room. It was at the end of the passage, as was Ritchie's; and the change of direction spoken of by Ritchie was easily discerned.

She had gone bravely on but now when she attempted to raise her voice to find if she could get an answer, the beating of her heart drowned the sound of her voice, and she rested gaspingly against the black wall until she could still it a bit.

There was a murmur of sounds in her ear. In an instant every sense was alert. It was Ritchie, and he was repeating the twenty-third psalm—

" 'Yea, though I walk through the valley of the shadow of death, I will fear no evil: for thou art with me;—' "

"Ay, Ritchie," she called, and her voice rang clear as a bell, "haud tae the Lord, an' we'll sune coom."

It was scarcely more than an hour before Ritchie was in his own house, and the doctor was there dressing the foot that alone had suffered in the cruel fall of slate. There was great rejoicing at Janet's fortunate remembrance, and regretting that poor Baily had been too drunk to give the information before.

"I canna understand what caused it." Ritchie was saying the next day. "I tapped the passage the whole way as I went in, an' there wasna a fa'se ring."

Janet knelt down by the couch and caught her husband's hand. "Ritchie, dae ye mean tae say ye didna grow heedless o' the props aifter thae awfu words o' mine?"

"Hoots, lass, did ye think I didna ken ye better than that—it was something ootside o' any power o' mine tae stay, caused it. But I doot," and he stroked Janet's hair gently; "wi' this foot tae hinder, the cab mayna be coomin' even next month."

Janet raised her head. "Ritchie, if ye hae forgiven those words o' mine, dinna ever speak o' the cab again. When the lad has sic a feyther spaired him—what dis he need o' a cab?"

Then!

By Christene W. Bullwinkle.

CONTENT I'll be, if when asleep
   And in that last repose,
Some little child will softly creep
   And lay a pale wild rose
On me, in mem'ry of the time
   When, sitting at my knee,
I sang for her a fairy's rhyme;
   Or, 'neath some lacy tree,
I charmed her ear with shepherd's tale
   And legends of the sea.

Content I'll be, dear heart, if thou
   Wilt say, when all alone
You sit beneath the apple-bough
   And see the blossoms blown
Across your path in perfumed flight,
   "Her songs were songs of cheer;
Where e'er she walked the way was bright,
   Where she walked naught was drear."
And so, a-dream, I'll smile, I know,
   If your dear voice I hear.

Westborough and Northborough

By Martha E. D. White

Illustrated from photographs by Mrs. O. W. Judd and others

"ONE generation shall praise thy works to another, and shall declare thy mighty acts'—the obvious import of which words is this, that the people who live in one age shall relate the works and mighty acts of the Lord to their posterity; and so shall each successive generation do, throughout all ages to the end of time." Thus did the Rev. Peter Whitney expound the text of his famous half-century sermon, delivered to his people in Northborough in 1796. "The works and mighty acts of the Lord" included the secular as well as the sacred relations of the people, and to relate them was to tell their history. Now at the end of another century the old minister's injunction is heard again; and the purpose of this article is to recall to this generation the works of their forefathers.

Sudbury had been settled eighteen years when thirteen of her young men, wearied of that "man-stifled town," coveted the land beyond the hills toward the sunset. These men had "lived long in Sudbury," their children were growing up, their cattle were increased, and, in short, they said, "Wee are so straightened that wee cannot so comfortably subsist as could be desired." The General Court was evidently moved by the pent-up conditions and wide aspirations of their petitioners, for it granted them a territory "six miles square, or its equivalent, under the name of the Whipsufferadge Plantation." Situated about thirty miles west of Boston at the head waters of the Sudbury and Assabet Rivers, this plantation was then the extreme outpost of civilization in the Massachusetts Bay territory. In 1660 the original thirteen families had increased to thirty-nine, and, having demonstrated their ability to maintain a "preached gospel" in their midst, the Plantation was incorporated as a town and named "Marlborow." Out of this wide domain were to grow the "borough towns;" and although the mother town gave to her offspring generously of her abundance, yet it is she who has "waxed exceeding," and to-day is an active manufacturing city, while her children are modest villages in the midst of rich farming lands.

In the western part of the Whipsufferadge Grant the settlers found a beautiful pond, surrounded by a broad, fertile plain, with wooded foothills, on its southern extremities. This pond was Naggawoomcom, so called by the Indians, meaning "great pond." But even before the "Marlborow" man had been the General Court, and the land around the pond had been set apart for President Chauncy of Harvard College. This was one of several similar farms given to Mr. Chauncy by the Court, which was richer in lands than in money.

The surveyor's description of this land is an interesting geographical document. Dated August 18, 1659, it reads: "Whereas John Stone and Andrew Belcher were appointed to lay out a farm for Mr. Charles Channcy, President of Harvard College, we have gone and looked on a place and there is taken up a tract of land bounded in this manner: On the east a little swampe, neare an Indian wigwam, a plaine runing to a great pond, and from thence to Assebeth River, and this line is circular on the north side, the south line runing circular to the South side of a piece of meadow and so to continue till it reach the said Assebeth River."

A college president is perforce a wise man, and doubtless President Chauncy could have found his farm, guided by this description; but there is no evidence that he even looked for it. A year later, having been "by them repaid all his charges expended," he relinquished his title to Marlborough; an obvious trace of his ownership still exists in the name of the pond, which was thenceforth called Chauncy. On the southerly slope of this pond grew up eventually a little settlement called Chauncy Village. In 1688 it was of sufficient importance to gain permission from Marlborough to build another meeting-house and maintain a minister, "if they found themselves able so to do." Chauncy seems to have doubted her ability, for she continued "at a considerable distance from the

Place of publick Worship," and ill accommodated, to attend it in Marlborow until 1718, when "a plat of the westerly part of Marlborough called Chauncy" was "erected into a township" called Westborough. This was Massachusetts's *one hundredth* town.

In the days of Indian occupation Channcy had been a border land between the Wamesits and Nipmucks. Hobomoc, then, as now, an uncanny pond, was the home of their "Evil Spirit." By another water course they held their corn dance. Their "great pond" smiled for them, and the many rounded hills offered sightly places for their wigwams. But pestilence, wars, and civilization had reduced their numbers so that the first settlers of Chauncy found only the residuum of the tribes once so powerful. The tribal relations were practically destroyed, and the individuals either joined one of the colonies of praying Indians fostered by John Eliot or lived in patriarchal simplicity, a solitary Indian in an isolated wigwam. In this manner old David Monanaow was living as late as 1737. Mr. Parkman then visited him, and writes in his diary that David "tells me he was 104 last Indian Harvest. Says the name of Boston was not Shawmut, but Shanwawmuck." What experiences had fallen to the lot of this centenarian! He had been with King Philip in his desperate attempt to win back the rights of the red men, and was one of the marauding party that sacked Medfield. After a term of imprisonment he came back to live out his life, an alien in the midst of his conquerors. It is not necessary to be an Indian apologist to see, in the swift, noise-

LAKE CHAUNCY

less raids that brought desolation and sorrow to the homes of the settlers, a grim kind of justice. What he could not effect by superiority and strength he would undertake through terrorism and treachery. From such warfare the Channcy settlers were heavy sufferers. The episode that had the most far-reaching results is graphically told by the Rev. Peter Whitney.

"On August 8, 1704, as several persons were busy in spreading flax on a plain about eighty rods from the house of Mr. Thomas Rice, and a number of boys with them, seven and some say ten Indians suddenly rushed down a wooded hill near by, and knocking the least of the boys on the head (Nahor, about five years old, son of Mr. Edmund Rice, and the first person ever buried in Westborough), they seized two, Asher and Adonizah, sons of Mr. Thomas Rice —the oldest about ten and the other about eight years of age—and two others, Silas and Timothy, sons of Mr. Edmund Rice, above-named, of about nine and seven years of age and carried them away to Canada."

Asher, four years after, was redeemed; Adonizah married and settled in Canada; but the two others lived Indian lives. One of them, years after, came back to Westborough under the imposing name of Oughtsorongoughton; and it appears from the record of his visit that he had become all that his name implies. He was taken to see the place "whence he was captivated," but he had forgot his English tongue and his memory of early days was very indistinct. This place "whence he was captivated" has been the centre of romance, as well as of history. The site of Mr. Thomas Rice's old garrison house was later occupied by the most imposing dwelling in Westborough, known for some years as the Whitney Place. The grounds are described by Mr. Howells in his novel, "Annie Kilburn": "The wall was overhung there by a company of magnificent elms which turned and formed one side of the avenue lead-

"ANNIE KILBURN" HOUSE

ing to the house. Their tops met and mixed somewhat incongruously with those of the stiff dark maples, which 7iore densely shaded the other side of the lane." Here Annie Kilburn tried the problem of life, and her ghost of fiction wrestles for supremacy in the imagination with the actors in the real tragedy enacted under the summer sky two centuries ago.

Westborough's first independent town action was "to resolve to build a meeting house forthwith the meeting house to Be fourty foot long, and thirty foot wide, and eighteen foot Between Joints." From this act stretches out during six years the devious way of meeting-house building. In 1718 the town meeting "resolves to put a place to vote to set ye meeting House upon;" and a site was agreed upon about midway of the town's area, near the present farmhouse of the Lyman School. The next step in progress is marked by the vote "to procuer Six Gallons Rhum and a Barrell and half of Syder for the raising the meeting house in sd town." Even the good spirit engendered by the raising did not accelerate the haste of the builders. Cautiously they proceeded to the next decision, "to have an Alley Between ye men and women through ye midel of the Mett house," and "to sell the space to be improved for

TOWN HALL, BAPTIST CHURCH AND SOLDIERS' MONUMENT, WESTBOROUGH

MAIN STREET, WESTBOROUGH

pews." In 1723 the vote "to compleate finishing the Meeting house" is recorded; and Westborough is henceforth provided with her civil and spiritual forum. During this troublesome time of building the set-tlers had not neglected to provide themselves opportunities to enjoy a "preached gospel." The Rev. David Elmer had ministered to them to their great dissatisfaction. He was never ecclesiastically settled, but through

CATHOLIC AND UNITARIAN CHURCHES, WESTBOROUGH

his possession of the ministerial farm he was enabled to stir the pool of church harmony for several years. He was finally deposed, and soon after the completion of the meeting-house the town settled their first minister, · the Rev. Ebenezer Park-man.

Parkman is a significant name in New England history. Ebeneezer was in the fourth generation of colonial Parkmans. His father, William, was a deacon of the New North Church in Boston. In Copp's Hill "lyes buried the body of Mrs. Eliza-beth Parkman, the virtuous and pious consort of Mr. William Parkman." Samuel Parkman was the minister's twelfth son. He became a merchant in Boston, famous alike for his shrewdness in business and the gen-erosity he showed toward the city. In Faneuil Hall are preserved two of his gifts to Boston, the portrait of Peter Faneuil and the Stuart portrait

of Washington.* Francis Parkman, the historian, was his grandson. Breck Parkman, the eleventh child of Ebeneezer, remained in Westbor-ough, and from him have descended all the local representatives of the family. Breck had the first and for many years the only store in West-borough.

Ebeneezer Parkman was a youth of twenty-three years, a recent graduate of Harvard College, and a bride-groom, when he accepted his call to Westborough, in 1724. His settle-ment was to be 150 pounds and his annual salary 80 pounds. Westbor-ough had then twenty-seven families, scattered over twice its present area. It was a long day's journey from Bos-ton, and the way difficult for any con-veyance. Wild beasts and Indian hostilities filled the settlers with ner-vous alarms. Mr. Parkman reached

*See NEW ENGLAND MAGAZINE, August, 1899.

ALONG THE ASSABET

his parish the first time on horseback, and walked to the meetinghouse pistol in hand. These apparently discouraging surroundings might have been regarded as temporal drawbacks at least; but Mr. Parkman had no eye for that side of the question. His own spiritual unworthiness seems to have been his only consideration. Filled with the sense of "my multiplied and heinous Iniquities and particularly unprofitableness under Y^e means of Grace, and Negligence and Sloth in ye Great Business God has been pleased to Employ me in," he prepared for "ye awful time approaching."

During Mr. Parkman's long pastorate of fifty-eight years, he remained the central imposing and impelling figure of the town. He was a stanch representative of the aristocratic type of Puritan minister, and Westborough under his guidance placed her ecclesiastical before her civil life, thus earning the title of "Westborough, pious." Mr. Parkman built his parsonage on the windswept top of the present Lyman School Hill, and in it centred the social, the spiritual, the intellectual life of Westborough. The church records, kept with much attention to minute detail, show that Mr. Parkman also kept the consciences of his people, and over their personal sins he sat in austere and absolute judgment. Sixteen times he records in red ink and large type the christening of a tiny lad or lassie born to the Parkman family. The hand drawn in the margin, with its index finger

727

singling out these particular and personal events, witnesses to the respect which he felt for his holy office, and also to a pardonable sense of his individual importance.

Early in life Mr. Parkman began to keep his secular history in a record called "Diurna, or the Remarkable Transactions of Every Day," while his soul history he confided to his "Natalita." Many of these volumes still exist. One volume of the "Diurna" has recently been published by the Westborough Historical Society. Its editor, Mrs. Harriette Forbes, added copious foot-notes explanatory of persons and places, making of the book a veritable gem of New England history. The temptation to quote from its pages is well-nigh irresistible; but once entered upon that narrative of "petty cares and economies, small jealousies and quarrels," there could be no turning away.

The serenity of ecclesiastical affairs in Westborough remained unclouded until about 1740. Then the settlers of the north part of the township began a movement looking to the division of the parish. In 1744 Mr. Parkman records: "A number of North Side people met those of ye South Side last night at Capt. Fay's to gather subscriptions to a petition to ye General Court that ye Town may be divided. At ye same meeting Eliezer Rice broke his legg by wrestling with Silas Pratt." This irrelevantly recorded "break" typified the disruption of the town. Northborough became a separate parish in 1744, and was incorporated two years later.

As a result of this division, Westborough's centre of population being changed, a new church became necessary and the village fathers decided to build it "on the North Side of the Country road where there is now a Pine Bush grows, about twenty-five or thirty rods easterly from the Burrying Place in Said Precinct." The "Country road" is now Main Street; and the meeting-house remained standing until a few years ago, under the name of "The Old Arcade." Like its predecessor the new meeting-house was guiltless of steeple and "culler." It continued thus unadorned until 1801. Mr. Samuel Parkman then gave the town a bell, cast in the foundry of Paul Revere; a concession was made to the pomps of life, the gift was accepted and the steeple built. This bell now hangs in the belfry of the Baptist Church, testifying weekly to Paul Revere's honest workmanship. Mr. Parkman soon followed the meeting-house, building himself an imposing house on the "Cuntry Road," whose timbers have thus far stanchly withstood the onslaughts of time. This house was thought to be somewhat vainglorious for a minister; and Mr. Parkman concedes that there is cause for criticism in the size of the window frames, and he "would they had been smaller." Happily they were not, for the old minister needed in the discouragement of the final years of his pastorate all the cheer that could be gained from wide windows. With a divided people, a multiplied family and a depreciated currency, the temporal trials of his last years were equalled only by the serenity of his spirit. He was a man of God; and the thought comes that perhaps he was a little too much a man of God to be in the highest de-

NORTHBOROUGH MEETING HOUSE

gree the benefactor of his community. He died in 1782. His tomb in Memorial Cemetery is covered with a horizontal slab bearing on its face an epitaph so deeply engraved that generations of Westborough boys have been unable to efface it. "He was a learned, pious, good man full of the Holy Ghost and faith unfeigned."

Mr. Parkman's death was followed by troublous ecclesiastical times. His successor, John Robinson, like "John

G. Robinson, he," in the "Biglow Papers," meddled in politics, and denounced the Democrats as "Knights of the halter." This outrage on a congregation largely made up of Democrats settled his fate, and he was soon succeeded by the Rev. Elisha Rockwood. During Mr. Rockwood's ministry, in 1825, the town ceased to act as an ecclesiastical parish and entered upon its modern era.

The Rev. Peter Whitney gives a graphic description of Northborough's early parish experiences. "The number of inhabitants was few (but 38 families) and their abilities small. They met with great difficulties from without (the particulars whereof we do not wish to perpetuate) and many difficulties from within. Nevertheless, such was their zeal in the cause in which they were engaged, and such their ardent desire to enjoy a preached gospel and divine ordinances among themselves, that they surmounted every obstacle thrown in their way; and the next spring, on April 30, 1745, they erected to the glory and for the worship of God this house in which we are now assembled."

From 1746 to 1766, the Rev. James Martin was satisfactorily their first minister. Closely associated with him in Northborough was a character unique in New England's early life. This was Mr. Judah Monis, known as Rabbi Israel Monis in his youth, and for many years instructor in Hebrew at Harvard College. Mr. Monis was some time converted from Judaism to Christianity, as its epitaph in the old Northborough cemetery has it:

"A native branch of Jacob see,
    Which once from off its olive broke,
Regrafted on the living tree,
    Of the reviving sap partook."

A curious legacy keeps the memory of this man alive. He left in care of the ministers of the First Church in Salem, in Hingham, in Cambridge and in Northborough a sum now equivalent to $400, the income of which was to be used to aid widows of indigent clergymen. This fund has survived the stress of financial storms, and at present four people are benefited by it. Northborough showed Mr. Monis great honor, voting him a "foor seat below in the meeting house." He in turn "left something very honourable and generous to the Church,"—"something" being two silver cups.

The Rev. Peter Whitney succeeded Mr. Martin in the ministry; and his pastorate continued for forty-nine years. He was a valiant, doughty man of stubborn principles and rigid practices. His "half-century sermon" is an example of the best in colonial sermon writing, and his History of Worcester County is a volume of unique value. He was also an aggressive patriot. It is recalled that he preached a sermon in which he convicted King George of twenty-six crimes. Many years after Mr. Whitney's death his successor wrote of him: "His mortal remains, and his monument, and the remembrance of his many virtues, are still with us." The house in which Mr. Whitney lived still stands, one of the oldest left in the town.

But it was left for Dr. Joseph Allen to make the abiding impression upon the life and character of the North-

borough people. Following Mr. Whitney, his pastorate extended from 1816 to 1873; and all good things seem to have come from this wise man's influence. A humanitarian, a "lover of flowers and of little children," a planter of trees and modern ideas, his influence brought about the "golden age" of Northborough. Nor was Dr. Allen's influence confined to local affairs. In connection with his wife, Miss Lucy Ware of Cambridge, he began an early crusade against intemperance, directing his efforts particularly toward a movement to enlist the clergy on the side of abstinence. An interesting incident of their temperance work in Northborough was the re-naming of "Licor Hill." With pomp and ceremony Mrs. Allen, accompanied by a party of school children, climbed to the summit of the hill and in a baptism of water re-christened it with "the gentler name of Assabet." Discouraged in an effort to win the Worcester Association of Ministers to pledge themselves to forego intoxicants, they turned their attention to the practical problem of relief for the pecuniary affairs of the drinking man. Out of the study of this problem Mrs. Allen conceived the idea of a provident institution for savings. In 1827 her idea—it was hardly a plan—was confided to the Worcester Association, and Dr. Bancroft, father of the historian, at that time a Worcester minister, struck with the practical side of Mrs. Allen's suggestion, undertook to work it out. The result was the Worcester County Institution for Savings, reputed to be the first institution of that character in this country.

Dr. Allen founded a lyceum which was for many years the intellectual forum of Northborough. He also became town historian and a very prominent participant in the town government. Early in his pastorate he evinced signs of a change in faith. As one who remembers him says, "he loved everything too much to remain a rigid Puritan." His growing liberalism resulted in the withdrawal of a portion of his congregation to found the Evangelical Congregational Society, in 1832. The town ceased then to be identical with the parish, and the old meeting-house became Unitarian, a character which it thenceforth maintained. In Westborough, under Mr. Rockwood, the same ecclesiastical change took place in 1825. It is an interesting coincidence that the parish churches of both towns should undergo the same change in theological belief and that the First Church in each instance should become the conserver of a liberal faith.

After these breaks in the solidarity of evangelical institutions, other changes soon followed. Already the Baptists had created a following, and in Westborough and Northborough churches were built, and societies formed, that are still doing valiant service. The Methodists established a church in Westborough in 1844. The Catholic Church came with the advent of a manufacturing population to both villages. An interesting Episcopal mission has recently been established in Westborough under the patronage of St. Mark's at Southborough. This mission has attracted much attention from having ingeniously transformed a stable into a well appointed chapel. The "mission of the converted stable" is not at all the irreverent title that it might at first sight appear to be.

After theology the New England man has ever considered education. In these "borough towns" the consideration was accorded the correct order, but there seems to have been no alacrity in proceeding to take the next step. In 1726 Westborough appointed a committee "to procure a suitable schoolmaster to teach children to Read, write and Sipher." Dominie Townsend was provided, and for thirteen years he taught those difficult branches, receiving in payment thirty-five dollars a year, part of the time paying for his "own diet." There was to be no schoolhouse for forty years, the school being held in the mean time in private houses. Provisions for a grammar school were made in 1753, but after "presentation" by the General Court the matter lapsed, and nearly a century passed before the grammar school became a part of the school system. Ten years later the first high school followed.

Northborough was somewhat more aggressive in educational matters. As early as 1779 several men who wished broader facilities for their children formed the "Seminary Association," a kind of coöperative arrangement which permitted the employment of a higher grade of teachers. The lyceum, established and continued for years, afforded the best type of University Extension work.

Libraries, perhaps not less important than schools, have been long established. In Northborough the "Social Library" was begun by the Rev. James Martin, and in 1793 greatly increased by young ladies who sewed straw to earn one hundred dollars with which to buy books. The present carefully selected library is

GALE LIBRARY, NORTHBOROUGH

beautifully housed in a building given by Cyrus Gale. In 1807 the nucleus of Westborough's present library was formed.

The church, the school, the library —those institutions so lovingly cherished and maintained, ofttimes with difficulty, have been in a great degree the nurseries of New England town life. To tell again of their influence is to rehearse a story that has been heard whenever a New England town has become articulate—the same story, but with many differences; everywhere the same end has been striven for, but nowhere have the steps been identical.

To treat of the honorable military and civic record of these towns adequately would take one into a long story of strong, simple, duty-doing persons, accomplishing in a homely, persistent spirit the feat of being true citizens of a noble republic. The first head of one of Mr. Parkman's sermons, delivered during the French and Indian War, prophesies that "God is not o' mind to destroy the land of his peculiar covenant people;" and it is evident that his hearers were eager to keep Providence in that state of mind. From all the "borough" places valiant young men went forth to do service for the king and gain the military spirit soon to be of such value in the Revolution. There was no disloyalty to Massachusetts when the time for independent action came; instead, every movement to protect the rights of the colonists was faithfully upheld, and the quiet preparation for conflict carried steadily on. Northborough showed the most aggressive spirit—a spirit doubtless due to the fiery, patriotic sermons of Rev. Peter Whitney, who was ill inclined to be ruled by a "Sinful Monster." Nine months before the Boston Tea Party, the young men of Northborough set the example Boston was to follow. The *Massachusetts Gazette* for February 17, 1773, relates that "one day last week a peddler was observed to go into a Shrewsbury tavern with a bag of tea. Information of which being had in Northborough, a company of (young men disguised as) Indians went from the Great Swamp or thereabouts and seized upon it, and committed it to the flames in the road in front of said tavern until it was entirely consumed."

On the nineteenth of April, Northborough's company of fifty minutemen, under command of Captain Samuel Woods, had assembled to hear a patriotic discourse by Mr. Whitney. "The hurry of hoofs in the village street" transformed the waiting company into active patriots, and with hasty words of farewell and a last pastoral blessing they were away to Lexington. From Westborough also before nightfall the march of the minutemen had begun. Their prompt action that day was fully continued in the subsequent events of the Revolution. Men, money, blankets—no call was ever unheeded. In six years Westborough enlisted 381 men, among them Henry Marble, who "enlisted for war or for life," fought in nearly every great battle of the war, achieving the rank of lieutenant. From Northborough men were sent in the same ratio; and to fill their empty places on the farm the women and boys were ever ready. These "borough towns" suffered severely from the evils of a depreciated currency; doubtless their being so entirely farming communities increased their liability to suffer from that cause. In Westborough attempts were made to control prices by legal enactments, the price of beef being fixed at $2\frac{1}{4}d.$ per pound, and corn $3s.$ $2d.$ per bushel. They were soon to learn that inevitable tendencies cannot thus be stayed. Three years later corn was worth fifty dollars a bushel, and beef four dollars a pound.

In the Civil War the part played by these towns was if possible even more loyal and energetic. Northborough furnished 140 men who saw active service; and Westborough, 337. Many of these were left on the battlefields, and others died in Southern prisons. It is idle to undertake to speak of the innumerable activites and sacrifices of these towns. Theirs was a heroic, silent service, loyally and reverently held in the hearts of those who have come after them.

The institution of slavery had not been unknown in Westborough. In 1737 Mr. Parkman bought a slave boy in Boston. A year later he records: "The sun of Maro's life is almost set." The rigors of a New England winter had been too severe for Maro. Stephen Maynard, the wealthiest farmer of the town, clung tenaciously to his slaves. A heavy stone wall inclosing the avenue that led to the old house was built by them, and is perhaps the last piece of slave labor performed in Massachusetts.

Two state institutions have been located in Westborough, thus adding to her own life this wider connection with the state. In 1846 the legislature appropriated $10,000 to build a Reform School* for boys, and the site for it was chosen on the beautiful northern slope of Lake Chauncy. The novel idea of reforming youthful citi-

*See NEW ENGLAND MAGAZINE, June, 1902.

zens appealed so strongly to that wise humanitarian, General Theodore Lyman, that he gave to this cause at various times, and in great fear lest his beneficence should be known, $72,000. To trace the history of this school would be to relate the evolution that has taken place in the policy the state maintains toward juvenile offenders. The buildings were partly destroyed by fire in 1859, the work of one of the inmates. This fire was the immediate cause of the first attempt to classify the boys according to their age and offences, which has finally resulted in the admirable system in use to-day. In 1885 the legislature transferred the buildings then in use and the site for use as an insane hospital, and moved the school across the lake, building on the hill which was the site of the first meeting-house and parsonage. Not till then was the name changed to the Lyman Schools for Boys.

The Westborough Insane Hospital, a homœopathic institution, was opened to patients in 1886. The admirable system of this institution and its high order of excellence need no comment.

To speak adequately of the "daily bread" side of these towns would require much more space than can here be commanded; for their industrial career has been sadly complicated and at times uncertain. The coming of the Boston and Albany Railroad, which passes through Westborough village, gave the first impetus to manufactures in these communities other than those purely domestic, and impressed upon that place the character of a manufacturing village, although its earlier characteristics were not effaced. This union of the two types makes the somewhat unusual appearance of the village described by Mr. Howells in "Annie Kilburn":

"The railroad tracks crossed its main street; but the shops were all on one side of them, with the work-people's cottages and boarding houses, and on the other were the simple, square, roomy old mansions, with their white paint and their green blinds, varied by the modern color and carpentry of French roofed villas. The old houses stood quite close to the street, with a strip of narrow door-yard before them; the new ones affected a certain depth of lawn, over which their owners personally pushed a clucking hand-mower in the summer evenings after tea. The fences had been taken away from the new houses; they generally remained before the old ones, whose inmates resented the ragged appearance their absence gave the street." In Annie Kilburn's time "over the track" was social perdition, but this aristocratic division has now been removed by the re-location of the railroad tracks a quarter of a mile further north, and Westborough's social life is reduced again to a harmonious democracy.

As early as 1828 Westborough began the manufacture of boots and shoes, which has since been a constant industry in the town. Straw sewing as a domestic industry appeared during the first half of the century. In 1863 the factory system was introduced, and soon after the "windowy bulk" of the present "straw shops" appeared just north of the Boston and Albany tracks, on Main Street. The manufacture of sleighs and bicycles has long been successfully carried on;

CHAPIN RESIDENCE, CHAPINVILLE

but bicycles "have had their day and ceased to be," giving away, as is sociologically if not practically logical, to the making of "locomobiles."

The Rev. Peter Whitney wrote that in 1796 the fulling mill in Northborough annually treated some 7,000 yards of cloth, "the work being most acceptable performed to the honor and advantage of the town." He further states that "great numbers of people are drawn to Northborough because of mills, forges and stores." In her later years this activity has been greatly lessened, and the abandoned mills are all that remain of her former industrial period. Large mills manufacturing satinet, located in Chapinville, still afford employment to a portion of the population.

Notwithstanding the various industries that have appeared in these "bor-

ough towns," they are still farming communities, as they were in their beginnings. At least the land is still the principal and the stable source of their wealth. But it is from the character and personality of their citizens that they have enjoyed the best degree of wealth, a competency—not a competency that merely enables one to get along easily, but with a generous margin ever ready to be used in the service of state and nation. "Old families" have persisted surprisingly, particularly in Westborough, the same names and faces constantly appearing in local affairs.

Northborough has furnished one governor to Massachusetts, "Honest" John Davis. He served the state two terms in the fifties. The Davis family was a pioneer family; the men it produced were strong, muscular, clear headed, men of power and great personal distinction.

The Gale family came into special prominence in early abolition days. Captain Cyrus Gale drew up the first call for the convention that resulted in the Free Soil party. Its signers included several Northborough men. This circumstance testifies again to the powers of leadership possessed by these people, and perhaps marks

THE WESSON PLACE, NORTHBOROUGH

DR. BALL'S HOUSE, NORTHBOROUGH

the difference between Northborough and the other "borough towns." They followed suggestions; Northborough initiated methods.

The Allen family has been and is famous in the educational annals of New England. Dr. Joseph Allen for many years tutored recalcitrant boys in his home. If the bad boy truly makes the brave man, Dr. Allen's mark must be on many a man who is making our present history.

Old Dr. Ball, Northborough's first medical practitioner, was an interesting character, who impressed his personality in no slight degree upon his contemporaries. When asked why he put so many different things into a prescription, he answered: "If you are going to shoot a bird you use plenty of shot."

Of the Westborough men who have made great names for themselves, Eli Whitney of cotton-gin fame, is preëminent.* On his ma-

See NEW ENGLAND MAGAZINE, May, 1890.

ternal side he descended from a first settler, John Fay. The farmhouse where he was born in 1765 was on a road toward Grafton, a mile or more from the centre of the town, now known as Eli Whitney Street. Nothing remains of the old house. In Memorial Cemetery the Whitney monument marks the graves of his parents. Eli passed his youth in Westborough, going elsewhere for his education; and subsequently Westborough knew him only as a visitor.

The Brigham family has especial claims to "honorable mention." David Brigham signed the First Church covenant. His grandson, Elijah, better known as "Judge" Brigham, took an active part in public affairs, serving as selectman, member of the legislature, state senator, and later as judge of the Court of Common Pleas for sixteen years. No generation since the "Judge's" day has been without its representative Brigham.

ELI WHITNEY MEMORIAL
Cyrus E. Dallin, Sculptor.

These few names might be augmented by many more, thus making a chronicle of faithful servitors and well doers that would bring prideful memories to the hearts of all who love the indigenous man of · New England. Civic, social, and industrial movements come and go, but much of the primitive man remains. In this fact rests the hope of our institutions.

I like to entertain the idea that on fine moonlight nights Parsons Parkman and Whitney mount their steeds for a gentle amble over the hills and through the valleys they loved so well.

Mr. Parkman would see in the chimneys and smoke of factories the blessing of God upon his chosen people whom He desired exceedingly to prosper. Mr. Whitney might grieve that Northborough had been seemingly left behind in the race toward riches, and he would look longingly for the independent creative spirit he had known. Perhaps in those shining steel rails that stretch out to the "new town of Worcester" and the "ancient town of Marlborow" and around to Southborough and Westborough, he would see the dawning of a new era—an era in which electricity will bind again together the "borough towns," as formerly they were bound by ties of love and common needs.

Westborough's first physician was Dr. Hawes. The house he built for himself still stands on East Main Street. He was a faithful practitioner, faithful to his one treatment, "visit and venesection." He served the town for many years as justice of the peace and town clerk, and was prominent in Revolutionary matters.

The Good Queen

By Charles Hanson Towne

PALE ruler of the heavens, with lavish hand,
    The spendthrift moon arose,
And spilt her silver out across the land,
    Alike on friends and foes.

A CAPE COD ROADWAY

Cape Cod Folks

By Clifton Johnson

With Illustrations by the Author

IT was densely dark when I arrived at Yarmouth one October evening. Viewed from the platform of the railway station the world about was a void of inky gloom.

"If you're looking for the town," said a man at my elbow, "you'll find it over in that direction;" and he pointed with his finger. "You follow the road, and turn to the right when you've gone half a mile or so, and that'll take you straight into the village."

"But I don't see any road," said I.

"Well, it goes around the corner of that little shed over thar that the light from the depot shines on."

"And how far is it to a hotel?"

"We ain't got no hotel in this place; but Mr. Sutton, two houses beyond the post office, he keeps people and I guess he'll take you in all right."

I trudged off along the vague highway, and at length reached the town street, a narrow thoroughfare solidly overarched by trees. Dwellings were numerous on either side, and lights glowed through curtained windows. How snug those silent houses looked; and how cheerless seemed the outer darkness and the empty street to the homeless stranger! I lost no time in hurrying up Mr. Sutton's, and the shel-

ter he granted brought a very welcome sense of relief.

When I explored Yarmouth the next day, I found it the most attenuated town I had ever seen. The houses nearly all elbowed each other for a distance of two or three miles close along a single slender roadway. Very few dwellings ventured aside from this double column. Apparently no other situation was orthodox, and I suppose the families which lived off from this one street must have sacrificed their social standing in so doing.

Yarmouth was settled in 1639 and is the oldest town on the Cape. Its inhabitants in the past have been famous sea-faring folk, and fifty years ago almost every other house was the domicile of a retired sea-captain, and in the days of the sailing vessels the Yarmouth men voyaged the world over. A certain class of them went before the mast, but the majority were ship's officers. A goodly number of the latter amassed wealth in the India and China

trade. This wealth has descended in many instances still intact to the generation of today, and accounts for the town's air of easy-going comfort. But fortunes are no more drawn from the old source, and at present the ambitious youth who aspires to riches turns his eyes cityward. The sea has ceased to promise a bonanza. Even the local fishing industry is wholly dead, though it is only a few decades since the town had quite a mackerel fleet; but the little craft are all gone now, and nothing remains of the old wharves save some straggling lines of black and broken piles reaching out across the broad marshes that lie between the long street and the salt water.

These marshes are of rather more economic importance to modern Yarmouth than the sea itself; for grass and rank sedges cover them and furnish a considerable proportion of the hay that is harvested. I liked to loiter on these wet levels and watch the men swing their scythes. I noticed that they left untouched the coarse grass that grew on the strips of sand. "That's beach grass," said one of the mowers with whom I talked. "The stock won't eat that, nor any other creatures won't eat it that I know of except skunks. Thar's plenty of them chaps along the shore on these ma'shes Me 'n' my dog kitch a lot of 'em here every winter."

The route back to the town from the marsh on which this skunk hunter was at work led across a low ridge of stony pasture-land where the blackberry vines displayed their ruddy autumn foliage and brightened the earth like flashes of flame. A most beautiful little lane threaded along the crest of the ridge. It was only about a dozen feet broad, and was hemmed in by stone walls overgrown with bushes among which rose an occasional tree. The paths trodden by the cows' hoofs wandered irregularly along, avoiding obstructions, and, as a rule, followed the line of the least resistance. There was, however, now and then, a deflection which the cattle had made purposely toward the thickest of the bordering brush, intent on crowding up against the twigs to rid themselves of flies. How shadowy and protected and pastoral the lane was! I envied the boys who drove the cows and thus had the chance to make a daily renewed acquaintance with its arboreal seclusion.

Not far from where the lane emerged on the village street stood a dwelling that I looked at with interest every time I passed. It was a low and primitive structure, and behind it was a little barn surmounted by a sword-fish weather-vane. Sword-fish, or ships, I observed, were the favorite vanes

everywhere for Cape Cod outbuildings. The attraction of this home with its serious air of repose under the shadowing trees, grew, until one day I ventured into the yard. Near the barn a gray-bearded ancient had just hitched a venerable horse into a wagon, and

was preparing to grease the vehicle's wheels. I spoke with him, and after some preliminaries said, "It appears to me that you have about the oldest house in town."

He gave me a sudden look of surprise out of the corner of his eyes. the purport of which I did not at the moment understand, and then went on with his work. "Ye-ye-yes," he replied in his hasty, stammering way; for his thoughts seemed to start ahead of his tongue, and the latter gained control with difficulty. "Ye-ye-yes, he is old, but he's a good hoss yet!"

"Oh, I didn't say horse," I remarked quickly, "I was speaking of your house."

"My h-h-h-house, hm-m-m! That —that's one of the old settlers. Must be two hundred year old; and do you see that pear tree thar with the piece of zinc nailed over the bad place in the trunk, and the iron bands around up where the branches begin, so't they wont split off? I s'pose that pear tree's as old as the house."

"What kind is it?"

"It-it-it it's wha-what we call the old-fashioned button pear. Uncle Peter Thacher that had this place years ago used to pick up the pears and sell 'em to the boys for a cent apiece. They ain't much larger'n wa'nuts. They're kind of a mealy kind of pear, you know—very good when they first drop off, but they rot pretty quick."

The man had finished applying the wheel-grease now, and he clambered into the wagon and drove off, while I walked on. I passed entirely through the village into a half-wild region beyond, where much of the land was covered by a dense pine wood. There were occasional farm clearings; but I noticed that the houses of this outlying district were generally vacant. Opposite one of the deserted homes was a corn-field that attracted my attention because the tops of the cornstalks had been cut off and carted away, and the ears left on the stubs to ripen. This was a common way of treating corn

years ago, but is seldom seen now. Here and there in the field were scarecrows,—sometimes an old coat and hat hoisted on a stake; sometimes a pole with a fluttering rag at the top and, suspended a little lower down on the same pole, a couple of rusty tin cans that rattled together dubiously in the breeze. As I was leaning over the roadside wall contemplating this cornfield, a man came along and accosted me, and I improved the opportunity to ask him why so many of the houses of the neigborhood were unoccupied.

"Wal," said he, "people don't like to live outside o' the villages nowadays. Sence the fishin' give out. the young folks all go off to get work, and they settle somewhar else, and the old folks move into the towns. In this house across the road, though, an old woman lived, and she died thar two years ago. She was kind o' queer, and some

say she wa'n't a woman at all. She wore women's clothes, but she had a beard and shaved every mornin', and her hair was cut short, and she carried on the farm and did the work just like a man."

My acquaintance spit meditatively and then inquired, "Have you seen Hog Island?"

"No," I responded.

"You'd ought to. It ain't fur from to'ther end of Yarmouth village. You go down the lane along the creek thar and ask the way of Jimmy Holton that lives by the bridge. He'll tell you. It aint really an island, but a bunch o' trees in a little ma'sh, and they grow so't if you see 'em from the right place they look just like a hog—snout, tail, and all."

The man had in his hand a large scoop with a row of long wooden teeth projecting from its base. This is the kind of implement used in gathering most of the Cape Cod cranberries, and the man was on his way to a berry patch he cultivated in a boggy hollow not far distant. I accompanied him and found his wife and children on their knees each armed with a scoop with which they were industriously scratching through the low mat of vines. Where they had not yet picked, the little vines were twinkled all over with ripe berries—genuine autumn fruit, waxen-skinned, ruddy hued, and acid to the tongue—as if the atmospheric tartness and coolness had helped the sun to dye and flavor them.

The bog was not at all wild. In preparing it for cranberry culture it had been thoroughly tamed. Brush and stumps had been cleared off and the turf removed. Then it had been leveled and coated with a layer of sand. It was encompassed and more

or less cut across by ditches; and, in the process of clearing, steep banks had been heaved up around the borders.

"Cranberries are a great thing for the Cape," said my friend. "They're the best crop we have, but it's only late years we've gone into 'em. When I was a boy, the only cranberries we used to have was a little sort that growed in the bogs wild; and we never thought nothin' o' dreamin' the marshes and goin' into the business the way we do now.

"My bog aint first class. A man's got to put a lot o' work into raisin' cranberries to do the thing just right; and when you only got a small bog you kind o' neglect it. There's one bog about a mile from here that's got sixteen acres in it, and they're always tendin' to it in one way and another the year around. They keep it clean

744

of weeds, and if there's any sign of fire-bug they steep tobacco and spray the vines. If there's a dry spell they rise the water, though that don't do as much good as it might. You c'n water a plant all you want to, but waterin' won't take the place o' rain.

"Pretty soon after we finish pickin' we flood the bogs, and they stay flooded all winter, if the mushrats don't dig through the banks. The water keeps the plants from freezin', and seems to kind o' fertilize them at the same time. The ponds make grand skatin'-places. They freeze over solid—no weak spots —and they aint deep enough to be dangerous, even if you was to break through."

This man's statement as to the importance of cranberry culture to the dwellers on the Cape was in no wise exaggerated. When I continued my journeyings later to the far end of the

ANCHORING THE HAYSTACKS

peninsula I saw reclaimed berry bogs innumerable. There was scarcely a swampy depression anywhere but that had been ditched and dyked and the body of it layed off as smooth as a floor and planted to cranberries. The pickers were hard at work—only two or three of them on some bogs, and on others a motley score or more. It seemed as if the task engaged the entire population irrespective of age and sex; and the picking scenes were greatly brightened by the presence of the women in their calico gowns and sunbonnets or broad-brimmed straw hats. Often the bogs were far enough from home so that the workers carried their dinners and made the labor an all-day picnic, though I thought the crouching position must grow rather wearisome after a time.

Aside from the fertile and productive bogs the aspect of the Cape was apt to be monotonous and sombre. The cultivated fields appeared meagre and unthrifty, the pastures were thin-grassed and growing up to brush, and, more predominant than anything else in the landscape, were the great tracts of scrubby woodland covered with dwarfed pines and oaks, often fire-ravaged, and never a tree in them of respectable size. Ponds and lakes were frequent. So were the inlets from the sea with their borderings of salt marsh; indeed, the raggedness of the shore line was suggestive of a constant struggle between the ocean and the continent for the possession of this slender ou'reach of the New England coast. The buffeting of the fierce sea winds was evident in the upheave of the sand dunes and the landward tilt of the exposed trees, which had a very human look of

PROVINCETOWN WHARF

small sailing-craft in and about the harbor, and always a number of schooners, and occasionally a larger vessel.

The inhabitants love the sea, or else are involuntarily fascinated by it. They delight to loiter on the wharves and beach, and to sit and look out on old ocean's wrinkled surface and contemplate its hazy mystery. One would fancy they thought it replete with beneficent possibilities and that they were willing lingerers dreamily expecting something fortunate or fateful would heave into view from beyond the dim horizon. The children seek the beach as assiduously as their elders. It is their playground, their newspaper. They poke about the wharves strewn with barrels and boxes, spars, chains, ropes, anchors, etc.; they find treasures in the litter that gathers on the sands; they dig clams on the mud flats; they race and tumble, and they learn all that is going on in the shipping.

The most exciting event while I was in town was an unexpected catch of squids in the harbor. Squids are the favorite bait of the cod fishermen, but at Provincetown there is rarely a chance to get this bait so late in the year. The squids sought the deepest portion of the bay, and a little fleet of small boats collected above and captured them by the barrel. One mid-day I stood watching the boats from a wharf. Two men who had come on to the wharf soon after I did were regarding the scene from near by. "It's queer how them squids hang in that hole thar," said one of the men.

"They bring a good price for cod bait. I believe." said I.

"Yes. Willie Scott that lives next door to me, he made seven dollars this

fear and seemed to be trying to flee from the persecuting gales, but to be retarded by laggard feet.

At the tip of the Cape is Provincetown snugged along the shore, with steep protecting hills at its back. It is a town that has an ancient, old-world look due to its narrow streets with houses and stores and little shops crowded close along the walks. It is a fishy place, odorous of the sea, and the waterside is lined with gray fish-shanties and store-houses. Many spindle-legged wharves reach out across the beach, and there are dories and

OVERHAULING THE FISHING TACKLE

mornin' and he has gone out again. I'll bet his eyes are full of squid juice this minute. The squids don't trouble much that way, but they'll flip up a smeller (that's what we call their arms) and give you a dose once in a while spite of all you can do. It makes your eyes sting, but it don't last long."

"How large are the squids?" I asked.

"Oh, they're small—not much more'n a foot and a half, smellers and all."

The other man now spoke. He was short and dark, had rings in his ears, and his accent was decidedly foreign. "Cap'n Benson," said he to his companion, "I seen the butt end of a squid smeller big as this barrel what I'm settin' on."

Cap'n Benson puffed a few times judiciously at his pipe. "Yes," he acknowledged presently. "there's a good many kinds of squids, and they do

kitch 'em large enough so one'll last a cod schooner for bait a whole v'yage. We only git a little kind here."

The wharf we were on was nearly covered with racks on which a great quantity of salted codfish had been spread to dry, and "Cap'n" Benson informed me there was plenty more fish awaiting curing in the hold of a slender-masted vessel that lay alongside the wharf.

"She's a Grand-Banker," he continued, indicating the vessel. "We aint got but six Grand-Bankers now, and only fifteen fresh fishermen. The fresh fishermen you know don't go farther'n the Georges and the West Banks. Forty years ago we had two hundred fishing schooners in the town and we had sixty-seven whale ships where now we got only three. Provincetown is played out. This mornin' me and this man with me didn't have

but one hour's work, and we won't
have over two hours this afternoon.
How you goin' to make a livin' at
twenty cents an hour with things goin'
on that way? Forty years ago you
couldn't get enough men at three dollars and a half a day."

The man with the earrings had
picked up a piece of shell and was attempting to drop it from the height of
his shoulder through a crack in the
wharf. He failed to accomplish his
purpose though he tried again and
again.

"Mr. Klunn, if you want to drop`
that shell through thar, just mention the minister," advised "Cap'n"
Benson.

He had hardly spoken when Mr.
Klunn let the shell fall, and it slipped
straight through the crack. "By Godfrey!" exclaimed the Cap'n, "I did it
for you. I never known that to fail.
When I been whaling, and we was
cuttin' up a whale, you couldn't
sometimes strike a j'int. You'd try
and try and you couldn't strike it, and
then you'd stop and say, 'Minister!'
and it was done already—you'd hit it
right off."

"I seen a whale heave up a shark
the half as big as a dory," remarked
Mr. Klunn after a pause.

"To be sure," the "Cap'n" commented. "Howsomever there's people say
a whale can't take nothin' bigger'n a
man's hand; but I guess that's after
he's been eatin' and had all he wanted.

"By gosh! a whale got a swallow so
big enough, if he hungry, he swallow
a man easy." Mr. Klunn declared.
"Some people ain't believe about Jo-
nah, but they believe if they seen as
much whales that I have."

"I'm thinkin' about them squids,"

PROVINCETOWN STREET

Cap'n Benson said as he shook his pipe
free from ashes and slipped it into the
pocket of his jacket. "I guess when
the tide comes in to-night I'll haul out
my boat and see if I can't get some of
'em."

"I aint had no boat sence the big
storm," observed the man with earrings.

"What storm was that?" I inquired.

"It was when the Portland went
down in November, 1899," explained
"Cap'n Benson. We had a awful time,
—wharves smashed, boat houses carried off, and vessels wrecked. It begun
to blow in the night. Fust thing I
knowed of it was my chimley comin'
down."

"I was sick that time," said the earring man. "The doctor had to give me murphine pills. I was in bed two three days, and I lose 187 dollars by the storm. You remember that schooner, Cap'n Benson, what the two old mens were drownded on?"

"Oh, I remember—washed overboard out here in the harbor, and the wind took the schooner bang up agin a wharf, and the Cap'n, he made a jump and landed all right; and he never stopped to look behind to see what become of the vessel nor nobody. He run up into the town and he took the next train for California."

"Yas, that's true," Mr. Klunn affirmed.

Later, while stopping over night at a Truro farmhouse a few miles back on the Cape, I heard more of the great storm. "Thar was three days of it," said my landlady, "startin' on Saturday. It thundered and lightened on Sunday and it snowed Monday. Everythin' that wa'n't good'n strong was blowed down. It blowed the shed off the end of our house, and it blowed a window in upstairs, and it blowed the saddle board off the roof and some o' the shingles. We had the highest tide we've ever had and there was places where the sea-water come across the roads. Monday the bodies begun to be washed ashore from the Portland, and they kept comin' in for two weeks."

Truro is a scattered little country place. Its homes dot every protected hollow. The only buildings that seemed independent of the smiting of the winter blasts were the town hall and the Baptist, Methodist, and Catholic churches. These stood in a group on a bare, bleak hilltop. The churchyards were thickly set with graves, and

VILLAGE WATCHMAKER'S SIGN

among the stones grew little tangles of sumachs and other bushes, but the sandy height had not a single tree.

On this hill, years ago, stood still another public institution—a windmill. "It sot high up thar so't it was in sight all over town," said my landlady. "You could see the miller puttin' the sails on the arms, and then when they got to turnin' we'd know which way the wind blowed. But some days there wouldn't be no wind, and the sails might hang there and not turn the whole day long. We used to raise this yaller Injun corn then a good deal more'n we do now on the Cape, and we raised rye, and we'd take the grain to the mill to grind. You can't buy no such corn meal or rye meal now as we used to get from that old mill. We e't hasty pudding them days, and it used to be so nice! and we had Johnny-cake and hasty-pudding bread."

"Hasty-pudding   bread — what's that?" I asked.

"It was made by putting some of the hasty-pudding into flour and mixing 'em up into dough together. We didn't have yeast then like we use now. Instead o' that we had what we called 'emptyin's' that I s'pose come from dregs of beer or other liquor got sometime at a distillery; but they kep' emptyin's fermentin' to use makin' bread at every farmhouse, and if yourn run out you could always get some at the neighbor's to start again. We'd stir up the dough and set it behind the stove to rise, and our emptyin's bread would be light as could be."

Of the churches on the hill the Catholic was the newest. It was a little shed of a building with a gilt cross surmounting the front gable. The attendants were chiefly Portuguese, the nationality which at present constitutes the great majority of the coast fisherfolk. Most of the fishing is done in rowboats, and the fish are caught in nets fastened to lines of stakes off shore. These fish-traps, as they are called, are visited daily. The crew of a rowboat usually consists of a "Cap'n" who is pretty sure to be a Yankee, and seven men who are likely to be all Portuguese. Truro had four rowboats thus manned. They started out at three in the morning and returned anywhere from noon to eight in the evening.

"It's hard work," explained my landlady, "and the Yankee men don't take up fishin' late years the way they did. I reckon they c'n make more money farmin'."

I wondered at this. The sandy soil did not look productive, and yet the houses, as a rule, were painted and in good repair and conveyed a pleasing impression of prosperity. The people with whom I talked seemed to be satisfied. "We git good crops," said a farmer I questioned about agricultural affairs. "We c'n raise most all kinds o' vegetables in the hollers, and good grass, too, though our heaviest crops o' grass we git off'n the marshes. The cows like salt hay fully as well as they do fresh hay, and they like sedge best of all, because its sweet; but you have to be careful about feedin' 'em too much of it, or the milk'll taste. Of course we got plenty o' pasture on the higher ground and plenty o' timber sich as 'tis. The trees don't flourish, though, and you won't find many that are much bigger'n your leg. This is a great country for wild berries,—blueberries, blackberries, and huckleberries. Our Portuguese here—land! they git half their livin' in the woods. Besides berries there's beach plums and wild cherries. But the cherries we don't use for common eatin'. We put 'em up in molasses and they kind o' work and are good to take for the stomach and the like o' that."

I climbed over the hills round about Truro and tramped the sandy, deeply-rutted roads faithfully. It was weary work to one used to solid earth. Such lagging progress! I could never get a good grip with my feet and slipped a little backward every time I took a step forward. Except along the watercourses nature's growths never attained the least exuberance. The grass on the slopes and uplands was very thin, and with the waning of the season much of it had become wispy and withered. It was mingled with goldenrod and asters that hugged the earth on such short, stunted stems as to be hardly recognizable.

The landscape, as viewed from a height, had a curiously unstable look. Its form had not been moulded by attrition, but the soil had been blown into vast billows that had the appearance of a troubled sea whose waves were on the point of advancing and overwhelming the habitations and all the green growing things in the vales. Some of the dunes really do advance, and the state has been obliged to make appropriations and devise means for checking their depredations. The work has chiefly been accomplished with the aid of beach grass. This has an affiliation for sand, and you can stick one of its coarse wiry tufts in anywhere and it will grow. It only needs to be methodically planted, and the shifting dunes are fast bound and the winds asail them in vain.

Some of the characteristics of this beach grass seem also to be characteristics of the people of the Cape. They have the same hardinesss and endurance, and, like the beach grass, have adapted themselves to their environment and thrive where most would fail. With its omnipresent sand and dwarf woods, the Cape, as I saw it at the fag end of the year, appeared rather

A LONE PICKER

dreary, but the prosperous look of the homes was very cheering. These are nearly all owned free from debt, and that nightmare of the agriculturists in so many parts of New England—a mortgage—is, happily, almost unknown among the Cape Cod folks.

NOTE COUNTERFEITER'S WORKSHOP

The Secret Service

By W. Herman Moran

CIVILIZED governments the world over maintain, as essential adjuncts, corps of trained investigators to cope with violators of the National or Federal laws. Under foreign governments this work is centralized—surveillance over criminals of every class being exacted of the one bureau— while in this country independent organizations, employing experts in the detection of specific offenses, are attached to the several executive departments. The effectiveness of this plan of pitting specialist against specialist has been satisfactorily demonstrated. Though the operation of all these bureaus are secret, but one such organi-

zation is entitled to the official designation "Secret Service"—a permanent and valuable branch of the Treasury Department, charged with the duty of keeping Uncle Sam's money clean from imitation.

Counterfeiting money is not original with this generation. Man's cupidity induced this crime in America as early as 1752; yet it does not appear to have become sufficiently prevalent to require recognition by the Government until 1860, when Congress appropriated ten thousand dollars for its suppression, to be expended under the direction of the Secretary of the Treasury. This sum was doled out as rewards to private detectives, municipal officers, and

NOTE COUNTERFEITER'S WORKSHOP—ENGRAVER'S ROOM

others instrumental in bringing to trial and punishment persons engaged in bogus money making. A similar course was pursued for several years. Meanwhile the Government was forced to issue paper money, or "Greenbacks," to meet the extraordinary expenses incident to the Civil War, and these notes were being counterfeited to such an alarming extent, it was realized that measures more effective must be employed. To that end, in July, 1864, the regular appropriation was increased to $100,000, and with this the Solicitor of the Treasury, who had been charged with the supervision and direction of the work, gathered about him a corps of men experienced in criminal investigations to be entrusted with the task of suppressing this output of spurious currency. So successfully did this plan operate that it resulted in the establishment of a permanent bureau to be thereafter known as the "Secret Service." Information as to the personnel and operations of this service is carefully guarded against publicity, a precaution to which much of its effectiveness is attributable.

The United States is divided into twenty-seven Secret Service districts, each in charge of an operative who has under his direction as many assistants as the criminal activity of his section demands. A written daily report, covering operations for twenty-four hours, is exacted of every operative. Many fascinating stories are contained in the bound volumes of these reports filed in

COIN COUNTERFEITER'S WORKSHOP

HEAVY PRESS FOR MINTING QUARTERS

the Chief's office at Washington, and the collection of photographs in the service "Rogues Gallery" would afford phrenologists and physiognomists ample opportunity to test their power.

It is not expected that the crime of counterfeiting will ever be wholly suppressed, but the Government depends upon the Secret Service to reduce it to a minimum, and, in its thirty-six years existence, this bureau has handled more than twenty thousand spurious money makers and distributors.

The development of modern processes of photo-lithography, photogravure, and etching has revolutionized the note counterfeiting industry. In the old days all counterfeiting plates were hand engraved, and it took from eight to fifteen months to complete a set. Now this part of the work consumes but a few hours. The famous Philadelphia-Lancaster conspiracy of two years ago is one of the rare instances in recent years of the employment of hand engraved plates, and, even in this case, photography laid the foundation for the work. This change of method on the part of the counterfeiter necessitated the abandonment of the old lines on which the Secret Service had conducted its investigations and the mapping out of new ones applicable to changed conditions; the fact that the yearly average of arrests has suffered no diminution would seem to indicate that these new lines are as effective as the old.

Counterfeiting is acknowledged to be the meanest of crimes, because the resultant loss most often falls on those least able to bear it. It is not confined to any particular locality, the officer operating in country districts being kept as busily employed as his city brother. The ranks of those who indulge in it are recruited from every race and condition of man. One day you may return home from your business to find that the neighbor with whom you had spent many pleasant social hours and who was considered in every way worthy your confidence and esteem, has been conducting a private mint, and is now under arrest with every prospect of a long term in the penitentiary before him.

Charles H. Smith, one of the most expert and prolific engravers of false money plates, was, until detected and arrested, a highly respected citizen of Brooklyn, New York. His residence adjoined that of a prominent city official, and the two men had frequently engaged in a friendly game of croquet on the lawn.

In the neighborhood where he resided in Detroit, Michigan, David Johnson was looked upon as a model of propriety in all that constitutes the honest, upright, dependable citizen, and as he was prominently identified with church work and musical affairs, the community was the more shocked and surprised when one morning, late in the summer of 1898, he and his brother Edmond, also highly respected, were placed under arrest charged with counterfeiting. The evidence found secreted in their homes, established beyond question their responsibility for the existence of certain dangerous counterfeit notes which the Government officers had been endeavoring to trace to their source for nearly eight years. The history of this case is interesting:—In September, 1890, one of the Treasury money experts discovered in a remittance from a Missouri bank a counterfeit two dollar silver certificate so nearly like the genuine as almost to defy detection.

The Secret Service went to work immediately, but, try as they might, could get no clue to the criminal. Every counterfeiter known to possess sufficient ability to do the work was located and investigated without results; the spurious notes meanwhile continued coming in with aggravating regularity. It was finally determined to recall the genuine issue of these counterfeits and replace them with notes of different design. The unknown culprit was not to be outdone, however, and it was but a short while after the first of these new bills was issued that its counterfeit was discovered in circulation. The counterfeiter had followed the government's move and refused to be checkmated.

On several occasions the officers felt assured that they were near a solution of the vexatious problem, only to discover in the suspect one of the numerous victims of the real culprit innocently assisting in circulating the counterfeits. One such incident occurred at Toledo, Ohio: The Secret Service agent on duty there was called to the telephone one morning in the Spring of 1898, and informed that a stranger had just passed a counterfeit two dollar note on a nearby tobacconist. On arriving at the place a few moments later, he was told of a tall, blonde, heavy-set, well-dressed man, sporting a large diamond stud in his shirt-front, coming into the store and paying for twenty-five cents worth of cigars with a two dollar bill which he abstracted from a large roll of notes taken from his right-hand trousers pocket. When shown the bill in question the agent immediately recognized it as one of the

troublesome silver ceritficates, and lost no time in going in search of the passer.

Hurrying in the direction taken by the man, he canvassed the various restaurants and business houses for several blocks without success, and was about to take a car for the depot to look through a train due to depart in ten minutes, when he espied the object of his search coming out of a haberdashery on the next block.

Quickening his pace, stopping long enough at the furnishing goods store to ascertain that a two dollar bill had been used in making some purchases, and to request that it be laid aside until his return, he was right behind his man when the latter turned into a saloon at the corner. While the suspect was drinking his glass of beer the officer stepped up to the bar and asked for change for a twenty dollar bill. The bartender could not accommodate him, but as had been hoped the stranger volunteered to make the change. Drawing from his pocket quite a roll of money he carefully counted out three fives, two twos, and a one, and adding the twenty to what remained, returned it to his pocket. The agent stepped outside to examine the change, and, much to his disappointment found all the bills genuine. He did not entirely abandon hope however, and when his man appeared in the doorway he was requested to accompany the officer back to the tobacco store and explain the possession of a counterfeit note. Disclaiming any knowledge of a counterfeit, the man readily agreed to return. En route a stop was made at the furnishing store. The bill here was also genuine. At the tobacco store, after the stranger had acknowledged paying the bill in question to the proprietor and had made good by substituting genuine money, he handed the officer his roll with the request that it be examined for other counterfeits at the same time, admitting his inability to discriminate between imitations so good as that he had just redeemed and the lawful currency. All his other money was genuine, and the officer, with visions of glory and promotion dispelled, returned to the office.

In July, following the above incident, Charles Johnson, an old and expert counterfeiter, who had just completed a term of twelve years in a Canadian prison for imitating the Dominion two and four dollar notes, arrived at the home of his sister, Mrs. Baylis, with whom Edmond was also residing, on McGraw street, Detroit. Then, for the first time, the friends and neighbors of David and Edmond learned of their relationship to this notorious individual.

As is customary in all such cases, the Secret Service was advised of Johnson's release and destination, and a few weeks later, when it was reported that a man whose description tallied with his had passed a counterfeit half dollar in a saloon on Woodward Avenue, the officers secured search warrants for the McGraw Street house, expecting to find the coin mill. Much to their astonishment, while looking through a closet on the second floor, a plank was discovered which bore unmistakable evidence of having been used in the process of "aging" notes. This find led to a more thorough inspection of the premises, and one of the officers, noticing that the baseboard in the closet was loose, inserted his knife in the space between the board and the floor, accidentally pressing against an ingeniously contrived lever, which forced a section of the board out from the wall, disclosing the hiding place of over two thousand dollars in spurious two dollar silver certificates.

Edmond and Charles Johnson and Mrs. Baylis were immediately placed under arrest, and enough information was obtained to warrant a search of David's residence. This was proceeded with at once, resulting in the finding of a panel like that in the other house, concealing the plates from which the first issue of counterfeits was printed and more than three thousand dollars of the notes. It was learned that David and his wife were visiting relatives near Blenheim, Canada, and an officer was dispatched to arrest and bring them back.

The mysterious source of these notable counterfeits had at last been discovered, and but one thing remained to complete the officers' work—to secure the plates from which the second issue was printed. These could not be found, though the two houses were thoroughly searched from cellar to garret. The hiding place of the plates might have been a mystery until to-day had it not been for a strange strain of chivalry in the natures of the Johnson brothers.

Realizing, as they did, that the women members of the family were apt to suffer from their connection with the case—remote though it might be—they notified the Government officers, after a consultation, that if an arrangement could be made looking to the release of Mrs. Baylis and Mrs. Johnson, they would surrender the plates. The offer was not a surprise to the Government. There had been previous exhibitions of this same sentiment. In 1864, when the entire family, consisting of father, mother, four sons and two daughters, were arrested at Indianapolis for dealing in spurious currency, the men persistently asserted the innocence of the women and, to obtain their release, one of the boys acknowledged responsibility for the existence of a counterfeit twenty dollar note and agreed to turn over the plates. A number of years later, when the family again came under the ban, the father, to insure freedom for wife and daughters, imparted to the Government information of the whereabouts of plates for several dangerous counterfeits.

In the Detroit case, while the evidence against the women was not conclusive, it was sufficiently suggestive to warrant their temporary detention; but when the Johnsons' proposition was presented, the Government promptly accepted it, and Edmond was turned over to the officers to act as guide.

Going first to the McGraw Street house he led the way to a bed-room on the second floor, and rolling the oak washstand out from the wall, proceeded to withdraw two of the screws which held the ornamental back piece in place. Raising the loose end of this back piece, he cut away some oak stained putty and removed a small piece of wood, disclosing a mortised space in the top board of the washstand. From this slot he drew out, by a string attached, the back and seal plates neatly wrapped in oiled linen.

For the face plate it was necessary to go to David's home. Mrs. Johnson's sewing machine was here used as

a hiding place. Lying on his back, under the machine, Edmond unscrewed a small cabinet of drawers and placed it on the floor. In a space hollowed out of the top board of the cabinet was the plate.

The history of this family of Johnsons might be advanced as an argument in support of the theory that the criminal instinct is hereditary. Three generations of counterfeiters is their record, and, with the arrest of David and Edmond, prison doors have closed upon the entire membership of this generation.

In a majority of cases arrests by the Service are so planned as to make resistance impossible, the element of surprise being employed to secure this result. But at times a show of force becomes necessary, calling for quick and determined action on the part of the officers. On several such occasions tragedies have been narrowly averted. A case in point was the breaking up of the notorious "Horse Market" gang of New York City: The Secret Service agents had succeeded in arresting individual members of this gang while engaged in "shoving the queer," but it yet remained to locate and shut off the source of supply. Frank, alias "Conkey" Carr, an ex-convict, was suspected as the maker, and when it was ascertained that he resided at No. 95 Fourth Avenue a close watch was placed upon the house. Albert Brown, better known as "Bill the Brute," a desperate character, and Harry Kingden spent much of their time at Carr's, and these two were, on several occasions, shadowed to Staten Island and other near-by places, where they passed counterfeit dollars.

At the end of three weeks it was

decided that ample evidence had been secured to warrant making the arrests. When the raiding party which included Operatives Bagg, Callaghan, and Flynn arrived in the vicinity of Carr's home they were informed by Assistant Stanley, who was on watch, that Kingden had just gone down Fourth Avenue, but that the others were upstairs. Leaving Stanley outside to pick up Kingden, the other three quickly ascended the stairs to the second floor, forced open the door to the rear room and surprised Carr, Brown, and Carr's wife, Belle, putting the finishing touches to a batch of coins. Carr bolted through an open window to the fire escape and Flynn started in pursuit. Brown and Belle Carr rushed at Callaghan and Bagg and for a few minutes there was a lively fight around the room, becoming so fierce that the woman was soon forced to retire. Brown, at last overcome, fell on the bed with both officers on top of him. During the lull which followed, the apparently much exhansted coiner called to the woman to bring him a drink of water, but when the officers relaxed their hold sufficiently to enable him to raise on his elbow he suddenly drew from his hippocket a revolver and placed the muzzle against Callaghan's stomach before it was realized what he was about. Striking the weapon aside just as the trigger was pulled, Bagg, with Calla-

ghan's assistance, quickly disarmed and handcuffed the infuriated criminal. Meanwhile, what had happened to "Conkey" Carr? Upon reaching the fire escape, he crawled along to the adjoining house and clambered into the window, closely followed by Flynn; breaking into the rear flat he reached a window opening on Third Avenue. Below was a grocery store with a vegetable stand on the sidewalk and projecting meat hooks. Taking in these difficulties and jumping far out to avoid them, Carr landed heavily on the pavement breaking both ankles. Thus disabled, Flynn found him and had him removed to the hospital.

After gathering up the counterfeit coins and other portable evidence, Bagg and Callaghan started with their prisoners down the stairs. About half way down they met Flynn returning from his chase after Carr. "Bill the Brute," taking advantage of the crowded condition of the stairway, made an effort to escape. Breaking away from Bagg he sprang at Flynn, who was in front of him, and struck the latter a heavy blow with his manacled wrists. But he reckoned without his host, for Flynn promptly returned the blow, flooring Brown, and he was landed in jail without further trouble. Stanley found Kingden in a near-by store, where he had been sent to purchase plaster of Paris, and had no difficulty in placing him behind the bars.

Aftermath

By Charlotte Becker

AH, faith that once I kept, belief
  Is hard to kill, and sorrow long—
Yet I was mute till after grief—
  I lost delight to gain a song!

Pygmalion

By Zitella Cocke

I WONDERED much that marble cold and stern
  Its obduracy could forget, and turn
To warm and palpitating flesh, and move
With life, responsive to Pygmalion's love,—
A fancy strange, methought, that subtle Greek,
Grown mad with thirst for beauty, fain would seek!

Yet Greek, thou'rt wise, and fond Pygmalion's love,
Though born of fable, doth thy wisdom prove,—
Thy thought, far-reaching, hath discerned the truth.
Immortal and eternal, hid forsooth
From surface resting sight, but plain to him
Who would God's writing read, though it be dim!

For in the wide and goodly universe,
Love's rule is mightiest, and primal curse
Shall from its priestly hands in blessing fall,
Since Love hath ever been, and shall be all!
Earth shall dissolve like pageantry of dreams,
Love only shall remain of all that seems!

Hartman

By Frank Baird

THE fact that Hartman taught the class in color should not be set down as a proof that he knew nothing about art. There were things Hartman knew, and things he did not know. But the really outstanding thing about Hartman was neither his knowledge nor his ignorance, but his ambition. That, to all sensible people, covered the multitude of his sins. And yet it was this commendable side of his nature that afterwards pushed him into strange difficulties.

The only other thoroughly ambitious man on the staff was Du Vernet. He liked Hartman because he understood him; and then most people hated him. Further, Hartman had pledged himself in a whole-souled, serious way to art; he hated men; women were an abomination to him. To Du Vernet this spelled genius. He believed in people who were strong enough to hate what most men loved. He took their part; they were true artists. He said they would do things before they died. In this latter contention Du Vernet was right—for Hartman did many things before he died—long before.

The term had slipped around to within a fortnight of its close. Du Vernet had wandered into Hartman's quarters where both comfortably smoked. A tourist map of Europe that lay on the table showed a long zig-zagging line drawn with a pencil.

It began at London, touched Paris, Rome, Naples, Florence, Milan, Munich, Dresden, and ended at The Hague.

"Claye," Du Vernet said, "was telling me last night it was generally believed you were to marry when abroad." Hartman swung his feet from the table and faced his friend.

"Claye," he said; "Claye told you that?"

Du Vernet laughed.

"Yes; was he right?"

"I had some regard for Claye once. Before that woman came he was an artist; now he's only a man."

Hartman replaced his feet on the table, drew himself a little lower into his deep chair, then for some moment he blew drifts of smoke at the ceiling

"Claye is of the class who think a man may be a papa—and a painter. Du Vernet laughed a low, pleased laugh.

Hartman's eyes found the range on the single picture in the room—a small Turner. When he had looked—and smoked—for a time, he spoke again.

"If they knew about Claye's new girl in heaven, she'd die wouldn't she?"

Du Vernet again filled the pause with a low, contented laugh. Hartman was at his best tonight. He would let him talk.

" 'Goodness is beauty! Beauty is a matter of æsthetic individualism—the thing for a time some men imagine to be beautiful!' And there are sane men as well as fools like Claye who think this. It's all drivel—Beauty is beauty." He rose quickly as if to emphasise his words. " 'Goodness is beauty!' "—the Devil! Beauty is beauty; and the man who is in earnest about art doesn't marry. Tell Claye that."

He threw his cigar-butt viciously towards the grate. Then he bent over the tourist map. He did not speak, but after a time he fumbled for his pencil. He drew a line from Interlaken to Grindlewald.

"Should be some subtle color effects there among those mountains," he said half to himself; "especially up where the air is thin. Something done up there would be new—sure."

He turned his back on the table and took a step or two towards the Turner on the wall.

"When is Claye to marry that divinity of his?" he said, still studying the picture before him.

"In the autumn I believe. She goes abroad some time during summer—to Paris I understand for —" Hartman waved his hand understandingly. A little later he said:

"Claye! the poor devil!"

As Du Vernet went home that night he settled on Hartman as one of the friends he intended to keep.

Three months later Hartman had come out of Italy into Switzerland. He had been faithful to art from The Louvre to Naples and from Naples to Lucerne. The sight of some Alpine peaks as the train emerged from the St. Gothard had set him on fire. He would go up and out-Turner Turner. He chose the Wetterhorn and went straight to Grindlewald. Pilatus, Jungfrau, even the Matterhorn, meant Railways,

crowds, no pleasure. But the chaste virginity of the Wetterhorn—that appealed to him. No shrieking locomotive panted up there to profane the place; there was no *funicalare*. Cameras did not go up thereon; no paper bags would be found there—for which reasons Hartman chose the aforesaid peak—the Wetterhorn.

"There are two ladies and a gentleman up as far as the Club House," the proprietor of "The Bear" said as the coach carrying Hartman drove off. "They went up yesterday."

When Hartman turned there was a severe look in his face. What he said did not really violate any of the canons of language; but it was not good English he spoke. What if some of these people wished to talk just when color effects were finest? Hartman spent two-thirds of the three hours it took the coach to climb the foot hills in silently swearing. The other third he swore audibly to the guides.

It was still early when he was set down near the small mountain hut that had been charitably dignified at the hotel below with the name of Club House. In a few moments the door opened and a woman came out. She advanced at once toward Hartman. "I—I—didn't we cross the Atlantic together—in March?—on the *Oceanic?*" She extended her hand. Hartman's face relaxed some. The artist in him swore; but the man smiled.

"Of course we did; but what in—blazes brings you up here?" I came here to be—to be—"

Wasn't there something subtle in the way the ground had been laid for her eyes? Wasn't there—?

"I came with Uncle and Aunt," she broke in vivaciously, while he hesitated. "I'm so glad of this. You'll help me to persuade them to go on up won't you?"

"I—" As he looked into her face more thoughts about color effects came to him. She was fresh from a long mountain sleep. She had the strong, pure look of wild things.

"I didn't—expect to find—" "But uncle must get up," she said. "I'll go and hurry him."

The next instant she was gone through the low door of the hut, and he was alone with his confusion. He thought some; but not profane thoughts.

The coach was sent back to the hotel, and the party gave themselves entirely into the hands of the guides. A single rope was used to which each person was securely tied, one of the guides leading and the other being in the rear. For some time the ascent was easy but it soon grew more difficult. Ice appeared and this in places was covered with mud. But in a short time this treacherous covering disappeared and the "footing" improved.

If Hartman had thought that his companions would soon tire and wish to return, by noon he had changed his mind. Mountain climbing has strange ambition-stirring effects. Each new point attained means new desires and still braver resolves. To each member of the party the wish to go on strengthened as the view widened. Then there were the keen, pure buoyancy of the delightful air, the newness of it all, the heroism, the danger!

Hartman grew momentarily more content. The thinning air, he noted, had strengthened and sharpened the lines about the mountain peaks. The light on the green and gray in the far-down valley was becoming more sensitive and elusive. The peep of a distant lake just coming into the picture between two horns of mountain away to the south half maddened him. He had seen many galleries—this effect never. It was new. To get it meant fame. That in the distance;—then this frank, unconventional, piece of breathing art beside him. He had not seen this in galleries either. Were the effects in this case due also to atmospheric conditions? Why had he not noticed before the large liberal way in which her face was cut? The perilous brevity of her gray, mountain-climbing skirt convinced him that her entire figure was done in the same spirit of splendid negligence that always meant perfection. Then there were the bold proportionings of the features, the sweeping Greek lines about the cheek and chin, the firm sure chisel with which the brow and neck had been done, the nervous delicacy in the cutting of the nose and lips, the full magnificent daring of the breast— these things were not due to altitude; they could not be. Was it because he had spent some days before masterpieces down in Italy that he now saw their counterparts in a woman—an American woman of his own City? Why was it that he was not alone with that distant lake—and yet he was content?

In mountain climbing time does not pass—it drops out in blocks. What Hartman said within himself was noon, his watch said was three o'clock. The party had come to the bottom of a long roof-like reach of ice. It was agreed to ascend this diagonally. At the top a stand would be made for rest and refreshment.

But not all plans made are carried out. This one was not. When a little more than half up the slope Hartman felt a fierce twitch at the rope about him. His companion—the American girl next to him on the line—had fallen. The next instant Hartman was off his feet. The guides drove their picks fiercely into the ice. For a moment the cord held—for a moment only—then snapped. The guides clung to the precipice but the others of the party were swept madly down the great glistening roof of ice.

Some five hundred feet below, a projecting horn of rock caught the rope about at its centre. It snapped again owing to the weight of Hartman and the American girl on one side and the other two of the party on the other. They were hurled on down the steeping slope. A few moments after the breaking of the rope and the final separating of the party into two, Hartman saw his companion plunge over a precipice; the next instant he was on its brink—then over. But it was less high than he had feared. The slope at its base was also less steep for a time than that above; but it dipped suddenly, and a glimpse down it showed jagged horns of rock protruding from the ice. Down this the two persons swept with terrific and accelerating force. Surely death lurked at the bottom. Might it not meet either—or both—by the way?

Hartman saw the tumbling figure in front of him pause for a moment then again disappear behind the rim of another precipice. She was still alive. He shuddered at the thought—of when he might see her—if he were alive to see her again. Was she—were they both—on the brink of doom? At any rate, that instant another savage twitch at the rope about him, brought him to the brink of a precipice. Some fifteen minutes later he was applying ice to the woman's forehead at the bottom of a gully over a thousand feet deep. He drew off his coat and pillowed her head upon it. Blood from a scalp wound oozed through her heavy hair. One hand was crushed and bloody. Mud and mountain slime almost hid the beautiful face. The shock had been tremendous; but there was still life. The lips quivered apart, the spirit of life that seemed to have gone out and hovered in the air above her for a time, not knowing whether to seek earth again—or heaven—stole back under the breast and sent it once more faintly ebbing and flowing.

At the sight Hartman's own pulse quickened. He felt his own blood throb warmly up about his temples. When the lids lifted showing the quiet blue grays of the eyes, the cold sick feeling left him. He felt to the full some of the joys of being alive—and of being there. But it was for her first to speak.

"Are you hurt?" she ventured, "I must get—".

But he forced her head gently back. He bent lower over her, and, with his handkerchief removed some of the mountain mud that threatened the red of her parted lips.

"You must remain quiet for a little," he said; "you are injured. I must bind this handkerchief about your head."

With a murmured protest she sunk back quietly abandoning herself to him. The pressure of her weight, the touch of her flesh, the warmth of her breath,—these things, instead of being the signal for the uprising of a host of wicked imaginings, now thrilled and elevated him to a plane of chivalrous nobleness, upon which it was not his habit to move. Something stung him suddenly into greatness. Why had these keen, delightful feelings not come to him before? He was not a man trained in ways of gentleness; but something within taught his manly fingers a soft nimbleness that made them feminine. He lifted the heavy hair from the high brow; then he bound up the wound.

"It is kind—good of you," she said softly, as he finished. At her words his heart throbbed up towards his mouth. More new feelings woke within him.

She made another attempt and raised herself to a sitting posture. With her unwounded hand she smoothed the folds of her dress, pushing her skirt further down. Then she drew her feet closer under it. But at this movement Hartman noticed symptoms of keen pain furrow her face. Were there bones broken? Must he —She sank suddenly back, cutting short what from a man would have been a groan.

"My ankle—my foot—oh—" She drew her right knee, slowly, painfully upward. The sharp marks of suffering again showed on her face.

"Your—foot—is it broken, do you think? May I?—I must take off your —boot," he stammered.

She drew both her feet still closer and again made to push her skirt lower.

"No, no," she said; "you must not— oh, my foot hurts drea—dreadfully.".

He drew his arm in a gentle rough way from beneath her head. He was frantic to do things.

"May I—"

"No, no, you must not do—anything. It would not be—and I do not know you."

"I must take off your boot," he said half sternly. "I must see what your injury is and help you."

The firmer note in his voice was not unwelcome to her. Now she might yield. A moment later her slender stockinged foot was warm in his hands. Was it pain—or what—that seemed to pluck it away from him? The dreadfulness of the situation made him sensible. "Your ankle is sprained," he said; "I must splinter it."

He released the foot, and the next instant the gray skirt hid it. He gathered some bits of wood, then ripped a sleeve from his shirt and quickly tore it into shreds. He placed the pieces of wood on either side of the quick swelling ankle and bound them strongly to it.

When Hartman tied the last knot, drops of sweat stood on his forehead. When she thanked him and repeated that he was kind he felt like leaping the precipice in front and dashing himself to pieces to show her how much more he was willing to do. But he didn't; he only felt like doing it.

"Will you now bind my hand?" she said; "the bleeding one—it's cold." He tied his other shirt sleeve awkwardly about her hand.

"Are you sure you are not hurt yourself? Could I not now do something—"

She suddenly fell silent. At the end of the pause he noticed her lip tremble. Her eyes wandered up the mountain slope.

"Uncle," she said—"and aunt are killed, I suppose." The tension of pain was gone. For a long time in a refined, subdued way, she wept.

Hartman was silent. It was his first opportunity for thinking since that savage twitch at the rope about his waist far up the mountain.

They were almost at the bottom of a great cup in the heart of the Alps. The rocks rose on every side but the one down which they had slid, steep as the walls of a Cathedral. The water from the melting ice above dripped continually. Now and then stones, clay, and immense ice boulders thundered down. Just in front, and far below, a few yards of a savage muddy stream showed as it raced along the bottom of the gorge. Conflicting cross-currents of warm and cold air drew fitfully up and down the great gully. Shattered tree-trunks, huge boulders of rock, blocks of ice, mountain herbs and grass that had been hurled down from the heights to the top of the glacier, branches of trees, sand, gravel, mud—the scarpings of the mountains for years—piled in the wildest confusion were the only things that met Hartman's eyes as he looked about. He hit upon a nook in the rock where it was both dry and safe from the falling débris. He collected some grass and branches of trees. Then he approached his companion.

"You are in danger here," he said; "you must move."

She did not speak, but she rose. Her breast still heaved; tears had cut white gruesome looking channels through the mud and blood stains on her face. She had come almost to an upright position, when, with a sudden shriek she sank limp and heavy back upon him. He bore her strongly to the sheltered nook in the cliff; then laid her gently upon the hurriedly made bed of twigs and mountain grass.

"I had forgotten—I put my weight on it suddenly. That was why I fainted. It was very stupid of me to—but how did I get here? Did I walk?"

He wiped the last of the blood and mud stains from her face.

"How did I get here?" and this time it was a demand.

"I carried you."

Her eyes looked a severe rebuke upon him. Then the sense of her helplessness came to her as not before.

"You will not leave me, will you," she said.

He wiped her high Greek brow in a gentle way that would have done for a caress.

"No," he said, softly; "No, I'll not go away. I'll stay here."

A silence fell again, and again Hartman felt and thought some. He hung above like a mother over the pillow of her sick child. Something whispered, "Pray;" but he would not be so womanly. Then Hartman never prayed. Night began to settle slowly. What about food, rescue—everything? He looked up. All about were rocks, mud, ice. Down below the stream bellowed louder than before; away at the top, a full mile above them, the sun still silver-plated the irregular brim of the giant cup down the side of which they had slid. On above that was the blue.

The woman fell into a tired sleep. When the moon climbed over the rim of the mountain and lit her face Hartman's breath came short and uncertainly. He had spent four of the greatest hours of his life in dumb enjoyment at Florence before Michael

Angelo's sleeping figure "La Notte." That was marble—this was flesh. That was cold—this was warm. That was art—this was art—and more. This needed him, depended upon him, trusted him. It was this latter sense that gave the keen intensity to his pleasure which he had not felt at Florence. Where had this new force that was overmastering him lain through the years? Had he not been wrong in thinking that art had stirred his nature to its depths? Was it her beauty, her suffering, her confidence in him— was it any one or all of these together that gave him this new wild joy? The delicate subtleness of his feelings eluded analysis. Why had not fate before thrown some woman—some beautiful breathing thing into his keeping where he might work, fight, die, that she might be protected or ministered unto? Why had he not earlier in life been permitted to come to his own— to himself? Might he not anywhere, and for a lifetime, enjoy what he was enjoying now? It was not in the mountain alone that beautiful women suffered, needed ministering unto, needed protecting. He had thought of marriage as a cramping, crippling, and restraining institution. But was it? Might it not enlarge and ennoble as he felt this woman's presence here beside him had enlarged and ennobled his nature in a way he had not looked for?

He thought of Claye, Du Vernet— Art; of the cold narrow empty loneliness of his life. What if he did go home with something new in color? What if he pushed on to the top in art? What if—

The breathing figure beside him twitched in uneasy sleep. He readjusted the clothing he had taken from himself closer about her. The warmth

of her breath blew once upon him. He felt she was his, but he drew back from her as something sacred. His regard for her was that of a miser for his gold—so great that he would not profane it by touching it. She turned her head and something from within pushed her lips apart. The moon had found better range now; he saw more than before. The lines about her face were done by a master, the oval mould of the cheek, the firm delicate chiselling about the chin, the brow, the lips, the peep of neck—any one of these would have made a sculptor immortal. And then when the colors came as he had seen them come—and go! From the deeps of Hartman's soul there sprang a great resolve. He rose from his leaning posture to the attitude reverent men assume when they pray. Then on his knees he vowed a vow.

It was July; but the night was cool up to the point of being cold. On other occasions when Hartman had been in danger he had thought of death—and had been afraid. But he was not afraid now. They had no food, death might come in a slow, awful form. He had seen one of the guides clinging to the slope of ice; but if he had saved himself would he not put those who had fallen down as dead? Hope of deliverance was small; and yet Hartman was not afraid. This woman had taught him things he had not known before. Was it her presence that now took away thoughts of death, sin—judgment—hell? To die was one thing; but to die here quite another.

All through the night the woman slept intermittently. Hartman watched her as a lion might his prey. During her sleeping moments he thought and planned. When she suffered pain he suffered also. Once when she sobbed out words regarding her uncle and aunt he comforted her. Oh the happiness of not only suffering but sorrowing with her! One new element of happiness followed another so quickly that the night hurried away like an hour. Once when he raised his head from bending over her in one of her quieter moods, and looked up, he saw the sun was again silver plating the peaks which had all night stabbed the blue black of the sky, and cut great triangular segments out of the starstrewn dome above. Before noon a party with appliances for removing dead bodies appeared on the cliff above. By sunset Hartman and his companion were in The Bear hotel at Grindlewald. And they had not been brought on stretchers either.

* * * * *

Three weeks later—when half way across the Atlantic—it came out that Hartman and Miss Inez Keppell both knew a man by the name of Claye.

"He wanted me to marry him," she said. "I was to give him my answer when I returned to New York."

"Claye! Marry you!" In the moonlight, on the Liner's deck she told him a long, low story.

"There was one thing I could never quite understand," she said in finishing. "Mr. Claye told me two of his friends had cast him off because he had made up his mind to marry. They were artists."

She had been looking off where the moon played on the sea; but she turned and suddenly looked him firmly in the face.

"Do you think they thought it a sin to marry?"

"I—I think—He didn't tell you their names, did he?"

"No; they were artists. That was all he said."

A broad band of silver ran from the ship away under the moon.

"I don't know anything about art—and artists," she went on. "Do you?"

"No," he said, "nothing." There was a tone in his voice that is always present when a man lies bravely.

The thresh of the far-away screws could be faintly felt.

"I like Mr. Claye. He was kind, but I felt sorry that he should have to lose his friends—for one—so I hesitated—and then—

"But—but what are you going to tell Claye when you get to New York?" he stammered.

Her eyes ran far out on the silver plated path towards the moon.

"I think," she said—and her eyes came slowly in from the moon; then found their way to his face; "I think, well, I have thought over all you have said—of how good you were on the mountain—and—and I have made up my mind to tell Mr. Claye, 'No.' "

* * * * *

Hartman and Claye are not on the same staff now. Du Vernet is back in France.

CPSIA information can be obtained
at www.ICGtesting.com
Printed in the USA
BVHW062101051118
532208BV00011B/503/P